Tolley's Tax Guide

2004–05

Tolley's
Tax Guide
2004–05

by

Arnold Homer

Rita Burrows

Tolley
LexisNexis™

Members of the LexisNexis Group worldwide

United Kingdom	LexisNexis UK, a Division of Reed Elsevier (UK) Ltd, Halsbury House, 35 Chancery Lane, LONDON, WC2A 1EL, and 4 Hill Street, EDINBURGH EH2 3JZ
Argentina	LexisNexis Argentina, BUENOS AIRES
Australia	LexisNexis Butterworths, CHATSWOOD, New South Wales
Austria	LexisNexis Verlag ARD Orac GmbH & Co KG, VIENNA
Canada	LexisNexis Butterworths, MARKHAM, Ontario
Chile	LexisNexis Chile Ltda, SANTIAGO DE CHILE
Czech Republic	Nakladatelství Orac sro, PRAGUE
France	Editions du Juris-Classeur SA, PARIS
Germany	LexisNexis Deutschland GmbH, FRANKFURT and MUNSTER
Hong Kong	LexisNexis Butterworths, HONG KONG
Hungary	HVG-Orac, BUDAPEST
India	LexisNexis Butterworths, NEW DELHI
Ireland	LexisNexis, DUBLIN
Italy	Giuffrè Editore, MILAN
Malaysia	Malayan Law Journal Sdn Bhd, KUALA LUMPUR
New Zealand	LexisNexis Butterworths, WELLINGTON
Poland	Wydawnictwo Prawnicze LexisNexis, WARSAW
Singapore	LexisNexis Butterworths, SINGAPORE
South Africa	LexisNexis Butterworths, Durban
Switzerland	Stämpfli Verlag AG, BERNE
USA	LexisNexis, DAYTON, Ohio

© Reed Elsevier (UK) Ltd 2004
Published by LexisNexis UK

A CIP Catalogue record for this book is available from the British Library.

[Twenty-third edition]

ISBN 07545 25082

Typeset by Letterpart Ltd, Reigate, Surrey
Printed and bound in Great Britain by CPI Bath
Visit LexisNexis UK at www.lexisnexis.co.uk

About this book

This is the twenty-third edition of Tolley's Tax Guide, which is one of the range of Tolley annuals on all aspects of taxation.

The Guide is updated annually to incorporate the changes in law and practice that occur each year, and is published soon after the passing of the Finance Act.

The aim of the book is to provide clear and concise guidance on all aspects of taxation that are likely to be encountered from day-to-day by businessmen, practitioners, professional advisers and private individuals. It deals with income tax (including self-assessment), corporation tax, capital gains tax, inheritance tax, value added tax and stamp duty. There are also chapters on council tax and business rates, tax credits, national insurance contributions and statutory sick pay, statutory maternity pay, adoption and paternity pay. There are numerous examples to demonstrate how the provisions work in practice.

The authors use their wide practical experience to bring out the tax planning opportunities in the various areas, and these are highlighted as 'tax points' at the end of most chapters.

This edition gives the position for the tax year 2004/05 and covers all legislation, statements of practice and other relevant sources of information including the provisions of the Finance Act 2004. Where appropriate the position for earlier years is also explained.

All chapters have been revised to incorporate the many changes that have taken place since the previous edition, and there is a useful summary of the main changes.

The general law, as opposed to tax law, is not always the same in Scotland and in Northern Ireland as in England and Wales. Except where otherwise stated, this book is concerned with the law in England and Wales. Readers in Scotland and Northern Ireland should take advice if in any doubt.

Any comments on this publication will as always be welcomed by the publishers.

LEXISNEXIS UK

Contents

Introduction

Chapter 1 Introduction

Outline of UK tax system

Chapter 2 Income tax and tax credits: general principles

Chapter 3 Corporation tax: general principles

Chapter 4 Capital gains tax: general principles

Chapter 5 Inheritance tax: general principles

Chapter 8 Council tax and business rates

Chapter 9 Dealing with the Revenue

CONTENTS

Employment

Chapter 13 National insurance contributions — employees and employers

Chapter 14 Statutory sick pay and statutory maternity pay

Chapter 15 Golden handcuffs and golden handshakes

Pensions

Chapter 16 Occupational pension schemes

CONTENTS

Chapter 17 Personal pension schemes

Trades, professions and vocations

Chapter 18 Sole trader, partnership or company?

Chapter 19 Starting up a new small or part-time business

Chapter 20 How are business profits calculated?

Chapter 21 How are business profits charged to tax?

Chapter 22 Capital allowances

CONTENTS

Chapter 27 Transfer of business to limited company

Chapter 28 Selling the family company

Chapter 29 Encouraging business investment, enterprise and efficiency

Land and buildings

Chapter 30 Your family home

Chapter 31 A country life: farms and woodlands

Chapter 32 Investing in land and buildings

Tax and the family

Chapter 33 Family matters

Chapter 34 Especially for the senior citizen

Chapter 35 Making a will and post-death planning

Choosing your investment

Chapter 36 Tax on your investments

Chapter 37 Investing in banks and building societies

Chapter 38 Investing in stocks and shares

Chapter 39 Chattels and valuables

Chapter 40 Sensible use of life insurance

Miscellaneous

Chapter 41 The overseas element

Chapter 42 Trusts and estates

CONTENTS

Abbreviations

ACT	=	Advance Corporation Tax
BES	=	Business Expansion Scheme
Board	=	Board of Inland Revenue
CAA 1990	=	Capital Allowances Act 1990
CGT	=	Capital Gains Tax
CTT	=	Capital Transfer Tax
DSS	=	Department of Social Security
EEA	=	European Economic Area
EIS	=	Enterprise Investment Scheme
ESC	=	Extra-Statutory Concession
EU	=	European Union
FA	=	Finance Act
FID	=	Foreign Income Dividend
FYA	=	First-year allowance
F(No 2)A	=	Finance (No 2) Act
IHT	=	Inheritance Tax
IHTA 1984	=	Inheritance Tax Act 1984
ISA	=	Individual Savings Account
ITEPA	=	Income Tax (Earnings and Pensions) Act 2003
MIRAS	=	Mortgage Interest Relief At Source
NIC	=	National Insurance Contributions
PAYE	=	Pay As You Earn
PEP	=	Personal Equity Plan
PPC	=	Personal Pension Contribution
RAP	=	Retirement Annuity Premium
reg	=	regulation
s	=	section
SA 1891	=	Stamp Act 1891
SAYE	=	Save As You Earn
Sch	=	Schedule
SI	=	Statutory Instrument
SMP	=	Statutory Maternity Pay
SP	=	Inland Revenue Statement of Practice
SSCBA 1992	=	Social Security Contributions and Benefits Act 1992
SSP	=	Statutory Sick Pay
TA 1988	=	Income and Corporation Taxes Act 1988
TCGA 1992	=	Taxation of Chargeable Gains Act 1992
TMA 1970	=	Taxes Management Act 1970
VAT	=	Value Added Tax
VATA 1994	=	Value Added Tax Act 1994

VCT	=	Venture Capital Trust
WDA	=	Writing-down Allowance
WDV	=	Written-down Value

Table of rates and allowances

(Correct to 1 July 2004)

Income and corporation tax

Personal allowances (see chapter 2 for full description)

	2002/03 £	2003/04 £	2004/05 £
Personal allowance			
general	4,615	4,615	4,745
aged 65–74	6,100	6,610	6,830
aged 75 and over	6,370	6,720	6,950
age allowance income limit	17,900	18,300	18,900
minimum where income exceeds limit	4,615	4,615	4,745
Married couple's allowance			
either spouse born before 6 April 1935 but aged less than 75	5,465*	5,565*	5,725*
either spouse aged 75 or over	5,535*	5,635*	5,795
age allowance income limit	17,900	18,300	18,900
minimum where income exceeds limit	2,110*	2,150*	2,210
Blind person's allowance	1,480	1,510	1,560

*These allowances attract tax relief at only 10%.

Income tax rates on taxable income (see chapter 2)

Rate	2002/03		2003/04		2004/05	
	Band	Tax	Band	Tax	Band	Tax
	£	£	£	£	£	£
Starting (10%)	0–1,920	192	0–1,960	196	0–2,020	202
Basic (22%)	1,921–29,900	6,155.60	1,961–30,500	6,278.80	2,021–31,400	6,463.60
Higher (40%)	Over 29,900		Over 30,500		Over 31,400	

See 2.19 and 2.20 for the rate of tax on savings and dividend income.

Car benefit scale rates (see chapter 10)

2002/03 onwards

The taxable benefit is the appropriate percentage of the list price of the car plus certain accessories, or of £80,000 if lower. The percentage for cars registered after 31 December 1997 which have an approved carbon dioxide emissions figure can be found using the table below.

Carbon dioxide emissions in grams per kilometre

2003/04	2004/05	2005/06	% of price taxable
155	145	140	15*
160	150	145	16*
165	155	150	17*
170	160	155	18*
175	165	160	19*
180	170	165	20*
185	175	170	21*
190	180	175	22*
195	185	180	23*
200	190	185	24*
205	195	190	25*
210	200	195	26*
215	205	200	27*
220	210	205	28*
225	215	210	29*
230	220	215	30*
235	225	220	31*
240	230	225	32*
245	235	230	33**
250	240	235	34***
255	245	240	35****

*Add 3% if car runs solely on diesel.

**Add 2% if car runs solely on diesel.

***Add 1% if car runs solely on diesel.

****Maximum charge, so no diesel supplement.

Cars first registered before 1 January 1998 and cars which have no approved carbon dioxide emissions figure are taxed as follows.

Engine size	% of price taxable	
	Pre-1.1.98 cars	Cars with no approved emissions figure
0–1,400 cc	15	15*
1,401–2,000 cc	22	25*
2,001 cc and over	32	35

*Plus 3% supplement for diesel cars.

Car fuel scale rates (see chapter 10)

2002/03

		Petrol £	Fuel benefit £	Diesel £
(a)	with a cylinder capacity of:			
	up to 1,400 cc	2,240		2,850
	1,401 cc to 2,000 cc	2,850		2,850
	2,001 cc or more	4,200		4,200
(b)	without a cylinder capacity		4,200	

2003/04 and 2004/05

For 2003/04 and 2004/05, the fuel benefit is calculated by reference to CO_2 emissions, where the car was new on or after 1 January 1998 and has an approved CO_2 emissions figure. The same percentage as for car benefit (ranging from 15% to 35% depending on CO_2 emissions) will be applied to the fixed sum of £14,400 (for a full year).

Where the car has no approved CO_2 emissions figure, the same percentage figure used to calculate company car benefit should be used.

Authorised mileage rates (*see chapter 10*)

Cars

	2002/03 to 2004/05 First 10,000 business miles	Additional business miles
All cars	40p	25p
Each passenger making same business trip	5p	5p

Advisory fuel rates for company cars

Cars

	Petrol (from Jan 2002)	Diesel (from Jan 2002)	LP6 (to 2003/04)	LP6 (from 2004/05)
1400cc or less	10p	9p	6p	7p
1401cc to 2000cc	12p	9p	7p	8p
Over 2000cc	14p	12p	9p	10p

Cycles

For 1999/2000 to 2001/02 the authorised mileage rate for cycles is 12p per mile for all business miles. For 2002/03 to 2004/05 the authorised mileage rate for cycles is 20p per mile for all business miles.

Motorcycles

For 2000/01 to 2004/05 the authorised mileage rate for motor cycles is 24p per mile for all business miles.

Official rate of interest—beneficial loans (see chapter 10)

From 6 January 2002	5% p.a.
From 6 March 1999 to 5 January 2002	6.25% p.a.
From 6 August 1997 to 5 March 1999	7.25% p.a.

Interest on overdue tax (income tax and capital gains tax) (see chapter 2)

From 6 December 2003	6.5% p.a.
From 6 August 2003 to 5 December 2003	5.5% p.a.
From 6 November 2001 to 5 August 2003	6.5% p.a.
From 6 May 2001 to 5 November 2001	7.5% p.a.
From 6 February 2000 to 5 May 2001	8.5% p.a.
From 6 March 1999 to 5 February 2000	7.5% p.a.
From 6 January 1999 to 5 March 1999	8.5% p.a.
From 6 August 1997 to 5 January 1999	9.5% p.a.
From 6 January 1994 to 5 October 1994	5.5% p.a.

Repayment Supplement (i.e. interest on overpaid tax) (income tax and capital gains tax) (see chapter 2)

From 6 December 2003	2.5% p.a.
From 6 August 2003 to 5 December 2003	1.75% p.a.
From 6 November 2001 to 5 August 2003	2.5% p.a.
From 6 May 2001 to 5 November 2001	3.5% p.a.
From 6 February 2000 to 5 May 2001	4% p.a.
From 6 March 1999 to 5 February 2000	3% p.a.
From 6 January 1999 to 5 March 1999	4% p.a.
From 6 August 1997 to 5 January 1999	4.75% p.a.

Note

The rates of interest on overdue and overpaid income tax and capital gains tax also apply, where applicable, to national insurance contributions (see CHAPTERS 13 and 24).

Interest on overdue corporation tax for company accounting periods ending after 30 June 1999 (Self-assessment) (see chapter 3)

From 6 December 2003	6.5% p.a.
From 6 August 2003 to 5 December 2003	5.5% p.a.
From 6 November 2001 to 5 August 2003	6.5% p.a.
From 6 May 2001 to 5 November 2001	7.5% p.a.
From 6 February 2000 to 5 May 2001	8.5% p.a.
From 6 March 1999 to 5 February 2000	7.5% p.a.

Interest on overpaid corporation tax for company accounting periods ending after 30 June 1999 (Self-assessment) (see chapter 3)

From 6 December 2003	3% p.a.
From 6 August 2003 to 5 December 2003	2% p.a.
From 6 November 2001 to 5 August 2003	3% p.a.
From 6 May 2001 to 5 November 2001	4% p.a.
From 6 February 2000 to 5 May 2001	5% p.a.
From 6 March 1999 to 5 February 2000	4% p.a.

Interest on overdue instalment payments for 'large companies' for company accounting periods ending after 30 June 1999 (Self-assessment) (see chapter 3)

From 21 June 2004	5.5% p.a.
From 17 May 2004 to 20 June 2004	5.25% p.a.
From 16 February 2004 to 16 May 2004	5% p.a.
From 17 November 2003 to 15 February 2004	4.75% p.a.
From 21 July 2003 to 16 November 2003	4.5% p.a.
From 17 February 2003 to 20 July 2003	4.75% p.a.
From 19 November 2001 to 16 February 2003	5% p.a.
From 15 October 2001 to 18 November 2001	5.5% p.a.
From 1 October 2001 to 14 October 2001	5.75% p.a.
From 13 August 2001 to 30 September 2001	6% p.a.
From 21 May 2001 to 12 August 2001	6.25% p.a.
From 16 April 2001 to 20 May 2001	6.5% p.a.
From 19 February 2001 to 15 April 2001	6.75% p.a.
From 20 April 2000 to 18 February 2001	7% p.a.
From 21 February 2000 to 19 April 2000	8% p.a.
From 24 January 2000 to 20 February 2000	7.75% p.a.
From 15 November 1999 to 23 January 2000	7.5% p.a.
From 20 September 1999 to 14 November 1999	7.25% p.a.
From 21 June 1999 to 19 September 1999	7% p.a.
From 19 April 1999 to 20 June 1999	7.25% p.a.
From 15 February 1999 to 18 April 1999	7.5% p.a.
From 18 January 1999 to 14 February 1999	8% p.a.
From 7 January 1999 to 17 January 1999	8.25% p.a.

Interest on overpaid instalment payments for 'large companies' and on early payments by other companies for company accounting periods ending after 30 June 1999 (Self-assessment) (see chapter 3)

From 21 June 2004	4.25% p.a.
From 17 May 2004 to 20 June 2004	4.00% p.a.
From 16 February 2004 to 16 May 2004	3.75% p.a.
From 17 November 2003 to 15 February 2004	3.5% p.a.
From 21 July 2003 to 16 November 2003	3.25% p.a.
From 17 February 2003 to 20 July 2003	3.5%p.a.
From 19 November 2001 to 16 February 2003	3.75% p.a.
From 15 October 2001 to 18 November 2001	4.25% p.a.
From 1 October 2001 to 14 October 2001	4.5% p.a.
From 13 August 2001 to 30 September 2001	4.75% p.a.
From 21 May 2001 to 12 August 2001	5% p.a.
From 16 April 2001 to 20 May 2001	5.25% p.a.
From 19 February 2001 to 15 April 2001	5.5% p.a.
From 21 February 2000 to 18 February 2001	5.75% p.a.

From 24 January 2000 to 20 February 2000	5.5% p.a.
From 15 November 1999 to 23 January 2000	5.25% p.a.
From 20 September 1999 to 14 November 1999	5% p.a.
From 21 June 1999 to 19 September 1999	4.75% p.a.
From 19 April 1999 to 20 June 1999	5% p.a.
From 15 February 1999 to 18 April 1999	5.25% p.a.
From 18 January 1999 to 14 February 1999	5.75% p.a.
From 7 January 1999 to 17 January 1999	6% p.a.

Interest on overdue corporation tax for company accounting periods ending before 1 July 1999 (Pay and File) (see chapter 3)

From 6 December 2003	5% p.a.
From 6 August 2003 to 5 December 2003	4.25% p.a.
From 6 November 2001 to 5 August 2003	5% p.a.
From 6 May 2001 to 5 November 2001	6% p.a.
From 6 February 2000 to 5 May 2001	6.75% p.a.
From 6 March 1999 to 5 February 2000	5.75% p.a.
From 6 January 1999 to 5 March 1999	6.5% p.a.
From 6 August 1997 to 5 January 1999	7.5% p.a.

Interest on overpaid corporation tax for company accounting periods ending after 30 September 1993 and before 1 July 1999 (Pay and File) (see chapter 3)

From 6 December 2003	2% p.a.
From 6 August 2003 to 5 December 2003	1.25% p.a.
From 6 November 2001 to 5 August 2003	2% p.a.
From 6 May 2001 to 5 November 2001	2.75% p.a.
From 6 February 2000 to 5 May 2001	3.5% p.a.
From 6 March 1999 to 5 February 2000	2.75% p.a.
From 6 January 1999 to 5 March 1999	3.25% p.a.

Interest on overdue corporation tax for company accounting periods ending on or before 30 September 1993 (see chapter 3)

From 6 December 2003	5% p.a.
From 6 August 2003 to 5 December 2003	4.25% p.a.
From 6 November 2001 to 5 August 2003	5% p.a.
From 6 May 2001 to 5 November 2001	5.75% p.a.
From 6 March 2001 to 6 May 2001	6.5% p.a.
From 31 January 1997 to 5 March 2001	—

Interest on overpaid corporation tax for company accounting periods ending on or before 30 September 1993 (see chapter 3)

From 6 December 2003	5% p.a.
From 6 August to 5 December 2003	4.25% p.a.
From 6 November 2001 to 5 August 2003	5% p.a.
From 6 May 2001 to 5 November 2001	5.75% p.a.
From 6 February 2000 to 6 May 2001	6.5% p.a.
From 6 March 1999 to 5 February 2000	5.75% p.a.
From 6 January 1999 to 5 March 1999	6.5% p.a.
From 6 August 1997 to 5 January 1999	7.25% p.a.

Corporation tax rates (see chapter 3)

Year beginning	1 April 2002	1 April 2003	1 April 2004
Full rate	30%	30%	30%
Small companies rate	19%	19%	19%
—upper profit limit	£300,000	£300,000	£300,000
—marginal relief upper profit limit	£1,500,000	£1,500,000	£1,500,000
—marginal relief fraction	11/400	11/400	11/400
—effective marginal rate	32.75%	32.75%	32.75%
Starting rate	0%	0%	0%
—upper profit limit	£10,000	£10,000	£10,000
—marginal relief upper profit limit	£50,000	£50,000	£50,000
—marginal relief fraction	19/400	19/400	19/400
—effective marginal rate	23.75%	23.75%	23.75%
—minimum rate for distributions to non-corporates	—	—	19%

Capital gains are included in profits and therefore chargeable at the corporation tax rate applicable.

Capital gains tax (*see* chapter 4)

Rate: Gains are chargeable to capital gains tax for individuals at the rates that would apply if they were non-dividend savings income and the top slice of income.

Annual exemption (Individuals)

1996/97	£6,300
1997/98	£6,500
1998/99	£6,800
1999/2000	£7,100
2000/01	£7,200
2001/02	£7,500
2002/03	£7,700
2003/04	£7,900
2004/05	£8,200

See 4.37 and 4.38 for the positions for personal representatives and trustees.

Taper relief

Gains on disposals of **business** assets after 5 April 2002

Number of whole years in qualifying holding period	Percentage reduction available	Percentage of gain chargeable
1	50	50
2	75	25

Gains on disposals of **non-business** assets

Number of whole years in qualifying holding period	Percentage reduction available	Percentage of gain chargeable
1	0	100
2	0	100
3	5	95
4	10	90
5	15	85
6	20	80
7	25	75
8	30	70
9	35	65
10 or more	40	60

See 4.16–23 for how to use the tables in calculating capital gains.

Note

Taper relief is not available to companies.

Retail prices index (*for indexation allowance*)

	1982	1983	1984	1985	1986	1987	1988
January		82.61	86.84	91.20	96.25	100.0	103.3
February		82.97	87.20	91.94	96.60	100.4	103.7
March	79.44	83.12	87.48	92.80	96.73	100.6	104.1
April	81.04	84.28	88.64	94.78	97.67	101.8	105.8
May	81.62	84.64	88.97	95.21	97.85	101.9	106.2
June	81.85	84.84	89.20	95.41	97.79	101.9	106.6
July	81.88	85.30	89.10	95.23	97.52	101.8	106.7
August	81.90	85.68	89.94	95.49	97.82	102.1	107.9
September	81.85	86.06	90.11	95.44	98.30	102.4	108.4
October	82.26	86.36	90.67	95.59	98.45	102.9	109.5
November	82.66	86.67	90.95	95.92	99.29	103.4	110.0
December	82.51	86.89	90.87	96.05	99.62	103.3	110.3

	1989	1990	1991	1992	1993	1994	1995
January	111.0	119.5	130.2	135.6	137.9	141.3	146.0
February	111.8	120.2	130.9	136.3	138.8	142.1	146.9
March	112.3	121.4	131.4	136.7	139.3	142.5	147.5
April	114.3	125.1	133.1	138.8	140.6	144.2	149.0
May	115.0	126.2	133.5	139.3	141.1	144.7	149.6
June	115.4	126.7	134.1	139.3	141.0	144.7	149.8
July	115.5	126.8	133.8	138.8	140.7	144.0	149.1
August	115.8	128.1	134.1	138.9	141.3	144.7	149.9
September	116.6	129.3	134.6	139.4	141.9	145.0	150.6
October	117.5	130.3	135.1	139.9	141.8	145.2	149.8
November	118.5	130.0	135.6	139.7	141.6	145.3	149.8
December	118.8	129.9	135.7	139.2	141.9	146.0	150.7

	1996	1997	1998	1999	2000	2001	2002	2003	2004
January	150.2	154.4	159.5	163.4	166.6	171.1	173.3	178.4	183.1
February	150.9	155.0	160.3	163.7	167.5	172.0	173.8	179.3	183.8
March	151.5	155.4	160.8	164.1	168.4	172.2	174.5	179.9	184.6
April	152.6	156.3	162.6	165.2	170.1	173.1	175.7	181.2	185.7
May	152.9	156.9	163.5	165.6	170.7	174.2	176.2	181.5	186.5
June	153.0	157.5	163.4	165.6	171.1	174.4	176.2	181.3	186.8
July	152.4	157.5	163.0	165.1	170.5	173.3	175.9	181.3	
August	153.1	158.5	163.7	165.5	170.5	174.0	176.4	181.6	
September	153.8	159.3	164.4	166.2	171.7	174.6	177.6	182.5	
October	153.8	159.5	164.5	166.5	171.6	174.3	177.9	182.6	
November	153.9	159.6	164.4	166.7	172.1	173.6	178.2	182.7	
December	154.4	160.0	164.4	167.3	172.2	173.4	178.5	183.5	

The index was re-referenced in January 1987 from 394.5 to 100. The figures above which relate to months before January 1987 have been worked back from the new base and are not, therefore, those produced at the time by the Department of Employment.

See 4.11 for how to use the retail prices index to calculate capital gains tax indexation allowance. The figures after April 1998 are relevant only for calculating capital gains of companies.

National insurance contribution rates

Employers and employees (see chapter 13)

	6/4/03–5/4/04	6/4/04–5/4/05
Lower earnings limit per week (LEL)	£77	£79
Upper earnings limit per week (UEL)	£595	£610
Primary threshold	£89	£91
Secondary threshold	£89	£91

2004/05

Not contracted out

Band of weekly earnings	Employee	Employer
£0 to £91	—	—
£91.01 to UEL	11%	12.8%
Over UEL	1%	12.8%

Contracted out

The 'not contracted out' rate for employees is reduced for earnings between £91 per week and the UEL by 1.6% to 9.4%. In addition, employees receive a rebate of 1.6% on earnings from the LEL up to £91 per week. Where the rebate exceeds the employee's liability, the excess goes to the employer. For employers the 'not contracted out' rate is reduced on the band of earnings from £91 per week to the UEL by 3.5% (to 9.3%) for employees in salary-related schemes and by 1% (to 11.8%) for employees in money purchase schemes. In addition, employers receive a rebate of 3.5% or 1% as appropriate, on earnings from the LEL up to £91 per week.

Reduced rate for certain married women and widows

Payable on earnings in the band £91.01 to UEL	4.85%
Over UEL	1%

2003/04

Not contracted out

Band of weekly earnings	Employee	Employer
£0 to £89	—	—
£89.01 to UEL	11%	12.8%
Over UEL	1%	12.8%

Contracted out

The 'not contracted out' rate for employees is reduced for earnings from £89 per week to the UEL by 1.6% to 9.4%. In addition, employees receive a rebate of 1.6% on earnings from the LEL up to £89 per week. Where the rebate exceeds the employee's liability, the excess goes to the employer. For employers the 'not contracted out' rate is reduced on the band of earnings from £89 per week to the UEL by 3.5% (to 9.3%) for employees in salary-related schemes and by 1% (to 11.8%) for employees in money purchase schemes. In addition, employers receive a rebate of 3.5% or 1% as appropriate, on earnings from the LEL up to £89 per week.

Reduced rate for certain married women and widows

Payable on earnings in the band £89.01 to UEL	4.85%
Over UEL	1%

Employers' national insurance contributions on benefits in kind (see chapter 13)

2004/05 (annual contributions due)

12.8% of the taxable benefit

2003/04 (annual contributions due)

12.8% of the taxable benefit

Self-employed (see chapter 24)

	2003/04	2004/05
Class 2 contributions per week	£2.00	£2.05
Small earnings exception	£4,095	£4,215
Class 4 contributions rate	8.0%	8.0%
on profits between	£4,615 and £30,940	£4,745 and £31,720
Class 4 contributions rate	1%	1%
on profits over	£30,940	£31,720

Voluntary (see chapters 13 and 24)

	2003/04	2004/05
Class 3 contributions per week	£6.95	£7.15

Statutory sick pay from 6 April 2004 (see chapter 14)

Average weekly earnings	£79.00 and over
SSP flat weekly rate	£66.15

Statutory maternity pay, statutory paternity pay and statutory adoption pay from 6 April 2004 (see chapter 14)

The lower of £102.80 and 90% of average weekly earnings.

Main state benefits (see chapter 10)

	2002/03 £	2003/04 £	2004/05 £
Taxable (weekly rates)			
Retirement pension*			
—single	75.50	77.45	79.60
—wife non-contributor	45.20	46.35	47.65
Old person's pension*			
—higher rate	45.20	46.35	47.65
Bereavement (widow's) benefits			
—widowed parent's (mother's) allowance	75.50	77.45	79.60
—bereavement allowance (widow's pension) (standard rate)	75.50	77.45	79.60

| | 2002/03 | 2003/04 | 2004/05 |
	£	£	£
Incapacity benefit			
short-term (weeks 29 to 52)			
—under pension age	63.25	64.35	66.15
—adult dependant	33.10	33.65	34.60
—over pension age	70.95	72.15	74.15
—adult dependant	40.80	41.50	42.65
long-term (after 52 weeks)			
—standard rate	70.95	72.15	74.15
—adult dependant	42.45	43.15	
Industrial death benefit***			
widow's pension			
—higher permanent rate	75.50	77.45	79.60
—lower permanent rate	22.65	23.24	23.88
Invalidity allowance**			
—higher rate	14.90	15.15	15.55
—middle rate	9.50	9.70	10.00
—lower rate	4.75	4.85	5.00
Carer's allowance (formerly invalid care allowance)			
—single	42.45	43.15	44.35
—adult dependant	25.35	25.80	26.50
Jobseekers allowance (taxable maximum)			
Single			
—under 18	32.50	32.90	33.50
—18–24	42.70	43.25	44.05
—25 or over	53.95	54.65	55.65
Couple			
—both under 18	32.50	32.90	33.50
—both under 18, one disabled	42.70	43.25	44.05
—both under 18, with child responsibility	64.45	65.30	66.50
—one under 18, one 18–24	42.70	43.25	44.05
—one under 18, one 25 or over	53.95	54.65	55.65
—both over 18	84.65	85.75	87.30

	2002/03 £	2003/04 £	2004/05 £
Non-taxable (weekly rates)			
(excluding income-related benefits)			
Child benefit			
—eldest child (couple)	15.75	16.05	16.50
—eldest child (lone parent)	17.55	17.55	17.55
—other children	10.55	10.75	11.05
Maternity allowance			
—higher rate	75.00	100.00	102.80
Child addition to benefits****	11.35	11.35	11.35
Incapacity benefit (first 28 weeks)			
under pension age			
—single	53.50	54.40	55.90
—adult dependant	33.10	33.65	34.60
over pension age			
—single	68.05	69 20	71.15
—adult dependant	40.80	41.50	42.65
Disability living allowance			
care component			
—higher rate	56.25	57.20	58.80
—middle rate	37.65	38.30	39.35
—lower rate	14.90	15.15	15.55
mobility component			
—higher rate	39.30	39.95	41.05
—lower rate	14.90	15.15	15.55
Attendance allowance			
—higher rate	56.25	57.20	58.80
—lower rate	37.65	38.30	39.35
Severe disablement allowance			
—single (standard rate)	42.85	43.60	44.80
—adult dependant	25.45	25.90	26.65

*   A taxable age addition of 25p per week is payable to persons aged 80 or over with any one of these benefits.

**   Taxable only if paid with retirement pension.

***   Payable for deaths before 11 April 1988 only.

****   Payable only to existing beneficiaries at 6 April 1987.

New Tax Credits

	2003/04 p.a.	2004/05 p.a.
Working tax credit		
— basic	1,525	1,570
—additional couple's and lone parent element	1,500	1,545
—30 hour	620	640
— disabled worker	2,040	2,100
— addition for severe disablement	865	890
— 50 plus return to work 16 to 29 hours	1,045	1,075
— 50 plus return to work 30+ hours	1,565	1,610
— childcare – maximum eligible cost	200	200
— maximum eligible childcare cost for one child	135	135
— percent of eligible costs recovered	70%	70%
Child tax credit		
— family (only one family element per family)	545	545
— addition for child under the age of 1	545	545
— child	1,445	1,625
— disabled child addition	2,155	2,215
— enhanced disabled child addition	865	890
For both working credit and child credit		
— first income threshold	5,060	5,060
— first withdrawal rate	37%	37%
— second income threshold	50,000	50,000
— second income withdrawal rate	1 in 15	1 in 15
— first threshold (those entitled to child credit only)	13,230	13,480

Value added tax (see chapter 7)

Standard rate (from 1/4/91)
17.5%

	from 10/4/03	from 1/4/04
Registration threshold taxable supplies		
—in last four quarters	More than £56,000	More than £58,000
—in next 30 days	More than £56,000	More than £58,000
Unless for next year not expected to be	More than £54,000	More than £56,000
Deregistration limits taxable supplies	from 10/4/03	from 1/4/04
—in the next year	£54,000 or less	£56,000 or less

VAT—fuel scale rates—private motoring (from 1/5/04)

Return period	Car's cc	Scale benefit (VAT inclusive)	Vat @ 17.5%
Petrol		£	£
Quarterly	to 1,400	232	34.55
	1,401–2,000	293	43.63
	over 2,000	432	64.34
Monthly	to 1,400	77	11.46
	1,401–2,000	97	14.44
	over 2,000	144	21.44
Diesel			
Quarterly	to 2,000	216	32.17
	over 2,000	273	40.65
Monthly	to 2,000	72	10.72
	over 2,000	91	13.55

Interest payable on VAT (default interest)

From 6 December 2003	6.5% p.a.
From 6 September 2003 to 5 December 2003	5.5% p.a.
From 6 November 2001 to 5 September 2003	6.5% p.a.
From 6 May 2001 to 5 November 2001	7.5% p.a.
From 6 February 2000 to 5 May 2001	8.5% p.a.
From 6 March 1999 to 5 February 2000	7.5% p.a.
From 6 January 1999 to 5 March 1999	8.5% p.a.
From 6 July 1998 to 5 January 1999	9.5% p.a.
From 6 February 1996 to 5 July 1998	6.25% p.a.

Repayment supplement

Repayment supplement of 5% of the tax due (or £50 if greater) is paid on overpaid VAT if the return was made by the due date, the return did not overstate the amount repayable by more than the greater of £250 and 5% of the amount due, and directions for repayment are not issued by Customs within 30 days from the day following the return due date, or the date the return was received if *later*.

Statutory interest payable by Customs and Excise in cases of official error

From 6 December 2003	3% p.a.
From 6 September 2003 to 5 December 2003	2% p.a.
From 6 November 2001 to 5 September 2003	3% p.a.
From 6 May 2001 to 5 November 2001	4% p.a.
From 6 February 2000 to 5 May 2001	5% p.a.
From 6 March 1999 to 5 February 2000	4% p.a.
From 6 January 1999 to 5 March 1999	5% p.a.
From 1 April 1997 to 5 January 1999	6% p.a.

Inheritance tax (see chapter 5)

Rate of tax

From 15 March 1988, there has been a single rate of inheritance tax of 40% (20% for lifetime transfers), applicable to the excess of gross cumulative chargeable transfers over a 'nil rate' threshold. The thresholds since that date have been as follows:

Transfers on and after 15/3/88 and before 6/4/89	£110,000
Transfers on and after 6/4/89 and before 6/4/90	£118,000
Transfers on and after 6/4/90 and before 6/4/91	£128,000
Transfers on and after 6/4/91 and before 10/3/92	£140,000
Transfers on and after 10/3/92 and before 6/4/95	£150,000
Transfers on and after 6/4/95 and before 6/4/96	£154,000
Transfers on and after 6/4/96 and before 6/4/97	£200,000
Transfers on and after 6/4/97 and before 6/4/98	£215,000
Transfers on and after 6/4/98 and before 6/4/99	£223,000
Transfers on and after 6/4/99 and before 6/4/00	£231,000
Transfers on and after 6/4/00 and before 6/4/01	£234,000
Transfers on and after 6/4/01 and before 6/4/02	£242,000
Transfers on and after 6/4/02 and before 6/4/03	£250,000
Transfers on and after 6/4/03 and before 6/4/04	£255,000
Transfers on and after 6/4/04	£263,000

Interest on overdue/overpaid inheritance tax

From 6 December 2003	3% p.a.
From 6 August 2003 to 5 December 2003	2% p.a.
From 6 November 2001 to 5 August 2003	3% p.a.
From 6 May 2001 to 5 November 2001	4% p.a.
From 6 February 2000 to 5 May 2001	5% p.a.
From 6 March 1999 to 5 February 2000	4% p.a.
From 6 October 1994 to 5 March 1999	5% p.a.

Stamp duty (see chapter 6)

Interest on overdue stamp duty

From 6 December 2003	6.5% p.a.
From 6 August 2003 to 5 December 2003	5.5% p.a.
From 6 November 2001 to 5 August 2003	6.5% p.a.
From 6 May 2001 to 5 November 2001	7.5% p.a.
From 6 February 2000 to 5 May 2001	8.5% p.a.
From 1 October 1999 to 5 February 2000	7.5% p.a.

Interest on overpaid stamp duty

From 6 December 2003	2.5% p.a.
From 6 August 2003 to 5 December 2003	1.75% p.a.
From 6 November 2001 to 5 August 2003	2.5% p.a.
From 6 May 2001 to 5 November 2001	3.5% p.a.
From 6 February 2000 to 5 May 2001	4% p.a.
From 1 October 1999 to 5 February 2000	3% p.a.

Main Tax Changes

In common with all the present Chancellor's additions to the tax legislation, this year's Finance Act is not only huge (the biggest ever) but also extremely complicated. Much of it is taken up with anti-avoidance provisions. Another massive section rewrites the whole of the pensions legislation, the changes coming into force on 6 April 2006.

A key feature of the Government's drive to block tax avoidance is the introduction of new provisions requiring promoters to give notification of tax avoidance schemes and requiring businesses to notify VAT avoidance schemes.

The main changes are outlined below. General points for each tax are shown separately, and points that relate to specific chapters bear the same chapter heading. Unless otherwise indicated, the changes apply from 6 April 2004 (1 April 2004 for companies).

Income tax

The 10% starting rate band has been increased from £1,960 to £2,020 and the basic rate band from £28,540 to £29,380, increasing the basic rate limit from £30,500 to £31,400. The tax rates up to that level payable by individuals remain unchanged at 22% for non-savings income, 20% for non-dividend savings income and 10% for dividend income. The rates for income above £31,400 also remain unchanged at 40% for non-dividend income and 32.5% for dividend income. Savings income is normally treated as the top slice of income, with dividend income being the highest part of that top slice. Non-taxpayers cannot claim a refund of dividend tax credits.

The income of personal representatives and trusts other than discretionary trusts is taxed at the same rates as for individuals, except that higher rate tax does not apply. The tax rate for discretionary trusts on income other than dividends has been increased from 34% to 40%, and the rate on dividend income from 25% to 32.5%.

The basic personal allowance has been increased to £4,745. Personal allowances for those over 65 have been increased to £6,830 for those aged up to 74 and £6,950 for those aged 75 and over. Married couple's allowance for those born before 6 April 1935 is £5,725, increased to £5,795 where either spouse is over 75. The personal and married age allowances are restricted to the extent that income exceeds £18,900, but the personal allowance will not fall below £4,745 and the married couple's allowance will not fall below £2,210. Maintenance relief where either spouse was born before 6 April 1935 is also £2,210. Tax relief on married couple's allowance and maintenance relief is at 10%. Blind person's relief has been increased to £1,560.

Corporation tax

For accounting periods starting on or after 22 July 2004, companies are required to notify the Revenue within three months after coming within the charge to corporation tax, and will be subject to penalties if they fail to do so.

Corporation tax rates and chargeable bands remain unchanged, with the corporation tax starting rate at 0%, the small companies' rate at 19% and the full rate at 30%. The marginal rates are therefore also unchanged, with the marginal starting rate being 23.75% and the marginal small companies' rate 32.75%. A new 'non-corporate distribution rate' (NCD rate) has, however, been introduced in relation to dividends paid to individuals, partners or trustees where the company's underlying corporation tax rate is less than the NCD rate. For the year to 31 March 2005 the NCD rate is 19%.

Capital gains tax

The annual exemption is increased to £8,200, with corresponding increases in the exemptions for trustees. Gains are charged at 10% to the extent that taxable income is below the starting rate limit (£2,020 for 2004/05). Where income exceeds £2,020, gains are charged at 20% up to the unused part of the basic rate band and 40% on the remainder. The rate of capital gains tax paid by personal representatives and trustees has increased from 34% to 40%.

Inheritance tax

The inheritance tax nil threshold is increased to £263,000.

Stamp duty

The stamp duty land tax provisions introduced from 1 December 2003 have undergone considerable changes, both before they came into force and afterwards. Various amendments have been made to the provisions relating to leases of land and buildings. The treatment of partnerships in relation to land transactions has been brought within stamp duty land tax from the day after 22 July 2004.

Value added tax

From 1 April 2004, the VAT registration limit is increased to £58,000 and the deregistration limit to £56,000. Those who register for VAT on or after 1 January 2004 and join the optional flat-rate scheme will get a 1% reduction in the flat-rate percentage for their trade sector for the first twelve months. The limits for using cash accounting and annual accounting have been increased.

Council tax (CHAPTER 8)

Councils have been given the right to reduce the discount for second homes and long-term unfurnished empty property from 50% to 10%. Most councils are opting for the minimum discount of 10%.

Employments — income chargeable, etc. (CHAPTER 10)

From 6 April 2005 up to £50 a week of childcare payments or childcare vouchers will be exempt providing the conditions are satisfied.

New rules will apply to employer-provided vans from 6 April 2005, which are expected to remove the tax charge from 85% of current van users. From 6 April 2007 the charge for unrestricted private use of vans will increase to £3,000.

Employee share options and awards (CHAPTER 11)

Last year's significant changes to tighten up the tax treatment of employee share schemes have been followed by more changes in the Finance Act 2004.

National insurance contributions — employees and employers (CHAPTER 13)

The lower earnings limit, from which employees have their rights to benefits protected even though they do not pay contributions until earnings reach the earnings threshold, has increased to £79 a week and the earnings threshold to

£91 a week. The upper earnings limit for contributions at the main rate has increased to £610 a week. There has been no change in the contribution rates.

Occupational and personal pension schemes (CHAPTERS 16 and 17)

From 6 April 2006 a new regime will be introduced covering both occupational and personal pension schemes. Most of the existing restrictions will be replaced by two overall limits, a maximum lifetime allowance for total pension savings and a maximum annual allowance for total contributions.

For 2004/05 the earnings cap/relevant earnings limit has increased from £99,000 to £102,000.

Capital allowances (CHAPTER 22)

The rate of first year allowance on plant and machinery for *small* businesses is increased from 40% to 50% for the tax year 2004/05 (year to 31 March 2005 for companies).

National insurance contributions for the self-employed (CHAPTER 24)

Class 2 contributions for 2004/05 have increased from £2 to £2.05 a week. The lower and upper limits for the band of earnings on which Class 4 contributions are payable at 8% is increased from £4,615 and £30,940 for 2003/04 to £4,745 and £31,720 for 2004/05.

Losses of sole traders and partners (CHAPTER 25)

New anti-avoidance provisions have been introduced for accounting periods ending on or after 10 February 2004 to prevent manipulation of tax relief for partnership losses. The provisions apply to the first four tax years of a partner's participation in a business in which he works for less than ten hours a week.

Encouraging business investment, enterprise and efficiency (CHAPTER 29)

The maximum amount on which income tax relief is available for investment in enterprise investment scheme and venture capital trust (VCT) shares is increased from £150,000 to £200,000 from 6 April 2004, and the rate of relief for investment in VCT shares is increased from 20% to 40% for shares issued in the tax years 2004/05 and 2005/06. Capital gains deferral relief is no longer available for gains reinvested in VCT shares issued on or after 6 April 2004.

The minimum amount of investment by small and medium-sized companies in research and development (R & D) to qualify for the 150% R & D relief, and for all companies to qualify for the extra 50% relief available for expenditure on vaccines research, is reduced from £25,000 to £10,000 for expenditure in accounting periods beginning on or after 27 September 2003. The same reduction applies for large companies to qualify for 125% R & D relief for accounting periods beginning on or after 9 April 2003.

Your family home (CHAPTER 30)

Anti-avoidance provisions have been introduced for disposals of private residences on or after 10 December 2003 where someone occupies the property under the terms of a trust. The private residence relief is not available if gifts relief on an earlier disposal is taken into account in calculating the gain.

Investing in land and buildings (CHAPTER 32)

A deduction from rents of up to £1,500 may be claimed by landlords for expenditure incurred between 6 April 2004 and 5 April 2009 on installing loft insulation and/or cavity wall insulation in residential property.

Family matters (CHAPTER 33)

Married couples jointly owning shares in close companies in unequal proportions will no longer be able to treat the income as split equally for income tax purposes, and will instead be taxed according to the beneficial ownership.

From 6 April 2005 the Government will provide a contribution of £250 (£500 for certain low income families) to a child trust fund for a child born after 31 August 2002 (and will make a further contribution when children reach age seven). Additional contributions of up to £1,200 a year in total may be made by parents and others. The child will have access to the fund at age 18. Income and gains from the fund will be exempt from tax.

Sensible use of life insurance (CHAPTER 40)

The tax charge on chargeable events in relation to life policies is now the excess of higher rate tax over the lower rate of 20% rather than the excess over the basic rate of 22%, thus increasing the amount payable.

Trusts and estates (CHAPTER 42)

The Government intends to modernise the tax treatment of trusts from April 2005. In the meantime, the tax rates on discretionary trusts have increased from 25% to 32.5% for dividend income and from 34% to 40% for other income and capital gains.

For disposals on or after 10 December 2003, gifts holdover relief is no longer available on disposals to a trust in which a settlor has an interest.

Subcontractors in the construction industry (CHAPTER 44)

A revised construction industry scheme is to come into effect from a date to be fixed, expected to be April 2006. Some of the changes will ease the regulatory burden on businesses, but a key new requirement will be for an 'employment status declaration' to be made, to ensure that a worker's status as self-employed rather than employed has been carefully considered.

Main anti-avoidance provisions (CHAPTER 45)

A considerable part of the Finance Act 2004 relates to anti-avoidance measures. Anyone who markets or promotes a scheme under which a main benefit is to obtain a tax advantage in relation to income tax, corporation tax or capital gains tax must disclose details to the Revenue and obtain a reference number, which must be notified to clients. Similarly, Customs will maintain a register of VAT avoidance schemes and businesses using such schemes must disclose their use to Customs.

Probably the most talked-about aspect of the Finance Act 2004 provisions is the introduction of a charge to *income tax* on the benefit of the use of 'pre-owned' assets. This is to block various *inheritance tax* avoidance schemes, and is widely regarded as unfair and inappropriate.

The rules relating to the tax treatment of transfer pricing and thin capitalisation, which previously applied only to transactions between UK and overseas companies, apply to transactions wholly within the UK as well from 1 April 2004.

1
Introduction

1.1   The general public would probably have thought that not much had changed in the tax system this year. Nothing could be further from the truth. So many changes are being made all the time, with previous changes being abandoned or even reversed, that those trying to cope with the tax system either on their own behalf or for their clients are faced with an almost impossible task. The editor of Taxation Magazine said recently that 'our tax system is under an unusual level of stress and there is no certainty that anything you can do today, however routine, will be equally valid tomorrow or indeed will remain tax effective in the future'. As always, this Tax Guide aims to outline the main features of the tax system and how they are relevant in common personal and business situations, and also where possible to indicate tax saving opportunities and potential pitfalls.

The rewriting of the tax law in simpler language is continuing. So far the law on capital allowances and employment and pensions income has been rewritten and the third rewrite bill now underway is dealing with trading and property income, savings and investment income and miscellaneous income. Having the law written in a simpler way is little comfort when set against the huge volume of new legislation which is being churned out year by year, with parts of last year's Finance Act being changed before they ever came into force.

1.2   UK tax law applies throughout the United Kingdom, but there are sometimes specific provisions that recognise the different legal systems in Scotland and to a lesser extent in Northern Ireland. These differences are not dealt with in this book.

The Scottish Parliament has the power to increase or decrease the basic rate of income tax (but not any other tax rates) by three pence. If this power was exercised, then even so income would in some circumstances be taxed at the normal basic rate instead of the Scottish rate.

UK tax law must comply with the regulations and directives of the European Union. EU member states must allow members of other EU states freedom of establishment and not tax them at higher rates than their own nationals. One EU state may require another state to take proceedings to recover both direct and indirect taxes owed in the first state. UK tax law must also be compatible with the European Convention on Human Rights and the Human Rights Act 1998.

There are presently two Government Departments that deal with tax, the Inland Revenue, who are responsible for direct taxes and national insurance, and Customs and Excise, who deal with excise duties (not covered in this guide) and value added tax. The Chancellor of the Exchequer has announced that the two departments are to be merged into a single tax service. The departments already work closely together to provide joint customer services and to combat tax evasion. They are allowed to disclose information to the police in the UK and abroad in connection with criminal investigations and also to the intelligence services. Information is also available to Government Departments as a result of the new money laundering regulations. Further comment on this aspect is included in CHAPTER 9.

1.3   Knowing how the UK system works, what taxes can be charged in particular circumstances, what deductions and allowances are available, and what the tax effect is of alternative courses of action, will help you to cope with the responsibilities placed upon you and to use the tax system to your best advantage. The first part of this book contains a brief outline of all the various taxes covered, including council tax. The following sections deal with specific subject areas, such as 'Employment', 'Pensions', 'Tax and the family', 'Choosing your investment' and 'Trades, professions and vocations'. Any special tax saving opportunities or possible problems are highlighted in the form of 'Tax points' at the end of each chapter.

If you need to look at a topic in more depth, there are statutory references to help you track down the relevant legislation. The main Acts dealing with taxation are the Income and Corporation Taxes Act 1988, the Capital Allowances Act 2001, the Taxation of Chargeable Gains Act 1992, the Value Added Tax Act 1994 and the Inheritance Tax Act 1984. The tax law relating to earnings and pensions has been rewritten under the tax law rewrite project mentioned above and is now contained in the Income Tax (Earnings and Pensions) Act 2003. In addition there are annual Finance Acts (sometimes two in a year) which alter some of the existing provisions and bring in new ones, and various statutory instruments. Statutory instruments are increasingly being used not only to provide detailed regulations on various aspects of the main Acts but to make changes to the provisions of the Acts, because so much legislation is being introduced with extreme haste and without all the details having been thought through. A major source of information is the explanatory booklets put out by the various Government Departments. And there are also published Statements of Practice and Extra-statutory Concessions, which explain the Revenue's views on particular aspects and sometimes allow matters to be treated more sympathetically than the strict letter of the law allows. This published material is also available on the various Government websites on the Internet, and the latest information is posted on the Internet well in advance of the paper versions. Indeed in some cases the websites are the only place to find the information. It is also the Government's declared aim to increase the use of electronic communication with taxpayers, and those filing and paying via the Internet have already been given small one-off discounts to do so. The Government has now gone much further, by introducing powers to force all employers, however small, to use electronic means to file their year-end PAYE returns. This will start in 2004/05 for larger employers and will apply to everyone by at the latest 2010 (cash incentives are being given to smaller employers in the meantime to encourage them to do so earlier).

1.4   Despite the vast array of tax statutes and supplementary material, it is not always clear what the law means. Alternatively, the meaning of the law may not be in doubt, but the facts of the case may be. You may therefore take a different view from the tax authorities either on the interpretation of the law, or on the facts, or a mixture of the two.

You may for example produce accounts which show a much lower rate of profit than that customary in your type of business. The Revenue may take the view that you have made more profit than you have declared. You have no disagreement with them about whether your profit should be taxed or not, only on the amount of profit that has actually been made. This is a dispute on a question of fact. On the other hand, you may have incurred expenditure in your business that you consider is allowable for tax purposes whereas the Revenue consider that it is not. The dispute is not about how much has been spent but whether or not it reduces your taxable profit, and this is a question of law.

Since income tax and capital gains tax are self-assessed, it is up to you to calculate how much tax you owe based on your view of the law, and if there are areas of doubt, you should draw these to the Revenue's attention. If you fill in a self-assessment tax return, the Revenue will initially deal with points of difference by raising an enquiry into the return, at the end of which they have the right to make amendments if they disagree with your figures. They also have the right to issue assessments themselves if you are fraudulent or negligent, or do not give them adequate information. You may appeal to a tribunal of Appeal Commissioners if you do not accept a Revenue amendment to your self-assessment, or if you disagree with a Revenue assessment. There are two types of Commissioners, the General Commissioners, who are usually local business people acting in a voluntary unpaid capacity, and the Special Commissioners, who are full-time civil servants who travel on circuit to the different parts of the country. Most appeals are heard by the General Commissioners, but some specialised appeals have to go to the Special Commissioners. You cannot make a non-specialised appeal to the Special Commissioners unless there are points in dispute. The General Commissioners hear appeals in private and their decisions are not reported. The Special Commissioners may hear appeals in public and reports of some of their decisions are published. The Special Commissioners may award costs if either the taxpayer or the Revenue has acted unreasonably.

The distinction between questions of law and fact is important, because what an appeal tribunal decides on questions of fact is generally binding on both the taxpayer and the Revenue. The tribunal's decisions on points of law, however, can be referred by the losing party to the High Court, then to the Court of Appeal (or the equivalent Scottish or Irish Courts) and finally, if leave is granted, to the House of Lords. You should, however, think very carefully before taking an appeal on a question of law to the appeal tribunal, because it may take a very long time before it is settled, it will cost you a lot of time and money, and at the end of the day you may find yourself on the losing side. In that event you may be required to pay the Revenue's costs, although they will not always ask for them, and may sometimes agree in advance not to do so if the case deals with a point of principle that is of widespread importance. But that could still leave the taxpayer with his own costs to bear. In addition, many taxpayer victories are short-lived, because the law is then changed to what the Revenue think it ought to be.

The Revenue have yet another weapon in their armoury, in that they can challenge 'a series of transactions with a tax avoidance motive' so that any intermediate steps are ignored and only the end result is taken into account. This has not only blocked some complicated tax avoidance schemes, but has also led to the need for caution to be exercised even when considering modest tax-saving plans. Advance planning by way of a series of transactions is still possible providing they are not so pre-planned and interlinked that they can only really be regarded as a single transaction. Such advance planning will, however, be affected by significant measures to counter tax avoidance that have been introduced in the Finance Act 2004. From 1 August 2004 those who 'promote' tax avoidance schemes, and in some cases taxpayers using such schemes, must provide details to the Revenue. Similar provisions will require businesses to disclose the use of VAT avoidance schemes to Customs and Excise. See 45.2 and 45.3 for further details.

As far as national insurance is concerned, most decisions on national insurance contributions are made by the Revenue and appeals against their decisions are dealt with by the tax tribunals, i.e. by the General or Special Commissioners (or by a social security appeal tribunal for appeals relating to contracting out of the State Second Pension Scheme — S2P). Further appeal is then possible, as for income tax, to the High Court, Court of Appeal and, where leave is granted, House of Lords.

Your tax dispute may be with Customs instead of with the Revenue. Appeals about VAT matters are dealt with in the first place by VAT tribunals, but there is the same possibility of taking the dispute to the Courts if you do not agree with the tribunal's decision.

There is the further possibility of going to the European Court if you think UK law is not in accordance with European Union rules. Most referrals to the European Court relate to VAT, but some relate to direct taxes. There is also the possibility of appealing to the European Court of Human Rights if you feel your rights under the European Human Rights Convention have been breached.

1.5   Most people do not want to be involved in disputes with the tax authorities, and merely wish to make sure that they comply with their obligations without paying more than is legally due. You need, however, to understand the difference between tax avoidance and tax evasion. Tax avoidance means using the tax rules to your best advantage, whereas tax evasion means illegally reducing your tax bills, for example by understating your income or overclaiming expenses, or by deliberately disguising the true nature of your transactions. Sometimes people distinguish tax avoidance from tax mitigation, the former being regarded as unacceptable and the latter acceptable. Much of the tax legislation is anti-avoidance legislation aimed at preventing 'unacceptable' reduction of your tax liabilities. The new measures mentioned in 1.4 requiring notification of tax and VAT avoidance schemes will enable swifter action to be taken to counter such schemes. But the legal position is that unless and until blocked by specific measures tax avoidance is permissible. As a judge once said a long time ago, no-one is required to arrange his affairs so as to enable the Revenue 'to put the largest possible shovel into his stores'. Similarly, in a recent VAT tribunal case, the chairman said that people don't run their businesses 'with a view to providing finance to the authorities. It is arguable that the correct economic activity for a trader is to retain as much of the funds he has earned for his own or shareholders' benefit as he legitimately can'. Where tax has been illegally *evaded*, you can not only be required to pay the tax you should have paid plus interest and penalties, but you could be facing a criminal prosecution. The tax authorities collect billions of pounds from their investigation, audit and review work, and undertake a number of major criminal prosecutions.

The UK also has wide-ranging international arrangements to help combat tax evasion, and information is exchanged with countries with whom the UK has double taxation agreements or tax information exchange agreements. A country with whom the UK has a double taxation or tax information exchange agreement may also ask the Revenue to require a UK taxpayer to provide information relating to tax liabilities with the overseas country.

The sensible course for taxpayers to follow is to try to understand what their liabilities are and to seek professional advice on non-straightforward matters. This book aims to explain the basic rules on how tax liabilities are calculated and how they can be reduced without falling foul of the law.

2

Income tax and tax credits: general principles

Basis of income tax charge

2.1   In order to deal with your income tax position you need to know what 'income' is. The tax law classifies amounts received under various headings, and an item must come within one of these headings to be charged as income. Until 2003 all of the headings were referred to as 'Schedules', some of the Schedules having subheadings which were labelled 'Cases'. Following the rewriting of the law on the tax treatment of earnings and pensions, the old 'Schedule E' heading for such income was dropped. Schedules B and C were abolished some time ago, and there are now only three income headings that are referred to as Schedules — Schedule A, Schedule D (subdivided into six Cases) and Schedule F. These Schedule headings will also be replaced at some time in the future under the tax law rewrite programme, although they will continue to apply for corporation tax purposes until the corporation tax legislation is rewritten. The present income headings are outlined in 2.5 under the heading 'Calculating your taxable income'.

Sometimes the tax law requires capital items to be treated as income. For example, when a landlord charges a tenant a lump sum for granting him a lease for up to fifty years, part of the lump sum is taxed as income. But unless there is a specific provision like that, an amount cannot be charged to income tax unless it has the quality of income rather than capital. There is a separate heading, Schedule D, Case VI, which deals with items of an income nature that are not covered elsewhere, and also certain capital items that the legislation regards as income. Usually commissions, cashbacks and discounts received by ordinary retail customers are not taxable, but such amounts may be taxable when received by employees or traders. See 37.3 for the tax treatment of cash received on building society mergers, takeovers etc.

Subject to what is said above, capital receipts are dealt with under the capital gains tax rules. Capital gains tax is dealt with in CHAPTER 4.

Child tax credits and working tax credits are social security benefits and as such do not enter into the calculation of taxable income, but they are dealt with by the Revenue and regarded by them as part of the tax system. They are dealt with briefly in 2.27–2.34.

Exempt income

2.2   Certain types of income are specifically exempt from tax, notably the following, which are dealt with in the chapter indicated:

	Chapter
The first £70 interest (husband and wife £70 each) from National Savings Bank ordinary accounts (new ordinary accounts no longer being available after 31 July 2004).	37
Income within individual savings accounts (ISAs).	36, 38
Income within personal equity plans (PEPs).	38
Increase in value of National Savings certificates.	36
Premium bond prizes.	36
Other prizes and betting winnings.	4
Bonuses and profits on life assurance policies (subject to detailed anti-avoidance rules).	40
The capital part of the periodical amount received from a purchased life annuity.	34
Financial support to adopters from local authorities and adoption agencies.	
Local authority home improvement grants.	
Some social security benefits (but others are taxable).	10
Benefits payable under sickness and unemployment insurance policies.	10
Damages and compensation for personal injury (whether received as a lump sum or by periodic payments).	
Save As You Earn account bonuses.	36
Shares and share options allocated to you by your employer under Revenue approved schemes.	11
Educational grants and scholarships.	
Statutory redundancy pay and certain larger amounts received from your employer on termination of your employment.	15
Maintenance payments following divorce or separation.	33
By concession, compensation paid by banks on frozen accounts of Holocaust victims.	

Persons chargeable

2.3   Each individual, whether man, woman or child, is responsible for tax on his/her own income, although a child's income may be treated as the parent's if it or the capital which produces it comes from the parent (see 33.7). Personal representatives and trustees pay tax on estate and trust income (see CHAPTER 42). Companies pay corporation tax instead of income tax (see CHAPTER 3).

Income tax is charged broadly on the income of UK residents, whether it arises in the UK or abroad, subject to certain deductions for individuals who are not ordinarily resident or not domiciled in the UK. Non-residents are liable to income tax only on income that arises in the UK. Double tax relief is available where income is taxed both in the UK and abroad. For detailed provisions on the overseas aspect, see CHAPTER 41.

Rates of tax payable by individuals

2.4   The rates of tax payable depend on the type of income, which for this purpose is divided into three classes, namely dividends, other savings income and non-savings income. The rates for 2004/05 on non-savings income are a starting rate of 10% on the first £2,020, the basic rate of 22% on the next £29,380 (the basic rate band), and the higher rate of 40% on income above £31,400 (the amount of £31,400 being known as the basic rate limit). On savings income other than dividends, the starting and higher rates are the same as for non-savings income, but the charging rate on income within the basic rate band is 20% (called the lower rate) rather than 22%. On dividend income, the charging rates are 10% on income up to the basic rate limit (called the Schedule F ordinary rate) and 32½% on income above the basic rate limit (called the Schedule F upper rate). See 2.17–2.20 for further details. The tax rates and income bands for 2002/03 and 2003/04 are shown in the Table of Rates and Allowances under 'Income tax rates on taxable income'.

Calculating your taxable income

2.5   The tax year runs from 6 April in one year to 5 April in the next, the current year from 6 April 2004 to 5 April 2005 being known as 2004/05.

Taxable income is broadly worked out by adding together the amounts under the headings referred to at 2.1, then deducting certain payments which reduce your taxable income and also deducting your personal allowance and blind person's allowance if relevant. Those deductions save tax at your highest rate. Certain other deductions and allowances save you a specified amount of tax. The detailed provisions are dealt with later in the chapter.

The following table outlines the income charged under each of the headings and how that income is normally measured (the basis of assessment).

Heading	Type of income	Basis of assessment
Schedule A	Rents from UK land and buildings	Rent for tax year less allowable expenses

Heading	Type of income	Basis of assessment
Schedule D		
Case I Case II	Profits of trade Profits of profession or vocation	Normally net profits of accounting year ended in current tax year, with special rules for opening and closing years and on change of accounting date
Case III	UK interest, annuities or other annual amounts received	Income received in tax year There is no relief for expenses
Case IV Case V	Income from foreign securities Income from foreign possessions	Normally the amount arising in current tax year but based on amount remitted to UK if taxpayer resident but not ordinarily resident and/or not domiciled in UK
Case VI	Income not assessable under any other heading	Amount arising in the tax year, less appropriate expenses
Schedule F	Dividends and distributions of UK-resident company	Dividends and distributions in the tax year plus accompanying dividend tax credits

Heading	Type of income	Basis of assessment
Earnings and pensions		
Employment income	Taxable earnings (including benefits) net of allowable deductions: Employees resident, ordinarily resident and domiciled in the UK	All earnings received in the tax year whether duties are performed in the UK or abroad (but special rules apply to seafarers)
	Employees resident and ordinarily resident but not domiciled in the UK	Earnings received in the tax year for UK duties *plus* overseas earnings from non-UK-resident employer that are remitted to the UK in the tax year
	Employees resident but not ordinarily resident in the UK	Earnings received in the tax year for UK duties *plus* foreign earnings that are remitted to the UK in the tax year
	Employees not resident in the UK	Earnings received in the tax year for UK duties
Pension income	UK pensions, including social security pensions, and foreign pensions	UK pensions either received in the tax year or accruing in the tax year, depending on type of pension; foreign pensions arising in the tax year *less* 10% deduction, except for those resident but not ordinarily resident or not domiciled in UK, who are charged on the full amount of foreign pension *remitted* to the UK
Social security income	Taxable social security benefits (see CHAPTER 10)	Benefits accruing in year, or chargeable to tax in year, depending on benefit

How is tax collected?

2.6   Tax is collected from most individuals without any direct contact with the Revenue. The most common sources of income are earnings from employment, interest from banks and building societies and dividends on shares. Tax on your earnings is collected through the Pay As You Earn (PAYE) scheme, whether the earnings are taxable at the starting, basic or higher rate. Tax on occupational pensions and personal pensions (but not retirement annuities) is collected in the same way. If you have some small items of other income that you have received in full (such as taxable interest on a National Savings Bank account) this is adjusted through your PAYE coding. Tax on retirement annuities (payable under pre-1 July 1988 pension contracts) is normally deducted at the basic rate (see 17.17).

Deduction of tax at source from savings income and dividend tax credits

2.7   Tax on bank and building society interest (except most interest from the National Savings Bank) is deducted by the bank or building society at the lower rate of 20%, and there is nothing more to pay unless you are liable to tax at the higher rate. (Tax is not deducted if you have certified that you are entitled to receive the interest in full because you are not liable to pay *any* tax on your income — see 37.2). Tax is not deducted from interest on any security issued by a company that is listed on a stock exchange (including building society permanent interest-bearing shares), nor from most interest on Government stocks — see 37.4 and 38.4.

2.8   UK dividends carry a tax credit of 1/9th (representing 10% of the tax credit inclusive dividend). Thus a dividend of £90 carries a tax credit of £10, giving income of £100. The tax credit of £10 covers the Schedule F ordinary rate tax of 10%, but a further 22.5%, amounting to £22.50, is payable by a higher rate taxpayer. Dividend tax credits are not repayable to non-taxpayers (although tax credits were payable until 5 April 2004 on shares held in Personal Equity Plans (PEPs) and Individual Savings Accounts (ISAs) — see 36.22 and 38.29).

Some companies give shareholders the opportunity of taking shares instead of dividends (scrip dividends). The shareholders are treated as having received dividends with a notional tax credit and their tax position is the same as on any cash dividends (see 38.3).

Paying tax direct to the Revenue

A minority of employees and pensioners, and all self-employed people, have to fill in tax returns and pay some or all of their income tax directly to the

Revenue. (Those with capital gains above the annual exempt limit are also required to fill in tax returns and pay the tax directly.) Tax that is due to be paid direct to the Revenue is normally collected by means of two half-yearly payments on account on 31 January in the tax year and the next 31 July, based on the total income tax payable directly for the previous tax year, with a balancing payment or repayment (plus the first payment on account for the following year) on the next 31 January. Any capital gains tax due is included in the balancing payment. This is dealt with in more detail at 9.7. See also 2.23.

Deductions from income and payments that reduce your tax bills

2.9   Certain payments you have made are allowable as deductions in arriving at your taxable income, thus saving tax at your top rate. The main category of such allowable deductions is allowable interest payments (other than on certain 'home income plan' loans to the over 65s — see below).

The allowable interest payments dealt with in 2.10 (other than home income plan interest) are made in full, and you get relief at your top tax rate by having your tax code adjusted or in working out your self-assessment.

You can also save tax at your top tax rate if you give quoted shares or securities, or land and buildings, to charity. The market value of such charitable gifts is deducted in arriving at taxable income.

You are also entitled to relief at your top tax rate on all 'gift aid' cash donations to charity, including covenanted payments. The gift aid provisions also apply to gifts to registered community amateur sports clubs. The cash amount donated is treated as being net of basic rate tax of 22% and you will normally retain the tax deducted as your tax relief. If you are taxable at the higher rate (either on your income or on capital gains), you will get the extra relief to which you are entitled by an adjustment in your coding or self-assessment. In exceptional circumstances you may not pay enough tax to allow you to retain all the tax relief on your charitable payments, in which case you may have to account for the shortfall. Both income tax and capital gains tax paid are, however, taken into account in deciding whether you have paid sufficient tax to retain the tax relief. For further details of the provisions relating to charities and community amateur sports clubs see CHAPTER 43.

You are entitled to tax relief at a specified rate, up to but not exceeding the rate of tax on your income, on certain other payments, as follows:

Interest on the first £30,000 of a pre-9 March 1999 loan to a borrower aged 65 or over to buy a life annuity, the loan being secured on the borrower's home (home income plans — see 34.9)	23%

Up to £2,210 maintenance payments to former or separated spouse where either spouse was born before 6 April 1935 (see 34.4)	10%
Venture Capital Trust (VCT) subscriptions up to £200,000 (see 29.6)	40%*
Enterprise Investment Scheme (EIS) subscriptions up to £200,000 (see 29.2)	20%
Amounts invested in Community Development Finance Institutions (see 29.10), relief being 25% of the investment spread over five years, giving an annual relief of	5%
*The 40% rate of relief for Venture Capital Trust subscriptions applies to shares issued between 6 April 2004 and 5 April 2006 inclusive, the rate thereafter being	20%

The tax relief for the over 65s on home income plan interest is usually given under the Mortgage Interest Relief At Source (MIRAS) scheme. You obtain the saving by deducting tax before you make the payment (so that, for example, if gross MIRAS interest is £1,000 you will pay £770 net). Non-MIRAS interest on home income plan loans, maintenance payments, VCT and EIS subscriptions and CDFI investments are paid in full and the tax saving is given by an adjustment in your coding or self-assessment.

If you have no earned income or you are self-employed, or are not in your employer's pension scheme, or you are in an occupational scheme but you earn less than £30,000 a year and are not a controlling director (see 17.4 below), you may pay premiums under a personal pension policy, which entitle you to tax relief. Employees pay the premiums net of basic rate tax at 22%, and any higher rate relief to which they are entitled is given by coding adjustment. Self-employed people and those without earned income also obtain basic rate relief by deducting it from their premiums, and higher rate relief where relevant is given in their self-assessments. Premiums on pre-1 July 1988 pension contracts (retirement annuity policies) are paid gross and reduce the taxpayer's taxable earnings, relief being given in self-assessments or by coding adjustment. For the detailed provisions, see CHAPTER 17.

Allowable interest (TA 1988, ss 353–379)

2.10   As indicated in 2.9, relief is available for pre-9 March 1999 home income plan loans to the over 65s, interest on the first £30,000 of such loans qualifying for tax relief at 23% (not the basic rate of 22%). Relief for such interest continues if you move home, or remortgage, or go into a nursing home (see 34.9).

You are usually entitled to deduct interest relating to let property from your rental income, saving tax at your top tax rate (see 30.12 and 32.4). You are also entitled to relief at your top tax rate on the following interest payments, the payments being deducted from your taxable income. Most of the items are dealt with in context in the appropriate chapter.

(a)   On a loan to buy a partnership share, to introduce capital to a partnership or to lend money to it, providing that you are not a limited partner or a partner in an 'investment' limited liability partnership (i.e. one whose business consists wholly or mainly of making investments) and providing you are still a partner when the interest is paid (see 20.10 and 23.7).

(b)   On a loan to buy shares in or lend money to a trading company controlled either by its directors or by five or fewer people (known as a close company), so long as, at the time the interest is paid, either you own more than 5% of the issued ordinary share capital or you own any part of the ordinary share capital, however small, and work for the greater part of your time in the management or conduct of the company or an associated company. (But if you or your spouse have claimed income tax relief or capital gains deferral relief in respect of shares acquired under the Enterprise Investment Scheme, you cannot also claim interest relief on a loan to buy the shares.)

(c)   On a loan to buy plant or machinery other than cars, vans, motor cycles or bicycles for use in your partnership or employment. Relief is available for interest paid in the tax year of purchase and the next three tax years. Where there is part private use, only the business proportion qualifies (see 10.11).

(d)   On a loan to personal representatives of a deceased person to pay inheritance tax (see 42.4).

(e)   On a loan to acquire shares in an employee-controlled trading company.

(f)   On a loan to acquire one or more shares in, or to lend money to, a co-operative.

Relief under (a), (b), (e) and (f) is restricted if the shares are sold or the partnership, close company or co-operative repays all or part of the loan, without your borrowing being reduced by an equivalent amount.

Interest is allowable on loans which replace existing qualifying loans.

Relief is only available as the interest is paid. It is not spread over the period of accrual and will not be allowed if it is never paid.

Bank overdraft interest is never allowed as a deduction from *total* income. Relief is only available where the overdraft is part of the funding of a trade or property letting and therefore allowable as an expense in arriving at trading or rental profits.

Personal allowances (TA 1988, ss 256–265; FA 2004, s 24; SI 2003/3215)

2.11   In addition to claiming a deduction for particular payments etc. as indicated above, you may reduce your taxable income by certain allowances, as detailed below. The amounts stated relate to the tax year 2004/05. For the rates of allowance for earlier years, see the Table of Rates and Allowances under 'Personal Allowances'. Personal allowances are available only to those resident in the UK, except for certain specified categories of non-resident (see 41.13).

The personal allowance and blind person's allowance are deducted from your income and save tax at your highest tax rate. The married couple's allowance saves tax at only 10% and is given by reducing the amount of tax payable (but it cannot create a repayment). For the way relief is given under PAYE, see 10.30.

Personal allowance

2.12   The personal allowance depends on your age, and is increased in and after the tax years in which you reach age 65 and age 75, the amounts for 2004/05 being as follows:

Under 65	Age 65 to 74	Age 75 and over
£4,745	£6,830	£6,950

Personal allowances are normally increased at least in line with inflation each year. The Chancellor has said that the over 65s allowances will rise at least in line with earnings rather than prices for the remainder of the current Parliament.

The higher allowances for those aged 65 and over are, however, subject to an income limit (see 2.15).

Blind person's allowance

2.13   An allowance of £1,560 is available to a registered blind person, which saves tax at the individual's highest tax rate. A married couple who are both blind may each claim the allowance. A married blind person may transfer unused blind person's allowance to the spouse (whether or not the spouse is blind).

Married couple's allowance for older couples

2.14   Married couple's allowance is available only to couples one of whom was born before 6 April 1935.

Where available the allowance is given to the husband (subject to any claim by his wife — see below). A higher rate of allowance is available in and after the tax year in which the older spouse reaches age 75, the allowance for 2004/05 being as follows:

	Elder aged 69 to 74	Elder aged 75 and over
	£5,725	£5,795
Tax saving	£572.50	£579.50

As with the personal allowance, the allowance is restricted if income exceeds a certain limit (see 2.15).

The married couple's allowance starts in the year of marriage, but in that year the available allowance (after taking into account the income restriction where appropriate) is reduced by one-twelfth for each complete tax month (ending on the 5th) before the wedding date. The married couple's allowance is given in full in the year of divorce, separation or death of either spouse. A widow will get the benefit of any unused married couple's allowance in the year of her husband's death.

A married woman is entitled as of right to claim £1,105 of the married couple's allowance. Alternatively the couple may jointly claim for an allowance of twice that amount, i.e. £2,210, to be given to the wife. In either case the allowance available to the husband is reduced accordingly. For detailed notes on claiming for part of the allowance to go to the wife, see 34.2.

If either husband or wife pays insufficient tax to use the married couple's allowance to which they are entitled, that spouse may notify the Revenue (not later than five years after the 31 January next following the relevant tax year) that the unused amount is to be transferred to the other. The unused amount is *not* transferred automatically. Provision for transferring surplus allowances is made in tax returns (see 9.28).

Income limit for age allowances

2.15   Your increased personal allowance because of age is reduced by £1 for every £2 by which your net total income (after any allowable deductions but before personal and blind person's allowances) exceeds £18,900, but the allowance cannot fall below £4,745.

The married couple's allowance is similarly reduced by half of the excess of the husband's total income over £18,900 which has not already been taken into account to reduce his personal allowance, but it cannot fall below £2,210. The wife's income is not taken into account, even if the allowance is given because of her age rather than the husband's, or if the tax saving is transferred to the wife because the husband's income is too low to use it.

For examples and detailed information on the tax treatment of the over 65s, see CHAPTER 34.

Life assurance relief (TA 1988, ss 266–274 and Schs 14 and 15)

2.16   Life assurance relief is no longer available for contracts made after 13 March 1984 but it continues for policies made on or before that date. The relief is 12½% of qualifying premiums, subject to a limit on allowable premiums of either one-sixth of total income or £1,500, whichever is greater. The relief is deducted when the premium is paid, and may be retained whether you are a taxpayer or not.

There were many restrictions on what policies qualified for relief, and there are anti-avoidance rules under which the Revenue recover excess relief. The provisions are dealt with in detail in CHAPTER 40.

Life cover for a limited period (term assurance) is available with tax relief on the premium at the highest rate you pay, under the 'personal pension scheme' provisions (see CHAPTER 17).

Calculating tax on your taxable income (TA 1988, ss 1A, 1B; F(No 2)A 1997, s 30; FA 1998, s 76)

2.17   As indicated in 2.4, there are different rates of tax payable depending on whether the income is dividend income, other savings income or non-savings income. The main types of income within each of these three categories are as follows.

Non-savings income (possible tax rates being starting rate of 10%, basic rate of 22%, higher rate of 40%)

2.18

Income from employment and self-employment
Pensions from the state and from occupational and personal pension schemes
Taxable social security benefits (see 10.3)
Rental income

Interest and dividends from abroad taxable on the 'remittances basis' (This applies to someone who is resident but not ordinarily resident in the UK and/or not domiciled in the UK, who is not taxed on such foreign income unless it is brought into the UK — see 41.6.)

Savings income other than dividends (possible tax rates being starting rate of 10%, lower rate of 20%, higher rate of 40%)

2.19

Interest arising on bank and building society accounts, government stocks, private loans etc., both in the UK and abroad (other than that charged on the remittances basis as indicated above)
The income element of a purchased life annuity (see 34.7)
Accrued income charges on the sale/purchase of interest-bearing securities (see 36.18)

Dividend income (possible tax rates being Schedule F ordinary rate of 10%, Schedule F upper rate of 32½%)

2.20   UK and foreign dividends (other than those charged on the remittances basis)

Composition of taxable income and treatment of deductions and allowances

2.21   The legislation treats savings income as the top slice of the taxable income, and furthermore, dividends are treated as the top slice of the savings income.

An illustration of how this works is in Example 1.

Example 1

In 2004/05 tax will be charged at the rates shown where a taxpayer's taxable income is as indicated (dividends shown being inclusive of tax credits and the non-savings income having been reduced by the personal allowance).

	(a) £		(b) £		(c) £	
Non-savings income	1,000	@ 10%	2,020	@ 10%	2,020	@ 10%
			14,480	@ 22%	17,980	@ 22%
			16,500		20,000	
Non-dividend	1,020*	@ 10%	5,000	@ 20%	8,000	@ 20%
savings income	3,480	@ 20%				
	5,500		21,500		28,000	
Dividends	3,000	@ 10%	6,500	@ 10%	3,400**	@ 10%
					31,400	
Dividends (balance)					600	@ 32½%
Taxable income	8,500		28,000		32,000	

*In (a) there is £1,020 of the starting rate band available for non-dividend savings income, giving rise to a tax refund claim if 20% tax has been deducted at source and tax has already been accounted for on the non-savings income.

** Total tax-credit inclusive dividends in (c) are £4,000, of which only £3,400 is within the basic rate band, so that an extra 22.5% is payable on £600.

There are two instances where savings income is not treated as the top slice of your income, namely when you receive a lump sum taxed under the 'golden handshake' rules (see 15.6) and when you have a chargeable event gain on a life policy (see 40.5).

Before applying the different tax rates to income in the order shown in Example 1, however, it is necessary to decide which sources of income have been reduced by deductions and allowances and to what extent. You are allowed to set deductions and allowances against your income in the order that saves most tax, which normally means setting them against non-savings income first, then savings income other than dividends, then dividends. If the taxable income remaining after deductions and allowances is less than the tax-credit inclusive dividend income, the dividend tax credit that can be set against tax payable is restricted to 10% of taxable income.

Effect of rate charging structure on marginal tax rates

2.22 The complex rate charging structure means that although the top rate of tax is 40%, the marginal rate of tax payable if taxable income increases may be higher than that, as illustrated in examples 2 and 3.

Example 2

Individual has taxable income in 2004/05 of £31,400 (i.e. equal to the basic rate band) as follows:

	£
Salary	34,145
Bank and building society interest	2,000
	36,145
Personal allowance	4,745
Taxable income	31,400

Tax payable:	Salary	2,020	@ 10%	202.00
		27,380	@ 22%	6,023.60
		29,400		
	Interest	2,000	@ 20%	400.00
		31,400		6,625.60

If his bank etc. interest increases by £100, an extra £40 tax will be payable (of which 20% will already have been deducted at source). If, however, his *salary* increases by £100, the extra salary will be taxed at 22%, but £100 of interest will be taxed at 40% instead of 20%, so that the total tax on the extra £100 would be £42, a marginal tax rate of 42%.

If the taxable salary had already been above the basic rate threshold, both extra salary and extra interest would cost extra tax of 40%.

Example 3

Using broadly the same situation as in Example 2, but with dividend income instead of interest, the position is as follows:

	£
Salary	34,145
Dividends (1,800 + tax credits 200)	2,000
	36,145
Personal allowance	4,745
Taxable income	31,400

				£
Tax payable:	Salary	2,020	@ 10%	202.00
		27,380	@ 22%	6,023.60
		29,400		
	Dividends	2,000	@ 10%	200.00
		31,400		6,425.60

If his dividends increase by £90, giving a tax credit inclusive amount of £100, an extra £32.50 tax will be payable (of which £10 is covered by the tax credit). If, however, his *salary* increases by £100, the extra salary will be taxed at 22%, but £100 of dividends will be taxed at 32½% instead of 10%, so that the total tax on the extra £100 would be £44.50, a marginal tax rate of 44.5%.

If the taxable salary had already been above the basic rate threshold, extra salary would cost extra tax of 40% and extra dividends would cost extra tax of 32½% (of which 10% would be covered by the tax credit).

Looked at from the opposite point of view, the marginal rates of tax illustrated in Examples 1 to 3 will be *saved* by making a payment qualifying for tax relief (such as a personal pension premium or gift aid donation) so that taxable income moves from above the basic rate limit to below it, and where the taxpayer is entitled to tax credit (see 2.27 onwards), the payment would also reduce income for credit purposes, possibly saving a further 37% (see Example 7 in 2.34).

Payment of tax, interest on overdue tax and repayment supplement on overpaid tax (TMA 1970, ss 55, 59A, 59B, 86 and Sch 3ZA; TA 1988, s 824)

2.23   As indicated in 2.6, much of the tax due on income is deducted before the income is received — under the PAYE (pay as you earn) system for employees and those receiving occupational and personal pensions and by retention from annuities and bank and building society interest. Dividends received are accompanied by a dividend tax credit. Tax that is not deducted or credited at source in this way is payable under the self-assessment system. Interest is charged on underpaid tax and repayment supplement is paid on overpaid tax. The rates are adjusted frequently in line with commercial interest rates — for details of recent rates see the TABLE OF RATES AND ALLOWANCES. You cannot deduct interest on unpaid tax in calculating your tax liability, and you do not have to pay tax on any repayment supplement you receive on overpaid tax.

An important point that needs to be recognised is that under the self-assessment rules, any claim that results in relief being given in relation to an earlier tax year (say because of a claim to carry back a trading loss in a new business — see CHAPTER 25) is *given effect* by an adjustment to the tax of the year of claim, so that a repayment supplement is payable only by reference to the balancing payment date for the claim year, e.g. where a claim is made in 2004/05 affecting the tax liability of 2001/02, the repayment would be calculated according to the 2001/02 tax position, but supplement would be payable only from 31 January 2006. Carry-back claims also have an anomalous effect in relation to payments on account (see 9.5).

Detailed calculations of interest and supplement are not shown on tax demands and statements. Mistakes do occur, so it is important that amounts charged or allowed are carefully checked.

2.24   If you are required to fill in self-assessment tax returns, you may work out your own tax or ask the Revenue to work it out for you and in either case this counts as self-assessment. The Revenue are able to 'determine' the tax you owe if you do not send in your return, but their tax figure will be replaced by your self-assessment when it is received, so that appeals are not relevant. If the Revenue enquire into your return, you have the right to appeal against any amendments they make to your figures, and also to apply to postpone payment of any disputed amount until the appeal is settled. In some circumstances claims are made separately from returns and you have the right to appeal against Revenue amendments to such claims, although not to postpone payment of the tax. There are some limited circumstances where the Revenue still issue assessments outside the self-assessment system and tax on such assessments is payable 30 days after the issue of the assessment. Interest on such assessments, however, runs from 31 January following the tax year to which the assessment relates, regardless of when the assessment was issued. Apart from such exceptions, the Revenue will not make assessments themselves unless they discover that tax has been underpaid through a taxpayer's fraudulent or negligent conduct, or because of inadequate disclosure of information (see 9.43). See CHAPTER 9 for detailed information on appeal and postponement procedures, claims made outside returns and Revenue enquiries.

2.25   The payment dates under self-assessment are outlined at 2.6. You are due to make payments on account on 31 January and 31 July, each equal to half the total net income tax and self-employed Class 4 national insurance contributions (and student loan repayments if relevant — see 9.3) payable for the previous tax year (unless the amount due is less than the limits stated below). You should then pay the balance of tax due, including capital gains tax if any, on the following 31 January, or claim a refund if tax has been overpaid. At any time before that 31 January date you may claim to reduce the payments on account (or get a refund if already paid) if you think your current year's tax will be lower (subject to penalties if you do so fraudulently or negligently). Interest is charged on underpaid payments on account and balancing payments from the due dates and repayment supplement is paid on overpayments from the date of the overpayment to the date the repayment order is issued. The interest or supplement is based on the correct amount of tax and Class 4 national insurance and student loan repayments if relevant that is finally due, taking into account all later adjustments (but see 24.12 re Class 4 national insurance contributions collected or refunded by the Revenue Contributions Office).

If you claimed to reduce your payments on account, you will in addition be charged interest from the half yearly due dates on any shortfall compared with the *lower* of half of the previous year's tax and half the current year's tax (excluding capital gains tax in each case). If the final income tax bill is less than the payments on account (net of any repayments already claimed), repayment supplement is payable on half of the difference from the date each payment on account was made. See example 4.

Example 4

Assume payments on account are made on due dates. Total income tax payable directly to the Revenue for 2002/03 is £15,000, so that the payments on account for 2003/04 should be £7,500 on each of 31.1.04 and 31.7.04. The due date for the final payment/repayment is 31.1.05. If no claim is made to adjust payments on account, no interest will be charged on them if final tax exceeds £15,000; if final tax is less than £15,000, interest will be allowed on half of the shortfall from each of the 31.1.04 and 31.7.04 payment dates.

Say the taxpayer, having made first payment on account of £7,500 on 31.1.04, applies to reduce the payments to £6,000 each because he thinks the 2003/04 tax will be around £12,000. The overpayment of £1,500 on the first instalment will be refunded with interest from the payment date to the date the repayment order is issued. If the final figure for 2003/04 (excluding any capital gains tax) turns out to be:

£16,000

A balancing payment of £4,000 will be due on 31.1.05 and interest will be charged from that date if it is paid late.

Interest will in any event be charged on the difference between the payments on account that should (with hindsight) have been paid, i.e. £7,500 each, and the £6,000 actually paid. The interest will therefore be:

On £1,500 re 1st payment on account from 31.1.04 to 30.1.05.
On £1,500 re 2nd payment on account from 31.7.04 to 30.1.05.

£14,000

The balancing payment due on 31.1.05 will be £2,000, and the interest charges re each payment on account will be based on £1,000 (since the payments should only have been reduced to £7,000 each instead of the £6,000 which has been paid).

£10,000

The taxpayer would be entitled to a refund of £2,000, with interest on £1,000 from 31.1.04 and £1,000 from 31.7.04 to the date the repayment order is issued.

Payments on account are not required if the previous year's income tax bill (excluding tax deducted at source) was below £500 or if more than 80% of the tax due was collected at source. A surcharge is payable if the balancing payment for the year is more than a month late. For further details see CHAPTER 9.

The Revenue will issue statements to keep you up to date with all payments made and all liabilities outstanding, including interest and surcharges.

Where there is a repayment of tax deducted at source (including over-deductions under PAYE), repayment supplement is payable from 31 January following the relevant tax year.

Repayment claims

2.26   People often overpay tax because, for example, tax has been deducted at source from much of their income and they have not received the full benefit of their personal allowances and/or lower rates of tax, or because they have incurred losses in their businesses that can be set against income on which tax has been paid. They are entitled to claim repayment of the overpaid amount, although many of those entitled do not put in claims. See Example 5. Repayment claims cannot be made in respect of tax credits on dividends.

Example 5

Income of taxpayer aged 67 in 2004/05 is £6,000 state pension, and £1,200 net building society interest.

Tax can be reclaimed as follows:

		£	Tax paid £
State pension		6,000	—
Building society interest (net)	1,200		
Tax deducted	300	1,500	300
		7,500	300
Age allowance		6,830	
Taxable income		670	
Tax thereon @ 10%			67
Repayment due			£233

Notes

(i)   The taxpayer was not entitled to apply to receive his building society interest in full, because this is only possible for someone who expects to pay no tax at all. Had he received the interest in full he would have owed tax of £67.

(ii) Had the savings income been dividend income, no repayment could have been claimed.

(iii) If the repayment was made after 31 January 2006, repayment supplement would be payable from that date.

The Revenue deal with repayment claims such as that shown in example 5 by issuing a repayment claim form outside the self-assessment system.

Repayments will also arise if your payments on account exceed the final tax liability shown in your self-assessment. The claim will usually be made in your tax return, but you may claim earlier if you believe an overpayment will occur (see example 4). Self-assessment returns state that the Revenue will normally carry forward overpayments of less than £10 against later tax bills. If you want immediate repayment you need to contact your tax office.

It is not necessary for either UK residents or non-residents to send in vouchers with repayment claims.

Tax credits (TCA 2002)

2.27   Two new tax credits were introduced from 6 April 2003, the child tax credit and working tax credit. The main legislation is in the Tax Credits Act 2002, but most of the detail is contained in statutory instruments, which

are continually being expanded and revised. The credits are being administered by the Revenue, who have issued a vast quantity of information on
their website, including a tax credits manual. They have also produced a
general guide WTC2.

The Civil Partnership Bill before Parliament at the time of writing will enable
same-sex couples to have their relationship legally recognised. For tax credits
this means such couples will have to make joint tax credit claims and other
provisions applicable to married couples will also apply to them.

To qualify for tax credits you must be aged 16 or over and must normally live
in the UK (although some non-residents qualify). For married couples and
couples living together as husband and wife, a joint claim must be made. The
credits are means-tested, so are progressively withdrawn from those with
higher incomes. Payments of tax credit will not be backdated for more than
three months, so claims for tax credit for 2004/05 should have been made (on
form TC600) by 5 July 2004. It is estimated that nine out of ten families with
children will qualify for one or both of the credits. Once a claim for tax credit
has been made, there is an automatic renewal process, as indicated below.

Credits are awarded for up to a year, the year ending on 5 April in line with
the tax year. Maximum credit entitlement is worked out on a daily basis
according to the circumstances during the year (see 2.30 for further details),
and is restricted where appropriate depending on income. For 2003/04 the
amount of credit was initially based on the income for 2001/02. For 2004/05
onwards it is initially based on the previous year's income. At the year-end
the Revenue will send claimants a renewal notice. For claimants entitled to
only the family element of child tax credit (see 2.33), the award will be
automatically renewed and they will only have to respond to the renewal
notice if their income and/or personal circumstances have changed. Other
claimants must send back a declaration confirming or amending the information in the notice by 30 September following the tax year (30 September 2004
for 2003/04). As far as income is concerned, where final figures are not
available at that date, an estimate must be given, with the final figures being
notified by the following 31 January at the latest (31 January 2005 for
2003/04). A penalty may be charged if the declaration is not submitted (see
2.31).

Definition of income

2.28   Income for tax credit purposes is defined in the Tax Credits (Definition and Calculation of Income) Regulations 2002 (SI 2002/2006) as amended
by later statutory instruments. Where there are joint claimants, the joint
income is taken into account. The definition of income equates fairly closely
with taxable income, but there are many differences both in the income and
the deductions that may be made, and the detailed provisions need to be
studied carefully.

Income is reduced by the gross amount of all pension contributions and gift aid donations to charity in the tax year (but there is no provision for carrying contributions and donations back). The first £300 of the total income (or joint total income for joint claimants) within five categories is ignored. The five categories are pension income, investment income (which includes chargeable event gains on life policies), property income, foreign income and notional income. Notional income covers amounts that are specifically included in taxable income, such as premiums on let property and scrip dividends, and also income someone has deliberately deprived themselves of, or failed to apply for, or could have received for services they provided (other than for voluntary or charitable bodies) at a cheap or nil cost. If a trading loss is incurred in the year, it is deducted from the total income of the claimant (or the combined total income where there are joint claimants) for that year. Any balance of loss not relieved against the total income of the current year is carried forward to set against the *trading* income in future years. (Note that losses may be treated differently for income tax — see CHAPTER 25 — and different rules also apply for Class 4 national insurance contributions — see 25.14.)

Notification of changes in income

2.29   You are not *required* to notify changes in income levels during the year, and if you do not, your entitlement will be revised at the end of the year using actual income if it is lower *or* actual income minus £2,500 if it is higher by more than £2,500. Any underpaid benefit will then be paid to you. Overpayments will normally be recovered from future benefits, or if that is not possible, by PAYE coding adjustments or by collecting the payment from you directly (see the Revenue's Code of Practice booklet COP 26). You may think it is preferable to notify changes in income levels when they occur, so that the credits may be adjusted to the correct levels and overpayments and underpayments will be avoided.

For self-employed people, the current income will not be known early enough to decide whether credits will be available, and as indicated in 2.27, awards are not backdated for more than three months. The self-employed should therefore make claims at the appropriate time, even though their previous year's income would not give them any entitlement. The Revenue will then issue a nil award, but this can then be adjusted appropriately when the actual income is known. A protective claim might indeed be appropriate for everyone, because no one knows how their circumstances may change. Whether the system would cope with the applications is another matter!

Calculation of entitlement

2.30   The calculation of the amount of tax credit available is relatively straightforward where the claimant's maximum entitlement remains unchanged throughout the tax year. Where entitlement starts part way through the year, or ends part way through the year, or circumstances change during the year, the year will be split into the appropriate number of 'relevant periods', with the maximum available credits for each period being calculated according to the daily amounts for the credits available in the period multiplied by the number of days in each period. Income, on the other hand, is not looked at according to the amounts arising in the relevant periods. It is calculated over the whole year and then apportioned on a time basis to each of the relevant periods. The relevant income thresholds for withdrawing credits are similarly reduced according to the days in each relevant period. The credits due for each period are then added together to give the total credit award for the year. For simplicity, annual figures are used in the rest of this section.

Changes in circumstances, interest and penalties

2.31   The following changes in circumstances *must* be notified within three months:

- A claimant no longer counts as a single claimant, or is no longer part of a claimant couple.

- One of a claimant couple goes abroad either permanently or for more than a specified period.

- Child care payments either cease or decrease by £10 or more a week for more than 4 consecutive weeks.

A penalty of up to £300 may be imposed for failure to notify within the time limit.

Other changes in circumstances need not be notified immediately, but if they increase the tax credits payable the increase will not be backdated for more than three months and if they decrease the credits they take effect from the date of the change. Examples of other changes would be changes in the number of children the claimant is responsible for, a child starting or ceasing full-time education, and changes in employment, including changes in hours of work that affect the amount of credit.

A penalty of up to £300 may also be imposed for failing to provide information or evidence relating to a claim, including failing to send in the year-end renewal notice. If the failure continues, a further penalty of up to £60 a day may be charged.

A penalty of up to £3,000 may be charged for fraudulent or negligent claims. An employer may be charged a similar penalty for fraudulently or negligently failing to pay an employee the correct amount, or refusing to pay tax credits.

Interest is chargeable on any unpaid penalties and also on any tax credit overpaid through the claimant's fraud or neglect.

Working tax credit

2.32   Working tax credit (WTC) is available to employees and the self-employed who usually do 16 hours or more paid work a week (the work being expected to last for at least four weeks), and who are aged 16 or over and are either responsible for one or more children or are disabled, or are aged 25 or over and usually work at least 30 hours a week, or are aged 50 or over and have recently been receiving a specified benefit. If both of a couple satisfy the conditions, there is only one credit and they must decide which of them will receive it. Where appropriate, WTC includes an amount for childcare.

WTC is calculated by adding together the following amounts (from 6 April 2004):

	Maximum annual amount £
Basic element	1,570
Disability element*	2,100
Couple/lone parent addition§	1,545
Extra element for those working 30 or more hours a week	640
Extra element if claimant has a severe disability*	890
Extra element (payable for 12 months only) for those aged 50 or over who have recently received a specified benefit* —	
working 16–29 hours a week	1,075
working 30 or more hours a week	1,610

*   Two elements are payable if both claimant and partner satisfy conditions.

§   Not available in addition to 50 plus element unless claimant or partner is *either* working 30 hours or more a week *or* responsible for a child *or* entitled to disability element.

The WTC may be increased by a childcare element for working claimants who pay for childcare (subject to detailed conditions). The claimant must work at least 16 hours a week (or for joint claimants each must work 16 hours a week unless one is incapacitated). The childcare element amounts to 70% of eligible costs up to £135 per week for one child (maximum £94.50 per week), or up to £200 per week for two or more children (maximum £140 per week).

The childcare element is not available after 1 September following the child's 15th birthday (or 16th birthday if the child is blind or disabled).

The WTC is reduced by 37p for every £ of income above an annual income threshold (which is the same amount for both single and joint claimants) of £5,060. The non-childcare element of WTC is withdrawn before the childcare element. For those entitled to both WTC and child tax credit (CTC — see 2.33), the same income threshold of £5,060 applies to the child element of CTC, and WTC is withdrawn first.

WTC is paid to eligible employees through the payroll and to the self-employed directly by the Revenue (into a bank, building society or post office card account), except for the childcare element, which is paid direct to the main carer along with CTC.

Child tax credit

2.33   Child tax credit (CTC) replaces all the previous child elements within social security payments, except child benefit, which will continue to be paid to anyone with eligible children regardless of income. You qualify for CTC if you are responsible for at least one child under 16 or under 19 if still in full-time non-advanced education. For children not in full-time non-advanced education CTC ends on 1 September after the 16th birthday unless they have ceased full-time education and registered for work or training with the Careers Service, in which case CTC will continue for up to 20 weeks. CTC comprises a family element and a child element. The family element is paid to any family responsible for one or more children, and it is paid at a higher rate (the baby element) if there is a child under the age of one. The child element is payable for each qualifying child, higher rates applying for children with a disability (the disabled child element). If a child dies, the entitlement for that child ends eight weeks after death. CTC is payable direct to the main carer — usually the mother.

The maximum amounts of CTC from 6 April 2004 are as follows:

	Maximum annual amount £
Family element (one only):	
*Either*Standard amount	545
*Or*Baby element for those with child under 1	1,090
Child element (per child):	

		Maximum annual amount £
Either	Standard amount	1,625
Or	Amount for disabled child	3,840
Or	Amount for severely disabled child	4,730

CTC is withdrawn progressively from those on higher incomes. There is a lower income threshold applicable only to the child element of CTC. As indicated in 2.32, for those entitled to both WTC and CTC, the annual income threshold for both WTC and the child element of CTC is £5,060, and WTC is withdrawn first. For those not entitled to WTC the child element annual income threshold from 6 April 2004 is £13,480 (previously £13,230). The child element of CTC is withdrawn at the rate of 37p for each £1 of excess income over the threshold. Once the child element of CTC has been fully withdrawn, there is no further withdrawal of CTC unless annual income exceeds a higher threshold of £50,000. The rate of withdrawal on income in excess of that amount is £1 for each £15 of excess income. This means that the upper cut-off point for CTC is income of around £58,000, or around £66,000 if the baby rate applies. But if CTC and/or WTC amounts to £26 or less no award is made. If the amount due exceeds £26 but is less than £2 a week it is paid in a lump sum.

Conclusion

2.34   The above summary only scratches the surface of the tax credits provisions, which represent a minefield for everyone involved — taxpayers, non-taxpayers and tax and social security advisers. Example 6 gives a very basic illustration of some of the principles. Example 7 illustrates the possible combined tax/tax credit effect of making payments, such as pension contributions or gift aid payments, that reduce taxable income.

Example 6

Married couple are both full-time employees and have two children aged 2 and 4. They make childcare payments of £240 a week. Their final entitlement to tax credits for 2004/05 will be as follows, given joint income (after excluding £300 of their investment income) at the following levels:

(a) £10,000   (b) £18,000   (c) £40,000   (d) £56,000

Tax credits maximum amount (worked on annual basis for simplicity):

	£
WTC:	
Basic	1,570
Couple addition	1,545
30 hour element	640
	3,755
Childcare element (max. 70% × £200 × 52)	7,280
	11,035
CTC:	
Child element (2 × 1,625)	3,250
	14,285
Family element	545
	14,830

	(a)	(b)	(c)	(d)
	£	£	£	£
Maximum credits excluding CTC family element	14,285	14,285	14,285	14,285
Restrict according to income:				
(10,000 − 5,060 =) 4,940 × 37%	(1,828)			
(18,000 − 5,060 =) 12,940 × 37%		(4,788)		
(40,000 − 5,060 =) 34,940 × 37%			(12,928)	
(43,668* − 5,060 =) 38,608 × 37%				(14,285)
	12,457	9,497	1,357	–
CTC family element	545	545	545	545
Restrict by $\frac{1}{15}$ × (56,000 − 50,000)				(400)
Tax credits payable	13,002	10,042	1,902	145
Payable by employer (3,755 − 1,828)	1,927	–	–	–
Payable to main carer	11,075	10,042	1,902	145

*   Income level at which all but family element of CTC is withdrawn

Notes

(i)   Credits would initially have been based on 2003/04 income, and adjusted to actual income after the year-end.

(ii)   If circumstances had changed in year, say because one partner became unemployed, the year would be split into separate 'relevant periods' and credits calculated separately according to the days in each period, with income for the year being split pro-rata between the separate periods.

Example 7

The couple in part (c) of Example 6, who had income of £40,000 in 2004/05, lost £12,928 of the maximum tax credits available, i.e. 37% of (£40,000-£5,060). If say the husband had paid a personal pension premium in the year of £2,000 gross, the tax credit entitlement would have increased by 37% of £2,000, i.e. £740. The payment would also reduce his tax bill by 40% (or possibly more depending on the mix of his income — see Examples 2 and 3), so that the net of tax cost of the pension premium would be around £660.

3
Corporation tax: general principles

Basis of charge (TA 1988, s 6)

3.1   Corporation tax is charged on the profits of companies and of unincorporated bodies that are not partnerships, for example members' clubs (see 3.26). The term profits includes all sources of income (other than dividends from UK companies) and also capital gains.

Corporation tax is charged on the world profits of UK-resident companies. Non-resident companies carrying on a trade in the UK through a 'permanent establishment', such as a branch or agency, are charged on the income arising from the permanent establishment and on capital gains on the disposal of assets in the UK used for the purposes of the trade or otherwise for the permanent establishment. Double taxation relief is available where profits are taxed twice. The overseas aspect is dealt with in CHAPTER 41.

From 8 October 2004, under the European Company Statute (an EU regulation), a new form of company known as a 'European Company' (Societas Europaea or SE) may be formed by businesses operating in more than one member state. This is intended to make it easier for businesses to carry out cross-border activities within the EU. Such companies will be subject to the tax law of their country of residence. Amendments to UK tax legislation will be introduced in the 2005 Finance Bill, although SEs will be able to operate under the existing rules until then.

Shipping companies may make an election to calculate their profits under a 'tonnage tax' regime rather than by reference to actual business results. Tonnage tax is not dealt with in this book.

Notification of liability (FA 2004, s 55)

3.2   For accounting periods starting on or after 22 July 2004, a company must give written notice to the Revenue when it comes within the charge to corporation tax. The notice must be given not later than three months after the beginning of the accounting period. Similar notice must be given of the beginning of any accounting period that does not immediately follow the end of a previous accounting period. A penalty may be imposed if the notice is not given as required, unless the company had a reasonable excuse for not doing so and complied without reasonable delay after the excuse ceased.

Self-assessment (TMA 1970, ss 59D, 59E, 87A, 91; FA 1998, s 117 and Sch 18)

3.3   Companies are required to self-assess their corporation tax and pay the amount due within nine months and one day after the end of the accounting period, except for certain large companies who are required to pay their tax by instalments (see 3.18). They must file a statutory return with supporting accounts and computations within twelve months after the end of the accounting period. Automatic penalties apply for late returns.

The provisions are broadly the same as those that apply for income tax self-assessment, except that companies do not have the option of asking the Revenue to work out the tax (see 9.31). The detailed provisions on returns, assessments and penalties are in CHAPTER 9. The payment provisions are dealt with at 3.18 and the provisions for charging interest on underpaid tax and adding interest to overpayments at 3.19.

Calculation of profits (TMA 1970, s 90; TA 1988, ss 9, 95, 208, 401, 826; TCGA 1992, s 8)

3.4   A company's taxable income is computed broadly using income tax rules (see CHAPTER 20), but different rules apply to interest paid and received by companies (see 3.6), profits and losses on derivative contracts (see 3.7), and profits and losses on intangible assets (see 20.21). Interest on underpaid corporation tax is allowable as a deduction and interest on overpaid corporation tax is taxable, and is taken into account under the 'loan relationships' rules (which are dealt with at 3.6).

Dividends paid by a UK resident company do not reduce the company's taxable profits. When such dividends are *received* by a company they are not charged to corporation tax (unless the company is a share dealer — see next paragraph). The tax treatment of dividends paid and received is dealt with at 3.14. Special rules apply to certain dividends from authorised unit trusts (see 38.15).

Dividends received by share dealers and others who hold shares as trading stock (such as banks etc.) are taxed as trading income. The chargeable amount does not include the tax credits.

In computing the company's trading profits, capital allowances are deducted as trading expenses, and balancing charges treated as trading income (see CHAPTER 22). Expenditure of a revenue nature (see 20.4) incurred not more than seven years before the trade started is treated as incurred on the first day of trading (see 21.8).

A company's chargeable gains are normally computed using capital gains tax principles, but the gains are charged to corporation tax and there is no annual exemption (see CHAPTER 4). Furthermore, profits and losses on a company's capital transactions relating to loans, certain derivative contracts and foreign exchange are brought into account in calculating income rather than chargeable gains (see 3.6 and 3.7). And from 1 April 2002 profits and losses on intangible assets created or acquired on or after that date, such as goodwill and intellectual property, are also brought into account in calculating income (see 20.21). A special 'substantial shareholdings exemption' applies where trading companies dispose of holdings of 10% or more in other trading companies (see 3.25).

From 6 April 1998 significant changes were made to capital gains tax, notably the introduction of taper relief, the freezing of indexation allowance and the abolition of share pooling. None of these changes apply to companies.

Charges on income (TA 1988, ss 338–338B, 339, 349–349D, 350, 587B; FA 2002, s 97)

3.5   Having arrived at the company's total profits (both income and capital), *charges on income* are deducted to arrive at the profits chargeable to corporation tax. Many of the items which used to be treated as charges on income are now brought into account under other headings, notably interest, which is dealt with under the loan relationships rules (see 3.6) and patent royalties, which are dealt with under the rules for intangible assets from 1 April 2002 (see 20.21). The main items that continue to be treated as charges and deducted from *total* profits are 'gift aid' cash donations to charity and certain gifts in kind to charity (see CHAPTER 43). The only other items within the definition of charges from 1 April 2002 are certain annuities or annual payments, but these will rarely occur. Income tax at the basic rate is deducted from some charges (see 3.17). The amount deducted from profits is the full amount of the charges paid in the accounting period (that is, before any income tax deduction at source, which will have been accounted for to the Revenue).

If the charges exceed profits, the excess may be carried forward as a trading loss to set against later profits from the same trade provided that the charges are wholly and exclusively for the purposes of the trade. No carry-forward is available for non-trade charges which exceed profits, such as charitable donations. The treatment of excess charges is dealt with in CHAPTER 26 on company losses.

Treatment of interest paid and received and profits and losses on loans (TA 1998, ss 349–349D; FA 1996, ss 80–105 and Schs 8–11, 15; FA 2004, ss 48, 52 and Schs 8 and 10)

3.6   Special rules apply to a company's 'loan relationships', which covers all loans made both by and to the company, excluding trading transactions for goods and services. Loans to the company include bank overdrafts and loans by the company include holdings of gilt-edged securities and corporate bonds. Gains and losses on building society permanent interest-bearing shares (PIBS, dealt with in 37.4) are included within the loan relationships rules. Subject to special provisions concerning particular types of security, all UK and foreign interest paid and received by companies is brought into account in calculating profits, normally on an accruals basis (i.e. taking into account amounts in arrear and advance). The accrued income scheme (see 36.18) does not apply to companies. As indicated at 3.4, interest on underpaid and overpaid corporation tax is taken into account in calculating profits, and it is treated as non-trading interest. Changes were made to the loan relationships provisions by FA 2002. Some aspects of the revised legislation were found to be defective and were corrected in FA 2003. Further amendments have been made in FA 2004.

Profits or losses made on loans (whether as borrower or lender) are treated as income or expenses, either on an accruals basis or, in very limited circumstances, on a 'mark to market' basis, which means that the profit or loss is worked out year by year according to market value. Any costs incurred are also taken into account. For accounting periods beginning on or after 1 January 2005, the legislation no longer prescribes these different accounting methods and requires instead that 'generally accepted accounting practice' is followed (see 20.2). Foreign exchange differences on loan relationships and other monetary debts are dealt with under the loan relationships rules. For brief notes on foreign exchange aspects see 41.38.

Amounts that relate to the trade are taken into account in arriving at the Schedule D, Case I trading profit or loss. (Interest receivable and profits/ losses on loans will not normally relate to the trade, except for financial businesses.) As far as non-trading profits, losses, interest paid and interest received are concerned, they are all aggregated and merged with any financial instruments non-trading debits and credits (see 3.8). An overall profit is chargeable under Schedule D, Case III. If there is an overall loss (a 'non-trading deficit'), relief is available similar to that available for trading losses. For the treatment of company losses in relation to money borrowed or lent, see CHAPTER 26.

Income tax is no longer deducted from most interest paid and received by companies. Where tax is deducted, it is at the lower rate of 20% (see 3.19).

Derivative contracts (previously referred to as financial instruments) (FA 2002, s 83 and Schs 26–28; FA 2003, s 177; FA 2004, s 49 and Sch 9)

3.7   There are separate provisions to deal with profits and losses on 'derivative contracts' (i.e. options and futures). This area is extremely complex and highly technical. It covers a wide range of instruments used by companies for managing interest rate and currency risk. The rules are closely aligned with the loan relationships rules dealt with in 3.6. Foreign exchange gains and losses on currency contracts are included within the provisions. Profits are charged (and losses allowed) in calculating income, being brought into account either as trading debits and credits or non-trading debits and credits as the case may be. Non-trading debits and credits are brought into account as if they related to loan relationships of the company (see 3.6). They are accordingly treated as part of an overall non-trading deficit on loan relationships where appropriate (see 26.5). There are detailed anti-avoidance provisions.

Periods of account and chargeable accounting periods (TA 1988, s 12; FA 2003, s 196 and Sch 41)

3.8   A company's taxable profits are computed for a chargeable accounting period, which normally means the period for which the company's accounts are made up, no matter how short it is. If, however, a company makes up an account for a period greater than twelve months, it is split into one or more chargeable accounting periods of twelve months plus a chargeable accounting period covering the remainder of the period of account.

In arriving at the split of profits for an account exceeding twelve months, the trading profit is usually split on a time basis. Capital allowances (see CHAPTER 22) are calculated for each chargeable accounting period, so that if for example an account was made up for the fifteen months from 1 July 2003 to 30 September 2004 and plant was bought in August 2004, the first allowance for the new plant would be given against the profit of the three months to 30 September 2004.

Interest received or paid that relates to the trade is taken into account in arriving at the trading profit of the period of account, and is normally time apportioned in the same way as the trading profit. Non-trading interest is also time apportioned if dealt with on an accruals basis. Where the 'mark to market' basis is appropriate (see 3.6), the relevant amounts to be included need to be established for each chargeable accounting period. Rental income is calculated in the same way as trading profits, so that it is split on a time basis (see CHAPTER 32 and also CHAPTER 41 for overseas aspects of rental income). If there are any other sources of income, such as isolated profits chargeable under Schedule D, Case VI, they are allocated to the chargeable accounting period in which they arise. Chargeable gains are similarly allocated to the chargeable accounting period in which the disposal occurs, and charges on income (see 3.5) to the chargeable accounting period in which they are paid.

If a company ceases to trade, the date of cessation marks the end of a chargeable accounting period even if the period of account continues to the normal accounting date. The commencement of winding-up also marks the end of a chargeable accounting period, accounting periods then running for successive periods of twelve months until the winding-up is completed. From 15 September 2003, these rules are varied in some circumstances for companies in administration. If a company enters administration, an accounting period will end immediately before that date. An accounting period will also end when the period of administration ends. If immediately before a company enters administration it is in the course of being wound up, the normal rule about accounting periods running for successive twelve-month periods during the winding up will not apply. See 3.20.

Losses (TA 1988, ss 393, 393A, 396; FA 1996, s 83 and Sch 8)

3.9   When a company incurs a trading loss, it may set the loss against any other profits of the same accounting period, both income and capital, and then, if it wishes, carry any balance back against the total profits of the previous twelve months so long as the trade was carried on in that year. Where the loss occurs in the last twelve months of trading, the carry-back period is extended to three years. The loss set-off is proportionately restricted to exclude profits of an accounting period falling partly outside the one year or three year carry-back period. For a continuing trade, any balance of loss remaining (or the whole loss if the company does not wish to claim the current set-off and carry-back) is carried forward to set against later profits of that trade. These loss reliefs are not available for trades carried on *wholly* abroad.

Where a loss arises under Schedule D, Case III (a non-trading deficit — see 3.6), the relief available is similar to that for trading losses.

Capital losses are set against capital gains of the same chargeable accounting period, any excess being carried forward to set against future gains. Capital losses cannot be carried back.

For detailed notes on trading losses and Schedule D, Case III deficits, including transferring loss reliefs within groups, see CHAPTER 26.

The treatment of losses on UK rented property is dealt with in CHAPTER 32. For foreign property letting businesses and losses on trades carried on wholly abroad see CHAPTER 41. Capital losses are dealt with in CHAPTER 4 and in context in other chapters.

Rate of tax (TA 1988, s 8; FA 2003, s 133; FA 2004, s 25)

3.10   Corporation tax rates are fixed for financial years ending 31 March. Financial years are identified by the calendar year in which they commence, so the financial year 2004 is the year to 31 March 2005. Since 1 April 1999 the rate has been 30% and that rate will also apply for the financial year 2005. (The main rate is fixed for the next following financial year because certain large companies have to pay corporation tax by instalments in advance — see 3.18.) A lower starting rate or small companies' rate applies where profits are below stipulated thresholds (see 3.11). For details of the rates in recent years, see under 'Corporation tax rates' in the TABLE OF RATES AND ALLOW-ANCES.

Where the tax rate changes during a company's chargeable accounting period, the total profits are apportioned on a time basis (in days) and charged at the respective rates in calculating the corporation tax payable for the period.

Small companies' rate (TA 1988, ss 13, 13ZA; FA 2004, s 26)

3.11   Where a company's profits are below a stipulated amount, but are above the upper limit for the starting rate (see 3.12), tax is charged at the small companies' rate, except for close investment-holding companies, whose profits are always charged at the full rate (see 3.21). The small companies' rate is 19% for the financial years 2002, 2003 and 2004. There is a special definition of profits for the small companies' rate. It includes not only the profits chargeable to corporation tax (which are called the 'basic profits') but also dividends received from other UK companies plus their related tax credits (the dividends plus the credits being called 'franked investment income'). The tax credit is at the rate of 1/9th of the cash dividend, so that a cash dividend of £900 carries a tax credit of £100 and thus represents franked investment income of £1,000. The inclusion of franked investment income in the calculations means that it is not possible for a company with a large amount of income in that form to obtain the benefit of the small companies' rate on only a small amount of profits chargeable to corporation tax.

Where the profits as defined lie between the stipulated level for small companies' rate and an upper maximum, marginal relief is available. The marginal relief is given by calculating tax on the basic profits at the full corporation tax rate and reducing it by an amount arrived at by the following formula:

$$(M–P) \times \tfrac{I}{P} \times F$$

where M = Upper maximum
        P = Profits as defined for small companies' rate purposes, i.e. income and gains chargeable to corporation tax plus franked investment income
        I = Basic profits, i.e. income and gains chargeable to corporation tax
        F = Small companies' marginal relief fraction

The current upper and lower limits are £1,500,000 and £300,000 and the marginal relief fraction is $^{11}\!/_{400}$ for the years to 31 March 2003, 2004 and 2005 (see under 'Corporation tax rates' in the TABLE OF RATES AND ALLOWANCES).

The marginal relief ensures that the corporation tax rate on the profits is gradually increased to the full level, but the effect is that profits lying between the lower and upper limits suffer a tax rate in excess of the full rate. This marginal rate is 32.75% for the years to 31 March 2003, 2004 and 2005. The marginal rate applies where there is no franked investment income; for companies with franked investment income the marginal rate is less. See Example 1.

Example 1

Year to 31 March 2005

Company with no franked investment income has the following profits chargeable to corporation tax:

		£
(i) £300,000 @ 19%		57,000
or		
(ii) £310,000 @ 30%	93,000	
Marginal relief		
$(1,500,000 - 310,000) \times \dfrac{310,000}{310,000} \times \dfrac{11}{400}$		
	32,725	60,275
Additional corporation tax on extra £10,000 profits (32.75%)		£3,275

To the extent that a company is able to reduce its profits within the marginal tranche, it can thus save tax at the marginal rate.

The lower and upper limits are annual limits and they are scaled down proportionately if an accounting period is less than twelve months. They are also scaled down where for any part of a chargeable accounting period a company has associated companies. Associated companies include both companies that are associated through being members of the same group and companies controlled by the same persons. If, for example, the same persons control five companies, the present limits for each company are £60,000 and £300,000. If four have profits of £70,000 and one £20,000 the small companies' rate will only apply to the last one, and the others will have profits subject to the marginal relief. On the other hand if, say, there were two companies associated with each other and one's profits were £1,800,000 and the other's £150,000, the company with £150,000 profits would qualify for small companies' rate even though the combined profits greatly exceeded the upper maximum.

If a company's accounting period does not end on 31 March and there is a change either in the marginal relief fraction or in the marginal relief limits or both, the profit figures have to be apportioned to apply the respective figures for the different financial years.

The small companies' rate or marginal relief must be specifically claimed in the company's return and, except for unincorporated associations such as members' clubs, the return should indicate how many associated companies there are. If there are none, this should be stated.

Starting rate (TA 1988, s 13AA; FA 2004, s 27)

3.12   Since 1 April 2000 a starting rate of corporation tax has applied following a claim by companies with profits of £10,000 or less. The rate was fixed at 10% for the years to 31 March 2001 and 2002 but has been reduced to nil for the years to 31 March 2003, 2004 and 2005. Marginal relief applies to companies with profits between £10,000 and £50,000. The starting rate and marginal relief operate in the same way, and are subject to the same restrictions, as for small companies' rate, and the marginal relief formula is the same. For the years to 31 March 2003, 2004 and 2005, the marginal rate on profits lying between £10,000 and £50,000 is 23.75% and the starting rate marginal relief fraction is $^{19}/_{400}$.

Example 2

Year to 31 March 2005

Company with no franked investment income has the following profits chargeable to corporation tax (no dividends having been paid in the year):

		£
(i) £10,000 @ nil		—
or		
(ii) £11,000 @ 19%	2,090.00	
Marginal relief		

$$(50,000 - 11,000) \times \frac{11,000}{11,000} \times \frac{19}{400}$$

	1,852.50	237.50
Corporation tax on extra £1,000 profits (23.75%)		£237.50

Non-corporate distribution rate (TA 1988, s 13AB and Sch A2; FA 2004, s 28 and Sch 3)

3.13   A new 'non-corporate distribution rate' (NCD rate) (19% for the financial year 2004) has been introduced for dividends paid on or after 1 April 2004 to shareholders who are not companies. The aim is to prevent people incorporating purely to take advantage of the nil starting rate on profits of £10,000. Where accounting periods straddle 1 April 2004, the parts before and after are treated as separate accounting periods. The NCD rate applies where dividends are paid to individuals, partners or trustees and the company's underlying corporation tax rate is less than the NCD rate. The part of the profits applicable to an NCD is charged at the NCD rate and the remainder at the underlying rate.

The underlying corporation tax rate is the rate that would otherwise apply on the profits chargeable to corporation tax, taking into account small companies' or starting rate marginal reliefs, and expressed as a percentage. (The reference in the legislation to small companies' rate marginal relief is presently irrelevant, since the tax rate on profits above the starting rate marginal relief limit of £50,000 is 19%, i.e. the same as the NCD rate. The NCD rate is, however, not linked to the small companies' rate, so presumably at some time the two rates may not be the same.)

Example 3

The underlying corporation tax rate of the company in Example 2 part (ii) above is:

$$\frac{237.50}{11,000} \times 100 = 2.159\%$$

If the company paid a dividend of £10,000 during the year to, say, its husband and wife shareholders, the corporation tax payable would be:

£10,000 @ NCD rate of 19%	1,900.00
£1,000 @ 2.159%	21.59
	£1,921.59

compared with corporation tax of £237.50 if no dividend is paid.

If the total dividends paid exceed the profits chargeable to corporation tax, the part of the profits charged at the NCD rate is the percentage of NCDs out of the total dividends paid. If the *NCDs* exceed the profits chargeable to corporation tax, the excess is referred to as excess NCDs. If a company with excess NCDs is part of a group, the excess must be allocated to other group companies that have profits in the corresponding accounting period, those companies then being treated as having made equivalent NCDs in the period. Any excess NCDs not allocated to another company are carried forward and treated as NCDs made in the next accounting period.

Dividends and other distributions (TA 1988, ss 14, 20, 231; FA 1998, ss 31, 32)

3.14   From 1973 to 5 April 1999, companies had to pay some of their corporation tax in advance (ACT) when they paid dividends. This changed from 6 April 1999, from which date ACT was abolished. To offset the loss to the Exchequer, the self-assessment rules require companies with profits above the upper limit for small companies' rate to pay their corporation tax by quarterly instalments (see 3.18). Many companies were not able to offset all the ACT they had paid against their tax bills, giving rise to surplus (unrelieved) ACT at 5 April 1999. They still have the right to offset surplus ACT even though ACT has been abolished, but only under the provisions of a shadow ACT system, which will still leave many companies with large unrecovered amounts. The detailed provisions of the shadow ACT system are dealt with in earlier editions of this book.

Treatment of dividends from 6 April 1999

3.15   From 6 April 1999, the tax credit on dividends was reduced from 1/4 to 1/9 (representing 10% of the tax-credit inclusive amount) and the tax credit is not repayable to *any* taxpayer, either individuals, trusts or companies (although special provisions enabled credits to be claimed up to 5 April 2004 on shares in Personal Equity Plans (PEPs) and Individual Savings Accounts (ISAs) — see 38.29 and 36.22 respectively). From the same date ACT was abolished as indicated above.

Qualifying and non-qualifying distributions (TA 1988, ss 14, 209–211, 233, 234)

3.16   The legislation distinguishes between 'qualifying distributions' and 'non-qualifying distributions'. Non-qualifying distributions are broadly those that confer a future rather than a current claim on the company's assets, such as a bonus issue of redeemable shares. The company has no tax liability on such a distribution, but the shareholder is liable where appropriate to the excess of the Schedule F upper rate of 32½% over the Schedule F ordinary rate of 10%. The company is required to notify the Revenue within fourteen days after the end of the quarter in which the non-qualifying distribution is made.

When the shares are redeemed, the redemption is a qualifying distribution, but any tax paid by the shareholder on the non-qualifying distribution may be set against any Schedule F upper rate tax due from him on the later qualifying distribution.

Where a company supplies goods or services to a shareholder for more than cost but at a price concession, this is not treated as a distribution because there is no cost to the company, as distinct from a reduction in profit margins, so that no part of the company profits has been distributed.

Deduction of income tax from charges on income, patent royalties and interest, and accounting for the tax deducted (TA 1988, ss 349–349D, 350 and Sch 16; FA 2004, ss 97–106)

3.17   As indicated in 3.5, charges on income comprise certain charitable donations and gifts and (rarely) certain annuities and annual payments.

Companies used to deduct and account for income tax on a wide variety of payments. Tax is no longer deducted from charitable donations and gifts, and companies (and local authorities) do not have to deduct tax from interest or patent royalties if they reasonably believe that the recipient is a company liable to corporation tax on the amount received, or a local authority, or a body exempt from tax, such as a charity, pension fund or an ISA, TESSA or PEP fund manager.

From 1 January 2004 the above provisions enabling payments to be made gross also apply (subject to various conditions) to payments of interest and royalties to companies of another EU state, or a permanent establishment in an EU state of such a company. (If it turns out that tax should have been deducted, the payer is liable to pay the tax plus interest, but no penalty will be charged unless it should have been clear to the payer that it should have deducted tax.) Tax must still be deducted from payments of interest and patent royalties by companies and local authorities that do not come within the above provisions, unless covered by a specific exception.

As far as payments to individuals are concerned, tax is not deducted from interest on 'quoted Eurobonds', which are interest-bearing securities issued by a company (or unincorporated association such as a building society) and listed on a recognised stock exchange. Nor is tax deducted from bank and building society interest paid to those who have certified that they are non-taxpayers (see 37.2). Tax at 20% is deducted from other interest paid to individuals, and tax at 22% is deducted from patent royalty payments to individuals and from retirement annuity payments under pre-1 July 1988 pension contracts. Where companies are required to deduct income tax from payments made, they have to account to the Revenue for the tax deducted.

Similarly, where a company *receives* patent royalties from an individual, they will be received net of 22% tax. Interest received from individuals will usually be received gross.

Any income tax deducted from a company's income may be retained out of income tax to be accounted for on the company's payments if any, as indicated below. Where income tax suffered on a company's income is not recovered in this way, it will be set against the company's corporation tax liability, or if that is insufficient it will be repaid.

Tax payable is accounted for at the appropriate rate of either 20% or 22% on form CT 61. Returns are made to 31 March, 30 June, 30 September and 31 December, the tax being due within fourteen days after the quarter ends. Where a company's accounting year does not end on one of the four calendar quarter days the company has five return periods, the first running from the first day of the account to the next calendar quarter day and the last ending at the end of the accounting period.

Date of payment of corporation tax (TMA 1970, ss 59D, 59DA and 59E, 98; SI 1998/3175)

3.18   Companies are required to self-assess their corporation tax, as indicated in 3.3. Companies with profits at or above the upper limit for small companies' relief, i.e. £1.5 million (reduced pro rata where there are associated companies and for accounting periods of less than 12 months — see 3.11

above), are required to pay their corporation tax by equal quarterly instalments (see below). Companies not required to pay by instalments are due to pay their corporation tax nine months and one day after the end of the accounting period. They must, however, account on a quarterly basis for any income tax they have deducted from charges on income and interest payments as indicated in 3.17. See Example 4.

Example 4

A company pays interest to and receives interest from other companies and pays patent royalties to an individual. The company's results for the year to 31 March 2005 are:

		£
Trading profits, net of allowable expenses other than interest and patent royalties (see below)		311,000
Rental income, net of allowable expenses		14,000
Interest received:	June 2004	15,000
	December 2004	15,000
Chargeable gains		104,000
Patent royalties paid (gross	May 2004	20,000
amount):	November 2004	28,000
Loan interest relating to the trade, paid February 2005		10,000

Patent royalties paid exceed patent royalties payable by £2,000.

Interest received and interest receivable are the same amounts. The interest payable for the year exceeds the interest paid during the year by £3,000.

The company paid a dividend of £100,000 in December 2004. There were no amounts brought forward from earlier years.

Corporation tax computation	£
Trading profits net of £13,000 interest and £46,000 patent royalties payable	252,000
Interest received	30,000
Rental income	14,000
Chargeable gains	104,000
Profits chargeable to corporation tax	400,000

	£
Corporation tax on £400,000 @ 30%	120,000
Less marginal relief for small companies' rate (1,500,000 − 400,000) × $^{11}/_{400}$	30,250
Corporation tax payable	89,750

How tax accounted for

CT 61 return for quarter to 30 June 2004

Income tax deducted from patent royalties paid May 2004 20,000 @ 22%	4,400
Income tax payable by 14 July 2004	4,400

CT 61 return for quarter to 31 December 2004

Income tax deducted from patent royalties paid November 2004 28,000 @ 22%	6,160
Payable by 14 January 2005	6,160

Corporation tax payment

Corporation tax as shown above payable 1 January 2006	89,750

No tax was deducted from the interest paid to and received from other companies. There were no taxed payments or taxed income in the quarters to 30 September 2004 and 31 March 2005, so CT 61 returns were not required for those quarters. The payment of the dividend does not affect the computation.

At any time before the corporation tax liability is finally determined, companies may claim repayments if they consider they have overpaid tax, but interest will be charged from the normal due date on any tax finally found to be due (or allowed on overpayments) — see 3.19.

The instalment paying provisions for companies with profits above the small companies' rate upper limit affect only around 20,000 out of 700,000 corporation tax-paying companies. The detailed provisions are in regulations, and companies are liable to penalties if they fail to provide, or provide incorrect, information, records, etc. The Revenue have issued guidance on estimating instalment payments and on penalties — see their August 2002 Tax Bulletin.

The first instalment is due fourteen days after the end of the sixth month of the accounting period and the remaining three instalments at quarterly intervals thereafter. The instalments are based on the company's estimated corporation tax liability for the accounting period (including, where appropriate, amounts payable under the provisions relating to loans to directors (see 12.12) and under the controlled foreign companies rules (see 45.14)). Companies can recover quarterly payments if they decide they should not have been paid. The instalment payment system has been phased in over a four year period which started with the accounting period ending between 1 July 1999 to 30 June 2000 as follows:

	Payable by equal instalments	*Payable 9 months and 1 day after end of accounting period*
Year 1	60%	40%
Year 2	72%	28%
Year 3	88%	12%
Year 4	100%	—

In year 1, companies also had to pay the corporation tax due for the previous year.

If a company's profits are below the small companies' rate upper limit in one year, they will not have to make quarterly payments in the following year if their profits in that year do not exceed £10 million (reduced pro rata where there are associated companies). A company with profits chargeable to corporation tax of less than £10,000 is not required to make quarterly payments, even though its profits exceed the marginal relief limits because of the number of its associated companies or because of its dividend income.

Groups of companies may pay their corporation tax on a group-wide basis, without needing to allocate instalments paid to particular companies until the respective liabilities are formalised.

Interest on overdue and overpaid tax (TMA 1970, ss 87A, 90; TA 1988, ss 826, 826A; FA 1989, s 178; SI 1989/1297)

3.19   Interest is charged on overdue corporation tax and allowed on overpaid corporation tax. The latest rates of interest are shown in the TABLES OF RATES AND ALLOWANCES. The interest is brought into account as non-trading interest under the 'loan relationships' provisions (see 3.6) in computing profits chargeable to corporation tax, subject to what is said at 3.20 re companies in liquidation or administration.

The fact that interest is taken into account in calculating profits is reflected in the formula for determining interest rates. For companies required to make quarterly payments, however, a different formula is used in order to reduce the differential between the two rates during the period from the first instalment date (14 days after the end of the sixth month of the accounting period) to the date nine months and one day after the end of the accounting period, after which the normal rates apply. This is intended to avoid penalising companies who make mistakes in their estimates. For companies not required to pay tax by instalments, interest on overdue tax runs from the normal due date of nine months and one day after the end of the accounting period, and interest on overpaid tax runs from the payment date. If, however, tax is paid early, repayment interest is not payable from any earlier date than the first instalment date for instalment paying companies, the interest rate from that date to the normal nine months due date being the same as for instalment paying companies.

If a company makes quarterly payments in the mistaken belief that its profits will exceed the upper small companies' rate limit, it will be entitled to interest on the overpayment from the payment date. Where a company is entitled to a refund of income tax suffered on its taxed income (see 3.17), interest will be paid on the refund from the day after the end of the accounting period.

A company that pays its instalments late may be liable to a penalty not exceeding twice the amount of interest payable, but this penalty is unlikely to be imposed other than in exceptional circumstances.

If a company is late paying the income tax due under the CT 61 quarterly accounting procedure (see 3.17), interest is charged from the due date for the quarterly return until the payment date. If any of the tax becomes repayable in a subsequent return period, some of the interest already charged is repaid, but only from the date the later return is due or, if earlier, from the date the later return is actually filed.

Company liquidations and companies in administration (TA 1988, ss 12, 342, 342A)

3.20   A company liquidation is usually preceded by a cessation of trade. The cessation of trade triggers the end of a chargeable accounting period, and a chargeable accounting period also ends at the commencement of winding-up (and at twelve-monthly intervals until the winding-up is completed, subject to what is said below about companies in administration). Self-assessment returns must be completed accordingly. To help liquidators who want to finalise matters before formal completion of the winding-up, the Revenue will accept an informal return, such as a letter, and will also, where appropriate, provide a clearance that they will not open an enquiry into the return. See also tax point at 28.12 re Revenue concession C16 on the use of the 'defunct company' procedure as an alternative to a formal liquidation.

From 15 September 2003, the above rules are varied if a company goes into administration. The changes result from recent changes to the insolvency procedures. Where a company goes into administration under the new rules, an accounting period will end immediately before the commencement of the administration and also at the date the company comes out of administration. Unlike the rule for companies in liquidation (see above), there is no requirement for accounting periods to run for twelve months during the administration period and the normal accounting date may be retained. Under the new insolvency procedures, certain creditors or the liquidator of a company that is in the process of winding-up may apply to the court for an administration order instead. If the order is granted the winding-up order will be discharged and the rule that accounting periods must end at twelve-monthly intervals until the winding-up is completed will cease to apply.

Under self-assessment, interest on underpaid and overpaid tax is taken into account in calculating taxable profits (see 3.19). If interest on overpaid tax is received or receivable by a company in liquidation in its final accounting period, however, the interest will not be included in taxable profits if it does not exceed £2,000. The same provisions will apply in respect of the final accounting period where a company is in administration if the company moves from administration to dissolution.

Problems can arise when a company that has been making trading losses realises chargeable gains on the sale of its assets, because if the gains are realised after the trade ceases there will be no current trading losses to offset them, but it is not possible to part with the assets until the trade has ceased. This problem can be avoided if an unconditional contract for sale of the assets takes place before ceasing to trade, with completion taking place subsequently. The contract date is the relevant disposal date for capital gains purposes, and any trading losses occurring in the accounting period in which the trade ceases will then be available to reduce the gains. The gains cannot, however, be reduced by trading losses brought forward (see CHAPTER 26 for the detailed provisions on company losses).

The liquidation of a trading company may also affect the capital gains tax taper relief to which individuals are entitled on their shareholdings in the company. Once a trade ceases, holdings that qualified as business assets may no longer do so, causing a proportionate part of the gain to qualify only for the non-business assets rates of relief (see 4.16 to 4.23).

Close companies (TA 1988, ss 13A, 414–422)

3.21   A close company is a company under the control of five or fewer participators (which broadly means shareholders, although it is defined more widely), or under the control of its directors. In considering what rights an individual has in a company, the rights of his 'associates' are included, which covers close family, business partners and the trustees of any family settlements.

As well as being subject to the normal corporation tax rules, close companies are subject to additional requirements.

Benefits in kind to participators are treated as distributions (except where already treated as earnings under the benefits rules, see CHAPTER 10) and loans to participators attract a tax liability. These provisions are dealt with in CHAPTER 12.

If the company is a 'close investment-holding company', tax is charged at the full rate of corporation tax (currently 30%) rather than at the lower small companies' or starting rate, whatever the level of the company's profits. A company is not a close investment-holding company if it is a trading company (including companies that deal in land, shares or securities) or a member of a trading group, or if it carries on the business of property investment on a commercial basis.

Close company liquidations

3.22   Where a close trading company ceases to trade and goes into liquidation, it will not be treated as a close investment-holding company for the accounting period beginning at the commencement of winding-up, providing it was within the definition of a close trading company for the previous accounting period. This provision will strictly only be of use when there is no gap between ceasing to trade and commencing winding-up, thus preventing that gap being treated as a separate accounting period (see 3.20). The Revenue may, however, ignore the strict rule if a company could not avoid a short gap and would suffer significantly if the rule were applied (see the Revenue's Company Tax Manual para 6708). Otherwise the full corporation tax rate will apply to the period in which the winding-up commences as well as to later chargeable accounting periods during the winding-up process.

Groups of companies (TA 1988, ss 402–413; TCGA 1992, ss 170–175, 179–181, 190 and Schs 7A, 7AA, 7AB; FA 1996, s 83; FA 1998, Sch 18 paras 66–77; FA 2000, s 98, Sch 28)

3.23   The Taxes Acts do not treat a group of companies as one taxable entity. The corporation tax position of each company in the group is computed independently (small companies' rate and various other limits being scaled down according to the number of associated companies). There are, however, various provisions as indicated below that recognise the group structure and give special treatment in the appropriate circumstances. It is also provided under the self-assessment regime that if group companies are required to pay their tax in instalments, the tax may be paid on a group-wide basis (see 3.18). See 6.25 for stamp duty provisions relating to groups.

The group provisions are not restricted to UK resident companies. Groups and consortia may be established through non-resident companies, enabling the benefit of the provisions to be claimed providing the companies concerned are within the charge to UK corporation tax. As a corollary, tax payable by a non-resident company may be recovered from another group company.

Holding company and its 75% subsidiaries

3.24

(a) Trading losses (and Schedule A rental losses and charges in excess of other profits) can be surrendered to other group members for use against total profits (including capital gains) of the corresponding accounting period. The same applies to an excess of non-trading losses/payments on loans over non-trading income on loans. (Trading interest paid and losses on trade loans are treated as trading expenses and thus form part of a trading loss.) These provisions — called group relief — are dealt with in CHAPTER 26.

(b) For capital gains purposes, assets transferred from one group company to another are treated as transferred on a no loss no gain basis.

Where a group company disposes of an asset outside the group, it may jointly elect with another group company within two years after the disposal that the asset be treated as first disposed of on a no gain no loss basis to the other group company and then disposed of by that other company. This enables groups to use capital losses of one group company against capital gains of other group companies without having to physically transfer ownership of the asset intra-group before making the outside disposal.

(c) Similar rules to (b) above apply to transfers of assets under the provisions for intangible fixed assets (see 20.21).

(d) A chargeable gain made by one group company on a business asset qualifying for rollover relief may be rolled over or held over against an acquisition by another group company. Rollover relief is dealt with in CHAPTER 4.

The group provisions have frequently been manipulated in order to make tax savings over and above what the provisions are intended to allow, and there are numerous anti-avoidance provisions. These include provisions denying group relief for losses where there are 'arrangements' under which some or all of a company's shares could be disposed of to another party and preventing groups reducing their capital gains liability by acquiring companies with capital losses or by bringing companies with capital gains into a group that has unrelieved capital losses. For the anti-avoidance provisions relating to trading and other losses see 26.16.

There are also anti-avoidance provisions deeming a gain to arise where a company leaves a group within six years after acquiring an asset intra-group on a no gain/no loss basis (known as the degrouping charge). All or part of the gain (or loss, if the event triggers a loss) may, however, be reallocated to one or more companies in the same group. A company that is chargeable in respect of a degrouping gain may defer the charge by claiming capital gains rollover relief (see 4.26) if the asset on which the charge arises is within the allowable rollover relief categories and replacement assets have been acquired within the appropriate period. Degrouping charges also apply under the intangible fixed assets provisions (see 20.21) and the same provisions apply to enable the charge to be rolled over or reallocated within the group.

Transfer pricing and thin capitalisation

To prevent groups reducing their taxable profits by having a high level of debt to equity, the thin capitalisation provisions require non-arm's length interest payments between connected companies to be treated as distributions and therefore not deductible in arriving at profits. Similarly, the transfer pricing rules require prices between non-arm's length companies to be adjusted to an arm's length price. The rules have not normally applied where the companies to be are wholly within the charge to UK tax. Changes have been made in FA 2004 to bring the two sets of provisions together and to introduce exemptions for most small and medium-sized companies, but also to make the provisions applicable between UK companies. They are covered briefly in 45.18.

Disposals of substantial shareholdings (TCGA 1992, s 192A and Sch 7AC)

3.25   Where a trading company (operating independently or as part of a trading group) disposes of all or part of a substantial shareholding in another trading company (or holding company of a trading group), any gain on the disposal is exempt from tax (and any loss is not an allowable loss). The exemption applies to qualifying holdings in overseas companies as well as UK companies. 'Substantial' means the company disposing of the shares must have owned 10% or more of the ordinary shares in the other company (and be entitled to 10% or more of the company's profits available for distribution and of its assets on a winding-up) throughout a period of at least 12 months in the two years before the sale. There are provisions to aggregate the shares held by companies and their 51% subsidiaries. The Revenue gave detailed comments on their understanding of the meaning of 'trading company' and 'trading group' in their December 2002 Tax Bulletin. The exemption is subject to anti-avoidance provisions, and the Revenue have issued Statement of Practice 5/02 in this connection.

Members' clubs

3.26   As stated at 3.1, the profits of members' clubs are chargeable to corporation tax. This does not apply to clubs that are registered as community amateur sports clubs, which are treated in a similar way to charities. For further details see 43.18.

The corporation tax charge on clubs applies only to profits from transactions other than between the club members themselves, so it covers such items as interest received on deposits of the club's funds, and any trading profits on transactions with non-members, no matter how small such income may be.

The fact that clubs are within the definition of companies for corporation tax means that banks and building societies are able to pay interest to them without deducting tax, so the clubs will be due to account for tax on the full amount of the interest at the appropriate rate (starting rate of nil, small companies' rate of 19% or full rate of 30% as the case may be). The Revenue may be prepared to treat a club as dormant if its profits are not expected to exceed the nil starting rate band. Clubs who feel they may qualify for this treatment should contact their tax office. Unless the Revenue have given written notification of dormant status, clubs must complete returns and account for any tax due under the self-assessment system. Where dormant status has been granted, clubs will not normally need to complete corporation tax returns, although the Revenue will periodically review the situation. Clubs must notify the Revenue within 12 months after the end of the relevant accounting period if their circumstances change.

The Revenue operate a special simplified scheme for investment clubs (i.e. people who join together to invest on the Stock Exchange), allowing them to submit less detailed calculations of members' gains and income than are strictly required by law if the club satisfies certain criteria.

The Revenue produce a booklet (IR 46 — Clubs, Societies and Associations) on the tax treatment of clubs.

Encouraging business investment, enterprise and efficiency

3.27   Various measures are available to enable companies to operate in a tax-efficient manner and to stimulate investment in new and expanding ventures, including:

Enterprise investment scheme.
Venture capital trusts.
Corporate venturing.
Community investment tax relief.
Purchase of own shares by company.
Demergers.

These are dealt with separately in CHAPTER 29.

4
Capital gains tax: general principles

Introduction

4.1   Capital gains tax was introduced with effect from 6 April 1965 to tax the gains of individuals, personal representatives and trustees. Most of the capital gains tax rules apply to companies as well, but there are some important differences, and a company's gains are charged to corporation tax and not capital gains tax (see 4.6). The law was consolidated in the Taxation of Chargeable Gains Act 1992 but has been substantially amended since then. All references in this chapter are to the 1992 Act unless otherwise stated.

Basis of charge for individuals, personal representatives and trustees (ss 1–6, 16(2A), 35 and Sch 3; FA 1995, s 113; FA 1998, s 122)

4.2   Capital gains tax applies when chargeable assets are disposed of. Gains and losses are calculated on each asset. In general, the cost of an asset acquired before 31 March 1982 is taken to be its value on that date, although there are provisions to use original cost in some circumstances.

An allowance, called indexation allowance, was introduced from March 1982 to adjust for inflation, the gains and losses then being aggregated to give the net chargeable gains or allowable losses for the year. If losses exceeded gains, the losses were carried forward without time limit, to set against later gains to the extent that they were not covered by the annual exemption (see 4.24). For individuals, personal representatives and trustees, however, the indexation allowance available on a disposal was frozen at the amount due up to April 1998 and no further allowance is due after that time. For periods from April 1998 a taper relief may be available instead. The treatment of brought forward losses remains the same, but the benefit of the losses is reduced because of the interaction with taper relief. See 4.24.

Relief for losses is usually claimed in tax returns, with an overall time limit to make the claim of 5 years 10 months from the end of the tax year in which the loss occurred (without, however, restricting the time for which the losses for which relief has been claimed may be carried forward). Where brought-forward losses are used to reduce gains, losses in years from 1996/97 onwards are regarded as set off before pre-1996/97 losses. This could delay, or at worst prevent, a pre-1996/97 loss on a transaction with a connected person being set off against later gains on transactions with that person (see 4.27), since any post-1996/97 losses would have to be set off first.

The first £8,200 of an individual's gains in 2004/05 is exempt. The balance is taxed at 10% to the extent that an individual's taxable income is below the starting rate limit, 20% to the extent of any unused part of an individual's basic rate band and 40% on the remainder. See Example 1.

Example 1

Net gains in 2004/05 £19,200 less annual exemption £8,200 = £11,000.

If taxpayer's taxable income is		Capital gains tax payable is			£	£
Nil, because income is equal to or less than available allowances		2,020	@	10%	202	
		8,980	@	20%	1,796	1,998
£6,000		11,000	@	20%		2,200
£21,000		10,400	@	20%	2,080	
		600	@	40%	240	2,320
£32,000		11,000	@	40%		4,400

The tax position of personal representatives and trustees is dealt with at 4.37 and 4.38.

Trading losses

4.3   Sole traders and partners may set off unrelieved trading losses against their capital gains in certain circumstances — see CHAPTER 25 for the detailed provisions.

Residence, ordinary residence and domicile (ss 2, 9–12)

4.4   Individuals who are resident or ordinarily resident in the UK are liable on all gains wherever they arise, if UK domiciled, and on gains arising in, or brought into, the UK if domiciled elsewhere. Non-resident individuals carrying on a trade, profession or vocation in the UK are liable on gains arising on the disposal of business assets in the UK. Other non-residents who are not ordinarily resident escape tax, unless (for those leaving the UK on or after 17 March 1998) they return to the UK and their period of non-residence is less than five complete tax years. In that event they will be liable to tax on gains arising during their absence. The overseas aspect is dealt with in CHAPTER 41. For the treatment of non-resident companies with interests in the UK see 41.29.

Husband and wife (ss 2, 58)

4.5   Gains of husband and wife are calculated and charged separately, each being entitled to the annual exemption (£8,200 for 2004/05). Losses of one may not be set against the other's gains. Disposals between husband and wife in a tax year when they are living together are, however, not chargeable. The acquiring spouse is treated as having acquired the asset at its original cost to the other spouse plus any addition for indexation allowance (subject to rules to ensure that the indexation allowance does not create or increase a loss when the other spouse disposes of the asset — see 4.36). It should therefore be possible through advance planning and transfers of assets between them to ensure that one spouse is not left with unrelieved losses while the other has gains in excess of the exemption. Taper relief from 6 April 1998 is calculated according to the combined period of ownership (see 4.22).

The above treatment of assets acquired from the other spouse has no relevance to assets acquired on a spouse's death. Any such assets are acquired at market value at the date of death. See 33.13 and 33.15 for the capital gains treatment on separation or divorce.

Companies (s 8 and TA 1988, s 6)

4.6   As indicated at 4.1, the capital gains of companies are broadly computed on capital gains tax principles but are charged to corporation tax and not capital gains tax. Companies are not entitled to an annual exemption. The capital gains tax changes introduced from 6 April 1998 in relation to the freezing of indexation allowance and the introduction of taper relief (see 4.2) do not apply to companies, for whom the pre-existing rules continue. Companies are also treated differently in relation to gains on stocks and shares (see CHAPTER 38). From 1 April 2002 a 'substantial shareholdings exemption' has been introduced for trading companies disposing of holdings of 10% or more in other trading companies — see 3.25 for brief details. Also from 1 April 2002 there are separate 'intangible fixed assets' rules under which gains and losses on such assets (notably goodwill) are dealt with in computing income profits and losses rather than capital gains and losses — see 20.21. Other differences in the capital gains provisions for companies are mentioned in context as they occur. See 3.24 in relation to the capital gains of groups of companies.

Chargeable assets and exempt assets (ss 21–27, 251–253)

4.7   All forms of property are chargeable unless specifically exempt and disposal of a chargeable asset may give rise to a chargeable gain or allowable loss. A chargeable gain or allowable loss may also arise when a capital sum is realised without any disposal taking place (for example if compensation is received for damage to an asset, although if the compensation is used to restore the asset no gain arises).

As far as the treatment of money lent is concerned, the rules are different for companies and for other taxpayers. Capital gains and losses on money lent by or to companies are brought into the company's computation of income (see 3.6). The rules for other taxpayers are dealt with below.

Where an asset is exempt no chargeable gain or allowable loss can normally arise, although there are some special rules about losses on chattels. See the table below for exempt assets and for the chapter in this book which deals with them. As indicated in 4.6, an exemption has been introduced from 1 April 2002 for the disposal by trading companies of substantial shareholdings in other companies. See also 37.3 for the treatment of cash payments on building society takeovers and conversions.

Exempt assets		
	TCGA 1992 reference	*See chapter*
An individual's only or main residence (providing various conditions are satisfied, otherwise part or all of the gain may be chargeable)	ss 222, 223	30
Chattels which are wasting assets, unless used in a business and capital allowances have been, or could have been, claimed	s 45	39
Non-wasting and business chattels where disposal proceeds do not exceed £6,000	s 262	39
Government securities and qualifying company loan stock	s 115	38
SAYE contracts, savings certificates and premium bonds	s 121	36
Prizes and betting winnings	s 51	4.7
Private motor cars, including veteran and vintage cars	s 263	39

	TCGA 1992 reference	See chapter
Sterling currency, and foreign currency for an individual's own spending and maintenance of assets abroad	s 21, 269	39
Decorations for valour if disposed of by the original holder or legatees but not by a purchaser	s 268	
Compensation or damages for personal or professional wrong or injury (and by Revenue concession D50, certain compensation from the UK or a foreign government for property lost or confiscated)	s 51	
Life assurance policies but only in the hands of the original owner or beneficiaries	s 210	40
Gifts of assets that are considered by the Treasury to be of pre-eminent national, historic or scientific interest, but breach of any conditions imposed will nullify the CGT exemption	s 258	
Gifts to charities and certain amateur sports clubs	s 257	43

If you win a lottery prize, it is exempt from capital gains tax, as indicated in the table. If you play as a member of a group, the group should draw up an agreement setting out how the group will operate, who will buy tickets and claim prizes, and how any prize money is to be shared. Otherwise a group claimant passing on shares of prize money to other group members could be regarded as making gifts for inheritance tax purposes. The same would apply to similar group arrangements, such as for football pools. There would not, however, be any inheritance tax to pay unless the person who passed on the shares of prize money died within seven years, and even then there may be exemptions available to cover the gifts. See CHAPTER 5 for the detailed provisions on inheritance tax.

Treatment of loans

4.8   For companies, capital transactions relating to loans are brought into account for income purposes (see 3.4). For individuals, trustees and personal representatives, a debt is not within the capital gains provisions unless it is a 'debt on a security' (which broadly means marketable loan stock). Even then, most loan stock is within the definition of a 'qualifying corporate bond' (see 38.23), and is exempt from capital gains tax. The effect is that if capital gains or losses arise on simple debts, or on qualifying corporate bonds, no relief is available for the losses (subject to some special rules for loans to UK traders — see 4.32 and 38.24), and gains are exempt. For the treatment of loan stock that is outside the definition of qualifying corporate bonds see 38.23. Where a simple debt has been assigned other than to someone with whom the creditor is 'connected' (see 4.27), the debt is a chargeable asset for the assignee, thus giving rise to a chargeable gain or allowable loss on a disposal by the assignee.

Computation of gains and losses (ss 2, 15–17, 35–57 and Schs 2–4)

4.9   Gains and losses on individual assets are worked out by deducting from the sale proceeds or, in some instances, from the market value at the time of disposal (see 4.27) the following amounts:

Original cost and incidental costs of acquisition
Expenditure that has increased the value of the asset
Incidental costs of disposal

For companies, an indexation allowance (see 4.11) may then be given to reduce or eliminate a gain, but the allowance cannot create or increase a loss. The indexation allowance used to be available to individuals, personal representatives and trustees, but it was frozen at April 1998 and taper relief is available instead from that date if the conditions are satisfied.

Taper relief depends on whether the asset is a business or non-business asset and the length of time it has been owned. The maximum taper relief on business assets is 75%, which applies after two years of ownership. On non-business assets the maximum relief is only 40%, and it does not apply until after ten years of ownership. Although the relief is calculated in relation to each asset, it is not taken into account until the gains otherwise chargeable to tax, after deducting allowable losses for the current and previous tax years, have been calculated. The detailed provisions are in 4.16 to 4.23.

Effect of capital allowances (s 41)

4.10   Gains on some assets that qualify for capital allowances are exempt from capital gains tax, such as on items of movable plant and machinery bought and sold for less than £6,000 (see 39.3). Where an asset is not exempt, capital allowances are not deducted from the cost in computing a gain, so that there will be a gain before indexation allowance or taper relief only if the asset is sold for more than original cost. Capital allowances are, however, taken into account in computing a loss, so that losses cannot normally arise, since the capital allowance system covers any drop in value.

For an example of a sale at a profit, see 22.24.

Indexation allowance (ss 53, 54; FA 1998, s 122)

4.11   Where available, the indexation allowance is calculated by applying to each item of expenditure the increase in the retail prices index between the month when the expenditure was incurred, or March 1982 if later, and the month of disposal of the asset or (except for companies) April 1998 if earlier. The index increase is expressed as a decimal and rounded (up or down) to three decimal places. The movement in the index is published monthly and the figure for each month since March 1982 is in the Table of Rates and Allowances under 'Retail prices index'. The formula for working out the increase is:

$$\frac{RD - RI}{RI} \text{ or put more simply}$$

$$\frac{RD}{RI} - 1$$

RD is the index for the month of disposal and RI the index for the month in which the expenditure was incurred. Using the figures in the 'Retail prices index' table in the Table of Rates and Allowances, the increase from November 1982 to April 1998 is

$$\frac{162.6}{82.66} - 1 = .967 \left(\text{or as a percentage, 96.7\%}\right)$$

For disposals on or after 30 November 1993, the indexation allowance can only reduce or eliminate a gain and cannot create or increase a loss.

Where the expenditure was incurred before 31 March 1982, the indexation calculation is made by reference to the value of the asset at 31 March 1982 if the taxpayer has elected to be treated as if he had acquired all the assets he owned on 31 March 1982 at their market value on that day (see 4.12). If the election has not been made, the 31 March 1982 value is still used to calculate the indexation allowance unless using original cost would give a higher figure, in which case the higher figure is taken.

Assets held on 31 March 1982 (ss 35, 36 and Schs 3, 4)

4.12   Originally, capital gains tax applied to gains or losses made on or after 6 April 1965, and there were special rules relating to assets already owned on that date to ensure that when they were disposed of, pre-6 April 1965 gains and losses were excluded. As from 6 April 1988, only gains or losses on or after 31 March 1982 are taken into account. Taxpayers may make an irrevocable election (a rebasing election) to regard all assets owned on 31 March 1982 (except plant and machinery on which capital allowances have been, or could have been, claimed) as having been acquired at their market value on that day. The time limit for making the rebasing election is two years after the end of the tax year or company accounting period in which the *first disposal* was made after 5 April 1988 (reduced for individuals from 1996/97 to one year from 31 January following the relevant tax year). Most disposals that normally result in no chargeable gain or allowable loss are not, however, treated as triggering the time limit (see Revenue Statement of Practice SP 4/92). For many people the time limit will have already expired because of earlier disposals, in which case if the election has not already been made it is no longer available. For disposals after 5 April 1998 by individuals, personal representatives and trustees, the rebasing calculations to arrive at the chargeable gain or allowable loss are made before considering taper relief.

If the election is not made, the 31 March 1982 value is still used to calculate gains and losses, unless using original cost would show a lower gain or lower loss, in which case the lower figure is taken. If one method shows a gain and the other a loss the result is treated as neither a gain nor a loss. In making these calculations indexation allowance is always based on the higher of cost and 31 March 1982 value (see 4.11).

For many assets it may be costly to find out their value at 31 March 1982, but this has to be done whether the election to use 31 March 1982 value is made or not. Examples 2 and 3 show the effect of making or not making the rebasing election.

Example 2

Chargeable asset was bought for £20,000 in 1980 and was worth £24,000 on 31 March 1982. It was sold in June 2004. Taxpayer had made no other disposals since 5 April 1988.

The retail prices index for April 1998 is 162.6. This gives an index increase from March 1982 of:

$$\frac{162.6}{79.44} - 1 = 1.047, \text{ i.e. } 104.7\%$$

Indexation allowance (based on 31 March 1982 value, since higher than cost) is therefore £25,128.

The position before taper relief is as follows.

If general rebasing election is not made

	(a)	(b)	(c)
	£	£	£
Sale proceeds, say	60,000	19,000	22,000
31.3.82 value (giving lower gain)	(24,000)		
Cost (giving lower loss)		(20,000)	
Unindexed gain (loss)	36,000	(1,000)	
Indexation allowance	(25,128)	—	
			No gain,
Chargeable gain (allowable loss)	10,872	(1,000)	no loss

If rebasing election is made

	(a)	(b)	(c)
	£	£	£
Sale proceeds as above	60,000	19,000	22,000
31.3.82 value	(24,000)	(24,000)	(24,000)
Unindexed gain (loss)	36,000	(5,000)	(2,000)
Indexation allowance	(25,128)	—	—
Chargeable gain (allowable loss)	10,872	(5,000)	(2,000)

Rebasing election is either neutral or favourable in relation to this asset, depending on sale proceeds.

Example 3

Using the same figures as in Example 2, but assuming that cost price was £24,000 and 31.3.82 value was £20,000, i.e. figures are reversed. The position before taper relief is as follows.

If general rebasing election is not made

The outcome will be the same as in Example 2, since the lower gain or loss is always taken, and there is no gain or loss where one computation shows a gain and the other a loss.

If general rebasing election is made

Cost of £24,000 becomes irrelevant. Indexation allowance on 31.3.82 value of £20,000 is £20,940.

	(a)	(b)	(c)
	£	£	£
Sale proceeds as above	60,000	19,000	22,000
31.3.82 value	(20,000)	(20,000)	(20,000)
Unindexed gain (loss)	40,000	(1,000)	2,000
Indexation allowance	(20,940)	—	(2,000)
Chargeable gain (allowable loss)	19,060	(1,000)	—

Rebasing election is unfavourable or neutral in relation to this asset, depending on sale proceeds.

Where the right to make a rebasing election is still available, you cannot be selective about making it. If it is made at all, it applies to all chargeable assets you owned on 31 March 1982 (except plant and machinery) and it cannot be revoked. The election does simplify the calculations and it makes it unnecessary to maintain pre-31 March 1982 records.

There are many instances in the capital gains legislation where tax on gains may be deferred to a later time, either by treating the gains as reducing other expenditure, or by treating them as arising at a later time. Where gains were deferred before 31 March 1982, the effect of using 31 March 1982 value to calculate later gains is that these deferred gains will escape tax altogether, since the cost from which the deferred gain was deducted is no longer used. Where an asset acquired after 31 March 1982 but before 6 April 1988 is disposed of after 5 April 1988, and the gain relates wholly or partly, directly or indirectly, to an asset acquired before 31 March 1982 (in other words, where a claim for deferral was made between 31 March 1982 and 5 April 1988 that related to an asset acquired before 31 March 1982), a claim may be made for one-half of the gain to be exempt from tax (see Example 4).

The main occasions when this relief applies are:

Rollover and holdover relief on replacement of business assets or compulsorily acquired land (see 4.26).

Holdover of gains where assets were acquired by gift, including the charge when the donee emigrates (see 4.27).

Rollover of gains on the transfer of a business to a company (see 27.6).

Example 4

| 1979 | Taxpayer acquires business asset No. 1 for £10,000. |
| 1984 | Asset No. 1 is sold at a gain of £4,000 and business asset No. 2 is acquired for £16,000. The gain is rolled over. |

1986	Asset No. 2 is sold at a gain of £10,000 (after taking into account gain rolled over on asset No. 1) and business asset No. 3 is acquired for £40,000. The gain is rolled over.
June 2004	Asset No. 3 is sold for £66,000. Available indexation allowance is 63.2%.

The taxpayer has no allowable losses for 2004/05.

Gain on sale of asset No. 3 is as follows:

	£	£
Sale proceeds June 2004		66,000
Cost 1986	40,000	
Less half of rolled over gain of £10,000 (other half being exempt)	5,000	
	35,000	
Indexation allowance 63.2%	22,120	57,120
Chargeable gain		£8,880

This gain could be rolled over if another qualifying business asset was acquired within three years. If rollover relief was not claimed, the gain would be charged to tax after deducting the available taper relief of £6,660 (75% for more than two complete years), and any available part of the annual exemption. This might eliminate the gain completely, in which case rolling over the gain against any further replacement would not be relevant.

Assets held on 6 April 1965 (s 35 and Sch 2)

4.13   Assets already owned on 6 April 1965, the original start date for capital gains tax, are treated as acquired at market value on 31 March 1982 if the rebasing election is made (see 4.12). If it is not, the position is more complicated, because the old special rules for those assets must be considered in conjunction with the new. The old rules for calculating the position on assets owned on 6 April 1965 contained separate provisions for land with development value, for quoted securities and for all other assets.

The gain or loss on land with development value was calculated by comparing the proceeds either with the original cost or with the value at 6 April 1965, whichever showed the lower gain or loss. If one method showed a gain and the other a loss, there was neither gain nor loss. The same rules applied to quoted securities, except that it was possible to elect for quoted securities to be treated as having been acquired on 6 April 1965 at their value on that date and pooled with later acquisitions of shares of the same class in the same company. The detailed provisions for shares are in CHAPTER 38.

Where an asset other than quoted securities or land with development value was acquired before 6 April 1965, only the time proportion of the gain falling after 6 April 1965 was chargeable, although the earliest date that could be used in a time apportionment calculation was 6 April 1945. You could elect to work out the gain by using the 6 April 1965 value as the cost instead of using time apportionment, but once made this election was irrevocable, even if it resulted in more tax being payable.

Following the 1988 changes in the legislation, if the rebasing election has not been made, the above rules are modified to bring the 31 March 1982 value into the calculation. The calculation is first made using the old rules for assets owned on 6 April 1965 but with indexation allowance based on 31 March 1982 value if higher. When making the time apportionment calculation for assets other than quoted securities and land with development value, indexation allowance is deducted before the gain is time apportioned. The resulting gain or loss is compared with the result using 31 March 1982 value. The lower gain or loss is then taken and if one calculation shows a gain and the other a loss, the result is neither gain nor loss. If, however, the old 6 April 1965 rules have already resulted in a no gain/no loss result, that position is not disturbed. See Example 5.

Example 5

Cost of antique 6.4.64	£4,000
Value at 6.4.65	£4,500
Value at 31.3.82	£15,000
Sale proceeds 6.4.2004	£44,705

Indexation allowance March 1982 to April 1998, 104.7%

If no election to use 31.3.82 value for all assets

Calculation using 6 April 1965 rules

	£	£
Sale proceeds	44,705	44,705
Cost	(4,000)	
6.4.65 value		(4,500)
Indexation allowance @ 104.7% on 31.3.82 value of £15,000	(15,705)	(15,705)
Overall gain	£25,000	

Time proportion since 6.4.65

$$\frac{39}{40} \times 25,000 =$$

	24,375

Gain	£24,375	or	£24,500

Therefore no election would be made to use 6.4.65 value and gain under 6 April 1965 rules is £24,375.

Calculation using March 1982 rules	£
Sale proceeds	44,705
31.3.82 value	(15,000)
Indexation allowance 104.7%	(15,705)
Gain under March 1982 rules	£14,000

Chargeable gain before taper relief is the lower of £24,375 and £14,000, i.e. £14,000.

If election made to use 31.3.82 value for all assets

Chargeable gain is not affected, since the 31 March 1982 value is used in any event.

Part disposals (ss 42, 242)

4.14   Where part only of an asset is disposed of, the cost of the part disposed of is worked out by taking the proportion of the overall cost that the sale proceeds bear to the sum of the sale proceeds plus the market value of what remains unsold. The indexation allowance is calculated on the apportioned part of the cost and not on the total.

Where part of a holding of land is sold for £20,000 or less, and the proceeds represent not more than 20% of the value of the land, the taxpayer may claim not to be treated as having made a disposal, but the amount received reduces the allowable cost of the remaining land for a future disposal. Any available indexation allowance on a subsequent disposal is calculated on the full cost in the usual way, but is then reduced to take account of the previous part disposal. This claim may not be made if other disposals of land are made in the same year, and the total proceeds for all disposals of land exceed £20,000.

Leases (s 240 and Sch 8)

4.15   The grant of a lease at a premium gives rise to a capital gains tax liability, and if the term is 50 years or less there is also an income tax liability. The calculation of the income and capital elements is shown in CHAPTER 32. Where a tenant assigns a lease at a premium to another tenant, the premium is charged to capital gains tax in the normal way if the lease has more than 50 years to run at the time of the assignment. If, however, it has 50 years or less to run, it is a wasting asset and the cost has to be depreciated over that 50 years according to a table in Sch 8 which ensures that the cost is depreciated more slowly during the early part of the 50-year period than during the later years.

Taper relief (s 2A and Sch A1)

4.16   For individuals, personal representatives and trustees, indexation allowance on assets held on 5 April 1998 is given only for the period of ownership up to April 1998 and no further indexation arises after that time. Instead, a taper relief may be available which reduces gains on a sliding scale according to the *complete* number of years that the asset has been held from acquisition or from 6 April 1998 if later. Unlike the indexation allowance provisions, taper relief dates from the date an asset is acquired (or 6 April 1998 if later), regardless of when any additional capital expenditure is incurred on the asset. The maximum period of ownership taken into account is ten years to the time of disposal. A higher rate of taper relief applies to business assets than to non-business assets, and the minimum ownership period before an asset qualifies for taper relief is one year for business assets and three years for non-business assets. It was originally provided that maximum relief was not obtained on either business or non-business assets until there were ten complete years of ownership and, except where the close company anti-avoidance provisions mentioned below applied, an extra year was added to the qualifying taper period for any asset owned before 17 March 1998. For example if an asset was acquired in February 1998 and disposed of in June 1999, the qualifying period was two years, i.e. one complete year between 5 April 1998 and June 1999 plus the extra year. Taper relief would only have applied in that case if the asset was a business asset.

For disposals between 6 April 2000 and 5 April 2002 the maximum taper relief for business assets applied after only four years, and this was further reduced to two years for disposals on or after 6 April 2002. From 6 April 2000 onwards, however, business assets acquired before 17 March 1998 no longer qualify for the extra year, so that if in the above example the asset had been disposed of one year later, in June 2000, the qualifying taper period for a non-business asset would be three years, but for a business asset it would be two years. Even though a business asset now qualifies for maximum relief after only two complete years, the maximum period of ownership which might have to be taken into account remains at ten years. This is important where the asset is not a business asset throughout the period (see 4.19).

The maximum rate of taper relief on business assets after two qualifying years is now 75%, leaving 25% chargeable. For non-business assets the maximum rate after ten qualifying years is 40%, leaving 60% chargeable. See tables below. Applying the present lower and higher tax rates of 20% and 40% to those chargeable percentages gives tax rates after maximum taper relief of 10% on business assets at the higher rate and 5% for gains below the higher rate threshold, compared with 24% and 12% respectively on non-business assets.

Gains on disposals of business assets on or after 6 April 2002

Number of whole years in qualifying holding period	Percentage reduction available	Percentage of gain chargeable
1	50	50
2	75	25

Gains on disposals of non-business assets

Number of whole years in qualifying holding period	Percentage reduction available	Percentage of gain chargeable
1	0	100
2	0	100
3	5	95
4	10	90
5	15	85
6	20	80
7	25	75
8	30	70
9	35	65
10 or more	40	60

Definition of business asset

4.17   For disposals on or after 6 April 2000 the definition of business asset was widened following changes in the Finance Acts 2000 and 2001. The following assets broadly qualify as business assets from that date:

(i)   Assets used for a trade carried on by the taxpayer (either alone or in partnership) or by a company that is within the definition of his qualifying company (see below)

(ii)   Assets held for use in his employment by an employee working for a trading employer

(iii)   Shares or securities in a qualifying company, i.e.:

(a)   a trading company or holding company of a trading group which is either an unquoted company*, or a quoted company in which the taxpayer is an officer or employee, or in which he holds 5% or more of the voting rights.

(b)   a non-trading company or holding company of a non-trading group in which the taxpayer is an officer or employee, where the taxpayer does not have a material interest in the company or a company controlling it.**

*   Unquoted companies include companies on the Alternative Investment Market (AIM).

**   An individual has a material interest in a company if he and/or one or more people connected with him control more than 10% of the company's issued shares or voting rights, or would be entitled to more that 10% of the company's income if the whole income were distributed, or more than 10% of the assets if the company were wound up.

Before 6 April 2000 an employee had to be a *full-time* employee under heading (ii), and for a company to be a qualifying company for headings (i) and (iii)(a) the taxpayer either had to hold 25% of the voting rights, or had to be a full-time officer or employee holding 5% of the voting rights. For heading (i), one effect of the changed definition is that if an asset other than shares is used by *any* unquoted trading company, the company is the taxpayer's qualifying company and the asset qualifies as a business asset. Taper relief is therefore available to a landlord with an unquoted trading company tenant with which the landlord has no connection. It was not, however, available before 6 April 2004 if the tenant was a partnership in which the landlord was not a partner. The definition has, however, been further amended from 6 April 2004 so that business assets taper relief applies from that date to any asset used wholly or partly for the purposes of a trade carried on by *any* individual, trustees of a settlement, personal representatives or a partnership of which an individual is a member. The anomaly regarding trading tenants who are not unquoted trading companies will accordingly not apply for periods of ownership from 6 April 2004.

Coupled with the reduction in the business assets taper period, the extended definition of business asset has significantly improved taper relief. The detailed provisions are, however, complex and great care needs to be taken to ensure that the necessary conditions are satisfied. The Revenue published guidance on the meaning of 'trading company' and related terms used in the legislation in their June 2001 Tax Bulletin, and they issued further guidance in their December 2002 Tax Bulletin.

Personal representatives and trustees

4.18   The business assets rates of taper relief are available in appropriate circumstances to personal representatives and trustees, the rules outlined above being adapted to refer to personal representatives, trustees, or trust beneficiaries with a life interest, rather than to individuals. A non-trading company is not, however, a qualifying company (see 4.17(iii)(b)) for personal representatives although it is for trustees. Where an individual acquires an asset as legatee, it is treated as a business asset for any period during which it was a business asset in the hands of the personal representatives.

Change in status of asset, mixed use etc.

4.19   Where an asset has not been a business asset throughout the period of ownership from the date of acquisition (or 6 April 1998 if later) to the date of disposal, or throughout the last ten years if shorter, the gain is apportioned according to the business and non-business periods and the respective amounts are then treated as separate gains qualifying for the relevant relief. Similar apportionment provisions apply to assets that are used partly for business and partly for other purposes.

Where the changed definition of business assets following Finance Act 2000 or 2001 results in an asset becoming a business asset from 6 April 2000, the proportion of the gain relating to the period from 6 April 1998 to 5 April 2000 qualifies only for the non-business assets taper relief. Since the relevant period taken into account for taper relief is a maximum of ten years, the effect is that even though business assets qualify for maximum relief after only two years from 6 April 2002, an asset that became a business asset only from 6 April 2000 cannot benefit from the maximum business assets taper relief of 75% until 6 April 2010. See Example 6. Similar apportionments will need to be made where an asset became a business asset from 6 April 2004 following FA 2003. Great care needs to be taken to ensure that the correct rate(s) of taper relief are applied.

Example 6

In 1995 shareholder buys 10% of the shares in an unquoted company with which he is not connected. On 6 April 2006 he sells the shares, making a gain after indexation allowance of £100,000. The chargeable gain (assuming there were no allowable losses and before considering any available annual exemption) is as follows:

Period from 6 April 1998 to 6 April 2006	8 years	
Non-business asset period	2 years	
Business asset period	6 years	
	£	£
Non-business asset gain (2/8)	25,000	
Less: 35% taper relief (9 years including extra year for pre-17.3.98 ownership)	8,750	16,250
Business asset gain (6/8)	75,000	
Less: 75% taper relief (maximum for 2 years or more)	56,250	18,750
Chargeable gain		35,000

If the facts were the same, but the disposal was on 6 April 2010, the asset would have been a business asset throughout the previous ten years, so that it would qualify for the full 75% relief, reducing the chargeable gain to £25,000.

If the shares had been acquired on 6 April 2000, then they would qualify for maximum relief on or after 6 April 2002.

When a company ceases to trade and goes into liquidation, this will similarly cause a restriction in the rate of taper relief available to individuals on their shareholdings (see 3.20).

Anti-avoidance provisions

4.20 There are anti-avoidance provisions to prevent abuse of the taper relief provisions. Broadly these provisions deny taper relief for periods when someone remains the nominal owner of an asset but has effectively ceased to hold it, or when the value of close company shares is artificially increased by shifting value from shares held for a shorter time into shares held for a longer time. There was previously an anti-avoidance provision to deny taper relief when the value of close company shares held for a long time was increased by switching an asset held for a short time into the company and then disposing of the shares. Taper relief was denied for the whole of the period from the date of acquisition of the asset (or 6 April 1998 if later) to the date of disposal of the shares. For disposals of shares on or after 17 April 2002 this provision has been replaced by one that excludes from the qualifying taper relief period those periods when a close company was not active (a company being, however, treated as active when preparing to carry on a business or when a business is being wound up). See the Revenue's Tax Bulletin of October 2002 for their comments on the revised provisions.

Way in which relief is given

4.21   Taper relief at the appropriate rates is applied to the chargeable gains net of allowable losses in the same year and also net of losses brought forward from earlier years or carried back from the year of death. Losses are set against gains so as to give the lowest tax charge, which means setting them first against any gains on which no taper relief is available, then against gains with less taper relief before other gains. See Examples 7 and 8. The set-off of losses brought forward or carried back is restricted so as not to waste the annual exemption, although such losses are still partly wasted where the losses are set against gains qualifying for taper relief (see 4.24).

Example 7

Non-business asset acquired in September 1989 at a cost of £10,000 is disposed of in June 2005 for £25,000. Indexation allowance up to April 1998 is 39.5%. Chargeable gain (assuming there are no allowable losses and before considering any available annual exemption) is as follows:

		£
Disposal proceeds		25,000
Cost	10,000	
Indexation allowance	3,950	13,950
Gain before taper relief		11,050
8 years' taper relief (including bonus year), 30%		3,315
Chargeable gain		7,735

Example 8

Total gains before deducting allowable losses of £5,000 are £27,000, spread over three assets as shown below, the optimum loss set-off being as follows:

Amount of gains £	Taper relief rate	Optimum loss set-off £	Taper relief £	Net gains £
2,000	—	(2,000)	—	—
10,000	10%	(3,000)	(700)	6,300
15,000	30%		(4,500)	10,500
27,000		(5,000)	(5,200)	16,800

Husband and wife transactions

4.22   Where an asset has been transferred between spouses (see 4.5), the taper relief on a subsequent disposal is based on the combined period of ownership.

Special rules apply, however, in relation to business use. Where an asset other than shares or securities has been transferred between spouses, it is treated as a business asset for taper relief for that part of the period of ownership of the transferor spouse during which it was in qualifying business use by either of them. The rate of relief for the period of ownership of the transferee spouse will depend on the use by that spouse. Where shares or securities are transferred, the business assets rate of taper relief applies only to that part of the combined period of ownership during which the *transferee* spouse satisfied the conditions for the business assets rate of relief. The relaxation of the definition of business assets will reduce the impact of these provisions. See Examples 9 and 10.

Example 9

Say property owned by a non-working wife has been used by her husband for his trade throughout her period of ownership. If the wife transfers the property to him, then when he disposes of the property it counts as a business asset for taper relief not only for his qualifying period of ownership but also for his wife's, since it was in business use by him throughout.

If on the other hand the property had been owned by the husband and used in his trade, and it was transferred to his non-working wife, she would qualify for taper relief only at the non-business assets rate for her own qualifying period of ownership, but relief at the business assets rate would apply to his period of ownership.

Example 10

Non-working husband owns 4% of the voting shares in an unquoted trading company in which his wife owns 4% of the voting shares and works full-time. Both shareholdings were acquired at the same time. If the husband had transferred his shares to his wife before 6 April 2000, they would qualify for the business assets rate of taper relief from the date of transfer (the holding then carrying 8% of the voting rights), but the non-business assets rate would apply to the earlier qualifying period of ownership of both spouses. Had the wife already owned 5%

---

or more of the voting rights, the whole of the gain on the holding would have qualified for the business assets rate of taper relief for the entire qualifying period.

If the holdings had been acquired after 5 April 2000, both holdings would have been business assets from the outset.

Effect of rollover/holdover reliefs

4.23   Where gifts holdover relief has been claimed on a gifted asset (see 4.27), only the holding period of the new owner is taken into account for taper relief. Where gains have reduced the cost of a replacement asset (such as with business assets rollover relief — see 4.26 or rollover relief on transfer of a business – see 27.6), taper relief will depend on how long the *replacement* asset has been owned. The time for which the asset which gave rise to the rolled over gain was owned is not taken into account.

Where gains are deferred, for example with business assets holdover relief on depreciating assets (see 4.26), taper relief will depend on the period of ownership of the asset on which the deferred gain arose. This means that where a gain had already been held over before 6 April 1998, no taper relief will be available on the deferred gain when it crystallises.

Careful planning will be needed to ensure that taper relief is not wasted. If, for example, existing business premises were extended instead of being replaced, taper relief would not be lost through claiming rollover relief, and furthermore when the premises were eventually disposed of, taper relief would run from the original acquisition date (or 6 April 1998 if later) even though the additional expenditure reflected in the calculation of the gain was incurred much later.

Annual exemption (s 3 and Sch 1)

4.24   The annual exemption is £8,200 for 2004/05, available to each of husband and wife. Provision is made for the exempt amount to be increased each year in line with increases in the retail prices index unless Parliament decides otherwise. The annual exemption reduces chargeable gains after taking into account taper relief. Gains and losses in the same year must be netted off before allowing taper relief on the net gains, so that both taper relief and annual exemption may be wasted. Brought forward losses are not set against gains covered by the annual exemption. If, however, the gains exceed the annual exemption, any brought forward losses that are used against gains must be set off *before* taper relief, so the annual exemption may be effectively wasted. See Example 11.

Example 11

The following example deals with three scenarios for an individual's only disposal in 2004/05.

	(a)	(b)	(c)
	£	£	£
Gain before 75% business taper relief	33,800	33,800	33,800
Losses brought forward	—	1,000	25,600
Net gain	33,800	32,800	8,200
Taper relief 75%	25,350	24,600	N/A
Gain before annual exemption	8,450	8,200	8,200
Annual exemption	8,200	8,200	8,200
Chargeable gain	250	—	—
Losses of		1,000	25,600
are used to eliminate gain of		250	250
Extent to which brought forward losses are effective		25%	1%

If the losses brought forward had exceeded £25,600, the excess over £25,600 would be carried forward. If the untapered gains of the year had been £8,200 or less, the full amount of the brought forward losses would be carried forward.

Note that losses brought forward from 1996/97 or later are regarded as set off before earlier losses (see 4.2).

For the annual exemption available to personal representatives and trustees, see 4.37 and 4.38. No annual exemption is available to companies.

Reliefs

4.25 Specific reliefs are available for:

(a) replacement of business assets;

(b) gifts of certain assets;

(c) transfer of a business to a company;

(d) assets of negligible value; and

(e) losses on certain loans.

These are dealt with in the following paragraphs, except for (c), which is dealt with in CHAPTER 27. Capital gains reliefs are also available under the

Enterprise Investment Scheme, Venture Capital Trusts and Corporate Venturing Scheme provisions. These are dealt with in CHAPTER 29.

Rollover/holdover relief on replacement of business assets and compulsorily purchased land (ss 152–159, 175, 247; FA 1993, s 86)

4.26   Where there is a chargeable gain on the disposal of a qualifying business asset and the proceeds (or deemed proceeds if the asset is given away) are matched by the acquisition of another qualifying business asset within the period commencing one year before and ending three years after the disposal, a claim may be made for the gain to be deferred. The Revenue have discretion to extend the time limit. The replacement asset need not be used in the same trade where one person carries on two or more trades either successively or at the same time. For holding companies and their 75% subsidiaries, the disposal and acquisition need not be made by the same group company. But an asset acquired intra-group on a no loss/no gain basis cannot be treated as a qualifying acquisition. For events on or after 1 April 2002, a group company that is chargeable on a gain when it leaves a group may claim rollover relief in appropriate circumstances (see 3.24).

The relief applies to land and buildings, fixed plant and machinery, ships, aircraft, hovercraft, satellites, space stations and spacecraft including launch vehicles, goodwill, milk and potato quotas, ewe and suckler cow premium quotas, fish quota and Lloyds syndicate rights. The replacement asset does not have to be in the same category as the asset disposed of, providing both are qualifying assets, and the proceeds of a single disposal could be applied in acquiring several qualifying assets or vice versa. For companies, disposals of goodwill and fish and agricultural quotas on or after 1 April 2002 no longer qualify for capital gains rollover relief unless the replacement asset(s) were acquired before 1 April 2002 and within twelve months prior to the disposal (and in that event the company has a choice whether to claim capital gains rollover relief or the rollover relief available under the new company rules for intangible assets). Disposals of other qualifying assets by companies on or after 1 April 2002 cannot be rolled over against acquisitions of goodwill and quotas on or after that date (unless the acquisitions are from related parties and are thus not within the new company rules for intangible assets). See 20.21 for details of the intangible assets rules. The rules for individuals remain unchanged.

If only part of the sale proceeds is used to acquire replacement assets within the rollover period, the remaining part of the gain is chargeable immediately, treating the gain as the last part of the proceeds to be used.

If the replacement asset has a life of more than 60 years (e.g. freehold land or, for individuals, goodwill), the gain is rolled over and treated as reducing the cost of the replacement asset (see Example 4 in 4.12). Where relevant, indexation allowance on the replacement asset is calculated on the cost less the rolled over gain. Taper relief, where appropriate, is given according to the time the *replacement* asset has been owned (see 4.23).

If a gain has been rolled over in this way against a replacement asset acquired before 31 March 1982, the effect of using 31 March 1982 value as the cost of such an asset is that the rolled over gain escapes tax altogether.

If the replacement is a depreciating asset with a life of 60 years or less (which in fact applies to most of the business assets qualifying for relief), the gain does not reduce the tax cost of the replacement (so the calculation of any available indexation allowance is not affected) but it is held over for a maximum of ten years. It becomes chargeable when the replacement asset is sold or ceases to be used in a business carried on by the taxpayer, or, at latest, ten years after acquisition of the replacement asset (see Example 12). The gain will not crystallise at that point, however, if at or before that time a non-depreciating asset has been acquired against which a claim is made for the gain to be rolled over instead. As far as taper relief is concerned, it is given where appropriate according to the length of ownership of the *original* asset on which the gain had been deferred (see 4.23).

Example 12

Qualifying business asset that cost £200,000 before 6 April 1998 is sold by a sole trader during 2004/05 for £300,000, with indexation allowance of £60,000, giving rise to a gain of £40,000. Qualifying replacement asset (freehold land) acquired within rollover period for:

£360,000	Full gain reinvested, therefore CGT cost of replacement reduced to £320,000. Taper relief will not be given until replacement asset disposed of and will be based on length of ownership of replacement asset.
£290,000	£10,000 of the proceeds (and hence the gain) not reinvested, so gain of £10,000 chargeable immediately (unless other qualifying assets acquired within rollover period). £30,000 of gain deducted from £290,000 cost of replacement, reducing CGT cost to £260,000. Taper relief of 75% (more than two complete years after 5 April 2002) will reduce gain of £10,000 to £2,500 (assuming no available losses). Taper relief position re remaining £30,000 gain as above.
£258,000	No part of gain reinvested therefore full £40,000 chargeable less £30,000 taper relief (unless other qualifying assets acquired within rollover period).

If the replacement had been a depreciating asset, there would be no change in the gains immediately chargeable. The CGT cost of the replacement asset would, however, not be reduced. Instead that part of

---

the gain that was reinvested would be deferred for not more than ten years. When it crystallised, taper relief of £30,000 would be given (assuming full gain of £40,000 reinvested and no available losses), based on the ownership of the original asset.

Both rolled-over and held-over gains escape tax completely on the taxpayer's death.

Rollover relief claims must give full details of assets disposed of and acquired, including dates and amounts (and where two group companies are involved, they must make a joint claim). For companies, the time limit for the original rollover or holdover claim is six years from the end of the accounting period to which the claim relates. The time limit for individuals is five years from the 31 January following the tax year to which the claim relates. The claim will normally be sent in with the tax return. There is a form for individuals to make the claim in Revenue Help sheet 290. Where the replacement asset(s) have not been acquired by the due date for the return, a provisional claim may be made with the return for the tax year or company accounting period in which the disposal took place, and the relief is then given as for an actual claim. The provisional claim will either be superseded by an actual claim, or will cease to have effect three years from the due date for the return for the period of disposal (e.g. for a disposal by an individual in 2003/04, the return for which is due by 31 January 2005, the provisional relief would no longer apply after 31 January 2008). All necessary adjustments to assessments and tax bills will then be made, including interest on underpaid tax from the date the tax would have been payable if no provisional claim had been made. Where a holdover claim is being replaced by a rollover claim as a result of the later acquisition of a non-depreciating asset (which could in fact be up to thirteen years after the disposal giving rise to the gain that had been held over), it is thought that the claim to switch from holdover to rollover relief would need to be sent in with the return for the year in which the non-depreciating asset was acquired.

The strict rules for rollover relief are relaxed by various Revenue concessions, notably D15, D16 and D22. Anti-avoidance provisions have been introduced to counter abuse of the concessions (see 45.12).

Rollover relief is also available where an asset owned personally and used in the owner's partnership or personal trading company is disposed of and replaced. A 'personal trading company' is one in which the individual owns 5% or more of the voting rights. The receipt of rent from the partnership or trading company does not affect the availability of the relief.

Apart from that exception, rollover relief is only available on investment property in two instances. If the property is the subject of compulsory purchase (or compulsory acquisition by a lessee), the relief is available provided that the replacement is not a capital gains tax exempt dwelling-house — see 32.18. (Companies in a 75% group can claim this relief if one company makes a disposal under a compulsory purchase order and another acquires the replacement.) The relief is also available on property let as furnished holiday accommodation (see CHAPTER 32).

See 4.12 for the treatment of disposals after 5 April 1988 that are affected by deferred gains on assets acquired before 31 March 1982. See CHAPTER 41 for the overseas aspect of rollover relief.

Gifts and transactions with connected persons (ss 17–20, 67, 165–169, 258–261, 281, 286 and Sch 7)

4.27   For capital gains purposes, a gift of a chargeable asset is regarded as a disposal at open market value (except for husband/wife transfers), and the chargeable gain or allowable loss is computed in the usual way, with indexation allowance to April 1998 and taper relief being taken into account to reduce or eliminate gains. There are, however, some special rules for both gains and losses.

Not only gifts but all transactions between connected persons, or not at arm's length, are regarded as at open market value except for husband/wife transactions, which are not normally chargeable (see 4.5). Broadly, a person is connected with his or his wife's close relatives and their spouses, with business partners and their spouses and relatives (except in relation to normal commercial transactions), and, if he is the trustee of a settlement, with the settlor (if an individual) and with any person connected with the settlor. The relatives that are taken into account are brother and sisters, ancestors (i.e. parents, grandparents, etc.), and lineal descendants (i.e. children, grandchildren, etc.). Companies under the same control are connected with each other and with the persons controlling them.

Where an asset is disposed of to a connected person (other than the individual's husband or wife) and a loss arises, the loss may not be set against general gains but only against a later gain on a transaction with the same connected person. (See 4.2 for the possible adverse effect of the set-off order for brought forward losses.) Where someone disposes of assets on different occasions within a period of six years to one or more persons connected with him, and their value taken together is higher than their separate values, then the disposal value for each of the transactions is a proportionate part of the aggregate value, and all necessary adjustments will be made to earlier tax charges.

4.28   Where a gain arises on the gift of an asset by an individual or trustees, it may be deferred if the asset qualifies for gifts relief (subject to various anti-avoidance provisions mentioned below). Gifts relief used to be available on virtually any asset, but the gifts that now qualify for relief are as shown below. Relief for gifts of shares or securities under (a)(iii) and (iv) is not available if the gift is to a company (unless the gift occurred between 6 April 2003 and 20 October 2003 inclusive — FA 2004, Sch 21.3).

(a)   Business assets, which comprise:

   (i)   assets used in the donor's business or in his personal trading company (i.e. one in which he owns at least 5% of the voting rights), or used by a company in a trading group of which the holding company is the donor's personal trading company;

   (ii)   farm land and buildings that would qualify for inheritance tax agricultural property relief — see 5.19; note that this enables relief to be claimed on agricultural land held as an investment, providing the appropriate conditions are satisfied;

   (iii)   unquoted shares or securities in trading companies;

   (iv)   shares or securities in the donor's personal trading company or personal holding company of a trading group (relief being restricted proportionately if not all the company's assets are business assets);

(b)   Gifts of heritage property (works of art, historic buildings, etc.);

(c)   Gifts to funds for the maintenance of heritage property;

(d)   Gifts to political parties;

(e)   Gifts that are *immediately* chargeable to inheritance tax or would be had they not been covered by the inheritance tax annual exemption. This mainly covers gifts into and out of discretionary trusts but also covers any other gifts that are within the inheritance tax annual exemption (see 5.3).

From 6 April 2003 the definitions of trading company, holding company and trading group for gifts relief are the same as for taper relief. See the Revenue's Tax Bulletin of December 2002 for their views on the meaning of trading company and related terms.

Subject to what is said below, gifts relief is available, where appropriate, on transfers into and out of trust, the relief under heading (a)(i) applying where the business is carried on by trustees or by a beneficiary with a life interest in the trust. For the detailed provisions, see CHAPTER 42.

Gifts relief is also available where assets are not given outright but are disposed of for less than their value. If, however, the amount received exceeds the original cost, the gain that may be deferred does not include the excess of the proceeds over cost.

4.29   Where gifts relief is claimed, the donor is not charged to tax on the gain and the value at which the donee is treated as having acquired the asset is reduced by the gain, so that the donee will make a correspondingly larger gain (or smaller loss) when he disposes of the asset. Taper relief is based on the *donee's* period of ownership (see 4.23). The Revenue have stated that in most circumstances it will not be necessary to agree market values at the time of the gifts relief claim. Establishing the market value at the date of the gift can normally be deferred until the donee disposes of the asset (Revenue Statement of Practice SP 8/92).

There are provisions to ensure that the gifts relief is not used to avoid tax altogether, for example where the donee is not resident in the UK. If a donee who is an individual is resident at the time of the gift but becomes not resident and not ordinarily resident before disposing of the asset and within six years after the end of the tax year in which the gift was made, the gain is then charged to tax (and no taper relief is available). This provision does not apply to trustees, because separate rules impose a tax charge on all trust assets when a trust becomes non-resident — see 41.40. For disposals on or after 10 December 2003, however, gifts relief is not available on disposals to trusts in which the settlor has an interest (see 42.9). Provisions have also been introduced to prevent the exploitation of the interaction between gifts relief and the private residence exemption dealt with in CHAPTER 30 (SEE 30.6).

4.30   Claims for gifts relief to apply must be made by the donor and donee jointly except where the donees are trustees, in which case only the donor need make the claim. Under self-assessment, claims will usually be sent in with tax returns. There is a form for making the claim in Revenue Help sheet IR 295. The overall time limit for claims is five years from the 31 January following the tax year to which the claim relates.

Where a gift on which the gifts holdover relief is claimed attracts inheritance tax, either immediately or as a result of the donor's death within seven years, the donee's base cost for capital gains tax is increased by the inheritance tax (but not so as to create a loss on future disposal). If, however, a lifetime gift does not qualify for holdover relief and capital gains tax is paid, there is no direct inheritance tax relief for the capital gains tax paid if the gift becomes chargeable for inheritance tax because of the donor's death within seven years (although the capital gains tax paid has reduced the wealth of the donor and therefore the amount liable to inheritance tax on his death).

Where tax remains payable after gifts relief, it may be paid by ten annual instalments on gifts of land, a controlling shareholding in a company, or minority holdings of unquoted shares or securities in a company. Interest is, however, charged on the full amount outstanding and not just on any instalment which is paid late.

See 4.12 for the treatment of disposals that are affected by deferred gains on assets acquired before 31 March 1982.

Assets of negligible value (s 24)

4.31   If an asset is lost, destroyed or extinguished, you are treated as disposing of it at that time, even if no compensation is received. This means, for example, that if you own shares in a company that goes into liquidation, you will be regarded as disposing of the shares when the liquidation is completed, and relief may be claimed for the loss.

It is, however, possible to get relief before the asset is lost or destroyed if its value has sunk to a negligible level. You may make a claim for the asset to be treated as sold and reacquired at that negligible value, establishing an allowable loss accordingly. You are treated as having disposed of the asset either on the date of the claim or, if you wish, on an earlier date indicated in the claim. The earlier date must fall within the two years before the tax year or company accounting period in which the claim is made, and the asset must have been of negligible value on that earlier date (whether or not it was of negligible value before then). You do not need to make a negligible value claim unless and until you wish to, so that, for example, a claim should not be made if it would mean wasting the annual exemption.

Relief for losses on loans (ss 251–253)

4.32   Special rules apply to the loss of money lent by companies (see 3.6). For other taxpayers, the normal rules for working out allowable capital losses do not apply to ordinary debts (unless the debt has been assigned to someone with whom the creditor is not 'connected' — see 4.27 — in which case the assignee may claim relief by reference to the amount he has paid for the assigned debt). The normal rules do, however, apply to the loss of money lent if the loan is marketable loan stock or a similar security *other than* a qualifying corporate bond (see 38.23). The loans qualifying for relief under the normal rules will therefore mainly be non-sterling loan stock, loan stock that is convertible into shares, and loan stock acquired before 14 March 1984.

Qualifying corporate bonds are exempt from capital gains tax, and if a loss arises it will not normally be an allowable loss (other than for companies). For QCB loans made before 17 March 1998, the relief described below may be claimed in certain circumstances — see 38.24.

Relief is available to the lender or guarantor for losses on loans or guarantees that do not qualify under the normal rules outlined above if the borrower is a UK resident and uses the money lent wholly for the purposes of a trade carried on by him. Upon an appropriate claim by the lender or guarantor, an irrecoverable loan or payment under guarantee gives rise to an allowable loss for CGT, provided that the debt or the rights acquired by the guarantor following the guarantee payment are not assigned. If any amount is subsequently recovered (whether from the borrower or from any co-guarantor) it will be treated as a capital gain. The loss under these provisions is treated as a loss at the date of the claim, unless the claim stipulates an earlier time falling not more than two years before the beginning of the tax year of claim, and providing the amount was irrecoverable at the earlier date.

Relief is not available if the loss arises because of something the lender, or guarantor, has done or failed to do, or where the amount has become irrecoverable in consequence of the terms of the loan, nor is it available where the claimant and borrower are husband and wife.

Returns, due date of payment, interest on overdue tax and repayment supplement (ss 3A, 283; TMA 1970, ss 59B, 86)

4.33 Under the self-assessment system, the annual tax return contains details of capital gains, although in some instances the capital gains pages of the return do not have to be completed. For further details see 9.20. The same payment date and interest rules apply for both income tax and capital gains tax (see 2.23), except that capital gains tax is not included in payments on account and is payable in full on 31 January following the end of the tax year. Interest on underpaid tax is charged from the due date and repayment supplement is paid on overpaid tax from the date of overpayment to the date the repayment order is issued. For the latest interest rates see the Table of Rates and Allowances.

Payment by instalments (s 280)

4.34 Capital gains tax may at the taxpayer's option be paid by instalments where the proceeds are being received by instalments over 18 months or more. The instalments run over eight years, or until the last instalment of the price is received if sooner, with relief for bad debts being available if part of the amount due proves irrecoverable. Interest is charged on any instalments paid late (but only on the instalment and not on the full amount outstanding).

Capital gains tax is also payable by instalments on certain gifts, but interest is then payable on the full amount outstanding, not just on overdue instalments — see 4.27.

Quoted and unquoted securities

4.35 Special rules apply to the treatment of both quoted and unquoted securities. As a result of the abolition of indexation allowance for individuals, personal representatives and trustees, and the introduction of taper relief, with the existing provisions being retained for companies, these rules have become even more complicated, since two different systems now run side by side. For the detailed provisions, see CHAPTER 38.

No gain/no loss disposals

4.36   Special provisions apply to certain disposals, the main ones being:

(a)   Transfers on company reconstructions (s 139).

(b)   Transfers within a 75% group of companies (s 171).

(c)   Husband/wife transfers (s 58).

The disposal is effectively treated as giving rise to neither gain nor loss, and the transferee's acquisition cost is the original cost plus any available indexation allowance. Any indexation allowance added to cost cannot, however, create or increase a loss on ultimate disposal. This does not apply to indexation allowance that had been added to cost up to the time of the last no gain/no loss transfer made before 30 November 1993, which may still create or increase losses.

For inter-spouse transfers, gains on ultimate disposal by the acquiring spouse will attract taper relief according to the combined period of owner-ship, although the position regarding business/non-business assets needs to be watched (see 4.22). See Example 13.

Example 13

A husband acquired a non-business asset in 1996 and transferred it to his wife in May 1999 at an indexed cost of £14,000. The wife then sold the asset in December 2004 for £26,000. The position would be as follows:

	£
Sale proceeds December 2004	26,000
Indexed cost taken over from husband	14,000
Untapered gain	12,000
Taper relief for 7 complete years 25%*	3,000
Chargeable gain (before any available annual exemption)	9,000

*   Using combined period of ownership, there are six complete years of ownership between 6 April 1998 and December 2004, and a further year is added since the asset was owned on 17 March 1998.

For disposals on or after 1 April 2000, companies in a 75% group may make a joint election under s 171A to set one group company's loss against another group company's gain without actually transferring assets intra-group under s 171 as indicated above (see 3.24).

Death (ss 3(7), 4, 62)

4.37   No capital gains tax charge arises on increases in value of assets up to the point of death. If losses arise in the year of death these may be carried back and set against gains chargeable to tax in the three previous tax years, latest first (with the set-off being made only against any gains not covered by the annual exemption in those years). Tax will be refunded accordingly, with repayment supplement where appropriate running from the payment date for the tax year of death (see 9.5).

The personal representatives or legatees are treated as acquiring the assets at the market value at the date of death. When personal representatives dispose of assets at values in excess of the values at death, gains arising will be charged to tax (and exemptions the deceased could have claimed may not be available, for example on a private residence) but they may claim the annual exemption, currently £8,200, in respect of disposals by them in the tax year of death and in each of the following two tax years. Any remaining gains have previously been charged at 34%, but from 6 April 2004 the tax rate is increased to 40%.

Where within two years after a death the persons entitled to the estate vary the way in which it is distributed, they may specify in the variation that it is to apply for capital gains tax. The variation is then not regarded as a disposal by those originally entitled but as having been made by the deceased at the date of death so that no CGT charge arises on any increase in value since death. See 35.10 for detailed notes on variations.

Trusts (ss 3, 4, 68–98 and Schs 1, 5)

4.38   Trustees are chargeable persons for capital gains tax. If, however, the settlor retains an interest in the trust, any gains are taxed as the settlor's gains (see 42.13). Where that does not apply, the trustees are entitled to an annual exemption of £4,100 for 2004/05 unless the trust is for a mentally disabled person or for a person receiving attendance allowance or the middle or higher rate of disability living allowance, in which case the exempt amount is £8,200. The exemption is divided where there are several trusts created by the same settlor, but with each trust getting a minimum exemption of £820. The exemption is usually increased each year in line with the retail prices index. The rate of tax payable on the remaining gains was previously 34%, but from 6 April 2004 it has increased to 40%.

When assets are placed in trust, and when they are transferred to beneficiaries other than on the death of a life tenant, a disposal at market value is treated as taking place, but gains may sometimes be held over under the gifts relief provisions dealt with at 4.27. New anti-avoidance provisions have, however, been introduced which prevent gifts relief being claimed by trustees on disposals on or after 10 December 2003 to trusts in which the settlor has an interest (see 42.7).

When a life interest ends other than on the death of a life tenant, but the property remains in trust, this has no effect for capital gains tax. When a life tenant dies and someone else becomes entitled to the life interest, or a beneficiary becomes absolutely entitled to trust assets following a life tenant's death, the trustees are not treated as making either chargeable gains or allowable losses (except to the extent of any gains held over under the gifts relief provisions when the assets were put into trust), but the market value of the trust property at that time becomes the future base value for capital gains tax, either in the hands of the trustees or of the beneficiary.

There have been various schemes used by trusts in order to reduce or avoid capital gains tax, and specific anti-avoidance provisions have been introduced to counter them (including the provision mentioned above in relation to settlor-interested trusts). The detailed provisions on the capital gains position of trusts, including brief notes on the anti-avoidance provisions, are dealt with in CHAPTER 42, except for the overseas element, which is dealt with in CHAPTER 41.

Options (ss 114, 143–148; TA 1988, s 127A and Sch 5AA)

4.39   There are special rules concerning options connected with employment (see CHAPTER 11). For companies, options in connection with financial instruments, such as currency options and interest rate options, are taken into account in calculating income (see 3.7) and are not subject to the capital gains provisions indicated below. Anti-avoidance provisions impose an income tax charge rather than a capital gains charge where transactions in futures and options produce a guaranteed return. Apart from these exceptions, the treatment of options depends on the type of option.

The following options are not treated as wasting assets:

Quoted options to subscribe for new shares (usually called share warrants);
Traded options to buy or sell shares or other financial instruments quoted on a recognised stock exchange or futures exchange and 'over the counter' financial options; and
Options to acquire assets for use by the option holder in his business.

This means that when they are disposed of or abandoned, an allowable loss or chargeable gain may arise.

Other options are treated as wasting assets, so that their cost wastes away over their life, restricting loss relief accordingly if they lapse or become valueless. If such options are abandoned, no allowable loss can arise. The forfeiture of a deposit is treated as the abandonment of an option.

Whether an option is treated as a wasting asset or not, it is generally treated as a separate chargeable asset, so that the full amount of the consideration for the grant of the option is chargeable as a gain. This separate treatment does not apply if the option is exercised. In that case the price paid for the option is incorporated with the cost of the asset to form a single transaction both as regards the seller and the buyer and taper relief runs from the date of the exercise of the option. In the case of a call option, the buyer's indexation allowance, where available, is calculated separately on the cost of the option from the date the option was granted and on the cost of the asset from the date of acquisition. In the case of a put option, the cost of the option is netted off against both the grantor's cost of acquiring the asset and the grantee's disposal proceeds. Where a call option is exercised and settled in cash, rather than by delivery of the asset, the grantor of the option is treated as having disposal proceeds equal to the price paid by the grantee for the option, less the cash payment made by the grantor, and the grantee is treated as having disposal proceeds equal to the cash received less the indexed cost of the option (but with indexation restricted so as not to create or increase a loss).

In relation to shares, the above provisions are modified for companies (and for individuals before 6 April 1998) to bring options within the share pooling provisions. Purchased options of the same series are pooled if an acquisition is not matched with a disposal on the same day or within the next nine days, and indexation allowance is then available. If an option is exercised, the shares acquired merge with any existing pool of shares of the same class in the same company, and the indexed cost of the option forms part of the pool cost. For disposals by individuals on and after 6 April 1998, the matching rules in 38.9 apply and indexation allowance is not given for periods after April 1998. The amount paid for an option will still merge with shares acquired if the option is exercised, but the acquisition will be a separate asset, taper relief running from the date the option is exercised.

For individuals, the disposal of an option to buy or sell gilt-edged securities or qualifying corporate bonds is exempt. For companies, such options are taken into account in calculating profits under the 'loan relationships' rules (as to which see 3.6).

This section does not deal with the special provisions that apply where an option was granted or acquired in a non-arm's length bargain.

Deferred consideration

4.40   Transactions are sometimes structured along lines where only part of the consideration is received at the time of the sale, with further amounts depending upon later events, for example profit performance in the case of the sale of a family company. This aspect is dealt with briefly in CHAPTER 28.

5
Inheritance tax: general principles

Introduction

5.1   Inheritance tax may be charged on certain lifetime gifts, on wealth at death and on certain transfers into and out of trusts. It used to be called capital transfer tax, and it was introduced in 1975 to replace estate duty. The law is contained in the Inheritance Tax Act 1984 (abbreviated in this book to IHTA 1984) and subsequent Finance Acts. All references in this chapter are to the Inheritance Tax Act 1984 unless otherwise stated.

Persons liable (ss 6, 48, 158, 159, 267)

5.2   UK domiciled individuals are chargeable to inheritance tax in respect of property anywhere in the world and non-UK domiciled individuals in respect of property in the UK. Husband and wife are chargeable separately, so any available exemptions apply to each of them and each can make transfers free of tax up to the nil threshold (see 5.6).

Domicile is a legal term that is not easy to define but essentially it means the country you regard as 'home'. The term has an extended meaning for inheritance tax, and you are treated as UK domiciled if:

(a)   you were UK domiciled on or after 10 December 1974 and within the three years preceding the transfer; or

(b)   you were resident in the UK on or after 10 December 1974 and in at least 17 of the 20 tax years up to and including the year of transfer.

Double taxation relief is given where the transfer of assets attracts tax overseas as well as in the UK.

Exempt transfers

5.3   Many gifts are completely exempt from tax. Others are exempt only if they are made in lifetime. The exempt lifetime gifts are as follows.

Small gifts to same person (s 20)

Any outright lifetime gifts to any one person in any one tax year if the total gifts to that person do not exceed £250 in that year.

Gifts in consideration of marriage (s 22)

Gifts of up to £5,000 by a parent, £2,500 by a grandparent, £2,500 by one party to the marriage to the other, or £1,000 by anyone else.

Normal expenditure out of income (s 21)

To obtain exemption the gift must be part of your normal expenditure, and must not, taking one year with another, reduce your available net income (after all other transfers) below that required to maintain your usual standard of living. The exemption will often apply to life assurance policy premiums paid for the benefit of someone else.

Waivers of remuneration and dividends (ss 14, 15)

A waiver or repayment of remuneration does not attract inheritance tax. Nor does a waiver of dividends made within twelve months before any right to the dividend arises.

Capital transfers for family maintenance (s 11)

You may sometimes need to make transfers of capital in order to provide for your family, for example, following divorce, when the usual exemption for transfers between husband and wife (see 5.4) no longer applies, or to make reasonable provision for a dependent relative. Such transfers are exempt.

Annual transfers not exceeding £3,000 (s 19)

The first £3,000 of lifetime transfers in any tax year are exempt. Any unused portion of the exemption may be carried forward for one year only for use in the following tax year after the exemption for that following tax year has been used.

5.4   Other exemptions are available whether the transfer is made in lifetime or on death, as follows.

Transfers between husband and wife (s 18)

These are exempt, except where a husband or wife domiciled in the UK transfers to a foreign domiciled spouse, when transfers are only exempt up to £55,000.

Gifts to charities etc (s 23; FA 2002, Sch 18.9)

Gifts to charities, either outright or to be held on trust for charitable purposes, and gifts to registered community amateur sports clubs.

Gifts to political parties (s 24)

Gifts to political parties that qualify by having either at least two MPs in the House of Commons, or one MP and at least 150,000 votes in their favour at the last general election.

Gifts of land to registered housing associations (s 24A)

Gifts for national purposes (s 25)

Conditional exemption for heritage property (ss 30–35A)

Providing various undertakings are given, for example public access, conditional exemption applies to the transfer of property which is designated by the Treasury as of pre-eminent national, scientific, historic, artistic, architectural or scenic interest (e.g. works of art and historic buildings). A claim for such designation must be made not later than two years after the date of the transfer, or where a potentially exempt transfer (see 5.7) becomes chargeable, the date of the transferor's death. If there is any breach of an undertaking, inheritance tax becomes payable by the donee.

Maintenance funds for heritage property (s 27)

Transfers into a settlement established for the maintenance, repair or preservation of heritage property are exempt providing a Treasury direction is made following a claim not later than two years after the date of the transfer.

Decorations awarded for valour

By Revenue concession F19, decorations awarded for valour or gallant conduct are exempt from inheritance tax in lifetime and on death providing they have never been sold. If they have been sold at any time, the exemption does not apply.

Late compensation for World War 2 claims

By Revenue concession F20, the £10,000 ex gratia payments made by the Government to British survivors of Japanese imprisonment or their spouses and various other modest amounts paid by European bodies to slave labourers and other World War 2 victims or their spouses will be excluded from the recipient's estate at death.

Mutual transfers

Where a potentially exempt transfer (see 5.7) or a chargeable transfer is made and the donee then makes a gift back to the donor, there are provisions to avoid a double charge to tax if the donor dies within seven years.

Excluded property (ss 3, 5, 6, 48)

5.5   Inheritance tax is not chargeable on lifetime transfers of excluded property nor is such property taken into account in valuing an estate at death. The most common forms of excluded property are:

(i)   property situated overseas where the owner is not domiciled in the UK; and

(ii)   reversionary interests in trust funds (which means the right to the capital when the rights to the income come to an end).

In limited circumstances, excluded property may need to be taken into account in valuing lifetime transfers of other property, but in general excluded property is treated in the same way as property that is exempt.

Basis of charge (ss 1–8 and Sch 1)

5.6   A running total is kept of chargeable lifetime transfers and no tax is payable either on the lifetime gifts or on your wealth at death until a threshold is reached. The threshold has been increased from £255,000 to £263,000 for transfers on and after 6 April 2004. The full rate of tax on transfers above the threshold is 40% (unchanged since 15 March 1988) but to encourage lifetime giving, chargeable lifetime transfers above the nil threshold are charged at only 20% (but see 5.11). The scales of rates for earlier years are shown in the Table of Rates and Allowances under 'Inheritance tax'. Transfers are excluded from the running total seven years after they are made.

The threshold is increased annually, at least in line with increases in the retail prices index, unless Parliament decides otherwise. Any annual increases do not enable tax paid on earlier transfers to be recovered.

Potentially exempt transfers (s 3A)

5.7   Most of the transfers you are likely to make in your lifetime are either wholly exempt from tax (see 5.3 and 5.4) or are 'potentially exempt', and will only be subject to tax if you die within seven years after making them (subject to what is said at 5.8 about retaining a benefit). Even then, there will be no tax to pay on a potentially exempt transfer unless, when added to reckonable chargeable transfers in the seven years before it (see 5.9), it exceeds the nil threshold at death. Potentially exempt transfers that become chargeable transfers will, however, be taken into account to decide how much, if any, of the nil band is available to set against the value of your estate at death. Clearly, a very wealthy individual who had made no chargeable transfers could make a series of annual gifts which, after exemptions, equalled the annual nil rate threshold, and if he survived the last of the series by seven years, a substantial amount would have been given away with no inheritance tax consequences. If, however, he died, say, within eight years after the first gift, an extremely large inheritance tax bill would arise before considering the estate at death (although tapering relief would apply on gifts made more than three years before death — see 5.12). For illustrations of potentially exempt transfers that become chargeable transfers see Examples 1 and 4.

Example 1

The only lifetime transfer made by a widower is a gift of £100,000 on 10 June 2002 to his daughter towards the cost of buying a house. He dies in May 2004, leaving an estate at death of £260,000.

After deducting two years' annual exemptions totalling £6,000 (see 5.3), there is a potentially exempt transfer of £94,000 on 10 June 2002, which becomes chargeable because of the widower's death within seven years. No tax is payable on that transfer because it falls within the £263,000 nil threshold. There is then, however, only £169,000 of the nil threshold remaining, so that £91,000 of the death estate of £260,000 is chargeable to tax at the rate of 40%.

> If the widower had survived until 10 June 2009 the lifetime gift would
> have been completely exempt, and tax would only have been payable
> if the estate at death had exceeded the nil threshold at that time.

Transfers into and out of trusts in which someone is entitled to the income
(called interest in possession trusts) are also potentially exempt. Trusts are
dealt with in CHAPTER 42.

A potentially exempt transfer which becomes a chargeable transfer because
of your death within seven years is brought into account at the value of the
gift when you made it, and tax is calculated taking into account any
chargeable transfers (including potentially exempt transfers that have
become chargeable) within the seven years before that transfer. The nil rate
threshold and rate of tax used are, however, those in force at the date of your
death.

It is therefore possible to fix the value of the transfer by giving in lifetime and
this may be particularly useful where there are appreciating assets, since any
later growth in value is in the hands of the donee. The capital gains tax effect
must also be considered, however, because a lifetime gift of a chargeable
asset will be liable to capital gains tax unless the gain can be deferred using
the gifts relief provisions (see 4.27), whereas if the asset is held until death the
increase in value up to that time escapes capital gains tax. Any capital gains
tax paid on a gift that is a potentially exempt transfer cannot be offset in
calculating the inheritance tax on the gift if it becomes liable to inheritance
tax, but the wealth of the donor will have been depleted by the capital gains
tax paid, thus reducing the inheritance tax payable out of his estate.

If the capital gains tax gifts relief *is* available, and the potentially exempt
transfer becomes liable to inheritance tax, that tax will be payable by the
donee and will be deducted in computing the donee's capital gain when he
eventually disposes of the asset.

See 5.11 for the treatment of a gift that has fallen in value by the time of the
donor's death.

*Gifts with reservation of benefit (FA 1986, ss 102–102C and Sch 20;
FA 2004, s 84 and Sch 15)*

5.8   Gifts of property on or after 18 March 1986 are still treated as
belonging to you if you continue to enjoy any benefit from the gifted
property. Where the property is an interest in land given away on or after
9 March 1999, you will be regarded as having retained a benefit if there is
some interest, right or arrangement which enables or entitles you to occupy
the land to a material degree without paying full consideration, and the gift
is made within seven years after the interest, right or arrangement is created

or entered into. If you still retain a benefit at the time of your death, the property is treated as remaining in your estate and is taxed accordingly. See Example 2.

Example 2

A donor gives away his house but continues to live in it. He will be treated as making a second gift at the time when he ceases to occupy the house or starts to pay a proper rent for his occupation so that inheritance tax may be payable if he does not then survive for a further seven years.

The same applies where a donor gives away £50,000, but continues to receive the interest on it. He will be treated as making a second gift when he ceases to receive the interest.

You will not be treated as still retaining an interest if you make an unconditional gift of a *share* in your home to, say, your son or daughter and you both continue to live there and each of you pays a *full* share of the outgoings.

The rules about retaining a benefit can result in a double inheritance tax charge and there are special rules to eliminate any double charges that occur.

Various schemes have been devised to circumvent the gifts with reservation rules. New provisions will be introduced from 6 April 2005 to impose an *income tax* charge where someone disposes of assets (or has disposed of assets since *18 March 1986*), but retains the right to use them. The charge will be based on the annual value of the use of the assets. If the total annual value amounts to £2,500 or less no tax charge will arise. See 45.27 for further details.

Chargeable lifetime transfers (ss 2, 3, 5)

5.9   The value of a chargeable lifetime transfer is the difference between the value of the donor's estate before and after the transfer, reduced by any available exemptions (see 5.3 and 5.4) and ignoring disposals of excluded property (see 5.5). This is referred to as the 'loss to the donor' principle. In many cases the value of the transfer will be the same as the market value of the asset transferred, but this is not always the case, particularly when unquoted shares are disposed of. In some instances other 'related property' also has to be taken into account (see 5.16).

The main category of transfers which are immediately chargeable in lifetime is transfers to a discretionary trust (i.e. a trust in which no-one has a right to the income, and it is up to the trustees how much of the income, if any, they distribute). The nil threshold of £263,000 is available providing it has not already been used against earlier chargeable transfers, and also the annual exemption. As with potentially exempt transfers, chargeable lifetime transfers are taken into account in the running total at death if the donor dies within seven years after making them and tax is recalculated on them at the full rate, taking into account any chargeable transfers (including potentially exempt transfers that have become chargeable) within the seven years before the transfer.

If the gifted asset was a chargeable asset for capital gains tax, and the gain had been deferred under the capital gains gifts relief provisions (see 4.27), any inheritance tax paid immediately or on the donor's death within seven years is deducted in computing the donee's capital gain when he eventually disposes of the asset.

The inheritance tax on a chargeable lifetime gift is usually paid by the recipient, but it may be paid by the donor. In that event, the amount chargeable to tax is found by grossing up the amount of the gift to allow for the tax which the donor has to pay.

Example 3

Donor makes a chargeable lifetime transfer of £8,000 when the nil threshold had already been used, so that the rate of tax is 20%. He pays the tax.

The value for inheritance tax is £8,000 × 100/80 = £10,000.

Being:	The chargeable transfer	10,000
	Tax payable @ 20%	2,000
	Leaving for the donee	£8,000

If the donor fails to pay the capital gains tax on a gift, it may be collected from the recipient, and in that event it is deducted from the value of the gift in calculating the value for inheritance tax.

Position on death (s 4)

5.10   When you die, you are treated as making a final transfer of the whole of your estate and the tax charged on the estate depends on the total of chargeable lifetime transfers and potentially exempt transfers within the previous seven years.

Your estate is the total of all the property to which you are beneficially entitled. Powers you may have over trust property are, however, excluded (see 42.11). As well as your own property, your estate includes:

(i)   an interest as a joint tenant. Such an interest is automatically transferred to the other joint tenant(s) on your death, but it still forms part of your estate for tax purposes (this differs from a share as a tenant in common, which means each person has a separate share which he may dispose of as he wishes, and which therefore counts as his own property for all purposes); and

(ii)   the capital value of a trust fund where you are entitled to the trust income (called an interest in possession).

The inclusion of the capital in a trust fund in your estate means that on your death, you are treated as making a chargeable transfer of the capital in the fund, although the tax on that amount is paid by the trustees.

On the other hand, there is no charge to tax when someone entitled to the income from a trust fund is allocated part of the supporting capital, because the capital is treated as being part of his estate already.

Where assets in your estate at death are left to your spouse, no tax is payable (unless the spouse is not domiciled in the UK, in which case the exempt amount is limited to £55,000). The other exempt transfers listed at 5.4 are also left out of account. For more detailed points relating to the death estate, see CHAPTER 35.

Transfers made within the seven years before death (s 7)

5.11   Where you have made a chargeable lifetime transfer, all or part of which has been charged at the 20% rate, and you die within seven years of making it, additional tax may be payable, because the tax is recomputed at the full scale rate applicable at the date of death, taking into account other chargeable transfers (including potentially exempt transfers that have become chargeable — see below) within the seven years before the transfer (and using the nil rate threshold applicable at the date of death).

If you have made any potentially exempt transfers in the seven years before your death, they become chargeable, and are taken into account in the running total, along with any chargeable lifetime transfers, according to the date each transfer was made. This may mean that the nil threshold is no longer available against a chargeable lifetime transfer, causing tax, or more tax, to be payable. See Example 4.

Example 4

Donor who died on 25 May 2004 made the following gifts in lifetime (after taking annual and other exemptions into account):

9 April 1997	To brother	£20,000
26 July 1997	To son	£70,000
15 September 1998	To daughter	£75,000
10 April 2002	To discretionary trust (tax paid by trustees)	£260,000
30 June 2003	To sister	£20,000

The only chargeable lifetime gift was the gift to the discretionary trust on 10 April 2002, on which, using the nil rate band at that date, the tax was

(£260,000 – £250,000 nil band) = £10,000 @ 20%   £2,000

On death:

Gift on 9 April 1997 is not taken into account, since it was more than seven years before donor's death. Gifts to son, daughter and sister become chargeable, but no tax is payable on gifts to son and daughter, since they are below nil threshold. Threshold remaining is, however, (£263,000 – £145,000) = £118,000.

Tax on gift to trust (£260,000 – £118,000) = £142,000 @ 40%			56,800
Less paid in lifetime			2,000
			£54,800
Tax on gift to sister	£20,000	@ 40%	£8,000

Tax @ 40% will also be paid on estate at death.

Had the gift on 9 April 1997 been to a discretionary trust, it would have been a chargeable transfer at that time, although no tax would have been payable since it would have been below the nil threshold. It would have been taken into account in calculating the tax on the other lifetime transfers, since it was made within the seven years before each of them. It would, however, have been excluded from the running total seven years after it was made, i.e. at 9 April 2004, and would not, therefore, have been taken into account in calculating tax on the death estate.

If the value of a gifted asset has fallen between the time of the gift and death, the lower value may be used to calculate the tax. If the donee had sold the asset before the donor's death in an arm's length, freely negotiated sale, to an unconnected person, the sale proceeds may be used instead if they are lower than the value when the gift was made. In neither case can the reduction be made where the gifted asset was tangible movable property with a predictable life of 50 years or less (for example, a car).

Tapering relief

5.12   When working out the tax, or additional tax, payable on gifts within the seven years before your death, the tax is reduced if you have survived the gift by more than three years. The percentage of the full scale rate payable following the reduction is as follows (see Example 5).

Time between chargeable gift and death	% payable
Up to 3 years	100
More than 3 but less than 4 years	80
More than 4 but less than 5 years	60
More than 5 but less than 6 years	40
More than 6 but less than 7 years	20

Example 5

The only chargeable transfer made by a taxpayer in lifetime is a transfer to a discretionary trust of £273,000 (after exemptions) on 30 September 2004. The tax payable by the trustees is (£273,000 – £263,000 nil band = £10,000 @ 20%), i.e. £2,000.

Assuming that the tax rate and threshold remain unchanged, so that £4,000 is in fact the amount of tax at the full scale rate, the effect of the tapering relief is as follows.

If taxpayer dies on	Time between gift and death	% of £4,000 payable	Amounting to
			£
10.10.2005	Less than 3 yrs	100	4,000
31.12.2007	3 to 4 yrs	80	3,200
31.1.2010	5 to 6 yrs	40	1,600

Extra tax if death occurs on 10.10.2005 will be £2,000.

Extra tax if death occurs on 31.12.2007 will be £1,200.

No extra tax will be due if death occurs on 31.1.2010 because the reduced tax of £1,600 is less than the tax already paid of £2,000.

The tax on death will usually not be double the earlier lifetime tax as in this example, because of the annual increase in the threshold.

If the lifetime gift had been to an individual, or an 'interest in possession' trust, it would have been potentially exempt, and no tax would have been paid on it in lifetime, but the calculation of the tax at death would be the same.

The donee has to pay the amount by which the tax at the appropriate percentage of the full scale rate exceeds any tax paid on the gift in lifetime. If, however, the lifetime tax exceeds the death tax, no repayment is available.

Valuation of property (ss 160–198)

5.13   The value of property for inheritance tax is the amount it might reasonably be expected to fetch if sold in the open market. The price is not, however, to be reduced on the grounds that the whole property is placed on the market at one time.

If the asset to be transferred will give rise to a capital gains tax liability, and the donee agrees to pay that tax, then the value transferred is reduced by the capital gains tax paid. However, capital gains tax may sometimes not arise on gifts because of the availability of gifts holdover relief. See 4.27.

Valuation on death

5.14   The way in which the death estate is valued, and the reliefs which are available, are dealt with below. The exemptions available are dealt with at 5.4.

Transfers of 'excluded property' are ignored in valuing the death estate (see 5.5).

Apart from life assurance policies (see 5.17), the value of property to be included in the estate at death is that immediately before death. Changes in the value of the estate as a result of the death are taken into account, for example the increased value of life assurance policies and the reduction in the value of goodwill which depends upon the personal qualities of the deceased. Allowance is made for reasonable funeral expenses. In the case of overseas property, allowance is also made for additional expenses incurred because of its situation, subject to a limit of 5% of the value of the property.

Quoted securities and land transferred on death

5.15   Where an estate on death includes quoted securities, and they are sold by the personal representatives within twelve months after death for less than their value at death, then the total sales proceeds before expenses may be substituted for the death value. A revised value may also be included for quoted securities that are cancelled, or in which dealings are suspended, within the twelve months after death. In claiming this relief, *all* sales in the twelve month period, including those at a profit, must be taken into account in the total proceeds figure. The relief is restricted if any purchase of quoted securities takes place in the period from the date of death to the end of two months after the last sale within the twelve months after death.

If the estate includes land which is sold by the personal representatives within four years after death, a claim may be made, subject to certain restrictions, to substitute the total sale proceeds before expenses for the value at death.

Related property

5.16   If you own part of an asset, and part is owned by your husband or wife, or you have made an exempt transfer of part of an asset to a charity, political party or national heritage body and it is still owned by that body or has been so owned at any time within the previous five years, the related property provisions apply. The related property provisions are mainly relevant to valuing transfers of unquoted shares and where freehold or leasehold property is owned jointly.

If it produces a higher value than its unrelated value, the value of a part of related property is taken as an appropriate portion of the total value of all the property. See Example 6.

Example 6

The shareholders of Related Ltd, an unquoted company, are Mr R 40%, Mrs R 25%, others 35%. Shareholdings are valued as follows:

65%	£117,000
40%	£48,000
25%	£30,000

Inheritance tax values are:

Mr R 40/65 × £117,000	£72,000 (being greater than £48,000)
Mrs R 25/65 × £117,000	£45,000 (being greater than £30,000)

If related property is sold within three years after death to an unconnected person, a claim may be made for the tax at death to be recomputed using its unrelated value (not its sale value).

Life assurance policies

5.17   The valuation of life assurance policies depends on whether the transfer is during the lifetime or on the death of the donor. Policies transferred in lifetime are valued at the greater of the surrender value and the premiums paid. Sometimes it is the policy premiums, rather than the policy itself, which are transfers of value (e.g. where a policy is written in trust for another person and the premiums are paid by the person whose life is assured) and in such cases each premium payment will be a potentially exempt transfer unless it is already exempt as a gift out of income or as a small gift or because of the annual exemption.

On death the maturity value of a policy taken out by a person on his own life will be included in his estate unless it has been assigned to someone else in lifetime, or it has been written in trust for the benefit of someone else.

Associated operations (s 268)

5.18   There are rules to enable the Revenue to treat a series of connected operations as a single transfer of assets made at the time of the last of them.

Business property relief (ss 103–114; FA 1987, s 58) and agricultural property relief (ss 115–124C; FA 1987, s 58)

Business property relief

5.19   Business property relief is available on the value of transfers of business property, providing certain conditions as to the length of ownership and type of business are satisfied. For transfers on and after 10 March 1992, and any recalculation of tax on earlier transfers following a death on or after that date, the relief is given at the following rates:

A business or interest in a business (including a partnership share)	100%
Transfers out of unquoted shareholdings	100%*
Transfers out of a controlling shareholding in a quoted company (including control through 'related property' holdings)	50%

Land or buildings, machinery or plant used for a business carried
on by:

a company of which the donor has control; or a   50%
partnership in which the donor was a partner; or the
donor, being settled property in which he had an
interest in possession

* The rate of relief for transfers out of unquoted shareholdings of 25% or
  less was previously 50%, but was increased to 100% for transfers on or
  after 6 April 1996, and for recalculating tax on earlier transfers where
  death occurs on or after 6 April 1996.

Shares on the Alternative Investment Market (AIM) are treated as unquoted
shares. Relief is not available on quoted or unquoted shares if the company's
business falls within those listed in the following paragraph.

The property transferred must normally have been owned by the donor
throughout the previous two years. For transfers out of unquoted shareholdings before 6 April 1996, the donor needed to have owned more than 25% of
the voting power *throughout* the two years before the transfer in order to get
the 100% rate of relief. Business property relief is not available where the
business consists of dealing in stocks and shares (except market makers on
the Stock Exchange and discount houses), dealing in land and buildings or
holding investments (including land which is let).

The relief is applied automatically without a claim and is given after
agricultural property relief (see below) but before available exemptions.

Agricultural property relief

5.20   Agricultural property relief is available on the transfer of agricultural property so long as various conditions are met. Agricultural property is
agricultural land or pasture (including short rotation coppice land and
farmland dedicated to wildlife habitats under Government Habitat
Schemes), woodland and buildings used for rearing livestock or fish where
the occupation of the woodland and buildings is ancillary to that of the
agricultural land, and cottages, farm buildings and farmhouses occupied
with the agricultural land. As with business property relief, the rates of relief
were increased to 100% or 50% for transfers on and after 10 March 1992, and
for any recalculation of tax on earlier transfers following a death on or after
that date. The relief only applies to the agricultural value of the property, and
in arriving at that value any loan secured on the agricultural property must
be deducted.

The agricultural property must at the time of the transfer have been either
occupied by the donor for agriculture throughout the two years ending with
the date of transfer or owned by the donor throughout the previous seven

years and occupied for agriculture by him or someone else throughout that period. Note that this enables relief to be given on agricultural investment property. In certain circumstances these rules are modified if the property transferred was acquired as a replacement for other agricultural property.

Relief is available both on the transfer of agricultural property itself, and on the transfer of shares out of a controlling holding in a farming company to the extent of the underlying agricultural value.

Relief is given at the rate of 100% where the donor had the right to vacant possession immediately before the transfer, or the right to obtain vacant possession within the next twelve months. By Revenue concession F17, the 100% rate is given on tenanted agricultural property where vacant possession is obtainable within twenty-four months, or where the property is valued broadly at vacant possession value despite the tenancy. For other tenanted agricultural property the relief is 100% for transfers of property where the letting commenced on or after 1 September 1995 (including successions to tenancies following the death of the previous tenant on or after that date) and 50% for transfers of property let before that date. Special provisions enable relief to be claimed at the 100% rate on tenanted agricultural property where the donor had been beneficially entitled to his interest in the property since before 10 March 1981 and would have been entitled to the higher rate of relief (then 50%) under the former provisions for agricultural relief which operated before that date.

Where agricultural property satisfies the conditions for business property relief, agricultural property relief is given first and business property relief is given on the non-agricultural value. As with business property relief, agricultural property relief is given without the need for a claim.

Binding contract for sale (ss 113, 124)

5.21   Property does not qualify for business or agricultural relief if it is subject to a binding contract for sale (except a contract relating to the conversion of an unincorporated business to a company, or a company reconstruction). A 'buy and sell' agreement made by partners or company directors to take effect on their death is considered by the Revenue to constitute such a contract, but not a double option agreement whereby the deceased's personal representatives have an *option* to sell and the surviving partners or directors an *option* to buy.

Calculation of tax on lifetime transfers following death within seven years (ss 113A, 113B, 124A, 124B; FA 1987, s 58)

5.22   Many lifetime gifts of agricultural and/or business property are potentially exempt when they are made. The gift will later become chargeable if the donor dies within seven years.

There are also occasions where the transfer was chargeable at the time (such as a transfer into a discretionary trust), but because the donor dies within seven years, the charge has to be recomputed at the full scale rates (allowing for tapering relief).

In computing the tax payable as a result of the death, business and agricultural property relief is applicable so long as:

(i)   the original property (or qualifying property which has replaced it) was owned by the donee throughout the period beginning with the date of the transfer and ending with the death of the donor; this condition will be regarded as satisfied if there is a period of up to three years between the sale of one qualifying property and the acquisition of another; and

(ii)   immediately before the death of the donor, the property (or any replacement property) is qualifying business or agricultural property (this may not apply because, for example, there might have been a change of use, or at the time of death there might be a binding contract for sale). In order for unquoted shares to be qualifying business property they must still be unquoted when the donor dies.

If the donee died before the donor, the periods at (i) and (ii) are from the date of the gift to the date of death of the donee.

Proportionate relief is available where only part of the property continues to qualify, for example, where part of the property has been sold.

Since any increase in the value of assets up to the date of death is also exempt from capital gains tax (see 4.37), the availability of the 100% business or agricultural property relief is an important influence in estate planning, because where it applies there will be no tax benefit from making potentially exempt transfers in lifetime. On the other hand, it cannot be certain that the tax regime will remain as favourable as it now is.

Growing timber (ss 125–130)

5.23   Where an estate on death includes growing timber, an election may be made to leave the timber (but not the land on which it stands) out of account in valuing the estate at death. The relief is dealt with in 31.23.

Quick succession relief (s 141)

5.24   Where a donee dies shortly after receiving a chargeable transfer, the transfer has increased his estate at death and therefore attracts tax in his estate as well as possibly having been taxed at the time of the earlier transfer.

Relief is given where the death occurs within five years after the earlier transfer. There is no requirement to retain the actual asset obtained by that transfer.

The total tax on the chargeable estate is calculated in the normal way and reduced by the quick succession relief. The relief is arrived at by first making the following calculation:

$$\frac{\text{Previous transfer net of tax}}{\text{Previous gross transfer}} \times \text{Tax paid on previous transfer}$$

The relief is the following percentage of the calculated amount:

Period between transfer and death	Percentage relief
Less than 1 year	100%
1–2 years	80%
2–3 years	60%
3–4 years	40%
4–5 years	20%

Example 7

Thomas, who died on 28 June 2004 leaving an estate of £300,000, had received a gift of £50,000 from his father on 30 October 2001, on which he had paid tax of £20,000 following his father's death on 26 May 2003.

Tax on Thomas's estate will be reduced by quick succession relief as follows (Thomas having died 2–3 years after gift):

$$\frac{\textit{Net transfer } 30,000}{\textit{Gross transfer } 50,000} \times \textit{Tax } £20,000 \times 60\% = £7,200$$

Quick succession relief is also available where there are successive charges within five years on trust property in which there is an interest in possession. The rates of relief are the same as those quoted above, with the percentage relief depending on the period between the successive charges.

It may be that at the time the donee dies, the transfer to him is still classed as a potentially exempt transfer because the donor is still alive, but the donor may then die, after the donee but within the seven-year period, so that the potentially exempt transfer becomes chargeable by reference to the donor's estate, with the personal representatives of the donee being liable to pay any tax. Quick succession relief will then be available in the donee's estate by reference to that tax.

Survivorship clauses (s 92)

5.25   Although the tax on successive transfers may be reduced by quick succession relief where death occurs within five years after the first transfer, this is not so beneficial as the value not being included at all. It is possible to include a survivorship clause in a will stipulating that assets do not pass to the intended beneficiary unless he/she survives the deceased by a prescribed period, limited to a maximum of six months (see 35.9). This avoids the double charge to tax.

Varying the distribution of the estate (ss 17, 142, 218A)

5.26   The way in which the estate liable to inheritance tax at death is distributed may be varied by those entitled to it, and legacies may be disclaimed wholly or in part. Where this happens within two years after the death, the variation or disclaimer takes effect for inheritance tax purposes as if it had applied at the date of death. The variation or disclaimer must not be for consideration. For variations (but not disclaimers) this is subject to the proviso that those making it (and the personal representatives if additional inheritance tax is payable) state in the variation that they intend it to have this effect. Where additional tax is payable, then within six months after the date of the variation the personal representatives must notify the Revenue of the amount of extra tax and send a copy of the variation. Following the variation/disclaimer inheritance tax will be payable as if the revised distribution had operated at death. Similar provisions apply for capital gains tax (see 4.37). For further details, see CHAPTER 35.

Interest-free loans

5.27   Where a loan is made free of interest, there is no transfer of capital and it is usually possible to regard the interest forgone as being normal expenditure out of income and thus exempt. If, however, a loan is made for a fixed period, or is not repayable on demand, it may be treated as a transfer of value equal to the difference between the amount lent and the present value of the future right to repayment.

Date of payment; interest on overdue or overpaid inheritance tax; penalties (ss 226–236)

5.28   The normal due dates of payment are as follows.

Chargeable lifetime transfers between 6 April and 30 September	Chargeable lifetime transfers between 1 October and 5 April	Death — including additional tax on chargeable lifetime transfers and tax on potentially exempt transfers which become chargeable
30 April in following year	6 months after end of month in which transfer was made	6 months after end of month in which death occurs

The personal representatives of a deceased's estate must, however, pay any tax for which they are liable at the time they apply for probate, even if this is before the due date as shown above. If the personal representatives take out a loan to pay the inheritance tax, relief for the interest paid on the loan is given against the income of the estate (see 42.4).

Interest is payable on overdue tax (or repayable on overpaid tax). For recent rates see the Table of Rates and Allowances under 'Interest on overdue/ overpaid inheritance tax'. Interest on overdue tax is not deductible in arriving at income tax payable by the personal representatives and interest on overpaid tax is tax-free. Overpayments carry interest from the date of payment.

Where tax has not been paid because a transfer was conditionally exempt, the due date is six months after the end of the month in which the event by reason of which it is chargeable occurs (e.g. breach of an undertaking in respect of heritage property).

Payment by instalments

5.29   Inheritance tax may be paid by equal yearly instalments over ten years on qualifying assets. This applies where the assets are transferred on death, and also to chargeable lifetime transfers if the *donee* pays the tax. The option to pay by instalments also applies to a potentially exempt transfer of qualifying property which becomes a chargeable transfer on the death of the donor within seven years after the gift, so long as the donee still owns the gifted property (or, for transfers of property qualifying for business or agricultural relief, replacement property) at the time of the donor's death. The first instalment is due on chargeable lifetime transfers on the normal due date and in the case of tax payable in consequence of death, six months after the end of the month in which the death occurred.

The instalment option applies to land wherever situated, to a business or interest in a business, to timber when it becomes chargeable after being left out of account on a previous death, to controlling shareholdings, and to unquoted shares if certain conditions are met. For unquoted shares, the instalment option is not available for tax payable as a result of the donor's death, unless the shares are still unquoted when the donor dies (or, if earlier, when the donee dies).

Interest normally runs only from the date the instalment falls due and not on the full amount of the deferred tax. This does not apply in the case of land, other than land included in a business or partnership interest and agricultural land, nor in the case of shares in an investment company. Interest in those two cases is charged on the total amount remaining unpaid after the normal due date, the interest being added to each instalment as it falls due.

If the property is sold, the outstanding tax becomes payable immediately.

Penalties

5.30   In addition to interest on overdue tax, various penalties may be charged. For details see 9.30.

Liability for tax (ss 199–214, 237)

5.31   On lifetime transfers of property which are immediately chargeable, other than transfers of property in a trust fund, primary liability for payment rests with the donor. The donor and donee may, however, agree between them who is to pay, the transfer having to be grossed up if the donor pays (see Example 3 at 5.9).

In the case of lifetime transfers of property which is within a discretionary trust, the primary liability is that of the trustees.

On death, the personal representatives are liable to pay the tax on the assets coming into their hands, while the liability for tax on trust property which becomes chargeable at death rests with the trustees. See the example at 42.17.

Where, as a result of the death of the donor within seven years, additional tax becomes payable on a lifetime transfer, or a potentially exempt transfer becomes liable to tax, the primary responsibility for paying the tax is that of the donee. The personal representatives are only liable if the tax remains unpaid twelve months after the end of the month in which the donor died, or to the extent that the tax payable exceeds the value of the gifted property held by the donee.

In addition to the persons mentioned, certain other people may be liable to pay inheritance tax, but usually only where tax remains unpaid after the due date. Where tax is unpaid the Revenue are usually able to take a legal charge on the property concerned.

The person who is liable to pay inheritance tax is not necessarily the person who ultimately bears the tax. The trustees of a settlement are liable to pay any tax arising on the transfer of trust funds, but the next person to enjoy the income or to receive the capital bears the tax because the trust funds are correspondingly lower. Personal representatives are liable to pay the tax on the assets of the deceased at death, but the residuary legatees (those who receive the balance of the estate after all other legacies) will suffer the tax by a reduction in the amount available for them, the other legatees receiving their legacies in full unless the will specifies that any particular legacy should bear its own tax.

Personal representatives, trustees and others liable to pay inheritance tax have to deliver an account to IR Capital Taxes (see 9.30).

Use of insurance

5.32   There are many instances in the inheritance tax provisions where the potential liability to tax is not known at the time of the transfer, notably when potentially exempt transfers are made, but also when chargeable transfers are made, because if the donor dies within seven years additional tax may be payable. Temporary insurance cover may be taken out by the donee on the life of the donor to provide for the possible tax liability, with the policies being tailored to take account of the reduction in potential liability once the donor has survived the gift by three years.

6
Stamp duty

Background

6.1   Stamp duty has been charged since the seventeenth century, and present legislation is based on the Stamp Act 1891 as amended by numerous subsequent Finance and other Acts. Stamp duty is a fixed or ad valorem charge on documents and duty is not payable if there is no document. A separate charge — stamp duty reserve tax — was introduced in 1986 to cover share transactions that escaped stamp duty (see 6.8). The Electronic Communications Act 2000 has now made it possible to remove the legal requirement for transactions to be evidenced by paper documents, and the Government has facilitated the introduction of electronic transfer of land and buildings by bringing in a separate tax — stamp duty land tax — to replace stamp duty on land and buildings from 1 December 2003 (or, in the case of certain partnership transactions, from 23 July 2004 – see 6.22). Following the introduction of stamp duty land tax, stamp duty applies only to stock and marketable securities and certain transfers of interests in partnerships (as to which see 6.23).

Legislation was passed fourteen years ago to abolish stamp duty reserve tax and to charge stamp duty only on land and buildings from an 'appointed day', which never arrived. Paradoxically we have now the reverse situation — retaining stamp duty reserve tax and abolishing stamp duty on land and buildings — except that another immensely complicated tax has been brought in to replace it.

Stamp duties are administered by Inland Revenue Stamp Taxes. Stamp duty is dealt with in 6.2 to 6.7, stamp duty reserve tax in 6.8 and 6.9, and stamp duty land tax in 6.10 to 6.21. Paragraphs 6.22 to 6.26 deal with topics affected by both stamp duty and stamp duty land tax.

Stamp duty

Instruments chargeable and rates of duty (FA 1999, ss 112, 113 and Schs 13–16)

6.2   Stamp duty is charged on certain documents completed in the UK or relating to UK property or transactions (other than land and buildings). No duty arises on transactions carried out orally.

Generally, documents should be stamped before they take effect, although in practice the Commissioners permit stamping within 30 days without charging any penalty.

Duty is either fixed or based on value depending on the heading under which the transaction falls. Following the introduction of stamp duty land tax from 1 December 2003, the only fixed stamp duty remaining is the £5 stamp duty on certain bearer securities. Ad valorem duties are rounded up to the nearest multiple of £5. Some of the main headings and rates of duty (some of which are on a sliding scale) are given in the table below. There are numerous exemptions and reliefs from each heading. There is no charge when shares are converted from certificated to paperless form on being deposited into CREST (the paperless share dealing system) (FA 1996, s 186).

Table of stamp duties **Heading**	**Rate of duty**
Bearer instruments (excluding those in foreign currency, but see 6.8)	
Bearer instruments issued in UK or by UK company, other than as indicated below	1½%
Deposit certificates in non-UK company and bearer instruments by usage issued by non-UK company	0.2%
Bearer instruments given in substitution for similar instrument stamped ad valorem	£5
Conveyances or transfers on sale	
Stock and marketable securities	½%
Certain partnership transfers (see 6.23):	
Up to £250,000	1%
£250,001 to £500,000	3%
Over £500,000	4%
Duty on 'certified transactions' not exceeding £60,000	Nil
Various share and convertible loan stock transactions	
Such as takeovers, mergers, demergers, schemes of reconstruction and amalgamation (except where there is no real change in ownership), purchase by a company of its own shares	½%
Shares converted into depositary receipts or put into duty free clearance systems	1½%*
* But see 6.8	

Adjudication and valuation (SA 1891, ss 12–13B)

6.3   Adjudication is the assessment by a Stamp Office of how much duty, if any, is payable on a document and also the amount of any penalty payable for late stamping (as to which see 6.6). Additionally, if after adjudication an unstamped or insufficiently stamped document is not duly stamped within 30 days, a penalty of up to £300 may be charged. Adjudication may be voluntary or compulsory. Anyone may ask a Stamp Office to state whether a document is chargeable, and if so, how much duty is payable. Sometimes, adjudication is compulsory, for example where exemption from duty is claimed on a company reconstruction without change in ownership.

Having considered the document the Stamp Office will either stamp it 'adjudged not chargeable with any stamp duty' or they will assess the duty and when it is paid, they will stamp the document 'adjudged duly stamped'. An adjudication stamp is normally conclusive evidence of due stamping.

An appeal may be made against an adjudication. Such an appeal must be made within 30 days and the duty plus any interest or penalty must be paid first. Appeals relating to late stamping penalties go first to the Special Commissioners and other appeals to the High Court.

Letters of allotment

6.4   Sales of renounceable letters of allotment are chargeable to stamp duty reserve tax at ½% (see 6.8).

Conveyances and transfers on sale (FA 1987, ss 50, 55; FA 1999, s 112 and Sch 13)

6.5   As indicated in 6.1, this heading is relevant only in relation to stock and marketable securities and certain transfers of interests in partnerships (as to which see 6.23).

No duty is payable in connection with British Government stock, including gilt warrants, nor on a conveyance, transfer or lease to the Crown. There are special exemptions from duty for financial intermediaries trading in UK securities and in connection with stock borrowing and sale and repurchase arrangements.

Interest and penalties (SA 1891, ss 15–15B; FA 1989, s 178; FA 1999, ss 110, 114 and Sch 17)

6.6   Where documents are submitted late for stamping, interest and penalties may be charged. There are separate interest and penalty provisions in relation to bearer instruments. The provisions for other documents are as follows.

Interest is chargeable on all documents liable to ad valorem duty that are not stamped within 30 days of execution, but rounded down to a multiple of £5 and not charging amounts of £25 or less. Interest is also chargeable on stamp duty penalties (other than late stamping penalties).

Interest will be paid on repayments of overpaid duty from 30 days after execution or from the date of payment if later (except for repayments of less than £25).

The rates of interest are the same as for income tax.

If documents are submitted for stamping more than 30 days after execution a (mitigable) penalty may be charged.

The maximum penalty is £300 or the amount of the duty if less for documents submitted up to one year late. For documents submitted later than that, the maximum is £300 or the amount of the duty if more. There is a penalty of up to £300, or up to £3,000 in cases of fraud, for various administrative offences.

Anti-avoidance provisions (FA 2000, ss 117–122 and Sch 33)

6.7   The sharply increasing rates of stamp duty over recent years have led to an increase in devices to avoid stamp duty. FA 2000 introduced a general provision that regulations may be issued to block such devices as they arise, where they relate to any extent to land, stock or marketable securities. Such regulations will cease to be valid after 18 months unless they have been included in a Finance Act. These anti-avoidance provisions are relevant only to stock and marketable securities and certain partnership transactions from 1 December 2003 following the introduction of stamp duty land tax.

Various specific anti-avoidance provisions were also introduced by FA 2000. For documents executed on or after 28 March 2000, duty is charged at the shares rate where marketable securities are transferred in exchange for property that is exempt from stamp duty reserve tax. For documents executed on or after 28 July 2000, stamp duty is also chargeable at the shares rate where the consideration for a sale is the right to a future issue of securities.

Stamp duty reserve tax (FA 1986, ss 86–99; FA 1990, ss 110, 111; FA 1997, ss 100, 101; FA 1999, s 122 and Sch 19; FA 2001, s 94; SIs 1986/1711; 1997/1156; 1999/3262; 2001/964)

6.8   Stamp duty reserve tax is dealt with mainly by Stock Exchange brokers and financial intermediaries, and comprehensive guidance notes have been issued for those concerned. The following is a brief outline of the tax.

Stamp duty reserve tax (SDRT) at the rate of ½% applies to share transactions which escape duty, for example, sales of renounceable letters of allotment and transactions within the same Stock Exchange account. Following the introduction of the CREST system of paperless share dealing on the Stock Exchange, CREST transactions that would have attracted stamp duty at ½% attract ½% SDRT instead.

Stamp duty reserve tax also applies to shares converted into depositary receipts or put into a duty free clearing system, and the rate of tax on these transactions is 1½%. The tax is only payable, however, to the extent that it exceeds any ad valorem stamp duty on the transaction, and where the ad valorem duty exceeds the amount of reserve tax, no reserve tax is payable. Clearing systems are able to elect to pay stamp duty or SDRT in the normal way on their transactions, and in that event the 1½% charge when shares are put into the system does not apply.

SDRT at ½% applies to transfers of units in unit trust schemes or shares in Open Ended Investment Companies (OEICs). From 6 April 2001 transfers of units in unit trusts and surrenders of shares in open-ended investment companies are exempt where they are held within individual pension accounts (see 17.1).

SDRT does not apply to gilt-edged stocks, traded options and futures, non-convertible loan stocks, foreign securities not on a UK register, depositary interests in foreign securities, transfers of units in foreign unit trusts, the issue of new securities and purchases by a charity. There are also special exemptions for financial intermediaries.

An anti-avoidance measure imposes stamp duty reserve tax at ½% on transfers of foreign currency bearer shares and of sterling or foreign currency bearer loan stock that is convertible or equity related. The charge does not apply if the securities are listed on a recognised stock exchange and the transfer is not made as part of a takeover. A further anti-avoidance measure imposes SDRT at 1½% on the issue or transfer by a UK company of foreign currency bearer instruments into a depositary or clearance service in connection with a merger or takeover of any company. SDRT at 1½% is also charged on the issue or transfer into a depositary or clearance system of foreign currency bearer instruments that would otherwise be exempt from duty, unless they are subscribed for cash and they either carry a right to a dividend at a fixed rate or are loan capital.

Liability to stamp duty reserve tax arises at the date of the agreement (or if the agreement is conditional, at the date the condition is satisfied). For transactions via an exchange (in particular CREST transactions), the tax is payable on a date agreed with the Revenue (or if there is no agreed date, the fourteenth day after the transaction). For other transactions the due date is the seventh day of the month following the month in which the transaction occurred and the person liable to pay the tax (i.e. the broker, dealer or purchaser) must give notice of the charge to the Revenue on or before that date. If duty is paid after reserve tax has been paid, the reserve tax is refunded (plus income tax free interest on refunds over £25). The tax is collected by market makers, brokers and dealers.

Interest and penalties (SI 1986/1711 reg 20 and Sch)

6.9   Interest is charged on overdue reserve tax (or paid on reserve tax repayments) from fourteen days after the transaction date for exchange transactions and otherwise from seven days after the end of the month of the transaction, and there are various penalties for defaults, including a mitigable penalty of £100, plus £60 a day following a declaration by the Commissioners, where the appropriate notice of liability has not been given and the tax has not been paid.

The rates of interest are the same as for income tax.

Stamp duty land tax (FA 2003, ss 42–124 and Schs 3–19; FA 2004, ss 296–305 and Sch 39–41)

6.10   Stamp duty land tax (SDLT) was introduced from 1 December 2003 to charge tax on transactions relating to UK land and whether or not any party to the transaction is present or resident in the UK and whether or not a document is used. If a document is used, SDLT is charged whether or not it is executed in the UK. If a contract for a land transaction is 'substantially performed' (broadly when most of the consideration is paid or possession is taken of the property) before being formally completed, SDLT arises at that time. Otherwise it arises at the time of completion.

The consideration for an SDLT transaction is the amount payable in money or moneys' worth. Where consideration is contingent, tax is payable on the assumption that the consideration will be payable. Where consideration is uncertain, a reasonable estimate must be made. Where all or part of contingent or uncertain consideration is payable more than 18 months after the effective date of the transaction, an application may be made to defer the appropriate amount of tax. Provision is made for the tax to be adjusted upwards or downwards when the contingency occurs (or it is clear it will not occur), or when uncertain consideration is ascertained. Where a company purchases land from a connected person, the purchase price is deemed to be not less than the market value.

Certain transactions are exempt from SDLT, as indicated in 6.19, 6.20 and 6.24.

Rates of tax etc

6.11   The rates of SDLT are as follow:

Non-residential property:	Up to £150,000	Nil
	£150,001 to £250,000	1%
	£250,001 to £500,000	3%
	Over £500,000	4%
Residential property:	Up to £60,000	Nil
	£60,000 to £250,000	1%
	£250,001 to £500,000	3%
	Over £500,000	4%

Because of Islamic rules, certain property financing arrangements have attracted additional stamp duty costs compared with conventional mortgages. Special SDLT provisions have been introduced to equate the SDLT payable with that on purchases made with conventional mortgages.

Leases of land and buildings (FA 2003, ss 55, 56, 120 and Schs 5, 17A; FA 2004, Sch 39; SI 2003/2914)

6.12   Stamp duty land tax (SDLT) applies both to lease premiums and to the rental element of a lease. Lease premiums are charged at the same rates as for freehold transfers, unless the annual rent exceeds £600, in which case there is no zero rate band for the premium and the 1% charging rate applies to premiums up to £250,000. All variations of a lease (whenever the lease was granted) that extend the lease or increase the rent (other than to reflect changes in the retail prices index) are treated as the grant of a new lease. SDLT will apply to a capital payment by the landlord where the term of a lease is reduced, and to a capital payment by a tenant to commute all or part of the rent. All other lease variations are ignored.

It was originally intended that the stamp duty charging provisions for the rental element of leases would be replaced by a 1% charge on the net present value (NPV) of the rental payments to the extent that the NPV exceeded £60,000 for residential property or £150,000 for non-residential property. It has now been provided that the 1% charge will apply only to the excess of the NPV over the £60,000 or £150,000 threshold.

6.13   Subject to anti-avoidance provisions, rent increases more than five years after the start of a lease are ignored in calculating NPV and the rent value used for later periods is the highest rent in any 12 months in the first five years. Where rent is uncertain (e.g. related to turnover), the NPV is originally based on a reasonable estimate. If the rent is still uncertain after five years, a single additional land transaction return is required in which the NPV will be based on the actual rent in the first five years and the highest rent in any 12 months during those years, as above, for the remaining years of the lease. If the rent becomes certain within the five years the single additional return will be required at that time.

6.14   Where a lease is surrendered, SDLT is payable on any consideration paid by the landlord as for a sale. If a reverse premium is paid by the tenant, SDLT is not chargeable. Where a lease is surrendered in return for a new lease, the grant of the new lease does not count as chargeable consideration for the surrender, and the surrender does not count as chargeable consideration for the new lease. Furthermore, credit is given in computing the SDLT on the new lease for the amount of rent due for the surrendered years.

6.15   The grant of a lease for seven years or less only has to be notified to the Stamp Office if there is tax to pay or a relief to be claimed. From 22 July 2004, this will also apply to the assignment of a lease. Other grants/ assignments of leases up to seven years may be self-certified.

Value added tax

6.16   The value on which stamp duty land tax is charged on sales and leases of land and buildings includes any value added tax on the transaction. Where, however, a landlord has the option to charge VAT, but has not chosen to do so by the date of the transaction, VAT will be excluded from the chargeable consideration for the lease. For further details on the VAT position on property, see CHAPTER 32.

Part exchanges, sale and leaseback and other reliefs (FA 2003, ss 57A, 58A and Sch 6A; FA 2004, s 296 and Sch 39)

6.17   Relief is available, subject to various conditions, where a builder takes a home in part exchange, or where someone buying a new home from a builder sells their old home to a property trader, or where a property trader buys a home from someone whose sale of the property has fallen through to enable that person to proceed with the purchase of another property. Where the conditions are satisfied, the acquisition by the builder or property trader is exempt from SDLT.

From 22 July 2004, relief for sale and leaseback transactions, previously restricted to commercial property, will be extended to other property to help those entering into 'home reversion plans'. The effect of the relief is that the 'leaseback' element of the transaction is exempt from SDLT.

Rents to mortgages scheme (FA 2003, Sch 9.6)

6.18   Where council house tenants buy their homes under a 'rents to mortgages scheme', stamp duty land tax is charged at the time they enter the scheme, on the then market value of the property, less any discount under the 'right to buy' provisions. If that amount is less than £60,000, no stamp duty is payable. 'Rents to mortgages' schemes enable tenants to buy their homes for an initial payment, which may be financed by a mortgage and repaid in place of rent, plus a balance provided by way of interest-free loan. The amount payable when the purchaser is ready to repay the loan depends on the market value of the property at that time.

Transfers and leases of land and buildings by and to Registered Social Landlords (FA 2003, ss 49, 71 and Sch 3)

6.19   Registered Social Landlords (RSLs), such as Housing Associations, provide social housing and are registered under the Housing Acts.

Land transactions under which property is acquired by RSLs in specified circumstances are exempt from SDLT.

Leases by RSLs for an indefinite term or terminable by notice of a month or less that are provided under contracts with local authorities to house the homeless, the RSL itself having obtained the property on a lease of five years or less, are also exempt from SDLT.

Transfers and leases of property in disadvantaged areas (FA 2003, s 57 and Sch 6; SI 2003/1056)

6.20   Sales and leases of non-residential property in designated disadvantaged areas (referred to as Enterprise Areas) are exempt from SDLT. Residential property is also exempt if the consideration, or the relevant rental value for leased property, does not exceed £150,000, unless in the case of leased property a premium is payable and the annual rent exceeds £600. In that event there is still no charge on the rental value but SDLT is chargeable on the premium. The part of the premium that would otherwise have fallen within the zero rate band is chargeable at the 1% rate. Provision is made for apportionment where only part of the property is within a disadvantaged area, or where property is only partly residential.

Returns etc

6.21   Purchasers must send the Stamp Office a return notifying a land transaction within 30 days after the effective date of the transaction. With limited exceptions this applies whether or not any tax is payable. From 22 July 2004, a return is not required for acquisition of interests in residential property for up to £1,000. Where tax is payable, the return must include a self-assessment and be accompanied by payment of any tax due (unless payment is made electronically or at a bank or post office). A further return will be required within 30 days after any event causing SDLT relief to be withdrawn under the groups or charities provisions, accompanied by the tax due.

It is possible in most circumstances to complete SDLT returns on the internet (www.ir-online.gov.uk/stamps/). Before doing so it is necessary to obtain book of paying-in slips from the Stamp Office, because the payslip contains the required reference number for the entire service. The system will calculate the tax due, and the return can then be printed, signed by the purchasers and posted. Later in 2004 it should be possible to submit returns using a full on-line service.

There are provisions similar to the income tax self-assessment rules providing for separate claims to be made where they cannot be made in an SDLT return or amended return, requiring records to be kept and providing for Revenue enquiries into returns, Revenue determinations and assessments, and appeals against Revenue decisions. There are also similar penalties for failing to deliver a return, fraudulently or negligently delivering an incorrect return, failing to preserve records, failing to comply with notices to provide documents or information, assisting in incorrect returns etc. Criminal proceedings may be taken for fraudulent evasion of SDLT. Interest is payable on overdue SDLT and on overdue penalties. Interest is payable to taxpayers on overpaid tax. The rates of interest are the same as for income tax.

When registering land transactions with the Chief Land Registrar, purchasers must produce either a Revenue certificate that a land transaction return has been delivered or a self-certificate that no land transaction return is required. There are provisions for records to be kept of, and Revenue enquiries into, self-certificates, and there are related penalty provisions.

Transfers of interests in partnerships (FA 2003, Sch 15, Pt 3; FA 2004, Sch 41)

6.22   From 23 July 2004, stamp duty land tax applies to the transfer of an interest in land into or out of a partnership and the transfer of an interest in a partnership where the partnership property includes an interest in land. The amount chargeable is the proportion of the market value of the land that has been transferred. Where existing partnership interests in land are transferred, the chargeable amount will be the appropriate proportion of the market value on which ad valorem or fixed stamp duty has not previously been paid.

6.23   Stamp duty will continue to apply to instruments effecting transfers of partnership interests, but the stamp duty payable will not exceed the amount that would have been payable on the value of any stock or marketable securities included in the transfer.

Distribution of a deceased's estate; transfers of property on break-up of marriage (FA 1985, ss 83, 84; FA 2003, ss 49, 58A and Schs 3, 6A; FA 2004, ss 296, 300 and Sch 39)

6.24   All qualifying variations of the distribution of a deceased's estate (see CHAPTER 35) and deeds conveying property under a divorce order or on separation are exempt from stamp duty and, from 1 December 2003, SDLT where the property concerned is an interest in land and buildings.

No charge to SDLT will arise when property passes to a beneficiary under a will or intestacy, nor (from 22 July 2004) when personal representatives dispose of a deceased's home to a property trader.

Intra-group transfers and company reconstructions etc. (FA 1930, s 42; FA 1967, s 27; FA 1986, ss 75–77; FA 2002, ss 111, 112 and Schs 34, 35; FA 2003, ss 62, 126 and Sch 7)

6.25   Stamp duty is not chargeable on transfers of property between companies within a 75% group, nor on company reconstructions without change of ownership. These provisions are subject to stringent anti-avoidance provisions. For transfers of shares and securities not within these provisions (takeovers etc.), stamp duty is charged at ½%, as indicated in the table at 6.2.

Similar reliefs and restrictions apply in respect of stamp duty land tax.

Foreign exchange currency rules (SA 1891, s 6; FA 2003, Sch 4.9)

6.26   All foreign currency amounts on which duty is payable are converted to sterling at the rate applying on the date of the document. For stamp duty land tax, foreign currency amounts are converted to sterling at the London closing exchange rate on the effective date of the transaction, unless the parties have used a different rate.

7
Value added tax: general principles

Basis of charge (VATA 1994, ss 1, 4)

7.1 Value added tax (VAT) is charged on the supply of goods and services in the UK and on the import of goods and certain services into the UK. It applies where the supplies are taxable supplies made in the course of business by a taxable person. Special rules apply to transactions within the European Union. These are outlined at 7.32. See 32.21 for the VAT position relating to land and buildings.

References in this chapter are to Value Added Tax Act 1994 unless otherwise stated, but many of the detailed regulations are by statutory instrument.

Taxable supplies (s 5 and Schs 4 and 6)

7.2 All supplies in the UK of goods and services to UK or overseas customers (including goods taken for own use) are taxable supplies, apart from items which are specifically exempt (see 7.3). There are special 'place of supply' rules to determine whether a supply is made 'in the UK'. Goods are normally supplied where they are physically located when they are allocated to a customer's order. Services are normally supplied where the supplier's business is established, although this general rule is subject to various exceptions, including special provisions for broadcasting and electronic services (see 7.33). Goods for own use are taxable supplies valued at cost. Business gifts are taxable supplies except where the total value of gifts given to the same person in the same year does not exceed £50. Where the limit is exceeded the gifts are valued at cost. There is not usually any VAT on gifts of services.

Exempt supplies (s 31 and Sch 9)

7.3 Supplies under the following headings are exempt, detailed rules applying as to what comes under each heading:

Betting, lotteries and gaming (except takings from gaming and amusement machines)

Burial and cremation
Charity fund raising events etc.
Cultural services etc.
Education
Finance services
Health and welfare services
Insurance
Investment gold
Land
Non-profit making sports competitions etc.
Postal services
Supplies of goods on which no input tax was recoverable
Supplies to members by trade unions and professional bodies
Works of art supplied to public bodies etc. under an inheritance tax or
capital gains tax exemption

Who is a taxable person? (Schs 1–3A)

7.4   From 1 April 2004 you are liable to be registered for VAT at the end
of any month if the taxable turnover of all your business activities in the year
ended on the last day of that month has exceeded £58,000 (previously
£56,000), unless you can satisfy Customs that your taxable turnover in the
next twelve months will not exceed £56,000 (previously £54,000). You are
required to notify Customs within 30 days of the end of the month in which
the yearly limit was exceeded and will be registered from the beginning of
the next month or such earlier date as is agreed with Customs.

Liability to register also arises at any time if your taxable supplies in the next
30 days are expected to exceed £58,000. You must notify Customs within the
30 days and you will be registered from the beginning of the 30 days.

Example 1

Your turnover for the twelve months ended 30 June 2004 was £59,000,
having been below the yearly limit at the end of previous months. You
should have notified liability to register by 30 July 2004 and been
registered from 1 August 2004 unless you could show that your
turnover in the year to 30 June 2005 would not exceed £56,000.

Example 2

On 16 December 2004 you start trading and expect your first month's
turnover to be £59,000. You must notify liability to register by 15 January 2005 and will be registered from 16 December 2004.

Registration may also be required in relation to EU acquisitions — see 7.32.

There is a penalty of up to 15% of the net tax due for failure to register, with a minimum penalty of £50. Farmers are able to avoid VAT registration if they opt to become 'flat rate farmers' — for details, see 31.10. Small businesses may join an optional flat-rate scheme, but they will still be required to be registered for VAT — see 7.19.

See also below as regards voluntary registration and selling a business as a going concern.

Notification is made on form VAT 1 and a certificate of registration VAT 4 is then issued showing the VAT registration number.

There are provisions for groups of companies to have group registration if they wish (see 7.31).

Customs have discretion to exempt you from registration if you make only zero-rated supplies (see 7.7), and do not wish to be registered. In that event you must notify Customs within 30 days of a material change in the nature of supplies made, or within 30 days after the end of the quarter in which the change occurred if it is not more precisely identifiable.

There are provisions to prevent the splitting of businesses in order to stay below the VAT registration threshold. Customs have the power to direct that where two or more persons are carrying on separate business activities which are effectively parts of the same business, they are to be treated for VAT purposes as the same business, e.g. where one spouse is a publican and the other runs the catering within the public house. Such a direction only affects future supplies and is not retrospective.

There are anti-avoidance provisions requiring non-UK registered overseas businesses to register in the UK if they sell goods in the UK on which they have claimed a refund of UK VAT under the EU or export/import provisions.

Cancellation of registration

7.5   From 1 April 2004, you will no longer be liable to be registered if your tax-exclusive turnover in the next twelve months will be £56,000 or less (previously £54,000), unless the reason for turnover not exceeding that amount is that you will cease making taxable supplies in that year, or will suspend making them for 30 days or more. You can, however, remain registered if you wish so long as you continue to trade.

You must notify Customs within 30 days of ceasing to make taxable supplies, and your registration will be cancelled from the date of notification or a later date agreed with Customs. VAT will be payable on the business assets at their value at the time of deregistration, unless no input tax was recovered on their purchase, or the business is transferred as a going concern (see 7.28), or the total VAT does not exceed £1,000.

Rates of VAT (s 2)

7.6   There are three rates of VAT, a standard rate of 17½%, the zero rate and a reduced rate of 5%. (See also 7.13 re imported antiques, etc.) The distinction between exemption and zero rating needs to be understood. Those who make exempt supplies do not charge VAT, but must recover any VAT suffered by including it in their selling prices. Those making zero-rated supplies are charging VAT, albeit at a nil rate, and can recover from Customs the VAT that has been charged to them. The VAT fraction on tax-inclusive supplies at the standard rate is 7/47 and on tax-inclusive supplies at the 5% rate is ½₁.

Zero rate (s 30 and Sch 8)

7.7   There are sixteen groups of zero-rated items, the main ones being as follows (see also CHAPTER 43 re charities):

Food, except where supplied in the course of catering, or where it is pet food, or a 'non-essential' item such as chocolate, ice cream, alcoholic and fruit drinks or crisps
Water and sewerage services, except where supplied for industrial purposes
Books (but not stationery)
Construction of buildings for residential or charitable use
Children's clothing and footwear
Transport (but not taxis or hire cars)
Drugs and medicines on prescription, and aids for the handicapped etc.
Exports (but see 7.32 re the European Union)

These are only broad categories and there are extremely detailed rules relating to what items fall under each of the headings, giving rise to many disputes between Customs and the taxpayer, a large number of which have to be settled by VAT tribunals or the courts.

Reduced rate (s 29A and Sch 7A)

7.8   The items charged at the reduced rate of 5% are:

Fuel and power for domestic or charitable use
Installation of energy saving materials (loft insulation etc. and, from 1 June 2004, ground source heat pumps) in residential or charity buildings

Grant-funded installation of central heating systems, water heating
systems, and home security goods (locks, security chains, spy holes, smoke
alarms)
Women's sanitary products
Children's car seats
Certain residential conversions, renovations and alterations (see 32.22)
See 43.5 re special grant scheme to cover VAT on repairs to and
maintenance of places of worship.

Mixed and composite supplies

7.9   Supplies may sometimes be a mixture of various elements. There is
a distinction between supplies treated as mixed supplies, i.e. a combination
of two separate supplies each taxable at the relevant rate for the item
concerned, and composite supplies, which are held to be a single supply,
with any ancillary elements being taxed at the same rate as the main supply.
Disputes as to the appropriate treatment have led to a large number of court
cases. The European Court has laid down various tests that need to be
considered.

How the system works (ss 24–26, 51B and Sch 10A)

7.10   Each person in the chain between the first supplier and the final
consumer is charged VAT on taxable supplies to him (input tax) and charges
VAT on taxable supplies made by him (output tax). He pays over to Customs
the excess of output tax over input tax, or recovers the excess of input tax
over output tax. The broad effect of the scheme is that businesses are not
affected by VAT except in so far as they are required to administer it, and the
burden of the tax falls on the consumer. All businesses, however, pay some
VAT that they cannot recover from Customs. Non–VAT registered businesses
cannot recover any VAT at all, partially exempt businesses cannot recover all
their VAT and there is some VAT that cannot be recovered by fully taxable
businesses, as indicated below. Apart from such specifically disallowed VAT,
any unrecovered VAT forms part of the business expenditure and will either
be an expense in arriving at profit or will be part of the cost of a capital item
that may qualify for capital allowances. VAT repayments are likely to arise
where most supplies are zero-rated, since the amount of VAT incurred on
purchases is likely to exceed the VAT (if any) charged on sales. If you make
both exempt and taxable supplies you can recover input tax under the partial
exemption rules — see 7.17.

If you offer a cash discount the VAT Guide 700 issued by Customs states that
VAT is charged only on the discounted amount whether the discount is taken
or not. This has recently been held by a VAT tribunal to be incorrect, so the
guidance may be changed..

The treatment of face value vouchers (such as gift vouchers and 'phone' cards) changed from 9 April 2003. The broad rules are as follows, but those issuing vouchers need to study the detailed rules carefully. As previously, retailers issuing vouchers which they will exchange for goods or services do not have to account for VAT until the vouchers are redeemed. Intermediate suppliers who sell vouchers are, however, liable to account for VAT when the vouchers are sold, subject to the normal recovery of input tax. Sales of postage stamps at or below face value continue to be disregarded for VAT purposes.

Output tax must be charged on all taxable supplies, including, for example, sales of fixed assets like plant and machinery. Special rules apply to second-hand goods — see 7.13. Where business cars on which no input VAT was recovered are sold, the sales are exempt. Where business cars on which any input VAT was recovered are sold, VAT is payable on the full selling price.

Input tax recovery

7.11   Subject to the restrictions for partially exempt businesses, you can recover input tax not only on goods purchased for resale but also on expenses such as telephones and stationery and on capital items. You cannot, however, recover input tax on business entertaining (subject to what is said at 20.8) or on cars (other than for resale, or use in a car hire or driving school business, or bought after 31 July 1995 exclusively for business purposes, for example leasing). Businesses paying leasing charges can normally recover the VAT element of the charges. If, however, the leased item is a car on which input tax has been recovered by the lessor, the lessee can recover only 50% of the input tax on the leasing charges if there is any private use of the cars. Companies cannot recover input tax on repairs, refurbishments and other expenses relating to domestic accommodation provided for directors or their families.

Where input VAT is not recoverable from Customs, it can be included as part of the business expenditure for income tax or corporation tax as indicated above, subject to any disallowance under the rules for measuring profit (so that, for example, business entertainment expenses cannot be included at all, and proprietors' car fuel expenses must be restricted by any private use — see CHAPTER 20). Disallowed VAT on cars forms part of the cost for capital allowances (see 22.2).

Business vehicle fuel bills

7.12   If your business vehicle fuel bills include fuel for private use by you or your employees, an adjustment must be made in respect of the non-business proportion unless, in the case of employees, they have paid for it in full, including VAT, in which case you have to account for the output VAT. For commercial vehicles, the adjustment is made by disallowing the private proportion of the input tax. For cars, a private use scale charge applies. The scale charges have been reduced from 1 May 2004 to reflect changes in fuel prices (see 'VAT—fuel scale rates—private motoring' in the Table of Rates and Allowances). Although employees earning less than £8,500 per annum are not charged to income tax on the benefit of private use of a car, employers have to pay the VAT fuel scale charge for *all* employees. Furthermore, it applies whether the car is provided by the employer or owned by the employee. The VAT charged on car fuel bills is fully recoverable, but a tax-inclusive supply equal to the car fuel scale charge is regarded as made in each return period for the appropriate number of cars. By concession, the scale charges do not apply if you notify Customs that you are not going to claim an input tax deduction for *any* fuel (including fuel used in commercial vehicles). The scale charges also do not apply if the input tax claimed relates only to business mileage (this being supported by detailed records). Input tax on repair and maintenance costs paid by the business is fully recoverable, and no private use adjustment is required, except that input tax cannot be reclaimed if a proprietor uses a vehicle solely for private purposes. (See 10.9 for the treatment of mileage allowances for business use of employees' cars.)

Second-hand goods (s 50A)

7.13   Many second-hand goods sold in the course of business have been obtained from the general public rather than from VAT registered traders, and if there were no special rules, the dealer buying the second-hand goods would have to charge VAT on the selling price without having any input tax to recover. EU countries operate a margin scheme which may be used for the sale of all second-hand goods, works of art, antiques and collectors' items except precious metals and gemstones, unless VAT was charged on the invoice under which the goods were acquired. Where goods are sold under the margin scheme, VAT is charged on each item only on the excess of the selling price over cost (i.e. the dealer's margin). VAT must not be shown separately on the invoice, and no input tax is recoverable by the purchaser. Where individual items cost £500 or less and are purchased in bulk, businesses may also adopt 'global accounting', under which they work out the margin on the difference between total purchases and sales rather than item by item. Global accounting cannot be used for aircraft, boats and outboard motors, caravans, horses and ponies and motor vehicles, including motor cycles. The margin scheme does not have to be used for all second-hand sales, so that VAT may be charged in full under a normal VAT invoice on sales to VAT-registered businesses.

Anti-avoidance provisions prevent the scheme being abused where goods that would not otherwise have been eligible are transferred under the provisions for transfers of going concerns (see 7.28) and where goods have been acquired through the assignment of rights under hire purchase or conditional sale agreements. Goods acquired under such transfers are not eligible unless they would have been eligible in the hands of the transferor.

EU margin scheme sales are charged to VAT in the country of origin rather than the country of destination. This means that UK margin scheme sales to someone from a country within the EU are taxed only in the UK (exports outside the EU are zero-rated). Acquisitions from countries in the EU are dealt with in the same way as purchases in the UK. VAT is not charged on acquisitions from private EU individuals, and the margin scheme may be used when the goods are sold in the UK. Acquisitions from EU VAT registered businesses may either be made through the scheme, so that the scheme may be used on resale, or outside the scheme, in which case VAT will be recoverable but the scheme cannot be used for the resale.

Imports of second-hand goods from outside the EU are subject to import VAT in the normal way (see 7.14), except that imports of certain works of art, antiques and collectors' items are charged at an effective import VAT rate of 5%.

Imports (s 37)

7.14   When goods are imported, the importer normally has to pay VAT on the goods at that time. Subject to any restriction for partial exemption etc., he then gets a credit for the input tax on his next return, thus cancelling or reducing the VAT cost to him. If the goods are for resale, output tax will be accounted for in the normal way when they are sold. There is a deferment scheme enabling importers to pay both customs duty and VAT monthly on paying an amount as security. From 1 December 2003 the scheme has been relaxed to enable a reduced (or sometimes nil) amount of security to be paid in respect of VAT. No VAT is payable on goods temporarily imported for repair, processing or modification, then re-exported. Goods which have been temporarily exported and are re-imported by the same person after repair, process, or modification bear VAT only on the value of the repair, etc. plus freight and insurance.

Separate rules apply to the European Union — see 7.32. See also 7.33 re Internet trading.

Voluntary registration

7.15   Customs will allow you to register voluntarily if your business makes taxable supplies even though your turnover is below the statutory limits. Once you are registered, you will then charge VAT on your supplies and recover input tax suffered. This may be beneficial if your customers are mainly taxable persons, but not where they are the general public. Registration will bring the burden of complying with the administrative requirements of the scheme, so may not be thought worthwhile even though a price advantage may arise. See Example 3.

Example 3

You are in business as a handyman and pay input tax of £750 on phone, stationery, etc. Your turnover is £20,000, of which £750 covers the VAT suffered.

If you register voluntarily for VAT, you need only charge £19,250 for the same supplies and your turnover will then be:

£19,250 + 17½% VAT £3,369 = £22,619.

You will pay Customs £3,369 less £750 = £2,619, leaving you with £20,000 (including £750 to cover the VAT you suffered) as before. If your customers are the general public your prices to them will be £2,619 higher, but if they are taxable persons they will recover £3,369, so that their net price will be £19,250. Your services will thus be more expensive to the general public but less expensive to the business community.

Intending trader registration

7.16   If you are in business and are not currently making taxable supplies, but intend to do so in the future, you may apply for registration and Customs are required to register you. This enables you to recover any input tax suffered even though no taxable supplies are being made. You may be required to provide evidence of your intention to trade.

Exemption and partial exemption (SI 1995/2518 Pt XIV)

7.17   If you make only exempt supplies you do not charge VAT but you cannot recover input tax charged to you, so your prices must include an element to recover the VAT suffered. Some businesses make both taxable and exempt supplies and are thus partially exempt.

If you are partially exempt you can still recover all input tax suffered despite the exempt supplies if your input tax on exempt supplies does not exceed 50% of total input tax and does not exceed £625 a month on average.

If these limits are exceeded, there are rules to determine how much of your input tax can be recovered. You can recover all the input tax directly attributable to your taxable supplies, and none of the input tax directly attributable to exempt supplies. As to the remainder of the input tax that relates to overheads, under the standard method input tax is deductible in the proportion that taxable supplies bear to total supplies. The proportion is expressed as a percentage, rounded up to the nearest whole number. Alternatively, a 'special method' can be agreed with Customs. Certain exempt supplies can be ignored in these calculations, for example where they are supplies of capital goods used for the business or are 'incidental' to the business activities. There is a right of appeal against the decision of Customs on the proportion of input tax which is recoverable.

Businesses using the standard method must adjust their deductible input tax if the method produces an amount which does not properly reflect the extent to which the goods and services are used to make taxable supplies, and the difference is substantial, defined as £50,000 or more, or 50% or more of the residual input tax, but not less than £25,000. This does not apply where the *total* residual input tax does not exceed £50,000 (£25,000 for a company that is part of a group that is not a VAT group – see 7.31).

From 1 January 2004, where businesses use a special method, and the method does not fairly and reasonably reflect the proportion of VAT relevant to taxable supplies, an override notice may be served either by Customs or by the business to correct the results of the special method until a replacement method is implemented. This will apply only where it is considered that a new method would not be agreed quickly and either Customs or the business would lose out.

Capital goods scheme (SI 1995/2518 Pt XV)

7.18   Input tax recovery on certain capital items does not depend just on the initial use of the asset but must be adjusted over a longer period where use changes between exempt and taxable supplies.

The assets concerned are computer hardware with a tax-exclusive value of £50,000 or more per item, and land and buildings (including refurbishment costs to existing buildings), or civil engineering works, with a tax-exclusive value of £250,000 or more. The adjustment period is ten years except for computers and leases for less than ten years, where the adjustment period is five years. The adjustments are reflected in the business capital allowances computations for the calculation of tax on your profits (see 22.28 below).

Optional flat-rate scheme (s 26B; SI 1995/2518 Pt VIIA)

7.19   Businesses with a taxable VAT-exclusive annual turnover of up to £150,000 (£100,000 before 10 April 2003) and total VAT-exclusive turnover of up to £187,500 (£125,000 before 10 April 2003) may join the flat-rate scheme (subject to certain exclusions, such as those using the second-hand or capital goods schemes, those convicted of VAT offences and group companies). Instead of calculating output VAT and input VAT, those using the scheme calculate the VAT payable by them by applying the appropriate flat-rate percentage for their trade sector to the VAT-inclusive value of all their business supplies in the period, including reduced rate, zero rate and exempt supplies. Businesses who register for VAT on or after 1 January 2004 and join the flat-rate scheme will pay 1% less than the flat-rate percentage for their trade sector for the first year from the date of their VAT registration. The rates for all sectors are being reduced from that date. Customs are providing an online ready reckoner to help businesses and their advisers decide whether the flat-rate scheme will be beneficial to them.

When invoicing supplies to their customers, flat-rate scheme traders add VAT in the normal way showing the normal VAT rate. The trader retains any VAT charged to his VAT registered customers but does not normally make a separate claim for input tax which is covered by the flat-rate percentage. If, however, the trader has acquired capital goods in the period with a tax-inclusive value of more than £2,000, he may recover the input tax on them. If such goods are subsequently sold, VAT must be accounted for at the full rate rather than the flat-rate. Those using the scheme cannot account for the flat-rate VAT under the cash accounting scheme, but they may use a cash-based turnover method which is very similar (see 7.23).

A trader may opt to leave the flat-rate scheme. He will have to leave the scheme if his total VAT-exclusive turnover in the previous year exceeded £225,000 (£150,000 before 10 April 2003) unless his turnover in the following year is not expected to exceed £187,500 (£125,000 before 10 April 2003), or his VAT-exclusive turnover is expected to exceed £225,000 in the next 30 days, or he becomes ineligible for the scheme.

See 20.16 for the way flat-rate scheme traders deal with VAT in their business accounts.

Tax point (time of supply) (s 6)

7.20   The basic tax point is normally when goods are made available or services are performed, unless they are invoiced and/or paid for earlier, in which case the earlier date is the tax point. Where goods or services are invoiced within 14 days after supply, the later date is the tax point, and if you invoice monthly you can adopt a monthly tax point, but in either case the tax point will be the date payment is received if earlier. For certain continuous supplies (including electricity, gas and water, management services) the tax point is normally the date of invoice or the payment date if earlier. To combat exploitation of these rules by connected businesses, some of which cannot recover all their input tax, new provisions applicable from 1 October 2003 provide for annual tax points for connected persons and groups of companies to ensure that VAT payments are not indefinitely or excessively delayed.

Special schemes for retailers

7.21   The normal VAT procedure requires records to be kept of every separate transaction. Some retailers would find it virtually impossible to keep such detailed records, so there are special schemes which enable retailers to calculate output tax in a way that suits their particular circumstances. Such schemes are restricted to businesses that cannot be expected to account for VAT in the normal way. There are three schemes, namely point of sale, apportionment and direct calculation. Any retailer with annual turnover in excess of £100 million is, however, required to arrange an individual scheme with Customs.

Lost goods (s 73) and bad debts (ss 26A, 36)

7.22   If goods are lost or destroyed before being sold, output tax is not chargeable. But once a supply has been made, VAT is chargeable. If a customer fails to pay, VAT may be reclaimed on any debt which is more than six months old and has been written off in your accounts. You must account for VAT on any part of the debt that is later recovered. If you have assigned the debt to someone else, payments received by the assignee are not taken into account unless, for debts assigned on or after 11 December 2003, you are connected with the assignee (for example you and the assignee are associated companies). If the debtor is declared insolvent, the claim in the insolvency will be the VAT-inclusive amount, because you have to account for VAT on any debt recoveries.

Debtors must repay to Customs input VAT they have reclaimed on supplies if they fail to pay the supplier within six months after the date of invoice (or after the date on which payment was due, if later), regardless of whether the supplier claims bad debt relief.

Cash accounting

7.23   Businesses with a tax-exclusive turnover of not more than £660,000 (£600,000 before 1 April 2004), can avoid the problems and delay in recovering VAT on bad debts by using the cash accounting system, providing they are up-to-date with their VAT returns and have either paid over all VAT due or have arranged to pay any overdue amount by instalments. Tax invoices still have to be issued but output tax does not have to be accounted for until cash is received. On the other hand, input tax is not recoverable until suppliers are paid. Businesses cannot use the scheme for hire purchase and similar transactions, goods and services invoiced in advance of the supply, or where payment is not due for more than six months after invoice, and Customs can refuse entry to the scheme if they think it necessary to protect tax revenue. A business must stop using the scheme if annual turnover exceeds £825,000 (£750,000 before 1 April 2004) but can leave it voluntarily at the end of any tax period. If they leave the scheme on or after 1 April 2004, they may continue for a further six months to account on a cash basis for VAT outstanding at the date they left the scheme.

VAT account, tax periods and tax returns, default surcharge (ss 59, 79; SI 1995/2518 Pt V)

7.24   The transactions for each tax period must be summarised in a VAT account. Returns are made to Customs on form VAT 100 for each tax period, showing the VAT payable or repayable and certain statistical information (including specific entries for European Union sales and purchases). The return is due within one month after the end of the tax period. Customs will automatically extend this period by seven days where payment is made electronically (e.g. by bank giro credit, BACS, CHAPS), except for businesses in the annual accounting and payments on account schemes (see 7.25, 7.26).

Businesses that register with the electronic VAT return service may file their VAT returns via the Internet.

A 'default surcharge' is payable if two or more returns within a year are not made on time. When a return is late, a 'surcharge liability notice' is issued. The notice remains in force for a period of one year, unless a further return is made late, in which case the surcharge liability period is extended for a year from the last day of the period covered by that return and so on. The surcharge is 2% of the tax due for the first late return in the surcharge liability period, then 5%, 10% and a maximum 15% for subsequent late returns. The 2% and 5% surcharges will not be collected if they are less than £400. The minimum surcharge at 10% or 15% is £30. If no VAT is due, or the VAT is paid on time even though the return is late, then although the late return affects the surcharge liability period, the surcharge does not apply and the rate for subsequent late returns is not increased. If Customs accept that a business has a reasonable excuse for late payment no default will be recorded. The Government has said that a business with turnover of up to £150,000 that is late with its VAT payments will first be offered advice and support rather than being subject to automatic surcharges.

Where there is an unreasonable delay on the part of Customs in making a VAT repayment, a repayment supplement amounting to an extra 5% (or £50 if more) will be added to the repayment, providing the return claiming the repayment was made on time (see 7.36).

A tax period is normally three months, but if you regularly claim VAT repayments (for example because you make mainly zero-rated supplies) you may have a one-month period if you wish. The advantage of earlier repayments in those circumstances must be weighed against the disadvantage of having to complete twelve returns annually.

Quarterly return dates are staggered over the year depending on your business classification. You can ask for the dates to be changed to coincide with your accounting period.

Annual accounting (SI 1995/2518 Pt VII)

7.25   Businesses with an annual tax-exclusive turnover of not more than £660,000 (£600,000 before 1 April 2004) that have been registered for at least one year may apply (on form VAT 600) to join the annual accounting scheme. They then agree a provisional VAT liability with Customs based on the position for the previous year. New businesses with a taxable turnover of £150,000 or less may join the scheme as soon as they are registered, their provisional figure being estimated.

For businesses with turnover above £150,000 the agreed provisional liability is divided by ten. Nine equal monthly payments are then made by direct debit starting four months after the beginning of the year. Businesses with a turnover of less than £150,000 are able to make quarterly instead of monthly interim payments, the quarterly payments being 25% of the provisional VAT liability.

The annual return and balancing payment have to be made within two months after the end of the year. Once in the scheme, a business may remain in it unless annual turnover reaches £825,000 (£750,000 before 1 April 2004).

Monthly payments on account for large VAT payers (s 28; SI 1993/2001; SI 1995/2518 Pt VI)

7.26   Traders who pay more than £2 million VAT a year have to make payments on account in the first two months of each quarter, based on 1/24th of their total liability for the twelve months to the previous 31 March, 30 April or 31 May, depending on their VAT return periods. The payments are calculated and notified to the trader by Customs, and the trader makes any necessary adjustment on his quarterly return. Traders may elect to pay their actual monthly VAT liability instead of the notified amount (which may be preferable where there are seasonal variations). Payments on account *must* be made by electronic means and there is no seven-day period of grace. Default surcharge (see 7.24) will apply if payments are not made on time.

Changes in circumstances

7.27 Where your circumstances change, you are required to notify Customs within 30 days of the change. Some changes require cancellation of your registration, others merely an amendment.

Your registration will require cancellation when you cease business, or take in a partner, or revert from a partnership to a sole proprietor, or incorporate or disincorporate your business, or cease to make taxable supplies. In some circumstances it is possible to transfer your registration number to the new business.

Many changes require amendment to your registration, such as changes in the composition of a partnership, change of business name, changes in a group of companies, change of address and so on.

Transferring a business as a going concern

7.28 If a VAT registered trader sells all or part of a business as a going concern, the seller does not normally have to account for VAT on the sale consideration, and the purchaser does not have any input tax to reclaim where the sale is to another taxable person or to someone who becomes a taxable person immediately after the sale. This does not apply to the transfer of land and buildings on which the option to charge VAT has been exercised or to commercial buildings and civil engineering works that are unfinished or less than three years old unless the purchaser has also opted to charge VAT and has so notified Customs by the date of the transfer. For transfers on and after 18 March 2004 the purchaser must also notify the seller that his option to tax will not be disapplied. (For details of the option to charge VAT, see 32.23.) If the purchaser is not already registered, the rules for deciding whether he is liable are the same as those outlined at 7.4, except that the seller's supplies in the previous twelve months are treated as made by the purchaser. The purchaser must notify his liability within 30 days of the transfer, and will be registered from the date of the transfer. If the seller was not, and was not required to be, VAT registered, his turnover would not have to be taken into account by the purchaser in deciding when registration was necessary.

These rules do not apply when you merely sell assets, rather than an identifiable part of the business which is capable of separate operation. The sale of a family company is dealt with in CHAPTER 28.

Anti-avoidance provisions apply to transfers to partially exempt groups (see 7.31). Further anti-avoidance provisions prevent the transfer of a business rules being used to enable businesses to give goods away without accounting for VAT on their value.

Records and returns (Sch 11)

7.29   VAT registered businesses must supply tax invoices in respect of taxable supplies, keep a VAT account showing the calculations of the VAT liability for each tax period, and make returns to Customs showing the VAT payable or repayable (see 7.24).

Vat invoices (SI 1995/2518 Pt III)

7.30   The rules for VAT invoicing have been harmonised throughout the EU as a result of the EC Invoicing Directive, the changes becoming operative by 1 January 2004. The changes are reflected in the following notes.

Where you make standard-rated supplies to another taxable person, you must provide and keep a copy of a VAT invoice showing the following:

Identifying number
Tax point (see 7.20)
Date of issue of the invoice
Your name, address and VAT registration number
Customer's name and address
Description of goods or services supplied, and for each type of goods, the quantity, rate of VAT and VAT-exclusive amount payable
Total amount payable excluding VAT and (from 1 January 2004), for countable goods or services, the unit price (for example, in the case of services, the hourly rate)
Rate of cash discount offered
Total VAT chargeable

It was previously necessary to show the type of supply (e.g. sale, hire-purchase or rental), but from 1 January 2004 this is no longer compulsory.

Retailers may provide a less detailed invoice omitting the customer's name and address and the amount (but not the rate) of VAT, if the VAT-inclusive price is £250 or less (£100 or less before 1 January 2004). Copies of these less detailed invoices need not be kept.

Provision is made for customers to self-bill their suppliers, subject to specified conditions. Provision is also made for electronic invoicing. Those who adopt electronic invoicing must notify Customs within thirty days of starting to do so.

There is a penalty of up to 15% of the amount charged as VAT for unauthorised issue of a VAT invoice, with a minimum penalty of £50.

Groups of companies (ss 43, 43A–43D, 44 and Sch 9A; FA 2004, s 20)

7.31   Two or more companies that are established or have a fixed establishment in the UK may apply to be treated as a VAT group if one of them controls each of the others, or if an individual, partnership or company controls all of them. Only one VAT return is then required and supplies between group members are disregarded for VAT purposes. Customs may remove companies from VAT groups if they are no longer eligible or if their membership poses a threat to tax revenue. There are provisions to ensure that unfair advantages are not obtained by group treatment, and Customs have powers to counter VAT avoidance involving group transactions. Additionally, changes have been made in the Finance Act 2004 enabling the Treasury to modify the eligibility rules for group membership, and preventing a company being a member of more than one VAT group at the same time.

Where there is no group registration, VAT has to be added to charges for supplies from one company to the other, such as management charges, and care must be taken to ensure that this is not overlooked.

Basic activities of holding companies, such as holding shares and acquiring subsidiaries, are not regarded under EU law as business activities and any associated input tax cannot be recovered. This only applies, however, to holding companies that neither trade themselves, nor have active trading subsidiaries making taxable supplies outside the VAT group, nor provide genuine management services to separate trading subsidiaries.

Where a business is transferred as a going concern to a partially exempt group, the transfer is treated as a supply to and by the group. The group therefore has to account for output tax, and is only able to recover its allowable proportion of input tax according to the partial exemption rules (see 7.17). This does not apply if the person who transferred the assets to the group acquired them more than three years previously. Nor does it apply to items covered by the capital goods scheme (see 7.16).

The group provisions are intended to reduce administrative burdens on businesses, but they also enable groups to improve the overall VAT position by including or excluding companies from the group registration. Where an application is made for a company to leave a VAT group, Customs may delay the removal of the company from the VAT group registration if VAT avoidance is involved.

European Union Single Market

7.32   On 1 May 2004 ten new countries joined the European Union, and those who have business dealings with customers in those countries must now apply the rules for EU transactions outlined below.

Supplies of goods between EU countries are not regarded as imports and exports, but as 'acquisitions' and 'supplies'. If a supplier in another EU country supplies goods totalling more than £70,000 in a calendar year to non-registered persons in the UK (known as 'distance selling'), the supplier is liable to register in the UK within 30 days of exceeding the limit, registration taking effect from the date the limit is exceeded. If a UK non-registered business makes acquisitions from other EU countries in excess of a stipulated threshold, the registration and deregistration provisions at 7.4, 7.5 apply, the limit for both registration and deregistration being £58,000 from 1 April 2004. The cumulative turnover limit for such acquisitions relates to the calendar year, i.e. to acquisitions from 1 January to the end of the relevant month. (For both the £70,000 and £58,000 limits, goods subject to excise duty and new means of transport are not taken into account, because they are subject to separate rules.)

When a VAT registered person acquires goods in the UK from an EU supplier, output tax must be accounted for on the next VAT return, but with an equivalent amount being deducted as input tax in the same return (subject to any partial exemption restriction). Supplies by a UK supplier to VAT registered EU customers are zero-rated, but VAT is accounted for by the customer at his country's VAT rate, i.e. the country of destination. (At a later stage it is intended to move to a charge based on the country of origin.) Special rules apply to new motor vehicles, motor cycles, boats and aircraft, under which VAT is charged at the rate of the purchaser's country. Other supplies to non–VAT registered EU individuals are at the rate applicable in the UK, although if sales to an EU country exceed that country's stipulated threshold the distance selling rules apply and the seller must register for VAT in that country or he may appoint a tax representative to act for him; that country will then become the place of supply. There are special rules where there is an intermediate supplier between the original supplier and the customer.

For supplies to VAT registered EU customers, a UK seller must state both his own and the customer's VAT number on VAT invoices. In addition to making his normal VAT returns, he also has to submit a return of all supplies to VAT registered customers in the EU for each calendar quarter (known as EC sales lists). Larger businesses (acquisitions or supplies above £233,000, decreased to £221,000 from 1 January 2004) have to submit monthly returns known as supplementary statistical declarations (SSDs) under the Intrastat system. See 7.13 for the EU treatment of second-hand goods, 7.30 for EU provisions relating to invoicing and 7.33 re Internet trading. See also 7.35 for new penalties applicable to those importing or exporting goods from or to countries outside the EU.

Internet and E-commerce

7.33   As well as business to business transactions, many private individuals are buying goods over the Internet, both from UK and foreign suppliers. The normal VAT rules apply in such circumstances, and where goods are bought from abroad, both customs duty and VAT have to be paid. If the goods are delivered by post, the Post Office will usually collect the amount due on delivery.

The development of business on the Internet raises significant problems for countries in terms of how those transacting such business are brought within the taxing rules of the country concerned. The intangible nature of Internet products leads to anomalies, for example in the UK books are zero-rated but an electronic 'book' is charged at the standard rate, all electronic products being supplies of services for VAT purposes. Countries round the world are worried about losing tax revenues through Internet trading and it is generally recognised that a global tax model needs to be developed. The EU have already taken action with the issue of an E-Commerce Directive relating to the place of supply of broadcasting and electronic services, which has been put into effect in the UK by statutory instrument. The new provisions took effect from 1 July 2003. In particular, services supplied by businesses outside the EU to private individuals and non-business organisations in the EU are now taxed in the EU state where the customer belongs. This strictly requires non-EU businesses providing such services to register and account for VAT in all EU states in which they make supplies. A new Special Scheme allows such businesses to register electronically in a single EU state of their choice and electronically declare the total EU tax due on a single tax return to that member state. The member state will then distribute the tax to the relevant member states.

Assessments (ss 73, 76, 77)

7.34   If a taxpayer fails to make returns, or Customs consider returns are incomplete or incorrect, they may issue assessments of the amount of VAT due. Such assessments must normally be issued before the expiry of two years from the end of the return period, or, if later, one year after the facts come to light. Assessments cannot be made later than three years after the end of the return period, except in cases of fraudulent or negligent conduct, when the period is increased to twenty years. Where the taxpayer has died, no assessment can be made later than three years after death, or relate to a period more than three years before death. If a taxpayer does not submit a return and instead pays the VAT shown on an estimated assessment, Customs may fix an estimated assessment for a later period at a higher figure than they otherwise would have done. Penalties for late submission may also arise.

Interest, penalties and surcharge (ss 59–72, 74; FA 2003, ss 24–41)

7.35   In addition to their right to take criminal proceedings (for other than regulatory offences) which could lead to a fine or imprisonment or both, Customs have the power to charge interest on overdue tax in certain circumstances, and there are severe penalties for late, incorrect or incomplete returns, for failure to notify liability to be registered for VAT or unauthorised issue of VAT invoices, for failure to keep proper records (which have to be retained for six years) and for various other breaches of the regulations. There is also a civil evasion penalty for conduct involving dishonesty (see below). As indicated at 7.24, there is a default surcharge for repeated late submission of VAT returns. Interest, penalties and surcharge are not allowable deductions for income tax or corporation tax.

Where there are errors in a VAT return, they will not normally be penalised if they are discovered and corrected in the next following return (even if the error was discovered by Customs). Nor will errors that are corrected by a compensating error in the next following return, such as input VAT claimed in the return before the correct return, or output VAT accounted for in the return following the correct return. Subject to these relaxations, the system works as follows.

If a taxpayer finds he has made mistakes in earlier returns causing tax to be overpaid or underpaid and the total net errors discovered are £2,000 or less, he may correct them by adjusting the amount of VAT payable or repayable in the current return (repayments being restricted to three years) or by notifying Customs. Providing this is done voluntarily, no penalty will apply and no interest will be charged on any overdue amount. If net errors totalling more than £2,000 are discovered, they cannot be adjusted in the current return and must be separately notified (on form 652) and if tax has been underpaid, interest will be charged on the overdue amount, but again no penalty will be charged if the errors are disclosed voluntarily. See 'Interest payable on VAT (default interest)' in the Table of Rates and Allowances for the latest interest rates.

Unless an underpayment is covered by this errors procedure, or the taxpayer can show a reasonable excuse, a penalty for serious or repeated misdeclaration may apply. The serious misdeclaration penalty of 15% will only apply where the underpaid or over-reclaimed VAT amounts to at least 30% of the total of the input and output tax figures that should have been stated on the return (or £1 million if less), and the penalty may be mitigated in appropriate circumstances. Smaller misdeclarations will be subject to a (mitigable) 15% repeated misdeclaration penalty where Customs have served a penalty liability notice following a material error and there are at least two further material errors within two years. A material error is one where the understated VAT is at least 10% of the combined input/output tax that should have been shown on the return (or £500,000 if less). If the error has been penalised as a serious misdeclaration (see above), it will not be double penalised but it will count in calculating whether repeated errors have occurred.

With such a wide range of possible penalties, taxpayers need to be careful that their VAT accounting procedures will enable them to account for VAT correctly and on time.

Where the taxpayer's conduct involves dishonesty, there is a civil evasion penalty, the maximum being 100% of the underpaid VAT, although Customs will usually mitigate this substantially if the taxpayer co-operates in ascertaining the correct liability. Customs are now adopting a less confrontational approach in many civil evasion cases. On the other hand, two new penalties have been introduced from 23 December 2003 — for evading certain duties or VAT, or for failing to comply with legal requirements under EU and national customs law. The penalties apply to customs duty, Community export duty, Community import duty, import VAT and customs duty of a country outside the EU that has made a preferential tariff agreement with the EU. The maximum penalty for evasion is an amount equal to the tax or duty evaded, and the penalty for contravening prescribed rules is an amount not exceeding £2,500.

Repayments, repayment supplement and statutory interest (ss 78–81; FA 1996, s 197; TA 1988, s 827)

Repayment supplement

7.36   Repayment supplement of 5% of the tax due (or £50 if greater) is paid on overpaid VAT if the return was made by the due date, the return did not overstate the amount repayable by more than the greater of £250 and 5% of the amount due, and repayment has been unnecessarily delayed by Customs. Unnecessary delay is defined as more than 30 days from the day following the end of return period, or the date the return was received if later. Repayment supplement is not chargeable to income tax or corporation tax.

Statutory interest

7.37   Where overpaid VAT has not been recovered through the normal accounting procedures, a claim may be made for a refund, which is increased by statutory interest where the overpayment is a result of error by Customs. Unlike repayment supplement, statutory interest is chargeable to direct tax, i.e. income tax or corporation tax. Before 18 July 1996 such repayments could go back as far as the start of VAT in 1973. The maximum carry-back period is now restricted to three years (which is mirrored by the three-year time limit for Customs to make assessments where no fraud or negligence is involved). A repayment will not be made if it would 'unjustly enrich' the claimant, i.e. the recovered VAT would not be passed on to the claimant's customers who originally suffered it.

For the latest rates of interest see 'Statutory interest payable by Customs in cases of official error' in the Table of Rates and Allowances.

Administration and appeals (Sch 12)

7.38   VAT is under the control of the Commissioners of Customs and Excise, operating through the VAT Central Unit and through local VAT offices under Collectors of Customs and Excise. If you disagree with a decision of Customs as to the VAT payable or various other matters, such as registration or cancellation of registration, use of a retailer's scheme, calculation of output tax, etc., you may appeal to an independent VAT and duties tribunal within 30 days of the decision. Normally, any tax in dispute must be paid before the tribunal hearing, but this requirement may be waived to avoid hardship. VAT tribunals normally hear appeals in public. If you are dissatisfied with the tribunal decision, further appeal is possible to the High Court, the Court of Appeal, and, where leave is granted, to the House of Lords. Taking an appeal to the courts may, however, result in costs being awarded against you if the appeal fails. Quite frequently, cases involving the interpretation of EU law and its incorporation into UK VAT law are referred by the courts (or are taken by the taxpayer) to the European Court of Justice.

The European Court of Human Rights has held that VAT civil evasion penalty proceedings are in the nature of a criminal charge. This has affected the way in which Customs conduct VAT investigations.

Combating VAT evasion and money laundering (VATA 1994, s 77A and Sch 11; SI 2003/3075)

7.39   Customs have extensive powers to combat VAT evasion, and these were strengthened from 10 April 2003. The revised provisions include enhanced powers to require security to be provided by traders reclaiming input tax if the traders deal with businesses in a VAT supply chain that are considered to be involved in tax evasion. In addition businesses receiving specified goods and services (currently, telephones, telephone parts and accessories, and computer equipment, including parts, accessories and software) in a supply chain in circumstances where they knew, or had reasonable grounds to suspect, that VAT would not be paid, are jointly and severally liable with their suppliers for unpaid VAT (see Customs Notice 726).

7.40   New regulations have been introduced requiring businesses that deal in goods and accept the equivalent of €15,000 (around £10,000) or more in *cash* for a single transaction (referred to as High Value Dealers — HVDs) to register with Customs and put anti-money laundering systems in place. The requirement to have anti-money laundering systems in place applies from 1 March 2004 and the registration requirement from 1 April 2004. The registration will be renewable annually and an annual fee (£60 for each outlet for the year to 31 March 2005) will be charged for each premises from which high value transactions are made. Details are in Customs' guides MLR6 and MLR7. Breach of the regulations may lead to a penalty of up to £5,000 for each breach or criminal proceedings. Businesses may avoid the rules by requiring such payments to be made by credit card or cheque.

VAT avoidance schemes

7.41   New rules have been introduced from August 2004 to combat what the Government regards as abusive VAT avoidance schemes. For details see 45.3.

8
Council tax and business rates

Introduction

8.1   This chapter gives an outline of council tax and business rates. Additional points of detail relating to specific areas are dealt with in the appropriate chapters, in particular employment aspects in CHAPTER 10 and let property in CHAPTER 32.

Council tax was introduced from 1 April 1993 in England, Wales and Scotland, replacing the poll tax, which had been introduced to replace domestic rates. Domestic rates are still payable in Northern Ireland. There are some differences in the system in Wales and Scotland and this chapter deals mainly with the system for England. There is a brief comment on the differences in Wales and Scotland at 8.10 and 8.11.

Business rates are paid by businesses at a uniform level fixed by central government except for businesses served by the City of London Corporation. The introduction of this system was preceded by a property revaluation and revaluations are to be made every five years, the first of which affected assessments from 1 April 1995 and the second from 1 April 2000. The third revaluation will take effect from 1 April 2005. Annual increases in the business rate will not exceed the increase in the Retail Prices Index, but the overall bill will be affected by valuation changes. Since the introduction of the uniform business rate, there have been transitional provisions to limit gains and losses for individual businesses. There are differences in the business rates provisions in Scotland and Wales. This chapter deals only with the position in England.

Council tax — the general rules

8.2   Council tax is payable on a 'dwelling', i.e. a house, flat, mobile home or houseboat, and there is a single bill for each dwelling. A self-contained unit within a dwelling is counted as a separate dwelling, but this does not apply where the unit is occupied by an elderly or disabled member of the family. Some properties are mixed private/business properties, and any part of a property that is wholly used for business purposes is subject to the business rate, with the council tax applying to the 'dwelling' part. Some dwellings are exempt (see 8.3).

Council tax bills may be reduced by one or more of the following:

The disability reduction scheme (see 8.6).
Discounts where there is only one occupier (see 8.5).
Council tax benefit for those on low incomes (see 8.7).

Where more than one of these reductions is relevant, they are applied in the order stated.

Legislation has been introduced giving councils flexibility over setting discounts and exemptions, to allow them to reflect local circumstances. This includes giving councils power to reduce discounts for second homes and long-term unfurnished empty properties and most councils have taken the opportunity to reduce such discounts (see 8.5).

The amount of the bill before any available deductions depends on the estimated value of the property at 1 April 1991, but taking into account any significant alteration to the property before 1 April 1993, such as an extension, and assuming that the property is in reasonable repair. Newly built property is similarly valued back to what it would have been worth at 1 April 1991. The bill is calculated according to which of the following valuation bands the property falls in:

Band	England	Scotland	Wales
A	Up to £40,000	Up to £27,000	Up to £30,000
B	£40,001–£52,000	£27,001–£35,000	£30,001–£39,000
C	£52,001–£68,000	£35,001–£45,000	£39,001–£51,000
D	£68,001–£88,000	£45,001–£58,000	£51,001–£66,000
E	£88,001–£120,000	£58,001–£80,000	£66,001–£90,000
F	£120,001–£160,000	£80,001–£106,000	£90,001–£120,000
G	£160,001–£320,000	£106,001–£212,000	£120,001–£240,000
H	Over £320,000	Over £212,000	Over £240,000

The council tax bills for the various bands vary according to proportions laid down by law. The full bill for a band H dwelling is twice that for a band D dwelling and three times that for a band A dwelling.

Properties will normally only be revalued when they are sold or let on lease for seven years or more, even if they have been substantially improved or extended. Such a revaluation takes effect from the date the transaction is completed. There is, however, provision for adjusting values downwards at any time if there is a major change in the area, such as a motorway being built nearby, or if part of the property is demolished, or if the property is adapted for someone who is disabled.

If, because of inaccuracies in the original list, a valuation is wrong, it can be corrected. If the effect of the correction is to *increase* the valuation, the revaluation takes effect only from the day the valuation list is altered. Decreases take effect from the date the valuation list was compiled.

You can appeal against the valuation in certain circumstances (see 8.8).

Council tax is calculated on a daily basis and is adjusted appropriately when a change of circumstances affects the bill, such as the property becoming or ceasing to be eligible for exemption or discount, and when you move from one house to another (the day you move in being a chargeable day but not the day you move out). This means that householders need to notify their councils of changes affecting their liability.

Council tax is normally paid by ten monthly instalments, but other payment methods may be offered. If you fail to pay on time, you may lose the right to pay by instalments and action may be taken against you for recovery. Collection may then be enforced in various ways, including an attachment of earnings order requiring your employer to deduct the outstanding tax from your salary and account for it to the council. If you do not pay at all, you may be sent to prison (except in Scotland).

Exempt dwellings

8.3   Exemption may be claimed in the following circumstances. The council must be notified if the exemption ceases to apply, otherwise penalties may be imposed.

A   Unoccupied property that needs structural alteration/major repair work, or is undergoing such work, or has undergone such work and less than six months have elapsed since the work was substantially completed, but the exemption is limited to a maximum period of twelve months.

B   Empty property owned and last used by a charity, exemption applying for up to six months.

C   Empty, unfurnished property, for up to six months (ignoring any period of reoccupation for less than six weeks).

D   Property left empty by someone in prison (other than for not paying fines or council tax).

E   Property left empty by someone now living in hospital or in residential care.

F   Property empty following the occupier's death, for up to six months after granting of probate or administration.

G   An empty property in which occupation is prohibited by law, e.g. after compulsory purchase (but there would be no exemption for squatters occupying such a building).

H   Property left vacant for a minister of religion.

I   Property that is empty because the occupier is now living elsewhere to receive care because of old age, disablement, illness, alcohol/drug dependence or mental disorder.

J   Property empty because the occupier is resident elsewhere to look after someone needing care as indicated in I above.

K   Empty property last occupied by a student whose main residence it was but who now lives elsewhere to be near to his place of education.

L   Unoccupied mortgaged property that has been repossessed by the lender.

M   Students' halls of residence.

N   Property wholly occupied by students as their full-time or term-time residence.

O   Properties used as accommodation for members of the Armed Forces.

P   Properties occupied by Visiting Forces.

Q   Unoccupied property for which someone is liable only as a Trustee in Bankruptcy.

R   A vacant caravan pitch or boat mooring.

S   Properties occupied only by people under 18 years of age.

T   Unoccupied annexes.

U   Properties occupied only by severely mentally impaired people.

V   Properties occupied by diplomats or members of certain international organisations.

W   Self-contained annexes and 'granny flats' occupied by elderly or disabled relatives.

Who is liable to pay?

8.4   There is only one council tax bill for each dwelling. The person liable is whichever resident (or residents) comes first on the following list.

(a)   An owner-occupier.

(b)   A resident leaseholder (including assured tenants under the Housing Act 1988).

(c)   A resident statutory or secure tenant.

(d)   A resident who has a contractual licence to occupy the property, such as someone living in a tied cottage.

(e)   A resident with no legal interest in the property, such as a squatter.

A resident is someone over 18 who lives in the property as his only or main home.

Where more than one person falls into the first category to apply, such as where there are several joint owners, they are jointly liable for the tax. Where only one of a married or cohabiting heterosexual couple owns or leases a property, the partner is also jointly liable. Homosexual couples are only jointly liable if they both fall into the first category to apply, for example, where they are joint owners/tenants. Where people are jointly liable, councils may choose to send the bill to just one or all of them.

Where there are no residents, the owner is liable. The owner is also liable instead of the residents in the case of the following dwellings.

(i)   Multi-occupied properties such as bed-sits where rent is paid separately for different parts of the property.

(ii)   Residential care homes, nursing homes, and some hostels providing a high level of care. (Where care home residents lived in self-contained units, the units were previously regarded as separate dwellings for which the residents had to pay council tax. This no longer applies from 1 January 2004.)

(iii)   Dwellings occasionally occupied by the owner whose domestic staff are resident there.

(iv)   Monasteries, convents, and dwellings occupied by ministers of religion.

(v)   Property occupied by asylum seekers under statutory arrangements.

Discounts

8.5   A council tax bill is regarded as having a 50% property element and a 50% personal element. The bill is reduced by 25% if there is only one householder. The bill has previously been reduced by 50% if the property is no one's only or main home. From 1 April 2004 councils have been given the power to vary the discount to a minimum of 10% for second homes, or even to give no discount at all in the case of long-term empty homes. Most councils have fixed the discount at 10%. The 50% discount still applies to caravans and boat moorings, and also where the owner lives in job-related accommodation.

The following are not counted in deciding how many residents there are, providing certain conditions are met.

A   People in prison, except for non-payment of fines or council tax, and those detained in hospital under the Mental Health Act 1983.

B   Those who are severely mentally impaired.

C   Full-time students and their non-British spouses or dependants, student nurses, apprentices and those undergoing Youth Training.

D   Long-term hospital patients and people being looked after in residential care homes, nursing homes, and hostels providing a high level of care.

E   Low-paid care workers employed by a government department, local authority or charity, or employed by the person being cared for, having been introduced by a charity.

F   Those with diplomatic privileges or immunity who are neither British citizens nor permanently resident in the UK.

G   Members of visiting forces and international headquarters and defence organisations and their families.

H   Monks and nuns.

I   Those for whom child benefit is payable, and 18 and 19 year-olds whose course of education ended between 30 April and 1 November (who are counted only from 1 November).

J   Those staying in certain hostels or night shelters, such as Salvation Army Hostels.

K   People caring for someone with a disability who is not a spouse, partner or child under 18.

Not being counted as a resident does not alter your responsibility for payment if you are the person liable to pay the tax (for example a student owner sharing with another adult). But where, after ignoring those who are not counted, the dwelling is no one's main home, the person liable to pay the tax would get a discount, usually of 10% from 1 April 2004 as indicated above.

You must notify the council if you are no longer eligible for a discount, or are only eligible for a smaller discount. Penalties apply if you do not.

Reduction for disabilities

8.6   Homes that provide one of the following special features for a substantially and permanently disabled adult or child who lives in the property qualify for a one-band reduction in the bill if they are in bands B to H. Band A properties qualify for a reduction equal to one ninth of the charge for a band D property. Any discounts and benefits then apply to the reduced amount. The special features are:

(a)   a room other than a bathroom, kitchen or toilet, that is mainly for the use of the disabled person (such as a ground floor bedroom in a two-storey property);

(b)   an extra bathroom or kitchen for the disabled person's use;

(c)   extra floor space for a wheelchair.

To qualify for the reduction, the additional feature need not be specially built, but it must be shown that the disabled person would be severely adversely affected if the feature was not available. A claim should be made each year to your council, who may require additional evidence that the conditions for the reduction are satisfied.

Council tax benefit

8.7   Those on low incomes may claim benefit of up to 100% of the bill, the amount of the benefit depending on their personal circumstances. Where the income of the person liable to pay the bill is too high for benefit, it may be possible to claim a 'second adult rebate' of up to 25% for someone on a low income sharing the home (but not for a spouse, partner or lodger). Anyone who disagrees with the amount of benefit allocated to them may appeal to a local review board if they cannot resolve the dispute with the council. Council tax benefit was previously restricted for those living in properties in bands F, G and H, the maximum benefit being calculated by reference to valuation band E. This restriction no longer applies from 1 April 2004.

Appeals

Valuation

8.8   You may appeal on the grounds that your home should or should not be shown on the valuation list. You may also appeal about your council tax banding if the value of the property has materially increased or decreased, or if the value has been affected by starting, stopping or changing business use. An upward revaluation because of extensions or improvements will only be made at the time of sale, so an appeal on those grounds will not be relevant until that time.

Valuation appeals are made initially to the Listing Officer at the local Valuation Office. If you cannot agree the appeal with him, it will be heard by a Valuation Tribunal.

Other grounds for appeal

8.9   Appeals may also be made where

(a)   you consider your home should not be liable to tax; or

(b)   you dispute your liability, either because you do not consider you are the liable person, or because of the calculation of available reductions; or

(c)   you disagree with a penalty imposed on you; or

(d)   you disagree with a completion notice identifying the date from which a new building becomes a dwelling, or when structural alterations are completed.

Appeal procedures differ depending on the nature of the appeal. Most disputes are settled between the taxpayer and the council, but where agreement cannot be reached they go to the Valuation Tribunal.

Wales and Scotland

Wales

8.10   Because of the high proportion of Welsh holiday homes, councils in Wales have always been able to restrict the discount for furnished dwellings that are no one's main home, or even to give no discount at all. These provisions now also apply in England as indicated in 8.5.

Scotland

8.11   In Scotland there are various differences in the way the council tax is administered and enforced. Scotland also has a separate council water charge, and those entitled to 100% relief from council tax still have to pay the water charge. Unlike taxpayers in England and Wales, Scottish taxpayers cannot be imprisoned for failing to pay the council tax.

Business rates

8.12   Businesses pay a uniform business rate (also called the national non-domestic rate) on their rateable values. (This does not apply to those served by the City of London Corporation, for whom there are special arrangements.) Rateable values are updated every five years, the current revaluation having been made as at 1 April 1998 and put into effect from 1 April 2000. The next revaluation will come into effect from 1 April 2005. At that time a new rate relief scheme will be introduced to help small businesses with rateable values below a limit which has been provisionally fixed at £8,000. Businesses will be able to register for the relief in October 2004.

The rate in the pound for England for 2004/05 has been fixed at 45.6 pence (compared with 44.4 pence for 2003/04). Annual increases cannot be more than the increase in the retail prices index.

Transitional arrangements have applied since the introduction of the uniform business rate for those facing large increases or decreases. From 2002/03 to 2004/05 annual increases are restricted to a maximum of 17.5% plus inflation. For properties with revised rateable values of less than £12,000, or £18,000 in Greater London, the maximum increase from 2002/03 to 2004/05 is 7.5% plus inflation. For those entitled to decreases there is a limit on reductions in liability, the available reductions for 2004/05 being 25% plus inflation for small properties, and 15% plus inflation for larger ones (12.5% and 7.5% plus inflation for 2003/04). Transitional relief will also be available following the April 2005 revaluations, details of which will be announced during autumn 2004.

If a property changes hands, the new owner is entitled to take over the previous owner's entitlement to transitional relief.

Empty property attracts only half the normal rates bill, and then only after it has been empty for three months. And no rates are payable on empty factories and warehouses, or on empty properties with a rateable value of less than £1,900.

Self-catering holiday accommodation is normally subject to the business rate if available for short-term letting for 140 days or more in a year.

If you offer bed and breakfast, you will not be liable to business rates if you intend to offer such accommodation for not more than six people, you intend to live in the property at the same time and the property's main use is still as your home.

Those in mixed business and private accommodation pay the business rate on the non-domestic part and council tax on the private part.

The business rate is collected by individual local councils but it is paid into a national pool and is then distributed on a formula basis to county and district councils. Councils have power to give business rates relief on hardship grounds. They may also give special reductions for limited periods to business in rural areas. For the position of charities, see 43.8.

9
Dealing with the Revenue

Structure of the Revenue

9.1   Income tax, corporation tax and capital gains tax are administered by the Commissioners of Inland Revenue (also called the Board of Inland Revenue). The Board operates through its appointed officers. The administrative structure is split between taxpayer service offices, taxpayer district offices and tax enquiry centres. Taxpayer service offices are the main offices the taxpayer deals with, handling PAYE codings, allowances, assessments and preliminary collection work. Taxpayer district offices handle the examination of business accounts, corporation tax, PAYE audit and tax recovery work. In many smaller towns and rural locations the functions of both offices are combined in a single integrated office. Tax enquiry centres handle enquiries and provide forms, leaflets, etc.

The Revenue also have responsibility for national insurance contributions, statutory sick pay, statutory maternity/paternity/adoption pay, State Earnings Related Pension Scheme contracted-out rebates and working tax credits and child tax credits. These are dealt with in other chapters.

Inheritance tax is administered by the Board of Inland Revenue through IR Capital Taxes. Stamp duties are administered by the Board through the Office of the Controller of Stamps.

Responsibility to provide information to the Revenue

9.2   The Revenue send out tax returns to individuals, trusts and companies when they are aware that tax may be due. As far as individuals are concerned, most people have their tax dealt with through the PAYE system, and only about 9 million out of around 29 million taxpayers receive tax returns. Where taxpayers are no longer required to complete a return they (and their advisers where relevant) will receive a letter from the Revenue. Nevertheless, if you do not receive a return and you have taxable profits or gains on which tax has not been paid and of which the Revenue are unaware, the onus is on you to tell the Revenue. Penalties apply if you do not, based on the tax unpaid at the normal payment date (see 9.46, which also shows the time limits for notification).

For individuals, the time limit for notification is 5 October following the end of the tax year, e.g. by 5 October 2004 for 2003/04. There is no obligation for employees or pensioners to notify if all their income is taken into account under PAYE. Employees who have a copy P11D from their employers may assume that the Revenue know about its contents unless they have reason to believe otherwise.

Apart from returns made by employers in respect of earnings of their employees, there are various reporting requirements, such as by banks and building societies as to interest paid, payers of commissions and royalties, and those who receive profits and income belonging to other people (for example, interest or rent collected by solicitors or other agents).

Stringent new regulations on money laundering (SI 2003/3075) came into force from 1 March 2004. The new regulations bring within the definition of money laundering any process of concealing or disguising the proceeds of *any* criminal offence — so tax evasion is brought within the provisions. Accountants and tax advisers, among others, will need to appoint a money laundering reporting officer (MLRO) if they do not already have one, and to implement appropriate systems and training of staff. Failing to report a knowledge or suspicion of money laundering is an offence punishable by imprisonment. The report has to be made to the National Criminal Intelligence Service (NCIS) or Customs. A particularly difficult problem is that it is an offence to warn the person concerned that a report is going to be made. Professional legal advisers are covered by a client's right to legal professional privilege, but this does not extend to non-legally qualified tax advisers. The new rules put tax advisers dealing with clients or prospective clients in Revenue investigation cases in a difficult position. The indications are that NCIS will refer matters that do not involve offences other than tax evasion to the Revenue (see the Revenue's Working Together Bulletin of June 2003). See 7.40 re new VAT money laundering regulations.

Self-assessment of income tax and capital gains tax — outline of the system (TMA 1970, ss 7–9ZB, 12, 28C, 30–33, 59A, 59B and Sch 3A; FA 2002, ss 135, 136; SI 2000/944; SI 2003/282)

9.3   This section deals with personal returns. For notes on partnership returns see CHAPTER 23. The UK operates a self-assessment system, under which the total amount payable comprises not only income tax and capital gains tax as calculated but also Class 4 national insurance contributions for the self-employed and, where relevant, student loan repayments. The provisions for interest, surcharges, penalties and appeals apply to the total amount payable. For employed students the loan repayments are collected through the PAYE system, but for those who self-assess they are included on returns in the same way as all other income. In the rest of this chapter, 'tax etc.' includes Class 4 contributions and student loan repayments.

Even though a self-assessment system is in operation, the Revenue will work out your tax etc. for you if you send in your tax return early enough. Self-assessment tax returns (forms SA 100) are normally sent out in April. If you want the Revenue to work out the tax etc. you will have to send in the return for the year ended 5 April 2004 by 30 September 2004 (or within two months after you receive the return if later). You will also have to get the return in by 30 September if you are an employee and want to have an underpayment of up to £2,000 collected in a later year through the PAYE scheme rather than having to pay it by the 31 January filing date, although if the Revenue receive the return before the end of November, they will still try to collect the underpayment through PAYE but cannot guarantee to do so. (Slightly later dates for coding out underpayments of up to £2,000 apply where returns are filed by the Electronic Lodgement Service (see 9.11) or over the Internet.) Otherwise you will have until 31 January 2005 (the filing date) to send in the 2003/04 return. (If you do not get a return until after 31 October 2004, the due date for the return is three months from the date it is issued.) There are automatic penalties for late returns (see 9.8). Although the normal filing date is 31 January, you will not be charged a penalty if your return is filed on 1 February.

Growing use is being made by the Government of the Internet, and the Revenue have the power to compel information to be submitted electronically. Compulsory internet filing is being introduced for PAYE returns (see 10.29) but the regulations relating to self-assessment returns presently permit, rather than require, internet filing. See 9.10 re filling in your tax return.

If you do not send in your return by the due date, the Revenue have the power to 'determine' the tax and Class 4 national insurance (but not student loan repayments) you owe, but their figure will be replaced by your self-assessment when it is received. If you work out your own tax etc. payments and you pay tax under PAYE, you will need your coding notices to know the amounts of underpayments dealt with by coding adjustment.

You do not include pence on the return (although pence will be included if your return is produced using commercial software), and income and gains should be rounded *down* and tax paid/tax credits rounded *up*. (If an entry in a particular box covers several different items, it is the *total* figures that should be rounded.) If your tax etc. is calculated either by the Revenue or by commercial software, it will be calculated in pounds and pence, but if you do it yourself you can round down if you wish. Resulting payments on account must, however, be calculated in pounds and pence. You will not be able to leave any blank spaces in the return if entries ought to be made, or to put 'to be agreed', but if you cannot establish the correct figure in time, you should include a 'best estimate' and indicate that you have done so. The correct figure should then be notified as soon as possible, together with an amended self-assessment. If the correct figure cannot be established within the one year time limit for amending the return (see below), and it turns out to be lower than the amount included, the Revenue will accept an error or mistake claim (see 9.33). Where estimated figures are included in a return, the Revenue cannot charge a late filing penalty, although the use of estimated figures may lead them to open an enquiry (see below). If a return is made close to the filing deadline and the Revenue send it back as unsatisfactory on or after 18 January before the deadline, then in cases of genuine oversight they normally allow 14 days for the return to be resubmitted without imposing a penalty. Note that you will be charged interest on underpaid tax etc. from 31 January following the tax year according to the amount of tax etc. finally found to be due (see 9.8).

The Revenue have nine months from the date they receive your return to correct obvious errors (although you have the right to reject the correction within 30 days), and you have a year from the filing date to make amendments yourself. Amending a return within the twelve-month period would not, however, stop you incurring a penalty for fraudulent or negligent conduct (as to which see 9.46) if the original return was made fraudulently or negligently, although your voluntary disclosure would help you when the Revenue were considering the extent to which the penalty would be mitigated. Where there are minor queries on a return, the Revenue may handle them by telephone contact with you or your agent.

The Revenue may open an enquiry into your return, providing they give you the appropriate notice (normally within one year after the filing date for the return). You may make amendments to your return while the enquiry is in progress. See 9.9 for details.

Claims for reliefs, allowances, etc. (TMA 1970, ss 42–43B and Sch 1A)

9.4   Where a claim is made for capital allowances (see 22.7), the claim must normally be in the return or an amended return, so the time limits indicated above for the return and amendments apply. Most other claims for reliefs and allowances are made in the same way. For claims that are not included in a return or amended return, a separate claims procedure is laid down, under which the Revenue have the same nine-month period after the claim to correct obvious errors and the taxpayer has twelve months from the date of the claim to amend it. Unless another time limit is stipulated in the legislation, the time limit for separate claims is five years from the 31 January filing date for the return (i.e. 5 years 10 months after the end of the tax year). See 9.9 re enquiries into claims and 10.30 re claims affecting PAYE codings.

Where capital losses are incurred, relief may be claimed either in the return or in a separate claim within the 5 years 10 months period (see 4.2). There is, however, no time limit during which carried forward losses have to be used (see 9.6 re retaining records).

Provisions have been introduced to enable certain information to be provided and claims to be made by telephone where appropriate. This applies only to individuals (or authorised third parties) and not to partners, trustees or personal representatives (Revenue Statement of Practice 2/98).

Backdated claims (TMA 1970, Sch 1B)

9.5   Where relief is claimed for a loss incurred or payment made in one tax year to be set against the income or gains of an earlier tax year, then although the tax saving from the claim is calculated by reference to the tax position of the earlier year, the claim is treated as relating to the later year and is given effect in relation to that later year. Repayment supplement (see 9.8) is therefore paid only from the balancing payment date for the later tax year (e.g. 31 January 2006 if the later year is 2004/05). This also applies to claims for averaging farming profits (see 31.4) and carrying back post-cessation receipts (see 21.9). In these latter two cases, the effect of the claim may be to *increase* the tax etc. payable for an earlier year. Interest on overdue tax etc. (see 9.8) similarly runs from 31 January following the later tax year. See 17.10 for the treatment of backdated personal pension premiums.

In calculating the revised tax position for the earlier year, the effect on claims and allowances that were made or could have been made is taken into account. For example, the effect of reducing income may be that age-related married couple's allowance becomes available, or that surplus married couple's allowance is available to transfer to a spouse, or following a loss carryback, the facility to pay personal pension premiums may be restricted, resulting in premiums already paid having to be refunded.

Keeping records (TMA 1970, s 12B)

9.6   You will not usually need to send accounts and supporting documents with your return (see 9.13). You must, however, keep all records relevant to your return for 22 months from the end of the tax year, unless you are in business or you let property, in which case you must keep the records for 5 years 10 months from the end of the tax year. If the Revenue have commenced a formal enquiry into a return before the expiry of the time limit (see 9.9), the records must be kept until that enquiry is completed.

Where a claim is made other than in a return (see 9.4), records relating to the claim must be kept until the day on which any Revenue enquiry into the claim (or amendment to a claim) is completed, or, if there is no such enquiry, until the Revenue are no longer able to open such an enquiry (see 9.9). (As far as claims for relief for capital losses are concerned — see 9.4 — this means that the time limit for retaining the records relating to the claim may have expired before the time when the loss is used to reduce a gain.)

Records may be kept on computerised systems providing they can be produced in legible form if required.

You may be charged a penalty of up to £3,000 for any tax year in respect of which you do not keep the required records, but this will only be sought in more serious cases.

Payment of tax (TMA 1970, ss 59A, 59B, Sch 3ZA)

9.7   Most of the tax etc. due is collected by those paying income to others, i.e. by employers under the PAYE system, by banks and others deducting tax from interest payments, patent royalties etc., and under the tax credit system for company dividends. The payment dates for the tax etc. remaining to be paid are dealt with below.

Two equal payments on account (calculated as indicated below) should be made on 31 January in the tax year and 31 July following, with the balance payable or repayable (taking into account any capital gains tax due) on the following 31 January. Payment may be made by post to the Accounts Office, by bank Giro, by cheque or cash at post offices, by electronic funds transfer through BACS or CHAPS, or by PC or telephone banking. The Revenue have had many problems with direct payments to Accounts Offices. It is essential that either the personal payslip is used or the payer's tax reference number, name and address are given and it would be sensible to keep a copy of the cheque. You do not have to make payments on account if the amount of income tax etc. you were due to pay direct to the Revenue for the previous year was less than £500, or if more than 80% of the previous year's income tax etc. was covered by PAYE and/or by deduction at source.

Under self-assessment, the Revenue will periodically send you statements of account (forms SA 300) telling you how much tax is owing or overpaid. The Revenue will not, however, routinely issue statements of account for amounts owing of less than £32, although they will send at least one a year. The delay before this is issued means that interest will be accruing on the underpaid amount (see below). If you have authorised an agent to receive copies of assessments etc., the Revenue should also provide the agent with details of your ongoing statements of account, and notify the agent if they start enquiries into your return (see 9.9).

Interest and possibly surcharges will be charged on underpaid tax etc. (see 9.8). If you are calculating your own tax etc., you will also calculate payments on account, and the Revenue's statements will be based on your figures (subject to any corrections made by them). If you send your return in by 30 September and the Revenue calculate your tax etc., they will also calculate and tell you the payments on account you need to make. They will still do so if asked even if you miss the 30 September deadline, but cannot guarantee to let you know the amount payable in time for you to avoid interest and surcharge. Interest is normally charged on underpaid tax etc. (including underpaid payments on account) from the due date. If, however, you sent in your return by 30 September and asked the Revenue to calculate the tax and they send the statement of account too late for you to make the first payment on account on the following 31 January, the payment date will be 30 days after the notification and interest is charged only from that date. Payments at local offices are credited on the date of payment. Payments by post are treated as made on the day the Revenue receive the payment. Bank giro payments are treated as made three working days before receipt and BACS/ CHAPS payments one working day before receipt. It is understood that PC and telephone banking payments are treated as made on the date the bank makes the transfer.

Each payment on account will normally be equal to half of the net *income tax* etc. liability of the previous tax year. (Capital gains tax is not taken into account.) Where income has fallen, you may make a claim to reduce or eliminate the payments on account at any time before the 31 January filing date for your tax return (and if one or more of the payments has already been paid the appropriate amount will be refunded with interest from the pay-ment date). The Revenue will send you a claim form (form SA 303) with your statement of account. If you have an agent dealing with your tax, he may make the claim for you. If you reduce your payments below what they should have been, you will have to pay interest on the shortfall from each payment date and possibly a penalty (see 2.23 and 9.8).

Example 1

The self-assessment timetable runs as follows:

31 January 2004	2003/04 1st payment on account due
April 2004	2003/04 return issued
31 July 2004	2003/04 2nd payment on account due
30 September 2004	2003/04 return to be filed if Revenue to calculate tax etc.
31 January 2005	2003/04 return to be filed if tax etc. self-assessed. Final payment/repayment for 2003/04, including capital gains tax, plus 1st payment on account for 2004/05 (based on half 2003/04 tax etc. paid directly on *all* income)

April 2005	2004/05 return issued
31 July 2005	2nd payment on account due for 2004/05
30 September 2005	2004/05 return to be filed if Revenue to calculate tax etc.
31 January 2006	2004/05 return to be filed if tax etc. self-assessed. Final payment/repayment for 2004/05, plus 1st payment on account for 2005/06

The total of the income tax etc. and capital gains tax for the year is shown in the tax return due to be sent in by the 31 January after the end of the tax year (or worked out and notified to you by the Revenue after they receive your return if you do not self-assess). This is compared with the tax etc. deducted at source and the payments on account. Any underpayment is due on that day and any overpayment will be repayable. The first payment on account for the next tax year is due at the same time. Although the balancing payment (if any) is due at the same time as the latest filing date for the return, the return is sent to the Tax Office and the balancing payment to the Accounts Office.

If you or the Revenue make an amendment to your return resulting in extra tax etc. payable, the additional amount is due 30 days after the amendment (although interest on overdue tax etc. runs from the original due date for the return — see 9.8).

Interest, repayment supplement, surcharges and penalties (*TMA 1970, ss 59C, 86, 93; TA 1988, s 824*)

9.8   Interest is charged or repayment supplement allowed from the payment dates on tax etc. paid or overpaid (subject to what is said at 9.5 and 9.7). For further details and an illustration see 2.23 and 2.26. Where an amendment is made to a return, interest is due on any additional tax etc. payable from the original due date for the return, even though the tax itself is payable 30 days after the amendment. Unpaid surcharges and penalties (see below) also attract interest.

If your balancing payment for a year is more than 28 days late, then unless you can show a reasonable excuse you will pay a surcharge on the late payment of:

5% of any tax etc. not paid by 28 February.
A further 5% of any tax etc. still not paid by 31 July.

If additional tax etc. becomes due following an amendment to your return, you have 30 days to pay the additional amount. Surcharges will only arise if the additional amount due is paid more than 28 days after the 30–day period, and the further surcharge only if the payment is not made within a further five months.

The surcharge is in addition to interest on the overdue tax etc. There is no surcharge, however, if you have incurred a penalty based on the same amount.

The following automatic penalties will be charged for late returns:

£100 if return is not made by 1 February (or day after filing date for return, if later), plus a further penalty of up to £60 a day if Revenue have applied for and received a direction from General or Special Commissioners to charge the daily penalty.
Further £100 if Commissioners have not imposed the daily penalty and return not made by 31 July (or six months from filing date, if later).
Further penalty if return is not made by next 31 January (or one year from filing date, if later) of an amount equal to the tax that would have been payable under the return.

The late return *fixed* penalties cannot exceed the amount of tax etc. for the year that remains outstanding at the return due date, and no fixed penalty can apply if a repayment is due. If a penalty has already been paid in these circumstances all or the appropriate part of it will be refunded. The daily penalties are not limited to the tax etc. payable. The Revenue have stated their intention of increasing their use of daily penalty proceedings. Where more than one return is outstanding the penalty applies to each return.

A penalty (not exceeding the amount of the shortfall in the payment) plus interest may be charged if you fraudulently or negligently reduce your payments on account.

Revenue enquiries (TMA 1970, ss 9A–9D, 19A, 28ZA–28ZE, 28A, 31, 31A–31D, 97AA and Sch 1A)

9.9   The Revenue will normally have a year from the filing date for the return to notify you that they intend to enquire into it (see 42.1 in relation to personal representatives and trustees). This gives them until 31 January 2006 to raise an enquiry into the 2003/04 return due to be filed by 31 January 2005. If you file the return late, or notify an amendment to it, the enquiry period extends for a year from the date the return or amendment is filed plus the period to the next quarter day, i.e. 31 January, 30 April, 31 July or 31 October as the case may be. You may make amendments to your return while the enquiry is in progress, although amendments to the amount of tax payable will not take effect until the enquiry is completed. Even then they may be rejected by the Revenue or be incorporated in their amendments rather than being dealt with separately. During the enquiry, questions arising may be referred to the Special Commissioners by joint notice from you and the Revenue.

On completion of the enquiry, the Revenue will issue a closure notice which will include making any amendments considered necessary. The taxpayer will have 30 days to appeal against those amendments. The normal appeal and postponement procedures will then apply (see 9.41 and 9.42).

The Revenue have similar powers to enquire into claims made separately from the return (see 9.4). The time limit for opening an enquiry into a claim made outside the return is the same as that for an enquiry into an amendment to a return, and the same procedures apply for appealing against Revenue amendments when the enquiry is completed. The Revenue have the power to require you to produce relevant documents in connection with an enquiry, and a penalty may be imposed if you fail to do so. You have the right to appeal against a notice requiring the production of documents.

If the Revenue do not start an enquiry within the time limit, the tax etc. as calculated will normally stand unless there has been inadequate disclosure or fraudulent or negligent conduct on your part. Although the implication is that the innocent taxpayer may regard the year as closed after the twelve-month period, this does not sit easily with the fact that in most cases the Revenue will not require business accounts and other documents to be sent to them. In order to be sure of finality, it seems that you will need to make sure that the Revenue are given all relevant information relating to your tax affairs, including accounts if appropriate, and furthermore that their attention is drawn to any contentious points (see 9.43).

Dealing with a Revenue enquiry will almost certainly involve extra costs, particularly accountancy expenses, which would not normally be allowable in calculating taxable profits (see 20.3). If the enquiry results in no addition to profits, other than to the year of enquiry, and there is no question of fraud or negligence, the expenses will be allowed.

Filling in your tax return

9.10   Completing your tax return cannot be described as a simple exercise and recent tax changes have made it even more difficult. The basic return form runs to ten pages, and this is supplemented by relevant additional pages according to your circumstances, together with a tax calculation guide for you to calculate your own tax if you want to. For those required to make student loan repayments this now requires calculation of the repayment due in addition to the tax calculation. The additional pages cover employment, share schemes, self-employment, partnership, land and property, foreign income, trusts and estates, capital gains and non-residence. You can also ask the Revenue for 'Help Sheets' that give more detailed guidance on particular topics. There is a standard tax calculation guide running to 16 pages that covers most circumstances and a comprehensive 34–page guide covering all circumstances. The Revenue ran a 'short tax return' pilot scheme for 2002/03 returns The scheme is being extended to over 400,000 taxpayers for 2003/04 returns and will be introduced nationally in April 2005. The short return is a four-page return with much shorter and simpler guidance notes. It will be used for those such as pensioners, low turnover self-employed people and employees who, on the basis of their last returns, have simple tax affairs. The pilot scheme will give a small number of people the option of completing the form by telephone.

Most taxpayers file their returns by post. Individuals, but not partnerships or trustees, may file their returns over the Internet. Returns cannot be sent in on disk or by e-mail. If you want to file via the Internet you need to register with the Revenue's Internet filing website (accessible from www.gateway.gov.uk). The Revenue have a free online web form but this is appropriate only for those who do not need any supplementary pages other than the employment and/or self-employment pages and the land and property pages. The Revenue's website, however, contains a list of all commercial tax return products that have passed their testing procedures.

9.11   All agents who have registered to use the Internet for self-assessment (at www.gateway.gov.uk) will be able to send clients' returns over the Internet providing the Revenue hold the agent's authorisation form 64–8 for the client. If the form is not held, the client may register with the Revenue and provide the appropriate authorisation. Agents must retain a signed hard copy (or electronically signed copy) of returns. The Internet filing system cannot cope with aspects of some returns (such as where the client has more than one accounting period) and it may therefore be necessary to supplement the return with paper information. Agents who have been granted Revenue approval may still file personal, partnership and trustee tax returns electronically using the Electronic Lodgement Service until at least April 2005 (thus covering 2003/04 returns).

9.12   The Revenue have a system of 'post-transaction rulings', under which you may get a ruling from them on the tax effect of transactions you have undertaken, before you send in your return. You may also ask them to check any valuations you have made for capital gains tax before you send in your return.

9.13   The self-assessment return is intended to be comprehensive and most taxpayers are not expected to need to submit accounts and other additional material. If, however, you do not provide the Revenue with full information and tax is consequently underpaid, they may make a 'discovery assessment' (see 9.33). You may send in any additional material you consider relevant with your return, but swamping the Revenue with information will not make you immune from a Revenue discovery assessment unless you have pointed out the relevance of the additional material.

The return requires details of your income, claims for reliefs and allowances, and, if relevant, capital gains details, for the year ended 5 April. Husband and wife get separate returns. It is sensible to keep a photocopy of the return so that you have a full record of the information you have provided. Remember that even though you will not usually need to provide supporting documentation with your return, you may be charged a stiff penalty if you do not keep detailed records relating to your tax affairs for the specified period (see 9.6). See 9.2 re notifying the Revenue if tax is payable and you do not receive a return form.

Various points relating to the return are dealt with below in the same order as the return, i.e. the sets of additional pages are covered first, then savings income, pensions, other income, reliefs and allowances, and other information.

Employment

9.14   This section of the return covers income as an office holder as well as that from a conventional employment. Thus an honorarium, or any excess of a general expenses allowance over the expenses incurred, should be declared.

A separate set of additional pages is needed for each employment. Your employer should provide you with details of your pay (and student loan repayments where relevant) on form P60 by 31 May and details of benefits and expenses on form P11D (or P9D if you earn less than £8,500 a year) by 6 July, so that you can complete the relevant entries. You should check the forms to make sure you agree with them. Expenses covered by a dispensation or a PAYE settlement agreement do not have to be shown on your return. Tips and income from activities associated with the employment should be shown, whether they are paid by the employer or by someone else. You may be entitled to a deduction for expenses incurred in doing your job that you have not reclaimed from your employer. See CHAPTER 10 for further details.

You may have to fill in extra pages or refer to specific help sheets if you have taxable benefits relating to share schemes, lump sum compensation payments, or earnings from abroad (see CHAPTERS 11, 15 and 41 respectively).

Self-employment

9.15   The self-employment additional pages are for sole traders — there are separate additional pages for income from partnerships. Even if self-employed accounts are sent with the return, the detailed headings dealing with income and expenses (referred to by the Revenue as 'Standard Accounts Information' — SAI) must be completed by *all* sole traders except those whose annual turnover is below £15,000. Separate figures must be shown if there are two relevant sets of accounts.

If your annual turnover is less than £15,000, you need only show your turnover, purchases and expenses, with the resulting net profit, in the spaces provided.

You need to fill in the self-employment pages if you use your home as a guest house or bed and breakfast business. You may be able to claim 'rent-a-room' relief (see 30.7). For details of how to fill in the self-employment pages where rent a room relief is claimed see Help Sheet IR 223.

Partnership

9.16   Your personal return has to include your share of partnership income, as detailed in the separate return made by the partnership. There are two versions of the additional pages for your partnership income, the shorter version being for those whose partnership income comprises only trading profits and taxed interest from banks and/or building societies. For details on partnership returns see 23.5.

Land and property

9.17   The additional pages for 'Land and property' deal only with UK property. Foreign property is dealt with under the 'Foreign' section.

If you are claiming the 'rent-a-room' relief for rooms let in your own home (see 30.7), fill in the appropriate part of the form. If you provide substantial services as part of the letting, for example where you run a guest house or bed and breakfast business, you need to fill in the self-employment pages instead (see 9.15).

Furnished holiday lettings are separated from other properties. Such lettings are treated as trades even though the income is declared under this section, providing the relevant conditions are satisfied. This affects the tax treatment. For details see 32.17. As with trades, if the gross rents are below £15,000 a year you may show a single total for all allowable expenses.

You then need to add to the furnished holiday lettings profit the total rents from all other furnished and unfurnished property for the year ended 5 April less allowable expenses on those properties. Chargeable amounts in respect of lease premiums are included in rental income. (See CHAPTER 32 for details.) Interest is an allowable expense, restricted if necessary for any private use of the property (and this also applies to foreign property). Again, a single figure may be shown for expenses if the total rents are below £15,000 a year.

If you are the landlord and you pay your spouse an amount for his/her assistance in rent collecting and administration, this payment should be shown as his/her income in the employments section of his/her return.

Foreign income and gains

9.18   The separate additional pages for foreign income and gains enable you to show details of foreign tax paid so that you may get the appropriate relief for it. See CHAPTER 41 for detailed points on overseas matters.

Trusts, etc.

9.19   The trusts pages cover both trust income and income from estates of deceased persons.

Trust income:

Include any income to which you are entitled in the year ended 5 April. The trustees should give you a certificate showing the amount, which will either have been paid to you or will be available for you to draw from the trust. You also have to give details of income received by some trust funds you have established yourself, for example where you have settled assets on your infant unmarried children, perhaps by making bank or building society investments in their name. Any such income remains yours for tax purposes and must be shown in your return, unless that and any other income on investments provided by you for the benefit of your children amounts in total to £100 or less per child.

If you have established a trust for your children under which the income is either to be accumulated or used for their maintenance, any payments from the trust for their maintenance while they are under 18 and unmarried count as your income and must be shown on your return. The amount to be treated as your taxable income in this instance is 100/66ths of the maintenance paid.

Income from estates (in the course of administration):

If you are entitled to a share of the capital from an estate, the amounts you receive will be a combination of that capital and the income which it has generated. The personal representatives, who will themselves have paid income tax on the income, will give you a certificate of the income and the tax deducted (some of which may be non-repayable, for example if it relates to dividends). For further details, see CHAPTER 42.

You may sometimes be entitled to income under a trust created by will rather than a share of the capital, in which case the personal representatives will first of all complete the administration of the estate then transfer the residue to a trust fund. You should show the gross amount of any income you receive during the administration period. Any income you receive from the trustees after the residue has been transferred to them will be entered under the trust income heading.

Capital gains (TCGA 1992, ss 3, 3A)

9.20   For returns for 2003/04 onwards, if your total proceeds from all disposals of chargeable assets did not exceed four times the exempt limit (amounting to £31,600 for 2003/04) and the chargeable gains were less than the exempt limit (£7,900 for 2003/04), you do not have to fill in the capital gains pages unless you have made capital losses (see 4.2). If you have disposed of your home, it is not always exempt and may need to be taken into account (see CHAPTER 30). (Assets disposed of to your spouse are not taken into account providing you were living together at some time in the tax year.) Similar provisions apply to personal representatives (see 4.37). For trustees the limit of proceeds is the same amount as for individuals and personal representatives, but the annual exempt limit depends on the type of trust (see 4.38).In the case of quoted securities it is helpful to maintain a schedule showing the movements through purchases, sales, scrip and rights issues, etc., thus reconciling opening and closing holdings. The calculation of the chargeable gains on these and other assets is dealt with in the appropriate chapters, the date of disposal being the contract date in all cases.

You may have chargeable gains in respect of payments made or benefits provided to you by trustees of non-resident or dual-resident settlements, or settlements in which you are the settlor (see 41.41 and 42.13). See 37.3 for the treatment of cashbacks on building society mergers etc.

It is important to retain precise records of acquisitions and additional expenditure on chargeable assets, so that the capital gains tax on a future disposal can be calculated. The indexation allowance to April 1998 and taper relief thereafter depend upon dates of purchase and sale, so make sure you record them accurately. You will often need to obtain valuations of assets when calculating your gains. You may ask the Revenue to check your valuations (using form CG34) before you send in your return.

Non-residence, etc.

9.21   Your residence status affects your UK tax position and these additional pages provide the relevant information. See CHAPTER 41 for details.

Income from UK savings and investments

9.22   Interest and dividends are dealt with under separate headings. (See below re unit trust distributions.)

Income from UK banks, building societies and deposit takers:

This heading covers interest from local authorities as well as banks and building societies. You may have registered to have interest paid gross (see CHAPTER 37). Some other interest is also paid gross (see 37.1 and 37.4). Remember to include any interest received on *current* accounts as well as on deposit accounts.

National Savings:

Show the interest received or credited on National Savings Bank accounts and on deposit or income bonds and capital bonds. The first £70 of interest on an *ordinary* account (not an *investment* account) is exempt from tax (for each of husband and wife). After 31 July 2004 ordinary accounts will become dormant (see 36.4), but so long as the accounts remain open the interest will still qualify for the exemption. If you have income from fixed rate savings bonds you need to show the amount of tax deducted from the gross interest.

Other income from UK savings and investments (except dividends):

Other interest received is shown under this heading. This will include interest received in full, such as on certificates of tax deposit and loans to private individuals, and interest from which tax has been deducted, such as on loans to companies. Interest on government stocks, which may be received gross or net (see 36.16), is also shown here.

This heading also covers accrued income charges and reliefs. Under the accrued income scheme (see 36.18), the amounts of any accrued income charges or accrued income reliefs on your purchases or sales of stock are dealt with in the return for the tax year in which the next interest payment on the stock fell due. The amounts will usually be shown on the contract notes. Do not show the accrued income amounts if you are exempt from the charge because the nominal value of all your stock does not exceed £5,000 in the tax year or years concerned. Accrued income reliefs are netted off against the related interest. If you have accrued income charges and reliefs relating to the same kind of stock with the same interest payment dates, they are netted off to give a single charge or relief figure.

If you have purchased an annuity from a life assurance company, it is dealt with under this heading. The income includes a non-taxable element to compensate you for having parted with capital in order to receive an income. This capital element should not be included in the amount entered on your return. The life assurance company and the Revenue will have agreed its amount and it will be clearly shown on the counterfoil accompanying your income. If you have entered into a life assurance contract in order in due course to replace the capital you have spent in purchasing the annuity, the life assurance company will only pay you the difference between the amount due to you under the annuity and the life assurance premium. This net amount is not the amount to show as income. The income is the income element of the annuity *before adding* the capital element and *before deducting* the life assurance premium.

Dividends from shares in UK companies:

The amount to show is the dividends received in the year to 5 April and the tax credits, which are shown on the dividend counterfoils. The total of the two is taken into account to see whether you are liable to higher rate tax. Dividend tax credits are not repayable.

Scrip dividends:

If you took any scrip dividends (see 38.3) instead of cash dividends, enter the appropriate amount notified to you by the company in the dividend column and an amount equal to ⅑ of the dividend in the notional tax credit column. The credit is treated in the same way as for cash dividends, i.e. it counts as tax paid when working out whether you are liable to higher rate tax, but it is not repayable.

Income from UK unit trusts:

Unit trust income distributions may be either interest distributions or dividend distributions and are entered under the appropriate heading. If you have acquired new units, you will usually have received with your income an amount called 'equalisation'. This is not income and should not be included. It should be deducted from the acquisition cost of the units for capital gains tax purposes, since it represents a reduction in the cost of your units to cancel the accrued income included in your purchase price when you bought them.

UK pensions, retirement annuities, Social Security benefits and Statutory Payments (*statutory sick pay, statutory maternity etc. pay*)

9.23   This heading covers both State benefits and pensions from employment and self-employment. Some State benefits are taxable and some are not. The taxable benefits are listed on the form and the tax return guide provides detailed information. Note that where a husband gets an addition to his State pension because he has a non-working wife under 60, that counts as his income. It is not counted as the wife's income until it is paid to her, i.e. when she is 60. The taxable part of incapacity benefit is notified to you by your Benefit Office (see 10.3).

Life policy gains, refunds of surplus additional voluntary contributions

9.24   Your life assurance company will issue a certificate of taxable gains which arise from your drawing a sum from a policy (partial surrender) or cashing it (maturity or complete surrender). The gains should be shown in the return of income for the year ended 5 April in which the policy year ends (see CHAPTER 40). Surplus additional voluntary contributions are dealt with at 16.9.

All other income

9.25   This section of the main return relates to any other income you may have. Examples are given in the notes sent with the return. If in doubt as to whether an item should be included you should either seek appropriate professional advice or clear the point in writing with the Revenue.

If you have ceased to trade in an earlier year but have received some late income which was not included in your accounts, the amount should be included here.

Income from personal activities, for example from writing the occasional article or from an occasional commission, where the extent is insufficient to be regarded as from a profession or vocation, should be included in this section. Where occasional profit items are included, relief may be available for losses on the same or other occasional activities (see 19.11). Ask the Revenue for the appropriate leaflet.

See 37.3 for the treatment of cashbacks on building society mergers etc.

Pension contributions and retirement annuity payments

9.26   These are dealt with in CHAPTER 17. Payments under pre–1 July 1988 contracts are called retirement annuity premiums and payments under later contracts personal pension contributions (which includes stakeholder pension contributions). All personal pension premiums are paid net of basic rate tax, whether they are paid by employees, the self-employed, or anyone else, so the payments have to be grossed up to establish the amount of the premium qualifying for relief. Any extra relief due to higher rate taxpayers is taken into account in calculating tax payable. Retirement annuity premiums are paid gross. Provision is made for personal pension contributions paid by 31 January in one tax year to be treated as paid in the previous tax year. This applies only if the carryback claim is made on or before that date. Less restrictive rules apply to retirement annuity premiums. The 2003/04 return provides for you to carry back 2003/04 personal pension contributions paid by 31 January 2004 to 2002/03, or 2004/05 contributions paid by 31 January 2005 to 2003/04. (You will need to make an entry in the 2004/05 return as well for a 2004/05 premium carried back to 2003/04.) You can make a carryback claim separately from the return if you wish and this would be sensible if you were planning to make a payment close to the 31 January deadline. You do not need to send in certificates from your pension provider with your claims, but you should keep evidence of your payments in case the Revenue enquire into your return. See 17.10 for the effect on your tax payments of carrying back premiums. Contributions by an *employer* to an employee's personal pension scheme are not shown in the return, although they are taken into account in calculating maximum allowable premiums. Such payments cannot be carried back (see 17.8).

Reliefs

9.27   Claims are made in the return for relief for various payments, some of which save you tax at your top tax rate and others at a lower rate (see CHAPTER 2 for further details). Some particular points are noted below.

Interest on pre–9 March 1999 home income plan loans:

Home loan interest no longer qualifies for relief, except for pre-9 March 1999 home income plan loans (as to which see 34.9). MIRAS home income plan loans do not have to be dealt with in the return, because the relief has been taken into account in your mortgage payments. Claims for relief for home income plan loan interest paid outside the MIRAS scheme are made in the return. The relief is given on the interest payable on a maximum loan of £30,000 at the rate of 23%.

Maintenance or alimony payments:

You can only claim relief for maintenance or alimony payments if you were born before 6 April 1935. For 2003/04 the relief is at 10% of £2,150, giving a tax saving of £215 (10% of £2,210 = £221 for 2004/05 — see CHAPTER 33).

Gift Aid donations and covenanted payments to charities etc.:

All such payments should be shown net of tax. If you calculate your own tax, the tax calculation form takes into account the extra relief due to higher rate taxpayers. If you wish, you may claim relief in tax year to which the return relates in respect of gift aid payments made between the end of that tax year and the date you send in the return. There is a box on the return for this to be done. See 43.9 and 43.10 for details. You should keep a note of any such donations to make sure that you do not claim relief again in the following year.

Allowances

9.28   Some particular points on allowances are noted below.

Married couple's allowance:

Married couple's allowance is available only where one of the couple was born before 6 April 1935 (see 2.14).

If you have married since the beginning of the previous tax year, give the date of marriage. This will enable the Revenue to work out, or check your own calculation of, your married couple's allowance. Married couple's allowance is not available for years after the year in which you separate, unless exceptionally you separated before 6 April 1990, you remain married and are still wholly maintaining your wife by unenforceable contributions.

All or half of a specified amount out of the available married couple's allowance (£2,150 for 2003/04) may be transferred to the wife (see 2.14), providing a written claim has been made to your tax office *before the beginning of the tax year*, i.e. before 6 April 2003 for 2003/04. For those who have not yet made a claim, the earliest year to which a claim may apply is 2005/06, the claim being required before 6 April 2005. Whether or not part of the married couple's allowance has been transferred to the wife, either spouse may claim for any unused balance of the allowance available to him/her to be transferred to the other spouse where income is too low to use it (see below under 'Surplus allowances').

Surplus allowances:

If your income may be too low to use your married couple's allowance (or blind person's allowance), you have to notify the Revenue in order to be able to transfer the surplus to your spouse. Put a tick in the appropriate boxes and show the spouse's name, address, tax reference, national insurance number and tax office in the 'Additional information' section on page 9 of the return.

Other information

9.29   Under self-assessment, you need to state whether you have had any tax refunded to you, and if you are calculating your own tax you need to provide other information about underpaid and overpaid tax for earlier years.

If you want to calculate your own tax etc., the Revenue provide a tax calculation guide which you may use (although it is not compulsory). If you do use the Revenue's form you need to follow the instructions carefully, transferring figures from various parts of your tax return. The calculation is necessarily complex, principally because the tax saving on some reliefs and allowances is at a restricted rate, whereas on others the tax saving depends on your top tax rate, plus the fact that on certain payments you may have deducted and retained all or part of the tax relief due when you made the payment. Further complexity has been introduced by treating student loan repayments as part of the overall 'tax' payable for the year. Many if not most taxpayers, and some agents, will probably decide to leave the formal calculation to the Revenue, making their own calculations, if appropriate, to check the Revenue's figures. This has the disadvantage, however, that the return has to be filed by 30 September.

The return then makes provision for you to claim repayment of any overpaid tax. You are asked to give various personal details. Your date of birth is relevant if you are over 65, or if you are paying self-employed pension contributions (because you might qualify for relief on a higher percentage of earnings than the minimum 17½% — see CHAPTER 17), or if you are claiming relief for venture capital trust subscriptions (because you need to be over 18 to qualify).

Various other boxes may need to be ticked, for example if you expect to receive a new pension, or do not want a tax underpayment dealt with through PAYE, or if you have included provisional figures in the return (see 9.3).

Inheritance tax (IHTA 1984, ss 216–225A, 245, 247–248; FA 2004, ss 293–295; SI 1981/880; SI 1981/1440)

9.30   Most lifetime transfers are 'potentially exempt' but an account (on form IHT 100) must be sent to IR Capital Taxes of those which remain chargeable, unless in the case of individuals they do not exceed £10,000 and do not bring the cumulative total to more than £40,000 and in the case of terminations of life interests in a trust the value of the interest is covered by the annual or marriage gift exemptions (see 5.3). Trustees of discretionary trusts normally need to send an account in respect of chargeable events (as to which see 42.20). For chargeable events on or after 6 April 2002, however, this does not apply in most cases to UK resident trustees providing the assets of the discretionary trusts have always comprised only cash and the total value of the trust assets at the time of the chargeable event is less than £1,000. Returns are strictly not required until twelve months after the end of the month in which the transfer takes place, but interest on overdue tax runs from earlier dates, so returns should be lodged accordingly (see CHAPTER 5).

In the case of death, the return is made (on form IHT 200) in conjunction with the application for a grant of probate (where there is a will) or of administration (where there is no will or where the named executors cannot or will not act). Again, a twelve-month return period is allowed, but interest on overdue tax runs from six months after the end of the month of death. There is a practitioners' guide (IHT 215) to completing forms IHT 200. See 5.28 for income tax relief where personal representatives take out a loan to pay inheritance tax, and 42.1 for provisions enabling personal representatives to arrange for banks etc. holding the deceased's funds to transfer sums direct to the Revenue to pay inheritance tax.

If a deceased's estate is varied (see 5.26 and 35.10) and the variation results in extra tax being payable, a copy of the variation, together with the additional tax, must be sent to the Revenue within six months after the variation.

Anyone liable to pay tax on a potentially exempt transfer that becomes chargeable as a result of the donor's death is required to submit an account. Personal representatives are required to include in their account details of earlier transfers, whether chargeable or potentially exempt at the time, which are required for the calculation of the tax payable (see CHAPTER 5). It is therefore essential that full records of lifetime gifts are kept.

Personal representatives need not submit an account if the estate is an 'excepted estate'. Before 1 August 2002 an estate that included an interest in a trust could not be an excepted estate, nor could an estate in which a chargeable gift of land and buildings had been made within the seven years before death, but these restrictions no longer apply. An account need not be submitted for a deceased's estate not exceeding £240,000 (this limit having been increased from £220,000 as from 1 August 2003 in relation to deaths on or after 6 April 2003). providing that the following conditions are satisfied:

- the deceased was domiciled in the UK (see 5.2)

- any trust assets in which the deceased had a life interest were held in a single trust and are not valued at more than £100,000;

- the value of the estate situated outside the UK does not exceed £75,000;

- any chargeable transfers within the seven years before death were only of cash, quoted shares or securities, or land and buildings (and contents given at the same time), the total value of such lifetime transfers not exceeding £100,000;

- the deceased had not made a gift in which he retained a benefit.

The excepted estates provisions also apply where the deceased was domiciled abroad and had never been (or been treated as) domiciled in the UK, providing the value of the UK estate does not exceed £100,000 and consists only of cash, or quoted shares or securities. The Revenue reserve the right to call for an account later.

A reduced Inland Revenue account may be delivered where, because of exemptions, most of the estate is free from inheritance tax. This applies where the deceased was domiciled in the UK, most of the property passes to exempt beneficiaries, and the *gross* value of property passing to non-exempt beneficiaries together with other property chargeable on death and the *chargeable* value of gifts within the seven years before death do not in total exceed the inheritance tax threshold. This reduces the information required in account form IHT 200, and enables the personal representatives to include their own market value estimates for property passing to an exempt beneficiary rather than getting professional valuations. If an estate is later found not to meet the conditions for a reduced account, or the distribution of the estate is varied so that the conditions no longer apply, the personal representatives must submit a corrective account. The detailed information is in Revenue booklet IHT 19.

Provision has been made in FA 2004 for regulations to be issued to extend the existing simplified procedures so that they will apply to the great majority of non-taxpaying estates (including larger estates covered by the exemptions for bequests to a spouse or charity). Personal representatives of estates covered by the new procedures will be able to provide the relevant details to a probate registry, such information being treated as provided direct to the Revenue.

The Revenue have power to issue a notice of determination in connection with various inheritance tax matters (for example the value of unquoted shares), against which there is a right of appeal. The Revenue also have power, with the consent of a Special Commissioner, to give notice requiring someone to provide information, documents etc. relevant for inheritance tax purposes. There is no appeal against such a notice. Similar notice (but without the need for a Special Commissioner's consent) may be given to those who are required to deliver an account, against which there is a right of appeal.

If an account is not submitted by the due date, the Revenue may impose an initial penalty of £100 plus a further penalty (on a direction by the Special Commissioners) of up to £60 a day until the account is delivered. If an account is delivered late before the Revenue have taken proceedings before the Special Commissioners, the penalty is increased to £200 if the account is more than six months late. Following FA 2004, if an account is delivered more than twelve months late, a penalty of up to £3,000 may be charged. The same applies if notification of a variation of a deceased's estate is made more than twelve months late. Fixed penalties (but not daily penalties) cannot exceed the tax chargeable and penalties will not be charged if there is a reasonable excuse for the delay.

Someone required to deliver an *account* who fails to comply with a Revenue information notice as indicated above is liable to a penalty of up to £50 plus a daily penalty of up to £30 once the failure has been declared by a court or the Special Commissioners. The penalties for anyone else who fails to comply with an information notice are up to £300 plus up to £60 a day.

Various other penalties may also apply. Those liable for tax (see 5.31) may be charged a penalty equal to the tax lost for negligence or fraud. No penalty will arise if no additional inheritance tax is payable. For information provided by someone not liable for the tax (for example solicitors), the maximum penalty for negligence or fraud is £3,000. Similar penalties apply where there is unreasonable delay in correcting information found to be wrong. As with penalties for income tax and capital gains tax (see 9.47), penalties will be reduced in a negotiated settlement.

Corporation tax returns (FA 1998, s 117, Sch 18)

Self-assessment

9.31   Self-assessment applies to accounting periods ending on or after 1 July 1999. In addition to self-assessing the tax on its profits, the company is also required to self-assess its liability for tax on close company loans (see 12.12) and under the controlled foreign companies rules (see 45.14).

The corporation tax payment date for companies with profits below the upper limit for small companies' rate is nine months and one day after the end of the accounting period. Companies with profits above the small companies' rate upper limit are required to pay their tax by instalments (see 3.18).

If a company with taxable profits does not receive a return, it must notify the Revenue within twelve months after the end of the accounting period. A penalty may be charged if it fails to do so, the maximum penalty being the tax remaining unpaid at that twelve months date.

Companies must keep records relating to information in their returns for six years from the end of the relevant accounting period, or sometimes longer in enquiry cases and where returns are late. A penalty of up to £3,000 per accounting period is payable if they do not, but this will only be sought in more serious cases. Normally the record keeping requirement will be satisfied by the same records that satisfy Companies Act requirements, except for transfer pricing purposes. Records may be kept on computerised systems providing they can be produced in legible form if required.

Most of the self-assessment provisions follow those for income tax, although companies do not have the option of leaving the tax calculation to the Revenue.

Between three and seven weeks after the end of the accounting period the company will receive a notice to deliver a corporation tax return (form CT 603), together with the return form CT 600. Where relevant, companies will need to send in supplementary pages, the main ones being loans to close company participators (CT600A), controlled foreign companies (CT600B), and group relief claims and surrenders (CT600C). The filing date for the return is twelve months after the end of the accounting period or three months after receiving the notice to deliver the return if later.

The Revenue are able to correct obvious errors in the return within nine months, and the company may notify amendments within twelve months after the filing date. The Revenue have twelve months from the filing date for the return to select returns for enquiry (extended as for income tax for returns delivered late and amended returns — see 9.9). A company may notify amendments to its return within the time limit stated above even when the Revenue are enquiring into the return, but the amendments will not take effect until the enquiry is completed. As with income tax, the company and the Revenue may jointly refer questions arising during the enquiry to the Special Commissioners. If the return is not selected for enquiry, the self-assessment will stand unless an underpayment of tax is subsequently discovered that arises because the company gave inadequate information or because of its fraudulent or negligent conduct. See 3.20 re returns for companies in liquidation.

If the return is not sent in by the due date, automatic fixed penalties are payable (although by Revenue concession B46 a penalty will not be charged if the return is received on or before the last business day within seven days after the due date), and also tax-related penalties if the return is more than six months late (see the table at 9.46). Where, because of exceptional circumstances, a company cannot produce final figures within the time limit, 'best estimates' may be used without attracting late filing penalties, or penalties for fraudulent or negligent conduct (see 9.46), but the figures must be adjusted as soon as the company is aware that they no longer represent the best estimate, and any late payment of tax will attract interest.

Claims for capital allowances and group relief must be made in the return or an amended return. If the Revenue enquire into the return, the time limit for claims is extended to 30 days after the enquiry is completed (see 22.7 and 26.14). The procedure for making other claims is the same as for income tax (see 9.4 and 9.10). Such claims are subject to a time limit of six years from the end of the accounting period, unless some other time limit is specified. Where a return is amended following a discovery assessment, provision is made for the company to make additional or amended claims (see 9.43). See CHAPTER 26 for further details on loss claims and group relief.

Companies may ask the Revenue (on form CG34) to check the valuations used to compute their capital gains before sending in their returns.

Companies involved in non-arm's length sales (see 45.18) are required to include any necessary transfer pricing adjustments in their returns.

Company law

9.32   Under company law, public companies must file accounts with the Registrar of Companies not later than seven months after the end of the accounting period, the time limit for private limited companies being ten months. Automatic late filing penalties apply for public companies, ranging from £500 if accounts are up to three months late to £5,000 if accounts are more than twelve months late, the figures for private companies being £100 to £1,000.

Tax returns must be accompanied by copies of accounts as prepared under the Companies Act (including directors' and auditors' reports).

Assessments and additional assessments; error or mistake claims

Position for income tax, capital gains tax and corporation tax under self-assessment (TMA 1970, ss 28C, 29, 33, 33A; FA 1998, s 117, Sch 18)

9.33   Under self-assessment, taxpayers work out their own tax etc. Taxpayers other than companies may ask the Revenue to work the tax etc. out for them, but the Revenue's calculation still counts as a self-assessment. The Revenue are able to make a 'determination' of the tax and Class 4 national insurance (but not student loan repayments) due in the absence of a return, but this is not open to appeal, because it is treated as the taxpayer's self-assessment until replaced by an actual self-assessment. The time limit for a Revenue determination is five years from the filing date for the return (with special provisions where a company filing date cannot be ascertained), and the taxpayer's superseding self-assessment can only be made within that time or, if later, within twelve months after the date of the determination. If the Revenue enquire into a return or into a claim made separately from the return (see 9.3, 9.9 and 9.31), taxpayers are able to appeal against any amendments required by the Revenue, and the appeal and postponement provisions at 9.40 onwards apply.

With some very limited exceptions, the Revenue will only issue assessments themselves if they discover that tax etc. has been underpaid through a taxpayer's fraudulent or negligent conduct, or because of inadequate disclosure of information (see 9.43) and the appeal/postponement procedures at 9.40–9.42 apply to such assessments. For corporation tax, the Revenue are also able to make 'discovery determinations' where a return incorrectly states an amount that affects another period or another company. Unless there is fraudulent or negligent conduct, the time limit for a discovery assessment is five years from the 31 January filing date for personal returns and six years from the end of the accounting period for company returns. The six-year time limit also applies to discovery determinations.

The Revenue previously took the view that error or mistake claims and claims made after the normal time limit for amending returns did not affect any interest, penalty and surcharge. They have now decided that the legislation does not permit such charges to be amended. Taxpayers may ask for claims relating to 1996/97 or a later year to be reviewed and any necessary repayments will be made, repayment supplement being added to the repayments.

Where there are errors or mistakes in returns, then, subject to certain conditions, claims for relief may be made within six years after the end of the accounting period for companies and within five years from the 31 January filing date for the return by individuals. Error or mistake claims cannot be made in respect of claims included in the return, for which the normal time limits relating to the return apply.

Inheritance tax *(IHTA 1984, ss 221, 240, 241)*

9.34   Notification of the amount of inheritance tax due is contained in a notice of determination issued by the Revenue. Adjustments for tax underpaid or overpaid, plus interest, may be made subsequently but not later than the end of six years from the date of payment, or if later, from the date payment was due. In cases of fraudulent or negligent conduct, the period of six years starts at the time the fraud, etc. became known to the Revenue. See 9.30 for the penalties chargeable in cases of fraud and negligence.

Stamp duties *(Stamp Act 1891, ss 12, 12A, 15; FA 2003, s 78 and Sch 10; SI 1986/1711)*

9.35   The Revenue may be required to state whether an instrument is liable to stamp duty and if so how much duty is payable, and also whether any late stamping penalty is payable. There is a right of appeal to the High Court. The detailed provisions are in CHAPTER 6. The provisions relating to stamp duty reserve tax and stamp duty land tax are also in CHAPTER 6.

Repayment and remission of tax because of official error (Extra-statutory Concession A19)

9.36   Unless a specific time limit is stated, the normal time limit for individuals to claim reliefs is 5 years 10 months from the end of the relevant tax year. Repayments will, however, be made on claims made outside the time limit where the overpayment was caused by an error by the Revenue or another Government department, providing the facts are not in dispute.

Where the Revenue discover that they have undercharged income tax or capital gains tax, although they have been given full information at the proper time either by the taxpayer, or by his employer, or (in relation to pensions) by the Department for Works and Pensions, they may, by concession, not collect the underpayment. This will apply only if the taxpayer could reasonably have believed his affairs to be in order.

Out-of-time tax adjustments in favour of taxpayer

9.37   The time limits for appealing against assessments, and for substituting a taxpayer's own self-assessment for a Revenue determination under the self-assessment provisions, are indicated at 9.40 and 9.33 respectively. If action is not taken within the time limits, the tax assessed or determined becomes payable. Where income tax (including tax due from employers under PAYE) or capital gains tax that has legally become due is higher than it would have been if all the relevant information had been submitted at the proper time, the Revenue may be prepared to accept an amount equal to what the correct liability would have been, providing the taxpayer's affairs are brought fully up to date. This practice is known as 'equitable liability'.

Due dates of payment and interest on overdue and overpaid tax (TMA 1970, ss 86, 91)

9.38   Due dates of payment and interest provisions vary for the different taxes and are dealt with in CHAPTERS 2 TO 7 and in this chapter. There are, however, special rules for interest where the taxpayer has been at fault — see 9.46.

Certificates of tax deposit

9.39   Certificates of tax deposit may be purchased by individuals, partnerships, personal representatives, trustees or companies, subject to an initial deposit of £500, with minimum additions of £250. The certificates may be used to pay any tax except PAYE, VAT, tax deducted from payments to subcontractors and corporation tax, and may also be used to pay Class 4 national insurance contributions. Interest accrues daily for a maximum of six years, and provision is made for varying interest rates during the term of the deposit. A lower rate of interest applies if the deposit is withdrawn for cash rather than used to settle tax liabilities. The interest accrued at the time the deposit is used or cashed is charged to tax under Schedule D, Case III. Tax deposit certificates are a way of ensuring that liquid resources are earmarked for the payment of tax when due. They also prevent the risk of interest charges when tax is in dispute, because when they are used to pay tax, interest on overdue tax will not be payable unless and to the extent that the deposit was made after the date the tax was due for payment.

Appeals (Income tax, corporation tax, capital gains tax — TMA 1970, ss 31, 31A–31D, 55; FA 1998, s 117, Sch 18; Inheritance tax — IHTA 1984, s 222; Stamp duties — Stamp Act 1891, ss 13, 13A, 13B; FA 2003, s 78 and Sch 10; SI 1986/1711)

9.40   Normally appeals must be made within 30 days after the date of issue of an assessment (or Revenue amendment to a self-assessment). The appeal must state the grounds on which it is made (for example that a Revenue amendment to a taxpayer's self-assessment is incorrect). Late appeals may be allowed if the Revenue is satisfied that there was a good reason for the delay.

Postponement of payment of tax

9.41   Tax etc. still has to be paid on the normal due dates even though an appeal has been lodged, except that in relation to income tax, corporation tax, capital gains tax and stamp duty land tax an application may be made to postpone payment of all or part of the tax etc. The postponement application is separate from the appeal itself and must state the amount of tax etc. which it is considered has been overcharged and the grounds for that belief. The amount to be postponed will then be agreed with the inspector or decided by the Appeal Commissioners (see 9.42). Any tax etc. not postponed will be due 30 days after the date of the decision as to how much tax etc. may be postponed, or on the normal due date if later.

The appeal itself may be settled by negotiation with the inspector or, failing that, by following the appeal procedure to the Commissioners and thence if necessary to the courts. Once the appeal has been finally settled, any underpaid tax etc. will be payable within 30 days after the inspector issues a notice of the amount payable. Any overpaid tax etc. will be repaid. Although a postponement application may successfully delay payment of tax, it will not stop interest being charged against the taxpayer on any postponed tax etc. which later proves to be payable (see the due date and interest provisions in CHAPTERS 2 to 4).

Appeal procedures

9.42   If an appeal is not settled between the taxpayer and the inspector, it is listed for hearing by the Appeal Commissioners. There are two types of

Appeal Commissioners, General Commissioners and Special Commissioners. Appeals before the General Commissioners are heard in private. Appeals before the Special Commissioners are heard in public unless the taxpayer (or the Revenue with the Commissioners' consent) asks for a private hearing. Selected decisions of the Special Commissioners are reported. Certain specialised appeals are heard by the Special Commissioners and other appeals normally by the General Commissioners. There are provisions for the transfer of proceedings between the two bodies of Commissioners.

The decisions of the Commissioners on matters of fact are normally binding on both parties. If either the Revenue or the taxpayer is dissatisfied with a decision on a point of law, further appeal is possible to the High Court, the Court of Appeal and, where leave is granted, the House of Lords. It should be noted, however, that the decision to take an appeal to the Commissioners on a point of law must be weighed very carefully because of the likely heavy costs involved, particularly if the taxpayer should be successful at the earlier stages and lose before a higher court. Costs may be awarded against the unsuccessful party, not only by the courts, but also (if the party has acted unreasonably) by the Special Commissioners (not the General Commissioners).

Additional and extended time-limit assessments to income tax, corporation tax and capital gains tax; interest and penalties re tax and national insurance (TMA 1970, ss 29, 34–36, 43A, 43B, 43C; FA 1998, s 117 and Sch 18)

9.43   The Revenue are able to issue an additional assessment for a year within the normal time limits of 5 years 10 months for individuals under self-assessment and six years for companies without alleging that the taxpayer is at fault. Under the self-assessment provisions for companies they may also make 'discovery determinations' (see 9.33), to which the same provisions apply as to discovery assessments. They may 'discover' that an assessment is inadequate through considering facts already in their hands, such as by comparing gross profit rates from year to year, or through new facts, or even because they change their minds on how something should be interpreted. They have, however, stated that they will not normally reopen an assessment they later believe to be incorrect if they had been given full and accurate information and either the point was specifically agreed or the view implicit in the computation submitted was a tenable one. Under self-assessment, the taxpayer is protected from further assessment after the Revenue period of enquiry expires (see 9.9 and 9.31) unless there has been fraudulent or negligent conduct, or the Revenue have not been supplied with full and accurate information. The protection given to the taxpayer by this provision has been seriously undermined by a recent Court of Appeal case concerning a property valuation relating to a director's benefit in kind. The Court held that a discovery assessment outside the normal enquiry period was possible unless the Revenue had been clearly alerted by the taxpayer or his representatives to the insufficiency of the taxpayer's self-assessment. Where a discovery assessment is made, other than one arising from the taxpayer's fraud or negligence, provision is made for claims, elections, notices etc. to be made, revoked or varied within one year after the end of the tax year or company accounting period in which the assessment is made.

To reopen years outside the normal time limit, the Revenue have to show fraudulent or negligent conduct. In that event, assessments may be made at any time up to 20 years after the tax year/company accounting period concerned. Under self-assessment for income tax and capital gains tax the time limit is 20 years from the 31 January filing date for the return.

If the Revenue suspect serious fraud, then unless they are considering a criminal prosecution the investigation will be handled by their Special Compliance Office under their code of practice COP 9. In such cases the taxpayer will usually be professionally represented. Interviews between the client and the Revenue will be conducted under caution following the rules of the Police and Criminal Evidence Act 1984. The Revenue will give the taxpayer a statement (known as 'Hansard') which indicates their practice in cases of suspected serious fraud and states that they will accept a money settlement and will not pursue a criminal prosecution if the taxpayer makes a full and complete confession of all tax irregularities. It is up to the taxpayer whether he co-operates with the investigation under the Hansard procedure. If he does not, and evidence of provable fraud is uncovered, the risk of prosecution will have been increased substantially. The Hansard statement is followed by five questions to the taxpayer. The interview, including the taxpayer's answers to the questions, will be tape-recorded. The Hansard procedure gives the client certainty that he will be able to put his tax affairs in order by making a full disclosure and paying the understated tax, interest and penalties.

Where serious fraud is not suspected, the Revenue will usually invite the taxpayer to co-operate in establishing the understated income or gains. Where co-operation is provided, the Revenue will then not normally have to resort to their statutory powers to call for documents and to enter and search premises. See 9.2 re problems caused for tax advisers in investigation cases as a result of the new money laundering provisions.

Establishing the tax etc. lost

9.44   A Revenue investigation will include some or all of the following for the appropriate period, the effect of one on another being considered:

(a)   A full review of the business accounts, often including verification of transactions by third parties such as suppliers.

(b)   A detailed reconstruction of the private affairs, establishing whether increases in private wealth can be substantiated; or a less time-consuming review ensuring that lodgements into non-business bank and building society accounts can be explained.

(c)   A business model based on a sample period, adapted for changing circumstances and compared with the results shown by the business accounts.

(d)   A living expenses review and comparison with available funds to establish the extent to which personal and private expenditure could not have been met out of disclosed income and gains.

At the conclusion of the review, if the need for a revision of profits, income or gains has been established, the calculation of tax underpaid follows automatically.

9.45   In advance of the formal joining together of the two departments, the Revenue and Customs are increasingly working more closely together, a joint enquiry on behalf of both departments being a possibility where underdeclarations of duties dealt with by either department are suspected.

Interest and penalties (TMA 1970, ss 86, 95–98A; FA 1998, s 117, Sch 18; FA 2000, s 144)

9.46   For both individuals and companies, interest on overdue tax etc. runs from the normal due date, whether the taxpayer has been at fault or not.

In addition to the payment of tax etc. and interest, the Revenue have statutory powers to impose penalties when it has been established that tax etc. has been lost through a taxpayer's fraudulent or negligent conduct. The maximum penalties are shown in the table below.

Non-compliance	*Maximum penalty*
Failure to notify liability within six months after end of tax year for income tax and capital gains tax, or twelve months after end of accounting period for corporation tax (TMA 1970, ss 7, 10; FA 1998, s 117 and Sch 18)	The equivalent of the tax etc. payable

Non-compliance	Maximum penalty
Failure to submit income tax or capital gains tax returns within required period (TMA 1970, s 93)	£100, plus £60 a day if so ordered by General or Special Commissioners, plus further £100 if return more than six months late, plus amount equal to tax charged if more than a year late (see 9.8)
Failure to submit corporation tax return (TMA 1970, s 94; FA 1998, s 117 and Sch 18)	*Automatic, non-mitigable penalties* £100 if return up to three months late (£500 for third consecutive late return), £200 if return over three months late (£1,000 for third consecutive late return) Plus following % of tax unpaid 18 months after end of accounting period: Return submitted 18 to 24 months after end of accounting period 10% Return submitted more than 24 months after end of accounting period 20%
Negligence or fraud in any return or accounts (TMA 1970, ss 95, 95A, 96; FA 1998, s 117 and Sch 18)	An amount equal to the tax etc. lost
Negligence or fraud in relation to a certificate of non-liability to tax, or failure to comply with any undertaking in such a certificate (TMA 1970, s 99A)	£3,000

The Revenue have power to reduce both interest and penalties. They will rarely reduce interest, but will usually accept a smaller penalty where a settlement is made with a taxpayer without formal proceedings being taken.

In addition to their powers to impose penalties, the Revenue have separate powers to take criminal proceedings. Criminal proceedings may be taken under the general provisions for serious fraud and there is a separate criminal offence of fraudulent evasion of income tax.

Alternative to interest and penalty proceedings

9.47 Instead of formal proceedings being taken for interest and penalties, the taxpayer will usually be invited to make an offer to the Revenue in consideration of their not taking such proceedings.

The amount of the offer will in fact be negotiated between the Revenue and the taxpayer and will comprise the calculated tax etc. and interest plus a penalty loading, the penalty being reduced principally on three counts:

(a) Whether the initial disclosure was voluntarily made by the taxpayer or induced or partly induced by communication from the Revenue.

(b) The size and gravity of the offence.

(c) The degree of co-operation by the taxpayer.

The acceptance of a taxpayer's offer by the Revenue creates a binding contract, and if the taxpayer fails to pay, the Revenue are able to proceed for the amount due under the contract itself without any reference to the taxation position, although the terms of the contract sometimes allow them to repudiate it if they wish in the case of non- or late payment (the Revenue then recommencing negotiations or taking proceedings), and further interest will be charged if payments due under the contract are delayed. This established procedure is used in the vast majority of cases, and has points both in the taxpayer's and in the Revenue's favour, in that the taxpayer may be treated less harshly than if proceedings were taken, and the Revenue are spared the trouble of taking those proceedings.

National insurance contributions

9.48 As indicated earlier in the chapter, Class 4 contributions payable by the self-employed are collected along with income tax through the self-assessment system and are subject to the same provisions in relation to interest on overdue and overpaid amounts, penalties and appeal procedures. The interest and penalty provisions in relation to employee/employer contributions are dealt with in CHAPTER 13.

Where employers or employees have a disagreement with the Revenue about a national insurance matter that cannot be resolved informally, the Revenue will make a formal decision and notify the employer/employee accordingly. An appeal against the decision may be made within thirty days and the appeal will be dealt with under the same procedures as an income tax appeal (as to which see 9.40–9.42). The disputed national insurance liability and interest thereon need not be paid until the appeal is settled, but if the appeal fails the amount payable will attract interest from 14 days after the end of the tax year in which it became due.

A penalty of £100 is payable by those who fail to register with the Revenue for Class 2 national insurance purposes within three months of starting business. The penalty is payable after three complete calendar months from the date the business started, e.g. someone starting in business on 10 August 2004 would be liable to the penalty if they did not register by 30 November 2004. The penalty is due for payment within 30 days. The penalty will not apply if profits were below the small earnings exception limit up to the date of registration, nor if there is a reasonable excuse for not registering, and the Revenue have the power to mitigate or waive the penalty.

Criminal proceedings may be taken for fraudulent evasion of national insurance contributions.

Death of taxpayer

9.49   Death of a taxpayer limits the Revenue's right to reopen earlier tax years to the six tax years before that in which he died, and moreover restricts their right to raise new or additional assessments to the three years from 31 January following the tax year in which the death occurs, whatever the reason for the unpaid tax, e.g. by 31 January 2009 for a death in 2004/05 (TMA 1970, s 40). Under the Human Rights legislation, however, tax geared penalties can possibly not be imposed on personal representatives in respect of tax evasion by the deceased. It is understood that the Revenue will still seek penalties in these circumstances, but on request they will issue a letter confirming that the penalty will be repaid with interest in the event of an adverse court decision or a change of Revenue view.

Companies and company directors

9.50   While the liabilities of a company and its directors are entirely separate, their financial affairs will be looked at together if they are suspected of being at fault. Unexplained wealth increases or funding of living expenses will generally be regarded as extractions from the company, and, under his duty to preserve the company's assets, the director must account to the company for the extracted funds. The director does not have to pay income tax on the extracted funds, but is required to account to the company for the extractions, the company's accounts having to be rewritten accordingly and the extractions being subject to tax at corporation tax rates where they represent additional company profits. The company is also accountable for tax at 25% of the extractions unless they are repaid, covered by an amount already standing to the credit of the director or written off (see 12.12). The tax liability attracts interest and is reckoned in the tax due to the Revenue when calculating penalties. The extractions may also affect the income tax payable by the director on the calculated benefit which he has enjoyed from the interest-free use of the company's money.

Tax points

9.51

- Where you expect a tax repayment in your self-assessment return for 2003/04 or a later year, the form enables you to nominate a charity to receive all or part of your repayment directly from the Revenue and to indicate that gift aid should apply to the donation. The donation will be regarded as made when the charity receives the payment and it is not possible to treat the gift as made in the tax year to which the return relates.

- Self-assessment is a difficult exercise even for those with straightforward tax affairs. Remember that you *do not have to calculate your own tax*, but you have to get your return in by 30 September to make sure that the Revenue will not only calculate the tax for you, but let you know in time for you to make your tax payments on the due dates.

- If you are working out your own tax, do not miss the 31 January deadline for sending in the return, otherwise you will have to pay an automatic penalty and possibly a surcharge.

- Companies must similarly pay their tax and file their tax returns promptly. If they fail to meet the deadlines, they incur automatic interest and penalties. Companies should also be aware of the company law penalties for late filing of accounts.

- You need to retain records relating to your tax affairs for a stipulated period — there is a maximum penalty of £3,000 for each relevant tax year if you do not (see 9.6 and 9.31). The Revenue give useful advice on the records to be kept in their booklet SA/BK4 Self Assessment — A general guide to keeping records. An additional booklet SA/BK3 is available for the self-employed and those who let property.

- An unwelcome feature of self-assessment is the fact that you have to pay interest on underpaid tax etc. from the return due date according to the finally agreed figures, no matter how long it takes to establish them. This is made worse by the large difference between the rate of interest you have to pay and the rate you get on overpayments. In addition, where a claim is made to backdate a loss incurred or payment made to an earlier year, the resulting tax etc. adjustment is made for the tax year of loss or payment, so there is no extra benefit in terms of interest on tax overpaid.

- The Revenue's self-assessment computer programme does not always work correctly, particularly where tax has been overpaid. You may find you have been wrongly charged interest on overdue tax because the overpayment was not allocated early enough to a tax liability. Make sure you check the Revenue's calculations carefully.

- If you have started a new business, the Revenue will probably need extra information from you, and they can only get this by making an enquiry into your return (see 9.9).

- If you are self-employed and your turnover is less than £15,000 a year, you need only show your turnover, allowable expenses and net profit on your tax return. The same applies if your rent income does not exceed £15,000 a year. You must still have detailed records in case the tax office want to see them.

- You can register to receive bank and building society interest gross if you are not liable to tax. But you must not certify that you are entitled to this treatment unless you expect to have *no tax liability at all*. Merely being entitled to a repayment of some of the tax paid for the year is not enough. There is a penalty of up to £3,000 for false declarations.

  If, having registered, you find you are no longer eligible, notify the bank or building society straight away, and let your tax office know if you think you may have some tax to pay.

- If you are aware of irregularities in your tax affairs, a payment on account of the tax eventually to be accounted for will reduce the interest charge and also possibly any penalty by helping to demonstrate your co-operation.

- You should also disclose such irregularities fully to the Revenue before they make a challenge. You will thereby obtain the maximum penalty reduction when an offer in settlement is eventually made.

- Whilst the Revenue will usually settle for a cash sum comprising tax, interest and penalties, they may also take criminal proceedings in cases which they believe amount to provable fraud. They may still seek a civil money penalty on those aspects not brought before the court or where the taxpayer has been acquitted of fraud and they feel able to prove negligence (Revenue Statement of Practice SP 2/88).

- Where the Revenue is conducting a criminal investigation into suspected tax fraud, they now have increased powers to require banks, lawyers, accountants etc. to produce documents that may evidence the fraud.

- The Revenue and Customs and Excise have jointly issued a 'Taxpayer's Charter' setting out what standards they expect from a taxpayer, those which the taxpayer should expect from them, and the taxpayer's rights.

- If your business accounts or taxation affairs generally are under Revenue investigation, the Revenue will issue you with appropriate leaflets and their Code of Practice. These are no substitute for appropriate professional representation but they do explain your rights and are helpful in explaining Revenue procedures.

10
Employments — income chargeable and allowable deductions

Introduction

10.1   As indicated in CHAPTER 1, the tax law relating to employment income has been rewritten under the tax law rewrite programme and is now contained in the Income Tax (Earnings and Pensions) Act 2003 (ITEPA 2003), which took effect from 6 April 2003. The use of the heading 'Schedule E' to deal with employment and certain pension income and social security benefits has been dropped and the Act deals with the various Schedule E income categories under the headings of employment income, pension income and social security income. Previously some pensions from overseas were charged under Schedule D Case V, but all pensions are now brought within the new legislation. This chapter deals with employment income and taxable social security benefits. Occupational pensions and state retirement pensions are dealt with in CHAPTER 16. Foreign pensions are dealt with briefly in 41.6.

Basis of charge (ITEPA 2003, ss 1, 3–13, 682–686)

10.2   The legislation covers the employment earnings of employees and directors. Tax on such earnings is normally collected through the Pay As You Earn (PAYE) scheme. It is often hard to decide whether someone is employed or self-employed. See CHAPTER 19 for further details. If an employer wrongly treats an employee as self-employed, he is liable for the PAYE and national insurance contributions that should have applied, with only limited rights of recovery from the employee of his share. The worker who is classed as employed rather than self-employed will find significant differences in his allowable expenses, the timing of tax payments and the liability for national insurance contributions. Most agency workers are required to be treated as employees. The agency is usually responsible for the operation of PAYE but the client is responsible if he pays the worker direct. An employment agency has not been required to account for VAT on the salary costs of an agency worker if the client pays the staff direct. This should strictly change as a result of new Department of Trade and Industry regulations which came into force on 1 July 2004, although Customs propose to operate a concession for

18 months from that date allowing agencies to continue to account for VAT only on their commission, after which the concession will be reviewed. Employment bureaux that hire out self-employed people cannot use the concession, but they may choose to act as agents or principals for VAT. Only if they act as principals will they be required to account for VAT on the total charges made to the client. A business (other than an employment agency) that seconds staff does not have to account for VAT on the consideration received providing it does not make any financial gain. Agencies are normally required to deduct PAYE tax and national insurance contributions from payments to construction workers supplied by them.

There are special rules to prevent the avoidance of tax and national insurance by operating through a personal service company rather than being employed directly (see 19.3).

Social security benefits; sickness and unemployment insurance benefits (ITEPA 2003, ss 663–667)

10.3   The tax treatment of social security benefits is extremely complicated, and the detailed rules are outside the scope of this Guide. Despite the Revenue's view that the working tax credits and child tax credits outlined at 2.27 onwards above are part of the tax system, they are included in the list of non-taxable social security benefits in ITEPA 2003. The tax treatment of work incentive payments under various short-term pilot schemes (usually of up to three years' duration) may be stipulated by Treasury Order instead of by Act of Parliament. Under the Government's 'New Deal' programme, employers may receive incentive payments to take on unemployed people. Employees pay tax and national insurance contributions on wages for a New Deal job. The table below indicates which social security benefits are taxable and which are exempt. Certain short term benefits are not shown. See the Table of Rates and Allowances for the current amounts payable.

SOCIAL SECURITY BENEFITS	
TAXABLE	EXEMPT
Bereavement allowance and widowed parent's allowance* Carer's allowance* Incapacity benefit* (except for first 28 weeks and except as opposite) Industrial death benefit paid as pension Jobseeker's allowance (up to a specified maximum)	Attendance allowance Bereavement payment Child benefit and child's special allowance Child tax credit Christmas bonus and winter fuel allowances for pensioners

SOCIAL SECURITY BENEFITS	
TAXABLE	EXEMPT
Statutory maternity pay, statutory paternity pay and statutory adoption pay Statutory sick pay *Excluding any addition for dependent children	Disability living allowance Guardian's allowance Housing benefit and council tax benefit Incapacity benefit to those who were receiving the former invalidity benefit at 12.4.95 for the same incapacity Income support (except where the claimant is involved in a trade dispute and is claiming in respect of a partner) Industrial injuries benefit Maternity allowance Pension credit Working tax credit

The working tax credit imposes significant burdens on employers. Credits for the self-employed and unemployed are paid by the Revenue. Credits for employees are paid by employers, as an addition to net pay. The credits are recovered by set-off against the amounts payable by the employer to the Revenue under the PAYE system. If the credits exceed the amount payable, employers may apply to the Revenue for advance funding. The Revenue notify the amounts payable, and when to start and stop payment. Working tax credits are awarded for up to a year, and may change during the year where the claimant's income or circumstances change.

Where incapacity benefit is taxable, the tax is collected by a coding adjustment if the claimant is paying tax under PAYE on an occupational pension. If that does not apply, Jobcentre Plus (part of the Department for Works and Pensions (DWP)) deducts tax from the benefit directly, under a modified version of the PAYE scheme.

Although jobseeker's allowance is taxable, tax is not deducted by the DWP, but the amount received is taken into account either by a new employer or in calculating the claimant's tax position for the year if he is still unemployed at the end of it.

If you take out insurance to cover periods of sickness or unemployment, benefits payable under the policy are exempt from tax. Such policies include mortgage protection policies, permanent health insurance and insurance to meet domestic bills etc. Various conditions must be satisfied, in particular you must not have received a tax deduction for the premiums. Details are in Revenue Leaflet IR 153.

Persons liable (ITEPA 2003, ss 3–41)

10.4   Your liability to tax on earnings depends on your country of residence, ordinary residence and domicile. Broadly, residence normally requires you to be in the country at some time in the tax year, ordinary residence means habitual residence and domicile is the country you regard as your permanent home.

If you are resident, ordinarily resident and domiciled in the UK, you are normally charged to tax on your world-wide earnings. If you are a visitor to the UK, you are liable to tax on the amount you earn in the UK. If you are not in the UK long enough to be classed as resident, you are not normally entitled to personal allowances, but certain categories of non-resident qualify (see 41.13). Your liability to UK tax may be varied by double taxation agreements.

The detailed treatment of earnings abroad for both UK citizens and visitors is dealt with in CHAPTER 41, which also explains residence, ordinary residence and domicile more fully and deals with the question of double taxation.

Assessable earnings (ITEPA 2003, ss 9–13)

10.5   Pay for income tax covers wages, salaries, commissions, bonuses, tips and certain benefits in kind. The earnings must be 'in the nature of a reward for services rendered, past, present or future'. (See CHAPTER 15 for lump sum payments received on ceasing employment or taking up employment.)

Pay for the purpose of Class 1 national insurance contributions is broadly the same as pay for income tax. There are, however, still a number of instances where the treatment differs, and it is essential to study carefully the employers' guides provided by the Revenue. The same applies to Class 1A employers' national insurance contributions, which are payable on virtually all benefits in kind on which employees earning £8,500 per annum or more and directors (see below) pay tax (except where the benefits are included in a PAYE Settlement Agreement and contributions are paid under Class 1B — see 10.36).

Some particular differences between pay for tax and Class 1 national insurance are that pay for Class 1 national insurance is not reduced by charitable payments under the payroll deduction scheme (see 43.13), nor by occupational or personal pension scheme contributions paid by the employee. Contributions by the employer to approved company pension schemes or to an employee's approved pension plan do not count as earnings either for tax or national insurance. For further details on company and personal pensions, see CHAPTERS 16 and 17.

If your employer pays a bill that you have incurred yourself and are legally liable to pay, this counts as the equivalent of a payment of salary. You are charged Class 1 national insurance contributions, but not income tax, at the time the employer pays the bill. The employer will show the payment on your year-end form P11D or P9D (see 10.35), and the tax on it will be included in the amount of tax you owe for the year.

Employers must deduct and account for tax and Class 1 national insurance contributions under PAYE when they provide pay in certain non-cash forms — see 10.15.

Tax is charged on the earnings received in the tax year, no matter what period the earnings relate to. Certain expenses incurred may be deducted in arriving at the taxable earnings, as indicated later in this chapter.

Employees earning £8,500 per annum or more and directors — P11D employees (ITEPA 2003, ss 216, 217)

10.6 If you are a P11D employee, you are taxed not only on cash pay but also on the cash equivalent of benefits in kind. All directors and employees earning £8,500 inclusive of benefits a year or more are P11D employees. Full-time directors earning less than £8,500 are not P11D employees unless they own more than 5% of the ordinary share capital. All part-time directors are P11D employees unless they work for a charity or non-profit making organisation and earn less than £8,500. The legislation used to refer to P11D employees as 'higher-paid' employees. Recognising that £8,500 a year might not now even cover the minimum wage for full-time employees, the position has been reversed in ITEPA 2003 by describing employees not in the P11D category as 'lower-paid'. (Form P11D is the form employers complete at the year end for those within the above definition – see 10.35.)

Lower-paid employees (P9D employees)

10.7 If you are not a P11D employee (i.e. you are a 'lower-paid' employee), you are not normally taxed on benefits unless they can be turned into cash, and the amount treated as pay is the cash which could be obtained. For example, if you are given a suit which cost your employer £180 but which is valued second-hand at only £20, you are taxed only on £20. You escape tax on the benefit of use of a car, unless you have the choice of giving up the car for extra wages. In that event, the car could be turned into cash at any time by taking up the offer, so you would be treated as having extra wages accordingly. Some benefits are chargeable on all employees — see later in this chapter.

Benefits provided by your employer must be distinguished from payments on your behalf by your employer for something you are legally liable to pay. Such payments do not escape tax — see 10.5. If the *employer* makes the contract, the payment comes within the benefits provisions.

Employers report taxable benefits and expenses for non-P11D employees at the year end on form P9D (see 10.35).

Allowable expenses and deductions (ITEPA 2003, ss 229–236, 316A, 333–360)

10.8   In arriving at taxable pay, you can deduct expenses that are incurred wholly, exclusively and necessarily in the performance of the duties of your employment. Relatively few expenses satisfy this stringent rule. Some expenses which would not are specifically allowable by statute or by concession.

You can also deduct qualifying travelling expenses. You are entitled to relief for the full cost you are obliged to incur in travelling in the performance of your duties or travelling to or from a place you have to attend in the performance of your duties, as long as the journey is not ordinary commuting between your home and your permanent workplace or private travel (i.e. travel for a private rather than business purpose). This means that site-based employees with no permanent workplace are allowed the cost of travelling to and from home (unless the job at the site is expected to last for more than 24 months, in which case the site counts as a permanent workplace). The 24–month rule does not cover the position of someone whose employment, as distinct from temporary place of work, is expected to last 24 months or less. The full cost of meals and accommodation while travelling or staying away on business is allowable as part of the cost of travel. Business travel includes travelling on business from home where the nature of your job requires you to carry out your duties at home (but doing work at home for convenience rather than because of the nature of the job does not turn your home into a workplace). Where a journey has both a business and a private purpose, the expense will be allowed if the journey is substantially for business purposes. As far as national insurance contributions are concerned, they will normally only be payable if your employer makes a payment to you that exceeds the cost of a business journey. Note that payment by the employer of congestion charges in London will only be an allowable expense if incurred on business travel.

Using your own transport for business

10.9   There is a statutory system of tax-free approved mileage allowances for business journeys in your own transport. You are taxable only on any excess over the approved rates. Employers will report any such excess on year-end P11Ds or P9Ds (see 10.35). The mileage rates are as follows:

Cars and vans:	First 10,000 miles in tax year	40p per mile
	Each additional mile	25p per mile
Motor cycles		24p per mile
Bicycles		20p per mile

10.10   For national insurance contributions, the NICs-free rates for motor cycles and bicycles are the same as for tax. For cars and vans, the NICs-free amounts are based on the 40p rate for 10,000 miles regardless of the business miles travelled. The *total* amount paid in the pay period (whether as a rate per mile or regular or one-off lump sum payment) is compared with the NICs-free amount for the number of business miles travelled and Class 1 contributions are payable on any excess.

As far as VAT is concerned, if your employer provides you with private fuel for your own car at less than its cost, the employer has to account for VAT using scale charges (see 7.12). Employers can reclaim the input tax on employees' own fuel purchases if they reimburse the cost to the employees. If you receive a mileage allowance, the employer can reclaim input tax on the fuel element (providing he has detailed records to support the claim), but not on the part of the allowance that is for repairs, etc. Customs will accept the Revenue's advisory fuel rates as stated in 10.19.

If you carry fellow employees on business trips, either in your own car or van or an employer's car or van, the employer may pay you up to 5p per mile for each fellow employee free of tax and national insurance contributions. You cannot claim any relief if your employer does not pay an allowance.

Other expenses

10.11   For various occupations, flat rate expenses allowances have been negotiated for the upkeep of tools and special clothing, although this does not stop you claiming relief for the actual cost if higher. The cost of normal clothing is not allowed even if it costs more than you would normally pay and you would not wear the clothes outside work.

If it is *necessary* for you to work at home, you may claim the appropriate proportion of the cost of light, heat, telephone calls, etc. If you use a room *exclusively* for work, a proportion of your council tax is allowable as well.

Reasonable expenses payments by employers on or after 6 April 2003 to cover additional household expenses where an employee regularly works at home under homeworking arrangements are exempt from tax. The Revenue have stated that up to £2 a week may be paid without supporting evidence of actual costs. There is no relaxation in the requirements relating to expenses met by the employee himself. See also 10.18 re exempt benefits, some of which enable employers to provide those working at home with computers, furniture, supplies etc, without a tax charge, where private use is insignificant.

Other allowable expenses include contributions to an approved pension scheme, charitable donations under the payroll giving scheme and most professional subscriptions that are relevant to your job. The cost of business entertaining is not allowed, but the disallowance may fall on you or on your employer depending on how payment is made. You cannot claim a deduction for entertaining expenses paid out of your salary or out of a round sum allowance. If you receive a specific entertaining allowance from your employer or are specifically reimbursed for entertaining expenses, you are not taxed on the amount received, but no deduction for it can be claimed by your employer (see 10.35 re the PAYE treatment).

You can claim a deduction against your earnings for:

Contributions to a personal pension plan (see CHAPTER 17).
Capital allowances if you buy equipment that is necessarily provided for use in your job (excluding a car, van, motor cycle or bicycle, for which mileage allowances are available instead – see 10.9), restricted by any private use proportion (CAA 2001, ss 15, 207) — see CHAPTER 22.
Interest on money borrowed to finance the purchase of such equipment (restricted by any private use proportion) — for the tax year of purchase and the three following tax years (TA 1988, s 359(3)).

You do not have to pay either tax or national insurance contributions on any payment by your employer to meet the cost of directors' liability insurance, professional indemnity insurance and work-related uninsured liabilities. If you meet the cost yourself you may treat it as an allowable expense. This treatment is extended to payments made by you or your employer at any time up to six years after the end of the tax year in which the employment ends.

Expenses payments and reimbursed expenses

10.12   The strict application of the rule for allowable expenses would require all expenses payments to employees to be treated as wages, leaving the employee to claim relief for the allowable part. To avoid a lot of unnecessary work, expenses payments that do no more than cover expenses that are 'wholly, exclusively and necessarily incurred in the performance of the duties of the employment' are not treated as pay under the PAYE scheme so long as the employer obtains from the Revenue a dispensation enabling them to be excluded. Dispensations are also effective for national insurance contribution purposes. Examples of expenses for which a dispensation may be granted are travelling and subsistence allowances on an agreed scale and professional subscriptions. Dispensations may be denied in respect of directors of family companies, unless the expenditure is vouched by independent documentation. An employee away from home overnight on business is exempt from tax and national insurance on payment or reimbursement by his employer of personal expenses such as newspapers and telephone calls up to a VAT inclusive amount of £5 a night (£10 if outside the UK) (ITEPA 2003, s 241). (See also 10.11 re expenses payments to homeworkers.)

For both P11D employees and other employees, there are special rules for payments connected with relocation, as follows.

Removal and relocation expenses (ITEPA 2003, ss 271–289)

10.13   When an employee moves home because of his job, qualifying removal expenses and benefits are exempt from income tax up to a maximum of £8,000 per move, providing they are incurred during the period from the date of the job change to the end of the next following tax year. In order for the expenses and benefits to qualify for relief various conditions must be satisfied. Allowable expenses include expenses of disposing of the old property and buying another, removal expenses, providing replacement domestic goods, travelling and subsistence, and bridging loan expenses (see 30.13). The Revenue produce a booklet IR134 giving detailed provisions.

Employers do not have to operate PAYE on qualifying expenses payments, even if they exceed £8,000, but PAYE applies to non-qualifying expenses payments. Qualifying expenses payments and benefits in excess of £8,000, and non-qualifying expenses and benefits must be reported on year-end forms P11D and P9D.

Where an employer makes a payment to an employee to compensate him for a fall in value when he sells his home, the payment is fully taxable as earnings. It does not qualify for relief as a relocation expense. See 10.14 re selling the home to the employer or a relocation company and sharing in a later profit.

As far as national insurance is concerned, employees are charged Class 1 contributions on all relocation expenses payments that are not eligible for tax relief. No contributions are payable on qualifying removal expenses and benefits up to £8,000. Class 1A employers' contributions are payable on non-eligible relocation benefits and on any excess of qualifying relocation expenses and benefits over £8,000.

Sale of home to relocation company or to employer (Revenue concession D37)

10.14   Where there is a guaranteed selling price scheme, the treatment depends on the precise details of the scheme. There will, however, be no taxable benefit where an employee sells his home to the employer or a relocation company at market value and pays his own selling expenses. Where the employee has a right to share in any later profits when the home is sold, he will be exempt from capital gains tax on any additional amount paid to him to the same extent as he was exempt on the original sale, providing the later sale occurs within three years. (Part of the original gain may have been chargeable because the home had not always been the main residence, or had been let, etc., in which case the same proportion of the later amount will be chargeable.)

As far as stamp duty land tax is concerned, the relocation company or employer will not have to pay stamp duty land tax on the acquisition from the employee providing certain conditions are satisfied (FA 2003, s 58A and Sch 6A introduced by FA 2004, Sch 39.17).

Benefits in kind for all employees — specific charges

10.15   All employees and directors, no matter how much they earn, pay tax on the provision of living accommodation and non-exempt vouchers (see 10.16 and 10.17). There is also a tax charge if a loan from your employer is written off by reason of your employment. For P11D employees, this applies even if the employment has ceased — see 12.12. Loans written off are reported on year-end forms P11D and P9D (see 10.35). Class 1 national insurance contributions are charged at the time of write-off.

Tax has to be accounted for under PAYE where pay is provided in the form of 'readily convertible assets'. Readily convertible assets are: stocks and shares, gold bullion, futures or commodities that may be sold on a recognised investment exchange such as the Stock Exchange; assets subject to a fiscal warehousing regime; assets that give rise to cash without any action being taken by the employee; assets in the form of debts owed to the employer that have been assigned to the employee, and assets for which trading arrangements exist or are likely to come into existence. From 10 July 2003, *all* shares and other securities are within the definition of readily convertible assets unless the employer company is entitled to a corporation tax deduction for them (see 11.1). The convertible assets provisions apply equally where vouchers and credit tokens are used to provide the assets, and they apply to agency workers and to those working for someone in the UK but employed and paid by someone overseas. Benefits chargeable under the convertible assets provisions are referred to as notional pay. They would have been taxable in any event, but charging tax under PAYE accelerates the payment date for the tax (see 10.31). Pay in the form of convertible assets is similarly charged to Class 1 national insurance contributions.

PAYE also applies where pay is provided in the form of the enhancement of the value of an asset owned by the employee (such as paying premiums to increase the value of an employee-owned life policy).

See CHAPTER 11 for the detailed provisions dealing with share options and share incentives provided by the employer. Where an employee is taxable under ITEPA 2003 when a risk of forfeiture of shares is lifted, or when shares are converted into shares of a different class, PAYE and Class 1 national insurance contributions must be applied if the shares are readily convertible assets. PAYE and, for options granted on or after 6 April 1999, Class 1 national insurance contributions must also be charged on any gains realised when a share option is exercised (other than under a Revenue approved scheme) or is assigned or released. Unapproved options granted before 6 April 1999 were liable to Class 1 national insurance when they were *granted*.

Living accommodation (ITEPA 2003, ss 77–113)

10.16   If your employer provides you with living accommodation, you are charged to tax on the amount by which its annual value, or the rent paid by your employer if higher, exceeds any rent you pay. The annual value is what the letting value of the property would be if you paid the taxes, rates and charges usually paid by a tenant and the landlord paid for repairs and maintenance. There is no charge, however, if

(a)   you are a representative occupier, for example, a caretaker, or

(b)   it is customary in your employment to be provided with living accommodation, or

(c)   the accommodation is provided for security reasons.

Except where the accommodation provided by a company falls within (c) above, a director cannot qualify for exemption from the charge unless he does not own more than 5% of the ordinary share capital and either he works full-time for the company or the company is a charity or an organisation which does not have a profit-making objective.

If you are exempt under one of the above headings, you are also exempt from both tax and national insurance on the payment of council tax and water charges by your employer. If you are not exempt, council tax and water charges paid on your behalf by your employer count as pay for both tax and Class 1 national insurance.

Lower-paid employees escape tax on the provision of other benefits such as heat and light (providing the *employer* entered into the contract with the supplier) and the use of furniture, because they cannot be converted into cash.

If you are a P11D employee, you are chargeable on the value of other benefits relating to the accommodation whether or not you are chargeable on the letting value, but if you are exempt from the charge on letting value the charge for other benefits cannot exceed 10% of your taxable earnings excluding those benefits. Taxable earnings means earnings after deducting allowable expenses and occupational pension scheme contributions or retirement annuity premiums (but not personal pension scheme contributions).

The charge for living accommodation is increased where the accommodation cost more than £75,000. The extra charge over and above the letting value is calculated as follows:

((Cost less £75,000) × appropriate %) less amount by which any rent paid exceeds the letting value.

The appropriate percentage is the official rate of interest chargeable on beneficial loans, as at the beginning of the tax year (for the latest rates, see 'Official rate of interest — beneficial loans' in the Table of Rates and Allowances). Both the basic and, where appropriate, additional charges are proportionately reduced if the property is provided for only part of the year, and also to the extent, if any, that any part of the property is used exclusively for business. Where the accommodation is provided for more than one employee at the same time, the total benefits charges are restricted to what would have been charged on a single employee.

Vouchers (ITEPA 2003, ss 73–96, 266–270A; FA 2004, s 78 and Sch 13)

10.17   The vouchers rules generally apply to all employees and are wide-ranging.

Cash vouchers and non-cash vouchers exchangeable for readily-convertible assets (see 10.15) are treated as pay under the PAYE scheme at the time the voucher is provided.

Most other non-cash vouchers are taxable, although not through the PAYE scheme. Where the Revenue use their power to exempt minor benefits from tax (see 10.18), non-cash vouchers in connection with such benefits are also exempt. Your employer has to provide details to the Revenue at the year end of the cost of providing non-exempt vouchers and the cost of goods or services obtained through the provision of employer's credit cards. Tax on the value of the vouchers is usually collected from you by a coding adjustment.

Exempt non-cash vouchers include transport vouchers for employees of passenger transport bodies (other than P11D employees), vouchers in connection with a works bus service, or to obtain a parking space for a car, motor cycle or bicycle at or near the workplace, or in connection with cycles or cyclists' safety equipment provided by the employer, vouchers provided by third parties for corporate hospitality, vouchers for incidental overnight expenses within the limits stated at 10.12, and vouchers used in connection with sporting or recreational facilities.

There is still a derisory exemption of 15p per day for luncheon vouchers, providing they are available to all employees, non-transferable and used for meals only. Any excess over 15p is taxable, details being shown on forms P11D and P9D. No tax arises on free canteen meals that are provided to staff generally, so the luncheon voucher rules discriminate against employers who are too small to have their own canteen.

Class 1 national insurance contributions are payable on most non-cash vouchers, subject to various exceptions in SI 2001/1004, Sch 3 Pt V, which mainly mirror income tax provisions such as those indicated above but also include childcare vouchers for children up to age 16. A limited income tax exemption for childcare vouchers will apply from 6 April 2005 (see 10.18).

Non-cash vouchers are valued for national insurance as for tax purposes, but unlike the tax position, they must be dealt with on a weekly basis rather than at the year end. Vouchers in connection with employer-provided cars and car fuel for such cars are charged under Class 1A rather than Class 1 (see 10.24).

See 10.36 re accounting for tax and national insurance on non-cash vouchers through the Taxed Award Scheme.

Benefits in kind for P11D employees (ITEPA 2003, ss 62–191, 201–220, 237–249, 261–265, 316–325; FA 2004, ss 78, 79, 81 and Sch 13)

10.18   If you are a P11D employee, you are charged to tax on all expenses payments received (unless covered by a dispensation, see 10.12) and on the cash equivalent of virtually all benefits provided either direct to you or to your family or household. Benefits in the form of accommodation, supplies or services used in performing the duties of the employment either on the employer's premises or elsewhere are exempt despite some insignificant private use unless they are motor vehicles, boats, or aircraft, or they involve extension, conversion etc. of living accommodation. See 10.22 for specific points on home telephones. The Revenue have the power to make regulations exempting minor benefits and they have used it to exempt private use of equipment, services or facilities provided to disabled people to enable them to do their work, other than the excluded items mentioned in the previous sentence. The charging rules include benefits provided by someone other than your employer, except for corporate hospitality (providing it is not arranged by your employer and is not in return for services rendered by you), and gifts costing not more than £250 in total from any one donor. See 10.35 for the year-end requirements for third parties providing benefits.

The main benefits that are not chargeable to tax are:

Meals in a staff canteen providing they are available to staff generally.

Employer's contributions to an approved occupational or personal pension scheme.

Directors' liability insurance, etc. (see 10.11).

Free parking facilities for motor vehicles, motor cycles and bicycles at or near your workplace.

Sporting and recreational facilities.

Counselling services to redundant employees and welfare counselling services available to employees generally.

Childcare for children under 18 (other than on domestic premises) provided by the employer alone or with other employers, local authorities, etc., but with each employer being partly responsible for finance and management. The exemption does *not* cover cash allowances, vouchers, or payment by the employer of the employee's childcare bills, which are taxable at present for all employees no matter what they earn. Note that there is a wider exemption of childcare (for children under 16) for both Class 1 and Class 1A national insurance purposes, covering not only workplace nurseries but also childcare vouchers and employers contracting for places in commercial nurseries or for the services of a childminder. From 6 April 2005 the tax treatment is to be broadly aligned with the national insurance treatment. The exemption for registered childcare provided by the employer on premises other than domestic premises will continue. In addition the first £50 a week of childcare or vouchers will be exempt providing the childcare benefit is made available to employees generally and the childcare is registered childcare (or childcare provided by a school) or approved home childcare. Approved home childcare will not include care by the employee's spouse or partner or by a relative in the child's home. Cash provided to cover employees' own childcare expenses is, however, subject to both tax and Class 1 national insurance.

Commissions, discounts and cashbacks available to employees on the same basis as to members of the general public (because such benefits do not arise from the employment). To escape tax, cashbacks must be provided under a contract separate from the employment contract and not be given gratuitously.

Mobile telephones (see 10.21).

Employer-provided cycles and cyclist's safety equipment, providing they are available to staff generally and used mainly for journeys between home and work and for business journeys. (The provision by the employer of 'cyclist's breakfasts' on official cycle to work days is also not taxable.)

Certain works bus services, providing the services are used mainly for journeys between home and work, free or subsidised travel on local public stopping bus services used by employees for journeys between home and work, and employer support for other bus services used for such journeys providing employees do not obtain the services on more favourable terms than other passengers. The use of works buses on workdays for trips of up to 10 miles to local shops is also not taxable.

The use of computer equipment with an annual benefit value (based on 20% of cost plus running expenses) of not more than £500, any excess over that amount being chargeable. This exemption does not include internet connection, but see 10.22. (The benefit does not escape tax if the equipment is provided only to directors, or on more favourable terms to directors.) The benefit also did not previously escape tax if the employee had the option to take salary instead of the benefit. This restriction no longer applies from 6 April 2004.

The benefit of one or more annual staff dinners, providing the cost to the employer for each person attending is not more than £150 a year (VAT-inclusive). If, say, there were three annual functions at £60 each, the exemption would cover two of them and you would be taxed on £60.

Long service awards for those with 20 or more years' service, providing no such award has been made within the previous ten years. The value of the award must not exceed £50 for each year of service. Such awards may be tangible assets or shares in the employer company (or a group company). Cash payments and cash vouchers are excluded.

No taxable benefit arises where benefits such as air miles, points to obtain gifts, etc. are obtained by employees in the same way as members of the public, even though the purchase relates to the business. If, however, employers distributed air miles, etc. under an incentive scheme tax would be charged.

From 6 April 2004 there is no taxable benefit when emergency personnel working for the fire, ambulance and police services have to take their emergency vehicles home when on call.

You are taxed on the provision of medical treatment or insurance unless it relates to treatment outside the UK when on a business trip. Payments for medical expenses abroad, and insurance against such expenses, also escape national insurance contributions.

The cash equivalent of a benefit is normally the extra cost to your employer of providing the benefit (including VAT where appropriate, whether recovered or not, except for gifts with a total cost in a 12–month period of £50 or less, which do not attract VAT — see 7.2) less any contribution from you.

Scholarships to employees' children are caught unless they are fortuitous awards paid from a trust fund or scheme open to the public at large under which not more than 25% of the total payments relate to employees.

Special rules apply to share option and incentive schemes (see CHAPTER 11), the use of cars and vans and the provision of cheap loans (see 10.19, 10.20 and 10.23).

Where you are allowed the use of any asset that belongs to your employer, other than living accommodation (see 10.16) or a car, van or cycle, you are charged to tax annually on the private use proportion of 20% of its cost. If such an asset is later given to you, you are charged to tax on the higher of its market value at the date of the gift and the original market value less the intervening benefits assessments, whether charged on you or on other directors/employees. See example 1.

Example 1

Television set cost employer £500. Used by director for two years, then given to him or any other P11D employee when market value is £50.

Tax will be charged on the following amounts:

For use of asset, 20% × £500 =		£100 per annum
On gift of asset, higher of	£50 and	
	£500 – (2 × £100) =	£300
	£300, i.e.	

If, as well as allowing you to use an asset, your employer meets expenses on it, for example, pays the running expenses of a boat or aeroplane, you are taxed on the private element of those expenses as well.

There is no charge for private use of a commercial vehicle of more than 3.5 tonnes gross weight (including the provision of private fuel), unless it is mainly used privately.

Motor cars (ITEPA 2003, ss 114–153, 167–172; FA 2003, s 137)

10.19   The benefit of private use of a car belonging to or leased by your employer is charged to tax according to the value of the car. An additional charge is made if, in addition to the provision of the car, you are also provided with car fuel for private use (see below). (See 10.18 for exemption in relation to emergency vehicles.)

The value of the car for the purposes of the private use charge is the list price (or £80,000 if lower). The list price is inclusive of VAT and includes delivery charges (but not road tax), extras supplied with the car and any accessory costing £100 or more that is added later (excluding mobile phones and excluding accessories designed only for use by the disabled). The extra cost of enabling cars to run on compressed natural gas or liquid petroleum gas is excluded from the price of the car in calculating the benefit. Cars valued at more than £15,000 and at least fifteen years old at the end of the tax year are taxed according to their open market value (up to the £80,000 ceiling) if more than the list price. Where an employee pays towards the initial cost of a car, a contribution of up to £5,000 reduces the cost on which the tax charge is based. Any contribution you make to your employer for the use of the car is deducted from the car benefit charge.

The car benefit charge covers the whole benefit obtained from the use of a car, except the expense of providing a chauffeur, which is charged in addition. No additional taxable benefit will accordingly arise for employees driving company cars in London if their employers pay their congestion charges. (Those using their own cars will, however, only be entitled to relief where the charge is incurred in the course of business travel – see 10.8.) If a car is provided for only part of the year (for example, in the year when you start or cease employment) the charge is proportionately reduced. It is also proportionately reduced if the car is incapable of being used for a period of 30 consecutive days or more. Where a car is replaced during the year, the appropriate proportion of each benefit figure is charged. See 10.34 for the requirements for employers to notify the Revenue about new or changed arrangements for car provision.

The car benefit charge is based on a percentage of the price of the car graduated according to the level of the car's carbon dioxide emissions. The charge is 15% of the car's price for cars with emissions at or below a qualifying level, rising in 1% steps for each five grams of emissions above the qualifying level to a maximum of 35%. As cars get more fuel efficient the qualifying emissions figure is being gradually reduced, being set at 155 grams for 2003/04, 145 grams for 2004/05 and 140 grams for 2005/06 and 2006/07. Diesel cars are subject to an extra 3% charge, but with the overall maximum remaining at 35%. The taxable benefit for cars registered before 1 January 1998 and cars with no approved carbon dioxide emissions figures is as follows:

Engine size	Pre–1.1.98 cars	Cars with no approved emissions figures
	% of price taxable	*% of price taxable*
0–1400cc	15%	15%*
1401–2000cc	22%	25%*
2001cc and over	32%	35%

*Plus 3% supplement for diesel cars

The taxable benefit for cars with no cylinder capacity and no approved emissions figure is 35% of the price, or 32% for cars registered before 1 January 1998, unless the car runs solely on electricity, in which case the charge is at 9%.

Very low emission diesel cars are not subject to a supplement and there are extra discounts for environmentally friendly cars, such as those running wholly or partly on road fuel gas.

Example 2 shows illustrative charges for a car costing £15,000 for 2002/03 to 2004/05.

Example 2

Car benefit charges for car costing £15,000

	2002/03		2003/04		2004/05	
		£		£		£
Petrol car with rounded emissions figure of 195g	21%	3,150	23%	3,450	25%	3,750
Diesel car with rounded emissions figure of 240g	33%*	4,950	35%*	5,250	35%**	5,250

* Including 3% supplement

** Including 1% supplement

As indicated above, an additional charge is made if, in addition to being provided with a car, you are provided with car fuel for private use. The car fuel scale charge is based on a set figure — £14,400 for 2003/04 and 2004/05 — which is multiplied by the same percentage as that used to calculate the car benefit (see above). The charge is proportionately reduced where an employee stops receiving fuel part way through the year, unless he again receives fuel in the same tax year, in which case the full scale will apply. There is no charge for power supplied to an electrically propelled vehicle.

There is no reduction in the car fuel charge for a contribution to the cost of fuel for private journeys. To escape the fuel charge you must reimburse the whole cost of private fuel to the employer, or pay for it yourself in the first place. The Revenue publish advisory fuel rates which may be used by your employer in relation to a company car, to reimburse business mileage where paid for by you or to recoup the cost of your private mileage where paid for by the employer. The advisory rates are 10p (petrol), 9p (diesel) and 7p (LPG) (6p before 6 April 2004) for cars of 1400 cc or less, 12p, 9p and 8p (7p before 6 April 2004) respectively for cars of 1401 cc to 2000 cc and 14p, 12p and 10p (9p before 6 April 2004) respectively for cars over 2000 cc. These rates will be accepted as not giving rise to taxable benefits or Class 1 NICs liability. Higher or lower rates may be acceptable if the employer can show that they represent the actual costs.

The provision of a car for private use and of private fuel for the car also attracts Class 1A employers' (but not employees') national insurance contributions — see 10.24. The tax figures for the car and fuel benefits are used to determine the Class 1A amounts payable. Employers also have to account for VAT on private fuel provided to both P11D and non-P11D employees whether the car is provided by them or owned by the employee — see 7.12 and also 10.10 re mileage allowances. VAT does not apply to the provision of the car itself, even if the employee makes a payment for private use (unless the employer recovered all of the input tax on the car, or leases it from a lessor who reclaimed the input tax on it — see 7.11 — in which case a payment by the employee would attract VAT).

It is possible to escape tax and Class 1A national insurance contributions on the benefit of use of a car if it is a pool car as defined, but the conditions are restrictive. A pool car is one where the private use is merely incidental to the business use, the car is not normally kept overnight at an employee's home, and the car is not ordinarily used by only one employee to the exclusion of other employees.

The increasing cost of providing employees with cars and private fuel has led some employers to offer employees extra salary instead. The tax and national insurance contributions are based on what the employee actually gets, either salary or use of a car.

Vans (ITEPA 2003, ss 114–118, 154–166; FA 2004, s 80 and Sch 14)

10.20   There is presently a fixed taxable benefit of £500 per annum for private use of a van with a laden weight of 3.5 tonnes or less (including the provision of private fuel), reduced to £350 if the van is four years old or more at the end of the tax year. The taxable benefit is reduced proportionately if the van is not provided for the whole year, or is unavailable for 30 consecutive days or more. (See 10.18 for exemption in relation to emergency vehicles.)

Where vans are shared between several employees, the total fixed charges are calculated and split evenly between those employees, regardless of variations in private use, but with no employee being taxed on more than £500. The shared vans benefit is not reduced for an employee who has the use of a shared van for only part of the year (for example, if he joins or leaves during the year). An employee may, however, claim to be taxed on £5 for each day of private use instead of the normal calculation.

Both for exclusive use and shared vans, the taxable amount is reduced by any payment by the employee for private use.

New rules will apply to employer-provided vans from 6 April 2005, which are expected to remove the tax charge from 85% of current van users. From that date there will be no charge where an employee merely takes a business van home with no other private use. Where there is unrestricted private use the present £500 or £350 scale charge will apply. Shared van calculations will be simplified and rules similar to those for cars will apply for periods when the van is unavailable and where the employee pays for private use. Where an employee has a choice between use of a van and salary, tax and national insurance will be based on what the employee actually gets.

From 6 April 2007 the discount for older vans will be removed and the unrestricted private use charge will be increased to £3,000. Where the employer provides fuel for unrestricted private use there will be a charge of £500 (reduced appropriately for shared vans).

Mobile telephones, home telephones and ss 316. 319 internet access (ITEPA 2003, ss 316, 319)

10.21   The provision of mobile phones, including line rental and private calls paid directly by an employer, is exempt from tax and national insurance contributions. If the employee contracts to pay the bills for the phone, but they are paid by the employer, or the employer reimburses the employee, the amount paid for private calls is liable to tax and Class 1 national insurance contributions. Private use of mobile phones by employees affects the input VAT that employers may recover. Input VAT may be recovered on the cost of the phone and on standing charges, and on the call charges if private use is not permitted (or is insignificant). If employees pay for private use, input VAT may be claimed in full but output VAT must be accounted for on the private use charge. If employees do not pay for private use, input VAT must be apportioned appropriately.

10.22   If your employer pays your home telephone bills, then unless private use is insignificant you are taxed on the payments, but you are entitled to a deduction for the proportion relating to the business calls (but not any part of the line rental). Class 1 national insurance contributions are payable on the amount paid by the employer for the line rental and private calls.

If your employer is the subscriber rather than you, then unless any private use is insignificant you are taxed on the cost of the line rental and calls, less any amount made good to the employer, and you may claim an expenses deduction for the business calls. The employer is liable for Class 1A national insurance contributions on the line rental and, unless you have made good the cost of private calls, the cost of all the calls. If on the other hand there is a clear business need for the telephone to be provided, and the employer has procedures to ensure that private calls are kept to a minimum, you may not be taxed either on the line rental or the calls if the cost of the calls is insignificant compared with the total cost. In this event Class 1A contributions would not be due either. Examples given by the Revenue of employees who might be in this position are ministers of religion, teleworkers, and care workers who may need daily contact with the relatives of those they care for or the emergency services.

Where a broadband internet connection is provided in an employee's home solely for work purposes, any private use being insignificant and no breakdown being possible between work and private calls, and the cost of the package is not affected by the private use, the cost of the connection will not be a taxable benefit.

These provisions are covered in more detail in the Revenue's Employment Income Manual at EIM 21615 and EIM 21616.

Cheap loans (*ITEPA 2003, ss 173–191*)

10.23   If your employer lends you money interest-free or at a rate of interest below the official rate, you are charged to tax on an amount equal to interest at the official rate less any interest paid. This does not apply if the loan is for a qualifying purpose for interest relief either in calculating your income (see 2.10) or as a deduction from business profits or rental income, and the *whole* of the interest would qualify for tax relief. Such wholly qualifying loans are exempt from the charge. If part of the interest on the loan would not qualify for relief, the tax charge on the full amount of the loan at the official rate is reduced by the appropriate tax saving on both the beneficial loan interest and any interest actually paid. The tax charge and the compensating tax saving are normally dealt with by a coding adjustment.

The official rate of interest is varied by Treasury Order and is kept in line with typical mortgage rates (see 'Official rate of interest — beneficial loans' in the Table of Rates and Allowances). The rate is normally fixed in advance for the whole of the tax year, but it may be reduced during the year to reflect significant reductions in mortgage rates. Subject to any such reductions, the rate has been fixed at 5% for 2004/05 (unchanged from 2003/04).

There is no tax charge on loans made to employees on commercial terms by employers who lend or supply goods or services on credit to the general public despite the interest paid being less than the official rate. Nor is there any charge if the total of all non-qualifying beneficial loans does not exceed £5,000 at any time in the tax year.

If the loan is written off, you are charged to tax on the amount written off whether you are still employed or not, with Class 1 national insurance contributions also applying (but see 12.12 for controlling directors of close companies).

Class 1A national insurance contributions (SSCBA 1992, ss 10, 10ZA, 10ZB and Sch 1; SI 2001/1004, Part III)

10.24   Class 1A national insurance contributions are payable only by employers, not by employees. The rate payable is 12.8%. The contributions are payable on virtually all taxable benefits in kind provided to P11D employees unless they have already been charged to Class 1 contributions (or to Class 1B contributions under a PAYE Settlement Agreement — see 10.36).

The amounts liable to Class 1A are taken from forms P11D, the relevant P11D boxes being colour coded and marked 1A. The total on which contributions are payable is shown on form P11D(b) and is then multiplied by the relevant percentage to give the amount payable. Payment is due by 19 July following the end of the tax year (19 July 2005 for 2004/05). Benefits covered by a dispensation (see 10.12) are not shown on forms P11D and are not liable either to tax or Class 1A contributions. If a benefit shown on form P11D is fully offset by a matching deduction for tax purposes (or is covered by the insignificant private use provisions at 10.18), Class 1A contributions are not payable and the total Class 1A amount shown on form P11D is adjusted accordingly. Where, however, there is both business and private use, Class 1A contributions are payable on the full amount, even though for tax purposes the employee will be able to claim a deduction for the business proportion.

Where private fuel is provided for use in an employee's own car from an employer's own pump, or is provided by means of an employer's credit card, garage account or agency card and the garage is told that the fuel is being bought on behalf of the employer, Class 1 contributions are not due but Class 1A contributions are payable. Where private fuel is supplied in other circumstances, Class 1 contributions are payable. See 10.10 for the treatment where a mileage allowance is paid.

Where goods or services are obtained through a company credit card for the personal use of the employee, Class 1 contributions are payable. Where the goods or services are obtained on behalf of the employer, and the supplier is told that that is the case, contributions are not payable unless the goods or services are then transferred to the employee, in which case Class 1A contributions are payable.

See 10.34 for the way in which Class 1A contributions are accounted for.

Training and education

Scholarship and apprentice schemes

10.25   Employees on full-time and sandwich courses at universities and colleges lasting one year or more may receive pay of up to £7,000 a year tax-free while they are on the course (Revenue Statement of Practice SP 4/86).

Work-related training courses (ITEPA 2003, ss 250–260)

10.26   An employee is not taxed on the payment or reimbursement by his employer of the cost of work-related training, including not only directly job-related training but also training in health and safety and to develop leadership skills. As well as the direct costs, the exemption covers learning materials, examination fees and registration of qualifications. Travelling and subsistence expenses are allowed to the same extent as they would be for employment duties. This exemption will rarely cover pre-employment training provided by a new employer (see the Revenue's Tax Bulletin of April 2003 for their views).

Retraining costs (ITEPA 2003, s 311)

10.27   Where a retraining course in the UK for up to one year is made generally available to appropriate employees, the employee is not assessed on the course costs and any incidental travelling expenses paid for by the employer. The employee must have been employed full-time for at least two years, must leave the employment within two years after the end of the course, and must not be re-employed within two years after leaving.

Summary of main benefits provisions

10.28

BENEFIT	AMOUNT CHARGEABLE TO TAX FOR P11D EMPLOYEES*
Use of car	Charge based on 35% of list price, reduced according to the car's carbon dioxide emissions
Car fuel for private motoring	£14,400 × percentage used to calculate benefit of use of car
Parking facilities	Not assessable
Use of van	Fixed charge of £500 (£350 if 4 years old or more at end of tax year), or proportionate charge for shared vans
Living accommodation	Letting value (unless job-related)
Provision of services and use of furniture in living accommodation	Cost of services plus 20% p.a. of cost of furniture (but charge cannot exceed 10% of other reckonable earnings from the employment if exempt from living accommodation charge)
Use of other assets (excluding heavy commercial vehicles)	20% of cost
Vouchers other than luncheon vouchers	Full value
Use of employers' credit cards	Cost of personal goods and services obtained
Medical insurance	Cost to employer
Beneficial loans	Interest at official rate (see 10.23) less any interest paid, but no charge if non-qualifying loans total £5,000 or less.
Loans written off	Amount written off
Creche facilities	Not assessable
Free or subsidised canteen meals	Not assessable if available to all employees

BENEFIT	AMOUNT CHARGEABLE TO TAX FOR P11D EMPLOYEES*
Pension provision under approved schemes	Not assessable

* Non-P11D employees escape tax on benefits except for the
following, which are taxed on the same basis as for P11D
employees:
Living accommodation (but not services etc. provided by employer)
Vouchers other than luncheon vouchers
Use of employers' credit cards
Loans written off

Example 3

An employee is paid a salary of £25,000 in 2004/05.

He is provided with a 2-year old 1500 cc petrol driven company car
with a list price of £12,000, and carbon dioxide emissions of 175g per
kilometre. The car is completely run by the employer, including the
provision of private petrol and a mobile phone for business and private
use.

He received an overnight allowance which amounted to £649 and in
respect of which a dispensation had been granted to his employer by
the Revenue.

He paid hotel and meal bills on business trips amounting to £1,540 and
spent £250 on entertaining customers. These expenses were reimbursed
by his employer. Home telephone bills amounting to £250 were paid by
his employer, of which the business use proportion of the calls, as
evidenced by the employee's records, amounted to £150.

He received a round sum expenses allowance of £1,200 out of which
allowable expenses of £200 were paid.

The assessable earnings are:

	£	£
Salary		25,000
Charge for use of car (£12,000 × 21%*)		2,520
Car fuel charge (£14,400 × 21%)		3,024
Mobile phone (exempt)		—
Overnight allowance (covered by dispensation)		—
Hotel and meal bills reimbursed		1,540
Entertaining expenses reimbursed		250
Home telephone account paid by employer		250
Round sum expenses allowance		1,200
		33,784
Less: Hotel and meal bills reimbursed	1,540	
Entertaining expenses reimbursed (disallowed to employer)	250	
Proportion of telephone account relating to employment	150	
Other allowable expenses	200	2,140
Assessable earnings		31,644

National insurance

As well as the salary, pay for Class 1 national insurance contributions will include the round sum expenses allowance (except to the extent of any identified business expenses).

A private telephone use figure that is supported by the employee's records is accepted for national insurance purposes, so that Class 1 contributions in this example will be due only on £100. If there are no such records, pay for Class 1 national insurance includes payment of telephone bills, unless the telephone contract is in the employer's name, in which case the employer will be charged Class 1A contributions.

The employer will also pay Class 1A contributions at 12.8% on the car and fuel charges of (2,520 + 3,024 =) £5,544. Class 1A contributions are not payable on expenses that are wholly offset by a matching expenses allowance for tax, so there is no liability on the reimbursed hotel and entertaining expenses.

Revenue dispensations are effective for Class 1 and Class 1A NI contributions as well as for tax, so there will be no NI on the overnight allowance.

Value added tax

The employer will pay output VAT on the car fuel of £43.63 per VAT quarter, unless no VAT input tax is being claimed on fuel for any motor vehicle. The input VAT on the mobile phone will be restricted according to the private use proportion, unless the employee pays for the private use, in which case the employer must account for output VAT on the amount paid by the employee (see 10.19).

* % charge for car with CO_2 emissions of 175g – see 10.19

PAYE (ITEPA 2003, ss 682–702; SI 2003/2682)

10.29   The regulations that deal with the administration of the PAYE system have been rewritten under the tax law rewrite project, and the revised regulations came into force on 6 April 2004.

The basic object of the PAYE system is to collect and account for tax on employment income and employers' and employees' national insurance contributions. This in itself is becoming virtually impossible for employers to cope with because of the complexity of the system. The system is, however, increasingly being used for other purposes which are nothing to do with tax and national insurance, such as paying working tax credits (see 10.3) and collecting student loan repayments. The Revenue notifies employers which employees are liable to make student loan repayments and the employers make deductions (on a non-cumulative basis) according to student loan deduction tables. A further burden for most employers is the requirement to offer stakeholder pension schemes. All employers who employ five or more people and do not offer a qualifying occupational pension scheme or personal pension scheme arrangement must provide employees with access to a stakeholder pension scheme chosen by the employer after discussion with employees. If an employee joins the scheme, the employer must deduct contributions from pay where the employee wishes and account for them to the stakeholder pension scheme provider (see 17.2 for details). Small employers particularly are finding all their new responsibilities very onerous, and yet they face heavy fines if they get things wrong and by 2009/10 they will be forced to file year-end PAYE returns via the internet or pay a payroll bureau to do this for them (see below).

The Revenue have been increasing the use of electronic communication and many larger employers use the electronic data interchange (EDI) service to send and receive much PAYE information electronically, such as coding notices, forms P45, P46 and P160, and year-end forms P35, P14 and P11D. Since 2000/01 all employers have been able to file year-end returns via the internet, and they were given a discount for 2000/01 if they did so. This process has now been taken much further. *All* employers will be required to file year-end returns electronically (using Revenue approved software), either by internet or EDI, commencing with returns for the following tax years:

2004/05 for employers with 250 or more employees
2005/06 for employers with 50 to 249 employees
2009/10 for employers with fewer than 50 employees

A penalty of up to £3,000 may be charged for non-compliance. A return by magnetic media (CD-ROM, cassette disk etc.) does not count as online filing. The Government view is that the new rules do not force small employers to use the internet because they can use a payroll bureau. There are apparently around 640,000 PAYE schemes with one or two employees, so payroll bureaux may be in for a field day!

Employers with fewer than 50 employees will get tax-free cash incentives for filing electronically of £250 for each of 2004/05 and 2005/06, £150 for 2006/07, £100 for 2007/08 and £75 for 2008/09, amounting in total to £825. These incentives will also be paid to those with fewer than 50 employees who already file by internet or EDI. In order to qualify for the incentives, the year-end form P35 must be accompanied by at least one P14 (which may be one on which no tax or national insurance contributions are due because, for example, the employee is paid above the national insurance lower earnings limit but below the earnings threshold — see 10.34 for details of the year-end procedure). The incentive will be credited to the employer's PAYE accounting record unless the employer asks the Revenue for a repayment.

The process of forcing employers to adopt electronic means has now been extended to PAYE payments. From 6 April 2004 employers with 250 or more employees are required to pay electronically using bank or building society internet or telephone banking services, debit card over the internet (BillPay), BACS or CHAPS. Surcharges will be imposed for late payment. A later due date of payment has, however, been introduced to compensate for the cash flow disadvantage compared with cheque payments (see below), and this later date applies for *all* employers.

The information required to operate PAYE tax and national insurance is available from the Revenue, although they supply minimum paperwork initially and leave it to employers to sort out and ask for those of the myriad tables, booklets, pamphlets and forms they need according to their particular circumstances. The employer's pack does, however, include a CD-ROM which contains most of the available material. Employers use tables supplied by the Revenue to deduct tax (usually on a cumulative basis) and Class 1 national insurance contributions (on a non-cumulative basis, subject to special rules for company directors — see 13.12) from the weekly or monthly pay (including statutory sick pay and statutory maternity/paternity/ adoption pay). Employers must make monthly payments to the Revenue of the total tax and student loan deductions due, net of amounts paid for working tax credits, and the total employees' and employer's Class 1 national insurance contributions net of recoveries relating to statutory sick pay and statutory maternity etc. pay and net of NIC rebate where relevant (re contracted out contributions — see 13.6). The payments must be made within fourteen days after the end of each income tax month (ending on the 5th), i.e. by the 19th of each month, or by the 22nd of the month for electronic payments, unless that date falls at the weekend, in which case the payment must be made by the previous Friday. Interest is charged on unpaid PAYE amounts for any tax year which remain outstanding after the following 19 (or 22) April. If during the tax year the cumulative tax paid by an employee exceeds the cumulative amount due, the excess is refunded to him by the employer, who then deducts it from the amount due to the Revenue.

Pay records will sometimes need to be kept even though no tax or national insurance contributions are payable, for example where the pay is above the national insurance lower earnings limit but below the earnings threshold, or where working tax credits are paid. In such cases year-end forms P14/P60 need to be completed (see 10.34).

Employers who expect their average net monthly PAYE payment to be less than £1,500 may pay quarterly instead of monthly. New employers must notify the Revenue accordingly but existing employers need not do so unless they receive a demand from the Collector.

For details on national insurance contributions, see CHAPTER 13. For details of statutory sick pay and statutory maternity etc. pay, see CHAPTER 14.

Code numbers

10.30   Employers calculate tax using code numbers notified by the Revenue on form P9 or using the specified emergency procedure where no code number is received. Once a code number is issued it remains in force from year to year until the Revenue notify a change. A change in code number may result from a claim by the employee for further reliefs or allowances. Under self-assessment, most claims are made in tax returns, but most employees do not get tax returns to fill in. The Revenue have stated that where claims are made other than in tax returns and are reflected in PAYE codings, the taxpayer will be able to regard a claim as final 22 months after the end of the tax year (except in cases of inadequate disclosure or fraudulent or negligent conduct).

Your code represents the tax allowances you are entitled to, such as personal allowances and allowable expenses in employment, less a deduction to cover other income like pensions and national savings bank interest or benefits from your employer such as cars or loans, or to adjust underpayments in earlier years. There is a coding adjustment described as the allowance restriction, which adjusts the tax relief on married couple's age allowance and maintenance relief to 10%.

The allowance restrictions vary according to whether the employee is expected to be paying tax at the basic or higher rate of tax.

Your code number is the amount of your allowances less the last digit. For example if your allowances total £4,745 your code number is 474. The code effectively spreads your tax allowances evenly over the tax year. This means that if in any pay period you earn some extra pay, there is no extra tax-free allowance to set against it, so that the whole of the extra suffers tax.

Most codes are three numbers followed by a suffix L, P, V, Y or T. Code suffix L denotes the basic personal allowance of £4,745. Code P denotes full personal allowance for those aged 65 to 74. Code V denotes full personal allowance and full married couple's allowance for those born before 6 April 1935 and aged under 75 who are estimated to be liable at the basic rate. Code Y denotes full personal allowance for those aged 75 and over. The code suffixes enable the Revenue to implement changes in allowances by telling employers to increase relevant codes by a specified amount. Suffix T means that the code is only to be changed if a specific notification is received from the tax office. A code T may be requested by a taxpayer who wishes his status to remain private.

Some codes have a prefix K instead of a suffix. Prefix K enables tax to be collected during the year where the amount of an employee's taxable benefits or an employed pensioner's state pension exceeds available allowances. The tax deducted under a K code cannot exceed 50% of cash pay (but see 10.31 re notional pay). Other codes are BR, which means basic rate tax applies, 0T, which means no allowances are available, NT, which means no tax is to be deducted and DO. Code DO is used if you have more than one employment and your total income will attract higher rate tax. Your allowances are given against the earnings from your main employment and tax is deducted in other employments according to the DO code.

Under self-assessment, employees are able to have underpayments of up to £2,000 dealt with by coding adjustment if their returns are sent in by 30 September after the tax year (see 9.3). Codings may also be adjusted to give effect to reliefs such as losses (see 25.6).

Payments in non-cash form (notional payments) (ITEPA 2003, s 696; FA 2003, s 143)

10.31   Where employers provide employees with certain assets that are readily convertible into cash (see 10.15), PAYE and Class 1 national insurance contributions must be charged on the amount which, using the employer's best estimate, is likely to be chargeable as employment income, and accounted for in respect of the pay period in which the asset is provided, whether or not the employee has sufficient pay in that period to enable the tax and employee's national insurance to be deducted. Any such tax and NI that is not deducted from pay should be made good by the employee within 90 days from the time the asset is provided. If the employee does not do so, the unrecovered amount must be shown as further pay on year-end forms P9D or P11D. The 50% overriding limit on deduction of tax under K codes (see 10.30) is ignored when dealing with the deductions for notional payments.

Tax tables

10.32   Tables A, SR, B and C work on a cumulative basis. Table A shows the cumulative free pay each tax week or month for the various code numbers, and it includes the adjustments needed to increase the tax collected from employees with K codes by increasing taxable pay. Tables SR and B show the tax due on taxable pay to date at the starting rate of 10% and the basic rate of 22% up to the basic rate limit and Table C the tax due at the higher rate. Table D is non-cumulative, and is a higher rate tax ready reckoner for use with Table C and for D codes.

Changing jobs or retiring

10.33   When you leave your job, then unless the employer will be paying you a pension, he should complete form P45, which is in four parts. He sends the first part to the Revenue and gives you the other three parts, parts 2 and 3 being for your new employer and part 1A for you to retain (you will need it if you have to fill in a tax return, and you need to retain it in any event as part of your tax records — see 10.37). The P45 shows the total pay, tax to date in the tax year, the code number in use and whether student loan deductions are to be made. Passing the form to your new employer when you start another job enables him to continue to deduct tax on the correct basis. Statutory redundancy pay and certain other amounts received when you leave are not normally treated as pay, but they may be subject to tax under special rules (see CHAPTER 15).

If you cannot produce form P45 to your new employer, he will ask you to complete and sign form P46, indicating whether this is your first job since leaving school and you have not claimed jobseeker's allowance, whether this is your only or main job and whether you are receiving a pension. You are also asked to give details of employments within the previous twelve months. The P46 procedure enables employers to deduct tax on a cumulative basis straight away for school leavers, so that they get the benefit of the personal allowance from the beginning of the tax year. New employees receiving a pension will pay tax at the basic rate. Other new employees earning above the PAYE threshold (£91 a week for 2004/05) will be allocated a single person's allowance, code 474L, on a non-cumulative basis (called week 1 or month 1 basis), which means they get only one week's (or month's) proportion of the allowance against each week's (month's) pay. The Revenue will notify revised codes as appropriate after receiving forms P46. If you do not sign form P46, the employer will send the form to the Revenue and deduct tax from your pay at the basic rate.

Forms P46 are sent to the Revenue unless the employee earns less than the PAYE threshold. Forms P46 for such employees must be retained by the employer, together with details of the employee's name, address and amount of pay. If the employee's earnings equal or exceed the national insurance lower earnings limit (£79 a week for 2004/05), a deductions working sheet must be prepared. Form P46 has a second part for the Revenue National Insurance Contributions Office, so that employers may be given correct national insurance numbers where the numbers are missing or wrong. A voluntary national insurance number tracing service is available where form P46 is not sent in.

If you are retiring on pension, your employer will send a retirement statement to the Revenue (using either form P160 or the employer's own form, the information being similar to that provided on form P45) and give you a copy, which you will need if you fill in a tax return. The employer will deduct tax from your pension on a week 1 or month 1 basis (see above) until the Revenue tell him what code number to use.

If an employee dies, all four parts of form P45 are sent to the Revenue, with 'D' marked in the box at the foot of the form. The employee copy of year-end form P60 (see 10.34) is scrapped.

Employers' records and year-end and other returns

10.34   Employers must keep records of their monthly payments in respect of net income tax and net Class 1 national insurance payments (see 10.29). The totals should be recorded monthly or quarterly either on form P32 or in the payslip booklet.

Details must be provided to the Revenue at the year end for all those who are or have been employed in that year at a rate of pay equal to or exceeding the Class 1 national insurance lower earnings limit (£79 for 2004/05), even if no tax or NIC payments have been made because the employee's earnings are below the level at which tax and national insurance contributions become payable (£91 for 2004/05). Details of all employees to whom working tax credits have been paid must also be provided, regardless of the level of pay.

Employers may either use deductions working sheets P11 supplied by the Revenue and official end of year return forms P14, or use their own pay records and notify the totals on forms P14, or use their own pay records with substitute end of year returns, or keep computerised records and make end of year returns on magnetic tape, or file via the internet. Internet filing is compulsory for large employers (see 10.29).

Form P14 is in three parts. Two parts are sent to the Revenue (one of which is for national insurance purposes) and the third is the form P60 which must be given to the employee showing the total pay (including any statutory sick pay and statutory maternity/paternity/adoption pay), student loan deductions, working tax credits and tax and national insurance contributions deducted in the year. P60s relating to former employees are scrapped. Employers were not previously able to issue duplicate P60s but the Revenue has now stated that duplicates (clearly marked as such) may be provided. Forms P14 also show separate figures for the total statutory sick pay paid in months for which the employer recovered part of it (see 14.12) and the total statutory maternity etc pay. The forms to be sent to the Revenue at the year end are —

Two copies of form P14 (or substitutes)
Form P35 showing for all employees and former employees the total tax, NICs and student loan deductions due, net of tax credits, and the amounts recovered by deduction from national insurance and tax payments or directly from the Revenue in respect of statutory sick pay and statutory maternity etc. pay (see 14.12 and 14.22). The amounts *paid* in respect of statutory sick pay and statutory maternity etc. pay do not need to be shown
Forms P11D and P9D for all current and former employees (for details see 10.35)
Form P11D(b), which is a combined return for employers' Class 1A contributions and for declaring either that forms P11D are attached for all relevant employees or that no expenses payments or benefits have been provided.

See 10.29 above re electronic and internet filing of returns.

The time limit for sending in forms P14 and P35 is 19 May (22 May for electronic payments), and for sending in forms P11D, P11D(b) and P9D, 6 July. Those who were in employment at the end of the tax year must be given year-end form P60 by 31 May after the tax year, and also a copy of form P11D or P9D as appropriate by 6 July. Copies for employees who left after 5 April may be sent to the last known address. Employers may consider it appropriate to provide copy P11Ds and P9Ds to employees who left *during* the tax year, but they are not *required* to do so unless the employee makes a written request (within three years after the end of that year).

Employers' Class 1A national insurance contributions (see 10.24) are calculated annually from the P11D entries, the boxes on the P11D relevant for

Class 1A contributions being colour coded. The total of the amounts liable to Class 1A contributions is recorded on form P11D(b) as indicated above and multiplied by the appropriate percentage (12.8% for 2004/05), and the payment is sent to the Revenue Accounts Office using a special Class 1A payslip. The due date for payment is 19 July after the relevant tax year, i.e. by 19 July 2005 for 2004/05. For earnings paid after 5 April 2004, payment may be made electronically if the employer wishes, and in that event the payment date is 22 July. The first Class 1A payment to which this will apply is that due in July 2005. When a business ceases, Class 1A contributions are due within 14 days after the end of the income tax month in which the last payment of earnings is made. If a business changes hands, the employer before the change must similarly pay over Class 1A contributions for any employee not continuing with the new owner within 14 days after the end of the final month. The liability for payment of the Class 1A contributions for continuing employees falls on the successor.

Employers have to give the Revenue details of new and changed arrangements for the provision of cars and car fuel to employees on form P46 (Car). The form must be submitted within 28 days after each quarter to 5 July, 5 October, 5 January and 5 April.

As stated at 10.29, interest is charged if PAYE and national insurance contributions for any year to 5 April are paid late. Except for Class 1A payments, interest runs from 19 April following the end of the tax year or 22 April for electronic payments (which is a month earlier than the due date for submitting the year-end forms P14 and P35). For Class 1A, interest runs from the due date of payment, i.e. from 19 July 2005 for the 2004/05 payment (or 22 July for electronic payments). For recent rates of interest, see the Table of Rates and Allowances.

Automatic penalties are payable by employers who do not send in end of year forms P14 and P35 by 19 (or 22) May, or who send in incorrect returns (although by concession a penalty will not be charged if the forms are received on or before the last business day within the following seven days). The penalty payable is £100 for every 50 employees (or part of 50) for each month or part month the return is late. For example, someone with 110 employees who does not send in his 2003/04 return until 10 September 2004 (between three and four months late) would be liable to a penalty of £300 × 4 = £1,200. The statutory penalty is, however, limited in practice to the *higher* of £100 and the total of the tax and national insurance contributions for the year that should be shown on the return. For fraudulent or negligent forms P35 a penalty of up to the underpaid amount may be charged. A director may be held personally liable for unpaid national insurance contributions due from a company if the non-payment is due to his fraud or negligence. Penalties are also charged for late filing of forms P11D and P9D. For *each form*, there is an initial penalty of up to £300 plus up to £60 a day if the failure continues. If an employer fraudulently or negligently provides incorrect information in a P11D or P9D he is liable to a penalty of up to £3,000 for each form.

The monthly penalties of £100 per 50 employees for late P14s and P35s also apply to late P11D(b) Class 1A national insurance contributions returns (due date 6 July as indicated above, although the form states that penalties may be charged if it is not submitted by 19 July). For fraudulent or negligent Class 1A returns a penalty up to the underpaid amount may be charged.

The PAYE regulations require employers to keep PAYE records for at least three years after the end of the relevant tax year. Under the income tax self-assessment rules, however, unincorporated businesses must retain records for longer (see 9.6). Companies have to retain records for six years under the corporation tax self-assessment rules.

Forms P11D and P9D

10.35   Under self-assessment, employees who complete tax returns must include details of expenses payments and benefits from their employers. Employers are therefore required to provide all current employees (and also former employees if they so request) with copies of forms P11D or P9D as appropriate (see 10.34).

Forms P9D show taxable benefits and expenses payments for those earning less than £8,500. The main items are expenses payments totalling more than £25 for the year (other than those wholly for business purposes), payment of an employee's bills, gifts (at second-hand value), non-cash vouchers (including the excess of luncheon vouchers over 15p a day), and living accommodation.

Forms P11D show the cash equivalents of benefits for employees earning £8,500 per annum or more and directors (see 10.6). The Revenue provide optional working sheets for working out the cash equivalents for living accommodation, cars and fuel, vans, mileage allowance payments and passenger payments, beneficial loans and relocation expenses. Employers do not take into account any reduction an employee is entitled to for the business proportion of an expense. These reductions are dealt with by employees on their tax returns. Employers' Class 1A contributions are based on the P11D figures, and employers therefore have to pay full contributions on benefits where there is mixed business/private use (see 10.24). This has the effect of costing the employer 12.8% on a business expense, albeit reduced by the income tax or corporation tax on that amount.

P11Ds and P9Ds do not have to show amounts covered by a dispensation (see 10.12) or by a PAYE Settlement Agreement (see 10.36), and employees similarly need not show such amounts in their own tax returns. It is sensible for employers to make sure employees know what items are covered in this way and the Class 1A liability makes it important for employers themselves to ensure that dispensations are obtained if appropriate.

Where employees receive a specific amount for entertaining expenses, employers must state on P11Ds or P9Ds whether the expense has been disallowed in their tax computations. In that event, the employee is able to offset the expenses payment received by an equivalent expenses claim (see 10.11).

An employer must include in P11Ds and P9Ds any benefits he has arranged for a third party to provide (for example, where another group company provides cars or medical insurance). The onus of providing the information falls on the third party rather than the employer if the employer has not arranged for the third party to provide the benefits, and the third party must provide the information to the employee by 6 July after the end of the tax year. The rules for benefits provided directly by third parties do not apply to gifts costing not more than £250 per year or to corporate hospitality. Third parties do not need to send details of the taxable benefits to the Revenue unless they receive a return requiring them to do so. Class 1A contributions are payable on taxable third party benefits, including non-cash vouchers (see 10.24). See 10.36 re the liability for paying the Class 1A contributions.

PAYE Settlement Agreements and Taxed Award Schemes

10.36   Employers may enter into a PAYE Settlement Agreement (PSA) with the Revenue, under which they make a single annual payment covering the tax and national insurance contributions on certain benefits and possibly expenses payments. Items covered by the PSA are not shown on year-end forms P35, P14, P11D and P9D and employees are not subject to tax or national insurance on them. The scheme covers items which are either minor or irregular, or are made in circumstances when it would be impracticable to apply PAYE (e.g. on shared benefits). Details are in Revenue Statement of Practice SP 5/96.

As far as national insurance is concerned, employers pay a special class of contributions, Class 1B, at 12.8% on the benefits etc. taxed under the PSA plus the tax thereon, to the extent that there would have been a national insurance liability under Class 1 or Class 1A. Both the tax payment under the PSA and the Class 1B contributions thereon are payable by 19 October after the end of the tax year to which the payment relates. For earnings paid after 5 April 2004, payment may be made electronically if the employer wishes, and in that event the payment date is 22 October. The first Class 1B payment to which this will apply is that due in October 2005. Interest is charged from the due date if the payment is not made.

Employers and third parties who operate formal incentive award schemes are able to enter into arrangements known as Taxed Award Schemes (TAS), which work in a similar way to PSAs. Employers operating such schemes directly (but not third parties) may use a PSA instead if they wish. Employers have to account for Class 1 or Class 1A national insurance contributions as the case may be on non-cash vouchers or other benefits provided to employees, where the vouchers/benefits are provided directly or where the employers arranged for them to be provided by a third party. They also have to pay Class 1 contributions on the tax paid under a TAS. Where non-cash vouchers or other benefits are provided by a third party (whether under a TAS or not), Class 1A rather than Class 1 contributions are payable. Where the employer has not arranged for the awards to be provided, third parties must pay the Class 1A contributions on the award, and if they also pay the associated tax, they are liable for the Class 1A contributions on the tax payment. Third parties may use the TAS accounting arrangements to make payment. Year-end returns are due from employers and third parties by 6 July after the end of the tax year and payment of tax and Class 1A national insurance by 19 July (or 22 July for electronic payments re 2004/05 onwards).

Employees' records and self-assessment

10.37   With the introduction of self-assessment, all taxpayers are required to keep records relating to their tax liabilities (see 9.6). Most employees will not need to fill in tax returns, because their tax will usually be dealt with through the PAYE system (see 9.2), but they should still keep records for the statutory period in case there is any query. Employees need to keep records for 22 months from the end of the tax year, unless they are also self-employed or receive rental income, in which case the period is 5 years 10 months. In both cases, if the Revenue are conducting an enquiry into the taxpayer's affairs (see 9.9), the period is extended until the enquiry is completed.

The main records employees need to keep are year-end certificates P60 and forms P11D or P9D, forms P45 when they change jobs or P160 if they retire on pension, and records, receipts and vouchers to support expenses claims. They should also keep any other records that relate to their employment income, such as coding notices, information relating to employee share schemes, information re earnings abroad (and proof of any foreign tax deducted), etc.

Tax points

10.38

- Employers are faced with an almost impossible burden in dealing with tax, national insurance, collecting student loans and paying working tax credits. Payroll software can alleviate the problem, but the mass of paperwork employers are required to wade through to ensure that they comply with their obligations imposes an unacceptable cost and diverts attention from their proper business activities. There are, however, severe penalties for getting things wrong, so businesses need to be sure that their systems can cope. *All* employers are going to be forced to send year-end PAYE returns by internet, but for employers with fewer than 50 employees this will not happen until 2009/10 and in the meantime they will receive incentive payments for internet filing from 2004/05 onwards.

- The imposition of employers' Class 1A national insurance contributions on taxable benefits has removed the main advantage of paying them. There will still be a tax and significant national insurance advantage in respect of non-P11D employees, and also a national insurance saving in employee contributions for P11D employees earning less than £610 a week. Even where there is no such saving, it may be possible to provide benefits for less than the employee would have paid himself, by use of in-house services, staff discounts, etc.

- Where tips are received, great care needs to be taken in relation to the PAYE, national insurance and national minimum wage treatment. The Revenue have given their views in Tax Bulletin 69 and have also issued a new leaflet E24.

- The 15p a day luncheon voucher concession used to buy you a three-course meal! Now that both tax and national insurance contributions are payable on the excess over 15p, the advantages are so minimal as to be worthless.

- Watch the 'pecuniary liability' trap. Tax (and national insurance contributions) may be avoided for non-P11D employees on certain payments providing the *employer* is legally responsible for paying them, for example, heat and light in employer-provided living accommodation and home telephones. Payment by an employer of an *employee's* debt counts as pay for *all* employees and must be reported on year-end forms P11D and P9D. Class 1 national insurance contributions are payable at the time of the payment.

- Travelling expenses from home to a permanent workplace are not deductible in calculating your taxable earnings unless the nature of your job requires you to carry out your duties at home. Area representatives and those holding part-time employments, such as consultants and tribunal members, should seek to establish when they accept their employments that their place of employment is at their home or other workbase, making their travelling expenses from that base deductible.

- The Revenue have a programme of visits to employers for the purpose of inspecting records to ensure compliance with PAYE and national insurance regulations, including reporting requirements. They have issued a leaflet IR71 and a Code of Practice (3) explaining their procedure, which are available from tax offices.

- The Revenue test payroll software packages and award a Payroll Standard kitemark to those that meet the PAYE requirements.

- The Revenue offer to help small businesses in various ways with PAYE problems, including offering a free payroll check to ensure that employee details and national insurance numbers are correctly recorded.

- Employers will find it costly if they do not comply with the requirements of the PAYE scheme. To give two examples, failing to apply the P46 procedure properly for new employees who do not produce form P45 could make the employer liable to pay the tax that should have been deducted from the amount paid; if forms P11D and P9D are not properly completed and sent in promptly for each current or former employee, employers face severe penalties.

- Forms P11D are increasingly subject to close scrutiny and testing by the Revenue as to their accuracy, for example through visits to business premises, knowledge of directors' personal circumstances and a close inspection of the position as regards loans to directors. Care should therefore be taken to ensure that all sections of the form are correctly completed, and in particular that all expenses of the employee met by the employer are declared (except those covered by a dispensation or PAYE settlement agreement), a claim being made by the employee in his annual tax return for a corresponding deduction if the expenses are allowable for tax.

- The definition of 'earnings at the rate of £8,500 per annum' includes certain car expenses met by the employer as well as the car and car fuel charges. This brings some employees whose salary is less than £8,500 into the P11D reporting net.

- The total cost in tax, national insurance and VAT of the provision of private car fuel to employees has risen dramatically. It will almost always be cheaper, as well as far more straightforward in terms of reporting requirements, to pay the employee extra wages to compensate him for buying his own private fuel.

- Remember that an employee's contribution towards the cost of a car (maximum £5,000) and for the private use of a car reduce the car benefit charge, but payments by the employee for car fuel are not taken into account unless they cover the whole cost.

- If a car is provided for a relative of a P11D employee, the benefit will be charged on the car user rather than the P11D employee if the car user is also an employee and the duties of the employment are such that the car is required in the performance of those duties (e.g. where the employee is a commercial traveller) and would be provided to any employee in equivalent circumstances.

- If you use your own vehicle, motor cycle or bicycle for business, mileage allowances based on the Revenue approved mileage rates (see the Table of Rates and Allowances) may be received from your employer free of both tax and national insurance. If you pay your own running expenses, you can claim the approved rates for the business miles, and if your employer pays you a mileage allowance below the approved rates you can claim an allowance for the shortfall.

- If an employer arranges for his employees earning less than £8,500 per annum to eat at a local café which sends the bill to the employer, the employee avoids tax on the provision of the meals. This will not work for P11D employees unless the café can provide a private room, which then effectively becomes the works canteen.

- There is no tax on an interest-free loan to a P11D employee to buy a season ticket unless the total loans at a nil or beneficial interest rate that are outstanding in that tax year from the employee exceed £5,000.

- You are charged to tax on benefits arising from your employment even though your employer is not the payer. The most common example is tips. Another example is where one of your employer's suppliers pays for you to have a foreign holiday as a sales achievement reward. Such a supplier may operate a 'Taxed Award Scheme' under which he accounts for your tax. You must be provided with relevant details of all third party benefits to enable you to complete your tax return, but you are responsible for the entries on the return.

- Third party benefits to employees in the form of corporate hospitality, such as entrance to and entertainment at sporting and cultural events, and non-cash gifts to an employee from a third party costing not more than £250 in a tax year, are exempt providing the benefits and/or gifts are not procured by the employer and are not related to services performed or to be performed in the employment.

- The Revenue frequently reviews the list of professional subscriptions which are allowable in computing the taxable pay of an employee. You should therefore keep a watchful eye on this if your own subscription has not so far been allowed.

- If you *occasionally* work very late, you are not charged to tax if your employer pays for your transport home. Those who regularly work late get no such exemption, although exemption applies if your employer pays for your transport home because of a temporary breakdown in regular home to work car sharing arrangements.

- 'Payment' for PAYE purposes can be triggered much earlier than when money changes hands, especially as regards directors.

- Under self-assessment, you need to keep records relating to your tax affairs — see 10.37. The Revenue give useful advice in their booklet SA/BK4 Self Assessment — A general guide to keeping records.

11
Employee share options and awards

Background

11.1 The legislation in this area provides tax incentives to encourage participation by employees (including directors) in their employing companies, but it is accompanied by stringent and lengthy anti-avoidance provisions which were significantly tightened up and added to in 2003 (and also in FA 2004). The legislation was entirely rewritten by Income Tax (Earnings and Pensions) Act 2003 which took effect on 6 April 2003, though the purpose of this was simply to make it more intelligible, and only minor changes were made to the law itself. Less than two weeks after this Act took effect, however, much of the legislation was again completely rewritten in the 2003 Finance Bill, this time making major changes to the law. This double rewriting has come in for some heavy criticism from MPs and professional bodies alike. The Government's answer is that the second rewrite was necessary to thwart avoidance schemes and stem the flow of funds from the Exchequer, but like all widely drawn anti-avoidance legislation it seems likely to also catch out the unwary. It has certainly turned the whole area into a minefield, the one saving grace being that the bulk of the changes do not affect the four types of approved scheme listed below. Nevertheless, some notable (and, in fairness, mainly beneficial) changes have been made to these schemes as well.

There are four sets of provisions designed to give favourable tax treatment to schemes to acquire shares if the necessary conditions are satisfied. These are generally known as the 'approved schemes' and are as follows:

SAYE linked share option schemes (see 11.11)
Company share option plans (also known as CSOP schemes) (see 11.12)
Share incentive plans (see 11.19)
Enterprise management incentive share option schemes (see 11.13)

Currently there are also approved profit-sharing schemes, but these are being phased out and no further shares can now be appropriated to employees under such schemes (see 11.31).

Except in relation to the approved schemes, the legislation applies to 'securities' rather than just to shares, so that it includes debentures, loan stock and other securities issued by companies, and it was extended by FA 2003 to cover a wide range of other financial instruments, including government and local authority loan stock. The approved schemes deal only with 'shares' as defined. The definition includes stock, except for CSOP schemes (although CSOP scheme shares may be exchanged for stock or other securities on a reorganisation). This chapter refers mainly to shares, but the wider scope of the provisions should be borne in mind.

Reporting requirements

11.2   Under all the approved schemes, employers are required to provide returns to the Revenue. The time limit for sending in annual returns is three months (thirty days in the case of approved profit sharing schemes) from the date the return is received from the Revenue (unless the Revenue specify a longer period in any individual case). Detailed information must also be provided where tax may be payable in connection with other shares or share options. There is a general requirement for details of shares acquired by a director or employee by reason of his employment to be given to the Revenue by the company before 7 July following the tax year in which the acquisition occurs. Options granted under the enterprise management incentive scheme are not qualifying options unless the company gives the Revenue notice within 92 days after the grant of the option. Where tax may arise on a chargeable event within the anti-avoidance provisions at 11.8, or on the discharge of a notional loan within 11.7, or in relation to an unapproved share option as in 11.9, companies must give details to the Revenue before 7 July following the tax year in which the event occurs. Penalties apply in each case if the company fails to comply. These reporting requirements were tightened up by FA 2003 and now impose obligations on persons other than the employer company, though in most cases, in practice, it will probably still be the employer company that complies (ITEPA 2003, ss 421J–421L; FA 2003, Sch 22 para 2).

PAYE tax and NI

11.3   In relation to shares that are *readily convertible assets* (see 10.15), employers must charge PAYE tax and Class 1 national insurance contributions when shares are acquired, by reason of employment, other than under approved share schemes, or are subject to a tax charge under the rules of an approved scheme. Shares are readily convertible assets if they may be sold on the Stock Exchange or arrangements exist or are likely to exist for them to be traded. These provisions apply to shares acquired directly and through the exercise of unapproved options that were granted on or after 27 November 1996. They also apply where tax is charged when a share option is assigned or released (see 11.9), or a risk of forfeiture of shares is lifted, or shares are converted into a different class (see 11.8). Where shares acquired in such circumstances are not readily convertible assets, neither Class 1 nor Class 1A national insurance contributions are payable, but tax is chargeable through the self-assessment system (see 11.36). From 10 July 2003, shares and other securities that would not otherwise be readily convertible assets are treated as such (except for the purposes of the share incentive plan rules at 11.27) unless they are shares (or stock) that attract a corporation tax deduction under the provisions at 11.33 (or *would* have done so if the company's accounting period in question had begun before 1 January 2003) (ITEPA 2003, s 702(5A)–(5D)). Following the implementation from 1 September 2003 of the major changes made by FA 2003 to unapproved schemes (see 11.8), PAYE and national insurance are extended to chargeable events within those new provisions. Where the chargeable event takes the form of a receipt of money, or of an asset which is a readily convertible asset, PAYE etc. applies regardless of whether or not the scheme shares are themselves readily convertible assets (ITEPA 2003, ss 698, 700).

The national insurance legislation previously charged share options relating to shares that are readily convertible assets when they were granted, but for options granted on or after 6 April 1999 contributions are payable when the options are exercised. Companies expressed concern about the unpredictable timing and amount of their liability to pay employer's secondary contributions on unapproved options. It is now possible in respect of options granted on or after 6 April 1999 for employees and employers to make formal joint elections to the Revenue for the employees to pay the employers' secondary national insurance contributions when the option is exercised. Such elections need Revenue approval. Alternatively the employer and employee may make an agreement for the contributions to be paid by the employee. In this event the formal liability remains with the employer. In either case, any amount paid by the employee will reduce the amount chargeable as employment income in respect of the option for tax purposes (but not for national insurance contributions). It will not affect the corporation tax deduction allowable to the company (see 11.33), nor the allowable cost of the shares for capital gains tax. From a date to be fixed by statutory instrument, similar provisions for the employee to pay the employer's national insurance contributions, with his employment income being reduced by the amount paid, will apply in relation to chargeable events in respect of restricted securities and convertible securities (see 11.8). As with share options, the amount deductible for corporation tax and the allowable cost for capital gains tax will not be affected. As an anti-avoidance measure, certain pre–6 April 1999 options are brought within the charge to national insurance when exercised after 9 April 2003; the charge applies where the value of the option shares has been increased by more than 10% by things done after 5 April 1999 otherwise than for genuine commercial purposes (SI 2003 No 1059).

Other provisions

11.4   There are provisions relating to Employee Share Ownership Trusts (see 11.34) which enable companies to set up trusts that have more flexibility than approved schemes, although without their tax benefits. Such trusts may be run in conjunction with approved schemes. Companies may transfer shares held in such trusts at certain dates into an approved share incentive plan trust without adverse tax consequences.

Subject to certain restrictions, employers can get tax relief for the costs of setting up approved share option schemes, approved share incentive plans, and employee share ownership trusts, and see also the relief at 11.33 for the cost of providing shares for employee share schemes. For capital gains purposes, on the grant of an option under an approved or unapproved scheme, the employer is treated as receiving the amount, if any, paid by the employee for the option (rather than market value, which usually applies to non-arm's length transactions — see 4.27), so no capital gains charge arises.

Shares acquired under SAYE linked share option schemes, approved share incentive plans or approved profit sharing schemes may be transferred free of capital gains tax into an Individual Savings Account (ISA) up to the annual limit of £7,000 (see 36.22) even if they are unquoted. There is no similar provision in relation to enterprise management incentive share options, but favourable capital gains treatment applies to such options. Shares acquired under SAYE schemes, share incentive plans or profit sharing schemes may be transferred into personal pension schemes and tax relief obtained thereon (see 17.8).

Limits on participation by close company members (ITEPA 2003, Sch 2 paras 19–24, Sch 3 paras 11–16, Sch 4 paras 9–14, Sch 5 paras 28–33)

11.5   A director or employee of a close company (see 3.21) cannot participate in any of the approved schemes if he and his associates have a material interest in the company, or have had one at any time in the previous 12 months. For SAYE share option schemes, share incentive plans and CSOP schemes, a material interest is defined as owning or controlling (with associates) more than 25% of the ordinary share capital. For enterprise management incentive share options the relevant percentage is 30% (and the restriction applies to non-close companies as well), but the rule about having held a material interest within the previous twelve months does not apply. An option over shares is treated as a right to control them. Apart from these limits, close companies may introduce appropriate schemes so long as the other conditions are satisfied.

Share awards outside the rules of approved schemes

Issue of shares at an undervalue (ITEPA 2003, Pt 3 Ch 1)

11.6   Unless covered by the provisions of an approved scheme, any shortfall between the price at which shares are issued to directors and employees and their market value is taxed as employment income. Where the shares are not readily convertible assets their market value may be difficult to ascertain.

Issue of shares partly paid up (ITEPA 2003, ss 192–197, 446Q–446W)

11.7   If shares are issued at a price equal to the current market value, with the price being paid by agreed instalments, no charge will arise under the general charging provisions since full market value is being paid, and this will apply even though the market value has increased by the time the shares are paid for. Any growth in value of the shares is liable only to capital gains tax.

A director or an employee who acquires shares other than under the approved schemes and does not pay the full price for shares immediately is, however, regarded as having received an interest-free loan equal to the deferred instalments, on which tax is charged at the beneficial loans interest rate (see page xxix in the Table of Rates and Allowances) unless the total of all beneficial loans outstanding from that director or employee in the tax year, including the deferred instalments, does not exceed £5,000 (see 10.23). The loan is regarded as being repaid as and when the instalments are paid. Any amount written off is taxed as employment income at that time; any amount so charged is deductible for capital gains tax purposes when the shares are disposed of.

Anti-avoidance rules

11.8   Various anti-avoidance provisions outlined below apply to employment-related shares and securities. These do not apply in relation to shares that comply with the provisions of approved schemes, but enterprise management incentive schemes (see 11.13) are not regarded as approved schemes for this purpose. As intimated at 11.1, these rules were substantially changed by FA 2003. Also, under the FA 2003 rules, advantages gained not just by the employee but by 'associated persons' are brought fully within the charge to tax. 'Associated persons' include the person who acquired the shares (if not the employee), persons connected with the employee (or with the person who acquired the shares) and members of the same household as the employee (or person who acquired the shares). (The definition of 'connected' is broadly the same as in 4.27.) There are exemptions from some of the rules below where the shares are acquired under a public offer, or are shares in an employee-controlled company or where the event in question affects all the company's shares of the same class and the majority of them are held by outside shareholders; these exceptions apply in respect of restricted shares, convertible shares and post-acquisition benefits.

Restricted shares (ITEPA 2003, ss 422–432 FA 2004 s 86):

If shares have certain restrictions or conditions attached to them, including risk of forfeiture, their value will be less than their true unrestricted value, which reduces the charge to tax on acquisition. To counter this, a chargeable event occurs when the restrictions are lifted or, if earlier, when the shares are disposed of. The charge is calculated using a complex formula which is designed to tax the effect the restriction had on the value of the shares at the time it was lifted. In cases where the shares may be forfeited within five years, the charge under 11.6 on acquisition is removed, but tax is still chargeable when the risk of forfeiture is lifted. There is no charge once seven years have expired after the employment ceases and no charge on death. These provisions apply from 1 September 2003 but only affect shares acquired on or after 16 April 2003.

The previous rules are contained in ITEPA 2003, ss 422–434 as originally enacted and ss 449–452 as originally enacted and still affect shares acquired before that date. Under the original ss 422–434, the charge to tax when a risk of forfeiture is lifted, or on earlier disposal, is on the market value of the shares at that time less anything paid for them and less amounts previously charged to tax when they were acquired or subsequently. The original ss 449–452 charge tax where the value of shares increases because of the creation or removal of restrictions or the variation of rights relating to the shares or to other shares in the company.

Whilst the new rules might be said to be broadly comparable with the old, they can result in very different amounts being taxed at different times. Various elections are now available which have the effect of charging amounts earlier than would otherwise be the case but possibly by reference to lower market values at that earlier time. Valid elections in such cases take the form of an irrevocable agreement between employer and employee, made within 14 days after a chargeable event; there is no requirement that they be submitted to the Revenue or that the Revenue's approval be sought. One such election possibility is to waive the exemption on acquisition (for shares subject to early forfeiture) in order to limit the potential charge on a subsequent chargeable event; this was not possible under the old rules.

Any amount charged to income tax forms part of the acquisition cost of the shares for capital gains tax purposes. Where the shares are held in trust until such time as the risk of forfeiture or other restriction is removed, they are usually treated as acquired at that time, rather than any earlier time, though this does depend on the exact terms of the agreement.

From a date to be fixed by statutory instrument, an employee will be able to pay the employer's national insurance contributions arising on amounts chargeable under these provisions (see 11.3).

Convertible shares (ITEPA 2003, ss 435–444 FA 2004 s 86):

Where shares are convertible into shares of a different class or description, or may become convertible if conditions are met, any tax due on acquisition (for example under 11.6) is computed by reference to what their market value would be without the conversion right. When they are converted, or on any other chargeable event (which could be a disposal, a release of the conversion right or a receipt of a benefit), the value of the conversion right is taxed at that time at its then value, with a deduction allowed for anything payable by the employee for the conversion itself. These provisions apply from 1 September 2003 and, except for the way tax is charged on acquisition, apply to all shares from that date regardless of when they were acquired.

Amounts charged to income tax form part of the acquisition cost of the shares for capital gains tax purposes.

From a date to be fixed by statutory instrument, an employee will be able to pay the employer's national insurance contributions arising on amounts chargeable under these provisions (see 11.3).

Post-acquisition benefits (ITEPA 2003, ss 447–450 FA 2004 s xx):

Tax is also chargeable on the amount or market value of any *benefit* received by virtue of the ownership of the shares. Apart from the extension of the charge to benefits received by associated persons (see above), the new rules, which apply from 16 April 2003, are fairly similar to the old. The previous rules were contained in ITEPA 2003, ss 457–460 as originally enacted.

Shares with artificially depressed market value (ITEPA 2003, ss 446A–446J FA 2004 s 87):

From 16 April 2003, if the market value of employment-related shares is depressed by 10% or more by means of non-commercial transactions, the reduction in value is charged to income tax as employment income. This applies at acquisition, and also applies in conjunction with the rules above for restricted shares and convertible shares to prevent the reduction of tax charges on chargeable events under those rules. In addition, in the case of restricted shares only, if any such non-commercial transaction has occurred in the previous seven years, a charge arises on 5 April in the tax year as if the restrictions had been lifted on that date. For national insurance purposes, these provisions apply from 1 September 2003.

Shares with artificially enhanced market value (ITEPA 2003, ss 446K–446P FA 2004 s 88, 89):

Also from 16 April 2003, provisions are introduced to ensure that where in any tax year the market value of employment-related shares is enhanced by

10% or more by means of non-commercial transactions, the increase in value is charged to income tax as employment income on 5 April in that year or, if earlier, on disposal. For national insurance purposes, these provisions apply from 1 September 2003.

Shares disposed of for more than market value (ITEPA 2003, ss 198–200, 446X–446Z):

When employment-related shares are disposed of for more than their market value, the excess is chargeable to income tax rather than capital gains tax.

Share options

Exercise, assignment, release etc. of share options (ITEPA 2003, ss 420, 471–484, TCGA 1992, ss 119A, 120, 144ZA)

11.9   Where a director or employee is granted a right to acquire shares (an option) by reason of employment (whether his own or someone else's), there are various circumstances in which a tax charge can arise. However, favourable tax treatment is given for options under approved schemes (see 11.11–11.18).

Where the option is granted other than under an approved scheme, an income tax charge arises when the option is *exercised* on the difference between the open market value at that time and the cost of the shares. If the shares are readily convertible assets, the tax will be collected through PAYE, and Class 1 national insurance contributions will also be payable, although the employee may agree to pay the employer's secondary Class 1 national insurance contributions (see 11.3). Following the FA 2003 changes, the reference above to an option being *exercised* includes the acquisition of shares which the director or employee has been given a right to acquire (for example after a specified period under a 'long-term incentive plan') without any need to formally exercise the right.

For both approved schemes and other options, where a right to acquire shares is assigned or released, an income tax charge arises on the amount received. The same applies where the option holder realises a gain or benefit by allowing the option to lapse, or granting someone else an option over the shares. The same comments apply as above if the shares are readily convertible assets.

From 1 September 2003, these tax charges apply on the exercise, assignment or release of the option by any associated person and not just by the employee (i.e. the person by reason of whose employment the option was granted). 'Associated persons' include the person to whom the option was granted (if not the employee), persons connected with the employee (or with the grantee) and members of the same household as the employee (or grantee). To some extent, this was always the case but the scope of the charge was narrower before 1 September 2003.

Also from 1 September 2003, a tax charge arises on the amount or market value of any benefit received, in money or money's worth, by the employee (or an associated person) in connection with the option, which might include, for example, sums received for varying the option or as compensation for its cancellation.

Whatever the reason for a tax charge, any amount paid for the option itself is deductible in determining the taxable amount. From 1 September 2003, expenses incurred in connection with the exercise, assignment, release or receipt of benefit are also deductible.

From 2003/04 onwards, no tax charge can arise by reason of an event taking place after the death of the employee, for example the exercise of the option by his personal representatives. This applied in most cases before 2003/04 as well, but there were some limited circumstances in which such a charge could arise.

The above provisions always applied not only in respect of options to acquire shares but also in respect of options to acquire most types of company security, for example loan stock, and as indicated in 11.1, FA 2003 extended the scope of the provisions even further. If an option is brought within the above provisions as a result of the extended definition, the above changes have effect from 16 April 2003 rather than from 1 September 2003.

For capital gains tax, the amount taxed as income on exercise of an unapproved employee share option counts as part of the cost of acquisition of the shares (as does anything paid for the option itself). The position was temporarily thrown into disarray, however, by the Court of Appeal decision in *Mansworth v Jelley* in December 2002 and the Revenue's reaction to it. It was decided in that case that the appellant could deduct for capital gains purposes the market value of the shares at the time he acquired them and not just their actual cost. In a statement on their website on 8 January 2003, the Revenue announced that following this judgment taxpayers could deduct *both* the market value of shares acquired *and* the amount charged to income tax. This was illogical and likely to result in a capital loss being incurred for tax purposes, even though in reality no such loss had occurred. For options exercised after 9 April 2003, FA 2003 restored the position to what it was understood to be before *Mansworth v Jelley*. For options exercised on or before that date though, the Revenue's interpretation of *Mansworth v Jelley* still applies, and taxpayers who feel they may be affected would be well advised to study the information on the Revenue's website or seek professional advice. In some cases, it may be possible to claim substantial capital gains tax repayments. The decision in *Mansworth v Jelley* did not affect options exercised under approved SAYE linked share option schemes and CSOP schemes (see 11.11, 11.12) in accordance with the rules of those schemes, but it does apply to options exercised under enterprise management incentive schemes (see 11.13) in the same way that it applies to unapproved options.

Capital gains taper relief runs from the date the shares are acquired under the option and not from the date the option was granted, *unless* the option is a qualifying enterprise management incentive scheme option (see 11.18).

Charge on grant of option (ITEPA 2003, s 475)

11.10   From 1 September 2003, no income tax liability arises on the *grant* of an option, unless exceptionally the option is granted at a discount under a company share option plan scheme (see 11.12). Before that date, if an option under an unapproved scheme was capable of being exercised more than ten years after it was granted (seven years for options granted before 6 April 1998), tax was chargeable at the time the option was granted on the excess of the then market value of the option shares over the price which, under the option, had to be paid for the shares. From 2002/03 onwards, the amount chargeable to tax when the option was granted is deducted from the amount chargeable when the option is exercised. Where the option is to acquire securities not previously within these provisions (see 11.9), the above change in the law has effect from 16 April 2003 instead of from 1 September 2003.

SAYE linked share option schemes (ITEPA 2003, ss 516–520, Sch 3)

11.11   An exemption from the option charging provisions is given for options exercised under approved savings-related share option schemes. No charge arises on the difference between cost and market value when a share option is exercised, nor at the time it is granted, where the cost of the shares is paid out of the proceeds of a linked SAYE scheme. Contributions of between £5 and £250 per month are paid under a SAYE contract with a building society or bank. The savings are usually deducted from pay. The option will normally be able to be exercised after three years, five years or seven years, when the SAYE contract ends. The shares to be acquired must be ordinary shares in the company that established the scheme or a company which controls it. If the employing company or the part of its business in which the employee works is sold or otherwise leaves the group operating the scheme, the scheme may provide for the employee to exercise the option within six months after that event, but if this results in the employee exercising the option within three years of joining the scheme, any gain arising is charged to tax and, for post–5 April 1999 options relating to shares that are readily convertible assets, Class 1 national insurance contributions (see 11.3). An employee who has been transferred to an associated company which is not participating in the scheme may nonetheless be permitted by the scheme rules to exercise his option within six months after the date his savings contract matures. If an employee dies before completing the contract, the option may be exercised within twelve months after the date of death. If an employee leaves through injury, disability, redundancy or retirement, the option may be exercised within the following six months. An option held by an employee leaving for any other reason must lapse, unless he had held it for at least three years, in which case he may be permitted to exercise it within six months after leaving.

Regardless of the treatment of the option, the SAYE contract itself may be continued by an employee after he leaves, by arrangement with the savings body, so that the benefit of receiving tax-free interest and bonuses at the end of the contract (see below) is retained. Contributions will then be paid direct to the savings body.

The scheme enables an option to be granted now to acquire shares at today's price, the shares eventually being paid for by the proceeds of a linked SAYE scheme. The price at which the option may be exercised must not normally be less than 80% of the market value of the shares at the time the option is granted. The employee does not get tax relief for the SAYE contributions but he gets the benefit of tax-free interest and bonuses at the end of the contract, and when the shares are taken up there is no income tax charge on the excess of the market value over the price paid. If the shares are not taken up, the employee retains the proceeds of the SAYE contract together with the tax-free interest and bonuses.

Various conditions must be complied with and in particular the scheme must be available to all directors and employees with a stipulated length of service which cannot be set at more five years (though certain close company members must be excluded — see 11.5). It must not stipulate a minimum monthly contribution higher than £5 and it must not have features that discourage eligible employees from participating. Part-time employees must be included, but part-time *directors* may be excluded. Companies may require scheme shares to be sold if an employee or director leaves the company, thus helping family companies who wish to ensure that their control is not diluted, and scheme rights can be exchanged for equivalent rights in a company taking over the employer company.

The capital gains tax base cost of the shares is the price paid by the employee so that when they are disposed of, the benefit of acquiring them at less than their market value is then partly lost, because the gain is charged to tax (except for the benefit of CGT indexation to April 1998, taper relief from the time the option was exercised and any unused annual exemption, which would not have been available if the gain had been charged to income tax). The employee has, however, had the benefit of the SAYE tax-free interest and bonuses. See 11.32 for the special capital gains tax rules for identifying share disposals with acquisitions. If the opportunity is taken to transfer the shares up to the available limit of £7,000 into an Individual Savings Account (ISA) (see 36.22), the capital gain on the transfer to the ISA is tax-free.

Company share option plans (CSOP schemes) (ITEPA 2003, ss 521–526, Sch 4, Sch 6 para 221; TCGA 1992, Sch 7D paras 11–13)

11.12   Tax advantages have been available for some time under approved, non-savings-related, discretionary share option schemes, but the advantages were significantly reduced for options granted on or after 17 July 1995. Pre–17 July 1995 schemes were referred to as executive share option schemes.

Under the revised rules (known as company share option plans or CSOP schemes), the option must not be granted at a discount (i.e. at an option price below the current market value of the shares) and the total market value of shares that may be acquired under the option and any other approved options held by the employee under the company share option plan provisions must not exceed £30,000. Providing the scheme complies with these and other conditions, there is no tax charge when options are granted. These provisions are regarded as included in all schemes from 29 April 1996, thus affecting options granted from that time no matter when the scheme was approved. If, exceptionally, an option *is* granted at a discount, the discount is taxed as employment income for the tax year in which the option is granted, though the amount taxed is deductible in computing any amount that falls to be taxed subsequently, for example on exercise of the option after the scheme has had its approval withdrawn, or in determining the amount of any interest-free loan under 11.7.

There is no income tax charge when the option is exercised, providing it is exercised between three and ten years after it was granted. For options exercised on or after 9 April 2003, there is also no income tax charge if the option is exercised within three years after it was granted but within six months of the employment coming to an end because of injury, disability, redundancy or retirement. Where the income tax exemption applies, tax (i.e. capital gains tax) is payable only at the time of disposal of the shares, when the total amount paid for the shares, including any discount charged to income tax when the option was granted and any amount paid for the option itself, is deducted from the proceeds in calculating any capital gain. See 11.32 for the special capital gains tax rules for identifying share disposals with acquisitions. (Taper relief runs from the time the option is exercised.) If options are exercised in breach of the stipulated time limits or at a time when the scheme is not an approved scheme, they are taxable in the same way as unapproved options, with PAYE tax and national insurance applying if the shares are readily convertible assets (see 11.9). PAYE also applies if the option is exercised more than ten years after it was granted.

Both full–time and part–time employees may be included in a scheme, but only full-time directors (i.e. working 25 hours or more a week) are eligible. (See 11.5 re the exclusion of certain close company members.) In contrast to SAYE linked share option schemes at 11.11, there is no requirement that the scheme be made available to all directors and employees who are eligible.

The shares to be acquired must be ordinary shares in the company that established the scheme or a company which controls it. Schemes may provide that participants must exercise their options when their employment ends but may also provide for options to be exchanged for equivalent options in a company taking over the employer company. The scheme may provide for options to be exercised within one year after the employee's death.

Enterprise management incentive share options (ITEPA 2003, ss 527–541, Sch 5, Sch 6 para 221; TCGA 1992, Sch 7D paras 14–16; FA 2004, s 96)

11.13   Small higher-risk companies may offer their employees enterprise management incentive (EMI) share options, subject to a limit of £3 million on the total value of shares in respect of which there are unexercised share options. Providing the scheme rules are complied with, there will normally be no income tax or employers' and employees' national insurance contributions to pay, and when an employee sells shares acquired under the scheme, capital gains tax taper relief will date from the time the option was *granted* rather than the date it was exercised. There is no requirement for the scheme to be registered, but notice must be given when options are granted (see 11.16).

Qualifying companies

11.14   For a company to be a qualifying company, the following conditions must be satisfied:

(i)   The company must not be a 51% subsidiary, or otherwise controlled by another company and persons connected with that company.

(ii)   If the company has subsidiaries, they must be 75% owned. For EMI options granted on or after 17 March 2004, subsidiaries need only be 51% owned, except for property managing subsidiaries, which must be 90% owned.

(iii)   The company's (or if relevant, the group's) gross assets must not exceed £30 million.

(iv)   The company or group must carry on one or more qualifying trades wholly or mainly in the UK. Qualifying trades exclude:

Dealing in land, commodities, futures, shares, securities or other financial instruments

Dealing in goods other than in an ordinary trade of wholesale or retail distribution

Banking, insurance, money-lending, debt-factoring, hire-purchase financing or other financial activities

Leasing or receiving royalties or licence fees (with certain exclusions)

Legal and accountancy services

Property development

Farming or market gardening, woodlands, forestry activities and timber production

Hotels, nursing homes or residential care homes.

Providing the conditions are satisfied, EMI share options may be offered by both quoted and unquoted companies.

Eligible employees

11.15   An eligible employee must be employed by the company or its qualifying subsidiary. He must be required to work, on average at least 25 hours a week or, if less, 75% of his working time (which includes time spent in both employment and self-employment) and he and his associates must not have a 'material interest' in the company (see 11.5).

Qualifying options

11.16   For an option to be a qualifying option, the company must be a qualifying company, the employee must be an eligible employee, notice of the option must be given as indicated below and the other requirements of ITEPA 2003, Sch 5 must be met. The principal additional requirements are:

(i)   The option must be granted for commercial reasons to recruit or retain an employee and not for tax avoidance purposes.

(ii)   An employee may not hold unexercised options in respect of shares with a total value of more than £100,000 at the time the options were granted. Where that limit has been reached, then whether or not the options have been exercised or released, any further options granted within three years of the date of the last qualifying option are not qualifying options.

(iii)   The total value of shares in respect of which there are unexercised qualifying options must not exceed £3 million.

(iv)   The shares that may be acquired under the option must be fully paid, irredeemable ordinary shares, and the option must be capable of being exercised within ten years from the date it is granted and must be non-transferable.

The company must give notice of the option to the Revenue within 92 days after it is granted, together with such supporting information as the Revenue require and also a declaration from the relevant employee that he meets the 'working time' requirement (see 11.15). The Revenue have the right to correct obvious errors in the notice within nine months, and to enquire into an option within twelve months after the 92 day period. The enquiry may be made to the company or, in relation to whether the 'working time' requirement is met, to the relevant employee. If at the conclusion of an enquiry, the Revenue decide that the qualifying option requirements have not been met, the company and the relevant employee have the right to appeal against the decision.

Income tax and national insurance

11.17   There is no charge to tax or national insurance when the option is granted. Providing the option is exercised within ten years after it was granted, there is also not normally a tax charge when it is exercised except to the extent that the market value when the option was granted (or when it was exercised if lower) exceeds the amount paid for the shares. There are, however, detailed provisions about disqualifying events. Where tax is charged on the exercise of the option, Class 1 national insurance contributions would be payable if the shares were readily convertible assets (see 11.3). The anti-avoidance rules at 11.8 apply to shares acquired under qualifying options as they do to shares acquired under unapproved schemes.

Capital gains tax

11.18   The excess of any sale proceeds for the shares over the sum of the amount paid for them plus any amount charged to income tax (see 11.17) is charged to capital gains tax, but see 11.9 for the effect of the decision in *Mansworth v Jelley*. See 11.32 for the special capital gains tax rules for identifying share disposals with acquisitions. For shares acquired under qualifying EMI options, capital gains tax taper relief dates from the date the option was granted (though special rules apply if a disqualifying event occurs). The shares will qualify for the business assets rate of taper relief (see 4.16), so the maximum tax payable once the option has been held for two years will be 10% (or 5% for a basic rate taxpayer).

Share incentive plans (ICTA 1988, ss 68A–68C, 251A–251D; TCGA 1992, Sch 7D paras 1–8; ITEPA 2003, ss 488–515, Sch 2, Sch 6 paras 10, 34, 221)

11.19   Companies may set up a share incentive plan (SIP — previously referred to as an all-employee share ownership plan), under which employees may allocate part of their salary to acquire shares in their employer company (known as partnership shares) without paying tax or national insurance contributions (NICs), nor will employers' NICs be payable. Employers may also award free shares to employees, including extra free shares (matching shares) for employees who have partnership shares.

The plans are operated through a trust and the trustees hold the shares for the employees until they are taken out of the plan or sold. A parent company may have a group plan for itself and its subsidiaries. The legislation is lengthy and complex, and what follows is only an outline.

General provisions

11.20   Revenue approval is required for the plan, and if it is refused, the company has the right to appeal to the Special Commissioners within 30 days. Provision is made for approval to be withdrawn if a 'disqualifying event' occurs, such as the plan being operated in a way that does not comply with the legislation. The company may similarly appeal within 30 days against the withdrawal of approval.

The plan must be available to all eligible employees and must not contain features which would discourage eligible employees from participating. Employees must be entitled to participate on the same terms (but taking into account remuneration, length of service and hours worked), and the plan must not have features likely to have the effect of conferring benefits wholly or mainly on directors and employees on higher levels of remuneration. The plan must not contain arrangements for loans to any of the employees. Shares must be withdrawn from a plan when an employee leaves the employment. The plan may provide for employees to lose their free or matching shares if they leave within three years, and for employees who leave to be required to sell their shares.

Eligible employees

11.21   Eligible employees must be employees of the company or a group company and, if so provided by the plan, must have been an employee throughout a qualifying period of (broadly) not more than 18 months. An employee within a group satisfies the qualifying period conditions even though he has worked for more than one group company during the period. Employees must not have a material interest in the company (see 11.5). An employee cannot participate *simultaneously* in two or more awards of shares under different plans established by the same company or a connected company. *Successive* participation in two or more awards in the same tax year is permitted but the limits on free shares, partnership shares and reinvested dividends (see 11.23, 11.24 and 11.26) apply as if all such plans were a single plan.

Eligible shares

11.22   There are detailed requirements for shares to be eligible shares, the main points being that the shares must be in a quoted company (or its subsidiary) or an unquoted company not controlled by another company, and the plan shares must be fully paid, non-redeemable ordinary shares. They may, however, be non-voting shares.

An anti-avoidance provision denies relief for shares in a company in which the employees provide services for a third party unless the employer company is an independent business.

Free shares

11.23   The company can award free shares in any tax year valued at up to £3,000 per employee at the time of the award. Plans may provide for the awards to be linked to performance, statutory rules being laid down for such performance allowances. Details of the relevant performance targets must be provided to employees. Free shares must normally be kept in the plan for a stipulated period, which may not be less than three years nor more than five years.

Partnership shares

11.24   Employees may authorise employers to deduct part of their salary to acquire partnership shares, such deductions reducing the pay for tax and national insurance purposes (but not reducing earnings for pension purposes). The maximum permitted deduction is £1,500 in any tax year, or 10% of salary if less. The minimum stipulated deduction on any occasion cannot exceed £10. From 10 July 2003 earnings of a kind specified in the plan, e.g. bonuses or overtime payments, may be excluded from 'salary' in applying the 10% rule. The amount deducted will be held by the plan trustees until used to acquire partnership shares. The plan may stipulate a maximum number of partnership shares that may be purchased. Employees may stop and restart deductions to the plan on giving written notice to the company, or may give notice to withdraw from the plan, in which case any money held will be refunded. Any money refunded will be liable to tax and national insurance contributions. Partnership shares may be withdrawn from the plan at any time (but see 11.27 for the tax position). Purchases by employees of partnership shares from the trustees are exempt from stamp duty and stamp duty reserve tax.

Matching shares

11.25   A plan may provide for employees who acquire partnership shares to be awarded matching shares at the same time, on the basis of not more than two matching shares for one partnership share. The same holding period requirements apply as for other free shares.

Reinvestment of cash dividends and rights shares

11.26   Plans may either provide that dividends on plan shares be reinvested in further plan shares or that they be paid over to employees. The total value of reinvested dividends cannot exceed £1,500 per employee in any tax year. Reinvested dividends do not carry a tax credit. The required holding period for dividend shares is three years. Acquisitions by employees of dividend shares from the trustees are exempt from stamp duty and stamp duty reserve tax.

Trustees must normally act on an employee's instructions in relation to rights issues. This may include selling some of the rights shares in order to raise funds to acquire the remainder. No capital gains tax is payable on the proceeds of such rights sales. Rights shares acquired in this way are treated as having been acquired when the plan shares were acquired. If rights shares are acquired using funds other than from such rights sales, they are not plan shares.

Income tax and capital gains tax

11.27   There is no income tax or national insurance charge at the time plan shares (including dividend shares) are awarded, nor will there be a charge on any free, partnership or matching shares held in a plan for five years. If such shares are held for between three and five years, income tax (and Class 1 national insurance contributions if the shares are readily convertible assets — see 11.3) will be charged on the initial value of the shares, or their value at the time of withdrawal if lower. If the tax charge is based on the initial value of the shares, it will be reduced by any tax charged on capital receipts (see below). Where the shares are held for less than three years, tax (and Class 1 national insurance contributions if the shares are readily convertible assets) will be payable on their value at the time when they cease to be held in the plan. Where the shares are readily convertible assets, the tax and national insurance will be collected from employers under PAYE. The employee's PAYE amount must be paid over to the employer either by the employee or the trustees (who are empowered to dispose of an employee's plan shares for this purpose). Tax payable in respect of shares that are not readily convertible assets will be payable through the self-assessment system (see 11.36).

If dividend shares are held in a plan for less than three years, an amount equal to the reinvested dividends is taxable under Schedule F (or Schedule D Case V for foreign dividends) and is deemed to carry a tax credit at the rate in force at the time of withdrawal. Any Schedule F upper rate tax is reduced by the tax on any capital receipts (see below).

The charges on plan shares do not apply if the employee leaves through injury, disability, redundancy, or retirement (at a specified age not less than 50), nor on the employee's death.

PAYE tax and Class 1 national insurance will be charged on capital receipts (sale of rights etc.) re plan shares acquired fewer than five years earlier (three years for dividend shares). This does not apply where the trustees sell some rights shares to raise funds to buy the remainder (see 11.26).

If shares are kept in a plan until they are sold, employees will not be liable to capital gains tax. If employees take them out of the plan and sell later, there will be a chargeable gain equal to the increase in value after the shares were withdrawn from the plan. Taper relief will apply from the date the shares are withdrawn.

Shares withdrawn from a plan may be transferred free of capital gains tax into the stocks and shares component of an Individual Savings Account (ISA — see 36.22) within 90 days from the date they cease to be plan shares.

Capital gains tax rollover relief (TCGA 1992, s 236A, Sch 7C)

11.28   A special rollover relief is available in relation to unquoted companies, which will be particularly relevant where family members and family trusts wish to transfer shares to employees. The relief applies where existing shareholders (other than companies) transfer ownership of shares they hold in the company to an approved share incentive plan that holds (either immediately or within twelve months after the transfer) 10% of the company's shares. Gains arising on the shares transferred may be treated as reducing the acquisition cost of replacement chargeable assets acquired within six months after the disposal (unless the replacement assets are shares on which enterprise investment scheme income tax relief is given (see 29.2) and subject to some special provisions relating to dwelling houses).

Shares held in existing qualifying employee share ownership trusts

11.29 Shares may be transferred into a plan from an existing qualifying share ownership trust (QUEST — see 11.34) without the trust or company suffering a tax charge. Such shares must be used as either free or matching shares under the plan rules.

Corporation tax (ICTA 1988, s 85B, Sch 4AA; ITEPA 2003, Sch 6 paras 12, 109)

11.30 In computing its taxable profits, the company is entitled to deduct the costs of setting up and running the plan. It is also entitled to deduct the market value of free or matching shares at the time they are acquired by the trustees, and the excess of the market value of partnership shares on acquisition by the trustees over the employees' contributions, such deductions being made in the accounting period in which the shares are awarded. Subject to the deduction for running expenses, no deduction is allowed for any expenses in providing dividend shares.

An earlier corporation tax deduction for the provision of plan shares may be claimed where on or after 6 April 2003 the company makes a contribution to the plan trustees to enable them to acquire the company's shares, providing that the shares are not acquired from a company, and that at the end of twelve months from the date of purchasing shares with the money contributed, the trustees hold at least 10% of the company's total ordinary share capital. Where that condition is satisfied, the deduction is given in the accounting period in which the twelve-month anniversary falls, and no deduction is then given when the shares are awarded to employees. There are further detailed conditions, including a requirement for at least 30% of the shares acquired with the contribution to be transferred to employees within five years, and all the shares to be transferred within ten years.

Approved profit sharing schemes (TA 1988, s 186 and Schs 9 and 10; FA 2000, ss 49, 50)

11.31 Favourable tax treatment was previously given to an approved profit sharing scheme under which a company appointed trustees and provided money for them to use to acquire shares in the company. The amount provided by the company was a tax deductible expense. Following the introduction of share incentive plans (see 11.19), approved profit sharing schemes are being phased out. No new schemes can be approved after

5 April 2001 and income tax relief does not apply to shares appropriated to employees after 31 December 2002. Corporation tax relief for companies' payments to schemes and administrative expenses applied only to payments up to 5 April 2002.

A director or employee is not charged to tax on shares allocated to him by the trustees under the scheme. He is regarded for capital gains tax purposes as being absolutely entitled to the shares even though they are still held by the trustees, and any dividends arising are regarded as his for income tax purposes. No income tax charge arises if the shares are transferred to the employee after three years.

The shares must remain in the hands of the trustees for a minimum period which is generally two years, and an income tax charge arises if the shares are disposed of within three years, equal to their market value when allocated to the employee or the sale proceeds if less (but no charge arises on an employee's death, no matter how long the shares have been held). The charge is reduced to 50% if the disposal occurs within the three years because the employee leaves as a result of injury, disability, redundancy, or reaching an age between 60 and 75 as specified by the scheme.

A similar tax charge arises if there is a capital receipt, as for example on a rights issue, within three years, but only if it exceeds a stipulated amount (broadly £20 per annum cumulatively up to a maximum £60).

Any amounts chargeable to income tax are normally paid by the trustees to the company, who then pay them to the employees after deducting tax under PAYE. Sometimes tax will be deducted directly by the trustees, and in this event the deduction is at the basic rate of tax. The amounts are not liable to national insurance. The trustees must give employees appropriate information relating to any income tax liability they may have if they dispose of scheme shares.

The income tax charge has no effect on the capital gains tax base cost. Whether shares are disposed of within or after the three-year period the capital gains tax base cost to the employee is the market value at the time the shares were appropriated to him (see 11.32 for the rules for matching disposals of shares with acquisitions). The employee may transfer the shares free of capital gains tax into an Individual Savings Account (ISA) within 90 days of their being transferred to him, or within 90 days of the end of the three-year period, if earlier (see 36.22).

Capital gains tax treatment of shares (TCGA 1992, ss 104, 105, 105A, 105B; FA 2002, s 50)

11.32   Where a shareholder makes several acquisitions of shares of the same class in a company, there are special rules for identifying which shares have been disposed of (see 38.9), which broadly match shares disposed of with shares acquired later rather than earlier, subject to special rules for shares bought and sold on the same day or within the following thirty days (see CHAPTER 38). Shares in approved share incentive plans and approved profit sharing schemes are treated as being of a separate class while they are retained by the trustees. This means that any disposals of shares owned outside the scheme by the employee will not be matched with scheme shares.

Unless they are subject to any special restrictions, shares acquired before 6 April 1998 under SAYE and other share option schemes (whether approved or not) are pooled with any other pre–6 April 1998 acquisitions of shares of the same class in the same company (acquisitions before and after 31 March 1982 being in separate pools — see 38.7, 38.8). Their cost is the price paid for them, plus the amount, if any, paid for the option, plus any amount that has been charged to income tax. The amounts paid for pre–6 April 1998 acquisitions attracted indexation allowance from the date of payment (but with no further indexation after April 1998). All acquisitions of shares of the same class in the same company on one day are normally treated as being a single asset. If some of the same day acquisitions are scheme shares they may have a lower capital gains cost than the other shares, which would reduce the average cost of any shares disposed of, and if there was a part disposal of the holding the capital gain would be correspondingly higher. Where shares are acquired on or after 6 April 2002 under any of the approved share option schemes dealt with in 11.11, 11.12 and 11.13 on the same day as other shares, the taxpayer may make a written election, on or before 31 January in the next but one tax year after the tax year in which he first makes a disposal of any of the same day acquisitions, to have the approved scheme shares and the other shares treated as two separate assets, the non-scheme shares being treated as disposed of first. This could reduce immediate gains on a part disposal, although the remaining shares would have a lower capital gains cost.

Shares acquired under an approved profit sharing scheme before 6 April 1998 are regarded as a separate pool while they are retained by the trustees, with the shares treated as acquired by the employee at market value at the date they are appropriated to him and indexed from that date (but with no further indexation after April 1998). After the three-year period of retention, the shares are transferred to the employee. If the transfer was before 6 April 1998, the transfer was into the employee's normal pool of shares of that class in that company. A sale at the end of the period of retention is not affected by the same day/thirty-day rules referred to above because the shares were treated as owned by the employee from the date they were allocated to him.

Corporation tax relief for cost of shares provided (FA 2003, Sch 22 paras 59–73, Sch 23)

11.33   A statutory corporation tax deduction has been introduced for the cost of providing shares (or stock) for employee share schemes where the employees are taxable in respect of the shares they acquire or would be taxable if the scheme were not an approved scheme. The relief applies in respect of shares acquired by employees in accounting periods of the employer company beginning on or after 1 January 2003. The deduction is normally based on the market value of the shares, at the time they are awarded or the share option is exercised (whichever is applicable), less any contribution made by the employee towards them. (Payment by the employee of the company's secondary national insurance contributions is not taken into account — see 11.3.) The deductions allowed for shares provided under share incentive plans (see 11.30) take priority over this relief. This relief relates only to the cost of providing shares; it does not displace reliefs for costs of setting up or administering schemes. The shares themselves must be fully-paid, non-redeemable, ordinary shares in a quoted company, a subsidiary of a quoted company or an unquoted company not under the control of another company. The relief is generally given for the accounting period in which the employee acquires the shares. There are, however, special rules for restricted shares and convertible shares (see 11.8) that also give relief, in subsequent accounting periods in which chargeable events occur, in amounts broadly equal to the amounts chargeable on employees as a result of such events, again ignoring any reduction of the amount taxable on the employee when he pays the company's national insurance contributions — see 11.3. Where the restricted shares rules introduced by FA 2003 do not have effect, special rules apply instead to shares subject to forfeiture; these give relief on the lifting of the condition for forfeiture rather than on acquisition.

Qualifying employee share ownership trusts (QUESTs) (FA 1989, ss 67–74 and Sch 5; FA 2003, s 142)

11.34   Provisions were introduced in 1989 to encourage companies to set up trusts to acquire shares in the company and distribute them to the employees. Revenue approval is not required but in order for the company's payments to the trust to be tax deductible the trust had to be a 'qualifying employee share ownership trust' (QUEST). Following the introduction of the relief at 11.33, payments to a QUEST in accounting periods beginning on or after 1 January 2003 are no longer tax deductible.

Beneficiaries under the QUEST cannot include anyone who owns 5% or more of the company's ordinary share capital. All other employees and full-time directors who have been employed throughout a period specified in the trust deed (not exceeding five years) must be included as beneficiaries. Distributions out of the QUEST must be on similar terms to all beneficiaries, but allowing for different distributions according to length of service and level of remuneration.

The trustees must, within nine months, use sums received for a qualifying purpose, principally to acquire the company's shares. The shares acquired must be distributed to employees within twenty years of acquisition (seven years for trusts established before 4 May 1994). If any of the conditions are breached, the QUEST will be charged to tax at 34% on the sums received by it on which tax relief has been given.

There are no special tax reliefs either for the QUEST or for the employees receiving shares out of it, but it was able to operate in conjunction with an approved profit sharing scheme trust (see 11.31), in which case shares allocated within the approved profit sharing scheme conditions are not charged to tax. QUESTs established on or after 29 April 1996 may also operate in conjunction with an approved savings-related share option scheme (see 11.11). Following the introduction of approved share incentive plans (see 11.19), trustees may transfer all shares held in the QUEST at midnight on 20 March 2000, or purchased with funds held at that time, to such a plan. All such shares must be used as either free or matching shares under the new plan. In these circumstances there will be no tax charge on the trustees or the company. Following the abolition of corporation tax relief for payments by companies to QUESTs (see above), trustees were given a further opportunity to transfer shares and cash to share incentive plans without adverse tax consequences, this time by reference to shares and funds held at midnight on 26 November 2002.

Priority share allocations for employees (ITEPA 2003, ss 542–548)

11.35   When shares are offered to the public, a priority allocation is often made to employees and directors. Where there is no price advantage, the right to shares in priority to other persons is not a taxable benefit, so long as the shares that may be allocated do not exceed 10% of those being offered, all directors and employees entitled to an allocation are entitled on similar terms (albeit at different levels), and those entitled are not restricted wholly or mainly to persons who are directors or whose remuneration exceeds a particular level. This treatment still applies where the offer to employees is strictly not part of the public offer, as a result of the employees' offer being restricted to shares in one or more companies and the public offer being a package of shares in a wider range of companies.

Where employees get shares at a discount compared with the price paid by the public, the discount is chargeable to income tax. The employee's base cost for capital gains tax is the amount paid plus the amount of the discount.

Self-assessment — employees' responsibilities

11.36   Employees who do not get tax returns must notify the Revenue by 5 October after the end of the year if they have income or gains that have not been fully taxed (see 9.2). If there is nothing to notify except taxable amounts relating to shares, and the tax payable is less than £1,000, employees can ask to have the tax collected through their coding. If that does not apply, a tax return must be completed.

There is a separate 'Share Schemes' section of the tax return for reporting taxable amounts arising from both approved schemes and otherwise. Options exercised within the conditions of approved schemes are not shown on the Share Schemes pages (since no tax is payable), nor are any taxable amounts relating to shares under a profit sharing scheme. Tax on the latter is collected by the employer or the trustees through PAYE (see 11.31) and is therefore included in pay in the 'Employment' section of the return. The same will apply to some of the taxable amounts under share incentive plans (see 11.27).

Where shares have been taxed under PAYE as *readily convertible assets* (see 11.3), the relevant amounts will be included in the pay figures in the Employment pages of the return, but they must also be included in the Share Schemes pages. The detailed provisions are in Revenue Help Sheet 218.

Employers tick a box on forms P11D if there are taxable benefits relating to shares, but do not give details of taxable amounts, so the employee needs to obtain the relevant information himself. Since employers are required to report details to the Revenue (see 11.2), they should be able to provide the appropriate figures. Trustees of profit sharing schemes are required to give employees the relevant information (see 11.31).

Tax points

11.37

- There is no clearance procedure under any of the anti-avoidance rules at 11.8 and to the extent that, under these rules, tax charges (and possibly national insurance contributions) arise on occasions other than acquisition and disposal, employment-related shares and securities falling within the rules are particularly vulnerable to uncertainty.

- In the case of unquoted companies, the value of shares has, when appropriate, to be agreed with the Revenue Shares Valuation Division.

- Group employees may participate in schemes through their parent company.

- If you acquire shares under an approved share option scheme and immediately dispose of them, the gain will be subject to capital gains tax (unless covered by reliefs or exemptions). Gains on shares acquired under SAYE-linked options (and also gains on approved share incentive plan shares) can be sheltered to the extent that shares valued at up to the annual limit are transferred into an ISA (see 36.22).

- If you have exercised an unapproved share option or an enterprise management incentive scheme option in recent years, but before 10 April 2003, and have sold the shares, you *may* be able to reclaim some capital gains tax as a result of the decision in *Mansworth v Jelley* (see 11.9).

- Employers face penalties if they fail to provide to the Revenue the returns and information required under the provisions outlined in this chapter.

- An approved SAYE share option scheme, company share option plan or share incentive plan cannot apply to a subsidiary company unless the parent is a non-close company listed on the Stock Exchange.

- Unquoted companies may see disadvantages to approved share incentive plans, because they cannot choose which employees may participate, there may not be a ready market for the shares if the employee wants to sell, an immediate market valuation is not available and the effect on existing shareholders must be considered. A condition can, however, be imposed that employees must sell their shares when the employment ends.

- Where you have a tax liability in connection with share schemes, make sure you include the appropriate entries on your tax return (see 11.36).

12
Directors of small and family companies

Directors and shareholders

12.1 In family companies, directors and shareholders are usually the same people, and they can benefit from the company in various ways, e.g.:

Payment of remuneration.
Provision of benefits.
Distribution of profits through dividends.

When considering to what extent, and in what form, to withdraw profits, the tax and national insurance treatment is an important factor. There are other considerations, in particular the effect on pensions. Remuneration and benefits are earned income in the hands of the shareholder, whereas dividends are unearned income. Only earned income is taken into account for pension purposes. Therefore, if you do not have a company pension scheme, taking a low salary means that personal pension contributions are correspondingly restricted (although you can contribute up to £3,600 a year to a personal pension scheme regardless of your earnings level, and you can base personal pension premiums on earnings of one of the previous five years — see 17.9). If you are in a company pension scheme, you presently need to watch the definition of final remuneration on which your pension will be based (see 16.11). The present restrictions on pension contributions will be replaced from 6 April 2006 by a new unified scheme covering both occupational and personal schemes. See 16.26 for details.

The introduction of the national minimum wage also needs to be taken into account. The Revenue have the power to enforce the national minimum wage legislation via employment tribunals or the courts, and severe penalties or even criminal sanctions may be imposed on employers who fail to pay the minimum rates or keep the proper records. Although the provisions do not apply to 'people living in a family and working in the family business', the wording of the regulations (SI 1999/584) makes it fairly clear that 'family business' does not include companies, so it would be prudent to ensure that family members who are employees of the company are paid at least the minimum wage and that this is supported by the records. The present minimum wage rate is £4.50 an hour, or £3.80 for those aged 18 to 21. These rates will increase to £4.85 an hour and £4.10 an hour respectively from 1 October 2004. From that date, 16 and 17 year olds will become entitled to the national minimum wage at the rate of £3 an hour. As far as working directors are concerned, a director who does not have an explicit employment contract is highly unlikely to be subject to the minimum wage legislation. Where such a contract exists, however, the legislation would apply, and the minimum wage would have to be paid even if, for example, the company was making losses. Pay for the minimum wage excludes benefits (other than accommodation). It should be noted that the minimum wage needs to be paid for the pay period, which cannot exceed one month. It is not therefore sufficient to make a single payment at the year end. The freedom to use company profits in the most tax-efficient manner is being attacked by the Revenue in some circumstances under the 'settlements' legislation (see 12.9), and after introducing provisions to enable companies with profits of up to £10,000 to distribute them as dividends at no tax cost only two years ago, the Government has now decided that this is unacceptable (see 3.13). Those who incorporated to take advantage of these provisions will find that disincorporating is not so easy (see 18.9). The treatment of shares in the joint ownership of husband and wife has also been changed from 6 April 2004. Dividend income has previously been split equally between spouses, but it will now be split according to the actual ownership (see 33.5). The right to decide how to deal with company profits has been removed completely for those caught by the new rules for personal service companies (see 19.3). The material in this chapter is therefore no longer relevant for such companies.

Where not constrained by the above considerations, companies need to be aware of the tax and national insurance cost of paying remuneration and dividends at different profit levels.

12.2   For 2004/05 profit taken as pay costs the company 12.8% Class 1 national insurance contributions on excess pay over £91 a week, but the contributions are deducted in arriving at taxable profits. Class 1 or Class 1A contributions are also payable on virtually all taxable benefits in kind (see CHAPTER 10). Employees do not have to pay contributions on the first £91 a week, but those earning £79 or more have their rights to benefits protected. From 6 April 2004, the rate of employees' contributions on earnings between £91 and £610 per week is 11% and employees must pay contributions at 1% on all earnings above £610 a week.

The additional net of tax cost of the employer's contributions on pay above £91 per week for the year to 31 March 2005 is as follows.

Company's tax rate		*Net cost of NI*
0%	(on profits up to £10,000)	12.8%
23.75%	(marginal starting rate on profits between £10,000 and £50,000)	9.76%
19%	(on profits between £50,000 and £300,000)	10.37%

12.3 DIRECTORS OF SMALL AND FAMILY COMPANIES

32.75%	(marginal small companies' rate on profits between £300,000 and £1,500,000)	8.6%
30%	(on profits of £1,500,000 and over)	8.96%

12.3 When profits are taken as dividends, the dividends are not deducted in calculating taxable profits, but the company's tax is effectively eliminated to the extent of the tax credits passed on to the shareholders. Tax credits are ⅑ of the cash dividend, representing a tax rate of 10% on the tax-credit inclusive amount. Basic rate taxpayers have no further tax to pay and higher rate taxpayers have to pay a further 22½%. Non-taxpayers, on the other hand, cannot claim a refund of the tax credits. The combined company/shareholder tax payable where profits are taken as dividends for a company liable at the small companies rate is 19% for a basic rate taxpayer and just under 40% for a higher rate taxpayer. It should be noted that the nil rate of corporation tax on profits up to £10,000 and the marginal rate of 23.75% on profits between £10,000 and £50,000 (which produces an *average* rate below 19% on the total profits) cannot apply to profits taken as dividends (see 3.13). The only rates applicable when dividends are paid are therefore the small companies' rate of 19%, the marginal small companies' rate of 32.75% and the full rate of 30%.

For 2004/05, the effective tax rate on a given amount of profits paid as salary or dividend to a director/shareholder liable to tax at 40% and already paying maximum NI contributions at the 11% rate is as follows.

Salary payment (not affected by company's tax rate, since taxable profits are reduced by the payment)

		£
Available profit		100.00
Employer's NI on salary (12.8% of 88.65)		11.35
Gross salary		88.65
Tax @ 40%	35.46	
Employee's NI @ 1%	0.88	36.34
Net income		52.31
Effective tax rate		47.69

Dividend payment

Company's tax rate	19%	32.75%	30%
Available profit	100.00	100.00	100.00
Corporation tax	19.00	32.75	30.00
Cash dividend	81.00	67.25	70.00
Tax credit ⅑	9.00	7.47	7.78
Shareholder's income	90.00	74.72	77.78
Tax @ 32½%	29.25	24.28	25.28
Net income	60.75	50.44	52.50
Effective tax rate	39.25%	49.56%	47.5%

Dividends for such director/shareholders are therefore more tax-effective than salary for companies paying at anything other than the small companies' marginal rate, but are less tax-effective for companies paying at the small companies' marginal rate. Where the dividend straddles different tax rate bands, detailed calculations need to be done to decide the most tax-effective position.

The position is different for those taxable at less than 40%. For 2004/05 employees' national insurance contributions are payable at 11% on earnings between £4,745 and £31,720 and at 1% thereafter. For those whose income does not exceed £31,720, taking dividends rather than pay will give a substantial extra saving (employees' national insurance contributions on pay of £31,720 for 2004/05 being £2,969), and also an extra 3% tax saving to the extent that salary is charged to income tax at 22% and dividends are paid out of profits charged to corporation tax at only 19% (the tax credit on the dividend covering the income tax liability for a basic rate taxpayer as indicated above). See Example 1.

Example 1

Company paying tax at the small companies' rate uses profits of £25,000 in the year to 31 March 2005 to make a payment to a director/shareholder who has no other income. Director does not have an explicit contract of employment. His available personal allowance is £4,745.

If profit is taken as	salary only £	salary and dividend £
Company's tax position on the payment is:		
Profits	25,000	25,000
Salary	(22,702)	(4,745)
Employer's national insurance	(2,298)	—
Taxable profits	—	20,255
Corporation tax at 19%		(3,848)
Cash dividend		16,407
Tax credit ⅑		1,823
Director's income		18,230
Director's tax position:		
Salary	22,702	4,745
Dividend, including tax credit	—	18,230
	22,702	22,975
Personal allowance	(4,745)	(4,745)
Taxable income	17,957	18,230
Tax payable (£2,020 @ 10%, £15,937 @ 22%)	3,708	
(dividends £18,230 @ 10%)		1,823
Tax credit on dividend		(1,823)
Tax payable		—
Disposable income:		
Salary	22,702	4,745
Employee's national insurance	(1,975)	—
Dividend	—	16,407
Tax	(3,708)	—
	17,019	21,152
Saving through paying dividend		£4,133

The saving through paying the dividend is made up as follows:

Extra income available as dividend through saving in		
employer's NI	2,298	
Less 19% corporation tax	436	1,862

Difference between corporation tax on balance of profits of (20,255 – 2,298 =) £17,957 taken as dividend compared with income tax on salary:		
17,957 @ 19%	3,412	
17,957 @ 10%/22%	3,708	296
Reduction in employee's NI		1,975
		£4,133

The salary in the second alternative has been fixed at the earnings threshold of £4,745, which attracts no employers' or employees' national insurance contributions even though rights to social security benefits are protected.

Retention of profits within the company or payment as remuneration or dividends

12.4   Retaining profits within the company will increase the net assets and hence the value of the shares if they are subsequently sold on the basis of underlying assets. Having already suffered corporation tax, the retained profits will thus swell the value of the shares for capital gains tax purposes.

Reducing retentions through paying remuneration or dividends may therefore ultimately reduce the shareholders' chargeable gains, but this must be weighed against the immediate tax cost, also bearing in mind the capital gains tax taper relief (see 4.16 onwards). Reducing taxable profit by a permissible contribution to a pension fund from which the director will benefit will often be a better alternative (see 12.7).

Effect on earlier years (TA 1988, s 393A)

12.5   A decision on whether to pay remuneration or leave profits to be charged to corporation tax should not be taken by reference to the current year in isolation. The payment of remuneration may convert a trading profit into a trading loss, which, after being set against any non-trading profits of the current year, may be carried back against the profits of the previous year, both from the trade and from other sources (see CHAPTER 26 for details).

Looking into the future

12.6   If all current-year profits are used to pay remuneration, there will be nothing against which to carry back trading losses of the next year. The expected future performance (including any imminent capital expenditure which attracts tax allowances) should therefore be taken into account in considering whether to reduce or eliminate taxable profits for the current year.

Pensions (TA 1988, Part XIV, Chapters I–IV; ITEPA Chapters 6–10)

12.7   From 6 April 2006 a new simplified regime will apply for both occupational and personal pension schemes. The new provisions are outlined in 16.26 onwards. The changes will need to be borne in mind when planning pension provision before that date.

The company may have its own pension scheme, either through an insurance company or self-administered. Provided that the benefits under the scheme are within the limits laid down by the Revenue, the company's contributions are allowable in calculating its taxable profit, and are not taxable on the director.

If there is no such scheme, a director may pay premiums himself under a personal pension plan. Although the allowable premium is presently limited annually to a percentage of earnings depending upon age (see CHAPTER 17), you can base the maximum premium calculation in a tax year on higher earnings in one of the previous five tax years. The premium payment might be funded by a loan-back facility arranged by or in conjunction with the pension company. Employees' pension contributions do not reduce earnings for employers' and employees national insurance contributions. Your company could itself contribute to your pension plan within the available limits, and neither tax nor national insurance would be payable on the amount contributed by the company.

Since the income and gains of both company and personal pension funds are usually exempt from tax (albeit the tax credits on dividend income cannot be reclaimed), paying pension contributions rather than taking salary and investing it privately will be a more tax-efficient method of saving for the future, although the pension benefits available will depend on the performance of the pension investments and on the changing legislation. With company schemes, the permissible benefits may depend upon remuneration, so that restricting salary unduly may affect the available benefits. With personal pension schemes, the benefits depend only upon contributions (which will themselves have been limited by relevant earnings or the earnings cap, although with the flexibility of using a higher earnings figure of one of the previous five years). For the detailed provisions on pensions, see CHAPTERS 16 and 17.

Limits on allowable remuneration and waiver of remuneration (IHTA 1984, s 14)

12.8   Remuneration, like any other trading expense, must be incurred wholly and exclusively for the purposes of the trade (see CHAPTER 20). If it is regarded as excessive in relation to the duties, part may not be allowed as a deduction in calculating company profits. This should be borne in mind when considering payments of remuneration, either by way of cash or as benefits in kind, to members of a director's or shareholder's family. On the other hand, the national minimum wage legislation may prevent wages being paid at too low a level (see 12.1).

Employing a spouse and children in the family company may be useful, particularly if they are not otherwise using their personal allowance, but the work done must be of sufficient quantity and quality to justify the amount paid. If children are under 16 you must also comply with the regulations as to permitted hours of work, which vary according to local bye-laws. Payments by a farmer to his very young children have been held to be 'pocket money' and disallowed in calculating the taxable profits of the farm.

There is no income tax on remuneration which is not received, so that (subject to the minimum wage legislation) an entitlement to remuneration can be waived to assist in a difficult period of trading, or because of a high personal tax rate. It is also specifically provided that no inheritance tax liability arises from such a waiver. The waiver might enable the company to pay higher remuneration to other directors or family members (provided always that it is justifiable under the 'wholly and exclusively' rule) or to increase its profits available for dividends. Dividends cannot, however, be used to generate tax refunds for non-taxpayers.

Tax planning and the 'settlements' rules (TA 1988, s 660A)

12.9   The rules relating to 'settlements' prevent someone gaining a tax advantage by arranging to divert his/her income to those taxable at a lower or nil rate. An outright gift of income-producing property (such as shares in the case of a family company) is not caught by the provisions unless the gift does not carry a right to the whole of the income or the property given is wholly or substantially a right to income.

The Revenue have recently increased their use of these rules to attack some tax planning measures in family companies and partnerships. A working party of representatives from all the main tax bodies in the UK has been discussing with the Revenue their serious concerns about the problems raised by the Revenue's new stance, not least of which is how taxpayers who may be affected are to make entries in their self-assessment returns.

The Revenue have given detailed comments on their interpretation of the rules, including how they affect family companies, in their Tax Bulletins of April 2003 and February 2004. Their illustrations include a main earner drawing a low salary from a family company so that there are higher profits out of which to pay dividends to family or friends. Many professional advisers disagree with the Revenue's stance and it may well be that one or more test cases need to be taken to see whether the Revenue's view is upheld. A case is due to be heard before the Special Commissioners in June 2004, but whatever the outcome, it is highly likely that the case will go before the courts. In the meantime great care needs to be taken not only where any new arrangements are being considered but also in relation to existing situations.

Employee benefits provided by the company

12.10   P11D employees, i.e. directors and employees with earnings of £8,500 or more per annum, are charged to tax on the cash equivalent of benefits provided either for them or for their family or household. Directors are caught by these provisions even if they earn less than £8,500, unless they do not own more than 5% of the ordinary share capital (including shares owned by close family and certain other people) and either work full-time or work for a charitable or non-profit-making body.

National insurance contributions are also payable on virtually all taxable benefits, either Class 1 contributions payable by both employer and employee or Class 1A contributions by the employer only depending on the benefit. In most cases, therefore, it will usually be equally tax/NICs efficient, and far more straightforward, to provide cash pay rather than benefits. See CHAPTER 10 for details.

If benefits are to be provided, care must be taken to distinguish benefits provided by the company from payments made on behalf of the director/employee for which the director/employee is legally responsible. Such payments are treated as pay for *all* employees (see 10.5), for both tax and national insurance.

Gifts of company assets (IHTA 1984, s 94; TA 1988, s 418)

12.11   Gifts of company assets to directors and employees are covered by the benefits rules mentioned above and explained in detail in CHAPTER 10. If an asset is given to a shareholder who is not a director or employee, the cost is treated as a dividend, and the total of the cost of the asset and the related tax credit is included in the shareholder's taxable income.

If a gift is made to someone who is neither a director/employee nor a shareholder nor connected with them, an apportionment of its value is made among the shareholders for inheritance tax purposes, the shareholders then being treated as having made personal transfers of the amount apportioned to them.

Loans from the company (TMA 1970, s 109; ITEPA 2003, ss 192–197)

12.12   P11D employees who overdraw their current accounts with the company or who receive specific loans from the company, either interest-free or at a beneficial rate, are treated as having received remuneration equivalent to interest at the 'official rate' (see 10.23) on the amount overdrawn or lent, less any amount paid to the company towards the benefit they have received. This does not apply if the whole of the interest on the loans qualifies for tax relief, nor if the total non-qualifying loans outstanding in a tax year do not exceed £5,000. The loans provisions apply to loans made to relatives of the director or employee, as well as to the director/employee himself. Where a director or employee receives an advance for expenses necessarily incurred in performing his duties, the Revenue do not treat the advance as a loan, provided that

(a)   the maximum amount advanced at any one time does not exceed £1,000,

(b)   the advances are spent within six months, and

(c)   the director or employee accounts to the company at regular intervals for the expenditure.

As well as the tax charge on the director or employee on interest-free or cheap loans, there are tax implications for the company if it is a close company in which the director or employee is a 'participator' or associate of a participator (see 3.21), and these provisions do not depend on whether any interest is charged. 'Participator' mainly means a shareholder, and is referred to as such in the rest of this chapter. Loans and advances to shareholders give rise to a tax liability on the company, except for loans not exceeding £15,000 made to a full-time working director or employee who does not own more than 5% of the ordinary share capital. The company has to notify the Revenue not later than twelve months after the end of the accounting period in which the loan is made, and must pay tax at 25% on the amount of the loan or overdrawn account balance.

The due date for payment of the tax is nine months after the end of the accounting period in which the loan is made (i.e. the same as the due date for the corporation tax of that period). (For companies required to pay tax by instalments under corporation tax self-assessment — see 3.18 — the tax on such a loan is to be taken into account in the instalment payments.) Under corporation tax self-assessment, companies show the tax on loans as part of the total tax due, but may claim an offsetting deduction if the loan has been repaid or if it has been released or written off. Where the loan is repaid after the tax falls due and has been paid by the company, the tax paid may be reclaimed. The tax repayment is due nine months after the end of the accounting period in which the loan is repaid, and will be increased by interest from that nine months date if relevant. See example 2.

Example 2

A close company with an accounting year end of 31 December makes an interest-free loan of £20,000 to a director/shareholder on 10 January 2003. The company is not liable to pay its corporation tax by instalments. The director repays the loan on:

(a)   10 September 2004

Since this is before 1 October 2004, when the company is due to pay its corporation tax for the year to 31 December 2003, the company will not have to pay tax at 25% of the loan, as the tax due is off set by the tax repayable.

(b)   10 October 2004

Since the loan has not been repaid by 1 October 2004, the company must pay tax on that date at 25%, i.e. £5,000, and cannot claim repayment of the tax until 30 September 2005.

The director/shareholder will in any event be taxed under the benefits rules on interest on the loan at the official rate from 10 January 2003 to the repayment date.

It should be noted that the loan in example 2 is in contravention of company law. Even so, the practicality is that many directors of closely controlled companies do borrow money from the company.

If a loan or overdrawing is written off or released by the company, the tax treatment is different for loans made to controlling shareholders by close companies and for other loans.

If a loan by a close company to a controlling shareholder is written off, the amount written off is not an allowable expense, although the company can recover the tax it paid when the loan was made. (For accounting periods starting on or after 1 October 2002, a close company cannot treat loans written off as an allowable expense if they are made to *any* shareholder, not just a controlling shareholder.) Loans written off by non-close companies are allowable expenses under the 'loan relationships' rules (see 26.5), except for loans between companies where one controls the other or both are under common control.

The write-off of loans does not affect the shareholder unless he is a higher rate taxpayer. Higher rate taxpayers are taxed as if the amount written off was income net of the Schedule F ordinary rate of 10% and tax is chargeable at the excess of the Schedule F upper rate of 32½% over 10%. A loan of £10,000 will thus be regarded as income of £11,111, on which an extra 22½% tax is payable, amounting to £2,500.

If the borrower is not a shareholder, but the loan was obtained by reason of his employment, whether or not it is at a rate of interest below the 'official rate', the borrower is treated as having received an equivalent amount of remuneration at the time of the write-off. For a P11D employee this applies even after he has left, but not if the loan is written off on death.

Liabilities in connection with directors' remuneration

12.13   Remuneration is regarded as paid not only when it forms part of the payroll but also when it is credited to the director's current account with the company and the liability of the company to account for PAYE and national insurance arises at that time. The credit to the current account should therefore be made net of employee's tax and national insurance contributions. Drawings from the account can be made without any further liability once the PAYE and national insurance have been accounted for to the Revenue. If a company pays remuneration to a director and bears the PAYE itself, the amount that should have been borne by the director is treated as extra remuneration and charged to tax and national insurance contributions accordingly (ITEPA 2003, s 223).

Where a director receives payments in advance or on account of future remuneration this has to be treated as pay for tax and national insurance purposes at the time of the advance, unless the advances are covered by a credit balance on the director's loan account or are on account of expenses as indicated at 12.12.

An advance payment of remuneration is not the same as a loan. The income tax treatment of loans is stated at 12.12. National insurance contributions are not payable unless a director's account becomes overdrawn *and* the director's earnings are normally paid into that account (see 13.5).

Directors' national insurance contributions cannot be reduced by paying remuneration at uneven rates and irregular intervals, because of the rules for calculating earnings limits. The detailed provisions are in CHAPTER 13.

If employers fail to deduct and account for PAYE and national insurance contributions when due, they may incur interest and/or penalties. Directors may also be personally liable to pay the tax on their remuneration if they knew of the failure to deduct tax.

Tax points

12.14

- Always look at the combined company/director/shareholder position in considering the most appropriate way of dealing with available profits, and consider past years and the following year as well as the current year.

- Make effective use of company or personal pension funds, which should grow faster than individual investments because of their available tax exemptions. Remember, in the case of company pension funds, that in calculating corporation tax, relief is only given in the accounting period when the pension premium is paid, so that it is not possible to reduce taxable profits of one year by making a payment in the next year and relating it back. It is therefore essential to anticipate the profit level if a pension contribution is to be used as a way of reducing corporation tax for a particular accounting period.

- When considering dividend payments, remember that they may affect the valuation of shareholdings.

- Dividend income on shares in family companies held jointly by husband and wife in unequal proportions is now split according to their actual ownership rather than being split equally.

- In considering the payment of a dividend instead of remuneration, remember to take into account the national minimum wage rules, which are enforceable by the Revenue. The legislation does not regard family companies as a special case, although directors who do not have an explicit employment contract are not covered by the rules.

- You are not charged either tax or national insurance contributions on pension contributions by your employer to an approved company scheme or to your own approved personal pension scheme. Your own contributions either to a company or private scheme reduce your income for tax, but not for employees' national insurance contributions.

- Director/shareholders taking a sizeable dividend from a company could avoid higher rate tax by investing in a commercial building in an enterprise zone (see 22.30–22.34). To retain the tax allowance, however, they would have to leave the money invested for at least seven years, and the commercial viability of the purchase must not be ignored.

- Remuneration is regarded as paid when it is credited to an account with the company in the name of a director. The fact that it is not drawn by him but left to his credit in the company (in other words, available for drawing) does not prevent the appropriate tax and national insurance being payable at the time the remuneration is credited. The director's account should be credited only with the net amount after tax and national insurance. If the gross amount is credited, whether or not it is drawn out, and the company fails to account to the Revenue for the tax and national insurance, the director may be personally liable for the failure under the PAYE regulations.

- Interest is charged on tax and national insurance contributions that remain unpaid 14 days after the end of the tax year, e.g. from 19 April 2004 for 2003/04.

- If your company has failed to pay over the PAYE tax and national insurance on your pay within 14 days after the end of the tax year, the Revenue may look to you for payment plus interest, providing you were aware of the company's failure to comply with the PAYE regulations. Additionally, you may be held personally liable as a director for *any* unpaid national insurance contributions due from your company if the non-payment is due to your fraud or negligence.

- If, before a director is credited with additional remuneration, his current account with the company is overdrawn, the Revenue will usually contend that the date on which the additional remuneration can be regarded as credited is that on which the accounts are signed (or the date when a clear entitlement to the remuneration was established — for example a properly evidenced directors'/shareholders' meeting) rather than the end of the accounting year for which the additional remuneration was paid. This can significantly affect the tax charge on the director in respect of beneficial loan interest (see 10.23) and can also affect the liability of the company to pay tax under the provisions for loans to directors (see 12.12).

- Where the Revenue discover that a director's private expenses have been paid by a company and not shown as benefits on form P11D, they will usually seek to treat the payments as loans to the director. Such payments, including any VAT, must be reimbursed to the company by the director or charged against money owed by the company to the director. They are neither allowable in calculating the company taxable profit nor assessable as income on the director.

- The Revenue Contributions Office take the view that if payment of a director's personal bills by his company is not covered by a credit balance on the director's account, and his earnings are normally paid into that account, national insurance contributions are due on the amount paid — see 12.13.

13
National insurance contributions — employees and employers

Introduction

13.1 A large part of the cost of the social security system is funded from contributions based on the present day earnings of employees and self-employed persons. The main legislation is the Social Security Contributions and Benefits Act 1992 (SSCBA 1992). The new National Insurance Contributions and Statutory Payments Act 2004 aligns the procedures for national insurance and statutory payments (as to which see CHAPTER 14) more closely with those for tax.

The amount of national insurance contributions payable and the rules for collecting it depend upon which 'class' of contribution is to be paid. The contribution rates are shown in the Table of Rates and Allowances. National insurance contributions are dealt with by the Revenue National Insurance Contributions Office (NICO). Social security benefits are dealt with by the Department for Works and Pensions. See CHAPTER 10 for employment aspects of national insurance and collection of contributions through the PAYE system.

Neither employers nor employees pay tax or national insurance contributions on pay up to an 'earnings threshold' (£89 a week for 2003/04 and £91 for 2004/05). Employees have their rights to State pensions and other contributory benefits protected by reference to a lower pay figure, because they are treated as paying notional contributions between a stipulated lower earnings level (£77 a week for 2003/04 and £79 a week for 2004/05) and the earnings threshold.

Classes of contributions

13.2 Unless they are 'contracted out' (see 13.6 and 16.3), employees and their employers pay Class 1 contributions under the State Second Pension Scheme (S2P), which replaced the State Earnings Related Pension Scheme (SERPS) from 6 April 2002. The contributions are based on a percentage of earnings. Payments made by employees are known as 'primary' contributions and those by employers as 'secondary' contributions. Before 6 April 2003 employees did not pay any contributions on earnings above an upper earnings limit, although there was (and is) no upper limit for employers. From 6 April 2003, employees' primary contributions are payable at two rates, a 'main primary percentage', applicable to earnings up to the upper earnings limit, and an 'additional primary percentage' of 1%, applicable to all earnings above that level. A separate category of contributions, Class 1A, is payable annually by employers (not employees) on taxable benefits provided to P11D employees that are not chargeable to Class 1 or Class 1B contributions — see 10.24. Class 1B contributions are payable only by those employers who enter into a PAYE Settlement Agreement with the Revenue and are payable at the same time as the tax payment (see 10.36). Class 1 contributions are collected through the PAYE system. Class 1A contributions are paid separately to the Revenue — for details, see CHAPTER 10. The self-employed pay Class 2 and Class 4 contributions (see CHAPTER 24). Voluntary Class 3 contributions may be paid by those who would otherwise not pay enough contributions to earn a full pension (see 13.3). Employees and the self-employed cease to pay contributions when they reach State pension age, but employers must still pay secondary Class 1 contributions and Class 1A and 1B contributions (see 13.9). Details of the various contribution rates are shown under 'National insurance contribution rates' in the Table of Rates and Allowances.

It is sometimes difficult to decide whether someone is employed or self-employed — see 19.1 for the national insurance implications.

Pensions

13.3 Occupational and personal pension schemes are dealt with in CHAPTER 16 and CHAPTER 17 respectively. There is an integrated system covering personal pensions and 'stakeholder pensions'. Those with no earnings may pay pension contributions up to £3,600 a year — for details see CHAPTER 17. As far as State pensions are concerned, the growing cost of the State pension scheme has been causing concern, while at the same time it is recognised that many pensioners are existing on very low incomes. Provisions are already in force for the equalisation of pension ages for men and women. In order to do this without considerably increasing the funding costs, the State pension age is to become 65 for both men and women from 2020. The change is to be phased in from 2010 to 2020. Women born after 5 April 1955 will be subject to the new retirement age of 65, but women born before 6 April 1950 will still qualify at 60. From April 2010 various provisions to give equality of treatment to men and women will apply. Men will be able to get a basic State pension based on their spouse's NICs contribution record (which already applies to widowers in certain circumstances) and women will be able to claim an increase for a dependent husband. From 6 April 2005 it is intended that both husband and wife will be able to defer claiming a pension for as long as they wish (compared with five years at present). The amount of extra pension earned through deferral will also increase and it will be possible to take a (taxable) lump sum instead of extra pension. Changes were made from 6 April 2002 to improve the earnings related element of State pensions for low earners and certain carers and long-term disabled people. From that date the State Earnings Related Pension Scheme was replaced by the State Second Pension, as indicated below. In general, in order to get a full basic State pension under the present rules, Class 1 contributions must be paid (or notionally paid — see 13.1) or credited on an amount equal to 52 times the lower earnings limit (see 13.1) in at least nine in every ten years of your working life from 16 to 65 for a man or 60 for a woman, or you must have paid 52 Class 2 or Class 3 (voluntary) contributions for those years. For the purpose of the basic pension, you are credited with contributions when you are registered as unemployed or receiving jobseeker's allowance, or unable to work through incapacity or disability, or because you receive carer's allowance for looking after someone who is disabled, or if you receive maternity allowance. If you are an unemployed man aged 60 to 64, you automatically get credits whether or not you are ill or on the unemployment register. Credits will usually be given to those aged 16 to 18 who would otherwise not have paid enough contributions, and also for certain periods of full-time training lasting up to twelve months, but not for longer courses such as university degree courses. Those who stay at home to look after children or sick or elderly people usually get Home Responsibilities Protection, which reduces the number of years needed to qualify for full pension.

If you do not earn enough, either as an employee or in your self-employment, to achieve the required level of Class 1 or 2 contributions, you may pay voluntary Class 3 contributions (£7.15 per week for 2004/05) to help you to qualify for the basic retirement pension and, for those under pension age, bereavement benefits. You can check with the Revenue Contributions Office to see whether your contribution record is good enough to earn you a full pension.

Class 3 contributions can be paid up to six years after the year to which they relate (but sometimes at a higher rate). The Revenue normally notify people annually if their contribution record is inadequate, but they failed to do so for several years owing to pressure of work. It was therefore decided that the time limit for paying Class 3 contributions for 1996/97 to 2000/01 would be 5 April 2008 (the same as the latest payment date for 2001/02 contributions). The Revenue have been sending out letters to those with gaps in their contribution record, but because this exercise may take longer than expected, they have announced a further extension to the time limit to 5 April 2009 for those whose letters are dated 6 April 2004 onwards.

Certain married women pay reduced contributions (see 13.8), and they are not entitled to contribution credits and cannot pay Class 3 contributions.

They get a pension equal to 60% of the husband's basic pension when the husband is over 65 and the wife is over 60. The same applies to other married women who have not paid enough full rate contributions to earn a higher pension in their own right. A husband with a wife under 60 gets an addition to his pension for her, unless she earns more than £55.65 a week. (This addition counts as his income, not hers.)

Under the State Second Pension Scheme (S2P) applicable from 6 April 2002 and its predecessor, the State Earnings Related Pension Scheme (SERPS), employees receive a higher pension than the basic amount depending on their earnings. For S2P, there is a 'low earnings threshold', set at £11,600 a year for 2004/05. Those with earnings below that amount but at or above the lower earnings level (£79 a week or £4,108 a year for 2004/05) will be treated as if they earned £11,600. In addition the rate of accrual of pension benefits on that band of earnings will be double that accrued under SERPS. Those with earnings below £4,108 (or no earnings) will be treated as earning £11,600 if they receive child benefit for a child under 6, or they are entitled to carer's allowance, or they get Home Responsibilities Protection because they look after a sick or disabled person. Those entitled to long term incapacity benefit throughout a tax year will also be treated as having earned £11,600 for that tax year providing that when they reach State pension age they have worked and paid Class 1 contributions for at least one tenth of their working lives since 1978.

The pension position of widows is complicated, and should be checked out with the Revenue Contributions Office. Widows aged 60 or over when their husband dies who are not already receiving the full rate of pension will be entitled to the full pension from that time (providing the husband had a full contribution record). The treatment of widows in relation to their late husbands' SERPS contributions is that those widowed before 6 October 2002 will inherit the deceased spouse's full SERPS entitlement. Where someone reached State pension age before 6 October 2002 their spouse will inherit up to 100% of their SERPS entitlement on their death. The surviving spouse of someone reaching State pension age after 5 October 2002 but before 6 October 2010 will be entitled to between 60% and 90% of the other spouse's SERPS entitlement. Where the contributor reaches State pension age on or after 6 October 2010 their spouse will inherit only 50% of their SERPS/S2P entitlement after their death.

Persons liable to pay Class 1 contributions (SSCBA 1992, ss 2, 6(1))

13.4   Unless specifically exempted (see below), all 'employed earners' and their employers must pay Class 1 contributions. An 'employed earner' is a person who is paid either as an employee under a contract of service or as the holder of an office with earnings chargeable as employment income (see CHAPTER 10).

Revenue leaflet IR 56 outlines various criteria which are taken into account in deciding whether a person is employed. For details, see 19.1.

Certain people are specifically brought within the liability to Class 1 contributions, including office and similar cleaners, most agency workers (including 'temps' but excluding outworkers), wives employed in their husbands' businesses and vice versa, ministers of religion paid chiefly by way of stipend or salary, and certain part-time lecturers and teachers.

Certain employees are exempted from payment of Class 1 contributions as indicated below. The exemptions also apply to employers' contributions, except for employees in category (a) who are over State pension age.

(a)   people aged under 16 or over State pension age,

(b)   people whose earnings are below the weekly lower earnings limit (£79.00 for 2004/05),

(c)   a wife employed by her husband for a non-business purpose and vice versa,

(d)   people employed for a non-business purpose by a close relative in the home where they both live,

(e)   returning and counting officers and people employed by them in connection with an election or referendum, and

(f)   certain employees of international organisations and visiting armed forces.

Special rules apply to those who go to work abroad — see 41.21.

Earnings (SSCBA 1992, ss 3, 4)

13.5   Class 1 contributions are calculated on gross pay, which is broadly the same as pay for income tax under PAYE and includes certain benefits in kind (see 10.5), but is before deducting:

Employees' pension contributions to occupational or private schemes; Charitable gifts under payroll giving scheme.

The employers' guides supplied by the Revenue need to be studied carefully to identify other differences between pay for PAYE and for national insurance.

Expenses payments to employees count as pay except to the extent that they are for proper business expenses, for which receipts or records must be available. Reimbursement of an employee's parking expenses, for example, must be for recorded business-related journeys. Where the Revenue have granted a dispensation allowing expenses payments to be ignored for tax purposes, the same treatment applies for national insurance, and the exemption for personal expenses of £5 a night (£10 if outside the UK) also applies (see 10.12). Similarly, contributions are not due on payments for directors' liability insurance, etc. (see 10.11).

Where benefits in kind do not attract Class 1 national insurance contributions, employers have to pay Class 1A contributions on virtually all taxable benefits, but only where they are provided to P11D employees. There is no Class 1A national insurance charge on the employee. For details see CHAPTER 10, in particular 10.24.

Class 1 contributions are not payable on benefits unless they have been made specifically chargeable (see below), so as well as non-P11D employees, P11D employees earning less than £610 a week will still get a significant advantage from receiving certain benefits rather than cash pay (the saving to those earning above £610 a week being 1% rather than 11%). It is, however, important to distinguish benefits from payments by the employer for which the employee is legally responsible. The key point is who made the contract. If it is the *employee*, contributions are payable (subject to deduction of any identifiable business proportion). If it is the *employer*, the payment is a benefit and is not liable to Class 1 national insurance unless it is for one of the specifically chargeable items. For example, if an employer contracts to buy an employee a television set, or groceries, Class 1 contributions are not payable (but the employer would have a Class 1A liability if the employee is a P11D employee). If the employee contracts to make the purchases, Class 1 contributions are payable. The detailed information in the Revenue guides for employers needs to be studied carefully.

As far as directors are concerned, payment of a director's bills where the payment is charged to the director's account with the company does not count as pay unless the account becomes overdrawn, and even then, only if the director's earnings are normally credited to the account.

Pay for Class 1 contributions specifically includes benefits that are in the form of 'readily convertible assets' (see 10.15). Readily convertible shares and share options (other than under Revenue approved schemes) come within these provisions (see 11.1 for details). Class 1 contributions are also payable on virtually all non-cash vouchers, the exceptions being broadly those that are exempt for income tax (see 10.17).

Contracted-out employees

13.6   Retirement pensions consist of two parts, a basic flat-rate pension, and an additional pension related to the level of the employee's earnings. The additional pension is paid under the State Earnings Related Pension Scheme (SERPS) and, for rights built up from 6 April 2002, the State Second Pension Scheme (S2P).

Employees who are members of occupational pension schemes may be 'contracted-out' of SERPS/S2P by their employers (see 16.3). Benefits under contracted-out schemes may be either related to salary (COSR schemes) or to the amount contributed, i.e. money purchase (COMP schemes). Contracted-out employees are still eligible for the basic pension from the State but obtain their additional pension from their employer's scheme. To help meet the cost of setting up and running a separate pension scheme, contracted-out employers and their employees are entitled to a rebate of Class 1 contributions on earnings between the lower and upper earnings limits (£79 and £610 a week respectively for 2004/05). The rebate payable through the PAYE scheme is 1.6% for employees for both COSR and COMP schemes. For employers the rebate is 3.5% for COSR schemes and 1% for COMP schemes. Employees in COMP schemes are entitled to a further age-related rebate, which is paid by the Revenue (see below). The treatment of the PAYE rebates is complicated, because the rebates are given on the band of earnings between £79 and £91 on which neither employers nor employees pay contributions. Where an employee's rebate exceeds the contributions payable by him, the balance reduces the employer's liability. See Examples 1 and 2.

Example 1

If an employer had a COSR scheme in 2004/05 and an employee's weekly earnings were exactly £100, the position would be:

		£
Employee	First £91	—
	Remaining £9 @ (11 – 1.6 =) 9.4%	0.85
	Rebate on (91 – 79 =) £12 @ 1.6%	(0.19)
	Contributions payable	0.66
Employer	First £91	—
	Remaining £9 @ (12.8 – 3.5 =) 9.3%	0.84
	Rebate on (91 – 79 =) £12 @ 3.5%	(0.42)
	Contributions payable	0.42

The total employee's/employer's contributions payable would be (66p + 42p =) £1.08.

Example 2

Facts as in Example 1 but employee's earnings were (a) £92 or (b) £82.

The position would be:

(a)		£
Employee	First £91	—
	Remaining £1 @ (11 – 1.6 =) 9.4%	0.09
	Rebate on (91 – 79 =) £12 @ 1.6% = (0.19) of	
	which amount allocated to employee is	(0.09)
	Contributions payable	nil
Employer	First £91	—
	Remaining £1 @ (12.8 – 3.5 =) 9.3%	0.09
	Rebate on (91 – 79 =) £12 @ 3.5%	(0.42)
	Balance of employee's rebate	(0.10)
		(0.43)

The total employee's/employer's contributions payable would be nil and the employer would be entitled to deduct 43p from his overall national insurance liability.

(b)		£
Employee	Contributions payable on £82	nil
	Rebate on (82 – 79 =) £3 @ 1.6% = 5p allocated to employer	
Employer	On £82	—
	Rebate on (82 – 79 =) £3 @ 3.5%	(0.11)
	Employee's rebate	(0.05)
		(0.16)

The total employee's/employer's contributions payable would be nil and the employer would be entitled to deduct 16p from his overall national insurance liability.

Employees may also contract out of SERPS/S2P by entering into personal pension arrangements, to which their employers may or may not contribute (see CHAPTER 17). Both employer and employee continue to pay full national insurance contributions, and the contracting-out rebate is paid by the Revenue into the personal pension scheme.

The Class 1 contributions rebate is age-related for both personal pension plans and contracted-out money purchase schemes (but not salary related schemes). The introduction of S2P has complicated the calculation of the combined employer/employee age-related rebates for personal pension plans (but not contracted-out money purchase schemes). Contracting-out rebates in respect of personal pension plans under S2P are biased to give lower earners a higher rebate. There are therefore up to three relevant percentages. For 2004/05 the first applies to annual earnings between the lower earnings limit of £4,108 and £11,600, the second to annual earnings between £11,600 and £26,600 and the third to annual earnings above £26,600, the relevant percentage in that case applying to earnings up to the upper earnings limit for employees' contributions of £31,720. The rebate percentage for the first earnings band is four times that for the second band, and twice that for the third band. The rebate is calculated by applying the respective percentages to the earnings in each band and then, for those earning over £11,600, adding the amounts together. For someone earning above £26,600 the effect is to give an overall percentage equal to that on the third band of earnings. See 17.11 for an example. The rebates system for contracted-out money purchase schemes has not changed under S2P. The range of combined employer/employee rebates for money purchase schemes is 2.6% at age 15 to 10.5% at age 53 or over. As indicated above, the rebate given on COMP schemes through the PAYE scheme is based on the lowest age-related rebates level of 2.6% (employee 1.6%, employer 1%). The relevant information is recorded on year-end forms P14 and the Revenue will pay the age-related rebate top-up when they receive the forms P14.

Contribution rates (SSCBA 1992, ss 1, 5, 8, 9)

13.7   National insurance rates for 2003/04 and 2004/05 are shown in the TABLE OF RATES AND ALLOWANCES. Although the earnings limits and thresholds have changed, there has been no change in the rates payable.

Employers' national insurance contributions are deductible in arriving at their taxable profits, so that the burden of employers' national insurance contributions is reduced by the tax saved on them. Tax on employees' earnings, on the other hand, is calculated on the gross pay before deducting national insurance contributions.

For 2004/05 employers pay Class 1 secondary contributions at 12.8% on the whole of the excess of an employee's pay above the earnings threshold of £91 a week. For employees there is a lower earnings limit of £79 a week and employees earning at or above that level must be brought within the PAYE system and a P11 deduction card (or substitute) made out for them. No contributions are, however, payable unless earnings exceed the earnings threshold of £91 a week. Employees who are not contracted out pay Class 1 primary contributions at the main primary percentage of 11% on earnings between £91 and £610 a week and at the additional primary percentage of 1% on earnings above £610 a week.

The rate of Class 1A contributions payable by employers on most taxable benefits in kind provided for P11D employees and directors (see 13.2) is 12.8%.

See 13.6 re rebates of contributions for contracted-out employees and see 13.8 for the reduced rate of employees' contributions payable by certain married women and widows.

Employee contributions

Reduced rate for certain married women and widows

13.8   Women who were married or widowed as at 6 April 1977 may have chosen on or before 11 May 1977 to pay Class 1 contributions at a reduced rate. If they are still entitled to pay the reduced contributions, they hold a certificate of election which must be handed over to the employer to enable him to deduct contributions at the correct rate.

If a married woman is self-employed, the election makes her exempt from paying Class 2 contributions, but not Class 4 contributions (see CHAPTER 24).

The reduced rate for 2004/05, which applies once earnings exceed £91 a week and is the same for both contracted-out and non-contracted-out employees, is 4.85% on earnings between £91 and £610 per week and 1% on earnings above £610 a week.

Although substantial amounts may be paid in reduced rate contributions, they do not entitle the payer to any contributory state benefits (but statutory sick pay and statutory maternity or adoption pay are payable where appropriate). Many married women and widows consider they were inadequately informed about the effects of not building up a contribution record of their own, but the Government does not accept that any compensation should be paid. A woman without a contribution record of her own may claim retirement pension or bereavement benefits based on the contribution record of her husband. The retirement pension a wife will get is 60% of the husband's basic pension if the husband is over 65 and the wife is over 60 (see 13.3). She will not get any earnings-related pension. Widows who are over 60 when their husband dies are entitled to a full pension based on their husband's contributions, including earnings related pension (but see 13.3 re the reduction of inherited SERPS entitlement after 5 October 2002). Bereavement benefits, comprising a lump sum bereavement payment plus widowed parent's allowance (including an earnings related supplement based on the husband's contributions) or bereavement allowance, are payable to widows under state pension age where the conditions are satisfied.

An election to pay reduced rate contributions is effective until it is cancelled or revoked. A woman loses the right to pay reduced rate contributions

(a)   if she is divorced, in which case the right is lost immediately after the decree absolute, or

(b)   if she becomes widowed and is not entitled to widow's benefit, in which case the right is not lost until the end of the tax year in which the husband dies, or the end of the following tax year if he dies between 1 October and 5 April, or

(c)   if she pays no reduced rate Class 1 contributions and has no earnings from self-employment for two consecutive tax years.

An election can be revoked in writing at any time and the revocation will, in most instances, take effect from the beginning of the following week. If the election is revoked, the wife will start earning a pension, including earnings-related pension, in her own right, and she will also be entitled to claim maternity allowance, jobseeker's allowance and incapacity benefit if appropriate. Those who are considering revoking may get a pension forecast to assist them in their decision. They should get form BR 19 from their local social security office. Women earning between the lower earnings limit of £79 and the earnings threshold of £91 a week would benefit from revoking the election, because they would become entitled to contributory benefits even though they would not have to pay any contributions (see 13.1). If their earnings increased to above the earnings threshold, however, they would pay 11% rather than 4.85% on the excess.

People over pensionable age

13.9   No contributions are payable by an employee who is over pension age (65 for a man, 60 for a woman), although the employer is still liable for secondary contributions where earnings reach the employers' earnings threshold, such contributions always being at non-contracted-out rates.

Employees who are not liable to pay contributions should apply for a certificate of age exception. This should be given to the employer as authority for Class 1 contributions not to be deducted from earnings.

More than one employment

13.10   Where a person has more than one employment, he is liable to pay primary Class 1 contributions in respect of each job. There is, however, a prescribed annual maximum contribution.

The maximum is based on 53 weeks' contributions. Before the introduction of the 1% charge on all earnings above the upper earnings limit the maximum was simply 53 weeks' contributions at the upper earnings limit. It is no longer a single figure because it depends on how much was earned in each employment and what part of the earnings was charged at the 1% rate. There is an eight-stage calculation in order to arrive at the figure in any particular case. The maximum for contracted-out contributions and reduced rate contributions by married women and widows is calculated by treating contributions payable at a lower rate as having been paid at 11%.

If at the end of a tax year an employee's contributions have exceeded the prescribed maximum by a stipulated amount (£3.80 for 2004/05), a refund is available. An employee may apply for a refund by writing to the NICO Refunds Group explaining why a refund is due and providing evidence of excess payments, e.g. certificates of pay, tax and NIC (forms P60).

To avoid having to pay contributions in all employments throughout the year and being refunded any excess after the end of the year, an employee may apply to defer some of his contributions. An application form for deferment of contributions can be found in Revenue booklet CA 72, and if deferment is granted, a certificate CA2700 is sent to the employers concerned (except those paying the earnings upon which the maximum contributions are payable) requiring them to deduct employees' contributions at 1% on any earnings above £91 a week (£395 a month). The amounts payable are shown in contributions Table J in booklet CA 38 (which also includes contributions Table A). The overall effect is that the employer collecting maximum contributions calculates the contributions at 1% on the excess of earnings over £4,745 a year. Deferment has no effect on employers' contributions, which are payable at 12.8% in each employment on the excess earnings over £4,745 a year. Employees who have or are considering having an appropriate personal pension plan into which the Revenue pay minimum contributions (see 17.11) should note that the Revenue take account only of employments in which full contributions are paid when paying minimum contributions, so deferring contributions in those employments would affect the pension entitlement.

To prevent abuse of the system, there are 'anti-avoidance' provisions as follows.

(a)   Where a person has more than one job with the same employer, earnings from those employments must be added together and contributions calculated on the total.

(b)   Where a person has jobs with different employers who 'carry on business in association with each other', all earnings from 'associated' employers must be added together for the purpose of calculating contributions.

These rules will not be enforced if it is not reasonably practicable to do so. See the Revenue's Tax Bulletin of August 2000 for their views on the meaning of 'not reasonably practicable'.

Income from self-employment

13.11 The position of the employee who also has income from self-employment is dealt with in CHAPTER 24.

Company directors

13.12 Directors sometimes receive a salary under a service contract and also fees for holding the office of director. They are often paid in irregular amounts at irregular time intervals, for example a fixed monthly salary together with a bonus after the year end, once the results of the company are known. To ensure that this does not lead to manipulation of liability to pay national insurance contributions, directors in employment at the beginning of a tax year have an annual earnings period coinciding with the tax year. Those appointed during a tax year have an earnings period equal to the number of weeks from the date of appointment to the end of the tax year. No Class 1 contributions are due unless and until the director's earnings reach the annual earnings threshold (2004/05 £4,732) or a pro-rata limit for directors appointed during a tax year (using the appropriate multiple of the weekly limit).

For directors who earn regular amounts, the annual earnings period causes an unnecessary distortion in their national insurance payments, but it is possible for contributions to be paid as if the special rules did not apply. The director still has an annual earnings liability, however, so that those seeking to manipulate the rules are still prevented from doing so.

All earnings paid to a director during an earnings period must be included in that earnings period (irrespective of the period to which they relate). Earnings include fees, bonuses, salary, payments made in anticipation of future earnings, and payments made to a director which were earned while he was still an employee.

If a director resigns, all payments made to him between the date of resignation and the end of the tax year that relate to his period of directorship must be linked to his other 'directorship earnings' of that tax year. If any such earnings are paid in a later tax year, they are not added to any other earnings of the year in which payment is made. Instead, they are considered independently on an annual earnings basis, and Class 1 contributions accounted for accordingly.

Many directors have payments in anticipation of future earnings, e.g. a payment on account of a bonus to be declared when the company's results are known. Liability for Class 1 contributions arises when the payments are made. The advance bonus payments are added to all other earnings of the annual earnings period. When the bonus is voted (probably at the annual general meeting) any balance will become liable to Class 1 contributions in the tax year in which the annual general meeting is held. Once a bonus is voted for a past period, it is deemed to be paid whether it is placed in an account on which the director can draw or left in the company, unless exceptionally it is not placed at the director's disposal.

To the extent that a director makes drawings against a credit balance on his director's loan account, no Class 1 liability will arise as these drawings simply reduce the balance of the loan account. If the loan account has been built up from undrawn remuneration, the Class 1 liability will have arisen at the time the remuneration was credited to it.

See 10.34 re a director's personal liability for both his own national insurance contributions and other contributions due from the company if he has been fraudulent or negligent.

Tax points

13.13

- Employees earning between £79 and £91 a week satisfy the contribution conditions for contributory social security benefits even though no contributions are payable.

- If an employee has several employments, he can get back national insurance contributions in excess of the annual maximum. Refunds are not, however, available in respect of employers' contributions.

- If your wife or husband pays maximum contributions at the 11% rate in a separate job and also does some work in the family business run by you, you cannot get back employers' national insurance on the earnings from the family business, so it may be more sensible to pay your spouse less than the earnings threshold of £91 a week. Remember, however, that earnings of either of you as an *employee* of the family business must be justified if relief for tax is to be given in calculating the business profits. On the other hand, remember that the national minimum wage legislation may apply (see 12.1).

- Except for company directors, who have an annual earnings period coinciding with the tax year, or for the remainder of the tax year in which they are appointed, national insurance does not work on a cumulative basis. If average earnings will not exceed the earnings threshold of £91, try to ensure that the actual earnings in any week do not do so, otherwise both the employee and the employer will be liable to pay contributions for that particular week even though on a cumulative basis the threshold may not have been reached.

- The annual maximum contribution liability is based on 53 weeks' contributions, although there are rarely 53 pay days in a year. If you have more than one job and earn more than £610 a week from one of them, make sure you apply for deferment. You should then not have any more to pay at the year end, whereas if you wait for a refund, you will only get back any excess over *53 weeks'* contributions. Even if you do not earn more than £610 a week from one job, applying for deferment where your *total* earnings exceed that amount is better than waiting for a refund after the year end. Note that the effect of deferment is that contributions will be payable at 1% rather than 11% on earnings above £91 a week in all jobs other than the main job.

- Dividends paid to shareholders do not attract national insurance contributions. It may be appropriate for shareholders/directors to receive dividends rather than additional remuneration (not forgetting the national minimum wage and personal service company legislation, and also the comments in 12.9 about the 'settlements' rules). It is important to ensure that dividends are properly documented so that they cannot be challenged as pay.

  The national insurance aspect must not, however, be looked at in isolation. Many other factors are important, e.g. the level of remuneration for company or personal pension purposes, and the effect of a dividend policy on other shareholders. See CHAPTER 12 for illustrations.

- If you have been paying the reduced married woman's rate of contribution, watch the circumstances in which you have to revert to the full rate, for example when you get divorced (see 13.8). If you underpay, even by mistake, you will probably have to make up the difference. But you do not have to pay contributions at all from age 60.

- Remember that if you have not satisfied the contribution conditions for a year to be classed as a qualifying year, your State pension may be affected (see 13.3). Class 3 voluntary contributions can be paid to maintain your contribution record.

- If an employer pays an employee's debt, it counts as pay for Class 1 national insurance contributions and for income tax. Where possible, make sure the contract is made by the employer. In that case, Class 1 contributions will not be payable unless the payment relates to a specifically chargeable item. If the employee is a P11D employee the employer will be liable to Class 1A contributions.

- Records are needed to prove business use in certain areas, such as for mileage allowances to those who use their own cars (see 10.9 re business mileage rates), and for contributions towards an employee's telephone bill, unless, in the case of telephones, there is an agreed business proportion for tax, which will also be accepted for national insurance.

- Where Class 1A contributions are payable on a benefit with mixed business/private use, the employer has to pay contributions on the full amount, without any offset for the business proportion.

14
Statutory sick pay and statutory maternity etc pay

Background

14.1   The provisions on statutory sick pay (SSP) and statutory maternity, paternity and adoption pay (SMP, SPP, SAP) are in the Social Security Contributions and Benefits Act 1992 as amended by the Employment Act 2002 (which introduced SPP and SAP). Most employees are entitled to receive SSP from their employers for up to 28 weeks of sickness absence. Employers are, however, entitled to opt out of the SSP scheme if they pay wages or sick pay at or above the SSP rates (see 14.13). SSP is paid at a single flat rate. From 6 April 2003 employers are required to pay statutory maternity pay, statutory paternity pay and statutory adoption pay where the conditions are satisfied (although they will be able to claim reimbursement of most or all of it). The period of paid maternity/adoption leave is six months, and employers must allow a further six months' unpaid leave. The period of paid paternity leave is two weeks. SMP, SPP and SAP are paid at two rates, the higher rate being dependent on the employee's earnings and the standard rate being a fixed amount. SSP, SMP, SPP and SAP all count as pay for income tax and national insurance contributions. Employers are entitled to recover SSP if and to the extent that it exceeds a stipulated monthly threshold — see 14.12. Employers are able to recover 92% of SMP/SPP/SAP, unless they qualify for Small Employers' Relief, in which case they can recover 100% of the SMP etc. plus a further 4.5% to compensate for the national insurance contributions on the SMP etc. (see 14.22).

Employers who fail to comply with the statutory requirements are liable to various penalties. For SSP and SMP these have previously been criminal penalties. From 13 May 2004, the date the National Insurance Contributes and Statutory Payments Act received Royal Assent, civil penalties will apply for all statutory payments.

Statutory Sick Pay (SSP)

Employees entitled to receive SSP

14.2   The definition of an employee is the same as that of an 'employed earner' for Class 1 national insurance contributions (see CHAPTER 13). Married women and widows paying reduced rate Class 1 contributions are therefore entitled to SSP.

An employee is entitled to SSP for each job he has, so that if an individual is employed by two different employers he will be paid SSP by each employer when off work through illness.

An employee is entitled to SSP unless he/she falls into one of the excluded groups (see 14.3).

When an employee is being paid SSP he is not entitled to State incapacity benefit. Employees who are not entitled to SSP and employees who have exhausted their SSP entitlement may claim incapacity benefit.

Employees excluded from SSP

14.3   Employees who, at the beginning of a 'period of incapacity for work' (see 14.6), fall into one of the following categories cannot claim SSP.

(a)   People under 16 or over 65.

(b)   Those who have claimed incapacity benefit or severe disablement allowance within the 57 days before falling ill. An employee who has received one of these benefits will receive a letter from the Department for Works and Pensions (known as a 'linking letter') notifying the employer of the period of exclusion. For certain claimants, the period of exclusion will be 52 weeks rather than the standard 8 weeks.

(c)   Those whose average weekly earnings* (usually calculated over the previous eight weeks) are below the lower earnings limit for national insurance contributions (£79 for 2004/05 — see CHAPTER 13).

(d)   A person who has not begun work under his contract.

(e)   Those who become ill while they are away from work because of a trade dispute, unless the employee can prove that he is not participating in, or directly interested in, the dispute.

(f)   A pregnant woman during her disqualifying period of 26 weeks (see 14.4).

(g)   Those who have received 28 weeks' SSP from their previous employer(s). This further exclusion does not prevent an employee receiving SSP if he should fall ill more than eight weeks after the end of the previous period of incapacity.

(h)   Those who fall ill while in prison or in legal custody.

* If an employee's average weekly earnings would otherwise be too low to qualify for SSP, but would qualify if the employer included that part of earnings on which Class 1B national insurance contributions (see 10.36) are paid by the employer in respect of the employee, then the employer must recalculate the earnings including the Class 1B amount.

Those who fall ill while working outside the European Economic Area (i.e. the EU plus Iceland, Liechtenstein and Norway) are eligible for SSP so long as the employer is liable to pay Class 1 national insurance contributions (see 41.21). If the employer's Class 1 liability ends during the incapacity, SSP will continue until stopped for another reason (e.g. reaching maximum entitlement).

Where an employer receives notification of illness from an employee who falls into an 'excluded' category, he must issue the employee with a change-over form SSP 1 (using either the official form or the employer's own version). The form must be issued within seven days of the notification of the illness or, if that is impracticable, on the first pay day in the following tax month. Form SSP 1 may also need to be issued when entitlement to SSP ends (see 14.9).

Pregnancy — disqualifying period

14.4   Statutory sick pay cannot be paid during a disqualifying period. For those entitled to statutory maternity pay or maternity allowance, the disqualifying period starts with the day the employee is first entitled to that payment and runs for 26 weeks.

For those not entitled to either of those payments and not already getting SSP, the disqualifying period runs for 18 weeks, normally starting on the earlier of the Sunday of the week in which the baby is born and the Sunday of the week the employee is first off sick with a pregnancy-related illness on or after the start of the fourth week before the baby is due. The starting date rules are sometimes slightly different if the baby is born early.

If SSP is already being paid to a pregnant woman not entitled to SMP or maternity allowance, the disqualifying period starts with the earlier of the day after the birth and the day after the first day she becomes sick with a pregnancy-related illness on or after the start of the fourth week before the baby is due.

Qualifying conditions for SSP

14.5   For SSP to be payable two qualifying conditions must be met:

(i)   there must be a 'period of incapacity for work' ('PIW'); and

(ii)   there must be one or more 'qualifying days'.

Incapacity for work

14.6   A PIW is a period of four or more consecutive days of incapacity for work, counting rest days and holidays as well as normal working days. A person may be deemed incapable of work on the advice of a doctor or medical officer of health (e.g. where a pregnant woman is advised to stay at home during an outbreak of German measles at her place of work), but a day counts towards a PIW only if the employee is, or is deemed to be, 'incapable by reason of specific disease or bodily or mental disablement of doing work which he/she can reasonably be expected to do under the contract of employment'. The incapacity must exist throughout the day, nightshift workers falling ill during a shift being treated as working only on the day on which the shift began.

If two PIWs are separated by 56 days or less, they are treated as one single PIW (called a linked PIW). See example 1.

Example 1

An employee is incapable of work through illness from Friday 7 May 2004 to Tuesday 11 May 2004 inclusive and from Sunday 27 June 2004 to Thursday 19 August 2004 inclusive.

The two PIWs are separated by 46 days and are therefore treated as a linked PIW.

Tables to help employers work out whether PIWs link are included in the SSP Tables issued by the Revenue.

Qualifying days

14.7   SSP is payable only in respect of 'qualifying days'. These are days of the week agreed between the employer and employee and will normally be those days on which the employee is required to work. Employer and employee may, however, come to other arrangements if they wish but qualifying days cannot be defined by reference to the days when the employee is sick. There is an overriding rule that there must be at least one qualifying day each week even if the employee is not required to work during that week.

SSP is not payable for the first three qualifying days in any PIW not linked to an earlier PIW. These are 'waiting days'. See example 2.

Example 2

An employee with qualifying days Monday to Friday each week, who had not been ill during May 2004, was ill on the days ringed in June, returning to work on 1 July.

M	T	W	Th	F	Sa	Su
	1	2	(3)	(4)	(5)	(6)
7	8	9	10	11	12	13
14	15	16	17	18	19	20
(21)	(22)	(23)	(24)	(25)	26	(27)
(28)	(29)	(30)				

There are three PIWs, from the 3rd to the 6th, from the 21st to the 25th, and from the 27th to the 30th.

In the first, there are two qualifying days which count as waiting days, and no SSP is payable.

In the second, which begins not more than 56 days after the end of the first and is therefore linked with it, the 21st is the third waiting day and SSP is payable for the other four qualifying days.

The third begins not more than 56 days after the end of the second and is therefore linked with it. As there are three waiting days in the linked PIWs, SSP is payable for each of the three qualifying days in the third PIW.

Amount of SSP

14.8   Providing the employee's average weekly earnings are at or above the national insurance lower earnings limit (£79 for 2004/05), SSP is payable on a daily basis at a flat weekly rate of £66.15 (from 6 April 2004).

The daily rate of SSP is the weekly rate divided by the number of qualifying days in the week (e.g. an employee who has five qualifying days in a week will receive SSP at a daily rate of £13.23 (£66.15 ÷ 5)).

SSP will usually be paid on the employee's normal pay day.

Wages paid to an employee can be offset against any SSP due for the same day. If the wages are less than the SSP due, the employer must make up the payment to the appropriate rate of SSP.

When SSP ends

14.9   SSP ends with whichever of the following first occurs:

(a)   the period of incapacity ends and the employee returns to work;

(b)   the employee reaches his maximum entitlement to SSP;

(c)   the employee's linked PIW has run for three years (which could only happen in exceptional circumstances where there were a large number of very short, four-day illnesses);

(d)   the employee's contract of employment ends;

(e)   the employee is taken into legal custody;

(f)   a pregnant woman employee starts her disqualifying period (see 14.4).

The maximum period for which the employer is liable to pay SSP is normally 28 weeks. Where, however, a new employee commences a PIW within eight weeks of the day when a PIW with a previous employer ended, the weeks of SSP shown on the leaver's statement provided by the previous employer (see 14.10) are taken into account to determine the new employer's maximum SSP liability. The previous period of sickness does not, however, affect the new employer's calculations in any other way and is not treated as a linked PIW.

Where entitlement to SSP ends while the employee is still sick, the employee will be able to claim incapacity benefit. To facilitate the change-over, the employer must issue change-over form SSP 1 to the employee at the beginning of the 23rd week of SSP (or, if sooner, two weeks before the employee's entitlement to SSP is due to end). If the employee's entitlement ends unexpectedly (e.g. through being taken into legal custody), the change-over form must be issued immediately. Form SSP 1 must also be issued at the start of the pregnancy disqualification period.

Leaver's statements

14.10   If an employee has a PIW which ends not more than 56 days before his employment ceases, and SSP was payable for one week or more, a leaver's statement SSP 1(L) (or the employer's own version of the form) must be issued if requested by the employee, showing the number of weeks' SSP payable (rounded to whole weeks, counting more than three odd days of payment as a week, and ignoring three odd days or less). The statement must be issued not later than the seventh day after the day the employee asks for it or, if that is impracticable, on the first pay day in the following tax month.

Notification and evidence for SSP

14.11   The payment of SSP is triggered by the employee notifying his employer that he is unfit for work. Form SC 2, available from Revenue offices, may be used for this purpose if employers wish. An employer can draw up his own procedure for notification subject to the following limitations:

(a)   reasonable steps must be taken to notify employees of the procedures;

(b)   it is not legal to insist that notification

    (i)   is made by the employee in person, or

    (ii)   is made by a particular time of day, or

    (iii)   is made more than once weekly for the same illness, or

    (iv)   is made on a form provided by the employer or on a medical certificate, or

    (v)   is given earlier than the first qualifying day; and

(c)   where the employee is a new employee with a leaving statement from his former employer, the statement must be accepted if it is produced not later than the seventh day after his first qualifying day of sickness.

If no notification procedures have been drawn up, the employee should inform his employer in writing by the seventh day after his first qualifying day of absence. If an employee fails to notify within the laid-down time limits, an employer may withhold SSP, but late notification may be accepted if there was good cause for delay.

Having been notified by an employee of his illness, the employer must satisfy himself that the illness is genuine before paying SSP. Employers usually obtain 'self-certificates' for the first week of illness and medical notes for longer absences. (The employer cannot insist on a medical certificate for the first seven days of a period of incapacity.)

An employer may withhold SSP when notification is late, and he may refuse to pay SSP if he feels that the employee is not in fact sick. In both these instances the employer, if required by the employee, must provide written reasons for withholding or refusing to pay SSP. An employee who disagrees with his employer's actions has the right to appeal for an official decision.

Recovery of SSP by employer

14.12   Employers may recover that part of the SSP paid in a tax month that exceeds 13% of their combined employer/employee national insurance contributions in that tax month (not including any Class 1A or Class 1B contributions but after deducting any contracted-out contributions rebate due — see 13.6).

Example 3

Total employer/employee national insurance contributions for August 2004 are £4,000. 13% thereof is £520. SSP would be recovered as follows:

SSP paid in month	£520 or less	£600	£1,000
SSP recovered	Nil	£80	£480

SSP is recovered from amounts due to be paid over to the Revenue Accounts Office in respect of national insurance and PAYE tax payable, and if it exceeds those amounts, the employer can either carry the excess forward or apply to the Accounts Office for a refund.

Opting out of SSP

14.13   Employers may opt out of the SSP scheme if they pay wages or sick pay above the SSP rates. They do not need to apply to do so, and may, if they wish, opt out for some but not all employees or periods of sickness. Records must be kept to enable form SSP 1 or SSP 1(L) (see 14.9 and 14.10) to be issued where appropriate, and various other details must be recorded as indicated in the employers' manual CA 30. Employers may recover the appropriate part of their sick pay as if it were SSP (see 14.12) and in that event they must show the relevant details on PAYE year-end forms P14 and P35 (see 10.34).

Statutory Maternity Pay (SMP)

Employees entitled to SMP

14.14   To be entitled to statutory maternity pay (SMP), an employee must satisfy the qualifying conditions (see 14.15). Self-employed and unemployed women, and employed women who cannot get SMP, may be able to claim maternity allowance from the Department for Work and Pensions. SMP is usually paid for 26 weeks, even if the employee is not returning after the baby has been born. Married women paying reduced national insurance contributions, and widows getting a State widow's benefit, are entitled to SMP if they satisfy the qualifying conditions. SSP and SMP cannot be paid at the same time, and SSP must cease on the last day before the maternity pay period (see 14.18) starts, even if for some reason the employee is not entitled to SMP.

Qualifying conditions for SMP

14.15   To qualify for SMP an employee must have been continuously employed (normally by the same employer) for at least 26 weeks into the 15th week before the baby is due. The 15th week is called the qualifying week. The employee's average weekly earnings in the eight weeks ending with the qualifying week must be not less than the lower earnings limit for national insurance contributions at the end of that week (currently £79). The employee must still be pregnant at the 11th week before the expected date of birth. There are special rules for premature births. If an employee satisfies the qualifying rules with more than one employer she can receive SMP from each employer.

If Class 1B national insurance contributions have been paid in respect of the employee, the earnings on which they are paid must be included in calculating average weekly earnings if the employee would otherwise fail to qualify for SMP, in the same way as for SSP (see 14.3). In that event they must also be taken into account to calculate the higher rate of SMP (see 14.19).

Notification and evidence for SMP

14.16   To get SMP an employee must normally give 28 days' notice of maternity absence in a manner prescribed by the employer, and must produce evidence of her expected week of confinement, normally on a maternity certificate form MAT B1 issued by a doctor or midwife, within 3 weeks after the start of the maternity pay period (this 3-week period can exceptionally be extended to 13 weeks).

Employees excluded from SMP

14.17   An employee is not entitled to SMP if:

(a)   she is not employed during the qualifying week (see 14.15);

(b)   she has not been continuously employed for 26 weeks;

(c)   the earnings rule (see 14.15) is not satisfied;

(d)   she has not given notice at an acceptable time of the date she is stopping work;

(e)   medical evidence of her expected confinement date is not provided;

(f)   she is in legal custody at any time in the first week of her maternity pay period.

An employee who is outside the European Economic Area (see 14.3) is not eligible for SMP unless the employer is liable to pay Class 1 national insurance contributions (see 41.21).

If an employee is not entitled to SMP at the start of the maternity pay period, she is not entitled to it at all.

An employee who is not entitled to SMP must be given form SMP 1 within seven days of the decision not to pay it, together with any maternity certificate she has provided. These forms will need to be produced to her social security office if she claims maternity allowance.

Payment of SMP

14.18   SMP is payable for a maximum of 26 weeks, called the maternity pay period. The maternity pay period may start at any time from the 11th week before the baby is due to the Sunday after the birth, but if a woman is on sick leave because of pregnancy she will be treated as on maternity leave if there are fewer than four weeks before the baby is due. For a non-pregnancy related sickness, the maternity pay period could be deferred and SSP could still be claimed instead in that last six weeks. The employee cannot do any work for the employer paying her SMP, but may continue to work or start work for another employer before the baby is born without affecting her entitlement. The employer will no longer be liable to pay SMP if, after the baby is born, the employee starts work for a new employer or returns to work for another employer who did not employ her in the qualifying week. SMP will also cease if the employee is taken into legal custody.

Amount of SMP

14.19   SMP is paid at the rate of 90% of the employee's average weekly earnings for the first six weeks and then at the standard rate, which is the *lower* of 90% of average weekly earnings and £102.80, for the remainder of the period.

Statutory Paternity Pay (SPP)

14.20   Statutory paternity pay (SPP) may be claimed by the baby's biological father, a partner/husband other than the biological father, or a female partner in a same sex couple. See 14.21 for SPP for adopting parents.

The same rule applies as for SMP for the SPP claimant to have a continuous period of employment of at least 26 weeks into the 15th week before the baby is due, and for SPP the claimant must continue to work for that employer until the baby is born. As with SMP, the claimant's averaged weekly earnings in the eight weeks before the 15th week before the baby is due must be at least £79.

The SPP claimant may choose to take either one or two (consecutive) whole weeks' leave within the eight weeks after the baby's birth (or for babies born more than 15 weeks before the original due date, within the period from the date of birth to the end of eight weeks from the Sunday of the week the baby was originally due). The employee must normally give 28 days' notice of the date he intends to take leave. The weekly amount of SPP payable is the same as the standard rate for SMP, i.e. either 90% of average weekly earnings or £102.80 whichever is lower.

The employee must tell his employer by the end of the 15th week before the baby is due (or as soon as reasonably practicable) that he is going to take paternity leave, and he must notify the employer of the date the baby is born. Employers must give SPP claimants a form SC3 (*Becoming a parent*) which explains the terms and conditions for SPP, and includes a tear-off slip for the employee to provide relevant information, including a 'declaration of family commitment' that the employee will be responsible for the child's upbringing and will take time off work to support the mother or care for the child. SPP cannot be paid unless the declaration is provided. If the employee does not qualify for SPP the employer must give him a form SPP 1.

An employee cannot get SPP and SSP at the same time.

Statutory Adoption Pay (SAP) and Statutory Paternity Pay (SPP) for adoptive parents

14.21   Providing the relevant conditions are satisfied, SAP may be claimed by male or female employees adopting a child aged up to 18. SPP may be claimed by anyone (male or female) who is the partner of someone adopting a child on their own or is adopting a child with their partner. Adopting couples must choose which will claim SAP and which will claim SPP.

The same rules broadly apply for both SMP and SAP, adapted appropriately by reference to the time when a child is matched for adoption (i.e. the adoption agency has decided that the person is suitable to adopt that child) and when a child is placed for adoption with the adoptive parents. The SAP period must start from the date of the child's placement, or from a fixed date up to 14 days before the expected date of placement. The SPP rules are similarly adapted to cover adoptive parents. The SPP period must start not earlier than the date of the child's placement and must be completed within eight weeks of the placement. The employer must give the employee form SC4 (*Becoming an adoptive parent*), which contains a tear-off slip for the employee to provide relevant information, including a 'declaration of family commitment'. If the employee does not qualify for SPP the employer must give him form SPP 1. The weekly rates of both SAP and SPP are the lower of 90% of average weekly earnings and £102.80.

Employees must give employers notice, 28 days before the adoption pay period starts or as soon as is reasonably practicable, of the date the child is placed with them for adoption, supported by a certificate from the adoption agency confirming the date they were told that they had been matched with a child. For SPP, the employee must provide a declaration of family commitment (see 14.20) and information on the dates when the parental leave is to be taken.

Recovery of SMP, SPP and SAP by employer

14.22   For 2004/05, employers other than 'small employers' are able to recover 92% of the gross amount of SMP/SPP/SAP paid in any month.

'Small employers' are those whose total annual employer/employee national insurance contributions (excluding Class 1A and Class 1B contributions but after deducting any contracted-out contributions rebate due — see 13.6) do not exceed £45,000. Such employers can recover all the SMP etc. paid, plus an extra 4.5% of the amount paid to compensate for the employer's Class 1 contributions on the payments. The annual contributions taken into account for 'small employers' are those for the tax year *before* that in which the SMP 'qualifying week' (see 14.15) starts, or in adoption cases, the tax year before that in which the adoptive parents were told by the adoption agency that they had been matched with a child.

The employer recovers the amount he is entitled to in the same way as for SSP (see 14.12), i.e. by deducting it from the total payments he makes to the Revenue Accounts Office in respect of national insurance and tax. If the employer calculates that he has insufficient money to cover all the payments he needs to make, he can apply to the Accounts Office for an advance payment.

Employer's records

14.23   Employer's records are particularly important, as the information required to be kept may have to be made available to Revenue inspectors.

Employers may use record sheets SSP 2, SMP 2, SPP 2 and SAP 2 available from Revenue offices, if they wish. The form the records take is up to the employer, but the following must be kept:

For SSP

14.24

(a)   records of dates of employees' PIWs;

(b)   all payments of SSP made during a PIW.

For SMP, SPP and SAP

14.25

(a)   records of payment dates and amount paid;

(b)   the date the pay period began;

(c)   for SMP and SAP, records of any weeks in 26 week period when payment wasn't made, with reasons, and for SPP, records of any unpaid SPP with reasons;

(d)   For SMP, maternity certificates (forms MAT B1) or other medical evidence, and copies of certificates returned to employees, for example when liability has ended;

(e)   for SPP, the declaration of family commitment (or a copy);

(f)   for SAP, the evidence your employee gave you from the adoption agency (or a copy).

For all statutory payments

14.26   Records must also be kept of the monthly amounts paid, and certain details need to be included on the end of year returns of pay, tax and national insurance (see 10.34).

Records must be kept for a minimum of three years after the end of the tax year to which they relate.

In addition to the records outlined above, the Revenue recommends that certain other records are also retained for further reference. For details see the various Revenue guides.

15
Golden handcuffs and golden handshakes

15.1   A 'golden handcuff' or 'golden hello' is the popular term for a lump sum payment received on taking up an employment, and a 'golden handshake' the term for a lump sum payment received when you leave an employment.

Lump sum payments on taking up employment (ITEPA 2003, ss 225, 226)

15.2   Where a lump sum payment is made to a prospective employee, it will be taxed as advance pay for future services unless it represents compensation for some right or asset given up on taking up the employment. It is difficult to show that a payment does represent compensation, and professional advice should be sought if you think a payment you are about to receive is in this category.

Sometimes a lump sum is paid in return for your agreeing to restrict your conduct or activities in some way, for example agreeing not to leave to join a competitor within a certain period of time. Any such special payments are treated as pay in the normal way, both for tax and for national insurance. If an employee makes such an agreement in return for a non-cash benefit, the value of the benefit still counts as pay for both tax and national insurance.

Lump sum termination payments and benefits (TA 1988, s 90; ITEPA 2003, ss 225, 226, 309, 393–416)

15.3   Lump sum termination payments and benefits are taxable under special rules (see 15.4), unless they are already taxable under the normal rules for earnings from employment.

A payment will be taxable as employment income if it is a payment for services rendered, i.e. it is really deferred pay. Wages in lieu of notice or compensation for loss of office are chargeable to both tax and national insurance in the normal way if they are provided for in the employee's terms and conditions of employment, even if the payment is discretionary, for example the employment contract provides for four weeks' notice to be given, or, at the employer's discretion, pay in lieu of notice. See the Revenue's Tax Bulletin of February 2003 for detailed comments on their views. To be within the special rules, payments must be by way of compensation because the employer has *broken* the employment contract, or be purely ex gratia payments that are not part of the employer's established practice. Even then, the Revenue may seek to tax them under another heading, if they are paid in return for an agreement by the employee to restrict his future conduct or activities. This will not normally apply where the only undertaking by the employee is that he will not pursue an action against the employer concerning the termination of his employment (unless a specific sum was attributed to the undertaking, which would be very unusual).

If the payment is made because the job no longer exists, for example redundancy pay over and above the statutory amount, it is not taxable as pay under the normal rules, even where it is covered by contractual arrangements. The important factor is whether the payment is for services rendered by the employee or because his job has ceased to exist.

In the case of an ex gratia payment, it will be more difficult to demonstrate to the Revenue that it was made because of the termination of employment rather than for services rendered. When employment is terminated by the employee's retirement (other than premature retirement through redundancy or disability) or death (other than as the result of an accident), the Revenue consider that ex gratia payments are fully taxable under the employment income rules as benefits under an unapproved 'retirement benefits scheme'. This will not apply if the employer gets tax approval for the payments, which will then become 'relevant benefits from an approved scheme', but approval will be subject to the normal rules limiting the maximum lump sum payable, and will not be given if the ex gratia sum is in addition to other lump sum entitlements, except any payable only on death in service. Alternatively, approval need not be sought if the lump sum is the only potential lump sum payable and does not exceed one-twelfth of the pensions earnings cap figure for the year of payment (£102,000 for 2004/05, giving a limit for that year of £8,500). (Revenue Statement of Practice SP 13/91).

For either compensation or ex gratia payments, the following circumstances may give rise to further complication:

(i)   Where the employee is also a shareholder, it may be difficult to show that the payment is not a distribution, for which no deduction would be given in calculating the employer's trading profit (see CHAPTER 3).

(ii)   Where the payment is made at the same time as a change in voting control, a clear distinction must be demonstrated between the payment and the share transactions if the payment is not to be regarded as part of the capital transaction.

(iii)   If the employee continues with the employer in a new capacity, either as an employee or perhaps under a consultancy agreement, it becomes that much harder to show that the payment was not for services rendered or to be rendered in the future.

Taxation of lump sum termination payments and benefits

15.4   Provided that the payment and/or benefit is not caught either as taxable earnings, or as a distribution, or as part of a capital transaction, it will be taxed according to the special rules for termination payments. Under these rules (subject to what is said below about wholly exempt payments), the first £30,000 is exempt and only the balance is taxable as earnings. Non-cash benefits are valued using the cash equivalents that apply in calculating employment income (see CHAPTER 10) unless, exceptionally, the 'money's worth' value is higher, for example where the asset's value has increased since the employer acquired it. Various benefits that would normally escape tax in a continuing employment are also excluded from the taxable termination payment. Statutory redundancy payments, whilst not themselves taxable, are included within the first £30,000.

The taxable amount is treated as income of the tax year in which it is received or (for non-cash benefits) enjoyed. This makes it easier to deal with cash amounts payable by instalments and continuing benefits. (Where the continuing benefit is a beneficial loan, then unless the taxable amount is covered by the £30,000 exemption, the notional interest charged to tax is treated as interest paid by the employee, so that tax relief is given if appropriate — see 10.23.) Employers deduct tax under PAYE on cash payments (see 15.7), and employees account for higher rate tax on such payments, and the whole of the tax on benefits, in their self-assessments.

Exemptions

15.5   Some payments are completely exempt from tax, for example those on death in service (subject to what is said above) or in respect of disability, or where the service has been predominantly abroad. Where service abroad does not qualify for complete exemption, there is a proportionate reduction of the taxable amount according to the time spent abroad.

Lump sums received under approved pension schemes are exempt. They may be boosted by agreed special contributions from the employer to the fund prior to the termination of employment so long as the permitted maximum lump sum is not exceeded (see CHAPTER 16). In view of the Revenue's view on ex gratia payments (see 15.3), this route provides an alternative where there is an approved pension scheme.

The £30,000 exemption applies after all other available exemptions, but it is taken into account before giving proportionate relief for foreign service that is not completely exempt.

Calculation of tax payable

15.6 Tax on the chargeable amount is calculated by treating it as the top slice of income (except for life policy gains — see 40.5), whereas under the normal rules savings income is treated as the top slice, with dividend income being the highest part of that top slice (see 2.21 above). This may reduce the tax payable (see Example 1).

Example 1

An individual's taxable income in 2004/05, after reliefs and allowances, comprises non-savings income of £18,000, dividend income of £10,000 (inclusive of tax credits) and £10,000 in respect of a taxable lump sum. The comparison of the tax position if the normal rules treating dividend income as the top slice of income applied with the special rules for dealing with lump sums is as follows:

	£		£	£
If no special rules applied				
Non-savings income	2,020	@ 10%	202	
(including £10,000 lump sum)	25,980	@ 22%	5,716	
	28,000			
Dividends (part)	3,400	@ 10%	340	
	31,400			
Dividends (balance)	6,600	@ 32.5%	2,145	
	38,000			8,403

	£		£	£
Lump sum of £10,000 treated as top slice of income				
Non-savings income	2,020	@ 10%	202	
other than lump sum	15,980	@ 22%	3,516	
	18,000			
Dividends	10,000	@ 10%	1,000	
	28,000			
Lump sum (part)	3,400	@ 22%	748	
	31,400			
Lump sum (balance)	6,600	@ 40%	2,640	
	38,000			8,106
Reduction in tax through treating lump sum as top slice of income				297

The reduction of £297 represents a saving of 22½% on dividends of £6,600 = £1,485, less the difference between the 40% and 22% rates (18%) on £6,600 of the lump sum = £1,188.

PAYE and reporting requirements

15.7   If the termination settlement is made before the employee leaves, the employer must deduct and account for PAYE tax on the excess of chargeable termination payments over £30,000 and also on ex gratia sums on retirement or death for which approval has not yet been granted (tax being refunded as and when approval is received). Cash payments will be shown on tax deduction sheets and forms P45. If payments are made after the employee has left and been issued with form P45, tax must be deducted under PAYE at the basic rate. Any higher rate tax due will then be collected directly from the employee on 31 January after the end of the relevant tax year, along with the tax on any non-cash benefits. Although this may give a cash flow advantage at the time, it may result in increased payments on account for the following year (see 9.7), because tax paid directly affects payments on account, whereas tax under PAYE does not.

Unless the package is wholly cash, or the total value of the package including benefits is estimated not to exceed £30,000, the employer must provide details of the termination package to the Revenue not later than 6 July following the end of the tax year in which the termination package was awarded (copies being provided to employees to enable them to complete their tax returns). The details should cover the total value of the package, the amounts of cash and the nature of the benefits to be provided and their cash equivalents, indicating which, if any, amounts and benefits are to be provided in later years. No further report needs to be submitted unless, exceptionally, there is a subsequent variation increasing the value of the package by more than £10,000, in which case a report must be sent to the Revenue by 6 July following the tax year of variation. If a report is not submitted because a package is originally estimated to have a value not exceeding £30,000, but the package is subsequently changed so that it exceeds that amount, a report and employee copy must be provided by 6 July following the tax year in which the change occurs. The employer is liable to a penalty of up to £300 if he fails to submit a report, plus up to £60 a day from the time the £300 penalty is imposed until the report is submitted. If an incorrect report is submitted fraudulently or negligently the maximum penalty is £3,000.

Calculating the employer's profits *(TA 1988, s 90)*

15.8   To be deducted in arriving at taxable profits, expenses must be wholly and exclusively for the purposes of the trade. Apart from statutory redundancy payments, which are specifically allowable, there is no special rule for termination payments, but it will usually be easier to show that they meet the 'wholly and exclusively' requirement when they are compensation rather than ex gratia payments, and when the trade is continuing rather than when it is not.

It may be particularly difficult for the employer to obtain a deduction where the payment is ex gratia and is associated with a sale of the shares or a change in voting control, or where it is an abnormally high payment to a director with a material interest in the company.

Where a trade is permanently discontinued, it is specifically provided that an additional payment up to three times any amount paid under the statutory redundancy pay provisions is allowable as a deduction in computing the employer's profits. Any payments in excess of this amount are disallowed unless they are made to an employee on cessation under a pre-existing contractual or statutory obligation (not ex gratia amounts).

National insurance position

15.9   Payments that are caught as earnings under the normal employment income rules are also liable to national insurance contributions, as indicated at 15.3. Otherwise, contributions are not payable.

Counselling services for redundant employees (ITEPA 2003, s 310)

15.10   The provision of counselling services by employers for redundant employees, or payment by the employer of an employee's costs for such counselling is specifically exempt from tax for employees, and the cost is fully allowed to employers.

Expenses incurred in obtaining a lump sum payment

15.11   Some employees may incur expenses, for example fees to advisers, in obtaining a lump sum payment. These will not reduce the taxable part of the lump sum as they will not have been wholly, exclusively and necessarily incurred in the performance of the duties of the employment. Where an employer pays an employee's legal costs in obtaining a compensation payment, the Revenue will not treat the payment as a taxable benefit if it is made direct to the employee's solicitor following an out of court settlement, or if it is made to the employee under a Court Order.

Tax points

15.12

- An ex gratia payment to a director or shareholder of a close company is especially vulnerable to Revenue attack, on either or both of the following grounds:

  (a)   it is not a deductible trading expense,

  (b)   it is a distribution of profits.

- If an ex gratia payment by a close company is not allowed in calculating profits, the Revenue may contend that each shareholder has made a proportionate transfer of value for inheritance tax. There is a specific exclusion where the payment is allowed in computing profits.

- Ex gratia payments may be taxed as non-exempt 'retirement benefits' — see 15.3. Such a charge takes precedence over a charge under the rules for termination payments.

- If an employee who receives a termination settlement is allowed to keep a company car as part of the package, the market value of the car will be taken into account for the purpose of the exempt £30,000 unless it is regarded as a reward for past services, in which case the full market value would be chargeable as pay. An alternative is to increase the lump sum and give the employee the opportunity to buy the car at market value. If the lump sum was taxable as an unapproved retirement benefit (see 15.3), the value of the car would similarly be taxable.

- If you pay one or more termination payments after an employee has left and been given his P45, tax only has to be deducted at the basic rate. The employee will then pay any higher rate tax due on 31 January after the end of the tax year. Under self-assessment, however, this may lead to increased payments on account for the following year (see 15.7).

- Unless you obtain new sources of income to replace your salary, the tax cost of a termination payment in excess of £30,000 may be lower if the termination occurs shortly after 6 April rather than before, because all or part of the payment may fall within the starting or basic rate bands, whereas it might have attracted 40% tax if it was received in addition to a full year's salary.

- It is essential that proper documentation and board minutes are available so that the nature of payments can be demonstrated to the Revenue.

- The tax reliefs for lump sum payments are only available to employees and not to those working under a contract for services, whose earnings are charged under Schedule D, Case I or II (see 19.1). If, exceptionally, employment income is included by agreement with the Revenue in the calculation of self-employed profits, e.g. directors' fees where the directorship is held in a professional capacity and the fees are included as income of the professional practice, this in itself will not prevent a lump sum qualifying for the reliefs outlined in this chapter.

- The chargeable part of a termination payment does not count as relevant earnings for the purpose of calculating maximum contributions to a personal pension plan taken out on or after 1 July 1988. (See CHAPTER 17.) It is included in calculating maximum contributions to retirement annuity contracts made before that date.

- A termination payment may affect the former employee's entitlement to social security benefits if he is then unemployed, but the employee will be entitled to unemployment credits for the period covered by the compensation payment so that his national insurance contribution record is not affected.

16
Occupational
pension schemes

Background

16.1 State pensions are recognised as providing an inadequate income in old age, even though employees' State pensions are boosted by an earnings-related addition. Rights to the earnings-related addition used to be built up under the State Earnings Related Pension Scheme (SERPS). From 6 April 2002 SERPS was replaced by the State Second Pension Scheme (S2P). Those earning up to a set figure (£26,600 for 2004/05) will receive better benefit levels than under SERPS. The aim is to provide a flat rate benefit for those on low incomes and to encourage middle and high income earners to make independent provision and contract out of the S2P by providing substantial national insurance rebates. For more details see 13.3.

Following a lengthy consultation process, the Government has now introduced a single integrated scheme for all occupational and personal pension schemes that qualify for tax relief, which will take effect from 6 April 2006. The new provisions are outlined in 16.26 to 16.32. Under the new scheme there will be no limit to the number of pension schemes of which an individual may be a member, and most of the restrictions currently applicable will be replaced by two overall limits, a maximum lifetime allowance for total pension savings and a maximum annual allowance for total contributions. This chapter and CHAPTER 17 deal with the existing legislation for occupational and personal pension schemes respectively, but the new scheme provisions are mentioned where relevant from a planning point of view. A number of simplified guides to the existing various pension options are available from the Government's Pension Service.

For those who wish to contribute to pensions other than under the State pension scheme, there are two main options — occupational schemes for employees who have an employer offering such a scheme, and personal pension schemes (which include stakeholder schemes), to which employers may or may not contribute. Contributions to personal pension schemes may be made by non-earners, as well as the employed and self-employed. Personal pension schemes are dealt with in CHAPTER 17.

From 6 April 2003 those in money purchase occupational schemes and personal pension schemes (including stakeholder schemes) will receive annual illustrations of what their future pension might be in present-day prices, so that people will have a more realistic idea about the value of their pension funds.

State pensions

16.2 State retirement and widows' pensions are taxable under the provisions of the Income Tax (Earnings and Pensions) Act 2003 (see 10.1). The amount chargeable is the pension accruing in the tax year. Wounds and disability pensions and war widows' pensions are exempt from tax. Tax on state pensions is collected either through the PAYE scheme or by self-assessment.

Taxable state pensions are earned by the payment of national insurance contributions. For employees, the entitlement is built up under the State Second Pension Scheme and is earnings related (see 13.2 and 16.1). For the self-employed, the pension is at a flat rate and there is no earnings-related addition (see 24.1). As indicated in 16.1, employers may arrange for their employees to be contracted out of the State scheme, an equivalent or better pension being paid instead from the employer's scheme (see 16.3).

Contracting out of the State Second Pension Scheme (S2P)

16.3 Employers may arrange for their employees to be contracted out of S2P (thus entitling both employers and employees to pay lower national insurance contributions) if they operate either a salary-related scheme (COSR) or a money purchase scheme (COMPS). The rules for contracted-out schemes changed from 6 April 1997. Pension rights built up under the earlier rules will still be payable. Salary-related schemes must now meet a new statutory standard of overall quality, which broadly requires benefits to be equivalent to or better than the State scheme, although there is no 'guaranteed minimum pension' for individual members. Scheme actuaries will regularly check that the standard is still met (usually at three-yearly intervals). Further changes were made from 6 April 2002 with the switch from SERPS to S2P. Once payable, pensions must be increased annually in line with inflation or by 5% if less. This is to be reduced to 2.5% when the provisions of the Pensions Bill now before Parliament come into effect. Rebates of national insurance contributions for salary-related schemes are 3.5% for employers and 1.6% for employees (see 13.6). Employers with money purchase schemes must make minimum payments into the scheme equal to the combined employer/employee rebates of 2.6% (employee 1.6%, employer 1%). The Revenue top up the payment by age-related rebates up to a maximum combined figure of 10.5% at age 53 or over for 2004/05 (see 13.6).

Employers may run combined salary-related/money purchase schemes (COMBS) (although a single member cannot be in both at the same time).

Many employers, particularly family companies, remain contracted in to the state scheme and provide their own pension scheme in addition. The employee then gets full benefits under the State scheme (and pays full contributions) plus the additional benefits provided by his employer's scheme. Family companies have the same facility as others for establishing schemes, but there are presently tighter rules on the calculation of maximum possible benefits where the employee is a shareholder holding 20% or more of the share capital. If a company is an investment company, the scheme must comply with the rules for automatic approval (see 16.5) if it is to include 20% directors or directors who are members of a family who control more than 50% of the company's shares. None of these restrictions will apply from 6 April 2006.

Employees in a contracted-in scheme are able to contract out of S2P independently while remaining in their employer's scheme, either by making a free-standing additional voluntary contribution (AVC – see 16.9) or through a separate personal pension plan (see 17.12). The rebates in such separate personal pension plans are calculated by applying different rebate percentages to bands of earnings so as to provide low earners with increased benefits (see 13.6). This weighting does not apply to the rebates for contributions to money purchase schemes, including free-standing AVCs, which are flat percentages depending on age as indicated above.

Membership of employers' schemes

16.4   Employees cannot be compelled to be members of their employers' schemes, unless the schemes are non-contributory and provide only death benefits. Employees are able to take out personal pension plans instead (see CHAPTER 17) or rely on the State pension scheme. Pension rights from an existing occupational scheme may be transferred to a personal pension plan, but if an employee remains in the employment, benefits accrued before 6 April 1988 cannot be transferred unless the scheme permits. See 17.5 re the position for mis-sold personal pensions. It is normally possible to transfer back from a personal pension plan to an employer's scheme if the scheme agrees or to a free-standing additional voluntary contribution scheme (FSAVCS, as to which see 16.9). If the employee transfers to a FSAVCS he will retain the right to take up to 25% of the transferred fund as a tax-free lump sum on retirement. The right to take a 25% tax-free lump sum will apply to all schemes from 6 April 2006.

An employee may pay up to £3,600 a year into a personal pension plan even though he is in an occupational scheme, providing he is not a controlling director, and has not been a controlling director in any tax year in the last five years (counting only years from 2000/01 onwards) and he has earned £30,000 or less in at least one of the last five tax years (counting only years from 2000/01 onwards) (see 17.4). These restrictions will not apply from 6 April 2006.

Revenue approval for employers' schemes (TA 1988, ss 590–612)

16.5   The present requirements for schemes to gain Revenue approval will be replaced from 6 April 2006 by simpler provisions for schemes to be registered (see 16.26). In the meantime the following provisions continue to apply. In order to obtain Revenue approval, the employer must contribute to the scheme but the employee need not (see 16.7).

A pension scheme gains automatic Revenue approval if it conforms precisely to the statutory conditions. The Revenue may, however, approve a scheme which does not precisely conform and nearly all schemes receive this discretionary approval under which greater benefits can be paid (but of course at a higher cost in contributions). The Revenue issue Practice Notes on the manner in which they exercise their discretion, and specialist pensions advisers are able to structure schemes so that they will receive the approval of Inland Revenue Savings, Pensions, Share Schemes (IR SPSS). Schemes may be either 'defined benefit' schemes, under which the benefits depend on final salary, or 'defined contribution' (money purchase) schemes, under which the contributions are fixed and the benefits depend on those contributions and on the investment performance of the scheme. Many employers have recently decided that they cannot afford to fund final salary schemes and have either closed them to new entrants or closed them completely. See 17.3 re transferring money purchase schemes to personal pension schemes.

A pension fund's investment in employer-related investments is limited to 5% of the current market value of the fund. Employer-related investments in the form of loans are not permitted at all, subject to various exclusions. The restrictions do not apply to small self-administered schemes — see 16.23.

Taxation advantages of Revenue approval

16.6

(a)   The employer's contributions reduce taxable business profits.

(b)   The employer's contributions are not treated as a taxable employee benefit, nor do they count as the employee's earnings for national insurance contributions.

(c)   An employee's own contributions reduce his earnings for tax purposes (but not for national insurance contributions).

(d)   A tax-free lump sum can be paid to the employee on retirement.

(e)   Provision can be made for a lump sum to be paid on an employee's death in service, which is usually free of taxation (see 16.17).

(f)   The investment income and capital gains of the fund are not taxed (although tax credits on dividends cannot be reclaimed).

Retirement age

16.7   Normal retirement age may be any age between 60 and 75. (For schemes approved before 25 July 1991, the normal retirement age is 55 for women and 60 for men, with an upper limit for both of 70.) Early retirement may presently be allowed from age 50 (or earlier for those in certain occupations, such as athletes) and is also permitted for incapacity. The minimum age will be 55 for all schemes from 6 April 2010 (see 16.26 and 16.31). See 16.9 for the special provisions for taking benefits from additional voluntary contributions.

Maximum contributions

16.8   Maximum contributions depend on an employee's earnings, which means the employment income on which he is chargeable to tax, including benefits but excluding taxable amounts under the rules relating to lump sum termination payments (see CHAPTER 15) and the acquisition and disposal of shares and share options (see CHAPTER 11). Earnings *include* amounts deducted from an employee's pre-tax pay to buy partnership shares under a share incentive plan (see 11.24).

The maximum combined contributions of employer and employee to an off-the-peg money purchase scheme are 17.5% of the employee's earnings from the employment concerned, of which the employer must contribute some and the employee cannot contribute more than 15%. For other money purchase schemes, contributions are normally required to be based on a percentage of salary, but they may be level annual contributions providing they do not produce funding levels above the maximum permitted.

For final salary schemes, there is no specific upper limit on the amount that an employer may contribute, subject only to the requirement that the benefits provided as a result are within the permitted levels and the contributions are not excessive in relation to those benefits. There are, however, regulations to prevent schemes being overfunded (see 16.20), although the reverse is the problem for many schemes in today's investment climate. If an employee joins a scheme late, it is possible to make contributions of several times the employee's current earnings in order to fund the maximum benefits.

Employers' contributions are deductible only in the accounting period in which they are paid, and not when provision is made in the accounts.

Special irregular contributions may be made by the employer in addition to the normal annual contributions. If such irregular contributions are £500,000 or more and they exceed the other contributions paid in the period, they have to be spread forward over a maximum of four years in calculating the employer's taxable profits, rather than all the relief being given in the year of payment. Special contributions to money purchase schemes cannot fund benefits in excess of the maximum justifiable by reference to the employees' service to date.

An employee need not be required to contribute to a scheme, but if he does, his contributions (including any additional or special contributions to obtain additional benefits) must not exceed 15% of his earnings as defined above from the relevant employment (see 16.11). For schemes set up on or after 14 March 1989 and for those joining existing schemes on or after 1 June 1989, there is a limit (referred to as the earnings cap) on the earnings on which contributions may be paid. This limit is usually increased annually in line with increases in the retail prices index (note — not in line with increases in average earnings), and has increased from £99,000 to £102,000 for 2004/05. From 6 April 2006 the earnings cap will no longer apply and an employee may contribute up to 100% of his total earnings from all sources, subject to a tax charge if contributions exceed the annual allowance — set at £215,000 for 2006/07 (see 16.26).

Additional voluntary contributions (AVCs)

16.9   The benefits available to an employee depend on the funds available in the employer's scheme. An employee wishing to increase his potential pension may pay additional voluntary contributions (AVCs) to the employer's scheme, or to a scheme of his choice to which only he makes contributions (free-standing AVCs). Free-standing AVCs are paid net of basic rate tax and the Revenue pays the tax to the pension scheme. Relief at the higher rate of tax, where appropriate, is claimed in the employee's tax return. Some employees were wrongly advised to enter into FSAVCs during the period 28 April 1988 to 15 August 1999 and may receive compensation. By concession, compensation in the form of a lump sum payment is exempt from tax.

Any AVCs paid must not take the employee's total contributions to more than 15% of his earnings from the employment concerned (the earnings being subject to the £102,000 limit where relevant). No part of the additional benefits earned may presently be taken as a tax-free lump sum, except for AVCs to an employer's scheme under a contract to purchase added years which will produce a precise level of pension and lump sum benefit, AVCs that are paid under arrangements made before 8 April 1987 and free-standing AVCs representing funds transferred from a personal pension scheme (see 16.4). Under the new rules applicable from 6 April 2006, lump sum benefits of 25% of the fund will be able to be taken from all AVC schemes, so those considering drawing AVC benefits may wish to delay the withdrawal until that date. Benefits from AVCs may presently be taken at any time between ages 50 and 75, irrespective of when the employee retires. Benefits may also be taken by income drawdown rather than all at once (see 16.15).

Some free-standing AVCs may have to be refunded on retirement or earlier death if the combined benefits from occupational and free-standing schemes are excessive. Tax is deducted from such refunds at 32%. Someone liable at the basic or starting rate is not, however, entitled to a refund of the tax deducted. A higher rate taxpayer is treated as having received a sum net of basic rate tax and is liable to higher rate tax on the gross equivalent. See Example 1. There is no higher rate liability if the repayment arises on death.

Example 1

Surplus AVCs of £1,000 gross paid to higher rate taxpayer. He receives £680 cash, which is treated as gross income of (680 x 100/78) = £872. Tax at 40% is £349, less £192 treated as paid, so that a further £157 is payable, leaving only £523 in the hands of the taxpayer.

A free-standing AVC may be used to enable an employee to contract out of S2P individually, even though his employer's scheme is contracted in. The AVC is boosted by the contracting-out rebate, which is equal to a percentage of earnings between the national insurance lower and upper earnings levels. The percentage depends on the employee's age and for 2004/05 ranges from 2.6% to a maximum 10.5% at age 53 (see 13.6). 1% of the rebate relates to the employer's contribution and the balance to the employee's contribution. With free-standing AVCs, the employee does not get the benefit of an addition for tax relief on the payment by the Revenue in respect of his share of the contracting-out rebate. If an employee wishes to contract out of S2P while remaining in his employer's scheme, it is therefore more sensible to do so by means of a personal pension plan, where the Revenue payment for the employee's rebate is grossed up for tax relief (see 17.11).

Employees earning not more than £30,000 per annum who are not controlling directors may now contribute up to £3,600 to a personal pension plan in addition to being in an occupational scheme. Such plans presently have the advantage over AVCs in that they allow a tax-free lump sum to be taken (see 17.4 and 17.6). From 6 April 2006 there will be no restriction on the number of schemes an employee may join. Tax relief will be available on contributions of up to 100% of total earnings, subject to the overall annual allowance, and a 25% tax-free lump sum may be taken from all schemes, subject to the lifetime allowance (see 16.26 and 16.27).

Sharing pension rights on divorce

16.10   There are provisions to enable a share in pension rights to be transferred on divorce. The provisions cover all pension rights, i.e. under occupational and personal schemes (including stakeholder pensions) and S2P. It is not compulsory for a divorcing couple to share pensions, but all schemes (whenever they were approved) are regarded as including pension sharing provisions. Although the legislation overrides the provisions of existing schemes in this respect, such schemes are expected to change their rules to incorporate pension sharing as and when they make other (non-trivial) amendments. Where the pension is shared, the spouse in a pension scheme will get reduced pension rights (a 'pension debit') and rights will be allocated to the other spouse (a 'pension credit'). The transferred pension credit rights may be held in the same scheme or transferred to another scheme. The benefits available to the ex-spouse will broadly follow those available to the scheme member. The scheme member's pension debit will be deducted from his benefits on retirement, or on leaving pensionable service if earlier. The debit will count in the calculation of maximum benefits, except for a member (other than a controlling director) who earns not more than one quarter of the earnings cap (i.e. £25,500 for 2004/05). This exception will no longer apply from 6 April 2006.

Maximum benefits for employees

Basis for calculating maximum benefits

16.11   For money purchase schemes (see 16.3), there is no restriction on the benefits, since the restriction is made in the amount contributed. For other schemes, maximum benefits are measured in terms of 'final pensionable remuneration'. Final pensionable remuneration is the greater of the remuneration (as defined at 16.8) in any one of the five years before retirement (with averaging for fluctuating payments) or the average of total remuneration for any period of three or more consecutive years ended in the last ten years before normal retirement date.

Unless the 'final remuneration' is that of the twelve months ending with normal retirement date, each year's remuneration included in the calculation may be 'dynamised', i.e. increased in proportion to the increase in the retail prices index for the period from the end of the year up to normal retirement date.

A director who, together with his defined family and trustees, has controlled 20% or more of the employing company's voting rights at any time in the last ten years cannot use a 'best of the last five years' final remuneration calculation and must instead use the three consecutive year averaging of earnings, but the increases from indexing may be taken into account. This averaging provision also applies to employees whose 'final pensionable remuneration' would otherwise exceed £100,000.

For schemes set up on or after 14 March 1989, and those joining existing schemes on or after 1 June 1989, there is an index-linked ceiling, £102,000 from 6 April 2004, on final remuneration taken into account for calculating benefits.

From 6 April 2006 maximum benefits will be limited only by the lifetime allowance (see 16.26 and 16.28).

Maximum pension

16.12   The maximum pension payable under final salary schemes is ⅔rds final remuneration, at the rate of ⅟₃₀th for each year's service up to 20 years (subject to what is said below about pensions from other schemes). For members of an existing scheme at 16 March 1987, the maximum can apply after 10 years' service. Inflation-proofing may be provided for within the funding of the scheme. Pension rights built up from 6 April 1997 under final salary schemes and money purchase schemes (other than from additional voluntary contributions) must be inflation-proofed in line with the retail prices index, up to a maximum of 5% per annum presently (to be reduced to 2.5% when the provisions of the Pensions Bill currently before Parliament come into effect). Part of the pension may be commuted for a lump sum (see 16.14).

Pensions from other schemes

16.13   Benefits at the ⅟₃₀th per year rate (or accelerated rate for members of pre-16 March 1987 schemes) may usually be provided in addition to any pension benefits from previous occupations or self-employed pension plans, providing the combined benefits do not exceed ⅔rds of final remuneration.

Lump sums

16.14   From 6 April 2006 all schemes may contain a provision for a lump sum up to 25% of the fund, subject to an overriding maximum of 25% of the lifetime allowance (see 16.26). Until that date the following provisions apply.

Under the present provisions, part of the maximum available benefits may be commuted to a lump sum. The maximum lump sum is normally 3/80ths final remuneration for each year of service up to 40, giving a maximum of 1½ times final remuneration, but this may be varied or restricted depending on when the employee joined the scheme.

For those joining schemes after 16 March 1987 but before 14 March 1989 (1 June 1989 for schemes in existence at 14 March 1989), there is an overall limit of £150,000.

For schemes set up on or after 14 March 1989 and those who join existing schemes on or after 1 June 1989, the lump sum cannot exceed 1½ times the 'earnings cap' figure giving a maximum lump sum of 1½ × £102,000 = £153,000 for 2004/05. There is also an alternative to the 3/80ths calculation. If it gives a higher figure, the lump sum is calculated as two and a quarter times the amount of the pension before commutation. This enables late entrants to get the maximum lump sum in appropriate circumstances.

In calculating the maximum lump sum payment, lump sums from earlier employments must be taken into account. If dynamised final remuneration is used to calculate the pension (see 16.11), it may also be used to calculate the lump sum. If a lump sum is to be taken, the maximum pension of ⅔rds final remuneration must be reduced.

Deferring pension benefits

16.15 Pension fund trustees may allow a member of a money purchase occupational scheme (but not a salary related scheme) to defer taking an annuity on all or part of the pension benefits until at latest age 75 and to make income withdrawals in the meantime (referred to as income drawdown). Income drawdown may apply to money purchase AVC arrangements, including free-standing AVCs. It is not appropriate for contracted-out money purchase schemes because of social security rules. The provisions broadly follow those outlined at 17.7 for personal pension plans, so that a member is able to take a tax-free lump sum and an income withdrawal of between 35% and 100% of the maximum annuity that could have been taken. If the member dies during the drawdown period, the fund can only be used to pay survivors' benefits (such benefits similarly being able to be taken by income drawdown), unless death occurs during a five-year guarantee period. In that event the balance payable up to the end of the guarantee period (based on what would have been received for 100% withdrawal) may be paid as a lump sum.

Provision for dependants

16.16 Provision for dependants may be made both for death in service and for death after retirement. Inflation increases may be provided for in both cases. A pension to a surviving spouse may continue for the spouse's lifetime, but children's pensions must normally cease when they reach age 18 or cease full-time education.

Death in service

16.17   When an employee dies in service, a lump sum not exceeding four times final remuneration (which is defined in a more generous way than for other benefits) may normally be paid without attracting inheritance tax. In addition, the employee's own contributions to the pension scheme may be repaid with interest. The pension scheme trustees usually have discretion as to who receives the death in service lump sum, but they generally act in accordance with the employee's known wishes. There may be an inheritance tax problem where the death benefit is to be held in trust for the employee's dependants, because if the employee dies in service after the earliest age at which he could have retired, the capital value of the pension he could have taken immediately before death may be taken into account for inheritance tax. The Revenue have, however, stated that this will not apply in genuine cases of deferred retirement, and will only apply where there is evidence that the intention of deferring benefits was to increase the estate of someone else.

Pensions may also be paid to the surviving spouse and/or dependants. The pension paid to any one person cannot exceed ⅔rds of the maximum pension the employee could have received if he had retired on incapacity grounds at the date of death (with potential service up to normal retirement age being taken into account). The total pensions to spouse and dependants cannot exceed the total incapacity pension the employee could have received.

Death after retirement

16.18   Provision may be made for an employee's pension to continue for a set period after retirement despite his earlier death. Separate pensions for spouse and dependants can also be provided, subject to the individual pensions not exceeding ⅔rds of the maximum pension that could have been approved for the employee and the total pensions not exceeding the whole of that maximum. Lump sum benefits are not normally permitted.

Changing employment (TA 1988, s 598)

16.19   When you change employment, then providing you have been in the pension scheme for at least two years, you may either have a preserved pension which will become payable on retirement, or a transfer payment to a new scheme (if the scheme will accept it) or to an insurance company or to a personal pension plan. Where there is a preserved pension under a final salary scheme, it must be increased each year in line with the increase in retail prices (or by a stipulated percentage if less – see 16.12). For contracted-out final salary schemes, the employer must ensure that the preserved pension must at least equal the guaranteed minimum pension under the State scheme for the period to 5 April 1997 and the statutory standard thereafter (see 16.3).

Refunds of contributions are not usually available except for periods of employment of less than two years, but where they are made tax is deducted at the rate of 20%.

Pension scheme surpluses (TA 1988, ss 601–603 and Sch 22)

16.20   There are special rules for pension scheme surpluses. A fund is in surplus where an objective actuarial valuation, in accordance with guidelines specified by the Government Actuary, shows that the projected value of the scheme's assets is more than 5% higher than the projected cost of paying pension benefits to members. The trustees are required to reduce the surplus at least to the 5% level by a combination of:

(i)   increases in pension benefits (within the permissible limits),

(ii)   a reduction or suspension of contributions by the employer and/or employees for up to five years, and

(iii)   a refund to the employer subject to stringent conditions, including, for final salary schemes, the need to first provide for inflation-proofing of pensions. Scheme members may ask the Occupational Pensions Regulatory Authority to look at a decision by trustees to make a refund to the employer, to ensure that the conditions have been met.

If a refund is made, it cannot reduce the surplus to below 5%. The trustees are required to deduct tax at 35% from any refund they make to the employer and pay it over to the Revenue within 14 days. Interest is charged for late payment. In no circumstances can a company obtain a repayment of the tax because of trading losses or other available reliefs.

Misuse of contributions by employer and scheme insolvency

16.21   The risk for an employee of his contributions being misused is significantly reduced by a compensation scheme. Where an occupational pension scheme's funds have been misappropriated and the employer is insolvent, compensation may be payable by the Pensions Compensation Board to cover 90% of the loss or to bring the fund up to 90% funding. The compensation scheme is paid for by a levy on occupational schemes.

Under provisions in the Pensions Bill presently before Parliament, a Pension Protection Fund is to be established to protect the pension rights of employees whose employers have become insolvent without funds having been misappropriated. This is also to be partly funded by a levy on occupational schemes.

Unapproved pension schemes (ITEPA 2003, ss 386–400; FA 1989, s 76)

16.22   It is possible to set up 'top-up' unapproved pension schemes alongside approved schemes (particularly to cover earnings above the 'earnings cap'), or to have just an unapproved scheme. Most unapproved schemes are funded schemes (FURBS). FURBS have both advantages and disadvantages. The employer's contributions are usually deductible in arriving at taxable profits. They are, however, taxed as a benefit on the individual employees (apart from the amount needed to establish and administer the scheme). Class 1 national insurance contributions are payable as well (although the legal basis for the Class 1 charge is not clear-cut). Most employees for whom employers make FURBS contributions would earn more than the upper earnings limit for Class 1 contributions, so that employees' contributions would be at 1%, with employers' contributions at 12.8%. For discretionary benefits schemes where there is no indication of the benefits each employee will receive, employers' payments are apportioned equally between scheme members in calculating the amount chargeable to tax on each individual.

Dividend income within the fund is charged at the Schedule F ordinary rate of 10%, other savings income at 20% and non-savings income at 22%. Capital gains are taxed at the trust rate of 40% (from 6 April 2004), and the fund is subject to the capital gains tax rules for taxpayers other than companies outlined in CHAPTER 4.

Death in service payments are usually free of inheritance tax, providing they are not paid to the employee's estate. The employee can take the benefits on retirement wholly as a tax-free lump sum. He could take a pension instead, but the pension would be taxable, so it would be better to take the cash and then choose whether to invest it or buy a life annuity, part of which would then be free of tax (see 34.7). Providing the employer's contributions are wholly and exclusively for the trade, there is no limit on the amount that can be contributed, and no limit on the tax-free lump sums that can be paid out.

There are anti-avoidance provisions to block the use of offshore funded schemes that pay little or no tax to provide increased tax-free lump sums to employees. For offshore schemes established or varied on or after 1 December 1993, tax will be charged at the employee's marginal rate on any difference between the lump sum received and the employer's and employee's contributions to the fund. See also 16.23 re the anti-avoidance provisions that apply if a small self-administered approved scheme becomes unapproved.

Under the new pension scheme provisions applicable from 6 April 2006, employers will not be restricted in the pensions that may be provided through a registered scheme, but a tax charge will apply when the annual or lifetime limits are exceeded. This will remove the need for unapproved schemes unless the employer wishes to provide benefits of a type that would not be permitted under the new regime. In that event there will be separate rules for 'employer-financed retirement benefit pension schemes'.

Self-administered pension schemes (SI 1991/1614; TA 1988, ss 591C, 591D)

16.23   A self-administered pension scheme is one where the contributions remain under the control of trustees appointed by the company, as distinct from being paid to a pensions provider such as a life assurance company. One of the trustees must be an independent person approved by the Revenue, known as a pensioner trustee. The limits on payment of benefits are the same as for other approved schemes, but the benefits are dependent on the funds within the scheme, so to that extent they are similar to money purchase schemes. While this type of scheme gives maximum flexibility in managing a fund, the pension scheme trustees must invest in the best interests of the members in order to provide their pension benefits. It is possible to have hybrid schemes where the funds are partly managed by a pensions provider. The fund will also usually hold life assurance cover on the scheme members so that its funds are not unacceptably diminished by the premature death of a member.

A small self-administered scheme — SSAS (i.e. one with less than twelve members) is subject to specific regulations that control its format, funding and investment powers. Contributions must normally be based on a percentage of salary rather than level annual contributions. To assist in the purchase of scheme assets, usually property, the trustees may borrow up to an amount equal to 45% of the scheme assets plus three times the normal annual contribution received from the company plus three times the members' contributions in the previous tax year. The borrowing is paid off by future annual contributions from the company, and in the meantime the interest cost is covered by the rent charged by the pension fund to the company.

Loans to pension scheme members or their families are forbidden, but loans to the company itself, or to buy shares in it, or the purchase by the trustees and leaseback of the company's premises, may be permitted (subject to certain restrictions and reporting requirements), providing each member of the scheme is a trustee, and has given written agreement in advance to the proposed investment.

Specialist advice is essential for such schemes.

Anti-avoidance provisions impose a tax charge at 40% on the market value of the scheme's assets if an approved scheme becomes unapproved (for example, by transferring offshore). The charge also applies to schemes with twelve or more members if a controlling director is a member. The tax may be collected from members with controlling interests in the company if both the pension scheme administrator and the company fail to pay.

See 16.24 for the position of self-administered schemes under self-assessment.

From 6 April 2006 there will be no special restrictions for self-administered schemes and they will be dealt with under the integrated scheme for all registered schemes — see 16.26 onwards.

Self-assessment

16.24   Trustees of approved occupational pension schemes, other than insured schemes, are within the scope of self-assessment, and trustees are required to notify the Revenue by 5 October following the tax year if they have a liability to tax and do not receive a return. Self-assessment returns are sent to all self-administered schemes. The same self-assessment rules and time limits apply to trusts as for individuals. Pension fund trustees may complete returns on an accounting year basis and accounts should accompany the return.

Self-assessment does not apply to scheme administrators (although they may be the same people as the trustees), who have separate responsibility for notifying liability on various chargeable events. The Revenue will issue assessments to collect the tax due.

Payment of pensions

16.25   Tax on pensions under occupational schemes is dealt with under the PAYE scheme, with coding adjustments being made where some or all of the available allowances have been used against other income, such as State pensions.

New regime for pension schemes from 6 April 2006 (FA 2004, ss 149–284 and Schs 28–36)

16.26   From 6 April 2006 the existing tax provisions relating to occupational and personal pension schemes will be replaced by a single scheme for all tax-privileged pension savings. The limits on contributions, the earnings cap, the ⅔rds of final remuneration limit for occupational schemes, and the lump sum restrictions will no longer be relevant. Occupational schemes will be able to offer flexible retirement, enabling employees to draw benefits while continuing to work for the employer.

The present complex requirements for obtaining approval for schemes will be replaced by a simpler process of scheme registration. Schemes that were approved schemes before 6 April 2006 will automatically become registered schemes. Individuals will be able to contribute to as many schemes as they wish. There will no longer be any provision for carrying contributions back or forward. Pension providers will be able to invest in all types of investment, including residential property. The minimum pension age will rise from 50 to 55 on 6 April 2010 (earlier retirement still being permitted on ill health grounds).

The new regime will have two key features:

- A single lifetime allowance on the amount of pension savings that can benefit from tax relief, set at £1.5 million for 2006/07, rising to £1.6 million for 2007/08, £1.65 million for 2008/09, £1.75 million for 2009/10 and £1.8 million for 2010/11. If benefits are withdrawn in excess of the allowance, tax will be charged on the excess as indicated at 16.28.

- An annual allowance for maximum 'pension inputs', i.e. contributions paid to money purchase schemes and/or increases in accrued benefits under defined benefit (final salary) schemes. The allowance will start at £215,000 for 2006/07 and increase at £10,000 a year for each of the next four years, reaching £255,000 for 2010/11. If pension inputs exceed the annual allowance, tax will be charged at 40% on the excess.

Both the lifetime and annual allowances will be reviewed every five years.

16.27   There will be no limit on the contributions an individual may make, but tax relief will only be given on contributions up to the higher of 100% of relevant earnings and £3,600 gross (the £3,600 limit applying to a scheme where contributions are paid net of basic rate tax). Tax will be charged at 40% as indicated in 16.26 when total 'pension inputs' exceed the annual allowance.

All schemes (including additional voluntary contribution schemes) will be able to offer a tax-free lump sum of up to 25% of the fund, subject to an overriding maximum of 25% of the lifetime allowance. The different provisions now applicable for retirement annuities and final salary schemes will no longer apply.

16.28   The lifetime allowance is considered at any time when benefits are withdrawn. On the first withdrawal of benefits, if the funds being used exceed the lifetime allowance, the excess will be taxed at 25% to the extent that it is used to buy a pension and at 55% where it is taken as a lump sum. On a later withdrawal, the *percentage* of the lifetime allowance used up when the first withdrawal was made is taken into account to calculate the lifetime limit remaining available at the time of the second withdrawal, and so on for further withdrawals. For example, say benefits were taken in 2006/07 amounting to £750,000, i.e. 50% of the 2006/07 lifetime allowance of £1.5 million. If further benefits were to be taken in 2008/09, the part of the lifetime allowance already used would be 50% of the *2008/09* limit of £1,650,000, i.e. £825,000. This would leave £825,000 of the lifetime allowance still available, rather than (£1,650,000-£750,000 =) £900,000.

16.29   Employers' contributions to registered schemes will continue to be tax deductible, with exceptionally large contributions being spread as now over two to four years.

16.30   As now benefits will have to be taken at latest at age 75. Someone in a money purchase scheme who does not wish to buy an annuity may, however, take his pension by way of income withdrawal from the pension fund (referred to as an 'alternatively secured pension'). The first withdrawal must not exceed 70% of the annuity available to someone aged 75. Subsequent annual withdrawals must not exceed 70% of the annuity available to someone of the relevant age. When the person dies, there is provision for annual payments to be made to dependants. The balance of the fund remaining on the death of the member or last dependant will either be gifted to a charity nominated by the member or dependant, or transferred to another member of the scheme nominated by the member or dependant, or in the absence of such a nomination, selected by the scheme administrator.

16.31   There will be transitional arrangements to protect pre-6 April 2006 pension rights and rights to lump sums. In respect of the lifetime allowance, there will be two options:

- Primary protection applicable to the excess value over £1.5 million. The pension scheme member will have to notify the Revenue that there is such an excess, and each year's lifetime allowance will be enhanced to the extent of that excess value. For example someone with funds totalling £1.8 million at 6 April 2006 will have an excess of £0.3 million, i.e. 20%, and their lifetime allowance for each year would be 120% of the standard amount.

- Enhanced protection available to those who cease membership of approved schemes before 6 April 2006 and do not resume membership of any registered scheme. All benefits becoming payable after 5 April 2006 will normally be exempt from the lifetime allowance charge, providing the member notifies the Revenue that enhanced protection is being claimed and thereafter all the relevant conditions are satisfied.

Employees who presently have the right to draw pensions earlier than the retirement age of 55 which will apply from 2010 may have that right protected, and there will be special protection for employees who are members of pre-6 April 2006 schemes with lower normal retirement ages, such as athletes. The available lifetime allowance for these protected groups will, however, be reduced.

16.32   If schemes do not register under the new provisions, they will not be subject to any restrictions, nor will they be entitled to any tax advantages. Transitional protection will apply to pension rights accrued within non-registered schemes at 6 April 2006.

Tax points

16.33

- Contributions by employers to approved pension schemes are one of the few benefits for employees earning £8,500 per annum or more and directors that are free of both tax and national insurance, so generous funding of a scheme within the permitted limits is particularly beneficial to them.

- A family company can have an approved pension scheme for its controlling directors. The contribution limits are less restrictive than those for personal pension plans and there will be no separate restrictions at all from 6 April 2006.

- A family company may be able to eliminate taxable trading profits by contributions to a pension scheme, and if the contributions exceed those profits, to carry the resulting loss back against the profits of the previous year. Some spreading forward of special contributions may be required — see 16.8.

- An unapproved scheme is presently worth looking at, particularly in view of the flexibility it gives on retirement. The whole benefit can be taken as tax-free cash, which can then be divided between husband and wife so as to make the best future use of available allowances and lower tax rates. There are, however, no longer any national insurance advantages of unapproved schemes. The new integrated scheme from

6 April 2006 gives much more flexibility than the existing rules and some unapproved schemes may decide to become registered schemes at that time.

- If you are young and highly mobile, a personal pension plan may be preferable to an employer's scheme because you will be able to take it with you from job to job, whereas there may be problems transferring a fund from one occupational scheme to another. But there is the disadvantage that when negotiating your employment contract you will have to agree with your employer how much the employer will contribute to your personal plan. The higher administration charges also have to be considered.

- If someone deliberately fails to exercise a right in order for someone else or a discretionary trust to benefit, this counts as a transfer for inheritance tax at the latest time the right could be exercised. The value of the transfer is the value of the rights not taken up. This rule may catch some death in service lump sums under pension schemes if the death benefit was held in trust for the family and the employee had deliberately deferred retirement so that the family could benefit. See 16.17.

- Although employee benefits may be treated as earnings for calculating maximum pension benefits, dividends received from family companies by working directors may not. This needs to be taken into account in considering whether remuneration or dividends should be paid.

- In the case of a small self-administered scheme, borrowing by the trustees could be helpful in boosting funds for, say, the purchase of premises for use by the company. The Revenue will not, however, approve the use of fund monies to acquire premises with private living accommodation or to buy assets from scheme members, nor may the trustees sell assets to scheme members.

- Where a director, before the normal retirement date provided by the scheme, ceases his full-time involvement with a company but continues in a much lesser role, the Revenue may seek to treat any lump sum retirement benefits paid to him as unauthorised benefits at that time on which tax must be charged. The House of Lords has, however, recently confirmed that a director/employee who retired as an employee but remained as a non-executive director was entitled to take his pension entitlement at that time. If the circumstances are not clear-cut it may be advisable to seek clearance from the Revenue before making any payment. From 6 April 2006 this problem will no longer arise, since benefits may be drawn without retiring.

- If sums are transferred from one pension scheme to another and commission is rebated to the customer, the fund's tax approval may be jeopardised, particularly if the rebated commission has been artificially increased.

- Those who retire before State pension age (65 for a man and 60 for a woman) may need to pay voluntary national insurance contributions to ensure that they get a full basic pension under the State scheme (see 13.2). But providing they are registered as unemployed and available for work, contributions will be credited, and unemployed men over 60 are automatically credited with contributions without the need to be registered.

- If you claim contribution-based jobseeker's allowance, it is reduced to the extent that you have an occupational pension (or personal pension) exceeding £50 a week.

17
Personal pension schemes

Background (TA 1988, ss 618–626 (retirement annuities), 630–655 (personal pensions)

17.1   Before 6 April 2001, one of the problems of building up an entitlement to a pension in addition to that provided by the State was that you could not get tax relief on pension contributions if you did not have any earnings. A period when your business was performing badly, or when you were unemployed, or when you were staying at home to look after a family, therefore left a gap in your pension provision. From 6 April 2001 an integrated regime was introduced for personal pension schemes (incorporating stakeholder pension schemes — see 17.2). This integrated regime will itself be replaced from 6 April 2006 by a single regime covering all tax-privileged pension schemes — see 16.26 to 16.32 for details. Under the new provisions the requirement for schemes to have tax approval is replaced by a simpler requirement for them to be registered. This chapter deals with the pre-6 April 2006 provisions, but reference is made to the new provisions where relevant, particularly for planning purposes.

Under both the existing and the 2006 provisions, those without earnings may pay up to £3,600 a year into a pension fund. The existing provisions enable contributions to be paid for up to five years after employment or self-employment ceases based on previous earnings. This facility is not available under the new regime. All personal pension premiums are paid net of basic rate tax, which is particularly beneficial to non-taxpayers (see 17.8).

The personal pension scheme provisions apply only to contracts starting on or after 1 July 1988. Pre-1 July 1988 contracts are called retirement annuity contracts. None of the provisions mentioned above apply to those contracts, and retirement annuity premiums continue to be paid gross. Otherwise, most of the rules are the same as for personal pension schemes, although retirement annuity contracts do not make provision for transfers on change of employment/self-employment. Other differences are indicated later in the chapter.

Personal pension schemes may allow members to direct where their funds are to be invested, subject to various restrictions to ensure that the scheme still meets the conditions necessary for tax approval. There are rules for regulating personal pension schemes and extra restrictions apply to self-invested personal pension schemes (SIPPS — see 17.16). The Government intended the benefits of SIPPS to be opened up to a wider market with the introduction of 'individual pension accounts' (IPAs). IPAs are aimed at providing a clear and simple way for individuals to identify their pension savings and possibly to make changes in the fund investments according to their particular requirements. The funds within an IPA may be invested in unit trusts, open-ended investment companies, investment trusts and government stocks. One of their advantages is that they make it easy to transfer from one pension scheme to another. IPAs have not, however been commercially successful. See 6.8 re exemption from stamp duty reserve tax when investments within IPAs are transferred.

As indicated in CHAPTER 16, from 6 April 2003 members of personal pension schemes (including stakeholder schemes) will receive annual illustrations of what their future pension might be in present-day prices, so that they will have a more realistic idea about the value of their pension funds.

Stakeholder pensions

17.2 The provisions relating to stakeholder pensions are in the Welfare Reform and Pensions Act 1999. A stakeholder pension scheme is one where annual charges cannot exceed 1% of the member's fund, members must be able to transfer into or out of the scheme without charge, minimum contributions cannot exceed £20, and the scheme must be run by trustees or by scheme managers authorised by the Financial Services Authority. Stakeholder pensions are presently regulated by the Occupational Pensions Regulatory Authority (OPRA). OPRA will be replaced by a new body called the Pensions Regulator when the Pensions Bill currently before Parliament comes into effect.

If an employer does not either have an occupational pension scheme that all employees are eligible to join within one year of starting work or provide employees with access to a personal pension scheme satisfying various conditions (in particular that the employer contributes an amount equal to at least 3% of the employee's earnings), he must offer access to a registered stakeholder pension scheme if he has five or more employees, of whom at least one meets the conditions to be provided with such access. Employees need not be provided with access if they have been employed for less than three months, or if they have earned less than the national insurance lower earnings limit (currently £79 a week) for one or more weeks within the last three months, or if they are ineligible to join a stakeholder scheme because they do not normally live in the UK.

Giving access means the employer must choose a stakeholder scheme, consult with employees, formally designate the chosen scheme, give details of the scheme provider to employees and give the scheme provider access to the employees. Employers are not required to contribute to the scheme. If employees joining a scheme so wish, the employer must deduct the contributions from pay and pay them over to the scheme provider by the 19th of each following month. As with all personal pensions, contributions are paid net of basic rate tax (see 17.1). Employers must keep detailed records of payments and must notify any changes to the scheme provider. Employers who fail to comply with the requirements of the stakeholder pension provisions are liable to fines of up to £50,000.

As indicated in 17.1, the tax treatment of stakeholder pension schemes is incorporated within the personal pension scheme provisions, and will be subsumed within the integrated scheme for all tax-privileged pension saving from 6 April 2006.

Converting occupational money purchase schemes to personal pension schemes (SI 2001/118)

17.3   Employers providing occupational money purchase schemes may apply to transfer those schemes to the personal pension regime. Benefits under the personal pension regime then include rights originally arising in the occupational scheme. Such conversions are subject to restrictions in relation to those who are or have in the previous ten years been controlling directors and those aged 45 or over who have in any of the previous six years earned more than the 'earnings cap' in force at the date of the conversion application (currently £102,000). There will be no such restrictions when the new integrated pension scheme comes into effect from 6 April 2006.

Qualifying individuals

17.4   Personal pension contributions within stipulated limits may be paid by someone aged under 75 who is:

A non-earner who is resident and ordinarily resident in the UK; or
Self-employed or in non-pensionable employment; or
An employee in an occupational scheme who is not a controlling director, and has not been a controlling director in any tax year in the last five years (counting only years from 2000/01 onwards), and who has earned £30,000 or less in at least one of the last five tax years (counting only years from 2000/01 onwards). This restriction will not apply under the new provisions from 6 April 2006.

Anyone within the above categories may make a contribution of up to £3,600 gross, £2,808 net, a year (referred to as the earnings threshold). The £3,600 limit includes any contributions by the employer if relevant. Higher contributions may be paid by those with 'relevant earnings' (see 17.8). Provision is also made for those who have ceased work or are temporarily out of work to make contributions in the next five years based on their previous earnings (see 17.9). This facility will not be available under the new provisions from 6 April 2006. The pension contributions are accumulated in a fund free of income tax and capital gains tax (although tax credits on dividends cannot be reclaimed).

Pension scheme administrators must ensure that applicants are eligible to join the scheme, and where necessary they must obtain evidence of earnings, or of eligibility to pay a personal pension premium at the same time as being in an occupational scheme (concurrency declaration). Legal guardians must complete application forms for those under 18.

Retirement annuity premiums have to be paid to an insurance company, but personal pension contributions can be paid to a life assurance company, friendly society, bank, building society, unit trust, or personal pension scheme trust established by employers and others. In both cases, the retirement benefits themselves are purchased from an authorised insurance company with the fund monies at retirement, and the 'best buy' available at that time can be selected.

See 16.4 re transferring personal pension plan funds on entering pensionable employment.

Mis-sold personal pensions (FA 1996, s 148)

17.5   It will not normally be beneficial for those eligible to be in an occupational scheme to which both they and their employer contribute to opt out of the employer's scheme and take out a personal pension plan funded by their own contributions. A review by the Securities and Investments Board found, however, that many people were wrongly advised to do so. Where as a result of the review someone receives compensation for that wrong advice, the compensation is exempt from tax. Furthermore, employees who rejoin their employers' schemes may be reinstated according to the tax rules that originally applied to them (so that, for example, they will not be subject to the earnings cap (currently £102,000) if their earlier membership started before 1 June 1989). They may also be allowed to pay contributions in excess of the normal 15% limit, although they will not get tax relief on the excess. Loss of tax relief may be avoided by paying back-contributions by instalments so that the limit is not exceeded.

Permissible benefits

17.6   The retirement benefits must commence not later than age 75 nor earlier than age 50 at present (60 for retirement annuity schemes), except in cases of ill health or where the occupation is one in which earlier retirement is customary, for example entertainers and athletes, for whom the Revenue may approve a scheme with an earlier retirement date. The minimum pension age is to be increased to 55 from 6 April 2006 (see 16.26 and 16.31).

At retirement the whole fund may be used to buy an annuity, which will be taxed as income, or a tax-free lump sum may be taken, with the balance used to buy an annuity. For personal pension plans, the lump sum may not exceed 25% of the fund (excluding that part of the fund consisting of 'protected rights' — see 17.11). For retirement annuity contracts, the maximum lump sum is presently three times the remaining annual pension, subject to an upper limit of £150,000 for contracts made between 17 March 1987 and 30 June 1988 inclusive. All schemes will be subject to the 25% limit from 6 April 2006, unless the transitional provisions apply (see 16.26 and 16.31).

Rather than taking all the benefits at one time, the taxpayer may defer taking an annuity, and make income withdrawals in the meantime, or buy an annuity with part of the fund and take income withdrawals from the remainder, or take benefits from part of the fund and leave the remainder invested until, at latest, age 75 (see 17.7).

It is possible for payment of the pension to be guaranteed for up to ten years even if the taxpayer dies within that time. Should death occur before retirement, the defined value of the fund may be refunded. The refund may be to the personal representatives or to any other person. Alternatively, the contract may provide for the death benefits to be held in trust, with the monies payable at the trustees' discretion. If paid to the personal representatives, the sum refunded will form part of the estate for inheritance tax purposes, but tax will not be payable to the extent that the estate is left to the surviving spouse. Inheritance tax will also usually be avoided where the proceeds are held in trust, but where someone works on past the earliest pension age under the policy with the deliberate intention of benefiting someone else, a charge to inheritance tax may arise as with an occupational scheme (see 16.17).

Deferring personal pension annuity purchase (income drawdown) and phased vesting (TA 1988, ss 634A, 638ZA)

17.7   Many people have suffered when they retired through having to use their pension fund to buy an annuity at a time when annuity rates were low, and this is still a major problem.

For schemes approved or amended after 1 May 1995, those with personal pension contracts may defer buying an annuity until, at latest, age 75. They can still take a tax-free lump sum at retirement date, and they may make taxable income withdrawals from the fund during the deferral period (known as income drawdown) up to a maximum that is broadly equivalent to the annuity they could have taken (with a minimum income withdrawal of 35% of the maximum). The fund will continue to build up tax-free, but further contributions may not be made once any benefits (including income withdrawals) have been taken. (Exceptionally, S2P contracting-out rebates may continue to be paid to an employee's personal pension plan — see 17.11 — for example if he retires below State pension age.) Although income drawdown may appear attractive, annuity rates might not improve, and you need to leave sufficient of the fund invested to retain a wide spread of investments to reduce risk. Many advisers consider that income drawdown is not suitable for those with pension funds of less than £250,000. (See 16.30 for a new option available from 6 April 2006 to take a form of income withdrawal referred to as an 'alternatively secured pension' from age 75.)

If the pension scheme member dies during the deferral period, a surviving spouse or dependant may take the fund in cash (subject to a tax charge of 35%), or buy an annuity immediately, or continue making income withdrawals and buy the annuity at latest when that person reaches age 75 (or when the pension scheme member would have reached age 75 if earlier). If the survivor dies before buying the annuity, the fund may be paid in cash to his or her heirs (net of tax at 35%). To the extent that a lump sum from the fund forms part of the estate of the deceased, inheritance tax may be payable unless the estate is below the nil threshold or is exempt because of being left to the surviving spouse.

These provisions only apply to those with personal pension contracts. Those with retirement annuity contracts are not able to defer taking the annuity unless they switch into a personal pension contract. A switch might presently result in a restriction on the lump sum taken at retirement (see 17.6) and might involve administration charges.

Another alternative is 'phased vesting' which enables the pension member to take a proportion of the fund to provide retirement benefits as and when he wishes, leaving the remainder invested until at latest age 75. On each such occasion the member may take a tax-free lump sum and either an annuity or income withdrawal payments.

Allowable contributions

17.8   As indicated in 17.4, personal pension contributions of up to £3,600 a year may be paid by non-earners, by the self-employed and those in non-pensionable employment, and by certain employees who are in an occupational scheme in respect of their earnings. Since basic rate relief is deducted and retained when paying the contribution, this means that a non-earner can establish a pension fund of £3,600 by making a payment of £2,808 (i.e. £3,600 less 22%). Anyone over the personal pension retirement age of 50 could in fact take benefits immediately, either by way of an annuity based on £3,600, or by way of a lump sum of £900 (see 17.6), reducing the net outlay to £1,908, and an annuity based on £2,700.

Higher contributions may be paid according to the individual's 'net relevant earnings'. Where personal pension contributions exceed the £3,600 earnings threshold, evidence of the relevant earnings must be supplied to the scheme administrator within thirty days from the payment date. For a self-employed person, net relevant earnings means his taxable profits, after deducting capital allowances, losses set against the profits and any excess of business charges (such as patent royalties paid) over general investment income. If a loss is set against income other than relevant earnings (see CHAPTER 25), later relevant earnings must be reduced by the amount of the loss. For an employee, net relevant earnings are those from an employment not carrying any pension rights. The earnings figure includes the cash equivalent of benefits, but is after deducting expenses allowable against those earnings. In line with occupational schemes, an employee's relevant earnings under personal pension plans exclude amounts treated as earnings under the rules relating to shares and share options and lump sum termination payments but *include* amounts deducted from an employee's pre-tax pay to buy partnership shares under a share incentive plan (see 11.24). An overall limit applies to net relevant earnings under personal pension plans (but not retirement annuity contracts), the limit being £99,000 for 2003/04 and £102,000 for 2004/05, which is the same as the limit for occupational pensions. This figure is usually increased annually in line with inflation. From 6 April 2006 contributions may be made up to 100% of total earnings, subject only to the annual allowance (see 16.26).

A scheme may provide for personal pension contributions to be made not only in cash but by way of transfer of shares received under approved SAYE share option schemes, share incentive plans and approved profit sharing schemes (as to which see CHAPTER 11). Such transfers must be made within 90 days of exercising the SAYE option or of shares being appropriated to the employee, and will be treated as contributions equal to the market value of the shares at the date of the transfer to the scheme. Tax relief will then be given on the contributions in the same way as for cash contributions.

For retirement annuity contracts, the maximum contributions allowed as a deduction from relevant earnings in any one tax year for someone aged 50 or under are 17½% of the net relevant earnings, plus any unused relief for the previous six years. Unused relief is the amount that could have been paid in an earlier year by reference to the net relevant earnings of that year, less what was actually paid in respect of that year's earnings. The percentage limit is increased for taxpayers over 51 at the beginning of the tax year, as follows:

Age at beginning of tax year	%
51 to 55	20
56 to 60	22½
61 and over	27½

Similar provisions apply for personal pension contributions, but with higher limits starting at age 36 as follows:

Age at beginning of tax year	%
36 to 45	20
46 to 50	25
51 to 55	30
56 to 60	35
61 and over	40

For personal pension contributions, however, it is not possible to utilise unused personal pension relief from the previous six years. Contributions may, however, be based on the relevant earnings of an earlier year (see 17.9).

As indicated above, individuals will be able to make contributions up to 100% of their earnings from 6 April 2006, subject only to the annual allowance (see 16.26). There will be no provisions for carrying relief back or forward.

Where someone has both personal pension and retirement annuity contracts (PPCs and RAPs), the PPC limits are reduced by any RAPs paid. For someone aged 53, for example, with net relevant earnings of £20,000, the maximum RAPs would be 20%, i.e. £4,000, and if premiums of that amount were paid, the amount available for PPCs would be reduced from £6,000 (i.e. 30% of £20,000) to £2,000.

Employees making personal pension plan arrangements may elect to con-tract out of the State Second Pension (S2P — previously the State Earnings Related Pension Scheme — SERPS), still, however, contributing for a basic retirement pension (see 17.11). It is also possible for an employee in a contracted-in pension scheme to remain in the scheme but contract out of S2P independently through a personal pension plan. See 17.12.

An employer can contribute to the personal pension scheme of an employee, and many employers offer group personal pension schemes rather than suffer the costs of running an occupational scheme. This number will probably increase now that employers with money purchase schemes have the option of switching to the personal pension scheme regime (see 17.3). The maximum contribution levels (17.5% or higher of earnings up to the £102,000 limit) cover the combined employee/employer contributions (but not those by the Revenue — see 17.11). Employers' contributions cannot be backdated to earlier years (see 17.10). Where, however, personal pension contributions are based on the earnings of an earlier year (see 17.9), the earlier year's figure would apply both to employers' and employees' contributions. As indicated in 10.5, neither employers' nor employees' national insurance contributions are payable on personal pension contributions paid by employers. This means that if the employee agreed to a salary sacrifice, and the employer made a pension contribution boosted by the employer's national insurance saving, the pension contribution would be higher than would result from an employee payment (see Example 1). Care must be taken with salary sacrifice arrangements to ensure that they are effective. The potential pay must be given up before being received and the legal outcome must be that the employee is entitled to lower cash remuneration and a benefit. Other effects of reducing the employee's earnings must not be ignored (in particular the effect on state pension entitlement under S2P — see 13.3).

Example 1

If a basic rate taxpayer earning £25,000 a year makes a personal pension contribution of £1,000 gross, £780 net in 2004/05, the amount of salary required to cover the contribution would be:

		£
Salary		1,164
Tax @ 22%	256	
NI @ 11%	128	384
Net Salary to cover PPC		780

If he made a salary sacrifice arrangement and agreed to receive a salary of (25,000 – 1,164 =) £23,836 plus a non-taxable benefit in the form of a pension contribution paid by his employer, the employer could contribute £1,164 + (12.8% x £1,164 =) £149 = £1,313. The employee's net pay would be £780 lower, leaving him in the same position he was before after paying the pension contribution, but the gross pension contribution would increase by £313.

Basing personal pension contributions on relevant earnings of an earlier year (TA 1988, ss 646B–646D)

17.9   It is possible (before 6 April 2006) to pay personal pension contributions based on the relevant earnings of one of the previous five tax years (known as the basis year) instead of the current tax year, providing evidence of the earnings is supplied to the scheme administrator not later than 30 days after paying a contribution based on those earlier earnings. For example, for 2004/05 an election could be made for the basis year to be any year from 1999/2000 to 2003/04. If 1999/2000 were chosen, another basis year would have to be chosen for 2005/06 unless the 2005/06 earnings themselves were to be used. If 2002/03 were chosen as the basis year for 2004/05 it would also be the basis year for 2005/06, so that maximum contributions for both years would be based on the 2002/03 earnings (although the allowable percentage would depend on the member's age in the current tax year). It is possible to change the election at any time by nominating a later basis year. The earnings cap figure of the *current* year is applied in considering whether earnings of the selected basis year are to be restricted in calculating the maximum contributions payable.

Where someone has relevant earnings in one tax year but not in the following year (the break year), for example because he is between jobs, or has retired, or has not drawn remuneration from his company, contributions may be paid for the five tax years starting with the break year based on the net relevant earnings of one of the six tax years before the break year unless, before the end of the five years, he joins an occupational scheme or again has relevant earnings. Since a person without relevant earnings may in any event pay contributions up to £3,600 a year, this is only relevant for those who want to pay contributions above that level. This option will not be available from 6 April 2006.

Backdating contributions to earlier years (TA 1988, ss 619(4), 641A)

17.10   A claim may be made (for years up to 2005/06) for a retirement annuity premium paid in one tax year to be treated as a payment for the previous tax year (or, if there were no net relevant earnings in the previous year, as a payment relating to the second year back). Backdating elections in respect of retirement annuity premiums normally have to be made by 31 January following the tax year in which the premium was paid, for example by 31 January 2006 in order to carry back a payment made in 2004/05 to 2003/04. Although premiums may no longer be carried back to an earlier year under the new pension provisions applicable from 6 April 2006, those with retirement annuity contracts may still elect before 31 January 2007 to carry back a retirement annuity premium paid in 2005/06 to 2004/05. Carryback claims may be made either in the tax return or separately.

More restrictive provisions apply for personal pension contributions. A contribution paid on or before 31 January in any tax year up to 2005/06 may be carried back to the previous year if an election is made at or before the time of payment. The election is irrevocable. As indicated in 17.8, where an employer contributes to an employee's personal pension scheme, the employer's contribution cannot be carried back.

The opportunity to carry back premiums to an earlier year gives a breathing space to establish what the maximum allowable contribution is for a particular year, and also to provide the cash resources to make the payment. Under self-assessment, however, carrying back has a serious disadvantage in relation to half-yearly payments on account (see below). Nevertheless, the carry-back provisions are useful, say where relief would be at a higher tax rate, or where relief would otherwise be wasted, or where you would otherwise have exceeded the maximum contributions for the year of payment. Such excess contributions cannot be carried forward. Indeed, any excess personal pension contributions (but not excess retirement annuity contributions) have to be refunded to the payer. If contributions have been paid by both employee and employer, the employee's contributions are refunded first.

The tax saving resulting from backdating is worked out by reference to the tax position of the earlier year, but the legislation provides that the claim is treated as relating to the later year and is *given effect in that year*.

The Revenue have issued guidance on their interpretation of what is meant by giving effect to carryback claims in the tax year in which the payment is made. The main points are as follows. Effect will not be given to the claim until the tax return for the earlier year has been submitted. There will be no *repayment* of tax unless the tax for the earlier year has been paid *in full* (i.e. both the payments on account and any balancing payment for the year). If any tax for the year in which the claim is made is due at the date of the claim (or will become due within 35 days from the date the claim is processed), the relief will be given by set-off against that tax. Only where there are no outstanding liabilities will a repayment be made. Repayment supplement is not payable unless tax is repaid after the 31 January following the *later* year, i.e. 31 January 2006 in Example 2. The most unacceptable feature of these rules is that the payment does not affect the *calculation* of payments on account for any year (although relief may be obtained by set-off against such payments). See Example 2.

Example 2

A taxpayer's payments on account for 2003/04 of £8,000 each are paid on the due dates of 31 January 2004 and 31 July 2004. The total tax due for the year before relief for pension premiums is £18,000. A pension premium of £10,000 entitling the payer to 40% relief, i.e. £4,000, is paid on 5 July 2004. If the premium is carried back to 2003/04, and relief is claimed before the 2003/04 tax return is sent in, the 2003/04 payment on account of £8,000 due 31 July must still be made (since the claim will not be put into effect before the return is filed). If the return is sent in, say, in September 2004, relief will be given by refunding £2,000 of the total amount paid on account (£16,000) and discharging the balancing payment. The pension premium does not affect payments on account for 2004/05, which will therefore be £9,000 each (half of £18,000), even though the net tax paid for 2003/04 was only £14,000.

If the claim related to a retirement annuity premium and it was delayed, say, until 10 July 2005, the relief would be given by set-off against the 2004/05 payment on account of £9,000 due on 31 July 2005,

---

but it would not be regarded as reducing the 2004/05 tax and would not therefore affect payments on account for 2005/06.

If carry-back relief is not claimed, the premium will reduce the 2004/05 tax. Say the total tax for 2004/05 before relief is £20,000, so that the relief will reduce it to £16,000. If, say, the final tax figure was known by June 2005, a claim could be made to reduce the payments on account to £8,000 each, so that £1,000 of the 31 January 2005 payment of £9,000 would be refunded, with interest from the date it was paid, the 31 July payment would be reduced to £8,000 and there would be no balancing payment. The 2005/06 payments on account would then be £8,000 each.

Contracting out of the State Second Pension (S2P) by employees not in an employer's scheme (SI 2001/1354; SI 2004/263)

17.11   Employees not in an occupational scheme may contract out of S2P by taking out a personal pension plan that satisfies conditions laid down in the legislation, referred to as an appropriate personal pension plan (APP) or appropriate personal pension stakeholder pension (APPSHP). The premium under the plan is paid net of basic rate tax and the Revenue pay the tax into the plan. The employee and his employer continue to pay full national insurance contributions, but the Revenue pay into the plan the contracting-out rebate. The calculation of age-related contracting-out rebates for appropriate personal pension plans (but not money purchase plans or salary related schemes) is made by applying different percentages to earnings in up to three bands (see 13.6 for further details). Since personal pension plans qualify for tax relief whereas national insurance contributions do not, the Revenue also pay in tax relief on the gross equivalent of the employee's share of the rebate. The contracting-out rebate and the tax relief on the rebate are known as 'minimum contributions'. The pension fund relating to the minimum contributions is known as 'protected rights'. See Example 3.

Example 3

Employee aged 33 in non-pensionable employment who earns £27,040 a year (£520 a week) contracts out of S2P by contributing £25 a week to an appropriate personal pension plan.

Weekly earnings on which contracting-out rebate is paid for 2004/05 are £520 less £79 lower earnings level, i.e. £441*, and the overall rate of rebate for 2004/05 at age 33 for someone earning £26,600 or more is 5%, of which the employee's share is 4%.

Weekly investment in plan in 2004/05 is as follows:

	£
Employee pays £25 less 22% tax (£5.50)	19.50
Revenue pays in the tax relief of	5.50
plus:	
Contracting-out rebate	
Employer's contribution 1% × £441*	4.41
Employee's contribution 4% × £441*	17.64
Tax relief on gross equivalent of employee's contribution	4.97
(£17.64 × 100/78 @ 22%)	
	£52.02

Had the employee earned between £4,108 and £11,600 a year the employer/employee rebate percentage would have been 10%, and it would have been calculated as if the annual earnings were exactly £11,600.

Had the employee earned between £11,600 and £26,600 a year, the overall rebate would have been somewhere between 10% and 5%, getting closer to 5% as the earnings approached £26,600.

*The contracting-out rebate is based on earnings between £79 and the weekly pay, even though national insurance contributions are payable only on earnings above £91 a week.

The protected rights part of the pension funded by the Revenue contracting-out payment can only be paid from State pension age. It cannot normally be commuted for a lump sum and it must include provision for index-linking and for widows'/widowers' pensions.

Contracting out of S2P and remaining in an employer's scheme

17.12   An employee who is in an occupational scheme that is contracted in to S2P may remain in the employer's scheme but opt out of S2P by means of an individual personal pension plan. The way that this is done is that the employee and employer continue to pay full national insurance contributions, and the payment into the personal pension plan is made solely by the Revenue, who contribute the same amount as indicated in Example 3 for employees not in a pension scheme, i.e. the age-related rebate percentage by reference to the employee's earnings between the lower and upper earnings levels plus tax relief on the employee's share of the contracting-out rebate.

Funding the contributions

17.13   Two often expressed objections to personal pension provision are, first, the cost and, second, the fact that you cannot use the fund until retirement. (From 6 April 2006 you will not have to retire to access your pension fund but you will still have to be of minimum retirement age.) Although it is not possible for a lender to take a charge on a personal pension fund, several pension providers have arrangements under which a lender will make an appropriate loan to a taxpayer with a sufficiently large accumulated fund, or who is paying regular contributions to a fund, usually in the latter case based on a multiple of regular contributions and the age of the taxpayer. The terms of the loan are usually that interest is payable year by year but capital repayments are taken from the eventual tax-free lump sum on retirement. Whether security for the borrowing is required often depends upon the trade or profession carried on by the taxpayer.

The loan could itself be used to fund contributions to the scheme, so that a significant part of the maximum allowable contribution might be funded from a loan made at the same time from the fund itself.

Tax relief is not available on the interest paid to the lender unless the borrowing is for a qualifying purpose, such as the relief for the acquisition of a business property or a partnership share (see CHAPTER 2). There will thus not be any relief for interest paid on a loan used to pay pension scheme contributions.

Term assurance and pensions for dependants (TA 1988, ss 621, 636, 637)

17.14   The refund of the defined value of the fund on death prior to retirement (see 17.6) is in itself a form of lump sum provision for dependants.

To cover the possibility that death might occur before a reasonable sum has been built up, the taxpayer may also pay a premium to provide a lump sum on death before age 75. The policy may be written in trust, which has the advantage of making the sum quickly available instead of waiting for probate, and also avoids the proceeds swelling the estate for inheritance tax. Relief for premiums paid is given at the payer's top tax rate, thus giving opportunity for life cover with tax relief, even though tax relief is not now available on ordinary life assurance policies taken out after 13 March 1984.

Alternatively or additionally, a premium may be paid to provide a pension for dependants.

The allowable premiums for the term assurance (and/or dependants' pensions for retirement annuity schemes) were previously subject to a limit of

5% of net relevant earnings, the 5% being part of, and not additional to, the 17½% (or higher because of age) limit (see 17.8). For term assurance contracts taken out after 5 April 2001 there is a much lower limit equal to 10% of the total contributions (including employers' contributions where relevant) paid otherwise than for life insurance (subject to the overall 17½% or higher limits). It is therefore no longer possible to take out a pension policy providing only life cover.

Way in which relief is given

17.15   As indicated in 17.1, retirement annuity premiums are paid gross and relief is given to the self-employed by deduction in the payer's self-assessment and to employees by coding adjustment. The premiums are deducted from earnings in calculating the tax liability.

Personal pension contributions are paid net of basic rate tax, which the pension provider reclaims from the Revenue. This enables non-taxpayers and taxpayers paying the starting or lower rate of tax to get basic rate tax relief on their payments. Higher rate relief must be claimed and will be given in the taxpayer's self-assessment or by coding adjustment for employees. The extra higher rate relief is given by extending the basic rate limit in the tax computation by the gross amount of the contribution. Strictly the extra higher rate relief only applies where *income* attracts higher rate tax, but by Revenue concession A101 it also applies in relation to capital gains (gains being charged at income tax rates — see 4.2). Where an employee contracts out of S2P, however, there is no higher rate relief on the part of the Revenue contribution that relates to the employee's contracting-out rebate. Example 4 shows the difference in treatment for personal pension contributions and retirement annuity premiums.

Example 4

Self-employed taxpayer entitled only to the single personal allowance has income in 2004/05 comprising earnings of £33,000 and interest of £5,000 gross. He paid a pension premium, the gross amount of which was £1,000. The treatment of the premium if it is either a retirement annuity premium or a personal pension contribution is as follows:

	Retirement annuity premium			Personal pension contri- bution		
	£			£		
Earnings	33,000			33,000		
Less: Retirement annuity premium	(1,000)					
	32,000					
Savings income	5,000			5,000		
	37,000			38,000		
Personal allowance	(4,745)			(4,745)		
Taxable income	32,255			33,255		
Tax thereon:						
Non-savings income	2,020	@ 10%	202	2,020	@ 10%	202
	25,235	@ 22%	5,552	26,235	@ 22%	5,772
	27,255			28,255		
Savings income (part)	4,145	@ 20%	829	4,145	@ 20%	829
	31,400			32,400		
(balance)	855	@ 40%	342	855	@ 40%	342
	32,255			33,255		
						7,145
Less: Basic rate tax retained 1,000 @ 22%						(220)
			6,925			6,925

*Basic rate limit increased by personal pension contribution.

Where personal pension contributions are made in the form of shares (see 17.8), the market value of the shares is treated as an amount net of basic rate tax, so that with basic rate tax at 22%, shares to the value of £780 would be treated as a gross contribution of £1,000.

See 17.10 for the treatment of premiums carried back to the previous year. Where a personal pension premium is carried back, the rate of tax deducted from the premium should be the basic rate of the *carry-back* year, which may be different from that of the year of payment.

Self-invested personal pension schemes and approval of pension schemes generally (TA 1988, ss 638A, 650, 650A, 651A, 653A, 658A; SI 2000/2316; SI 2001/117)

17.16   Self-invested personal pension schemes (SIPPS) are schemes which allow members to direct where their funds are to be invested. There are regulations affecting all personal pension schemes requiring them to provide certain information to the Revenue and to allow inspection of records. The regulations include specific provisions in relation to SIPPS, which require them to provide details of investments and borrowing transactions. All personal pension schemes must keep relevant documents and records for six years from the end of the relevant scheme year, and there is a penalty of up to £3,000 for failure to comply. There are also regulations relating to personal pension scheme investments which permit SIPPS to invest in a wide range of assets, including equities, collective investments and commercial property. There are, however, restrictions in relation to investments involving the member of the SIPPS and to the scheme's borrowing powers.

The Revenue have power to withdraw approval either from a scheme or from an individual member's arrangements under the scheme if the conditions for approval cease to be met. If approval is withdrawn from an individual member's personal pension arrangements tax will be charged at 40% on the value of the member's fund.

From 6 April 2006 the same registration provisions will apply to all pension schemes, and all schemes will be subject to the same criteria in relation to investments and borrowing powers.

Payment of pensions (TA 1988, s 648A)

17.17   Retirement annuities are normally paid net of basic rate tax, and any under- or overpayment of tax must be dealt with in the taxpayer's self-assessment (or, for repayments, by a separate repayment claim — see 2.26). Non-taxpayers may ask their pension provider for form R89 which will enable payments to be made gross. Under the new pension regime from 6 April 2006 annuities under a retirement annuity contract will continue to be paid net of basic rate tax unless the Treasury issue an order to the contrary.

Annuities under a personal pension plan are taxed through the PAYE scheme in the same way as occupational pensions, with tax being charged at the appropriate rate and coding adjustments being made where some or all of the available allowances have been used against other income, such as State pensions.

Late assessments and investigation settlements (TA 1988, s 625; Revenue Statement of Practice SP 9/91)

17.18   Assessments are sometimes made more than six years after the tax year to which they relate, usually owing to the fraudulent or negligent conduct of the taxpayer (see CHAPTER 9). Where an assessment becomes final and conclusive more than six years after the tax year to which it relates, a taxpayer may presently utilise any unused relief created by the assessment to cover a retirement annuity premium in excess of the 17½% (or higher because of age) limit (see 17.8) for the year of payment, provided that he both makes the additional contribution and makes an election within six months after the assessment becomes final and conclusive. Relief is then given against the earnings of the year of payment. (Only the contribution related to the unused relief need be made within the six-month period. The contribution under the normal rules could presently be made in the following year and carried back.) Strictly, this relief is only available where assessments are *formally* determined, but the Revenue will allow it where an investigation settlement is concluded in the more usual way by their acceptance of an offer in settlement of tax, interest and penalties.

The above provisions are not relevant for personal pension contributions because unused personal pension relief cannot be carried forward. They will not be relevant for retirement annuities either from 6 April 2006 when the new single regime for pensions comes into force.

Tax points

17.19

- Contributions to personal pension plans attract tax relief at your top rate making them a highly tax-efficient means of providing for the future. The available pension at retirement will, however, be determined by the investment performance of the funds into which the pension contributions are paid.

- You may receive commission on your personal pension contributions. Providing this is under a separate contract from the pension contract, it will not jeopardise the tax approval of the fund. Your pension contribution will be treated as the net amount paid if you deduct the commission from the contribution or you pay a discounted premium. If you pay the contribution gross and receive the commission separately, tax relief will be given on the gross amount.

- Consider tax-efficient term assurance within the personal pension scheme rules as an alternative to life assurance. But remember that a term assurance can only provide a lump sum on death before age 75, not on surviving to a certain age as with an endowment policy.

- Also bear in mind that life assurance contracts taken out before 14 March 1984 will probably still entitle you to 12½% income tax relief on the premium payments, so if you are considering replacing existing life cover, it may be more appropriate to surrender later policies.

- An inheritance or unexpected windfall may be used to fund an exceptional pension contribution supported by current or previous earnings and, for retirement annuity contributions, unused past relief.

- Most people are entitled to pay a personal pension contribution of up to £3,600 a year whether or not they have any earnings. You will retain basic rate tax relief out of your contribution whether or not you are a taxpayer. If contributions are paid for your children (of whatever age), you need to remember that they cannot take benefits until at earliest age 50 (to be raised to 55 from 6 April 2010). Retired people under 75 can similarly get the tax saving from paying net contributions and can take the benefits immediately — but although this buys you an annuity at a low cost you need to live long enough to reap the benefit.

- Self-assessment contains some harsh and unreasonable rules about carrying back pension premiums. Carry-back may still be appropriate in some circumstances, for example where tax relief would be at a higher rate, or where you want to avoid wasting retirement annuity relief brought forward. Carry-back will not be possible from 2006/07 onwards.

- There are special rules for doctors and dentists, who, despite having to pay pension contributions under the National Health Service Acts, can also make personal pension contributions along the lines of this chapter, subject to certain modifications because of the NHS pension contributions. The calculation rules are complicated and should be considered very carefully in deciding to what extent relief is available.

- Some building societies and other lenders will allow the borrower to pay only interest during the period of a loan, with an undertaking that the loan itself will be repaid from the tax-free lump sum from a pension fund on retirement.

- You can delay buying an annuity with your personal pension fund when you retire until at latest age 75, which may be useful since annuity rates are presently at a very low level. You are, of course, taking the risk that the annuity rates may have fallen even further at the time when you want to buy the annuity. You can hedge your bets by keeping part of your fund invested, either by income drawdown or by phased vesting, but you need to have a substantial fund for this to be appropriate.

- You may presently go on paying personal pension contributions for five years after you cease work if you want to, based on your pre-retirement earnings, but this will not apply from 2006/07 onwards.

After that time you can pay a personal pension contribution of up to £3,600 a year so long as you are under 75.

- If a person works on after the earliest permitted retirement age under a pension contract and dies before drawing the pension, there is a possibility that the value of the pension rights immediately before his death may be taken into account as part of his estate for inheritance tax — on the same grounds as those indicated at 16.33 for employees in occupational schemes.

- Trading losses set off against other income (see CHAPTER 25) must even so be taken into account by reducing the next available profits from the trade in order to establish earnings for the purpose of calculating maximum pension contribution and any unused retirement annuity relief.

- If you retire early and register as unemployed, contribution-based jobseeker's allowance is reduced to the extent that a personal pension or occupational pension exceeds £50 a week.

18
Sole trader, partnership or company?

Non-tax considerations

18.1   The alternatives when you start in business or need to consider a change in how you operate are to become a sole trader, to form a partnership with others or to form a limited liability company. A sole trader is liable for the debts of the business to the full extent of his personal assets, and can in the extreme be made bankrupt. The same applies to partners, unless they have formed a limited liability partnership, which enables them to restrict liability to the assets of the business (see 23.23). A company shareholder's liability is normally limited to the amount, if any, unpaid on his shares. Protection of private assets is usually one of the main reasons for trading through a company (and this is also the reason for forming limited liability partnerships). However, lenders, landlords and sometimes suppliers often require directors to give a personal guarantee in respect of the company's obligation, which reduces significantly the benefit of limited liability. There are also major compliance requirements for a company under the Companies Acts, including the need to produce accounts, which must be sent promptly to the Companies Registry (see 9.32). Companies whose turnover is £5.6 million or less need not, however, have their accounts audited unless their gross assets exceed £2.8 million. Limited liability partnerships have similar reporting obligations to companies.

The general commercial and family considerations must be weighed alongside the comparative tax positions when choosing what form the business is to take.

Comparative income tax and national insurance position for the unincorporated trader and the company director

18.2   There are so many variables to take into account in comparing the tax/national insurance position for the unincorporated trader and the company director that it is impossible to draw hard and fast conclusions, and detailed calculations need to be made in every case. Simplified assumptions and comments on some of the variables are made in the illustrations which follow.

18.2 SOLE TRADER, PARTNERSHIP OR COMPANY?

As a sole trader or partner, you will pay combined income tax and national insurance contributions for 2004/05 at 41% on all your profits (after personal allowances) in excess of £31,400, whether you leave the profits in the business or withdraw them. The £31,400 threshold is available to each of a husband and wife partnership. If you are a controlling director/shareholder you can decide how much profit to take in the form of remuneration or dividends (on which you will pay income tax) and how much to leave to be taxed at corporation tax rates. (Your net of tax remuneration or dividend need not be withdrawn from the company, it can be left to your credit on loan account.)

Special rules apply, however, to personal service companies (and also to certain partnerships). Where the company acts as an intermediary providing the services of a director/employee to clients, and the nature of the work done by the director/employee for the client is such that he would have been an employee of the client if he had contracted directly with the client, the intermediary company is deemed to make a salary payment on the last day of the tax year equal to the difference between the amount received from the client and the amount paid out as remuneration to the director/employee (less certain deductions). For details see 19.3. Personal service companies are therefore unable to allocate profits to remuneration or dividends as they see fit.

For those not caught by the personal service company rules, national insurance contributions are one of the most significant factors in comparing the liabilities under the respective formats. Sole traders and partners pay much lower national insurance contributions than the combined employee/employer contributions for a company director.

In a husband and wife partnership both have to pay Class 4 national insurance contributions. They also both have to pay Class 2 contributions unless the wife elected not to do so on or before 11 May 1977 and holds a certificate of exemption. The national insurance contributions are not an allowable deduction from the business profits. The national insurance contributions on remuneration paid by a company depend on the earnings (see 13.7). From 6 April 2003 the national insurance cost of drawing remuneration from a company has increased by 2% (reduced in respect of the company's share by the corporation tax thereon), whereas the increase in Class 4 contributions for unincorporated businesses from that date is 1%, so the extra cost of taking remuneration from a company will be higher. If in 2004/05 remuneration is taken at £610 a week (the upper limit for employees' contributions at the 11% rate), i.e. £31,720 over the year, the combined employer's and employee's contributions would be £6,420. The employer's share (£3,453) is, however, allowable as a deduction in calculating the profits of the company which are liable to corporation tax (reducing the figure to £5,764 if corporation tax is at 19%). The national insurance cost for a sole trader with profits of £31,720 is:

Class 2 contributions 52 × £2.05	106	
Class 4 contributions 8% × (31,720 − 4,745)	2,158	£2,264

The extra national insurance cost of operating through a company at that profit level would therefore be (5,764 − 2,264 =) £3,500.

The overall comparative tax position is significantly affected by whether profits are withdrawn as salary or dividends, since paying dividends saves national insurance contributions and the shareholder pays no extra tax on the dividend unless his taxable income exceeds the higher rate limit (£31,400 for 2004/05), and pays tax at only 25% of the cash dividend (32½% of the tax credit inclusive amount) on the income above that level. The tax effect of making dividend payments out of modest profits has been changed by new provisions charging corporation tax at a minimum rate of 19% from 1 April 2004 where profits are paid out as dividends to individuals or trustees (see 3.13 and Example 2 below).

Four other points should be borne in mind. First, some benefits, in particular jobseeker's allowance and earnings-related retirement pension, are not available to the self-employed. Second, to obtain a deduction in calculating taxable profits, earnings as a director or employee are required to be 'wholly and exclusively for the purposes of the trade', so particularly where a wife or husband does not work full-time in a business, the earnings may be challenged by the Revenue as excessive in calculating the taxable profit of the company. There is no such requirement for a wife or husband who is an active partner, albeit working less than full-time, although artificial arrangements will not work (see 23.24). Third, the Revenue are attacking some commonly used tax planning measures in family companies under the rules for 'settlements' (see 12.9). Although outright gifts between spouses are not normally within the settlements rules, this exception does not apply if the gift is wholly or substantially a right to income. A gift of ordinary shares from one spouse to another has traditionally been considered by tax advisers to be outside this exception, because ordinary shares carry other rights in addition to income rights, for example rights to a share of the assets if the company is wound up. This would obviously be particularly relevant if the couple separated. The Revenue consider, however, that in some circumstances gifts of ordinary shares are caught as settlements. They have issued detailed information on their views in their Tax Bulletins of April 2003 and February 2004. Anyone who is considering such tax planning measures needs to be aware of the Revenue's attitude. The fourth point is that the rate of inheritance tax business property relief may be lower when operating through a company (see 5.19).

The profit level at which the retentions after tax and national insurance will be less operating through a company than as a sole trader or partner is not a static figure but one which will vary according to whether there are other sources of income, how much remuneration is paid by the company, and whether any dividends and pension contributions are paid. Example 1 shows that in 2004/05 if an individual with no other income is paid a salary of £36,145 by a company to leave him with taxable income equal to the basic rate threshold of £31,400, the profit level at which the tax burden using the company format equates with that of an individual trader is £47,663. (If pension contributions were being paid, this would need to be taken into account in the calculations.) The turning point would be at a lower profit level on a salary of less than £36,145 and a higher level on a salary above £36,145 (and would in any event be double for a husband/wife partnership). There could, however, be further tax liabilities on the company retentions at a later date, but these may never materialise, through changes in tax rates, exemptions, etc., and in the meantime cash will have been conserved in the company. Example 2 illustrates that the company format can be more tax-effective even at much lower profit levels if most of the profits are extracted by way of dividend, even though the minimum corporation tax rate from 1 April 2004 on profits taken as a dividend is the non-corporate distribution rate of 19% (see 3.13). The other disadvantages of incorporation would, however, probably outweigh the tax/national insurance advantage at that profit level.

Example 1

Business profits before tax and national insurance are £47,663 and there are no other sources of income. A sole trader is liable to income tax on the full amount. If a company director was paid a salary of £36,145 during 2004/05 (which after the personal allowance of £4,745 leaves income of £31,400 to use the starting and basic rate income tax bands), the comparative position is:

[continued on page 353]

			Trader		Company director
Profits/ remuneration			47,663		36,145
Personal allowance			4,745		4,745
Taxable income			42,918		31,400
Tax thereon:	2,020	@ 10%	202		202
	29,380	@ 22%	6,464		6,464
	11,518	@ 40%	4,607		
	42,918				
			11,273		6,666
Class 2 NI (flat rate)			106	Employee's NI**	3,011
Class 4 NI*			2,317		
Total personal tax and NI			13,696		9,677
Company's tax and NI:					
Profits				47,663	
Less: Director's remuneration				(36,145)	
Company's NI thereon				(4,019)	4,019
Taxable profits				7,499	
Tax thereon @ 0%				—	—
				7,499	
Total tax and NI liabilities			13,696		13,696
Drawn or undrawn profits			33,967		33,967
			47,663		47,663

		£
*	On (31,720 – 4,745) @ 8% 2,158	
	On (47,663 – 31,720) @ 1% 159	2,317
**	On (31,720 – 4,745) @ 11% 2,967	
	On (36,145 – 31,720) @ 1% 44	3,011
†	On (36,145 – 4,745) @ 12.8%	4,019

Each extra £1 of profit would cost the sole trader 41p in tax and national insurance and the company nil on £2,501 (undrawn profits up to £10,000), then 23.75% on the next £40,000 (see 3.12).

Possible further tax liabilities if company retentions of £7,499 are paid out:

If distributed as dividends*, income tax of (32.5 – 10)% on £8,332 (i.e. £7,499 plus tax credit £833)   £1,875

If taxed as capital gains, 40% on £7,499 (reduced by any available taper relief, possibly to 10%, i.e. £750)   £3,000

* The company's underlying tax rate in the period in which dividends were distributed would need to be at least equal to the non-corporate distribution rate, presently 19%, otherwise there would be corporation tax of that amount on the profits applicable to the dividend as well as income tax payable by the shareholder.

Example 2

Say total profits are £25,000 and there are no other sources of income. The comparative position for a sole trader compared with a company director who is paid a salary of £7,000 and the balance after corporation tax as a dividend is as follows:

			Trader				*Company director*
			£				£
Profits/ remuneration			25,000				7,000
Personal allowance			4,745				4,745
Taxable income			20,255				2,255
Tax thereon:	2,020	@ 10%	202	2,020	@ 10%		202
	18,235	@ 22%	4,012	235	@ 22%		52
	20,255		4,214	2,255			254
Class 2 NI (flat rate)			106		Employee's NI		
Class 4 NI (25,000 − 4,745 = 20,255 @ 8%)			1,620		(2,255 @ 11%)		248
Total personal tax and NI			5,940				502
Company's tax and NI:							
Profits						25,000	
Less: Director's remuneration						(7,000)	
Company's NI thereon (2,255 @ 12.8%)						(288)	288
Taxable profits						17,712	
Tax thereon*						3,097	3,097
Dividend (tax covered by tax credit)						14,615	
			5,940				3,887
Saving through operating as company							2,053

* The company's underlying rate of tax on £17,712 (see 3.12 and 3.13) is:

		£
17,712	@ 19%	3,365
Less:	Marginal starting rate relief (50,000 – 17,712) x $^{19}/_{400}$	1,533
	Corporation tax payable	1,832

Underly-
ing rate
$$\frac{1,832}{17,712} \times 100$$
$$= 10.34\%$$

Tax rate payable on profits used as dividend is
NCD rate of 19%.
Maximum dividend payable out of profits can be calculated
as £14,615, giving corporation tax payable of:

		£
14,615	@ 19%	2,777
3,097	@ 10.34%	320
17,712		3,097

Thus the dividend and the corporation tax payable are equal to the
taxable profits.

Paying tax on the profits (TMA 1970, ss 59A, 59B, 59D, 59E)

18.3   Directors' remuneration is subject to tax and national insurance
under the PAYE scheme immediately it is paid or credited to the director's
account, with corporation tax on any profits left in the company being
payable nine months after the end of the accounting period.

An unincorporated business makes tax payments on account half-yearly on
31 January in the tax year and 31 July following. The payments on account
are based on the total income (not just the business profits) of the previous
tax year, with an adjustment to the correct figure, including any tax due on
capital gains, on the following 31 January. The extent to which the unincorporated business will be better off than the company from a cash flow point
of view will depend on whether directors' remuneration has been taken (and
if so, how much and when), and whether the tax payments on account are
significantly less than the full amount due. See Example 3.

Example 3

Say accounts of a business that started in 1995 were made up for the
year to 31 December 2004. The profits of that year would be part of the

total income of 2004/05 and tax on that total income would be payable provisionally in two equal instalments on 31 January 2005 and 31 July 2005, based on the previous year's income. The correct figure of tax on the income plus capital gains of 2004/05 would be notified by 31 January 2006, and a balancing payment or repayment would be made accordingly. The first provisional payment for 2005/06 would also be due on 31 January 2006.

If the business had been a company, tax on the profits of the year to 31 December 2004 (after paying directors' remuneration) would have been due on 1 October 2005, with PAYE tax and national insurance being payable at the time when any remuneration was paid. For income tax purposes, the additional tax on dividends for higher rate taxpayers is payable as part of the balancing payment when the dividends are received for the first time, but is then taken into account in arriving at payments on account for subsequent years.

There is an additional flexibility open to unincorporated businesses. By choosing an accounting date early in the tax year, say 30 April, they may benefit from lower tax rates and higher thresholds in the year of assessment compared with those in force when most of the profits were earned (although the rates can of course go up as well as down, as they did for 2003/04 with the imposition of the extra 1% national insurance charge). The possible advantage of an accounting date early in the tax year may, however, be counterbalanced by the rules for taxing profits when the business ceases. For the detailed rules on how profits are charged to tax, see CHAPTER 21.

Losses (*TA 1988, ss 380–385, 393, 393A, 574–576; FA 1991, s 72; TCGA 1992, s 253; FA 2002, s 48*)

18.4   If a new business is expected to make losses in its early years, it is essential to bear in mind the different loss reliefs available to individuals and to companies. (These are dealt with more fully in CHAPTERS 25 and 26.)

Individuals can claim generous reliefs for trading losses in a new business. Losses in any of the first four tax years of a new business may be carried back to set against *any* income of the previous three tax years, earliest first. The tax liability of the earlier years is recalculated accordingly to establish the tax saving. Effect is, however, given to the saving in the tax year in which the loss is incurred rather than the tax year in which the loss has been set off, so the tax saving is not boosted by interest on overpaid tax (repayment supplement). For losses in later years (or instead of a carry-back claim for opening year losses) a claim may be made to set them against the total income of the tax year in which the loss is sustained or the previous tax year, and tax will be discharged or repaid. The losses may have been boosted, or indeed created, by capital allowances. In some circumstances, trading losses may be set against capital gains. Unrelieved trading losses may always be carried forward to set against future trading profits of the same trade.

If a new company makes trading losses, they may only be set against any current profits of the company, such as bank interest or chargeable gains, or carried forward against the company's later *trading* profits. Trading losses of an established trading company may be set against the profits from other sources, if any, in the same accounting year, then against the total profits of the previous year, with any balance being carried forward against trading profits. The relief for established companies is thus similar to that for established unincorporated businesses.

Funds introduced to a limited company to support losses, either as share capital or on loan, do not qualify for any immediate relief (but see 2.10 as regards relief for interest payable on any borrowing to enable the funds to be introduced). There are two relieving measures for shares and loans, but they are only available when shares are disposed of or when money lent becomes irrecoverable. The provisions are as follows:

(a)   An individual can set a capital loss on the disposal of shares that he had *subscribed for* in an unquoted trading company against any of his income in the same way as a trading loss, as an alternative to setting the capital loss against capital gains.

(b)   The loss of money loaned to the company (or paid to cover a bank guarantee) may be deducted against the lender's capital gains.

To get the first relief, you need to dispose of the shares, or they need to have become virtually worthless, probably because the business has failed. The second relief is also only likely to be available because the company is in financial difficulties. The distinction between the shares relief being given against income and the loan relief only against capital gains is important, because relief against income gives more flexibility and the opportunity for early relief.

These two relieving measures are available both to working directors and to others providing funds to a company.

Pensions

18.5   If you are self-employed, you are entitled to relief at your top rate of tax on contributions to an approved pension scheme. The maximum allowable contribution is presently between 17.5% and 40% of your profits (subject to a £102,000 ceiling for 2004/05 — see 17.8), depending on your age, or £3,600 if higher. Where earnings fluctuate, however, you are able to base the maximum personal pension contribution calculation in a year on higher earnings in one of the previous five years. Company directors/employees in non-pensionable employment can also take advantage of the personal pension provisions, but it is often preferable for a family company to operate its own pension scheme. The ability to base personal pension contributions on the earnings of one of the previous five years does, however, give an extra advantage to incorporated businesses, because after having established an appropriate level of earnings in one year, dividends may be taken instead of pay in later years, giving a significant national insurance saving.

Company pension schemes are less restrictive than personal pension schemes in that the only limit on the company's contributions to an approved scheme is that the retirement benefits provided must not exceed certain limits and the scheme must not be overfunded, although the same £102,000 earnings ceiling often applies in calculating maximum benefits. The company scheme can be contributory or non-contributory, the company's contributions reducing the company's taxable profits and not being charged either to tax or national insurance on the employee, and the individual's contributions, if any, being allowed in calculating tax on his earnings from the company (although not deducted from pay in calculating employers' and employees' national insurance contributions).

For details on company and personal pension schemes, see CHAPTERS 16 and 17. The pension scheme provisions for both company and personal pension schemes are being drawn together under a new simplified regime from 6 April 2006. Pension planning in the intervening period will need to take the new provisions into account. They are outlined in 16.26 onwards.

Capital gains

18.6   Where realised chargeable gains are not covered by available reliefs, the first £8,200 of the total gains in 2004/05 is exempt from tax for individuals (£8,200 each for husband and wife), tax being charged at the appropriate income tax rate of 10%, 20% or 40% on the remainder. Companies are not entitled to any exemption and pay corporation tax on the full amount. The rate of tax on a company's gains for the year to 31 March 2005 could therefore be anything between the starting corporation tax rate of 0% and the marginal rate of 32.75% on profits between £300,000 and £1,500,000. This means that the effect of gains being realised within a company depends on the company's tax rate and the way in which the gains are passed to the shareholder.

The possible effect if the gains are passed on as a dividend is shown in Example 4. The corporation tax on profits paid out as dividends cannot be less than 19% (see 3.13), so the 0% starting rate on profits up to £10,000 and the marginal starting rate of 23.75% on profits between £10,000 and £50,000 (which gives an *average* rate below 19%) are not relevant.

If the gains are retained within the company until the shareholder disposes of his shares or the company is liquidated, the shareholder will be liable to capital gains tax on the increase in value of his shareholding, and since the gain made by the company will have borne corporation tax when it was made this would effectively give a double tax charge. Reliefs may, however, be available at the time the shares are disposed of (see below).

Example 4

Company makes a gain of £10,000 in year to 31 March 2005, which is passed on to shareholders as a dividend.

Rate of tax on profits

	19%	Marginal rate of 32.75%*	30%
	£	£	£
Company gain	10,000	10,000	10,000
Corporation tax	(1,900)	(3,275)	(3,000)
Leaving for cash dividend	8,100	6,725	7,000
Tax credit on dividend at ⅑	900	747	778
Shareholder's income	9,000	7,472	7,778
Maximum income tax @ 32.5%	2,925	2,428	2,528
Leaving shareholder with net cash of	6,075	5,044	5,250
Combined company and personal tax	3,925	4,956	4,750
i.e.	39.25%	49.56%	47.5%

* For details of the marginal rate on profits between £300,000 and £1,500,000 see 3.11.

Whether or not a business is incorporated, the increase in the value of its chargeable assets may lead to chargeable gains in the future, and in the case of a company there is the possibility of further personal chargeable gains where the share value is increased by profit retentions. Death is an effective, albeit unwelcome, way of escaping capital gains tax liabilities. Legatees effectively take over the assets at their market value at the date of death and thus get a tax-free uplift in base cost where values have risen.

Less drastically, there are important reliefs which lessen the capital gains tax impact, and these reliefs are available to sole traders, partners and company shareholders.

Taper relief is available to reduce chargeable gains, and the relief is at a much higher rate on business assets. Furthermore, the taper period for business assets is only two years, so that the maximum charging rate after that time is 25% x 40% = 10% (see 4.16). The definition of business assets has also been widened (see 4.17). The taper relief replaces indexation allowance, which was frozen at April 1998. Taper relief will often be more beneficial than indexation allowance where business is carried on through a company, because base costs of shares are often low. Where, however, profits are retained in the company rather than being distributed, care must be taken not to jeopardise the company's trading status for taper relief by building up large cash balances.

There is also a holdover relief if you make gifts of chargeable business assets. The gifts are treated as disposals at open market value, which may give rise to chargeable gains. You and the donee may, however, jointly claim to treat the gain as reducing the donee's capital gains tax cost, and thus avoid an immediate tax charge. Taper relief is, however, based only on the *donee's* period of ownership.

A further relief is available under the enterprise investment scheme where gains (whether arising through the business or otherwise) are wholly or partly reinvested by subscribing for ordinary shares in a qualifying unquoted trading company. Tax on the reinvested gains is deferred until the new shares are disposed of.

See CHAPTERS 4 and 29 for a fuller treatment of these provisions.

Inheritance tax (IHTA 1984, ss 103–114)

18.7   There is usually no inheritance tax to pay on gifts of all or part of your business in lifetime or on death, whether you operate as an individual or through a company. Business property relief is available at the rate of 100% on transfers of all or part of an individual's business and on transfers out of unquoted shareholdings (providing the company carries on a qualifying business — see 5.19 — and providing any lifetime gifts of such property, or qualifying replacement property, are still retained by the donee when the donor dies). Shares on the Alternative Investment Market are unquoted shares. The rate of inheritance tax business property relief on assets owned outside a partnership or company but used within the business is only 50% and in the case of a company the relief is only available to a controlling director. For details, see CHAPTER 5.

If you want to pass on your business gradually to other members of the family, the company format has the edge in terms of flexibility, since it is easier to transfer shares than to transfer a part of an unincorporated business.

Raising finance and attracting high calibre employees

18.8 The enterprise investment scheme gives a qualifying company an advantage over an unincorporated business in attracting funds from outside investors. Individuals may obtain tax relief at 20% on up to £200,000 invested for at least five years in shares of qualifying unquoted trading companies, and gains on disposal of the shares are exempt from tax. Similar provisions apply to investments in venture capital trusts, which are quoted companies that invest in unquoted companies. The rate of relief on venture capital trust investments is 40% rather than 20% for shares issued between 6 April 2004 and 5 April 2006.The enterprise investment scheme, also enable chargeable gains that are matched by equivalent investments in scheme shares to be deferred until the scheme shares are sold. Smaller, high risk companies have two further advantages over unincorporated businesses in the form of 'enterprise management incentives' and 'corporate venturing relief'. (This deferred relief used to be available for gains reinvested in venture capital trust scheme shares, but it does not apply in relation to such shares if they are issued after 5 April 2004.) Under the management incentives provisions qualifying companies may provide employees with share options worth up to £100,000 per employee (up to an overall maximum of £3,000,000). Corporate venturing relief gives corporation tax relief at 20% to companies who subscribe for shares in smaller, high risk companies. The detailed provisions on these schemes are in CHAPTER 11 for enterprise management incentives and CHAPTER 29 for the other schemes.

Changing from one format to another

18.9 It is a simple matter for an unincorporated business to change from a sole trader to a partnership or vice versa (see CHAPTER 23). Where an unincorporated business is to be incorporated, careful planning is necessary to ensure the best tax position and to minimise the disadvantages — see CHAPTER 27. Unfortunately there are no special tax provisions to help companies who wish to disincorporate. If the company has accumulated trading losses, these cannot be transferred to the shareholders. If the shareholders take the company's assets into personal ownership in order to use them in a new unincorporated business, the disposal by the company will be an open market value disposal for the purpose of calculating a taxable gain, and where there are trading losses, any capital gains can only be reduced by current and not by brought forward losses. Corporation tax will then be payable on any remaining gains. The consequences of either paying out gains as dividends or as capital distributions in a liquidation are illustrated in CHAPTER 28. If the company's disposal of any of the assets should yield a capital loss, no relief would be available unless the company had gains in the same accounting period against which to set it, and the shareholders would be acquiring the assets at a lower capital gains tax base cost than was paid by the company.

Tax points

18.10

- Don't let the tax tail wag the commercial dog. Consider *all* aspects of alternative business forms.

- The loss rules for individuals, particularly the three year carry-back of new business losses, make an unincorporated start an attractive proposition where there is heavy initial expenditure, particularly on revenue items but also on capital items which attract tax allowances. The business can later be converted to a company if appropriate.

- To get income tax relief on a capital loss where you dispose of shares in an unquoted trading company, the shares must have been issued *to you* by the company. Shares acquired by transfer from a previous shareholder do not qualify.

- The possible double tax charge where a company first sells chargeable assets at a profit, thus paying corporation tax on the profit and also increasing the value of its shares, can be avoided by shareholder/directors retaining personal ownership of assets such as freeholds or leaseholds and allowing the company to use them. But inheritance tax business property relief at 50% is only available on those assets where a shareholder *controls* the company, whereas the 50% reduction is available to any partner who personally owns assets which are used by the partnership.

- Although chargeable gains are taxed at income tax rates, they are none the less still chargeable gains. Thus, any available income tax deductions, such as allowances for buildings in enterprise zones, cannot be set off against them. But a dividend from a company, even if payable out of a capital profit, counts as income in the hands of the shareholder, enabling available deductions to be set off and saving tax at higher rates accordingly, although dividend tax credits cannot be repaid.

- The ability to base personal pension contributions on the earnings of one of the previous five years enables incorporated businesses and their employees to save national insurance contributions by the payment of dividends, while still making substantial contributions to personal pension plans based on earlier earnings – see 17.9.

19
Starting up a new small or part-time business

Is it a self-employment?

19.1   It is essential to establish at the outset whether your activities amount to self-employment or whether you are an employee. You may be neither employed nor self-employed but receiving casual sums taxable under the 'any other income' provisions (for example receiving payments for writing the occasional article, but not often enough to be regarded as an author). Exceptionally, the activity may not be taxable at all.

The distinction between employment and self-employment is important in deciding whether PAYE tax and employees' national insurance should be deducted from payments (and employers' national insurance paid), what expenses may be deducted from the income in calculating the tax liability, and whether the recipient should register for VAT. In the case of those operating through their own personal service companies, the Government has decided to look through the legal structure to ensure that those in what they regard as disguised employment pay the same tax and national insurance as someone employed directly. See 19.3 below for details.

An important distinction between employment and self-employment is whether payment is under a contract of *service* and thus chargeable under the PAYE rules or a contract *for services* entitling you to payment against your invoice or fee note, to be included in your self-employed accounts. But the decision is not clear-cut, and depends on the overall circumstances rather than just the form of the contract. There is a Revenue booklet IR 56 outlining the main points to be looked at. (A separate version of the booklet — IR 148 — is published for contractors in the construction industry and the Revenue have provided some additional guidance for such workers — see CHAPTER 44.) Factors pointing to employment are that you work wholly or mainly for one business, you need to carry out the work in person, you have to take orders as to how and when to do it, to work where those providing the work tell you to, and to work set hours at an hourly, weekly or monthly rate, and you get paid for overtime, sickness and holidays. Factors pointing to self-employment are that you risk your own capital and bear any losses, you control whether, how, when and where you do the work, provide your own equipment, are free to employ others to do the work and are required to bear the cost of correcting anything that goes wrong. None of these factors is conclusive — indeed many of them will be irrelevant in particular cases — and all the circumstances have to be taken into account. The decision on your status both for income tax and national insurance is taken by the Revenue but the tax and national insurance rules are not always the same. The tax/national insurance treatment is not, however, conclusive for VAT.

You can challenge a ruling by the Revenue or Customs that you are an employee, and some taxpayers have recently had some success, but it could be costly and time consuming. The Revenue have twice changed the treatment of entertainers, first requiring them to change from self-employed status to employment status and then reversing the treatment, except for entertainers who are permanent members of an orchestra, opera, ballet, theatre company or similar body. (Such people may nonetheless have other earnings that are treated as being from self-employment.) Where entertainers remain taxable as employees, the fees they pay to their agents (including VAT) are specifically allowed as a deduction from their earnings (subject to an overall maximum deduction in any tax year of 17½% of the employment earnings) (TA 1988, s 201A). Anyone (in any business) who has been reclassified as self-employed is normally also treated as such for national insurance purposes. Where Class 1, 1A or 1B contributions have wrongly been paid in the belief that someone was an employee, then after the end of the next following tax year (e.g. after 5 April 2005 for contributions paid in respect of 2003/04) the contributions will be treated as having been correctly paid for the relevant period, which means there will be no need for the contribution record of the employee to be amended and repayments will not be made. The two year time limit for refunds does not apply if a categorisation decision or a tax appeal relating to Class 1B national insurance contributions remains unsettled at the end of the two year period.

Special national insurance provisions apply for entertainers. From 6 April 2003 an entertainer not employed under a contract of service or in an office with earnings chargeable as employment income is nontheless liable to Class 1 contributions unless his remuneration does not include any payment by way of salary. Between 17 July 1998 and 6 April 2003 this provision applied only where the remuneration did not consist wholly or mainly of salary. Yet again some entertainers have been wrongly categorised since 17 July 1998 and claims may be made for refunds of Class 1 employees' and employers' contributions. The normal two year time limit will not apply until a cut-off point is announced (see the Revenue's Tax Bulletin of June 2003 for details).

For VAT, particular care is needed with licensing and franchise arrangements, and even if someone is regarded as self-employed, they may be treated as the agent of the licensor/franchisor, so that the VAT liability depends on the licensor's/franchisor's VAT status. VAT tribunals have often come to conflicting decisions about people doing similar work, particularly in cases relating to driving instructors and hairdressers, some of whom have been held to be self-employed principals and some to be acting as agents. Even if regarded as a principal, a hairdresser will usually be treated as paying for composite supplies chargeable at the standard rate of VAT rather than merely renting space.

Many businesses which use part-time assistance are justifiably wary of paying fees in full, since they could be held liable for the PAYE and national insurance they should have deducted if someone is later held to be an employee, and possibly interest and penalties as well. Some businesses will, however, accept a written assurance from a tax office or from a professional representative (accompanied by a self-assessment and national insurance number) that the income is included in self-employed accounts of the recipient and that the payment should not be taxed under PAYE.

Someone who occasionally buys and sells may contend that his activities are not a trade but remain a hobby, a collector's activity or an investment, such as collecting and restoring antique furniture, sometimes selling the occasional piece at a profit. Self-assessment tax returns tell you to contact your tax office if you are unsure whether you are carrying on a business or not. If you do not do so, and the Revenue subsequently enquire into your tax position, you could be faced with interest and penalties for non-disclosure. It may be the Revenue rather than the taxpayer who take the view that an activity is a hobby, particularly where there are losses, because to accept that it is a commercial activity would open the way for loss reliefs against other income. Each case depends on the facts, with appropriate rights of appeal if the Revenue do not see it in the same way as the taxpayer.

Registering for tax, national insurance and VAT (SI 2001/1004)

19.2   Where a self-employment has been established, you will have responsibilities in relation to tax, national insurance and possibly VAT. The Revenue have a leaflet P/SE/1 setting out the basic requirements for those who have started, or are thinking of starting, in business, and you can telephone a helpline for the newly self-employed (08459 15 45 15) to ask for a more detailed booklet 'Starting up in business', which deals with record-keeping, employing staff and other points. A free video is also available. You may register for tax and national insurance by telephoning the helpline for the newly self-employed or completing form CWF1 which is in leaflet P/SE/1. There is a box to tick if you expect to be liable to register for VAT. There is a penalty of £100 if you fail to register for Class 2 national insurance within three months of starting business. See 9.45 above for details. You need to register even if you are going to claim deferment of Class 2 contributions because you pay maximum Class 1 contributions at the main primary rate (see 24.12 below).

The Revenue will provide ongoing advice and information after the business has started, and you can ask to see an adviser from one of their local Business Support teams. Help on payroll matters for new employers is also available from a special helpline 0845 60 70 143.

Personal service companies (FA 2000, s 60 and Sch 12; FA 2002, s 38; FA 2003, s 136 SI 2000/727; SI 2002/703)

19.3   There are special rules (known as the IR35 rules) to prevent people paying substantially less tax and national insurance by operating through a personal service company or other intermediary rather than being employed directly. The rules apply where a worker provides services under a contract between a client and an intermediary company or partnership that meets certain conditions, and the income would have been treated as employment income if the worker had contracted directly with the client. The rules have not previously applied if the client is a private individual rather than a business, so that they did not apply to domestic workers such as nannies provided by a service company. Such workers are brought within the scope of the personal services rules for services provided after 9 April 2003. The existing tests to differentiate employment from self-employment outlined at 19.1 above still apply. The Revenue will give an opinion on whether they consider a contract to be one of employment or self-employment. They will not, however, comment on draft contracts. They have published a leaflet IR175 *'Supplying services through a limited company or partnership'* and also a separate Employment Status Manual which is available on the Revenue's website (www.inlandrevenue.gov.uk). The status tests set out in the Manual were, however, criticised by the judge in a judicial review of the IR35 rules, although the judge found that the rules were not a breach of the human rights legislation and European law, and following an appeal on the European issue the Court of Appeal also found that European law was not contravened. Other cases on the personal service company rules are being brought but it seems unlikely that any definitive guidance will be gleaned from them, since each will depend on the particular circumstances.

A company is within the IR35 provisions if the worker (together with his close family) controls more than 5% of any dividends from the company, or receives or could receive payments or benefits which are not salary but which could reasonably be taken to represent payment for services provided to clients. A partnership is within the provisions if the worker (together with his close family) is entitled to 60% or more of the partnership profits, or where most of the partnership profits come from work for a single client, or where a partner's profit share is based on his income from relevant contracts.

Where the rules apply, and the intermediary is a company, the company operates PAYE and Class 1 NICs on its employee's earnings during the tax year in the normal way, and pays Class 1A NICs on any benefits provided. At the end of the year, the excess of the amount of cash and non-cash benefits that the company has received from clients for the employee's services (net of VAT and net of allowable expenses paid by the company) over the amount the company has paid to the employee as earnings plus non-cash benefits (including mileage allowance payments for use of the employee's own car and 5p per mile passenger payments if relevant — see 10.10 and 10.11 above) is treated as pay on 5 April and liable to PAYE and Class 1 NICs accordingly. This means that the extra tax and NICs are payable by 19 April after the year-end and interest will be charged on underpayments from that date. The deemed payment is included in the employee's year-end earnings certificate P60 and will be shown on his self-assessment return.

The allowable expenses broadly comprise a flat rate allowance of 5% of the net of VAT payment for the relevant contracts, expenses paid by the intermediary (or by the employee and reimbursed by the intermediary) that would have been allowable to an employee of the client (including travelling expenses from home to the client's premises plus subsistence expenses, providing the job is expected to and does last less than 24 months), capital allowances that could have been claimed by the employee, employer pension contributions, and the amount of Class 1 and Class 1A employer's national insurance contributions paid by the company in respect of the employee's earnings. Allowable expenses include mileage allowances, on the same basis as if the personal service company employee had been employed direct by the client and had used his own car for the client's business (see 10.10 above).

The excess amount arrived at is treated as inclusive of employer's Class 1 national insurance contributions, which are then deducted to arrive at the deemed Schedule E payment. See example 1.

Example 1

During 2003/04 client pays £50,000 to company for worker's services. Contract is caught by IR35 rules. Company pays worker salary of £18,000 through PAYE and provides taxable benefits of £2,000. It also pays pension contributions of £4,000.

Deemed Schedule E payment is:

		£	£
Total from client			50,000
Less:	5% × 50,000	2,500	
	Pension contributions	4,000	
	Employer's NIC on £20,000		
	(Class 1 £1,713, Class 1A £256)	1,969	8,469
			41,531

Less:	Salary actually paid and benefits provided	20,000
Excess amount		21,531
Less:	Employer's Class 1 NIC therein (12.8/112.8)	2,443
		19,088

Company is deemed to pay employee £19,088 on 5 April 2004 and must account for PAYE tax and NIC thereon by 19 April 2004.

Similar provisions apply where the intermediary is a partnership receiving gross payment under a contract. The worker will be deemed to receive Schedule E income on 5 April, and liable to tax and national insurance accordingly, and such income will be excluded from the worker's share of the partnership profits (although the present practice of including small amounts of Schedule E income in partnership profits will continue).

The deemed Schedule E payment and the intermediary's national insurance thereon are allowable deductions in computing the intermediary's profits of the accounting period in which the deemed payment is treated as made for corporation tax purposes or, if earlier, the accounting period in which the trade ceases.

It is important to realise that later salary payments of amounts included in the deemed salary at 5 April *cannot* be made free of tax and NICs. Actual salary payments reduce the deemed payment of the tax year in which they are *paid*. The only way to avoid double taxation on the deemed payment is to pay a dividend. The company may make a claim (by 31 January following the tax year in which the dividend is paid) to regard the dividend as reduced by the deemed salary payment (net of tax and employee's national insurance). This relief applies to dividends paid to the worker before dividends paid to anyone else, and to dividends paid in the same tax year as the deemed payment before dividends paid in later years. When the relief is claimed the worker's taxable income is reduced accordingly. For more detailed information on calculating deemed payments see the Revenue's booklet IR 2003.

The time frame for paying the tax and NICs due on deemed payments is ridiculously short. The Revenue have said that providing estimated payments are made on time, with a covering letter accompanying the P35 stating that the company is within IR 35 and that the payment is provisional, and a supplementary return is made and the correct tax/NICs paid by the following 31 January, penalties will not be charged, although interest will be payable. Unpaid amounts may be collected direct from the worker if the company does not pay.

One final twist is that the deemed Schedule E payment is not wages for the purposes of the national minimum wage, so that actual pay (excluding benefits other than accommodation) must be sufficient to meet the minimum wage requirements (see 12.1 above).

Computation of taxable profits

19.4 The detailed rules for calculating profits are in CHAPTER 20. CHAP-TER 22 deals with capital allowances for the purchase of buildings, equipment, etc. A newly-established business is often run from your home, perhaps using your existing car for any business travelling that is required. You can claim for the business proportion of car expenses, and also the business proportion of capital allowances on the value of the car at the time you started using it for business (or what you paid for it if less). You can also claim a deduction for business use of your home telephone. Where you run the business from your home, expenses of part of the home can be allowed against taxable profits if they are wholly and exclusively for the business, so that a proportion of, for example, the light and heat can be charged for the part of the residence used for the business, such as a study/office, surgery, workshop, etc. You will be liable to pay business rates on that part of the property, as well as paying the council tax on the rest of the property, unless you can show that the business use does not stop you continuing to use that part of the property for domestic purposes. If paid, business rates are allowable against your profits. Where business rates are not paid, you are able to treat as a business expense an appropriate proportion of the council tax according to the business use of the home.

Under self-assessment you have to show details of your business income and expenses under specified headings in your tax return. If your turnover is below £15,000, however, you can just show your turnover, expenses and net profit (see 9.12 above). This does not mean that you do not need to have the detailed information available. Keeping records is often not a strong point for many small businesses, but under self-assessment it is vital that you do keep adequate records relating to your business expenses (and indeed your other tax liabilities — see 9.6 above), and that you would be able to justify, if challenged, the way you have worked out the allowable part of mixed expenses.

If no part of your home is used wholly and exclusively for the business, your capital gains tax owner-occupier exemption will not be affected. If part of your property is so used, that part will be outside the capital gains tax owner-occupier exemption. Any gain need not be charged to tax immediately if you sell the property and continue the business from a new residence, because a claim may be made for the gain to be regarded as reducing the cost for capital gains tax of the business part of the new residence (see 4.19

above), although it would not be necessary to make that claim if the chargeable gain was covered by the annual capital gains tax exemption (see example 2).

Example 2

House bought June 1992 for £60,000, sold June 2003 for £150,000, indexation allowance £10,020.

Used to June 1997 wholly as residence then 1/6th for self-employment for remainder of period

Total gain (150,000 – (60,000 + 10,020))	£79,980
Chargeable gain: Business use 1/6th for 6 years out of 11, 1/6 × 6/11 × £79,980	7,271
Less maximum business assets taper relief 75%	5,453
	£1,818

Covered by 2003/04 annual exemption of £7,900 unless already used against other gains.

Employing staff (FA 1989, s 43)

19.5 If you employ staff in the business, you will need to operate the PAYE scheme (see CHAPTER 10). You must also make sure you comply with the national minimum wage legislation, which requires you to pay hourly rates of at least £4.20 for those aged 22 and over (or £3.60 for the first six months if they are starting a new job and undertaking accredited training) and £3.60 for those aged between 18 and 21. From October 2003 the £4.20 rate is increased to £4.50 and the £3.60 rate to £3.80. Further increases from October 2004 to £4.85 per hour and £4.10 per hour have been provisionally agreed. You do not have to pay the minimum wage to certain apprentices and trainees. There is also an exception for family members who live at home and work in the family business (but not if the business is a company). The Revenue is responsible for enforcing the legislation (see 12.1 above). If you employ five or more people, you may need to offer access to a stakeholder pension scheme (see 17.2 above). As far as PAYE is concerned, the Revenue will supply you with all the necessary documentation (and see 19.2 above re getting help from a Revenue Business Support team). It is important to make sure that PAYE is operated properly, particularly where you take on casual or part-time employees. Even if you pay someone less than the tax and national insurance threshold, you must still deduct tax if they have significant other earnings. Form P46 must be completed for any employee who does not produce form P45 (employee's leaving certificate). In a new small business, the first employees are very often members of the family and the PAYE rules apply equally to them. In addition, the salary payments must be both justified and paid. If the Revenue open an enquiry into your self-assessment return (which they may well do for someone who has just started in business), they will be unwilling to accept that an amount drawn for housekeeping or personal use includes family wages. They will also be better able to challenge the validity of the expense if it is left as an amount owing rather than having actually been paid. Payments of wages must in any case be made within nine months after the end of the accounting period if they are to be allowed for tax against the profits of that period rather than a later period.

If family wages can be justified for the work done, they enable personal allowances to be used if not already covered by other income. Now that neither employers nor employees pay national insurance contributions on pay up to the income tax threshold (£89 for 2003/04), paying wages to family members at the level of the personal allowance of £4,615 will reduce tax bills unless the personal allowances are already used against other income (see example 3). Even though national insurance contributions are paid only on earnings above the income tax threshold, employees earning at or above the national insurance lower earnings limit of £77 have their rights to benefits protected (see 13.1 above).

Example 3

If a husband pays his wife a justifiable wage of £4,615 in 2003/04 and she has no other income, she will pay no tax or national insurance contributions and the payment will reduce the husband's taxable profits, saving tax at say 22% = £1,015. The reduction in the husband's profits may also save Class 4 national insurance contributions (payable at 8% on profits between £4,615 and £30,940 and 1% thereafter). If the whole of the £4,615 would otherwise have been liable to Class 4 contributions at the main rate the extra saving would be 8% of £4,615 = £369.

How are profits charged to tax?

19.6   The first profits usually form the basis of the first two years' tax bills (see 21.4 below). A part-time start may therefore help to reduce the tax burden for those years so long as the transition from the part-time activity to full-time self-employment cannot be argued by the Revenue as the start of an entirely new trade. Linking a slow start with a 30 April year end may be particularly helpful (see example 4), although the initial and ongoing advantage where profits are rising needs to be set against the possible disadvantage of a higher taxable profit when the business ceases (see 21.5 below).

Example 4

Trader starts business on a part-time basis on 1 May 2001 and makes up accounts to 30 April 2002, showing a profit for the first year of £12,000. He then devotes all his time to the business and makes a profit of £24,000 in the year to 30 April 2003. The tax position on those profits is as follows:

2001/02	1.5.01 – 5.4.02	$^{11}/_{12} \times £12,000$	£11,000
2002/03	1.5.01 – 30.4.02		£12,000
2003/04	1.5.02 – 30.4.03		£24,000

Although £11,000 of the £12,000 profit is taxed twice, a deduction of £11,000 will be given against profits when the business ceases (or sometimes earlier).

The effect of choosing a 30 April year end is that the profits taxable in the current year were largely earned in the previous year. The actual profit in 2002/03 was $^{1}/_{12}$ of £12,000 and $^{11}/_{12}$ of £24,000 = £23,000, whereas the taxable profit is £12,000.

Loss relief

19.7 If you make losses in the first four tax years of a new business, they may be treated as reducing any income of the previous three tax years, earliest first, or set off against any other income and chargeable gains of the tax year of the loss. You will then either get a tax refund or an equivalent amount of tax owed will be discharged. If a loss is carried back, the tax saving from the claim is calculated according to your tax position in the earlier year, but it is still regarded as a claim relating to the loss year, so that you will only be entitled to interest on the repayment from the 31 January following the tax year in which the loss occurred. See CHAPTER 25 for details of the claims.

Pension provision

19.8 Earnings from a small business can support a personal pension premium, both in respect of the self-employed earnings and for the family employees. It does not matter that the self-employed taxpayer or family employee is also in separate pensionable employment. You can claim tax relief on premiums up to £3,600 a year even if you have no earnings and if your earnings fluctuate you may claim relief by reference to higher earnings in one of the previous five years. See CHAPTER 17 for details.

VAT registration

19.9   From 10 April 2003, you need to register for VAT at the end of any month if your turnover in the previous twelve months exceeded £56,000 (previously £55,000). You are required to notify Customs and Excise and you will then be registered unless you can show that your turnover will not exceed £54,000 (previously £53,000) in the coming twelve months. If you expect your turnover in the next 30 days to exceed £56,000, you must register immediately. You need to watch these limits carefully because there are severe penalties for not complying with the rules. Even if your turnover is below the limit you may wish to register voluntarily in order to recover VAT input tax on your purchases. But this will not be to your advantage unless most of your customers are VAT registered. There is a special VAT flat-rate scheme for small businesses. See CHAPTER 7.

National insurance

19.10   For the tax year 2003/04, a self-employed person pays Class 2 contributions of £2 a week, and also Class 4 contributions, at 8% on profits between £4,615 and £30,940 and 1% on profits above that level. The detailed provisions are in CHAPTER 24. Note particularly the provisions for deferring contributions if you are both employed and self-employed. Neither deferment nor a refund affect the liability of the employer to pay employers' contributions.

If your self-employed earnings were below £4,025 in 2002/03 and your circumstances have not materially changed, or are expected to be below £4,095 in 2003/04, you can apply for a certificate of exception from Class 2 contributions (see CHAPTER 24). This will, however, affect your contribution record for social security benefit purposes, particularly retirement pension. Since Class 2 contributions are now only £2 a week it is worth paying them to maintain your right to benefits. See 9.46 above re the penalty of £100 if you fail to register as self-employed within three months of starting business.

Occasional earnings not treated as from self-employment

19.11   If you are not treated as self-employed, occasional earnings are taxed under Schedule D, Case VI according to the amount earned in the tax year, with a deduction for justifiable expenses. You should account for the tax in your self-assessment along with the tax on your other income. If you are also an employee, the Revenue will sometimes, for convenience, offset small amounts of occasional earnings against your tax allowances when arriving at your PAYE code number.

Any losses can be set off against any income from other sources charged under Case VI, but it is unlikely that there will be any, in which case the losses are carried forward to reduce any future Case VI profits.

Tax points

19.12

- When you start a new business, you will have a tax liability for the tax year in which the business starts, unless the profit is covered by reliefs and allowances. If you do not get a tax return, you have to let the Revenue know that you have taxable profits by 5 October following the tax year-end of 5 April (see 9.2 above), otherwise you will be liable to an income tax penalty. Unless you expect your profits to be below the national insurance exemption level, however, you will need to register with the Revenue within *three months* of starting business otherwise you will be liable to a Class 2 national insurance contributions penalty of £100 (even though at £2 a week the Class 2 contributions for a whole year are only £104). You also need to make arrangements to pay Class 2 contributions (quarterly or by direct debit — see 24.2 below).

- If your turnover is below £15,000 you can complete a simple three-line account in your return — see 9.12 and 19.4 above.

- Do not take people on without making sure of their employment status. If you make a mistake you have only limited rights to recover underpaid tax and national insurance from the worker, and you may have to pay interest and penalties as well.

- A useful test on the self-employed status is whether there is a risk of loss as well as gain, normally implying self-employment; and whether the worker has to carry out corrective work without payment.

- The new rules for personal service companies bring enormous practical problems for those affected. The Revenue publish answers to frequently asked questions on the Internet (www.inlandrevenue.gov.uk).

- A deemed payment under the personal service company rules is generally treated in the same way as actual pay, so that it counts as relevant earnings for personal pension contributions and will be included in remuneration for determining permissible benefits under occupational pension schemes.

- Do not forget to register for VAT if appropriate. You need to check at the end of every *month* to make sure that the annual turnover limit has not been exceeded. See CHAPTER 7.

20
How are business profits calculated?

Background (TA 1988, ss 18, 832)

20.1　Taxable profits from trades, professions and vocations are all calculated in the same way (but see 23.22 and 23.23 re limited partners and partners in limited liability partnerships). The legislation refers to income from trading profits as taxable under Schedule D Case I and from professions and vocations as taxable under Schedule D Case II. It is usually obvious that a trade is being carried on, but the charge under Case I is extended beyond what would normally be regarded as trading and can cover occasional transactions and those to which an investment motive cannot be attributed, where the circumstances point to a trading intention.

Important indicators of possible trading, when there is any doubt, are the nature of the asset itself (whether it is income producing, or something you get enjoyment from owning, which will indicate investment rather than trading), your reason for acquiring it, how long you owned it, whether you worked on it to make it more saleable, your reason for selling and how often such transactions were undertaken.

General rules for computing trading profits (TA 1988, s 74; FA 2004, ss 50–52 and Sch 10)

20.2　Whether the business is that of an individual trader, a partnership or a company, profits are calculated so as to give a true and fair view in accordance with generally accepted accounting practice, unless that practice conflicts with the tax legislation as interpreted by the courts. For accounting periods starting on or after 1 January 2005, the term generally accepted accounting practice means either UK generally accepted accounting practice (UK GAAP) or, where appropriate, generally accepted accounting practice in accordance with international accounting standards (IAS). There are provisions to prevent groups of companies gaining a tax advantage through one company using UK GAAP and the other using IAS.

The two most important rules for expenses are first that they must be wholly and exclusively for the purposes of the trade, and second, that they must be of a revenue, and not capital, nature. There is guidance on computing business profits in the Revenue's new Business Income Manual available on their website.

There are special 'transfer pricing' rules for businesses that are connected with one another, in particular companies in the same group, to require an arm's length price to be used on transactions between them. These are dealt with in 45.18.

In recent years, different rules have been introduced for companies compared with unincorporated businesses in relation to the tax treatment of certain expenditure. The main areas are the treatment of 'loan relationships' (see 3.6 and 26.5), intangible assets, including goodwill (see 20.21), cleaning up contaminated land (see 20.22), and various reliefs related to research and development (see 29.16 to 29.19). The amount deductible from profits for tax purposes under the contaminated land and research and development provisions is greater than the amount of the expenditure, and loss-making companies may claim a cash payment in respect of the appropriate part of their unrelieved losses.

'Wholly and exclusively'

20.3   If you are a sole trader or partner, you cannot claim a deduction for an expense that is for both business and private purposes, such as clothing bought primarily for business but also for private purposes. Part of a mixed expense may, however, be wholly and exclusively for the purposes of the trade and thus be a valid deduction in calculating profits, such as the charges for business telephone calls from your home telephone. (In fact the Revenue are prepared to allow a proportion of the *total* bill, including the line rental.) The same applies to mixed business and living accommodation, where again it may be possible accurately to separate the business and private areas (see 19.4). Where meals are taken while working away from the place of business, the cost is not generally regarded as wholly and exclusively for business. The Revenue accept, however, that those who travel regularly in their work, and those who make occasional business journeys outside the normal pattern, are entitled to claim for reasonable expenses incurred. Where one or more nights need to be spent away from home, reasonable costs of overnight accommodation and subsistence are allowed.

If you are a sole trader or partner, some of your car mileage is wholly and exclusively for business, some is purely for private purposes, and some may be partly both. Where expenditure is for the sole purpose of the business, any incidental private benefit would be ignored. But if you undertake a trip both for business and private purposes, you cannot strictly claim a deduction for any part of the expenses, even though the business derives benefit from the trip. Providing the trip has a genuine business purpose, however, you are in practice allowed to claim an expenses deduction based on the time spent on business. See Example 1.

Example 1

A trader's recorded mileage in a twelve-month period of account was as follows:

Purely business journeys		5,000
Purely private journeys	4,000	
Home to business	2,000	
Journeys for combined business/private purposes	1,000	
	7,000	
	12,000	

Allowable business proportion is 5/12ths. In addition, a deduction could usually be claimed for an appropriate proportion of the expenses for the mixed purpose journeys.

Allowable car expenses are strictly required to be worked out by taking the business mileage proportion of the actual expenses incurred. If your turnover is below the VAT threshold (£58,000 from 1 April 2004, previously £56,000), you may, however, use the Revenue authorised mileage rates (see the Table of Rates and Allowances and 10.9) instead. In that event you cannot claim capital allowances as well, but, unlike the rules for employees, you may also claim relief for the business proportion of interest on a loan to buy the car.

In the case of a company, there can be no private use by the company itself. Where a company or unincorporated employer incurs expenses that benefit employees or directors, the usual treatment is that the expenses are allowed in calculating the taxable profits of the employer, but are treated as taxable earnings of the employee or director (see CHAPTER 10). Sometimes, directors' fees, wages paid or the cost of benefits provided to members of the family who do not work full-time may not be allowed in full if the payment is considered excessive in relation to the work done, because it would then not be regarded as wholly and exclusively for the business. It is also particularly important where a business employs family members that the wages payment is properly made (see 19.5).

In the case of family and similar companies, a distinction must be drawn between company expenditure which benefits a shareholder who is a director and the payment by the company of the personal debts of the shareholder/director, for example school fees, private entertaining, or expenses of a private residence. A payment for personal debts should be treated as a payment of salary, and declared on form P11D (see 10.5). (Class 1 national insurance contributions should have been accounted for at the time of the payment.) If the Revenue discover that the payment has not been properly dealt with, they will normally treat the amount as a loan which the shareholder/director must repay to the company and it is then neither an allowable business expense nor taxed as a benefit on the shareholder/ director. The loan has tax consequences both for the company and the director — see 12.12, and possible national insurance consequences — see 12.13.

In family companies, loans to directors and employees may sometimes be written off. For non-controlling shareholder directors and employees, the amount written off is treated as taxable pay and is allowed as a deduction to the company, subject to what is said above about remuneration that is excessive for the work done. See 12.12. If the director or employee is a controlling shareholder, special rules apply to prevent the company obtaining a deduction for the write-off, and to treat it as dividend income of the shareholder net of 10% tax (see 12.12).

Where an employer takes out insurance against loss of profits arising from the death, accident or illness of a key employee, the premiums will usually be allowable to the employer and any policy proceeds treated as a trading receipt. If in the event of accident or illness the benefits of the policy were passed on to the employee, they would be taxed either as normal pay if the employee had a contractual right to them or as sick pay.

Any of your accountancy expenses that relate to calculating the tax on your profits rather than calculating the profits themselves are incurred in the capacity of taxpayer rather than trader, so they are not strictly deductible in calculating taxable profits. In practice such expenses are allowed, except where they arise as a result of a Revenue enquiry into your tax affairs. Even then, they will be allowed if adjustments arising from the enquiry are made to the current year only and they do not arise through your fraudulent or negligent conduct.

The costs of preparing your tax return or calculating capital gains are not allowable, but if your affairs are straightforward these costs are likely to be fairly low. Where a business is run through a company, and the company's accountants deal with the directors' tax returns, it is preferable for the work for the directors to be billed to them directly. If the bill is actually paid by the company, then unless the amount has been charged to the director's loan account the company would be settling the director's personal liability and the director should be charged to tax and Class 1 national insurance through the PAYE system on the amount paid. If the company has contracted with the accountant for dealing with directors' tax returns, the fees, including VAT, should be treated as a benefit in kind to the directors (as to which see

CHAPTER 10). The company would be allowed a deduction for the amount paid, so long as the total remuneration falls within the wholly and exclusively rule(see 20.3 above).

Capital or revenue

20.4 Revenue expenditure is an allowable expense in calculating your taxable profit unless specifically prohibited, such as business entertaining expenses (see 20.8).

A capital expense cannot be deducted in calculating profits, although many items of capital expenditure may attract capital allowances (see CHAPTER 22). The usual definition of a capital expense is one made 'not only once and for all, but with a view to bringing into existence an asset or an advantage for the enduring benefit of the trade'. One person's stock in trade will be another person's fixed assets. Your business premises are clearly a capital item, but if you build and sell factories, the factories will be trading stock and the cost will be taken into account in calculating your profit. Cars used by you and your employees are capital items, but cars held for sale by a motor dealer are trading stock. Normally, repair expenditure is revenue expenditure and is allowable, but if you buy a capital asset that cannot be used in your business until it is renovated, the cost of renovating it is part of the capital cost. The distinction is often hard to draw, and has led to many disputes between the taxpayer and the Revenue which have had to be settled by the courts.

Similar considerations apply in deciding whether a particular item is income chargeable under Schedule D, Case I or II or a capital profit.

The categorisation of expenditure as capital or revenue now differs in certain respects for companies and unincorporated businesses, as indicated in 20.2.

Again as indicated at 20.2, generally accepted accounting principles may be used to arrive at profits for tax purposes unless they conflict with tax law.

Provisions for future liabilities

20.5 Provisions for future liabilities are normally allowable for tax purposes, so long as they do not conflict with the tax legislation as interpreted by the courts and they follow accepted accounting practice.

The accepted accounting treatment changed following the issue by the Accounting Standards Board of accounting standard FRS 12, which deals with 'Provisions, Contingent Liabilities and Contingent Assets'. The standard requires a provision to be made if, at the balance sheet date, a *present* obligation exists as a result of a *previous* event and a *reliable estimate* can be made of the expenditure which will probably be required to meet the obligation. With some exceptions for smaller businesses, the standard needs to be followed for tax purposes, so that appropriate tax adjustments must be made.

Any reductions of earlier provisions that have been allowed in calculating taxable profits increase the taxable profit of the period in which the adjustment is made.

Allowable and non-allowable expenses

20.6   The principles outlined above provide a broad guide to what expenses are allowed, and points of detail relating to certain expenses are covered below. The table at 20.19 lists some specific examples, including items specifically allowed or disallowed by the tax legislation.

Payment of remuneration (FA 1989, s 43)

20.7   Directors' and employees' pay may only be taken into account as an expense of the accounting period to which it relates if it is paid during or within nine months after the end of the period. Otherwise it may only be deducted in the accounting period in which it is paid.

Business entertaining (TA 1988, s 577)

20.8   The cost of business entertaining and business gifts (apart from the £50 gifts exemption noted in the table at 20.19) is not allowable. Expenditure on entertaining staff (and their guests) is normally allowable, unless it is incidental to entertaining those with whom the employer does business, but there will be a benefits charge on P11D employees (subject to the exception noted at 10.18).

The VAT position is slightly different. Input VAT on business entertaining is not recoverable, but where proprietors or employees act as hosts at meals with clients, etc. while away from work on business, input VAT other than that relating to the clients is recoverable (unless business entertainment was the main purpose of the trip). As far as staff entertainment is concerned, the proportion of input VAT relating to *guests* at a staff function is not recoverable, but you can recover the proportion relating to staff. In the same way as for income tax, there is a £50 gifts exemption (see 7.2).

Any unrecovered input VAT on entertaining expenditure is not allowable when calculating taxable profit.

Bad and doubtful debts (TA 1988, ss 74(1)(j)(2), 94)

20.9   Normal trading bad debts and specific provisions for bad debts may be deducted from profits for tax purposes. In accordance with the principles outlined above, however, a *general* provision for bad debts cannot be allowed in calculating taxable profits. Any specific debts written off or provided for that are subsequently recovered must be included in profits for tax purposes.

A creditor may treat a debt as bad if he has released the debt in a voluntary arrangement under the 1986 Insolvency Act. The debtor in a voluntary arrangement will not have to bring into his trading profit debts that have been released in this way but debts released other than under such arrangements must be brought in as trading receipts.

For companies, bad debts that do not relate to ordinary trading transactions are dealt with under the loan relationships rules — see 26.5. See also 12.12 re losses on loans to close company directors, employees and shareholders.

Interest paid (TMA 1970, ss 86, 87, 87A, 90; TA 1988, 349, 360, 362, 363, 787, 826, 826A; FA 1996, ss 80, 82)

20.10   Interest paid on business borrowings must be wholly and exclusively for the purposes of the business.

Companies pay interest in full in a wide range of circumstances. Other interest paid by companies is paid net of income tax at 20%, and the company pays over to the Revenue the income tax it has deducted (see 3.17). Interest relating to the trade is deducted from the company's trading profits. All other interest is taken into account in arriving at the profit or loss on the company's non-trading loan relationships. See 3.6 for details.

Individuals normally pay interest in full and deduct interest relating to the trade as a trading expense. Partners may obtain tax relief for interest on a loan used for lending money or introducing capital to a partnership by deducting the interest from their total income (see 2.10 and 23.7). So may those who introduce funds into their family company (see 2.10).

Where interest is paid on borrowing to acquire a property that is partly private and partly business, the interest has to be split to arrive at the part that is allowable as a business expense and the part that is for the living accommodation. This will depend on the respective values of the parts of the property. Where part of the property is sometimes but not always used exclusively for business, the period of business use will also be taken into account.

Since interest on home loans does not qualify for tax relief, individuals should consider business borrowings instead, or if they are partners, borrowing money individually to lend to the firm (see 2.10), rather than leaving undrawn profits in the business in order to boost the business capital. Capital can also be withdrawn (except to the extent that it represents asset revaluations), leaving the business to obtain funding from partners' loans or from other sources. If, however, withdrawing funds leads to a proprietor's capital/current account with the business becoming overdrawn, interest on business borrowings that had enabled the drawings to be made would not be wholly and exclusively for the trade. And partners must not withdraw their capital *after* making loans to the business, because to that extent they would be regarded as merely withdrawing what was introduced, with relief for interest on the loans being restricted accordingly.

There are some anti-avoidance provisions affecting both individuals and companies, and professional advice is essential.

Where interest arises on overdue or overpaid tax, the treatment is different for individuals and companies. For an individual, interest on overdue tax is not allowed in calculating profits and interest on overpaid tax is not taxable. For a company, interest on overdue and overpaid tax is taken into account in computing profits and losses on the company's loan relationships (see 3.6).

Lease of cars (TA 1988, ss 578A, 578B)

20.11   If you buy a car costing more than £12,000, capital allowances are usually restricted (see 22.20), but the full cost will be allowed to you eventually, except to the extent that the car is used privately by a sole trader or partner. There is no private use restriction for a company, but the car user is taxed on the benefit. As far as expenditure on repair and maintenance is concerned, the cost of the car does not affect the allowability of that expenditure, so that sole traders and partners get relief for the business proportion and companies get relief in full.

If instead you lease a car with a retail price when new of more than £12,000 (a 'car' for this purpose includes a motor cycle), part of the leasing cost is not deductible in calculating taxable profits. You can only deduct from profit the proportion of the total hire charge that £12,000 plus the retail price bears to twice the retail price, and for cars used by sole traders and partners, the allowable amount must be further restricted by the private proportion. (If there is a subsequent rebate of rentals, the amount brought in as a taxable receipt is reduced in the same proportion.) See Example 2. Lease contracts may either be operating leases (contract hire), under which the lease rental covers repair and maintenance as well as the provision of the car, or finance leases, under which only the car is provided and repair and maintenance costs are borne by the lessee (see 20.12). Where you acquire a car on contract hire, you should try to get the contract hire company to split the lease rental between the amount paid for the car and the repair and maintenance charge. The £12,000 restriction will then only apply to the car hire payment.

Example 2

Car with retail value of £30,000 leased on 1 May 2004 for £9,000 a year.

Allowable hire charge:

$$9,000 \times \frac{12,000 + 30,000}{60,000} = £6,300$$

The £6,300 will be further restricted if the car is used privately by a sole trader or partner.

No tax relief is available for the remaining £2,700.

The above restriction on allowable hire charges does not apply to the hiring of an electric car, or car with low CO_2 emissions, providing the car is first registered on or after 17 April 2002 and the hire begins before 1 April 2008. 'Car' in this case does not include a motor cycle.

See 20.16 for the VAT position on leased cars.

Finance leases (FA 1997, s 82 and Sch 12)

20.12   Although for accounting purposes you are treated as owning an asset acquired under a finance lease, it is in law owned by the lessor so the lessor is entitled to the capital allowances and the lease rental payments are a revenue expense allowable against your profit, restricted as indicated above if the leased asset is a car costing more than £12,000. You must take all relevant circumstances into account when allocating the lease rental payments over the term of the lease for tax purposes (Revenue Statement of Practice SP 3/91).

There are, however, special provisions to prevent exploitation of the tax treatment and to align it more closely with the recognised accounting treatment. The rental income for tax purposes will normally be the higher of the actual rent and the earnings recognised in the lessor's accounts. There are also special rules for capital allowances (see 22.2).

Goods and services for private purposes

20.13 Goods taken from stock for private purposes are reckoned for tax purposes at selling price. Services are valued at cost, so no notional profit has to be included for services provided free of charge to, say, a relative. Where business is carried on through a limited company, the directors are charged on goods and services taken for their own use under the benefits rules (see CHAPTER 10) and the cost is allowed in calculating the company profits, unless some of the directors' total remuneration including benefits is considered not to be wholly and exclusively for the trade (see 12.8).

Stock and work in progress — valuation (TA 1988, ss 100–102)

20.14 Stock is valued at the lower of cost or realisable value, opening and closing stock being brought into the accounts in determining profit. Work in progress is similarly brought into account, and an appropriate addition for direct or indirect overheads must be included in its value. The Revenue do, however, accept that the amount to include in work in progress for overhead costs is likely to be nil or minimal in most professional firms of up to four partners, although this may depend on the ratio of partners to productive staff.

The value of a proprietor's or working partner's own time is not a contributory part of cost, so this element need not be included in a work in progress valuation, only being reflected in profit when it is billed out.

New barristers need not bring in work in progress for their first seven years of business. They must include it thereafter, but they may spread the amount brought in (called the catching-up charge) over ten years, with the flexibility of increasing the amount of the charge in any of the earlier tax years, an appropriate reduction then being made in later years.

When a trade ceases (other than because of the death of a sole trader), stock is valued at the price received, if sold to an unconnected UK trader. Where the stock is transferred with other assets, the total price is apportioned between the assets on a just and reasonable basis. If the UK trader is connected with the vendor (e.g. through a family link, or as companies in the same group), then the stock is valued at an arm's length price. If, however, that value is greater than both the actual sale price and the cost of the stock, the two parties may make a claim to use the higher of cost and sale price instead of arm's length value. Stock that is disposed of other than by being sold to a UK trader, for example taken by a trader for his personal use, is valued at open market value.

Where a business ceases because of the death of a sole proprietor, the closing stock and work in progress is valued at the lower of cost and market value.

Its acquisition value for executors or beneficiaries is, however, its market value at the date of death, both for capital gains purposes and for income tax purposes if they carry on the business.

Change in basis of computing profits (FA 1998, ss 42–46; FA 2002, ss 64–66 and Sch 22)

20.15 Where a valid basis of accounting is changed such that income is not included or expenditure is included more than once, then in calculating taxable profits the excluded income is brought in and the double counted expenditure is reckoned only once. Such changes might occur because of the adoption of generally accepted accounting practice or court decisions.

Reliefs already obtained may be retained, rather than being withdrawn and allowed in a later period, and effect of reckoning an uplift within profits is spread forward in certain circumstances.

This legislation does not cover a change from an invalid basis to a valid basis of accounting, where the tax consequences of having adopted an invalid basis have to be corrected, often with interest and penalties being incurred.

Value added tax

20.16 If you are VAT registered, VAT is not normally taken into account either as part of your turnover or part of your expenses. You collect VAT for Customs on your supplies of goods and services and recoup any VAT that anyone has charged you subject to an adjustment where there is non-business use. Where there is non-business use, the input VAT is normally apportioned. Alternatively you may claim input VAT in full and account for output VAT on non-business use as it arises. This second alternative is only available in specified circumstances. See Customs' Business Brief 22/03 for the detailed provisions. Where an asset on which input VAT was restricted is sold, output VAT is not charged on the non-business proportion of the sale proceeds.

These general rules are subject to various specific provisions. VAT on business entertaining expenditure (subject to what is said in 20.8) and on the purchase of cars cannot be recovered from Customs unless, in the case of cars, they are used *wholly* for business purposes, e.g. by private taxi firms, self-drive hire firms, driving schools and leasing companies — see 7.11. The unrecovered VAT on entertaining cannot be allowed in calculating your taxable profit either, because business entertaining itself is not so allowed (subject to what is said in 20.8). But disallowed VAT on cars forms part of the cost for capital allowances (see CHAPTER 22). Where assets are acquired on lease, the VAT included in the leasing charges is normally recoverable, but if there is any private use of a leased car on which the lessor recovered the input VAT, the lessee may only recover 50% of the input VAT on the leasing charges. The balance, restricted by the actual private use proportion, would then form part of the lease charges deducted from profits. (There would be no 50% restriction on any input tax relating to a charge for repairs and maintenance if the charge was made in a separate contract as mentioned in 20.11.) Private car fuel is subject to a VAT scale charge (see 7.12). Unlike the provisions for income tax and national insurance, the VAT scale charge applies to private fuel provided for any employees, no matter what they earn, and no matter whether the car is provided by the employer or belongs to the employee. The VAT accounted for to Customs on the fuel may be included as part of the travelling expenses allowed against your profit, except any relating to private use by a sole trader or partner, which will be disallowed along with the private expenditure itself (see 20.3). There is no disallowance of the input tax on car repair and maintenance expenditure, providing there is some business use (see 7.12).

If you are not registered for VAT, any VAT you have suffered on business expenditure (other than on business entertaining expenses, which are wholly disallowed) forms part of your expenditure in calculating taxable profits. It will either qualify for capital allowances as part of the cost of a capital item or it will be an expense in arriving at your profit. The same applies where, although you are VAT registered, some of your supplies are exempt from VAT. You may then not be able to recover all your input VAT from Customs, and the non-deductible amount is taken into account as part of your expenditure for income tax or corporation tax.

If you have joined the VAT flat-rate scheme (see 7.19), your accounts will normally show your turnover and expenses inclusive of output and input VAT. The amount of flat-rate VAT paid may either be deducted from the turnover figure or treated as an expense. Under the scheme, input VAT may be recovered on capital items with a VAT-inclusive value of more than £2,000. Any such input VAT would be recovered by set-off against the flat-rate VAT payable, but it would not reduce the flat-rate VAT charged as an expense in the accounts. It would instead be deducted from the cost of the capital item. Where input VAT on capital items is not recovered, it forms part of the cost of the asset for capital allowances purposes.

National insurance

20.17   The Class 1 national insurance contributions you pay on your employees' wages, Class 1A contributions on the provision of taxable benefits to P11D employees and Class 1B contributions under a PAYE Settlement Agreement (see 10.36) are allowable in calculating your taxable profit. No deduction is allowed for a sole trader's or partner's own Class 2 and Class 4 contributions.

Foster carers etc (FA 2003, s 176 and Sch 36)

20.18   Previously those providing foster care services to local authorities were taxable on payments their local authority identifies as 'reward' payments. A new tax exemption was introduced from 6 April 2003 for foster carers whose gross receipts do not exceed an individual limit. The limit is a fixed amount of £10,000 a year plus an additional amount per child (£200 a week for a child under eleven and £250 a week for a child aged eleven or older). Where the limit is exceeded, foster carers may either compute their profits in the normal way or they may make a written election to treat their taxable profits as being the excess over their individual limit. Such an election must be made by 31 January next but one after the relevant tax year (31 January 2007 for 2004/05).

A non-statutory tax relief is available to adult placement carers, who look after vulnerable adults who are placed with them by local authorities or charities. Those who care for up to three adults may calculate their profits on a fixed expenses basis, with no taxable profit arising if the expenses are within the stipulated level.

Both foster carers and adult placement carers are liable to Class 2 and Class 4 national insurance contributions where appropriate, although no Class 2 contributions are payable if the profits are exempt, or fall within the small earnings exception. Carers may wish to pay Class 2 contributions in any event to maintain their right to various benefits, including incapacity benefit and state pension (the amount payable for 2004/05 being only £2.05 a week). The Revenue's help sheet IR236 deals with both the tax and national insurance position for carers.

Examples of allowable and non-allowable expenditure

20.19

Allowable	*Not allowable*
Staff wages and benefits in kind	Profit shares in the form of interest on partners' capital
Employer's Class 1 national insurance contributions on employees' wages, Class 1A contributions on the provision of taxable benefits to P11D employees and Class 1B contributions under a PAYE settlement agreement	Self-employed national insurance contributions

Allowable	*Not allowable*
Cost of staff temporarily seconded to charities and educational establishments	Cost of improvements, extensions, additions to premises and equipment
Counselling services for redundant employees	Depreciation (capital allowances are available on certain assets — see CHAPTER 22)
Rent and rates of business premises	Expenses of private living accommodation (unless assessable on directors or employees as a benefit in kind)
Repairs	Legal expenses on forming a company, drawing up partnership agreement, acquiring assets such as leases
Premium for grant of lease for 50 years or less, but limited to the amount taxed on the landlord as extra rent (see CHAPTER 32), spread over the term of the lease	Illegal payments such as bribes (including payments overseas that would be illegal in the UK)
Interest on business borrowings	Payments made in response to threats, menaces, blackmail and other forms of extortion
Cost of raising loan finance (excluding stamp duty), for example debentures (not share capital)	Fines and any legal expenses connected therewith
Advertising	Business entertaining expenses including the VAT thereon (except on a reasonable scale when entertaining staff)
Business travel	Gifts to customers, except gifts with a conspicuous advertisement that cost not more than £50 per person per year and are not food, drink, tobacco or gift vouchers
Bad debts written off and provision for specific bad debts	Charitable subscriptions, and charitable donations unless exceptionally the donation satisfies the wholly and exclusively rule (but see CHAPTER 43 re gift aid donations)
Accountancy expenses (see 20.3)	Donations to political parties

Allowable	*Not allowable*
Legal expenses on debt recovery, trade disputes, defending trade rights, employees' service agreements and, by concession, renewing a short lease (i.e. 50 years or less)	Taxation (but see above column as regards VAT)
Contributions to local enterprise agencies and training and enterprise councils (see 29.15)	
Contributions to the running costs of Urban Regeneration Companies	
Research and development expenditure (see also 29.16 to 29.19), and sums paid to scientific research associations etc. undertaking scientific research related to the trade	
Gifts to educational establishments or charities of equipment manufactured, sold or used in the donor's trade	
Gifts of medical supplies and equipment from a company's trading stock for humanitarian purposes	
Non-recoverable VAT relating to allowable expenses, for example where turnover is below VAT threshold, or VAT partial exemption applies	

Non-trading income and capital profits

20.20   Any non-trading income of sole traders and partners included in the business accounts is not charged to tax as part of the business profits. The precise nature of the income determines under what head it is taxed, for example interest under Schedule D, Case III and rent under Schedule A. By concession, the Revenue allow small amounts of rental income to be included in the trading income if they are from subletting a part of business premises that is temporarily surplus to requirements. Under self-assessment, tax on all sources of income (and capital gains) is calculated as a single figure. It is still necessary to keep different sources of income separate, however, particularly because of the treatment of losses. In the case of a partnership, non-trading income has to be shown separately from the trading profit in the partnership return, and partners show their shares of trading income and non-trading income in their personal returns (see CHAPTER 23).

A company's non-trading income is excluded in calculating the trading profit, but the company is chargeable to corporation tax on all its sources of income plus its chargeable gains, tax being payable by self-assessment. See CHAPTERS 9 and 21.

Capital profits of sole traders and partners are liable to capital gains tax, subject to any available reliefs and to the annual exemption (see CHAPTER 4).

Treatment for companies of intangible fixed assets (FA 2002, s 84 and Schs 29, 30; FA 2004, s 52 and Sch 10)

20.21   From 1 April 2002 new rules apply for companies in relation to the tax treatment of goodwill, intellectual property (which includes patents, trade marks, copyrights, know-how, licences etc.) and other intangible assets (intangible assets being as defined in FRS 10 issued by the Accounting Standards Board). The rules generally apply to expenditure on the creation, acquisition or enhancement of intangible fixed assets on or after 1 April 2002, to abortive expenditure on the assets, and to expenditure on their preservation and maintenance. Certain intangible assets are excluded, for example rights over land, financial assets and rights in companies. Computer software treated as part of the cost of the related hardware is excluded except to the extent of any royalties payable in respect of the software. The company may *elect* to exclude capital expenditure on computer software, enabling capital allowances to be claimed instead (see 22.10). Where a company reclassifies an asset as an intangible asset, and capital allowances had been given on it when it was treated as a tangible asset, the asset is not dealt with under the intangible assets rules despite the reclassification.

Expenditure on research and development is excluded from the rules so as to preserve the special research and development tax reliefs (see 29.16 to 29.19). Profits from the exploitation of research and development are, however, brought into account, and in calculating gains on realisation of assets, expenditure on research and development is excluded from the allowable cost.

There are the anti-avoidance provisions to prevent the rules being manipulated and these were widened from 20 June 2003 to close perceived loopholes, particularly in relation to groups of companies.

Gains and losses on intangible fixed assets are brought into account in calculating a company's income. There are rules similar to those for loan relationships (see 3.6) for bringing such amounts into account. Amounts relating to a trade are brought into account in calculating trading income, amounts relating to a property business in calculating Schedule A income, and non-trading amounts are taxed under Schedule D Case VI. If there is a non-trading loss, the company may claim, not later than two years after the end of the accounting period, to set it against the total profits of the same period. Any loss not relieved in that way and not surrendered under the group relief provisions (see 26.12) will be carried forward to set against later non-trading profits.

The cost of intangible fixed assets will in most cases be depreciated for tax purposes according to the amounts charged in the accounts. This will often be by way of straight line depreciation over the asset's useful life. The company may, however, make an irrevocable election, not later than two years after the end of the accounting period in which the asset was acquired or created, to claim allowances at a fixed rate of 4% per annum, which would be beneficial for assets with an indefinite life and long-life assets. Payments for the use of intangible assets, such as royalties, are also within the new rules whether they relate to assets acquired before or after 1 April 2002. Gains and losses when intangible fixed assets are disposed of are brought into account in calculating income, although companies may claim a special rollover relief where the proceeds for the assets are reinvested in new intangible fixed assets that are capitalised in the accounts. This rollover relief follows the same rules as the capital gains relief, i.e. the proceeds must be reinvested within one year before and three years after the date of disposal.

Where a company changes its accounting policy, for example because it has changed from using UK generally accepted accounting practice to using international accounting standards, an adjustment must be made where the closing and opening values of intangible assets are different, unless the company has elected to claim 4% fixed rate allowances as indicated above.

Apart from the royalty treatment indicated above, assets acquired or created before 1 April 2002 are still subject to the previous rules. (Internally generated goodwill is treated as created before 1 April 2002 if the business was carried on at any time before that date by the company or a related party, as to which see below.) When such assets are disposed of on or after 1 April 2002, they will qualify for the rollover relief referred to above. Where such a disposal is of goodwill, or fishing or agricultural quotas, which previously qualified for capital gains rollover relief, the asset does not qualify for that relief unless the reinvestment under the capital gains rules was made before 1 April 2002 and within twelve months before the disposal. In such a case, a disposal could qualify both for capital gains rollover relief (in respect of a reinvestment before 1 April 2002) and intangible assets rollover relief (in respect of a reinvestment in an intangible asset on or after that date). Where this applies, the company may choose to claim either under the capital gains rules or the intangible assets rules, or partly under one set of rules and partly under the other. Purchases of goodwill and quotas on or after 1 April 2002 (except certain acquisitions from related parties as indicated below) are outside the capital gains rollover relief rules.

Special provisions apply to 75% groups. Assets may be transferred from one group company to another on a no loss/no gain basis, subject to a degrouping charge (as in 3.24) if the acquiring company leaves the group within six years. The intangible fixed asset rollover relief provisions apply where one group company makes a qualifying disposal and another acquires a qualifying replacement, and the same provisions apply as in 3.24 to allow a degrouping charge to be reallocated to another group company and for the company chargeable in respect of the degrouping gain to claim the intangible assets rollover relief against replacement assets where appropriate.

There are special provisions dealing with company reconstructions and also for transfers between related parties. The definition of related parties is complex, but is broadly as follows. Companies are related where one controls the other or the same person controls both or (from 20 June 2003) both companies are members of the same group. A person is related to a company if the company is a close company and the person is a participator or associate of a participator in the company (see 3.21 re close companies). A company's acquisitions of intangible assets on or after 1 April 2002 from a related party will only be within the new provisions if the asset was within the provisions in the hands of the related party, or the related party acquired the asset on or after 1 April 2002 from an unrelated party, or the asset was created on or after 1 April 2002 by the related party or someone else. Even so, on disposal by the company, such assets no longer qualify for the capital gains rollover relief.

Tax relief for companies for cleaning up contaminated land (FA 2001, s 70 and Sch 22)

20.22 A special relief may be claimed by companies that acquire contaminated land for the purposes of a trade or Schedule A letting business. The relief is equal to 150% of qualifying expenditure incurred on cleaning up the contaminated land ('land remediation expenditure'). The expenditure must be additional to normal site preparation. If the deduction results in a trading or Schedule A loss, then to the extent that the loss is not relieved against profits of the company (or where relevant, a group company), the company may claim a 'land remediation tax credit' equal to 16% of the amount of the deduction (i.e. 24% of the corresponding expenditure), or 16% of the unrelieved loss if lower. Losses available to be carried forward are reduced accordingly. The claim for the tax credit must be made in the company's tax return or an amended return. The tax credit will be paid to the company by the Revenue (subject to set off against any outstanding tax liabilities). It does not count as income for tax purposes.

Films (F(No 2)A 1992, ss 40A–43; F(No 2)A 1997, s 48; FA 2002, ss 99–101; FA 2004, ss 119–123; ESC B54)

20.23   Expenditure on the production and acquisition of films, tapes and discs is treated as revenue expenditure and not capital expenditure, with the cost being written off over the income-producing life of the film. This does not apply to qualifying British films providing the films are genuinely intended for theatrical release in the commercial cinema. For qualifying British films, pre-production expenditure up to 20% of the total budgeted expenditure, and abortive expenditure, may be written off as it is incurred. Except as indicated below, production expenditure and expenditure on acquisition of qualifying British films is written off at a flat rate of 33⅓% a year from completion of the film. Alternatively, an election may be made for allowances to be given under the normal plant and machinery rules, but this would give lower allowances.

For expenditure incurred between 2 July 1997 and 1 July 2005 on the production or acquisition of qualifying British films completed on or after 2 July 1997 with a total production expenditure of £15 million or less, the whole of the production expenditure not already relieved may be written off in the period in which the film is completed, or the acquisition expenditure is incurred, if later. This only applies to production expenditure which, when the film is completed, has either been paid or is unconditionally payable within the next four months, and acquisition expenditure only qualifies if the acquisition is by or directly from the producer of the film. If the qualifying acquisition expenditure exceeds the production expenditure, allowances for the excess not qualifying for the 100% allowance may be claimed at 33⅓% a year under the normal rules. The same will apply where some of the production expenditure is incurred after 1 July 2005. The Revenue have given guidance on the treatment of expenditure on films in Statement of Practice 1/98.

Anti-avoidance provisions have been introduced from 10 December 2003 to prevent the acceleration of tax relief available under the above provisions being turned into a permanent tax advantage. This has been occurring particularly with sale and leaseback arrangements, under which schemes have been devised to enable an investor in the leasing business to create losses to set against other income in the early years, but to dispose of the investment before taxable rental income arises.

Profits averaging for authors and creative artists (TA 1988, s 95A and Sch 4A)

20.24   Special averaging provisions are available for authors and creative artists that follow the same rules as those that apply to farmers (see 31.4). The essence of the special rules is that claims may be made by individuals and partners to average the profits of two consecutive tax years if the profits of the lower year are less than 70% of the profits of the higher year or are nil, with marginal relief if the profits are more than 70% but less than 75%. The time limit for averaging claims is twelve months after the 31 January following the end of the later of the two years, i.e. by 31 January 2007 for a claim to average 2003/04 and 2004/05. The effect of the claim on Class 4 national insurance contributions needs to be taken into account, where all or part of the higher profits were above the Class 4 upper limit, thus attracting contributions at only 1%, whereas averaging brings profits below it, attracting contributions at 8%.

Tax points

20.25

- Try to avoid mixing business and private expenditure. Make sure you do not cloud a genuine business expense with a private element.

- If you are a retailer, use your business connections to make private purchases at lower cost, rather than taking goods out of your own stock and suffering tax on a figure equivalent to the profit you would have made if you had sold them to a customer.

- Since any expense for the benefit of staff is normally allowable in computing profits, it is sometimes more appropriate to provide acceptable benefits than to pay higher salaries. The employee will usually be taxable on the benefit but may prefer the tax charge to having to fund the purchase himself. As far as national insurance contributions are concerned, Class 1 contributions are payable on some benefits by both P11D employees and lower-paid employees, and also by employers (see CHAPTER 10). Other benefits are chargeable to Class 1A contributions, which apply only for P11D employees, and are payable only by employers. There is therefore an 11% national insurance saving on benefits within the Class 1A category for employees paying contributions at the main rate, and a 1% saving for employees earning above the upper earnings limit of £31,720.

- If you claim a deduction that is not commercially justifiable, you may have to pay interest on tax underpaid as a result, and possibly a penalty as well. This is very important when considering the 'wholly and exclusively' business element of a mixed expense, such as accommodation and motor expenses. An inaccurate claim and/or providing insufficient information to the Revenue may be costly in the long run.

- Wages payments to a spouse must not only be commercially justifiable for the spouse's participation in the business but must be properly made and the payment entered in the business records. If the Revenue enquire into your tax return, they will usually challenge the charge if it has not been separately paid, but has instead been regarded as included in the amount drawn by the trader or for housekeeping, with an accounting entry being made to create the wages charge.

- Similar considerations apply where mature children are able genuinely to participate in the business, for example in farming, retail and wholesale trades.

- Remember that wages paid after the end of an accounting period must be paid within nine months if they are to be deducted from the profits of that period, otherwise they will be deducted from profits in the period of payment.

- Although expenses incurred by a company from which a director or employee derives a personal benefit are allowable in computing trading profit and taxed as earnings of the director or employee, this must be distinguished from using company funds to meet the private expenditure of a director/employee who is a shareholder and not treating the amount as pay. This will usually be treated as a loan from the company, which will have tax and sometimes national insurance consequences both for the director and the company — see 12.14.

- Where you use part of your home for business, you will usually pay business rates. If you do not, you can claim the appropriate part of your council tax as a business expense — see 19.4.

- If you pay congestion charges incurred by you or your employees while travelling on business in Central London, they are allowable against your profit. For employees who have private use of company cars, the taxable benefit covers congestion charge payments (see 10.19).

- You must make sure you keep all business records relating to your tax affairs for at least 5 years 10 months after the end of the tax year, and sometimes longer. Penalties of up to £3,000 per tax year apply if you do not. See 9.6. The Revenue have issued a useful booklet SA/BK3 on record-keeping for the self-employed.

21

How are business profits charged to tax?

Companies (TMA 1970, ss 59D, 59DA, 59E; TA 1988, ss 8–12; FA 1998, s 117 and Sch 18)

21.1   Although taxable business profits for individuals and companies are calculated on similar lines, the way company profits are taxed is much more straightforward. A company's trading profits are taxed with its other profits, such as interest, rents and chargeable gains, by reference to chargeable accounting periods (see 3.8). A chargeable accounting period can be as short as the company wishes but cannot exceed twelve months. If a company makes up an account for say fifteen months it is split into two chargeable accounting periods for tax purposes, the first of twelve months and the second of three months. Capital allowances (which are available on certain assets, notably plant and machinery and industrial buildings — see CHAPTER 22) are then deducted in arriving at the trading profits. The capital allowances are not calculated for the fifteen-month period and divided pro rata. They are calculated for the separate periods of twelve and three months according to the events of those periods.

Companies are within the self-assessment system, under which they are required to file their returns with supporting accounts and computations within twelve months after the end of the accounting period. Assessments will not normally be issued by the Revenue except in cases of fraudulent or negligent conduct. For details, see 9.31.

Example 1

A company makes trading profits of £150,000 in the 15 months to 30 June 2004. The profits will be charged to tax as follows:

	12 months to 31.3.2004	3 months to 30.6.2004
	£	£
12/15, 3/15	120,000	30,000
Less capital allowances (say)	10,000	8,000
	£110,000	£22,000
Tax payable:	£	£
1.4.2003 – 31.3.2004, £110,000 @ 19%	20,900	
1.4.2004 – 30.6.2004, £22,000 @ 19%		4,180

The due date for payment of corporation tax is nine months and one day after the end of the chargeable accounting period, i.e. 1 January 2005 for the twelve-month account and 1 April 2005 for the three-month account in Example 1. Under corporation tax self-assessment, large companies have to pay corporation tax by quarterly instalments (see 3.18).

If companies delay payment it will cost them interest, because when the tax for the period is finally determined, any shortfall between that amount and the amount paid suffers interest from the original due date (see 3.19).

Individuals (TA 1988, ss 60–63A)

Current year basis of assessment

21.2   All sources of income are charged to income tax on the income of the tax year. For business profits this does not mean that accounts have to be made up for the tax year itself, because businesses are free to choose their annual accounting date. Apart from special rules for the opening years and when the accounting date is changed, the taxable profits of a tax year are taken to be those of the accounting year ending in the tax year.

There is no stipulation as to the length of the first accounting period, or indeed of subsequent accounting periods. The consequences of having a first accounting period shorter or longer than twelve months are dealt with in 21.4 and the change of accounting date rules are dealt with in 21.7. It should be realised, however, that if accounts are not available at the time when the tax for the relevant tax year is due for payment, tax must be paid on an estimated basis, and interest will be charged from the original due date on any underpayment (or allowed on any overpayment) when the correct figures are known.

Capital allowances

21.3   Capital allowances are treated as a trading expense and balancing charges as a trading receipt of the accounting period. If the accounting period is shorter or longer than twelve months, the annual writing-down allowances are reduced or increased proportionately. The detailed provisions are in CHAPTER 22.

Taxable profits in the early years

21.4   In their first tax year, new businesses are taxed on their profit from the start date to the end of the tax year. The second year's charge is normally based on the profits of the accounting year ended in the second tax year. Part of that profit has usually already been taxed in the first year, and this is called the 'overlap profit' (see Example 2). Overlap profits can also occur on a change of accounting date. Businesses that were in existence at 5 April 1994 may also have 'transitional overlap profits', which arose when the rules for taxing business profits and some other income changed from the 'previous year basis' to the current year basis. The transitional overlap profits normally cover the period between the annual accounting date in 1996/97 and 5 April 1997, that period also having been included in the taxable profits for 1997/98. For example, a pre-6 April 1994 business that makes up accounts to 30 June would have a transitional overlap period from 1 July 1996 to 5 April 1997. The detailed transitional provisions are covered in earlier editions of this book.

Example 2

Business started 1 January 2004 and made up its first accounts for 12 months to 31 December 2004, then annually to 31 December.

The taxable profits are arrived at as follows:

2003/04	1.1.04 – 5.4.04	3/12 × 1st year's profits
2004/05	1.1.04 – 31.12.04	1st year's profits
2005/06	1.1.05 – 31.12.05	2nd year's profits
Overlap profits are:		3/12 × 1st year's profits

Where profits need to be apportioned, the apportionment may be made in days, months, or months and fractions of months providing the chosen method is used consistently. If a business makes up accounts to 31 March, the Revenue are prepared to treat the year to 31 March as being equivalent to the tax year itself, so that for such a business starting on say 1 April 2004 the result of the first five days would be treated as nil, giving a nil profit for 2003/04. The profit of the first twelve months to 31 March 2005 would be taxed in 2004/05 and there would be no overlap profits and no overlap relief. Similarly, if a business changes its accounting date to 31 March, relief for all overlap profits is given at that time.

If the first accounts are made up to a date in the second tax year, but for a period of less than twelve months, the charge for the second tax year is based on the profits of the first twelve months.

Example 3

Business started 1 January 2004 and made up its first accounts for 9 months to 30 September 2004, then annually to 30 September.

The taxable profits are arrived at as follows:

2003/04	1.1.04 – 5.4.04	3/9 × 1st profits
2004/05	1.1.04 – 31.12.04	Profits of 1st 9 months plus 3/12 × profits of yr to 30.9.05
2005/06	1.10.04 – 30.9.05	
Overlap		3/9 × 1st profits plus 3/12 × profits
profits are:		of yr to 30.9.05

If accounts are made up to a date in the second tax year, and are for twelve months or more, the charge for the second tax year is based on the profits of twelve months to the accounting date (see example 4 and also Example 2 at 23.3 re the admission of a new partner).

Example 4

Business started 1 October 2003 and made up its first accounts for 15 months to 31 December 2004, then annually to 31 December.

The taxable profits are arrived at as follows:

2003/04	1.10.03 – 5.4.04	6/15 × 1st profits
2004/05	1.4.04 – 31.12.04	12/15 × 1st profits
2005/06	1.1.05 – 31.12.05	
Profits of 1st 15 months		
have therefore been used to		
charge tax for 18 months,		
so overlap profits are:		3/15 × 1st profits

If the first accounts are made up for more than twelve months and no accounting period ends in the second tax year, the charge for the second tax year is based on the profits of the tax year itself, and the charge for the third tax year is based on twelve months to the accounting date.

Example 5

Business started 1 January 2004 and made up its first accounts for 16 months to 30 April 2005, then annually to 30 April.

The taxable profits are arrived at as follows:

2003/04	1.1.04 – 5.4.04	3/16 × 1st profits
2004/05	6.4.04 – 5.4.05	12/16 × 1st profits
2005/06	1.5.04 – 30.4.05	12/16 × 1st profits
Profits of first 16 months have therefore been used to charge tax for 27 months, so overlap profits are:		11/16 × 1st profits

Taxable profits when business ceases

21.5   When a business ceases, it is taxed on its profits from the end of the basis period for the previous tax year to the date of cessation (unless it ceases in its second tax year, in which case it is taxed in that final year on the profits from 6 April to the date of cessation). See Example 6. Depending on the dates to which accounts are made up, there may be two accounts that together form the basis for the final taxable profit (see Example 7).

Overlap profits and overlap relief

21.6   The effect of the rules for overlaps is that the business is taxed over its life on the profits made. There is, however, no provision for any inflation-proofing of overlap profits. A record needs to be kept not only of the amount of overlap profits but also the length of the overlapping period. If an overlapping period shows a loss, it must be recorded as an overlap of nil for the appropriate period (relief for the loss being available separately). This is important because overlap relief is given either when the business ceases, as in Examples 6 and 7, or partly or wholly at the time of an earlier change of accounting date to the extent that more than twelve months' profit would otherwise be chargeable in one year (see Examples 8 and 9 at 21.7).

Example 6

Business started 1 January 2000 and makes up accounts annually to 31 December. It ceases on 30 June 2004. Profits after capital allowances were as follows:

		£
Year to 31 December	2000	24,000
	2001	30,000
	2002	28,000
	2003	34,000
6 months to 30 June	2004	20,000
		136,000

The profits are charged to tax as follows:

			£
1999/2000	1.1.2000 – 5.4.2000 ³⁄₁₂ × £24,000		6,000
2000/01	1.1.2000 – 31.12.2000		24,000
	(Overlap profit £6,000)		
2001/02	1.1.2001 – 31.12.2001		30,000
2002/03	1.1.02 – 31.12.02		28,000
2003/04	1.1.03 – 31.12.03		34,000
2004/05	1.1.04 – 30.6.04	20,000	
	Less overlap profit	6,000	14,000
			136,000

Thus the business is taxed over its life on the profits earned.

Example 7

Facts as in Example 6 but business ceases on 31 March 2004, i.e. in the tax year 2003/04. The accounts for the three months ending on that date show profits of £10,000, so that the total profits are £126,000.

The taxable profits from 1999/2000 to 2002/03 are the same as in Example 6, totalling £88,000. The final taxable profit for 2003/04 is as follows:

1.1.03 – 31.12.03	34,000	
1.1.04 – 31.3.04	10,000	
	44,000	
Less overlap profit	6,000	£38,000

Total taxable profits are therefore equal to the profits earned, i.e. (88,000 + 38,000 =) £126,000.

Change of accounting date

21.7   Notice of a change of accounting date has to be given to the Revenue by 31 January following the tax year of change. The fact that the Revenue do not recognise a change unless notice is given means that accounts may be made up to an intermediate date for commercial reasons, say when a partner leaves, without the annual accounting date being altered. The rules also provide that a change of date will not be recognised if the first accounting period to the new date exceeds 18 months. This does not mean that accounts cannot be prepared for longer than 18 months, but tax has to be computed according to the old date (apportioning results as necessary) until the rules can be satisfied.

Example 8

Accounts were made up for 12 months to 30 June 2002, then for the 21 months to the new accounting date of 31 March 2004 and annually thereafter. Taxable profits will be calculated as follows:

2002/03	12 months to 30 June 2002
2003/04	12 months to 30 June 2003 (i.e. $^{12}/_{21}$ × accounts to 31 March 2004)
2004/05	21 months to 31 March 2005 (i.e. $^{9}/_{21}$ × accounts to 31 March 2004 and 12 months to 31 March 2005)
	Less relief for all previous overlap profits*

* The full amount of available overlap relief is given if the accounting date is changed to 31 March — see above.

Example 9

Business starts on 1 January 2004 and makes a loss in the year to 31 December 2004, profits arising thereafter. There is no taxable profit in 2003/04 or 2004/05, but the overlap period is from 1 January 2004 to 5 April 2004, i.e. (to the nearest month) 3 months, the overlap profit being nil. If the accounting date was later changed to 30 June, this would give a further overlap of 6 months. The combined overlap period would be *9 months,* with an overlap profit of nil plus a 6 months' proportion of the profit at the time of the later overlap.

If the accounting date was subsequently changed again to, say, 30 September, 15 months' profit would be charged at that time, less a deduction for a 3 months' proportion of the overlap profit, but this would amount to *3/9ths* not 3/6ths.

The rules for dealing with the change broadly ensure that twelve months' profit is charged in each tax year, except the first year and the last year. If accounts are made up to a date earlier in the tax year than the previous date, profits of *twelve* months to the new date will be charged, but this will result in overlap profits for which relief will be due later. The overlap profits and period to which they relate will be combined with any earlier overlap profits (including transitional overlap profits on the change from previous year to current year basis) and overlap period to give a single figure for a single period. If accounts are made up to a date *later* in the tax year, more than twelve months' profits will be charged in the year of change, but a proportion of the available overlap relief will be deducted, according to how many more than twelve months' profits are being taxed. If the earlier overlap period(s) showed a loss rather than a profit, however, there would be no overlap relief due (relief for the loss having been given separately), so that the charge on more than twelve months' profit would stand. The *length* of the total overlap period is not affected by the fact that one or more earlier overlap periods showed a loss (see 21.6). This is particularly important when calculating how much relief may be given when more than twelve months' profit would otherwise be charged in one year.

Even where losses are not involved, the overlap profit may have been seriously eroded by inflation, so that the amount deductible when more than twelve months' profits would otherwise be charged, or on cessation, may be of much less real value than the profits currently being charged to tax.

Example 10

Say a business started on 1 January 2000, making up accounts to December, and the overlap profit for the 3 months to 5 April 2000 amounted to £6,000. If the business had continued with a 31 December year end until 31 December 2008, making profits in that year of £96,000, and had then made up a 9-month account to 30 September 2009, the assessment for 2009/10 would be based on the profits of *12* months to 30 September 2009, so that ³⁄₁₂ths of the profits of the year to 31 December 2008, i.e. £24,000, would be taxed twice. That amount would be an additional overlap profit, which would be combined with the earlier overlap profit of £6,000, giving total overlap profits of £30,000 for 6 months. Overlap relief for that amount would be given either on cessation or in an earlier year to the extent that more than 12 months' profit would otherwise be taxed.

Alternatively, say that instead of making up accounts to 30 September 2009, the business had made up a 14-month account to 28 February 2010, showing a profit of £112,000. The profits of the year to 31 December 2008 would be taxed in 2008/09. The profits of the 14 months to 28 February 2010 would be taxed in 2009/10, reduced by 2 months' overlap relief, i.e. ⅔ of £6,000 = £4,000 (although 2 months at the then

---

> profit rate represents profits of £16,000). The balance of the overlap relief of £2,000 would be given on cessation or when tax was again being charged for a period exceeding 12 months.

Changes of accounting date are not permitted more than once in every five years unless the Revenue are satisfied that the change is for commercial reasons. In the absence of Revenue approval, the taxable profits are calculated using the previous accounting date, with the figures being apportioned on a time basis.

Pre-trading expenditure (TA 1988, s 401)

21.8   Some expenditure, for example rent, rates and interest, may be incurred before trading actually starts. So long as it is a normal trading expense and is incurred not more than seven years before the trade starts, it may be treated as an expense of the first trading period. These provisions apply to sole traders and partners and also apply to companies, except in relation to interest paid. Pre-trading interest paid by a company is brought into the calculation of the company's Schedule D, Case III *non-trading* profit or loss at the time of payment (see 3.6). If this results in a loss, it is deducted from the taxable profits of that period, or carried back against the Schedule D, Case III profits of the previous twelve months, or carried forward against later non-trading profits. The company may, however, make a claim, within two years after the end of the period in which the deduction was taken into account, to treat the interest as an expense of the first *trading* period instead, and it will be deducted in that period providing the trade starts within seven years after the end of the period in which the non-trading deduction was originally taken into account.

Post-cessation receipts (TA 1988, ss 103–110)

21.9   Income may arise after a business has ceased which has not been included in the final accounts. Any such income is charged to tax under Schedule D, Case VI. The chargeable amount may be reduced by any expenses, capital allowances or losses that could have been set against the income if it had been received before the business ceased. The taxable amount is treated as income of the tax year in which it is received, unless it is received within six years after cessation, when the taxpayer can elect to have it treated as arising in the tax year when trading ceased. The carry-back election must be made within one year after the 31 January following the tax year in which the income was received. The amount of tax payable on the additional income will be calculated by reference to the tax position of the earlier year, but it will be treated as additional tax payable for the tax year in which the amounts were received.

Post-cessation expenses (TA 1988, s 109A; FA 1995, s 90)

21.10   Certain expenditure incurred by sole traders or partners in the seven years after a trade or profession has ceased that has not been provided for in the final accounts and cannot be set against any post-cessation receipts may be set against the total income and capital gains of the tax year in which it is incurred. This applies to professional indemnity premiums, cost of remedying defective work plus any related damages and legal expenses, bad debts and debt recovery costs. For the relief to apply, a claim must be made within one year after the 31 January following the tax year in which the expenditure was incurred.

Tax points

21.11

- Choosing an accounting date early in the tax year in an unincorporated business gives more time for planning the funding of tax payments. It also means that you are paying tax each year on profits that were largely earned in the previous year, giving an obvious advantage if profits are rising. When the business ceases, however, the final tax bill may be particularly high, because the profits then being earned may be very much higher than the early overlap profits for which relief is given on cessation.

- This chapter contains examples of claims which are available to tax-payers. There is always a time limit involved, which depends on the type of claim being made. The legislation should be checked for the time limit whenever a claim is available. There is a general time limit under income tax self-assessment of approximately five years ten months after the end of the tax year where no other time limit is specified.

- The time limit for notifying liability to income tax or capital gains tax if a return is not received is six months from the end of the tax year, e.g. by 5 October 2004 for someone who started a new business between 6 April 2003 and 5 April 2004. The taxpayer may have to complete his self-assessment on an estimated basis and amend it later, because the information may not be available in time (see next tax point). There are penalties for late notification of liability, and also penalties for late returns, together with interest and surcharges on late payments (see 9.8). See also 9.48 for the penalty of £100 payable in respect of Class 2 national insurance contributions if you fail to register within three months of starting business.

- New unincorporated businesses may often incur interest charges on underpaid tax under self-assessment, because interest runs from the 31 January filing date for the return (or three months after the return is issued, if later) on what the tax finally turns out to be. If you started business say on 1 January 2003 and make up accounts to 31 December 2003, tax (and Class 4 national insurance) was due on 31 January 2004 (i.e. the return filing date) on the profit from 1 January to 5 April 2003. You were unlikely to have completed the December 2003 accounts by that date. If you underestimated the tax and Class 4 national insurance due, interest will run on the underpayment from 31 January 2004 (although the tax and national insurance payment itself will not be due until 30 days after you file an amendment to your return).

22
Capital allowances

Background

22.1 Capital expenditure cannot be deducted in calculating income profits, but taxable profits may be reduced by capital allowances on certain assets. The law on capital allowances is contained in the Capital Allowances Act 2001, as amended by subsequent legislation.

The most important allowances available are those in respect of expenditure on:

Plant and machinery
Industrial buildings
Agricultural buildings
Hotels
Buildings in enterprise zones, other than dwelling houses
Patents
Know-how
Research and development
Mineral extraction

These allowances are available to sole traders, partnerships and companies, except that for companies, capital allowances are no longer claimed on patents and know-how acquired on or after 1 April 2002. Relief in those cases will be given by a deduction in computing income under the 'Intangible assets' provisions (see 20.21). See also 22.10 re computer software.

Agricultural buildings allowances are dealt with in more detail in CHAPTER 31.

100% capital allowances are available in respect of expenditure on renovating or converting space above qualifying shops and commercial premises to provide flats for rent. The details are in 32.12. It is intended that 100% allowances will be available from 2005 for renovating business premises in designated Enterprise Areas (see 32.13).

Plant and machinery allowances are available not only to businesses but also to employees who have to provide plant and machinery for use in their employment (see 10.11), and to those who let property and/or equipment, in respect of fixtures, fittings, etc. (see 22.23). As well as claiming allowances on fixtures, landlords of let property may claim industrial and agricultural buildings allowances when qualifying buildings are let. An example of qualifying expenditure on plant and machinery by an employee might be a musical instrument purchased by an employee of an orchestra. The most common example used to be cars, but employees can no longer claim capital allowances on cars, being entitled to mileage allowances instead.

If an asset is used partly for private purposes by sole traders or partners, or by employees claiming allowances for their own plant and machinery, allowances are given only on the appropriate business fraction. There is no restriction where company assets are used privately by directors or employees, but the director/employee is taxed on the benefit obtained.

Expenditure qualifying for relief (CAA 2001, ss 67–69, 219, 290, 291, 532–543)

22.2   Capital allowances are available when expenditure is incurred on a qualifying asset, even if the expenditure is funded by means of a loan or bank overdraft. Interest on such funding is, however, allowed as a business expense and not as part of the cost of the asset. Where an industrial building is let at a premium on a long lease (more than 50 years), the landlord and tenant may elect for the premium to be treated as the purchase price for the building, so that industrial buildings allowances may be claimed by the tenant. If the tenant himself incurs capital expenditure on a qualifying building, he is entitled to allowances on that expenditure.

When an asset is purchased under a hire-purchase agreement, the expenditure is regarded as incurred as soon as the asset comes into use, even though the asset is not strictly owned until the option-to-purchase payment is made. The hire-purchase charges are not part of the cost but are allowed as a business expense, spread appropriately over the term of the agreement.

Where plant and machinery is acquired on a finance lease, then although for accounting purposes the assets are treated as owned by the lessee, they belong in law to the lessor and it is normally the lessor who gets the capital allowances. Finance lessors are normally entitled only to writing-down allowances (see 22.11 for exceptions), and the allowances are restricted on a time basis according to when in the accounting period the plant and machinery was acquired. For the treatment of the lease payments see 20.12. There are extensive anti-avoidance provisions in relation to finance leases, and to sale and leaseback or lease and leaseback transactions, which are outside the scope of this Guide.

Subsidies or contributions from third parties must in general be deducted from the allowable cost. Regional development grants, however, are specifically excluded from this requirement and do not have to be deducted. If the qualifying expenditure on an asset is restricted because the owner has received a contribution or subsidy from someone else, the third party may claim allowances on the contribution, even though strictly he does not have an interest in the asset.

Where value added tax has been paid and cannot be recovered, for example on motor cars or, in the case of other asset purchases, because of the partial exemption rules or because the trader is not VAT registered, it forms part of the allowable expenditure for capital allowances. Capital allowances computations have to be adjusted where input VAT on buildings and computers is later adjusted under the capital goods scheme (see 22.28).

Chargeable periods (CAA 2001, s 6)

Corporation tax

22.3 For a company, the chargeable period by reference to which capital allowances are given and balancing charges are made is the company's chargeable accounting period, so that where a period of account exceeds twelve months, it is split into a twelve-month chargeable accounting period or periods and the remaining period, and relief for capital expenditure is first available according to the chargeable period in which the expenditure is incurred. Writing down allowances are proportionately reduced for accounting periods of less than twelve months.

Income tax

22.4 For individuals, capital allowances are treated as trading expenses, and balancing charges as trading receipts, of the period of account. If the period of account is longer or shorter than twelve months, writing-down allowances are increased or reduced accordingly (the £3,000 maximum allowance for cars costing more than £12,000 — see 22.20 — being similarly increased or reduced). If a period of account exceeds eighteen months, however, capital allowances are calculated as if it was one or more periods of account of twelve months plus a period of account covering the remainder of the period. The aggregate allowances for the separate periods are then treated as a trading expense of the whole period. This prevents undue advantage being gained as a result of the long account. See Example 2 at 22.17.

Chargeable periods for non-trading individuals

22.5 For employees and landlords who are individuals, the chargeable period is the income tax year itself.

Date expenditure is incurred (CAA 2001, s 5)

22.6 This is generally the date on which the obligation to pay becomes unconditional (i.e. normally the invoice date), but if any part of the payment is not due until more than four months after that date, that part of the expenditure is regarded as incurred on the due date of payment. The due date of payment is also substituted where the unconditional obligation to pay has been brought forward to obtain allowances earlier. It sometimes happens that, under large construction contracts, the purchaser becomes the owner at an earlier date than the time when the obligation to pay becomes unconditional, e.g. on presentation of an architect's certificate. Where, in those circumstances, ownership passes in one chargeable period, but the obligation becomes unconditional in the first month of the next, the expenditure is regarded as incurred in the earlier period.

Way in which capital allowances are given (CAA 2001, ss 3, 247–262, 352, 353, 432, 450, 463, 478–480; TA 1988, s 379A; FA 1998 Sch 18 Pt IX)

22.7 As indicated at 22.3 and 22.4, the allowances claimed are treated as trading expenses of the period of account for sole traders and partners and of the chargeable accounting period for trading companies. They may therefore form part of a loss or turn a profit into a loss. For the reliefs available for trading losses see CHAPTER 25 for individuals and CHAPTER 26 for companies.

Allowances claimed by individual or corporate property investors are given against rent income, and for both individuals and companies, they are deducted as an expense in arriving at the profit of the 'Schedule A business' — see 32.11.

If the Schedule A business makes a loss then an individual investor may claim to set an amount equal to the capital allowances included in the loss against any income of the same tax year or of the following tax year. See Example 6 at 22.30. The time limit for such a claim is one year from 31 January following the tax year in which the loss arises. Any loss not relieved in this way is carried forward against future income from the Schedule A business (see 32.6).

A corporate investor cannot make a separate claim relating to capital allowances included in a Schedule A loss, but more generous relief for a Schedule A loss is available to a corporate investor than an individual investor (see 32.9).

Both individuals and companies must make a specific claim for capital allowances in a tax return or amended return.

For companies, the normal time limit for making or amending claims is two years after the end of the accounting period, but if the Revenue enquire into the return the time limit is extended to 30 days after the time when the profits or losses of the period are finally settled. If the effect of a claim following an enquiry is to reduce the allowances available for a later period for which a return has been submitted, the company has 30 days from the settlement of the enquiry to make any necessary amendments to the return, failing which amendments will be made by the Revenue. If the Revenue make an assessment under their 'discovery' powers (see 9.43), then providing the company had not been fraudulent or negligent, further claims may be made within one year from the end of the accounting period in which the assessment is made. See CHAPTER 9 for further details.

For individuals, capital allowances are subject to the same time limits as for other entries in returns, i.e. any amendment must normally be made within twelve months after the 31 January filing date for the return, although special rules apply to fixtures (see 22.23). If the Revenue enquire into the return, amendments may be made up to 30 days after the settlement of the enquiry, providing the original return was submitted within the time limit. If the Revenue make an assessment under their 'discovery' powers (see 9.43), then providing the taxpayer had not been fraudulent or negligent, further claims may be made within one year from the end of the tax year in which the assessment is made. See CHAPTER 9 for further details.

You may claim less than the full allowances available if you wish. This may enable you to make better use of other available reliefs and allowances (see Tax points at 22.39).

Balancing allowances and charges (CAA 2001, ss 55, 56, 314, 417, 418, 441, 442, 457, 458, 471, 472)

22.8 When an asset is sold, a 'balancing allowance' is given for any amount by which the sale proceeds fall short of the unrelieved expenditure on the asset. If the proceeds exceed the unrelieved expenditure, the excess is included in taxable income by means of a 'balancing charge'. If the proceeds exceed the original cost, however, the excess over cost is dealt with under the capital gains rules (see 22.24), except for sales of know-how where special rules apply (see 22.36).

For plant and machinery, balancing allowances and charges are normally dealt with on a 'pool' basis for most assets (see 22.17).

There are provisions to prevent businesses obtaining increased allowances on disposal of certain assets, in particular industrial and agricultural buildings and certain flat conversions, as a result of a tax avoidance scheme. These are dealt with briefly in 22.27, 31.8 AND 32.12.

Connected persons, etc. (CAA 2001, ss 61, 265–268, 567–570, 573, 575; TA 1988, ss 343, 344)

22.9   If an asset is withdrawn from a business for personal use or sold to a connected person for use other than in a business, the amount to be included as sales proceeds is usually the open market value. (The definition of 'connected person' is broadly the same as that for capital gains tax — see 4.27 — although it is slightly wider.)

On a sale of plant and machinery between connected persons, open market value is not used for the seller if the buyer's expenditure is taken into account for capital allowances (so that, for example, intra-group transfers are taken into account at the price paid). On a sale of assets other than plant and machinery, open market value is used, except that providing the sale was not made to obtain a tax advantage, a joint claim may be made by seller and buyer, within two years after the sale, for the sale to be treated as made at written-down value.

Where the transfer of an asset to a connected person takes place at the time when the business itself is transferred, the assets are treated as being sold at open market value. But the predecessor and successor may make a joint election, within two years from the date of the transfer, for it to be treated as made at the tax written-down value, so there will be no balancing adjustment on the predecessor and the successor will take over the allowances from that point. The most common example of the application of these rules is when a business is transferred to a company (see 27.2).

Special rules apply where a trade is transferred from one company to another, and at some time within one year before the transfer and two years after the transfer, the same persons own three-quarters or more of the trade (see 26.15). These rules enable the predecessor's capital allowances computations to continue. First year allowances on plant and machinery are claimed by whoever incurred the expenditure and balancing adjustments are made on the company carrying on the trade at the time of the disposal. Writing-down allowances are split on a time basis.

Plant and machinery

What is plant and machinery? (CAA 2001, ss 21–33, 71)

22.10   There is no overall definition of plant and machinery in the legislation, although there are certain items that are specifically stated to be within the definition, for example certain expenditure by traders on fire safety, heat insulation in industrial buildings, and expenditure on safety at sports grounds. In addition the legislation explicitly lists certain expenditure on buildings and structures that cannot be treated as plant or machinery, and lists other items of expenditure which are not affected by the exclusions and which will in general be accepted by the Revenue as plant and machinery. Most of these items derive from court decisions.

Deciding what 'machinery' is does not pose much of a problem, but the question of what is and is not plant has come before the courts many times. The main problem lies in distinguishing the 'apparatus' *with* which a business is carried on from the 'setting' *in* which it is carried on. Items forming part of the setting do not qualify for allowances unless they do so as part of the building itself and not as plant, for example where it is an industrial building, or unless the business is one in which atmosphere, or ambience, is important, but, even so, allowances for plant are not available on expenditure on an asset which becomes part of the premises, such as shop fronts, flooring and suspended ceilings. (Although initial expenditure on a shop front is disallowed, the cost of a subsequent replacement is allowed as a revenue expense against the profit, but excluding any improvement element.) Lifts and central heating systems are treated as plant, while basic electricity and plumbing systems are not. Specific lighting to create atmosphere in a hotel and special lighting in fast food restaurants have been held to be plant. A tenant who incurs expenditure on items that become landlord's fixtures can nonetheless claim allowances — see 22.23.

Expenditure on computer hardware is capital expenditure on plant and machinery. Except for expenditure by small businesses that qualifies for 100% first year allowances (see 22.13) allowances will usually be claimed under the 'short-life assets' rules (see 22.18). Unless it is developed 'in house', computer software is usually licensed for lifetime to a particular user or users rather than being purchased outright. Despite the fact that a licence to use software is an intangible asset, it is specifically provided that capital expenditure on licensed software and electronically transmitted software qualifies for plant and machinery allowances. Where computer software is treated as part of the cost of the related hardware, it is not affected by the rules for companies relating to intangible assets (see 20.21) and it remains within the capital allowances regime. Where it is not so treated, it will be dealt with under the intangible assets provisions unless the company elects, within two years after the end of the accounting period in which the expenditure was incurred, for the capital allowances provisions to apply. Such an election is irrevocable.

If licensed software is acquired on rental, the rentals are charged against profit over the life of the software. Where a lump sum is paid, the Revenue normally take the view that the cost of software with an expected life of less than two years may be treated as a revenue expense and deducted from profit. Otherwise, subject to what is said above about the intangible assets provisions for companies, it will usually be treated as capital expenditure for which plant and machinery allowances may be claimed (under the short-life asset rules if appropriate — see 22.18). The treatment of in-house software is broadly similar, being either treated as capital or revenue depending on the expected period of use.

Allowances available (CAA 2001, ss 39–49, 52, 55, 56; FA 2002, ss 59, 61 and Schs 19, 20)

22.11   The allowances available on plant and machinery are writing-down allowances and, in some circumstances, first year allowances. There are also balancing allowances and balancing charges which arise when the business ceases or sometimes when a particular asset is disposed of.

Writing-down allowances are given at 25% per annum on the reducing balance method (except for long-life plant and machinery — see 22.21). For companies, the writing-down allowance is reduced proportionately in respect of accounting periods of less than twelve months. For individuals, the writing-down allowance is proportionately reduced or increased if the period of account is less than or more than twelve months, but with special rules if it exceeds 18 months (see 22.4 and Example 2 at 22.17).

First year allowances are available in the circumstances indicated below, the allowances being instead of the first year's writing-down allowance. Any available first year allowance may be claimed in full regardless of the length of the chargeable period. The allowances cannot be claimed for the chargeable period in which the trade is permanently discontinued. Nor can they be claimed on transactions between connected persons (as to which see 22.9), or on plant and machinery used for other purposes before being brought into the trade or obtained as a gift, or where obtaining capital allowances is the main benefit of the transaction. Subject to what is said below, first year allowances are not available for expenditure on plant and machinery for leasing or letting on hire, cars, motor cycles, taxis, sea-going ships and railway assets.

The range of assets on which first year allowance is presently available is now quite wide, the allowance under some of the headings being restricted to expenditure within a specified period. The headings are as follows:

Certain expenditure by small or medium-sized businesses
Expenditure by small businesses on information and communications technology
Expenditure on energy-saving equipment*
Expenditure on electric and low CO_2 emissions cars*
Expenditure on natural gas/hydrogen refuelling equipment*
Expenditure on environmentally beneficial plant or machinery.

* Expenditure incurred on or after 17 April 2002 on such plant and machinery for leasing qualifies despite the general exclusion stated above for plant and machinery for leasing.

The detailed provisions are as follows.

22.12   First year allowances at the rate of 40% may be claimed for expenditure incurred by small or medium-sized businesses on new or second-hand plant and machinery (other than long-life plant and machinery). For *small* businesses, the rate is increased to 50% for expenditure incurred in the tax year 2004/05 by individuals and in the financial year to 31 March 2005 by companies. (See 22.13 for the definition of *small*.)

Businesses qualify as small/medium-sized if they satisfy two of the following conditions (taking into account other companies in the same group, or for unincorporated businesses, other businesses carried on by the same sole trader or partnership):

Turnover not more than £22.8 million*
Assets not more than £11.4 million*
Not more than 250 employees
* Increased from £11.2 million and £5.6 million respectively for accounting periods ending on or after 30 January 2004

22.13   First year allowances at the rate of 100% have been available for expenditure incurred by 'small' businesses between 1 April 2000 and 31 March 2004 on information and communications technology. After 31 March 2004 the rates in 22.12 apply. The main qualifying assets for the 100% relief were computers and associated equipment, internet-enabled mobile phones and computer software. For expenditure on or after 26 March 2003, computer software did not qualify for the 100% allowance if it was acquired for licensing to others. (Software acquired for leasing was already excluded under the general provisions indicated above, but there was a loophole in relation to licensing.) The conditions for businesses to qualify as small are that, taking into account other companies in the same group, or for unincorporated businesses, other businesses carried on by the same sole trader or partnership, two of the following conditions are satisfied, i.e. there are not more than 50 employees, the turnover is not more than £5.6 million and the assets total is not more than £2.8 million (increased from £2.8 million and £1.4 million respectively for accounting periods ending on or after 30 January 2004).

22.14   100% first year allowances are available for expenditure on new plant and machinery within stipulated categories (heat and power systems, lighting, refrigeration etc.) that have been certified as meeting energy efficiency criteria. Businesses such as energy service companies may claim the allowance on such equipment provided and operated on a client's business premises under an energy management contract if the company and the client make a joint election. The first year allowance is also available to leasing businesses where the expenditure is incurred on or after 17 April 2002.

22.15   100% first year allowances may be claimed for expenditure incurred between 17 April 2002 and 31 March 2008 (inclusive) on new electric cars and cars with low CO_2 emissions (i.e. not more than 120g/km). 'Car' in this case includes a taxi but does not include a motor cycle. 100% first year allowances may also be claimed for expenditure between the same dates on new plant and machinery for refuelling stations used to refuel vehicles with natural gas or hydrogen fuel. These first year allowances are available to leasing businesses.

22.16   100% first year allowances are available for certain expenditure on or after 1 April 2003 on environmentally beneficial plant and machinery (other than long-life plant and machinery). The allowances will apply to expenditure on designated plant and machinery to reduce water use and improve water quality. The qualifying technologies and products are detailed in the Water Technology List, which is available on the internet at www.eca-water.gov.uk.

Pooling expenditure (CAA 2001, ss 53, 54, 57–59)

22.17   Qualifying expenditure on plant and machinery is pooled for the purpose of calculating writing-down allowances, balancing allowances and balancing charges. There are three types of pool; single asset pools, class pools and a main pool covering all assets not included in one of the other pools. Where a first year allowance has been claimed, the balance of the expenditure, if any, is not part of the relevant pool until it is 'allocated' to the pool. The legislation provides that this allocation does not occur until (at earliest) the next following period, unless the asset is disposed of in the period of acquisition, in which case any remaining expenditure is allocated in that period. The latest time for allocating the balance of expenditure, including where relevant a 'nil' balance, is the period in which the asset is disposed of. Even so, it makes practical sense to include any unrelieved balance in the written down value carried forward at the end of the period of acquisition, and to regard any 'nil balance' assets as being incorporated in the appropriate pool at that time.

Single asset pools are required for:

At the taxpayer's option, any asset that is expected to be disposed of within five years ('short-life assets' — see 22.18).
Any asset with part private use by a sole trader or partner (see 22.19).

Any 'car' costing over £12,000 (see 22.20). 'Cars' are defined as all motor vehicles (including motor cycles) except those primarily suited for carrying goods, those not commonly used as private vehicles and unsuitable to be so used, those let on a short lease (i.e. where the car is normally hired to the same person for less than 30 consecutive days and for less than 90 days in any twelve months), those let to someone receiving mobility allowance or disability living allowance, and electric and low CO_2 emissions cars qualifying for 100% first year allowance (see 22.15).

Class pools are required for:

Long-life assets (see 22.21).
Assets for foreign leasing (see 22.22).

The writing-down allowance at the rate of 25% per annum (reducing balance method) is calculated on the unrelieved expenditure brought forward from the previous period, plus expenditure in the period (excluding expenditure on which first year allowance has been claimed, unless the asset has been disposed of in the same period, in which case any unallowed expenditure is included), less any sales proceeds (up to, but not exceeding, the original cost — see 22.24). If the proceeds exceed the pool balance, a balancing charge is made. Any available first year allowance is calculated separately and the remainder of the expenditure is then included in the pool balance carried forward (unless already included as indicated above). See example 1. Where a first year allowance is available, it will sometimes be possible to avoid a balancing charge by not claiming the allowance on all or part of the qualifying expenditure and including the expenditure in the pool instead.

A balancing allowance will not arise on the main pool, except on a cessation of trade where the total sales proceeds are less than the pool balance. The same applies to long-life asset pools (see 22.21). See 22.22 for assets for foreign leasing. For single asset pools, a balancing allowance or charge is made when the asset is disposed of. If the single asset is disposed of in the period in which it is acquired for less than cost, there will be a balancing allowance on the shortfall. If it is disposed of in that period for more than cost it will not be brought into account for capital allowances at all and the capital profit will be dealt with under the capital gains legislation (the gain being exempt if the asset is a car).

The general rules, and the way in which a balancing charge may be avoided by not claiming first year allowance, are illustrated in Example 1. See also Example 2, which illustrates the special rules mentioned in 22.4 for income tax accounting periods that exceed 18 months.

Example 1

A trader whose business qualifies as small has the following transactions in 'main pool' plant in the years ended 31 December 2003 and 2004 (plant purchases qualifying for FYA where appropriate):

		£
March 2003	Arm's length purchase	10,000
June 2003	Proceeds of sales	3,000
August 2003	Purchase from associated business	5,000
January 2004	Proceeds of sales	8,500
February 2004	Arm's length purchase	10,000
December 2004	Arm's length purchase	7,000

The main pool balance brought forward at 1 January 2003 is £8,000.

The allowances are calculated as follows:

	£	£
Year to 31 December 2003		
Pool balance brought forward		8,000
Additions not qualifying for FYA:		
August 2003 from connected person (cost not based on market value since dealt with as a sale in the computations of the associated business — see 22.9)		5,000
		13,000
Less sales proceeds June 2003		(3,000)
		10,000
Writing-down allowance 25% (reduces taxable profit)		(2,500)
		7,500
Additions March 2003 qualifying for FYA	10,000	
FYA 40% (reduces taxable profit)	(4,000)	
Balance allocated to main pool		6,000
		13,500
Year to 31 December 2004		
Sales proceeds January 2004		(8,500)
		5,000
Writing-down allowance 25% (reduces taxable profit)		(1,250)
		3,750
Additions qualifying for FYA:		
February 2004	10,000	
FYA 40% (reduces taxable profit)	(4,000)	6,000
December 2004	7,000	
FYA 50% (reduces taxable profit)	(3,500)	3,500
Balance allocated to main pool		9,500
Pool balance carried forward		£13,250

If the sale proceeds in January 2004 had been, say, £17,500, they would have exceeded the pool balance of £13,500 by £4,000. The balancing charge of that amount that would have arisen could have been avoided by not claiming the 40% first year allowance on £4,000 of the February 2004 expenditure, as follows:

	£	£
Year to 31 December 2004		
Balance brought forward		13,500
Additions on which FYA not claimed		4,000
		17,500
Sale proceeds		(17,500)
Additions on which FYA claimed:		
February 2004 (remaining expenditure)	6,000	
FYA 40%	(2,400)	3,600
December 2004	7,000	
FYA 50%	(3,500)	3,500
Balance allocated to main pool		7,100
Pool balance carried forward		£7,100

Thus taxable profits would be reduced by FYAs of £5,900 instead of being reduced by FYAs of £7,500 and increased by a balancing charge of £4,000. The net immediate benefit of not claiming full FYAs would be an additional allowance of £2,400, although the balance carried forward would be correspondingly reduced.

Example 2

22–month account is made up from 1 January 2003 to 31 October 2004. Main pool balance brought forward is £100,000. The only addition was new plant qualifying for 40% FYA that cost £20,000 in March 2004. The allowances will be calculated as follows:

		£
Year to 31.12.2003		
Pool balance brought forward		100,000
WDA 25%		25,000
		75,000
10 mths to 31.10.2004		
WDA 25% x 10/12		15,625
		59,375
Additions qualifying for FYA	20,000	
FYA 40%	(8,000)	
Balance allocated to main pool		12,000
Written down value carried forward		71,375
Total allowances for period treated as trading expense (25,000 + 15,625 + 8,000)		£48,625

Without the special rule for accounts longer than 18 months, allowances would have been:

	£
WDA 100,000 @ 25% x 22/12	45,833
FYA	8,000
	£53,833

Short-life assets (CAA 2001, ss 83–89)

22.18   Some assets have a very short life and depreciate very quickly. Pooling them within the main pool would not give relief for their cost over their life span because when they are disposed of, any unrelieved expenditure remains in the pool to be written off over future years (unless the business has ceased, when a pool balancing adjustment is made — see 22.17). An election may be made to have the capital allowances on specified items of plant and machinery calculated separately in single asset pools under the 'short-life assets' provisions. A balancing allowance or charge will then arise if the asset is disposed of within four years from the end of the accounting period in which it is acquired. If the asset is still held at the end of that period, the tax written-down value is transferred into the main pool. Cars (including hire cars other than those hired to someone receiving mobility allowance or disability living allowance) and any other assets which would not in any event have been included in the main pool of expenditure cannot be dealt with under the short-life assets rules. The election for this treatment is irrevocable, and must be made within two years after the end of the accounting period in which the expenditure is incurred for companies and

421

within one year after the 31 January following the tax year in which the period of account in which the expenditure was incurred ends for individuals. The Revenue have issued guidelines (Statement of Practice SP 1/86) on practical aspects of the short-life assets rules, including provisions for grouping classes of assets where individual treatment is impossible or impracticable.

Assets with part private use (CAA 2001, ss 205–208)

22.19   Any asset that is privately used by a sole proprietor or by a partner in a business is dealt with in a separate single asset pool. This does not apply to assets used by directors of family companies. The use of company assets for private purposes by directors or employees does not affect the company's capital allowances position, but results in a benefits charge on the director/employee (see CHAPTER 10).

Allowances and charges for each privately-used asset are calculated in the normal way, but the available allowance or charge is restricted to the business proportion. An individual balancing adjustment is made when the asset is disposed of.

Cars costing more than £12,000 (CAA 2001, ss 74–77)

22.20   Each car (as defined at 22.17) that costs more than £12,000 when acquired is dealt with in a separate single asset pool, and the available writing-down allowance is £3,000 per annum or 25% of the unrelieved balance, whichever is less. If such a car is used privately by a sole trader or partner the available amount is further restricted by the private proportion. When the car is sold a balancing allowance or charge arises. See 20.11 for the treatment of a car with a value of more than £12,000 that you lease instead of buy.

Long-life plant and machinery (CAA 2001, ss 90–104)

22.21   Plant and machinery first bought new on or after 26 November 1996 with an expected working life of 25 years or more normally qualifies for writing-down allowances at only 6% per annum (on the reducing balance) throughout its life rather than 25% per annum (total expenditure on such assets being included in a separate 'class pool'). For businesses that qualified as small/medium-sized, however (see 22.12), a special first year allowance of 12% was available for expenditure between 2 July 1997 and 1 July 1998 inclusive. The long-life asset provisions do not apply to cars (including hire cars), taxis, or to certain ships or railway assets bought before the end of 2010, or to assets used in a dwelling-house, retail shop, showroom, hotel or office. Nor do they apply where total expenditure on such long-life assets does not exceed £100,000 a year (divided pro rata for associated companies). Most of the plant and machinery affected by these rules would alternatively qualify for industrial buildings allowances and businesses may choose which allowances to claim.

The reduced rate of writing-down allowance does not apply to second-hand assets if the pre–26 November 1996 rules applied to the vendor.

When all or any of the long-life assets are disposed of, a balancing charge will arise if the total proceeds exceed the pool balance brought forward. If the total proceeds are less than the pool balance, writing-down allowances will continue to be given on the remaining expenditure. A balancing allowance will not arise until the trade ceases, even if all the assets are disposed of before that time.

Assets for foreign leasing (CAA 2001, ss 107, 109)

22.22   Assets leased to non-UK residents who do not use them for a UK trade are kept in a separate class pool, normally attracting writing-down allowances at 10%, balancing charges where the total sales proceeds exceed the tax written-down value of all such assets, and a balancing allowance where the tax written-down value exceeds the total proceeds in the final chargeable period (i.e. the period after which there can be no more disposal receipts). In some circumstances, no allowances at all are available.

Fixtures (CAA 2001, ss 172–204)

22.23   Complex rules apply in relation to allowances on fixtures. Those who let property can claim allowances on expenditure incurred on fixtures and fittings (subject to what is said below). Where a business tenant incurs the expenditure, and the fixtures become the landlord's property in law, the tenant can nonetheless claim allowances. Where fixtures are provided by equipment lessors, the lessee (who may be the owner or tenant of the property) and the equipment lessor may elect for the equipment lessor to claim the allowances. See 22.14 re elections by energy service companies and their clients to enable the companies to claim 100% first year allowances on energy saving plant and machinery. See that section also for the entitlement of equipment lessors to claim 100% first year allowances on certain assets.

Allowances cannot be claimed on fixtures leased to non-taxpayers, such as charities, unless the lessor has an interest in the relevant land. Nor can they be claimed by equipment lessors or landlords on fixtures in dwelling-houses. An exception is made for expenditure incurred by equipment lessors between 28 July 2000 and 31 December 2007 on boilers, radiators, heat exchangers and heating controls installed in low income homes under the Government's Affordable Warmth Programme. Where capital allowances are not available, landlords will usually be able to claim a wear and tear allowance instead under the provisions of Revenue concession B47 (see 32.11).

Allowances are not available on any amount in excess of the original cost of the fixtures when new. Vendors and purchasers may make a joint election (within two years of the date of the contract) fixing how much of the purchase price of a building relates to fixtures, the agreed amount being limited, however, to the vendor's original cost. Where a claim in a return becomes incorrect, for example because of such an election, the claimant must notify an amendment to the return within three months after becoming aware of that fact.

There are anti-avoidance provisions to prevent allowances on fixtures being artificially accelerated.

Effect of capital allowances on capital gains computation (TCGA 1992, ss 41, 55(3))

22.24   Capital allowances are not deducted from the cost of an asset in computing a capital gain, but are taken into account in computing a capital loss. There will only be a gain if an asset is sold for more than cost, and in that event any capital allowances given will be withdrawn by the cost being taken out of the capital allowances computation (except for certain industrial buildings allowances — see 22.27 — and agricultural buildings allowances — see 31.8) and will not therefore affect the computation of the gain. There will not normally be a capital loss, since any amount by which the sale proceeds for an asset fall short of the written-down value will be taken into account in the capital allowances computation.

For plant and machinery that is moveable rather than fixed, there is no chargeable gain if it is sold for £6,000 or less. Where the proceeds exceed £6,000, the chargeable gain cannot exceed 5/3rds of the excess of the proceeds over £6,000 (see 39.3). If plant and machinery is fixed rather than moveable, gains are not exempt but they may be deferred if the item is replaced (see 4.26). See Example 3.

Where the asset was acquired before 31 March 1982, plant and machinery is not covered by a general 31 March 1982 rebasing election (see 4.12) so computations have to be made both under the pre- and post-March 1982 rules.

Example 3

Plant which cost a trader £50,000 in December 2001 is sold in September 2004 for £65,000.

Since the plant is sold for more than cost, the capital allowances will be fully withdrawn by deducting £50,000 from the pool balance. There is a capital gain of (65,000 − 50,000 =) £15,000, subject to taper relief. If the plant is fixed plant, the gain will be eligible for rollover relief, and if rollover relief is claimed, taper relief will be available only when the replacement asset is sold, based on the period of ownership of the replacement asset. If rollover relief is not claimed, business assets taper relief for two years' ownership or more, i.e. 75%, would reduce the gain to £3,750, providing the gain was not reduced by allowable losses. If the plant is moveable plant, the gain will be fully chargeable, again reduced to £3,750 by available taper relief. See CHAPTER 4 for detailed capital gains provisions.

Industrial buildings

Buildings qualifying for relief (CAA 2001, ss 271, 274, 277, 283)

22.25   Industrial buildings allowances in respect of qualifying construction expenditure are available under four headings: buildings in use for a qualifying trade, qualifying hotels, qualifying sports pavilions, and commercial buildings and structures in enterprise zones. Qualifying hotels are dealt with in 22.29 and enterprise zone buildings in 22.30. A sports pavilion qualifies for the allowances indicated below if it is provided by a person carrying on *any* trade for the welfare of employees.

As far as qualifying trades are concerned, the most common examples are manufacturing or processing goods or materials. Businesses which provide services such as transport, water, sewerage or electricity are also within the definition. Buildings used to store goods and materials before and after manufacture or processing are included. Offices, shops, hotels, wholesale warehouses and buildings used as retail shops (including repair shops), and buildings used for ancillary purposes, are not qualifying trades (but see 22.29 below re qualifying hotels). The Revenue treat a vehicle repair workshop as an industrial building if it is completely separate from the vehicle sales area, does not have a reception, and public access is discouraged. Allowances would be restricted to the extent that vehicles for resale were repaired in the workshop. Where part of a building is outside the definition (for example offices in a factory), the whole building qualifies for allowances providing the expenditure on the non-industrial part does not exceed 25% of the total cost. This applies only where the non-industrial part is housed within the same building, not where it is a separate building. Where a building is in an enterprise zone, there is no restriction on the use to which it may be put (except that a private dwelling does not qualify) and much more generous allowances are available (see 22.30).

Allowances for new buildings and additional capital expenditure on existing buildings (CAA 2001, ss 272, 285, 292–297, 309–313)

22.26   Allowances are given on the cost of construction and no allowances are available for the cost of the land, although site preparation works qualify. Where a building is bought from the builder, allowances are available on the amount paid. Where additional capital expenditure is incurred on an existing qualifying building, the additional expenditure qualifies for allowances as if it were a separate building. This enables a tenant to get allowances on any capital expenditure he incurs on a qualifying building, and it is specifically provided that if any repair expenditure on a qualifying building does not qualify as a business expense for tax purposes, it is treated as qualifying capital expenditure. Furthermore, expenditure on items that become part of the building does not qualify for plant and machinery allowances and counts instead as part of the building expenditure — see 22.10.

The allowances available are writing-down allowances at the rate of 4% of the construction cost per annum, starting in the chargeable period in which the building is brought into use. (Writing-down allowances are at the rate of 2% per annum on capital expenditure incurred before 6 November 1962, such buildings having a tax life of 50 years.)

In earlier years, initial allowances have been available from time to time in addition to writing-down allowances, the allowances being given in the chargeable period related to the incurring of the expenditure. For companies this meant the chargeable accounting period as it does now. For individuals, under the 'previous year basis' rules that then applied, the allowances for a tax year normally related to expenditure in the accounting year ended in the previous tax year (e.g. the 1994/95 allowances related to expenditure in the year to, say, 31 December 1993), with special rules applying for the opening and closing years of the business. Initial allowances first started on 6 April 1944, the rates of allowance from 11 March 1981 being as follows:

Date construction expenditure incurred	*Rate*
11 March 1981 to 13 March 1984	75%
14 March 1984 to 31 March 1985	50%
1 April 1985 to 31 March 1986	25%
1 November 1992 to 31 October 1993*	20%

*Buildings bought new in that year also qualified for the allowance, even if they were constructed earlier.

Initial allowances have not been available in respect of expenditure on or after 1 November 1993.

You need not claim all of the writing-down allowance you are entitled to (or initial allowance when available). The effect of claiming reduced amounts would be to extend the writing-down period beyond the building's normal tax life of 25 or 50 years, unless the building was disposed of in the meantime.

Example 4

A factory built in Spring 2004 is bought from the builder for £500,000 in October 2004 by a trader making up accounts to 31 December. The building is brought into use immediately. The annual writing-down allowance at 4% is £20,000. Unless there is a change of accounting date, or the building is sold, allowances of that amount will be given from 2004/05 to 2028/29.

Had the building not been brought into use until say February 2005, the first writing-down allowance would have been given in 2005/06.

If a building is sold before the expenditure has been fully relieved, there is a balancing adjustment between the seller and the buyer, and the buyer is entitled to writing-down allowances over the remainder of the building's tax life (see 22.27). Second-hand purchasers were not entitled to initial allowances.

Sale of the building (CAA 2001, ss 314–331, 354)

22.27   On sale, there will be a balancing adjustment on the seller (unless the building is sold after the end of its tax life — see below) and a possible claim for relief by the purchaser (but see below re anti-avoidance provisions).

Whilst there are rules to deal with periods of non-industrial use, the basic adjustment is to give the seller a balancing allowance to make up any shortfall between the unrelieved expenditure and the sale proceeds, or to make a balancing charge to withdraw excess allowances if the sale proceeds exceed the unrelieved expenditure. If a building is disposed of after the trade has ceased, any balancing allowance is treated as if it were an expense of a Schedule A business, so the treatment for such businesses in 22.7 would apply. A balancing charge is similarly treated as Schedule A income, but it may be reduced by any amounts that could have been set against it if it had been received before the trade ceased, in the same way as for post-cessation receipts (as to which see 21.9).

Providing he uses the building for a qualifying trade, the purchaser gets allowances on the part of the original building cost remaining unrelieved after the balancing adjustment on the seller. This amount is relieved by way of equal annual allowances over the remainder of the 'tax life' of the building. No matter how much the purchaser pays for the building, the maximum amount on which he can claim relief is the original building cost, which may have been incurred many years earlier and bear little relation to current prices. No relief is available for the cost of the land whether relating to new or used buildings. The tax life of industrial buildings is 25 years from the date the building is first used for expenditure on or after 6 November 1962 and 50 years for expenditure before that date. See example 5. If a building's tax life has already expired, there is no balancing adjustment for the seller and the purchaser cannot claim any allowances at all, unless additional capital expenditure on the building had been incurred at a later date, in which case that expenditure would be treated as if it related to a separate building with its own tax life (see 22.26). Despite the fact that once a building's tax life has expired, the seller does not lose the capital allowances claimed, the full cost of the building is taken into account in the computation of the capital gain on disposal.

Example 5

The construction costs of an industrial building in December 1992 were £400,000, the land cost being £50,000. Initial allowance of £80,000 and annual allowances of £16,000 for 12 years, totalling £272,000 in all, have been claimed.

The building (including £100,000 for the land) is sold in November 2004 for

(a) £200,000   (b) £380,000   (c) £960,000

The vendor's position is

	(a) £	(b) £	(c) £
Sale proceeds	200,000	380,000	960,000
Land included	100,000	100,000	100,000
Building proceeds	100,000	280,000	860,000
Building cost	400,000	400,000	400,000
Cost of owning building	300,000	120,000	Nil
Allowances already given	272,000	272,000	272,000
Balancing allowance/(charge)	£28,000	£(152,000)	£(272,000)

In the case of (c) there would also be a capital gain:

	(a)	(b)	(c)
Proceeds (land and buildings)			960,000
Cost (land and buildings)			450,000
Chargeable gain (before any available indexation allowance and taper relief)			£510,000

The purchaser would get reliefs as follows.

	(a)	(b)	(c)
Cost to him (building only)	£100,000	£280,000	£860,000
Restrict to original cost if less than purchase price			£400,000
Annual allowance ⅟₁₃th*	£7,692	£21,538	£30,769

(*13 years of 25-year life remaining, ignoring fractions of year for illustration.)

If the building had been built in 1975, there would have been no balancing adjustment for the seller and no allowances to the buyer, because it would be over 25 years old. The capital allowances given would not be deducted from the cost to calculate the capital gain.

If the building had been built in 1960, there would still be 6 years remaining out of the writing-down life of 50 years (for expenditure incurred before 6 November 1962), but the allowances would relate to any unallowed balance of the *1960* building cost.

Where plant and machinery is purchased with a building, the purchase price needs to be apportioned and plant and machinery allowances can then be claimed on the appropriate part of the purchase price. There is no restriction of plant and machinery allowances to the original cost of the items, except for fixtures (see 22.23).

Anti-avoidance provisions apply to certain sales of buildings within the industrial buildings definition (see 22.25). Where the sale price has been artificially depressed as a result of a tax avoidance scheme, the seller is not entitled to a balancing allowance, but the buyer's allowances are calculated as if the balancing allowance had been made.

Interaction with VAT capital goods scheme (CAA 2001, ss 234–246, 345–351, 446–449, 546–551)

22.28   Input tax adjustments under the VAT capital goods scheme (see 7.18) are reflected in capital allowances computations. Changes to VAT paid in respect of an industrial building are added to or deducted from the unrelieved expenditure on the building and writing-down allowances recalculated over the remainder of the building's tax life. Similarly, adjustments for VAT on computers are made in the plant and machinery main pool or short-life asset pool in the period in which the VAT adjustment is made. Where the original expenditure qualified for the special 20% initial allowance on industrial buildings (see 22.26) or the first year allowance on plant and machinery (see 22.11 ONWARDS), any additional VAT liability is treated as additional expenditure qualifying for extra initial or first-year allowance, the extra allowance being given in the adjustment period.

Hotels (CAA 2001, s 279)

22.29   Relief is available for construction costs in respect of a qualifying hotel or hotel extension. The hotel or extension must be of a permanent nature, be open for at least four months between April and October, and when open must have at least ten letting bedrooms offering sleeping accommodation. It must provide services of breakfast, evening meal, making beds and cleaning rooms. The relief works in the same way as that for industrial buildings (see 22.26). The annual writing-down allowance is 4% of cost, and the 20% initial allowance was available for qualifying expenditure in the year to 31 October 1993. If the hotel is in an enterprise zone, it qualifies for the allowances described below, with no restriction on months of opening or number of bedrooms, etc.

Buildings in enterprise zones (CAA 2001, ss 298–313, 327–331)

22.30   When an area has been designated as an Enterprise Zone by the Secretary of State, expenditure incurred or contracted for within ten years after the creation of the zone on any buildings other than dwelling houses qualifies for an initial allowance of 100%, or whatever lower amount is claimed. (If part of a building is used as a dwelling, the whole expenditure still qualifies, providing the expenditure on that part does not exceed 25% of the total building cost.) Any expenditure on which initial allowance is not claimed qualifies for writing-down allowances of 25% of cost (straight line method) until it is written off in full. See 22.7 for the way in which an investor may get relief for the allowances he claims, which is illustrated in Example 6 below. Where fixed plant or machinery is an integral part of the building, it can be treated as part of the building for the purposes of claiming enterprise zone allowances.

Example 6

In September 2003, i.e. in the tax year 2003/04, a single man purchased a workshop in an enterprise zone from a developer for £72,000 (including land £6,000), the first letting taking place in the following tax year,

---

i.e. 2004/05. He had rent income from another property of £10,000 in 2003/04 and he had other income of £43,000. His total income in 2004/05 was £60,000 and is expected to continue at that level. The allowance he can claim in 2003/04 is any amount up to a maximum of 100% of £66,000. The amount claimed can be set against just his rent income of that year and later years, or alternatively the loss created by the claim may be set against his total income of either 2003/04 or 2004/05 or both years, any unrelieved balance then being set only against rental income in later years. If he claimed the maximum of £66,000, however, and claimed relief for the resulting loss against his income of 2003/04 he would waste his personal allowance in that year and there would be an unrelieved balance of £13,000 carried forward to 2004/05. He could instead claim allowances as follows.

Initial allowance	18,000
Which will be set against rent income of 2003/04	10,000
	8,000
Loss relief which may be claimed against other 2003/04 income of £43,000	8,000
Leaving taxable income (just above basic rate threshold after personal allowance) of (53,000 − 10,000 − 8000)	£35,000

The unrelieved expenditure would be £48,000 (£66,000 − £18,000) and this could be relieved as follows:

2004/05 (25% × £66,000)	16,500
2005/06 (25% × £66,000)	16,500
2006/07 (the remainder)	15,000
	£48,000

If he wanted to eliminate his taxable income in 2003/04 he could instead claim initial allowance of £48,385 for that year and writing-down allowances for the next two years, the effect on his taxable income after making loss claims where appropriate being as follows.

	2003/04	2004/05	2005/06
Total income	53,000	60,000	60,000
Initial allowance	48,385		
Writing-down allowance		16,500	1,115
Leaving taxable income (before personal allowance) of	£4,615	£43,500	£58,885

This would save starting and basic rate tax in 2003/04 at the expense of additional higher rate tax in 2005/06 and 2006/07.

Balancing allowances or charges apply on the disposal of buildings in enterprise zones using the same rules as for industrial buildings (see 22.27), and treating the life of the building as being 25 years. This means that if the building is sold in the early years, the seller will usually lose all or a large part of the benefit of the 100% allowances. Furthermore, if a lease is granted for a capital sum within seven years after the date of the contract to acquire the interest in the building, the receipt of the capital sum triggers a balancing charge on the lessor (or if he has not claimed the maximum allowance, a reduction in the unrelieved expenditure qualifying for writing-down allowances). This treatment does not apply to leases granted after more than seven years unless the lessor has a guaranteed exit arrangement, in which case a balancing charge is made on the granting of a lease at *any* time within the building's 25-year life. If the lease is for 50 years or less, the amount already charged as additional rent (see 32.15) is excluded from the capital sum in calculating the balancing charge. If the lease is for more than 50 years, these special rules do not apply if the landlord and tenant have *elected* to treat the capital sum as sale proceeds so that the tenant may claim allowances (see 22.2).

Purchase within two years after first use

22.31   Someone who acquires an enterprise zone building within two years after it is first used is treated as if he had acquired an unused building, so that he can claim the 100% initial allowance or 25% writing-down allowance as indicated above. As far as any subsequent second-hand purchaser is concerned, the position is the same as for purchasers outside the first two years (see 22.32), but the 25-year life of the building dates from the date of first use by the person who acquired it within the first two years of use.

Purchase more than two years after first use

22.32   Where the first disposal of an enterprise zone building occurs more than two years after it is first used, the purchaser cannot claim the 100% or 25% enterprise zone allowances. He gets writing-down allowances only, normally on the lower of the price paid by him and the original construction cost. The writing-down allowance is calculated by spreading the unrelieved expenditure over the balance of the building's 25-year life which is unexpired at the date of purchase. Where, however, a building is transferred between connected persons (say husband and wife), they may make a claim to treat the transfer as being at written-down value (see 22.9), so that the benefit to the vendor of the higher enterprise zone building allowances is not lost as a result of the transfer.

Limits on enterprise zone allowances

22.33   Where part of the expenditure on a building was incurred neither within the ten-year life of the enterprise zone, nor under a contract entered into within the ten-year period, that part of the expenditure qualifies only for the normal level of buildings allowances (i.e. for industrial buildings or hotels), or not at all if it is a non-qualifying building.

Enterprise zone allowances cannot be claimed on expenditure incurred more than 20 years after the site was included in the enterprise zone, no matter when the contract was entered into.

Way in which allowances are given

22.34   Enterprise zone allowances may be claimed both by traders and investors. The treatment is dealt with at 22.7.

Patents (CAA 2001, ss 464–483; TA 1988, s 524; FA 2002, s 84 and Sch 29)

22.35   Expenditure incurred in devising and patenting an invention (or an abortive attempt to do so) is allowable as a business expense (and qualifies for the new research and development reliefs — SEE 29.16 to 29.19). Where, however, patent rights are purchased, capital allowances are available to individuals as follows. These provisions also apply to companies in respect of expenditure incurred *before* 1 April 2002. From that date, patents are dealt with for corporation tax under the 'Intangible assets' provisions outlined at 20.21.

The capital allowances available are writing-down allowances at 25% on the reducing balance method, with all expenditure on patent rights being pooled.

Balancing charges arise in the usual way, and a balancing allowance is given on any unallowed expenditure if the last of the rights come to an end without subsequently being revived or on the permanent discontinuance of the trade.

Although a balancing charge can never exceed the allowances given, there are specific provisions to charge a capital profit on patent rights as income rather than as a capital gain. The profit is not dealt with as part of the business profits but is charged to income tax under Schedule D, Case VI over six years in equal instalments, commencing with the tax year in which it is received, unless the taxpayer elects to have the whole sum charged in the year of receipt.

Patents allowances granted to non-traders can only be set against income from the patent rights and not against any other income.

Know-how (CAA 2001, ss 452–463; FA 2002, s 84 and Sch 29)

22.36 'Know-how' is defined as any industrial information or techniques which are likely to assist in a manufacturing process, or the working of a mine, or the carrying out of agricultural, forestry or fishing operations. Revenue expenditure on creating know-how related to a trade is allowable as a business expense (and qualifies for the new research and development reliefs — see 29.16 to 29.19).

For companies, know-how is dealt with in respect of expenditure incurred on or after 1 April 2002 under the 'Intangible assets' provisions outlined at 20.21. In respect of company expenditure before that date, and expenditure by individuals, the treatment is as follows.

Capital expenditure on the acquisition of know-how for use in a trade qualifies for an annual writing-down allowance of 25% on the reducing balance method. Any additional expenditure is added to the unrelieved balance and any sale proceeds are deducted from it before calculating the writing-down allowance. If the sale proceeds exceed the tax written-down value, a balancing charge is made and this is not restricted to the allowances given, so that the balancing charge will include any excess of the proceeds over the original cost.

If know-how is sold as part of a business, the payment is regarded as being for goodwill and thus dealt with under the capital gains rules, unless both seller and buyer elect within two years of the disposal for it to be treated as a sale of know-how.

If the trade ceases during the writing-down period but the know-how is not sold, relief for the unallowed expenditure is given by way of a balancing allowance.

Research and development (CAA 2001, ss 437–451; TA 1988, s 837A; FA 2000, s 69 and Sch 20)

22.37 The term 'research and development' has been substituted for the earlier term 'scientific research' in the capital allowances legislation. Subject to any express provisions to the contrary, research and development means activities that would be treated as such in accordance with generally accepted accounting practice. Detailed guidelines are published by the Department of Trade and Industry, and these have recently been updated.

Capital allowances are available at 100% on capital expenditure on research and development. The allowance need not be claimed in full. Expenditure on land and dwelling houses does not generally qualify for relief. On disposal, a balancing charge is made equal to the amount by which the disposal value (i.e. sale proceeds, compensation for destruction etc.) exceeds the allowance given, or the allowance claimed if less. If there is a capital profit it is dealt with under the capital gains rules.

If the sale takes place in the same chargeable period as that in which the expenditure is incurred, then if the proceeds are less than the expenditure the allowance is equal to the shortfall, and if the proceeds exceed the expenditure no allowance is given and the excess is dealt with under the capital gains rules.

Revenue expenditure on research and development is allowed in full as a business expense, as are amounts paid to scientific research associations etc. undertaking scientific research related to the trade. Special reliefs apply to revenue expenditure on research and development by companies (see 29.17 and 29.18).

Mineral extraction (CAA 2001, ss 394–436)

22.38   Expenditure on mineral extraction qualifies for writing-down allowances on a reducing balance basis at the following rates:

	Rate
Acquisition of a mineral asset (mineral deposits, land comprising mineral deposits, etc.)	10%
Other qualifying expenditure	25%

A balancing charge is made if sales proceeds exceed tax written-down value. A balancing allowance is given in the chargeable period when the mineral extraction trade ceases, or when particular mineral deposits cease to be worked, and in the case of pre-trading expenditure, when trading commences or exploration is abandoned before then.

Tax points

22.39

- A specific claim for capital allowances must be made by individuals, partnerships and companies, so it is important to ensure that the appropriate entries are made on the tax return.

- If claiming the maximum capital allowances means wasting personal allowances, you can reduce your capital allowances claim, or not claim allowances at all — see 22.7. In the case of plant and machinery, you will then get writing-down allowances on an increased amount in future years. If you do not claim all or part of an industrial buildings writing-down allowance, the period over which the cost is written off is extended (unless you dispose of the building in the meantime).

- Both individuals and companies can revise capital allowances claims within the period allowed for making returns or amendments to returns.

- Companies will benefit by not taking allowances, where they want to leave profits high enough to take advantage of reliefs which are only available in the current period, such as group relief for losses or double tax relief. The amount on which writing-down allowances will be available in later years is increased accordingly.

- Companies will also benefit by not taking allowances, and thus increasing the amount available for allowances in later years, if they would otherwise have taxable profits of less than £10,000, because the rate of corporation tax on profits of up to £10,000 is nil. To the extent that the company pays dividends to non-corporate shareholders, however, the nil rate does not apply (see 3.13).

- Allowances available on capital expenditure incurred on commencing trading on your own or in partnership may contribute to a trading loss, which may be carried back against the income of earlier years (see CHAPTER 25).

- Whereas you get only 25% writing-down allowance when you buy cars, if you lease a car instead, you can set the whole of the leasing charge against your profit, subject to disallowance of any private element and the restriction on the allowable hire charge where the car cost the leasing company more than £12,000 — see 20.11.

- When you buy or sell a group of assets, such as goodwill, plant and machinery and trade premises, some will be subject to capital allowances at different rates and some will not qualify for allowances at all, with the tax treatment of goodwill depending upon the status of the buyer and seller (see 20.21). It is essential that the price apportionment is realistic and is agreed with the other party at the time of purchase or sale in order to avoid complications when you submit tax returns. See also 22.23 for the special provisions relating to fixtures.

- If there is doubt as to whether a contract for the purchase of plant or machinery is a hire-purchase contract or a leasing contract, it is advisable to check with the finance company as to the nature of the payments to them to ensure the correct treatment in tax computations.

- Writing-down allowances at 25% on the reducing balance method will write off about 90% of the expenditure in eight years. The option to keep short-life assets out of the plant and machinery main pool enables you to shorten this time to five years or less if the assets are sold or scrapped within that period.

- One of the main categories of short-life assets is computer equipment. If computer equipment was bought by a small business as defined (see 22.13), between 1 April 2000 and 31 March 2004, the expenditure qualified for 100% first year allowances, so it was better to have the equipment in the main pool, so that a balancing charge would not be triggered on disposal. Now that 100% allowances are no longer available, short-life asset treatment will again be appropriate.

- For companies, expenditure on patents and know-how from 1 April 2002 is dealt with under the 'Intangible assets' rules (see 20.21) rather than by way of capital allowances. In general the cost will be written off over the economic life of the assets, which will not normally be as generous as the capital allowances regime.

- If you take over a business from someone with whom you are connected, the election to continue the predecessor's capital allowances computation has to be made within two years after the change (see 22.9). Do not forget the time limit.

- Plan the expenditure on any non-qualifying parts of a new industrial building (for example, offices) to ensure, if possible, that it does not exceed the allowable 25% for non-qualifying expenditure.

- Since the purchase of land does not qualify for industrial buildings allowances, more tax-efficient use of capital expenditure can be achieved by constructing on leasehold land.

- If you want to invest in an enterprise zone building but the cost is too high, you can participate on a co-ownership basis or through an enterprise zone property trust.

- The allowances for buildings in enterprise zones are available for any commercial buildings and not just industrial buildings — see 22.30.

23
Partnerships

Nature of partnership

23.1   Partnership is defined in the Partnership Act 1890 as 'the relation which subsists between persons carrying on a business in common with a view of profit'. An ordinary partnership is not a separate legal entity except in Scotland. Under the Limited Liability Partnerships Act 2000, partners may form a separate corporate entity known as a limited liability partnership, which as the name implies, limits the liability of the partners for the firm's debts. See 23.23.

Assessment (TA 1988, s 111; TCGA 1992, s 59)

23.2   Under self-assessment a partnership must send in a partnership tax return and the individual partners must show their partnership income in their personal returns (see 23.5).

Partners are separately liable for their own tax on all sources of income and the Revenue cannot proceed against other partners if a partner fails to pay. Partners would, however, be affected by the irresponsible conduct of their fellow partners which caused partnership profits to be understated, in that they would be liable for tax on any consequent increase in their profit shares even though the normal time limit for a Revenue challenge to their self-assessments had expired (see 9.43).

Although partners do not have joint liability for tax on the partnership trading profits, partnership profits still have to be agreed globally, no partner being able to agree an adjustment to his share of profits independently of the others. It is only the liability for the tax that is separated under the self-assessment rules.

Sharing profits and losses

23.3   The profits of the accounting period, as adjusted for tax purposes, are divided between the partners according to the sharing arrangements in the period. Each partner's share of the profit is then treated as arising to him individually, and the rules for opening and closing years and for overlap relief depend on when he joins and leaves the firm (see Examples 1 and 2). Losses are similarly shared on an accounting period basis and treated as arising to the partners individually, loss claims being made accordingly.

Example 1

A, B and C, who have been in business for many years, shared profits equally in the year ended 30 November 2003. From 1 December 2003 they amended the profit-sharing ratio to 2:1:1.

The profits for tax purposes will be shared in the same way as the accounts profits, the profit of the year to 30 November 2003 (taxable in 2003/04) being shared equally and that of the year to 30 November 2004 (taxable in 2004/2005) being shared 2:1:1.

Example 2

D and E commenced in partnership on 1 January 2002, making up accounts annually to 31 December and sharing profits equally. F joined them as an equal partner on 1 July 2003 and E left the partnership on 28 February 2004. Profits and their division between the partners for the first three years are as follows:

Year ended	Profits	D	E	F
	£	£	£	£
31.12.02	40,000	20,000	20,000	
31.12.03	60,000	25,000	25,000	10,000
31.12.04	90,000	42,500	5,000	42,500
Total profits for period		87,500	50,000	52,500

Assessments and overlap profits available for relief are:

	D	E	F
	£	£	£
2001/02			
1.1.02 – 5.4.02	5,000	5,000	
2002/03			
1.1.02 – 31.12.02	20,000	20,000	
Overlap profits	(5,000)	(5,000)	
2003/04			
1.1.03 – 31.12.03	25,000		
1.1.03 – 28.2.04 (25,000 + 5,000)		30,000	
Less overlap relief		(5,000)	
		25,000	
1.7.03 – 5.4.04:			
To 31.12.03	10,000		
To 5.4.04 $\frac{3}{12}$ × £42,500	10,625		20,625
2004/05			
1.1.04 – 31.12.04	42,500		42,500
Overlap profits			(10,625)
Profits assessed over 4 tax years and overlap profits available for relief			
Total assessable profits	92,500	50,000	63,125
Overlap profits	(5,000)	—	(10,625)
Tax adjusted accounts profits	87,500	50,000	52,500

Any non-trading partnership income is divided according to the sharing arrangements in the accounting period in the same way as the trading profits (see 23.4).

A change in partners is not regarded as a cessation of the partnership unless none of the old partners continues after the change.

Non-trading income

23.4 Partnership non-trading income is shared for tax purposes according to the sharing arrangements in the accounting period. If the income is received net of tax (or, in the case of dividends, accompanied by a tax credit), the partners' shares for the relevant accounting periods are then allocated to the appropriate tax year, those amounts being shown in the partnership tax return (see 23.5) and each partner shows his income for the tax year in his personal tax return. If the income is untaxed income, it is treated as if it arose from a separate trade that commenced when the partner joined the firm and taxed according to the same periods as the trading income, so that normally the taxable amount for each partner will be his profit share in the accounting year ending in the tax year. There may be overlap relief on commencement and possibly on a change of accounting date. The overlap relief for non-trading income will be allowed to the extent that more than twelve months' income would otherwise be charged in one year as a result of a change of accounting date, and otherwise in the tax year in which a partner ceases to be a partner (even if the source of income ceased earlier). The deduction will be given against the untaxed non-trading income of the relevant tax year. If it exceeds that untaxed income it will be relieved against other income of that tax year.

Self-assessment tax returns (TMA 1970, ss 12AA–12AE, 28B, 30B, 31, 33A)

23.5   A partnership tax return (form SA 800) must be sent to the Revenue each year, incorporating a statement showing the names, addresses, tax districts and references of each partner, and each partner's share of profits, losses, charges on income and tax deducted or credited. There is a short version of the partnership statement for partnerships with only trading profits and taxed interest and a full version for partnerships with other types of income and/or capital gains.

Accounts details must normally be shown in the partnership return by completing the relevant boxes (known as 'Standard Accounts Information' — SAI). Where turnover is below £15,000, however, only the turnover, expenses and net profit need be shown. If turnover is above £15 million, accounts must be submitted (and the SAI need not be completed). Otherwise, accounts need not be sent in unless the Revenue ask for them, although it is advisable to submit them to make sure the Revenue have full information (see 9.10). The return includes details of income other than from the trade and of disposals of partnership chargeable assets. The details provided normally relate to the accounting year ended in the tax year. Details of *taxed* income, partnership charges, such as an annuity to a retired partner (see 23.11), and disposals of chargeable assets are, however, shown for the tax year itself rather than for the accounting year ended in the tax year, so that the partners will have the information they need to complete their own returns. The partnership tax return states that the taxed income of the relevant accounting periods should be apportioned to arrive at the figure for the tax year. A straight time apportionment would, however, give anomalous results if tax rates changed. It is acceptable, and probably more appropriate, to enter the taxed income actually received in the tax year itself. Similarly, where profit shares change, the partners' actual shares of the taxed income may be shown rather than time apportioning the total for the tax year. The return will not include calculations of tax payable, because these will be in each partner's separate return.

The partnership return must be submitted by the 31 January following the tax year, e.g. by 31 January 2005 for 2003/04. (Different dates apply to partnerships with corporate partners.) There are automatic penalties for late returns, chargeable on the partners rather than the partnership. A fixed penalty of £100 is charged on each partner, and a further fixed penalty of £100 each if the return is more than six months' late. The Revenue may ask the Commissioners to impose a daily penalty of £60 in substantial cases, in which case the further penalty after six months does not apply. There are no tax-geared penalties for partnership returns. The provisions for amending returns and for Revenue enquiries into them are the same as for individual returns (see 9.3 and 9.9). If the Revenue enquire into a partnership return, this automatically means that the enquiry extends to partners' personal returns, since the personal returns must reflect any changes to the partnership return. An enquiry into a personal return relating to non-partnership matters does not affect the other partners.

Relief may be claimed where there is an error or mistake in a partnership statement. Claims may be made within five years of the filing date for the partnership return. When the claim is accepted the Revenue will make appropriate adjustments to the self-assessments of each partner affected by the claim.

Each partner's personal return will include his share of the partnership income and charges as shown in the partnership statement, and gains on his share of partnership assets. Any expenses paid personally by partners and capital allowances on partners' own cars must be included in the *partnership* return, the expenses being added to the 'Standard Accounts Information' figures. They cannot be separately claimed in the personal return. (A corresponding adjustment should be made to the partnership net profit figure shown in the balance sheet, or alternatively a reconciliation shown in the 'Additional Information' box.) Again, there is a short version of the partnership pages in the personal return if the partnership has only trading profits and taxed interest.

Class 4 national insurance contributions are included in partners' personal returns. The return makes provision for a partner to indicate that he is excepted from contributions or that contributions have been deferred. From 2003/04, where deferment applies, Class 4 contributions remain payable at 1% on the excess of the total profits over the lower earnings limit, £4,745 for 2004/05. Contributions at the 1% rate will therefore be included in returns.

Work in progress (FA 1998, ss 42–46; FA 2002, ss 64–67 and Sch 22)

23.6 For accounting periods of established professional practices up to and including the period ending in the tax year 1999/2000, the Revenue accepted that work in progress did not need to be included in the accounts. If it was not included, it had to be brought in and treated as income arising on the first day of the first accounting period beginning *after* 6 April 1999, with tax being payable on the amount of the adjustment, known as the 'catching-up charge', over a maximum of ten years, normally starting in 1999/2000, but exceptionally in 2000/01. The detailed rules are in earlier editions of this book. The catching-up charge is limited to ¹⁄₁₀th of the taxable profit before deducting capital allowances in the first nine years, with the balance taxable in the tenth year. The charge is made on partners according to their profit shares in the accounting year before the anniversary of the date on which work in progress was brought in. This means that partners leaving the partnership during the ten-year period will escape tax and partners joining will pay tax on part of the charge.

If the business ceases, the charge continues for the remainder of the ten year period with the subsequent annual charges split between the former partners according to the profit sharing arrangements of the period prior to the cessation.

An election may be made to pay tax on all or part of the charge earlier, for example if there are allowable losses which could be set off, but it must be made by all who were partners in the relevant twelve-month period, unless the partnership has ceased, in which case it is made by each former partner separately.

The amount charged to tax counts as earnings for the purposes of calculating personal pension contributions. It does not, however, attract Class 4 national insurance contributions.

Changes both in the way work in progress is valued and in the way it is accounted for often need to be considered in the interests of consistency when two firms merge. This is a complex area, on which professional advice is essential.

Introducing funds to a partnership (TA 1988, ss 362, 363)

23.7 If a partner who is neither a partner in an investment LLP (see 23.23) nor a limited partner (see 23.24) borrows to introduce funds to a partnership, either as capital or on loan, interest on the borrowing is allowable as a deduction from his total income at his top tax rate (see 2.10). If, however, a partner then withdraws all or part of his capital, the introduced funds will be treated as repaid up to the amount of the withdrawal, restricting or eliminating the amount on which interest relief is available. This provision does not apply if the partner withdraws his capital *before* introducing new funds. The partnership would, however, need to be able to bridge the gap between the withdrawal of the existing funds and the introduction of the new. See 20.10.

If borrowings are made by the partnership itself, the interest is allowed as a business expense.

Consultancy

23.8   An outgoing partner may perform consultancy services for the partnership. He is taxed on the income either as employment income, if he is an employee of the partnership, or under Schedule D, Case I or II, if the payments to him are in his capacity of self-employed consultant (see 19.1). The payments are an allowable deduction in calculating the taxable profits of the partnership so long as they satisfy the 'wholly and exclusively' rule (see CHAPTER 20).

Trading losses (TA 1988, ss 380–390)

23.9   CHAPTER 25 deals with the calculation of the available loss reliefs and ways in which relief may be given. Relief for partnership trading losses may be claimed by each partner quite independently of the others. Thus one partner may decide to carry forward his share of the loss, another to set his against other income of the same tax year, another to set it against any income of the previous tax year, another to carry back against the income of the previous three tax years in the early years of his being a partner, and so on.

The carry-back loss rules for the first four years of a new trade only apply to a new partner, not to the continuing partners. There is an anti-avoidance provision blocking carry-back claims by a new partner if he is joining his spouse in a continuing business.

New anti-avoidance provisions have been introduced in relation to partnership losses — see 25.13.

Partnership assets (TCGA 1992, ss 59, 286; Revenue Statements of Practice D12 (10/2002), 1/79 and 1/89)

23.10   When partners join or leave a partnership, this usually involves a change in the persons who are entitled to share in the partnership assets.

There is no capital gains tax consequence if an incoming partner introduces cash which is credited to his capital account. Nor is there normally any capital gains tax consequence when an outgoing partner withdraws his capital account. In the first instance, an incoming partner is paying in a sum which remains to his credit in his capital account, whilst in the second instance, an outgoing partner is only withdrawing what belongs to him.

If, however, before an outgoing partner withdraws his capital account, that capital account has been credited with a surplus on revaluation of partnership assets (e.g. premises or goodwill), his leaving the partnership crystallises a chargeable gain in respect of the excess on revaluation, and whether or not the capital is withdrawn or left on loan to the partnership, there is a charge to capital gains tax. The chargeable gain will be reduced by indexation allowance to April 1998 and taper relief for later periods.

This charge will arise not only when a person ceases to be a partner, but whenever a partner's capital account includes a revaluation of chargeable assets and his entitlement to share in the assets is reduced. He is treated as having disposed of a proportion of the chargeable assets equivalent to the drop in his entitlement. The change will usually correspond with the change in the profit-sharing ratio, except where income and capital profits are shared differently, when the capital ratio will apply.

A payment by an incoming partner to the existing partners for a share in the chargeable assets such as goodwill or premises constitutes a disposal by the existing partners for capital gains tax, and a cost for capital gains tax to the incoming partner. The same applies where there is a payment, whether in cash or through an accounting adjustment, on a variation of profit-sharing arrangements without a change in partners. It makes no difference whether the amount is left in the partnership (by a credit to the capital account of those disposing) or is withdrawn by them, or indeed is dealt with outside the partnership itself. The test is whether a partner receives consideration for reducing his share in the partnership. Conversely, if he does not receive consideration, whilst there is still a disposal in the sense that his partnership share is less than it was, then, unless the partners have a family connection, the market value of the assets is not substituted for the purpose of calculating and charging the gain that could have been made, and thus no chargeable gain arises.

Example 3

X and Y are in partnership. Z is admitted as a partner in July 2004, sharing equally in both capital and income. He introduces £45,000 as capital which is credited to his account. The £45,000 is neither a capital gains tax base cost for Z nor a disposal by X and Y. The partnership assets include premises worth £180,000, which cost £63,000 when acquired in 1990.

Consider the following alternatives:

(1)   Before Z's admission, X and Y revalue the premises up to £180,000 by crediting each of their capital accounts with £58,500.

On Z's admission they each make a chargeable gain of:

	£	£
Value of premises reflected in their capital account (½ each)		90,000
Share of premises retained after Z's admission (⅓ each)		60,000
Disposal proceeds		30,000
Less cost:		
Cost was ½ each × £63,000	31,500	
Cost is now ⅓ each × £63,000	21,000	
Cost of part disposed of		10,500
Gain (subject to indexation allowance to April 1998 and taper relief)		£19,500

The £19,500 gain is the ⅓rd of the increase in value of £58,500 which has been realised by the reduction in the partnership share from ³⁄₆ths to ²⁄₆ths. The other ²⁄₃rds which remains unrealised is not charged to tax until realisation.

The cost of Z's share in the premises is £60,000 (⅓ × £180,000), equivalent to the disposal proceeds of X and Y.

(2)   The premises are not revalued on the admission of Z.

There is then no deemed gain by X and Y, and the cost for capital gains tax purposes for each of X and Y is ⅓ × £63,000 = £21,000. Z's cost will be £21,000 and he will be entitled to indexation allowance from April 1990 to April 1998. On future disposals, X and Y will also each get indexation allowance from 1990 to April 1998 on £21,000.

(3)   Z privately pays £60,000 (£30,000 each) to X and Y, for a ⅓rd share in the partnership premises.

X and Y are treated as receiving £30,000 each as in (1).

The capital gains cost for future disposals in the case of (1) and (3) is:

	X	Y	Z
	£	£	£
Original cost	31,500	31,500	—
On introduction of Z	(10,500)	(10,500)	21,000
Gains on which X and Y are assessable (subject to indexation allowance to April 1998 and taper relief)			39,000
	21,000	21,000	60,000

On future disposals, X and Y will each get indexation allowance on £21,000 from 1990 to April 1998.

Annuities to outgoing partners (Revenue Statements of Practice D12 (10/2002) and 1/79)

23.11   An outgoing partner may be paid an annuity by the continuing partners when he retires. He will not be charged to capital gains tax on the capitalised value of the annuity so long as it is regarded as reasonable recognition for past services to the partnership. For this purpose, the average of the partner's best three years' assessable profit shares out of the last seven is calculated and the annuity is considered reasonable if it does not exceed the fraction of that average amount obtained from the following table:

Years of service	Fraction
1–5	1/60 per year
6	8/60
7	16/60
8	24/60
9	32/60
10	2/3

The paying partners can deduct their share of the annuity in calculating their taxable income. They deduct basic rate income tax when making the payment and claim relief at the higher rate where appropriate by an adjustment in their personal tax returns. The annuity forms part of the recipient's taxable income. Since it is received net of basic rate tax, the recipient may have further tax to pay or tax to reclaim depending on his tax position.

An annuity paid by the continuing partners must be distinguished from a sum paid by them to an insurance company with which to purchase an annuity for the outgoing partner. The cost of such annuity counts as proceeds of the disposal of the outgoing partner's share.

Capital gains tax reliefs

Length of ownership for taper relief (Statement of Practice D12 (10/2002))

23.12   Since each partner entitled to share in a capital surplus on a chargeable asset is regarded as owning a fractional share of that asset, it follows that the date of acquisition for taper relief is when that fraction is acquired.

So far as goodwill is concerned, the statement of practice distinguishes that generated by a partnership in the conduct of its business from that acquired by a partnership for consideration.

In each case, the interest of a partner who disposes of his share for actual consideration is regarded as the same asset as was originally acquired by that partner when first becoming entitled to a share in the goodwill of that partnership, so long as the generated goodwill is not recognised in the balance sheet and the purchased goodwill is not at any time so recognised at a figure greater than the cost of acquisition, and in both cases no higher value is placed on goodwill in dealings between the partners.

Thus increases and decreases in profit shares do not affect the length of time for which the asset has been held when calculating the length of ownership for taper relief, but the self-generated goodwill is regarded as a separate asset from the purchased goodwill, so that on a disposal for actual consideration of the purchased goodwill, the taper relief period starts on the later of the date of purchase and the date when the partner disposing first became entitled to share in it. For the taper relief position where shares in partnership assets are transferred between husband and wife, see 4.22.

Replacement of business assets (TCGA 1992, ss 152–157)

23.13   Rollover relief for the replacement of business assets (see 4.26) is available where an asset owned personally by a partner and used in the partnership is disposed of and replaced. This is not affected by the payment of rent by the partnership.

Partner acquiring asset from the partnership (Statement of Practice D12 (10/2002))

23.14   When a partner acquires an asset from the partnership, he is not regarded as disposing of his fractional share in it. See 23.12 for the date of acquisition for taper relief.

Death of a partner

23.15   Where a partner dies in service:

(a)   any gains arising on the disposal of his share in partnership assets by reason of the death are exempt from capital gains tax, like gains on any other chargeable asset held at death;

(b)   the annuity dealt with in 23.11 may be paid to his widow or dependants.

Inheritance tax

23.16   The amount of a deceased partner's capital account, plus his share of any increase in the value of partnership assets, qualifies for the 100% business property relief unless the surviving partners are obliged to acquire his partnership share, in which case it is regarded as an entitlement under a contract for sale and not therefore eligible for relief. Relief is not lost where there is an option, as opposed to an obligation, for the share to be acquired by the surviving partners.

The amount on which the 100% relief is available may be restricted if the partnership assets include any not required for the trade (for example excessive cash balances).

Although the option to pay tax by ten annual instalments applies to the transfer of a partnership share, the instalment option is irrelevant for such transfers where the 100% relief is fully available. The instalment option is still relevant for transfers of land owned by an individual partner and used in the business, the rate of business property relief for such land being 50% (see CHAPTER 5). Interest is, however, charged on the full amount of tax outstanding rather than just on overdue instalments.

23.17   A gift of an interest in a partnership, including the whole or part of the partner's capital account, will qualify for business property relief so long as it is made whilst the donor is a partner and the partnership assets all qualify for relief because of their use in the trade.

A gift of the balance on the capital account after ceasing to be a partner will not qualify for business property relief since the amount will have become a partnership creditor rather than part of the business capital.

Value added tax

23.18   Customs need to be notified of a change of partner within 30 days, but not of a change in profit-sharing arrangements. The registration number will normally continue. A retiring partner remains liable for VAT due from the partnership until the date on which Customs are notified of his retirement. See 23.23 re limited liability partnerships.

National insurance

23.19 For the national insurance position of partners, see 24.10 (and see 23.24 re sleeping partners).

Stamp duty

23.20 There is no stamp duty on a partnership agreement, nor does stamp duty normally apply on the document effecting the division of assets when a partnership is dissolved.

The treatment of transfers of interests in a partnership for stamp duty and stamp duty land tax is dealt with in 6.22 and 6.23. Stamp duty does not arise where an incoming partner merely introduces capital to his own capital or current account. See 23.23 re limited liability partnerships.

Husband and wife partnerships (TA 1988, s 660A)

23.21 Many husbands and wives form business partnerships because of the practical and commercial advantages such a partnership can bring. The effect on their respective tax and national insurance positions will be an important factor.

The national insurance cost of employing a spouse is usually greater than if the spouse were a partner. The tax advantages of being a partner must be weighed against a partner's legal liability, which includes the possibility of being made bankrupt if the partnership cannot pay its debts.

Taking a spouse into partnership may be regarded as an appropriate way of maximising tax reliefs and use of the starting and basic rate bands, but it must be genuine, with the spouse's share being appropriate to his or her contribution to the business, otherwise there is the risk of the partnership arrangement being treated under the provisions of TA 1988, s 660A as a settlement, in which case the income would remain that of the other spouse. The Revenue have recently increased their use of the settlements provisions to attack husband/wife partnerships where, in their view, there is a bounteous arrangement. They have given various examples in their Tax Bulletins of April 2003 and February 2004. There is widespread disagreement with the Revenue's view by tax professionals. Under self-assessment the Revenue's approach places an unacceptable burden on taxpayers. Husband and wife partners who feel they may be affected need to take professional advice.

Partnerships which include a limited liability company as a partner (TA 1988, s 114; FA 2004, ss 131, 132)

23.22 A *company* may be a partner with individuals. In this case the profit share of the company for the relevant accounting period is liable to corporation tax, whilst the share applicable to the partners who are individuals is charged to income tax. There are, however, differences in the way profits are calculated for companies and individuals, so separate corporation tax and income tax calculations must be made.

Where a money debt is owed to or by the partnership, the corporate partner computes loan relationship debits and credits on its share, and brings the result into its corporation tax computation.

Anti-avoidance provisions apply from 17 March 2004 to amounts received by corporate partners. These are aimed at schemes where income is allocated to non-UK partners and capital to UK company partners. A UK company partner is charged to corporation tax on any amount that it realises as capital where the capital represents partnership profits on which the company would have been charged to corporation tax if the partnership profits had been allocated in proportion to shares of partnership capital. There are provisions to ensure that any amounts chargeable under these provisions will not also be taxed as capital gains.

Limited liability partnerships (TA 1988, ss 118ZA to 118ZD, 842B; TCGA 1992, ss 59A, 156A, 169A; IHTA 1984, s 267A; FA 2003, s 65; FA 2004, Sch 41; SSCBA 1992, s 15; SP D12 (10/2002))

23.23 Partners may register as a 'limited liability partnership' (LLP) under the Limited Liability Partnerships Act 2000. An LLP is a corporate entity and the liability of the partners is limited to the amount of their subscribed capital, although partners in LLPs will be liable in the same way as company directors for fraudulent trading and there are provisions to protect creditors. LLPs have to file annual accounts and an annual return with the Companies Registry. An LLP partner may be either a company or an individual. Corporate partners are liable to corporation tax on their profit shares, with individual partners being generally treated for tax and national insurance purposes in the same way as partners in any other partnership. The actions of an LLP are regarded for tax purposes as those of its members. The transfer of an existing partnership to an LLP will normally be on a tax neutral basis. If the LLP goes into formal liquidation, however, it is treated as a company

451

rather than a partnership for capital gains purposes. Any gains held over by partners under the business assets or gifts rollover provisions will be treated as realised by those partners at the start of the formal liquidation and will be chargeable on them accordingly. Taper relief is not available in respect of such gains.

Partners in LLPs are broadly subject to the same restrictions on reliefs for losses, interest etc. as limited partners under the Limited Partnership Act 1907 (see 23.24). An LLP partner's undrawn profits cannot, however, be added to his subscribed capital in working out whether reliefs are restricted, unless the partnership agreement unconditionally treats such profits as part of the partner's capital. Where the amount of loss set off against other income is restricted to the amount of the partner's subscribed capital, the unrelieved amount may be carried forward and treated as a loss available for relief against other income under Sections 380 and 381 (see 25.6 and 25.8), or where the partner is a company, Sections 393A(1) and 403 (see 26.3 and 26.12) in subsequent years — subject to the 'subscribed capital' restriction in those years. It should be noted that reliefs are not restricted where the LLP carries on a profession rather than a trade. As with limited partners, a partner in an 'investment LLP' cannot claim relief for interest on a loan to buy into the partnership (see 2.10). New anti-avoidance provisions have been introduced in relation to partnership losses, which apply both to ordinary partnerships and LLPs — see 25.13.

Stamp duty is not charged on property transferred to an LLP within one year after its incorporation if the partners' shares remain unchanged. The same applies to stamp duty land tax from 1 December 2003 where the property transferred includes land. The exemptions do not strictly apply if partners join or leave at the time the LLP is formed, but a charge can be avoided if the change takes place immediately before or after incorporation (providing evidence is available to that effect). See 6.22 and 6.23 for the general stamp duty/stamp duty land tax provisions for partnerships, which apply equally to LLPs.

Inheritance tax business and agricultural property reliefs are available for shares in appropriate partnership assets.

For VAT purposes, an LLP will be registered as a separate entity. While there will be a VAT liability on the transfer of assets if an existing partnership becomes an LLP, this will be subject to the rules for transfers of going concerns. The partnership's VAT number may be transferred to the LLP.

See the Revenue's Tax Bulletin of December 2000 for detailed points on LLPs.

Miscellaneous

23.24   A *salaried partner* must be distinguished from a partner who is allocated a salary as part of the profit-sharing arrangement. Senior employees are often described as partners in professional firms whilst retaining their salaried employee status. They remain liable to income tax as employees, receiving a salary for the duties of their employment, with national insurance being payable appropriately.

There is a further distinction where a partner is on a fixed share of profit, not because he is a salaried partner but his profit share being certain rather than depending on results. So long as the circumstances do not imply an employment, such a partner pays tax and national insurance as a self-employed person.

The share of a *sleeping partner* ranks as unearned income and cannot therefore support a pension premium higher than the £3,600 a year limit available to anyone under 75 who is resident and ordinarily resident in the UK, regardless of their income (see CHAPTER 17). On the other hand a sleeping partner is not liable either to Class 2 or Class 4 national insurance contributions, since he is not 'gainfully employed' for Class 2 and does not have Schedule D Case I or II earned income for Class 4.

A partnership may include a *limited partner* under the Limited Partnership Act 1907, whose liability is limited to the amount of the partner's agreed capital contribution. The limited partner, who may be either an individual or a company, cannot take part in the management of the partnership, although he is not barred from taking part in a non-managerial capacity. If the profit share of a limited partner ranks as unearned income, it cannot be used to support a pension premium higher than the £3,600 limit available to all UK residents under 75 (see above). Certain reliefs available to a limited partner cannot exceed the amount of the partner's agreed capital contribution plus undrawn profits (TA 1988, ss 117, 118). The reliefs concerned are reliefs for trading losses against income other than trading income from the partnership (see 25.6, 26.2 AND 26.12), interest paid in connection with the trade by an individual, and trade charges on income paid by a company but there are hardly any company payments that now fall within this category – see 3.5. A limited partner is not entitled to relief for interest on a loan to buy into the partnership (see 2.10).

Partnership itself, and matters arising, need not be governed by *formal written agreement*. In the absence of such agreement, sometimes indeed despite it, the Revenue will require other evidence of partnership, for example the name of, and operating arrangements for, bank accounts, VAT registration, names on stationery, contracts, licences, etc.

The overseas aspect of partnerships is dealt with in CHAPTER 41.

Tax points

23.25

- The requirement for profits to be computed on a true and fair view basis does not mean that time spent by partners must be included in a valuation of work in progress.

- The Revenue accept that the overhead content of work in progress is likely to be minimal for professional firms of up to four partners and can normally be ignored in calculating the work in progress figure.

- Since, in the case of spreading, the work in progress catching-up charge is allocated to partners by reference to their profit shares in the ensuing years, financial arrangements on the retirement and admission of partners will have to seek to match the tax burden with the benefit.

- A merger of two or more firms is strictly a cessation of each firm and the commencement of one new firm. The converse applies where one firm splits into two or more new firms. In both cases it may not be clear whether the rules for partnership changes apply. The Revenue issued a Statement of Practice (SP 9/86) explaining their view and issued further guidance covering the change to the current year basis in their SAT 1 (1995) guide. This area is one where professional advice and consultation with the Revenue is essential.

- Calculate annuities to retiring partners within the allowable capital gains tax limits, leaving them taxable only as income in the hands of the recipient and allowable for income tax to the payers. An inflation-linked increase to an annuity which is initially within the allowable limits does not affect the capital gains exemption.

- A pension payment by continuing partners to a retired partner, whilst assessable as income on the recipient, is not regarded by the Revenue as deductible in calculating the partnership taxable profits. The annuity arrangements in the previous tax point are a more tax-efficient way of providing income to a retired partner.

- Under self-assessment, partners are responsible for paying their own tax, and the half-yearly instalments due on 31 January and 31 July are on account of a partner's total income tax liability, not just his partnership share — see 9.7. In some circumstances it is prudent for partnerships to retain part of a partner's profit to meet the tax liability on partnership income, releasing it to the Revenue as part of each partner's personal liability on the due dates. Many partnerships find it best to adopt this procedure.

- If you have the choice of borrowing to buy your home and borrowing to introduce funds to a partnership (other than as a limited partner or partner in an investment LLP), interest on the partnership borrowing will save you tax at your highest rate, whereas that on the home loan will not save tax at all.

- If one spouse takes the other into partnership as an active partner, it should not be forgotten that the new partner has to pay Class 2 national insurance contributions. A penalty of £100 applies for failing to register for Class 2 national insurance contributions within three months.

- A capital gain may arise where partners sell partnership assets (e.g. land and buildings) to raise funds to pay out a retiring partner. Rather than pay tax on that gain, the partners will be able to deduct it from the cost of acquisition of the outgoing partner's share of any of the remaining business assets of the partnership that qualify for rollover relief. An alternative to paying out the retiring partner's share in land and buildings might be for him to retain that share as a co-owner with his former partners. There will not have been a disposal of his share in these circumstances, since he retains what he had before, albeit it will no longer be a qualifying asset for inheritance tax business property relief and will change its status from business to non-business asset for capital gains tax.

- Income and capital profit-sharing ratios need not always be the same. Established partners can retain the right to the whole of the future increase in value of partnership premises, to the exclusion of incoming partners, by excluding the incoming partners from the capital profit-sharing ratio.

  Any running expenses of those premises, including interest on borrowing, remain allowable in calculating trading profit, which is divided in the income-sharing ratio.

- If you are thinking of giving away the balance on your capital account, do so whilst you are still an active partner and at a decent interval before you propose ceasing to be a partner. In this way, business property relief for inheritance tax will be available on the gift. It will not be available if you make the gift after ceasing to be a partner.

24
National insurance contributions for the self-employed

Background

24.1   National insurance contributions are the responsibility of the Revenue and are dealt with by the Revenue National Insurance Contributions Office (NICO). Benefits are dealt with by the Department for Work and Pensions. The legislation is in the Social Security Contributions and Benefits Act 1992 (SSCBA 1992) and statutory instruments.

A self-employed person over the age of 16 must, unless specifically exempted, pay both Class 2 and Class 4 contributions. Class 2 contributions are payable at a flat weekly rate and entitle the contributor to all contributory benefits except contribution-based jobseeker's allowance and the earnings-related supplement to retirement pension. Class 4 contributions are payable on all profits in excess of a specified limit that are chargeable to income tax under Schedule D, Case I or II (see CHAPTER 21). They carry no entitlement to benefits of any kind. See 13.3 for the position on receiving contribution credits in order to satisfy the contribution requirements for State pensions and 19.1 re retaining Class 1 contributions on your record if you have wrongly been treated as an employee. See also 9.48 for the national insurance position in relation to interest, penalties and criminal evasion of liability.

Class 2 contributions

Payment (SSCBA 1992, s 11; SI 2001/1004)

24.2   If you become self-employed, you must notify the Revenue within three months that you are liable to pay Class 2 contributions, even if you are going to apply for deferment because you pay maximum Class 1 contributions as an employee at the main primary rate of 11% (see 24.12). You are liable to a penalty of £100 if you fail to do so (see 9.48). You must also make arrangements to pay your Class 2 contributions, unless you are not liable to pay (see 24.3 and 24.4). The weekly rate is £2. Payment is made either by monthly direct debit or quarterly in arrear. If you pay quarterly, you will get a bill from the Revenue showing the amount payable.

If Class 2 contributions are paid late, they may affect your entitlement to benefits. If they are paid after the end of the tax year following the one in which they were due, they normally have to be paid at the highest rate applicable between the due date and the payment date. See also 9.48 re penalties for late payment.

Exempt persons

24.3   Class 2 contributions are payable by 'self-employed earners', which means those who are 'gainfully employed' other than as employees. The Class 2 net is wider than Class 4, because it includes a 'business', whereas Class 4 only covers a trade, profession or vocation.

The following people are, however, not liable to pay Class 2 contributions:

(a)   men and women over state pension age (men 65, women 60);

(b)   married women who chose on or before 11 May 1977 to pay reduced rate Class 1 contributions or to pay no Class 2 contributions (provided that this election has not been automatically revoked by divorce or possibly revoked by widowhood — see 13.8);

(c)   someone with small earnings who obtains a certificate of exception or is told by NICO that a certificate is not needed (see 24.4 and 24.5);

(d)   someone who, for a full week, is

   (i)   incapable of work, or

   (ii)   in legal custody or prison, or

   (iii)   receiving incapacity benefit or maternity allowance;

(e)   someone who, for any day in a particular week, receives carer's allowance or unemployability supplement.

In the case of (d) and (e), the exemption is applicable only to the particular week concerned.

Special rules apply to those who go to work abroad — see 41.21.

Small earnings

24.4   You need not pay Class 2 contributions if your earnings are small, but since the amount payable is presently only £2.05 a week, then unless you also have earnings on which you pay Class 1 contributions it is probably sensible to pay Class 2 contributions and maintain your contribution record for social security benefits, particularly the State retirement pension. Your contribution record could alternatively be maintained by paying Class 3 voluntary contributions (see 13.3), but these are now at a much higher rate than Class 2, being £7.15 a week for 2004/05.

If you decide to apply for a certificate of exception for a tax year you need to show that:

(i)   your net earnings for that tax year are expected to be less than a specified limit; or

(ii) your net earnings for the previous tax year were less than the limit specified for that year and that circumstances have not materially altered.

In this context 'net earnings' are earnings shown in the profit and loss account as opposed to taxable earnings, but excluding income under the New Deal scheme. If employed earnings on which Class 1 contributions have been paid are included in the accounts, these are not counted in net earnings. Where an accounting period overlaps 5 April, earnings are strictly apportioned on a time basis between tax years but in considering (ii) above, the Revenue will normally take the accounts year ended in the previous tax year.

The small earnings exception limits are:

2002/03	£4,025
2003/04	£4,095
2004/05	£4,215

Certificates of exception can be applied for on form CF 10 in leaflet CA 02 obtainable from your local tax office. Exception from payment cannot apply from a date earlier than 13 weeks before the date of the application. A certificate issued on registration for self-employment expires at the end of that tax year, but later certificates last for three years. NICO automatically invites existing holders to apply for renewal.

If you paid contributions but could have claimed exception, you may apply for a refund. Refund claims must be made by 31 January after the end of the relevant tax year. Where repayments are concerned, the earnings will be calculated strictly over the tax year, which means claims may have to be made before the exact earnings are known.

Persons not 'ordinarily' self-employed (SI 1978/1689)

24.5   When someone applies for a certificate of exception from paying Class 2 contributions, he may be told that he does not need a certificate. This is because NICO consider that he is not ordinarily self-employed and that there is therefore no liability to pay contributions. There is no statutory definition of 'not ordinarily self-employed' but the example quoted in leaflet

CA 02 is of a person employed in a regular job whose earnings from spare-time self-employment are not expected to exceed £1,300 in a tax year.

More than one self-employment

24.6   People who are self-employed have to pay only one weekly Class 2 contribution no matter how many self-employed occupations they may have. In deciding whether you are entitled to a certificate of exception on the grounds of small earnings, self-employed earnings from all sources are added together.

Class 4 contributions

Payment (SSCBA 1992, ss 15–17 and Sch 2 paras 2, 3)

24.7   Class 4 contributions are payable at a main percentage rate of 8% on profits chargeable to income tax under Schedule D, Case I or II, which fall between specified upper and lower limits and at the additional Class 4 percentage rate of 1% on profits above the upper limit. The lower and upper limits for 2003/04 and 2004/05 are:

2003/04	£4,615 and £30,940
2004/05	£4,745 and £31,720

If you have more than one self-employment, all the profits are added together when calculating your Class 4 liability.

In general, 'profits' are computed in the same way for Class 4 contributions as for income tax but certain special rules apply, for example trading losses allowed under TA 1988, ss 380, 381 (see CHAPTER 25) against non-trading income and capital gains for tax purposes are set only against trading income for national insurance, and may thus be carried forward against future profits for calculating Class 4 contributions. Losses on furnished holiday lettings and retirement annuity and personal pension premiums cannot be deducted in calculating Class 4 contributions.

Class 4 contributions are collected along with income tax under self-assessment, so that the half-yearly payments on account made on 31 January and 31 July include Class 4 contributions based on the previous year's figures, with any balancing adjustment shown in the tax return and payable or repayable on the following 31 January. Provision is made in returns for the taxpayer to indicate that he is exempt from Class 4 contributions (see 24.8), in which case no contributions are shown, or that deferment applies (see 24.12), in which case contributions are payable at the 1% rate on all profits above the lower profits limit. If any further Class 4 contributions are payable, they are collected by the Revenue directly rather than through the self-assessment system.

Exempt persons

24.8   The following people are not liable to pay Class 4 contributions:

(a)   men and women over state pension age (men 65, women 60) at the beginning of the tax year;

(b)   individuals who are not resident in the UK for income tax purposes;

(c)   trustees and executors who are chargeable to income tax on income they receive on behalf of other people (e.g. incapacitated persons);

(d)   'sleeping partners' who supply capital and take a share of the profits but take no active part in running the business;

(e)   divers and diving supervisors working in connection with exploration and exploitation activities on the Continental shelf or in UK territorial waters;

(f)   someone who is under 16 on 6 April in a particular tax year and holds a certificate of exception for that year. Application for an exception certificate should be made on form CA 2835U; application need only be made once as any certificate granted will cover all the relevant tax years;

(g)   someone who is not 'ordinarily' self-employed (see 24.5).

Late payment or overpayment of contributions

24.9   The income tax rules for charging interest (see 2.23) apply if Class 4 contributions are paid late and also the penalties in cases of fraudulent or negligent conduct (see 9.46). The income tax repayment supplement provisions also apply where contributions are refunded.

Partnerships (including husband and wife partners)

24.10   Each active partner is liable to both Class 2 and Class 4 contributions (unless a wife is exempt from Class 2 contributions — see 24.11), the Class 4 profit limits applying to each partner's profit share.

A partner's Class 4 contributions are entered in the partner's personal return. Where a partner carries on a further trade or trades, the profits of all such businesses are considered together when calculating his overall Class 4 liability.

Married women

24.11   If you are a woman who was married or widowed before 6 April 1977, you could elect on or before 11 May 1977 not to pay full national insurance contributions. If you have made the election, you pay Class 1 contributions as an employee at a reduced rate, and you do not have to pay Class 2 self-employed contributions. You do, however, have to pay Class 4 contributions.

You lose the right to pay no Class 2 and reduced rate Class 1 contributions in some circumstances. For details, and further points on the reduced rate election, see 13.8.

Self-employed and employed in the same tax year

24.12   If you are both self-employed and an employee, you are liable to pay Class 1, 2 and 4 contributions, and if you have more than one employment you are liable to Class 1 contributions in each employment. There is, however, a maximum figure above which contributions will be refunded.

Before 6 April 2003 the maximum was worked out in a straightforward way and was the same for all taxpayers. Now that contributions at 1% are chargeable on all earnings/profits above the upper earnings/profits limit (£31,720 for 2004/05), the calculation is very complicated and has up to nine stages. The maximum figure is not a fixed amount and will vary according to the mix of employment/self-employment and the amounts earned. If there are several employments no contributions are payable on the first £4,745 in each employment. For self-employed profits there is only one £4,745 nil rate band on the total profits from all self-employments. The calculation of the maximum then includes contributions on the band of earnings/profits between £4,715 and £31,720 either at the 11% employees' rate or if there are insufficient employed earnings, at the 8% Class 4 rate. All other earnings/profits above the £4,745 lower limit are charged at 1%. When calculating the maximum for the self-employed, 53 weekly Class 2 contributions of £2.05 are included. If your contributions for 2004/05 exceed the maximum by £3.80 or more, you may claim a refund of the excess from NICO. Any such refund is made outside the income tax self-assessment system and no adjustments are made to payments on account, interest etc.

Where you expect your contributions to exceed the maximum, you should apply to defer payment of contributions. Application for deferment of Class 4 and 2 contributions must be made on form CA 72B, which is part of leaflet CA 72 — 'NI contributions — deferring payments'. Where deferment is granted, Class 4 contributions remain payable at 1% on all profits above the lower profits limit of £4,745. Application for deferment of Class 1 contributions should be made on form CA 72A, which is also part of leaflet CA 72.

If you feel you have overpaid contributions you may apply to NICO for a refund. This could happen, for example, if you have several businesses and the profits of those businesses have been totalled incorrectly in arriving at your overall Class 4 liability, or if you have paid Class 1 contributions that have not been taken into account in calculating your Class 4 liability. You will not be able to get a refund of Class 4 contributions until your Class 4 self-assessment for the year has been finalised and fully paid.

Tax points

24.13

- Make sure you notify the Revenue of any weeks for which a Class 2 contribution is not due, for example when you are receiving incapacity benefit, so that an adjustment can be made.

- If you are both employed and self-employed, make sure you claim deferment if you are eligible. This is better than waiting till after the year end for a refund.

- Remember that trading losses set off against non-trading income for income tax purposes are carried forward against trading profits for Class 4 contributions purposes. If you calculate your own liability under self-assessment, the worksheet in the tax return guide provides for you to make the appropriate adjustment to the profits.

- Make sure you notify the Revenue as soon as your self-employment commences. You are liable to a penalty of £100 if you do not notify within three months. A national insurance small earnings exception may be asked for at the same time if the early profits are anticipated to be minimal, although you may not think this worthwhile, since the Class 2 contributions rate is only £2.05 a week.

- If you take your wife or husband into partnership do not forget that a liability to Class 2 contributions will almost certainly arise. The arrears will have to be paid later if this is overlooked, together with the £100 penalty referred to above.

- If you are a married woman who has elected not to pay Class 2 contributions, watch the circumstances in which contributions become payable, for example following widowhood or divorce.

25
Losses of sole traders and partners

Introduction

25.1   Losses may arise in a trade, profession or vocation carried on in the UK or abroad, or in a business of property letting. Capital losses may arise on the disposal of chargeable assets. Losses relating to rented property may normally be relieved only against rental income, and are dealt with in CHAPTER 32. Relief for losses relating to businesses controlled abroad is restricted to profits from the same source (see CHAPTER 41). Capital losses are normally set against capital gains of the same tax year, with any balance carried forward against later gains (see CHAPTER 4), although capital losses on certain unquoted shares may be set against income (see 38.21). Other aspects relating to capital losses are dealt with in context in other chapters. The remainder of this chapter deals with losses of UK trades. The rules for trading losses apply equally to professions or vocations.

Calculation of losses and reliefs available

Calculation of loss

25.2   Losses are calculated using the same basis periods as those used for calculating profits. So a loss of the year to 31 August 2004 would be regarded as a loss of 2004/05 in the same way as a profit of that year would be taxed in 2004/05. The loss basis period could be longer than twelve months if the accounting date has been changed (see 21.7), subject to the rules mentioned below for overlapping basis periods. Furthermore, a basis period of more than twelve months would result in the loss being increased by an appropriate proportion of available overlap relief (see Example 1).

Example 1

Trader started business on 1 July 2000, making up his accounts to 30 June annually, and made profits each year until 2003. He then made up a 15-month account to 30 September 2004 showing a loss. The position is as follows:

Basis periods

2000/01	1.7.2000 – 5.4.01
2001/02	1.7.2000 – 30.6.01 (overlap profits 9 mths to 5.4.01)
2002/03	1.7.01 – 30.6.02
2003/04	1.7.02 – 30.6.03
2004/05	1.7.03 – 30.9.04 (loss)

Relief may be claimed for the 2004/05 loss of the 15 months to 30 September 2004, augmented by overlap relief of ⅗ths of the overlap profits.

The basis period rules apply on cessation as they do in a continuing business. Any available overlap relief is taken into account in computing the result of the final accounting period. If a business that had made up accounts annually to 30 June ceased trading on 30 April 2004, making a loss in the final ten months, the loss of that ten months would be treated as a 2004/05 loss and would be increased by any available overlap relief (but see 25.9 re terminal loss claims). Where a loss would be taken into account in two successive tax years (for example, in the first trading period of a new business or on a change of accounting date), it is only taken into account in the first year. See Example 2.

Example 2

Trader starts in business on 1 August 2002 and makes a loss of £24,000 in the year to 31 July 2003 and a profit of £15,000 in the year to 31 July 2004. The assessments for 2002/03 and 2003/04 are therefore Nil.

⁸⁄₁₂ths of the loss, i.e. £16,000, is treated as the loss of 2002/03 and ⁴⁄₁₂ths, i.e. £8,000, as the loss of 2003/04. The profit of £15,000 is assessed in 2004/05.

Loss reliefs available

25.3 There are various ways in which relief for trading losses may be claimed:

Carry forward against later profits of *same trade* (TA 1988, s 385).
Set against *total* income of tax year of loss and/or the previous tax year (TA 1998, s 380). The claim for either year may, if the taxpayer wishes, be extended to include set-off against capital gains (FA 1991, s 72).
In a new trade, carry back against *total* income of previous three tax years, earliest first (TA 1988, s 381).

When a loss occurs on ceasing to trade, set against *trading* income of final tax year, then carry back against *trading* income of previous three tax years, latest first (TA 1988, ss 388, 389).

Loss claims are taken into account to the maximum possible extent against the relevant income (i.e. total income under Sections 380 and 381 and trading income for Section 385 and terminal loss claims). Since the set-off is made *before* deducting personal allowances, in many cases personal allowances will be wasted.

See 25.13 re anti-avoidance provisions in relation to a partner's losses in the early years of joining a partnership.

Capital allowances

25.4   Capital allowances are treated as trading expenses, and therefore form part of the trading result. There is some flexibility, however, because the capital allowances claim can be reduced to whatever amount is required (see 22.7 and 22.39).

Loss carried forward (TA 1988, s 385)

25.5   The most straightforward way of obtaining relief for a loss is by carrying it forward to reduce later income of the same trade, so that in Example 1 the total available losses, including the overlap relief, would be carried forward to reduce trading profits of 2005/06 and later years. In Example 2 the total losses of £24,000 would eliminate the 2004/05 assessment of £15,000 leaving £9,000 still to carry forward. The set-off can only be made against profits of the *same* trade, so that a change in activity will cause relief to be denied.

There are obvious disadvantages in carrying forward a loss. The trade may cease, or its nature change, before the loss is fully relieved. There is also a considerable delay before the loss results in a cash saving by reducing or eliminating a tax bill.

Loss set against other income (TA 1988, s 380)

25.6   Earlier relief may be obtained by setting off the loss against any other income of the tax year in which the loss is incurred or of the previous tax year, or, if the loss is large enough, of both tax years. If claims are to be made for both available years, the taxpayer may decide which claim comes first. If there are losses in successive years, and both a current year loss and a carried back loss are to be relieved in the same tax year, the earlier year's loss is set off first. If there were other sources of income, Section 380 claims could be made for the 2004/05 loss in Example 1 against the income of 2004/05 and/or 2003/04. Section 380 claims could be made in Example 2 for the 2002/03 loss of £16,000 in 2002/03 and/or 2001/02, and for the 2003/04 loss of £8,000 in 2003/04 and/or 2002/03. If, however, the taxpayer claimed against 2002/03 income in respect of both the 2002/03 loss and the 2003/04 loss, the 2002/03 loss would be set off first. See 25.8 re the claims possible in Example 2 under Section 381.

A Section 380 claim cannot be made for losses incurred in 'hobby' trades as distinct from commercial activities. A claim is also specifically prohibited for the sixth year of a consecutive run of farming and market gardening losses (reckoned before capital allowances) (TA 1988, s 397) (see 31.3).

Extending Section 380 claim to capital gains (FA 1991, s 72; FA 2002, s 48)

25.7   A Section 380 claim may be extended to include set-off against capital gains, in either or both of the tax year of loss and the previous tax year. The claim against income of the year must be made first (personal allowances therefore being wasted, except where married couple's age allowance is transferred) and the loss available to set against capital gains is also reduced by any other loss relief claimed, for example under Section 380 in the previous year or by carry-back under Section 381 in a new business (see 25.8). From 2004/05, the maximum amount of capital gains available to relieve the trading loss is the amount of the capital gains after deducting any capital losses of the relevant year and unrelieved capital losses brought forward from earlier years but before deducting taper relief and the annual exemption. The amount available for relief is the lower of the available loss and the available amount of capital gains. The available amount is treated as an allowable capital loss of the relevant year and is therefore set off against capital gains in *priority* to brought forward capital losses and also before deducting taper relief. Depending on the levels of gains and losses, the claim may leave trading losses carried forward even though there are gains chargeable to tax, or may mean wasting both taper relief and all or part of the annual exemption. The way in which the loss available for relief against gains is arrived at and the interaction with taper relief and the annual exemption make the calculations quite complicated.

For tax years before 2004/05, the loss available for set-off was calculated by reference to the gains *after* taper relief. For losses made in 2002/03, a trader could elect that the revised provisions should have effect in relation to claims relating to gains of either 2001/02 or 2002/03 or both years. An election may similarly be made in respect of a loss of 2003/04 for the revised provisions to operate in relation to gains of either 2002/03 or 2003/04 or both years. The time limit for the election is the same as the time limit for extending the

Section 380 claim to capital gains (see 25.10). An illustration of when the election would be beneficial is given in Example 3.

Example 3

Trader makes loss of £60,000 in year to 31 December 2003, and claims Section 380 relief for 2003/04 against his other income for that year of £10,000, and against his capital gains. His capital gains of the year (net of capital losses of the year) were £80,000 (eligible for 50% taper relief). There were no capital losses brought forward. The gains available to cover unrelieved trading losses are therefore £80,000 less taper relief of £40,000 = £40,000.

The Section 380 claim against income covers £10,000 of the loss, and wastes personal allowances (although if he is entitled to married couple's age allowance, the allowance may be transferred to his wife). The unrelieved trading loss is therefore £50,000. The amount that may be set off against capital gains is, however, restricted to the net gains *after* taper relief, i.e. £40,000. This reduces the net capital gains *before* taper relief to (80,000 – loss 40,000 =) £40,000, which is then reduced by 50% taper relief of £20,000 and the annual exemption of £7,900, leaving net chargeable gains of £12,100 and an unrelieved trading loss carried forward of £10,000. Tax on the gains would be £1,960 @ 10% and £10,140 @ 20%.

The trader could *elect* to calculate the relief for the trading loss by treating the available capital gains as the amount *before* taper relief, i.e. £80,000. After setting off the loss of £50,000 this would leave gains of £30,000, reduced by taper relief of £15,000 and the annual exemption of £7,900 to £7,100. Tax on that amount would be £1,960 @ 10% and £5,140 @ 20%. Following the election the tax payable would be reduced by £5,000 @ 20% = £1,000, but there would be no unrelieved trading loss carried forward.

The election in the above paragraph was only relevant for trading losses of 2002/03 and 2003/04. If the trading loss had occurred in the year to 31 December 2004, the available capital gains would be the capital gains *before* taper relief, as in the second alternative above.

Where there are capital losses brought forward that already reduce gains to the exempt level, the trading loss claim would give no immediate tax saving and it would be a question of whether it would be preferable to have unrelieved trading losses carried forward or unrelieved capital losses carried forward. See Example 4.

Example 4

After setting a trading loss of the year to 30 June 2004 against other income under Section 380, a trader has an unrelieved loss of £10,000. He claims to extend the claim to his capital gains of 2004/05. His capital gains of that year (in respect of which taper relief of 50% was available) were £21,000 and he had capital losses of £2,000 in 2004/05 and capital losses brought forward of £9,400.

The gains available to offset the unrelieved trading loss of £10,000 are £21,000 less £2,000 current capital losses less £9,400 brought forward capital losses = £9,600. Since this is less than the available trading loss, the loss set off against capital gains is restricted to £9,600. The effect of claiming or not claiming relief for trading losses against capital gains is as follows:

	Without loss claim £	With loss claim £
Capital gains of year	21,000	21,000
Capital losses of year	(2,000)	(2,000)
Trading loss		(9,600)
Brought forward capital losses	(9,400)	
Restricted to leave gains covered by annual exemption	—	(1,200)
Covered by taper relief/annual exemption	£9,600	£8,200
Capital losses carried forward	—	8,200
Trading losses carried forward	10,000	400
Total losses carried forward	£10,000	£8,600

Without the trading losses claim, the effect of having brought forward capital losses of £9,400 is that they are fully used to offset taxable gains of only (19,000 − taper relief 9,500 − annual exemption 8,200 =) £1,300 (see 4.24 for further illustrations). With the trading loss claim, losses of £10,800 need to be used to achieve the same result, and the combined capital and trading losses to carry forward are £1,400 less.

New trades — carry-back of losses (TA 1988, s 381)

25.8   Where a loss occurs in any of the first four tax years of a new sole trade, or of a new partner's membership of a partnership, relief may be claimed against that person's general income of the three previous tax years, *earliest* first. A Section 381 claim is a single claim and the loss must be set off to the maximum possible extent against the income of all three years. See Example 5. There is no set-off against capital gains in those previous three years. As with Section 380 (see 25.6), this carry-back claim cannot be made unless the trade is carried on commercially. Where a loss is large enough, a claim under Section 380 may be preceded or followed by a Section 381 claim.

Example 5

In Example 2 at 25.2, the trader incurred losses of £16,000 and £8,000 respectively in his first and second tax years of trading, 2002/03 and 2003/04.

As an alternative to claiming relief under Section 380 (or in addition to a Section 380 claim, depending on the level of other income) relief could be claimed under Section 381 as follows:

2002/03 loss of £16,000
Against total income of 1999/2000, then 2000/01, then 2001/02.

2003/04 loss of £8,000
Against total income of 2000/01, then 2001/02, then 2002/03.

Any losses not relieved under either Section 381 or Section 380 would be carried forward under Section 385.

Because of the way losses are calculated where basis periods overlap (see Example 2 at 25.2), choosing an accounting date early in the tax year may restrict the Section 381 claims available. See Example 6.

Example 6

New business started 1 May 2002. If there are losses in the early years and accounts are made up annually to 31 March, Section 381 claims will be possible in respect of losses made in the 11 months to 31 March 2003, and the years to 31 March 2004, 2005 and 2006. If accounts are made up annually to 30 April, Section 381 claims will only be possible in respect of the loss of the year to 30 April 2003 (the claim being split as to $^{11}\!/_{12}$ths in 2002/03 and $^{1}\!/_{12}$th in 2003/04), and the years to 30 April 2004 and 2005.

Although the tax saving from Section 381 claims is *calculated* by reference to the tax position of the carry-back years, repayment supplement runs from 31 January following the loss year (see 25.11).

Loss on cessation of trade (terminal loss) (TA 1988, ss 388 and 389; CAA 2001, s 354)

25.9   Losses towards the end of a business clearly cannot be carried forward against future profits. A claim may be made to set the loss of the last twelve months of trading (called a terminal loss) against the *trading* income (after capital allowances) of the tax year in which the business ceases, then the three tax years prior to that tax year, *latest* first. The terminal loss is calculated in two parts, splitting the last twelve months at the tax year end, i.e. at 5 April. If the *result* of either part is a profit, it is treated as nil in the calculation. Profits must, however, be taken into account in arriving at the figures for each part, as shown in Example 7. The full amount of any available overlap relief is included in the terminal loss. The tax saving flowing from carrying back the loss is calculated by reference to the tax position of the earlier years, but it is given effect in relation to the loss year, with a consequent reduction in the amount of repayment supplement payable (see 25.11).

Where there is other income, a Section 380 claim (see 25.6) may be made in addition to (or instead of) the terminal loss claim. Unlike the terminal loss calculation, a loss of the final tax year for Section 380 is on an accounting period basis, as shown in Example 7. Where both claims are made, the taxpayer may choose which claim is to be dealt with first.

Example 7

Trade ceases 30 September 2004.

Previous accounts have been to 31 December, recent results up to the cessation being:

Year to 31 December 2001	Profit £17,500
Year to 31 December 2002	Profit £12,000
Year to 31 December 2003	Profit £7,200
Period to 30 September 2004	Loss £27,000

Overlap relief brought forward is £3,000.

Assessments will be (see CHAPTER 21):

	£
2001/02 (year to 31.12.2001)	17,500
2002/03 (year to 31.12.2002)	12,000
2003/04 (year to 31.12.2003)	7,200
2004/05 (9 months to 30.9.2004)	—

Terminal loss of year to 30 September 2004:

		£	£
1.10.03 to 5.4.04			
First 3 months	Profit	1,800	
Next 3 months	Loss	(9,000)	(7,200)
6.4.04 to 30.9.04	Loss	(18,000)	
Overlap relief (in full)		(3,000)	(21,000)
			(28,200)

Since there is no trading income in 2004/05, the terminal loss may be carried back and set off against trading assessments as follows:

2003/04		7,200
2002/03		12,000
2001/02	(balance, reducing assessment to £8,500)	9,000
		28,200

If there had been insufficient trading income to obtain relief for the terminal loss (or as an alternative to a terminal loss claim), a Section 380 claim could be made to set the 2004/05 loss against *any* income or chargeable gains of that year and/or 2003/04. The 2004/05 loss for a Section 380 claim is the full £27,000 loss to 30 September 2004 plus the overlap relief of £3,000, totalling £30,000, less any terminal loss relief claimed.

Where an industrial building, qualifying hotel or enterprise building is sold after the cessation of a trade and a balancing charge arises, unrelieved trading losses, expenses and capital allowances may be carried forward to set against the balancing charge.

Time limits for claims

25.10

TA 1988, s 380	Set off against income and gains of same tax year or previous tax year	Within one year from 31 January after the end of the tax year in which the loss occurs
TA 1988, s 381	Set off new business losses against income for three previous tax years, taking earlier before later years	Within one year from 31 January after the end of the tax year in which the loss occurs

| TA 1988, s 385 | Carry forward against future profits of same trade | Within five years from 31 January after the end of the tax year in which the loss occurs |
| TA 1988, ss 388, 389 | Carry-back of terminal losses | Within five years from 31 January after the tax year in which the business ceases |

Repayment supplement (TMA 1970, Sch 1B para 2; TA 1988, s 824)

25.11   A loss claim will either prevent tax being payable or cause tax already paid to be repaid. Repayment supplement runs from the date of an overpayment, but the rate of interest is significantly lower than that charged on unpaid tax (currently 2.5% compared with 6.5%). Furthermore, where a loss is carried back and set against the income of an earlier tax year, then although the tax saving is calculated by reference to the tax position of the earlier year, the adjustment is made by reducing the tax liability of the loss year (see 9.5) and supplement runs from the 31 January payment date for that year. This significantly affects the benefit of carrying back new business losses for up to three years (see 25.8).

Losses of limited partners and partners in limited liability partnerships (TA 1988, ss 117, 118 and 118ZB–118ZD)

25.12   Some partnerships have 'limited partners', whose liability for partnership debts is limited to a fixed capital contribution (see 23.24). These limited partners may be either individuals or companies. A loss claim by such partners in any year against income other than from the trade cannot exceed the total of the limited partner's fixed capital contribution plus undrawn profits to the end of that year less loss relief already given against non-trading income. The loss claims referred to are those under Sections 380 and 381 for individuals, and under TA 1988, s 393A(1) or the Section 403 group relief provisions for companies (see 26.3 and 26.12). There is no restriction on the right of limited partners to carry forward their unused losses against later profits from the same trade.

Similar rules apply in relation to partners in limited liability partnerships (LLPs — see 23.23). Undrawn profits cannot, however, be included in a partner's subscribed capital unless such profits are unconditionally treated as part of the partner's capital. Losses unrelieved in one tax year against income other than from the trade because of the restriction are available for relief against non-trading income in subsequent years, similarly restricted by reference to the subscribed capital of the later year. New anti-avoidance provisions apply to losses of partners in LLPs in the first four tax years (see 25.13). These rules operate for those years instead of the provisions in this section.

Anti-avoidance provisions re partnership losses in early years (TA 1988, ss 118ZE–118ZK; FA 2004, ss 119–124)

25.13   New anti-avoidance rules have been introduced to prevent manipulation of the tax reliefs for partnership losses. They apply to trading losses for accounting periods ending on or after 10 February 2004, subject to transitional provisions which exclude losses in the part of the accounting period before that date, and make appropriate adjustments for capital allowances. They only affect partners who do not spend at least ten hours a week actively working in the business when the losses arise, and apply to losses arising in the first four tax years in which the partner carried on the trade.

The provisions prevent such partners in general partnerships and limited liability partnerships (LLPs) claiming relief for losses against non-trading income and capital gains (see 25.6 to 25.8), or relief for interest against non-trading income (see 2.10) to a greater extent than the amount of their capital contribution and profit share. They also impose an 'exit charge' where such partners share in large early losses in trades that acquire a licence which entails significant expenditure before any income arises, obtain relief for the losses against their other income or gains, and then dispose of their share of the benefit of the income from the licence without attracting an income tax charge.

National insurance

25.14   Losses reduce your profit for Class 4 national insurance as well as for income tax. If you claim income tax relief for your loss against non-trading income or against capital gains, you can still set the loss against future trading income for Class 4 national insurance purposes.

Where a loss claim results in Class 4 contributions being refunded, the refund attracts repayment supplement.

Tax points

25.15

- When considering how to claim relief for losses, the key questions are how much tax will you save, when will you save it and how much tax-free repayment supplement will be received. Watch the effect of changes in tax rates and allowances in the various years.

- More than one claim will frequently be possible and your tax position may be different according to the order in which claims are taken into account. You may generally stipulate which claims take priority.

- If you are liable to tax under PAYE, coding adjustments are made not only to collect tax on untaxed sources of income but also to take into account reliefs to which you are entitled. It was held in a recent tax case concerning a Lloyds underwriter that if the taxpayer so wished, the Revenue should adjust codings on a provisional basis to take into account loss relief to which the taxpayer would become entitled during the tax year. This decision was, however, overruled in the Court of Appeal.

- Claiming carry-back relief under Section 381, instead of current year relief under Section 380, for a first year loss leaves other income of the loss year available for a possible carry-back claim under Section 381 for a loss in later years.

- Loss relief against general income is restricted to those losses incurred in a demonstrably commercial trade and this may be difficult to prove. This is particularly so in the case of a new trade, so that a viable business plan is often essential to support a carry-back claim under Section 381.

- A loss in the opening years carried back under Section 381, in preference to a claim under Section 380, must be fully relieved under Section 381 before the balance of available losses can be relieved under Section 380. It is not possible to carry back sufficient of the loss to relieve income of the third year back and then not to proceed against the income of the second year back and then the first. The carry-back facility must be exhausted if claimed at all, before a Section 380 loss claim is made in respect of the balance remaining unrelieved.

  If there is a loss in the next year of trading this forms an entirely new claim. Relief for that loss can be claimed under Section 380 in preference to Section 381, but if a Section 381 claim is embarked upon first, the same remarks as above apply, so that the carry-back facility must be exhausted in respect of that particular loss before the balance can be relieved under Section 380.

- Under self-assessment, there are time limits both for making claims and for amending them (see 9.4 and 25.10). Claims do not have to be agreed by the Revenue within the time limits, but they may challenge the validity of the claims if they open an enquiry (see 9.9).

26
Company losses

Introduction

26.1 Companies may incur losses in their trades, in the course of letting property, in relation to investment income if expenses exceed the income, and in their capital transactions. In some cases the losses will relate to activities outside the UK. The overseas aspect is dealt with in CHAPTER 41. The treatment of losses on rented property is dealt with in CHAPTER 32. The treatment of non-trading losses on intangible assets is dealt with in 20.21. The treatment of capital losses is dealt with in CHAPTER 4 and in context in various other chapters (including CHAPTER 3 in relation to capital losses within a group of companies). The loss of money lent is regarded as an income loss rather than a capital loss. Such losses are dealt with in this chapter at 26.5.

Reliefs available for trading losses

26.2 Trading losses of companies are calculated in the same way as trading profits. The following alternatives are available for obtaining relief for such losses:

Set-off against current profits from other sources (TA 1988, s 393A(1)).
Carry-back against earlier profits from all sources (TA 1988, s 393A(1)(2)(2A)(2B)).
Carry-forward against future trading profits (TA 1988, s 393(1)).
Group relief (TA 1988, ss 402–413).

Set-off against current profits (TA 1988, s 393A(1))

26.3 A trading loss of a company can be set against any profits of the same chargeable accounting period, thus reducing or eliminating the corporation tax bill. Profits for this purpose include not only all sources of income (other than UK dividends, which are not liable to corporation tax) but also capital gains (see 3.1). A claim against current profits in respect of a non-trading deficit relating to loans takes priority over this claim (see 26.7). See 26.8 for the treatment of charges on income.

Carry-back against previous profits and carry-forward (TA 1988, ss 393(1), 393A(1)(2)(2A)(2B))

26.4 After a trading loss has been set against all profits of the current period, any balance may be carried back and set against the total profits of accounting periods falling wholly or partly within the previous twelve months, so long as the trade was carried on in the earlier period. If the loss period is less than twelve months this does not restrict the carry-back period. Where a trade has ceased, the carry-back period for losses of accounting periods falling wholly or partly within the last twelve months of trading is extended to three years before the loss period. Where an accounting period falls only partly within the last twelve months, the carry-back period for the part of the loss within the last twelve months is three years, the normal twelve month carry-back applying to the remainder of the loss. As far as the carry-back period is concerned, results are similarly apportioned as necessary where an accounting period falls only partly within the twelve-month or three-year period.

As with the claim against current profits, the set-off in the carry-back period is not limited to trading profits and is made against profits of any description. See Example 1. If in the period of set-off there is a non-trading deficit relating to loans for which relief is claimed against the profits of that period, that claim takes priority over the claim to set off carried back trading losses (see 26.7). See 26.8 for the treatment of charges on income.

Example 1

In its year to 31 March 2005 a company made a trading loss of £72,000. It has no associated companies. Its other results and loss claims arising are:

	Year ended 30.9.03 £	6 months to 31.3.04 £	Year ended 31.3.05 £	Loss and Loss claims £
Trading profits	46,000	12,000	—	(72,000)
Investment income	7,000	4,000	3,000	
Capital gains	5,000	3,000	1,500	
Total profits	58,000	19,000	4,500	
Loss set off:				
Against profits of same period			(4,500)	4,500
Against previous profits for up to 12 months				
6 mths to 31.3.04		(19,000)		19,000
6/12 × yr to 30.9.03	(29,000)			29,000
Profits remaining in charge	29,000	—	—	
Losses carried forward				19,500

Any loss not relieved against current or previous profits may be carried forward for set-off against future trading profits of the same trade, without time limit on its use unless there is a change of ownership to which the anti-avoidance provisions outlined at 26.16 apply. Although any carried-forward losses cannot normally be relieved after a trade ceases, where a building is sold after the cessation and a balancing charge is made to withdraw excess capital allowances, unrelieved trading losses may be set against that balancing charge (see 22.27).

Claims to set off losses against current and previous profits of any description are only permitted if the company carries on business on a commercial basis with a view to the realisation of profit (and see 31.3 for additional restrictions for farming companies). There is no commercial basis restriction for carrying losses forward, since the permitted set-off is only against trading profits of that same trade.

Losses relating to loans and derivative contracts (TA 1988, s 403; FA 1996, ss 83, 84A and Sch 8; FA 2004, s 52 and Sch 10)

26.5 Special rules for 'loan relationships' apply to interest paid and received by companies, and to profits and losses on loans (see 3.6). Foreign exchange differences on loan relationships are included within the general loan relationships rules rather than being dealt with separately. The loan relationships rules cover the treatment of the loss of money lent both for trading and non-trading purposes (excluding normal trading transactions for goods and services). Relief may not be claimed for loans written off if the borrower and lender are 'connected persons'. A person (including another company) is connected with a company if the person holds shares, voting power or other rights that enable that person to control the company. See 12.12 for detailed notes on writing off loans to controlling shareholders. Where the parties are not connected, the following treatment applies.

Losses arising out of loans for the purposes of the trade are taken into account in arriving at the trading result.

The rules for loans that do not relate to a trade also apply to derivative contracts that do not relate to a trade (see 3.7). For such non-trading loans and derivative contracts, interest, expenses and profits and losses on disposal are aggregated. If there is an overall profit it is taxed under Schedule D, Case III. If there is a loss, i.e. a 'non-trading deficit', relief for *all or part of the loss* may be claimed as follows:

(a)   By way of group relief (see 26.13).

(b)   Against any other profits (including capital gains) of the deficit period.

(c)   Against any Schedule D, Case III profits of the previous twelve months.

Treatment of any remaining non-trading deficit

26.6   Any part of the deficit for which relief is not claimed under (a) to (c) above is carried forward automatically and set against the *total* non-trading profits of later accounting periods. A claim may, however, be made for all or part of any carried forward amount not to be set against the non-trading profits of the next accounting period. This enables all or part of the carried forward deficit effectively to 'leapfrog' the period in which it would otherwise be set off which could in appropriate cases avoid loss of double tax relief in that period, such relief being available only to the extent that there are chargeable profits.

Priority of reliefs

26.7   Relief against the other profits of the same accounting period under 26.5(b) is given *after* relief for brought forward trading losses but *before* relief for current or carried back trading losses (see 26.3, 26.4) or for carried back non-trading deficits under 26.5(c).

Carry-back relief for any accounting period under 26.5(c) is given against the profits of the period of set-off *after*:

Relief for a deficit incurred in an earlier period,
Relief for trade charges,
Relief claimed against the profits of the set-off period under 26.5(b),
Group relief under 26.5(a),
Current or carry-back relief for trading losses (see 26.3, 26.4).

Charges on income (TA 1988, ss 338, 338A, 338B, 393(9), 393A)

26.8   There are very few payments and amounts that are within the definition of charges on income. Charges comprise gift aid donations and gifts of shares to charity (see 43.11 and 43.12), and certain annuities and other annual payments, excluding payments in respect of loan relationships (see 3.6) and royalties relating to intangible assets (see 20.21).

Charges may be deducted not just from trading profits but from total profits, including capital gains. The treatment of charges and the way they interact with loss claims is different according to whether or not they are paid wholly and exclusively for the purposes of the trade. If there are trading losses and/or non-trading deficits (see 26.5), the losses and/or deficits are set off in priority to both trade and non-trade charges of the same period. Where losses and/or non-trading deficits are carried back, they are set off *after* trade charges, but *before* non-trade charges, such as charity donations. Where *trade* charges exceed the available profits, the excess may be *carried forward* as a trading loss. In a continuing business, excess charges, whether trade charges or non-trade charges, may never be carried back against previous profits. When a business ceases, however, unrelieved *trade* charges (but not non-trade charges) of the final twelve months may be treated as part of the trading loss that may be carried back under the provisions at 26.4.

If the charges are not paid wholly and exclusively for the purposes of the trade (for example, charity donations), and the company has insufficient profits against which to set them in the accounting period in which they are paid, they may not be carried forward for relief against later profits. They may, however, be the subject of a group relief claim (see 26.13).

Effect of carry-back of losses on tax paid

26.9   Loss relief may be obtained at one or more of five possible corporation tax rates depending on the rate(s) charged on the profits against which the loss is set: at the starting or marginal starting rate, the small companies' or marginal small companies' rate or the full rate. For the years to 31 March 2003, 2004 and 2005 the starting rate is 0%, the marginal starting rate 23.75%, the small companies' rate 19% and the marginal small companies' rate 32.75%. The full rate is unchanged at 30%. Where a company pays dividends to non-corporate shareholders on or after 1 April 2004, the rate of corporation tax on the amount of profits equal to such dividends cannot be less than 19%, referred to as the non-corporate distribution (NCD) rate (see 3.13). Carry-back loss claims will result in corporation tax already paid being repaid, or in tax otherwise due not having to be paid. Where carried back losses are set against profits that were charged at the NCD rate, excess NCDs will arise which will have to be allocated to a group company or carried forward (see 3.13).

Interest calculations (*TA 1988, ss 825, 826*)

26.10   Repayments attract interest from nine months after the end of the relevant period or, if later, from the actual date of payment of tax for that period (see 3.19) (although the interest rate is lower than the rate charged on overdue tax). This is illustrated in Example 2. The latest available interest rates are set out in the Table of Rates and Allowances.

For calculating interest on repayments resulting from current and carried back losses, a repayment is normally treated as relating to the *loss* period, but a repayment relating to an accounting period falling *wholly* in the twelve months before the loss period is treated as relating to that accounting period.

Example 2

A company has the following results up to the date it ceased to trade on 31 March 2005.

Year ended 31 March	2003 £	2004 £	2005 £
Trading profit (loss)	50,000	20,000	(40,500)
Investment income	3,000	3,000	3,000
Chargeable gains	4,000	2,500	2,000
Total profits	57,000	25,500	5,000
If loss relief under TA 1988, s 393A(1) is claimed:			
Profits	57,000	25,500	5,000
Less loss	(10,000)	(25,500)	(5,000)
Total profits	47,000	—	—

Any tax repayment for the year to 31 March 2004 resulting from carrying the loss back 12 months will attract interest from the corporation tax payment date for that year, i.e. from 1 January 2005. The repayment for the year to 31 March 2003 will attract interest from 1 January 2006 (the payment date for corporation tax for the *loss* year to 31 March 2005).

Time limits for claims

26.11

TA 1988, s 393A; FA 1996, s 83(2)(a)(c)	Set off trading losses or non-trading deficits against profits of same accounting period and previous accounting periods	Within two years after the end of the accounting period of loss or deficit, or such further period as the Board allow
TA 1988, s 393(1)	Carry forward trading losses against later trading profits from same trade	No claim is required. Losses are entered on the corporation tax return and any unrelieved amounts are carried forward automatically

FA 1996, s 83(3A)	Carry forward non-trading deficit against later Schedule D, Case III profits	No claim is required
FA 1996, Sch 8 para 4	Restrict set-off of non-trading deficit against total non-trading profits of next accounting period	Within two years after the end of that next accounting period

See Revenue Statement of Practice 5/01 in relation to the circumstances in which they may admit late claims.

Group relief for losses etc. (TA 1988, ss 402–413; FA 1996, s 83; FA 2002, s 84 and Sch 29)

Trading losses

26.12   In a group consisting of a holding company and its 75% subsidiaries, trading losses may be surrendered from one company to one or more other companies within the group, provided the necessary conditions are satisfied. This enables the company to which the loss has been surrendered to reduce its taxable profits by the surrendered amount. The loss available to be surrendered must relate to an accounting period of the loss-making company that corresponds with that of the claimant company. This will not pose any difficulty when accounts within the group are prepared to the same date, but where accounts are prepared to different dates, part of the loss period will correspond with part of one accounting period of the claimant company and the remainder with part of the next accounting period. The loss available for relief and the profits against which it may be set must be apportioned as indicated below. Relief is also proportionately restricted if the parent/ subsidiary relationship does not exist throughout the accounting period, usually on a time basis, but by reference to what is just and reasonable where a time basis would give an unreasonable result.

The set-off rules are quite flexible, and broadly the loss-making company may surrender any part of its trading loss (without first claiming other reliefs available), up to a maximum of the available total profits of the claimant company or companies for the corresponding period. The rules enable the loss to be divided among several group companies in order to obtain the maximum loss relief. A claimant company cannot, however, claim more *in total* than an amount equal to its profits of the period that overlaps with the accounting periods of surrendering companies, and a loss company cannot surrender more *in total* to fellow group companies than its loss in the overlapping period(s). If a company with a loss in the year to 30 June 2004 had two fellow group companies making up accounts to 31 December, the *total* surrender to the two companies for their year to 31 December 2003 could not exceed 6/12ths of the loss, leaving the loss of the second half of the year to be surrendered against a maximum of 6/12ths of the profits of each of the companies for the year to 31 December 2004. The profits of the claimant company available for relief are profits from all sources, including capital gains, but after deducting charges on income.

A significant factor in deciding the optimum loss claim is the rate of tax saving. Other things being equal, it will be best to surrender the loss against profits being charged at the small companies' marginal rate (or indeed not to surrender it at all if the company's own profits are charged at that rate). See Example 3.

Example 3

Company A has been the wholly owned subsidiary of Company B for many years. (Small companies' rate marginal relief limits are therefore reduced for each company to £150,000 and £750,000 and starting rate marginal relief limits to £5,000 and £25,000.) Both companies prepare accounts to 31 March, and for the year to 31 March 2004, results are as follows:

Company A has a trading loss of	£80,000
and other profits of	£10,000
Company B has total profits of	£205,000

In the year to 31 March 2003, Company A had total profits of £170,000. Company A's profits for the year to 31 March 2005 will be between £100,000 and £150,000.

Company A may claim its own available loss reliefs and not surrender any part of the loss to Company B; or it may surrender the full £80,000 and pay tax on its own profits of £170,000 in 2003 and £10,000 in 2004; or it may surrender any amount up to £80,000, as the companies wish, and claim its own loss reliefs on the balance.

Rates of tax at which relief is available for the loss:	On Company A's profits	On Company B's profits
Year to 31 March 2004	23.75% on £5,000	32.75% on £55,000
	0% on £5,000	19% on £25,000
Year to 31 March 2003	32.5% on £20,000	No relief available
	20% on next £50,000	
Year to 31 March 2005	19%	

By a combination of claims against Company A's own profits and group relief, tax can be saved on £70,000 of the loss at the marginal small companies' rate. Interest on overpaid tax will arise from 1 January 2005 for claims in respect of the year to 31 March 2004 and from 1 January 2004 for claims in respect of the year to 31 March 2003.

The most tax-efficient claim is to surrender £50,000 of the loss to Company B, achieving a 32.75% tax saving thereon against Company B's profits, and to claim relief for £30,000 against Company A's own profits, giving relief on £5,000 at 0% and £5,000 at 23.75% in the year to 31 March 2004 and £20,000 at 32.5% in the year to 31 March 2003. (Despite the fact that there is a nil saving on £5,000 of the £30,000 loss relieved in Company A, the overall rate of tax saving on the £30,000 is 25.6%.)

Where a loss would otherwise be unrelieved, it might be appropriate for a profit company in a group to disclaim some of the allowances on its plant and machinery, to give it a higher profit against which to make a group relief claim (see 22.7 and 22.39). The profit company would then have a higher pool balance carried forward on which to claim capital allowances in the future, whereas if it has insufficient current profit to cover the loss available for surrender, the surrendered loss has to be restricted.

The group relief provisions are also available in certain circumstances to a consortium of companies that owns at least 75% of the ordinary share capital of a trading company or of a holding company with 90% trading subsidiaries, with the consortium members each owning at least 5% of that ordinary share capital. Losses in proportion to the consortium member's shareholding in the consortium-owned company can be surrendered both from the trading companies to the consortium companies and from the consortium companies to the trading companies.

To satisfy the requirements for group or consortium relief, claiming and surrendering companies must either be resident in the UK or carrying on a trade in the UK through a permanent establishment. The overseas aspect is dealt with in CHAPTER 41.

Group relief for other unrelieved amounts

26.13   In addition to trading losses, group relief may also be claimed in respect of excess charges on income, Schedule A losses (see 32.6), excess management expenses of companies with investment business, non-trading losses on intangible assets (see 20.21) and all or part of a non-trading deficit relating to loans or derivative contracts (see 26.5). As with trading losses, a company may surrender a non-trading deficit relating to loans or derivative contracts without claiming other reliefs available. The other amounts eligible for group relief can only be surrendered to the extent that they exceed the company's profits of the surrender period.

Procedure for group relief claims (TA 1988, Sch 17A; FA 1998, Sch 18 Pt VIII; SI 1999/2975)

26.14   Under self-assessment, companies may make, vary and withdraw group relief claims up to the latest of one year from the filing date for the claimant company's return (see 9.31), 30 days after the completion of a Revenue enquiry into the return, 30 days after the notice of Revenue amendments to the return following an enquiry, and 30 days after the final determination of an appeal against such an amendment. Each group company makes initial claims for specified amounts of group relief and shows amounts available for group relief surrenders on its own individual corporation tax return or amended return. Claims must show the name and tax district reference number of the surrendering company and be accompanied by a copy of the surrendering company's consent. The surrendering company will send the notice of consent to its own tax district. Where a group has non-resident company members, group relief claims must identify non-resident claimant or surrendering companies and any non-resident companies through which common group or consortium membership is established. Where original claims are to be varied, the original claim must be withdrawn and replaced by a new claim. Groups dealt with mainly within one tax district may enter into simplified arrangements under which group companies may authorise one company to amend returns on behalf of all group companies in relation to making and withdrawing claims and surrenders of group relief.

Company reconstructions without change of ownership (TA 1988, ss 343, 344)

26.15   Where a trade is transferred from one company to another and, at some time within one year before and two years after the transfer, the same persons own three-quarters or more of the trade, it is treated as transferred to the successor company rather than being discontinued. This prevents the predecessor carrying trading losses back under the terminal loss rules, and enables the successor to take over the unrelieved losses of the predecessor (subject to special rules restricting the available loss where the successor does not take over all the predecessor's assets and liabilities). The successor also takes over the predecessor's capital allowances computations (see 22.9).

Anti-avoidance provisions

26.16   There are provisions to prevent a purchased company being used to obtain relief that would not otherwise be available for trading losses. The provisions apply if either:

(a)   within a period of three years there is both a major change in the nature or conduct of a trade carried on by a company and a change in its ownership; or

(b)   after the scale of activities in a trade carried on by a company has become negligible and before any considerable revival, there is a change in ownership (TA 1988, ss 768, 768A).

The provisions prevent losses incurred before the change of ownership being carried forward, and prevent losses in an accounting period *after* the change of ownership from being carried back to an accounting period *before* the change. The Revenue have issued Statement of Practice SP 10/91 giving their views on the meaning of a 'major change in the nature or conduct of a trade'.

Where there is a change in ownership of a company with investment business, there are provisions to prevent the company carrying forward unrelieved management expenses, charges on income, non-trading deficits on loans and derivative contracts, and non-trading losses on intangible fixed assets (TA 1988, ss 768B, 768C 768E and Sch 28A). There are similar provisions preventing losses being carried forward on a change in ownership of a company carrying on a property business (TA 1988, s 768D).

The 75% link for group relief purposes (see 26.12) is defined very much more restrictively than simply 75% of ordinary share capital, to prevent companies taking advantage of the provisions by means of an artificial group relationship (TA 1988, s 413 and Sch 18).

Group relief is not available for a part of an accounting period in which arrangements exist whereby the loss-making company could cease to be a member of the group (TA 1988, s 410).

Tax points

26.17

- When considering loss claims, always look at the amount of tax saved. For the years to 31 March 2003, 2004 and 2005, set-off of losses will save tax at 30% if profits are charged at the full rate, 32.75% where the set-off is within the marginal small companies' tranche of profits, 19% if profits are charged at the small companies' rate, 23.75% if profits are charged at the marginal starting rate and 0% if profits are charged at the starting rate.

- Where dividends have been paid to non-corporate shareholders, and the profits of the period when the dividends were paid are reduced by a loss claim, the special NCD rate and the provisions on excess NCDs need to be borne in mind (see 26.9 and 3.13).

- Remember that group relief for losses is not available if there is less than a 75% link between holding and subsidiary companies.

- If two or more companies are controlled by the same individual(s), group relief is not available. But unused trading losses are still available against the future profits of a trade if that trade is transferred from one company to another under the same control (see 26.15).

- Watch the anti-avoidance provisions on group relief. An arrangement made part-way through an accounting period to sell a loss-making subsidiary will prevent group relief being claimed for the remainder of the accounting period even though the parent/subsidiary relationship exists throughout.

- Exceptional revenue expenditure, such as extraordinary repairs, or establishing or boosting a company pension scheme within permissible limits, may result in a normally profitable trade incurring a loss. When a company is planning such expenditure or considering when, or indeed whether, it should be incurred, the carry-back of losses against earlier profits, resulting in tax not having to be paid, or being repaid, is an important consideration.

27
Transfer of business to limited company

Choice of date

27.1   When the trade of an individual or partnership is transferred to a company the trade has ceased for income tax purposes, so that the closing year rules dealt with in CHAPTER 21 apply.

Under the income tax rules, there is no opportunity to vary the profits that escape tax on cessation. The amount of any overlap profit is calculated at the time of the overlap, and that is the amount that is deducted from the profits of the final trading period. The timing of the cessation still needs to be considered in the light of expected income in the years affected, for example the deduction of the overlap profit may reduce higher rate tax, or possibly create a loss to be relieved against other income of the current tax year or carried back against earlier income. The effect of capital allowances also needing to be considered. See 27.2.

Capital allowances (CAA 2001, ss 265–268, 567–570)

27.2   Normally the cessation of trade would involve a balancing allowance or charge by reference to the proceeds of disposal to the company of plant and equipment.

The sole trader or partners and the company may usually, however, jointly elect within two years after the transfer date for the assets to be treated as transferred at the tax written-down value (see 22.9) even though the justifiably higher market value is used for accounting purposes. The company gets writing-down allowances (but not first year allowances) on the price it pays or the tax written-down value as the case may be (see 22.11).

In neither case is there a writing-down allowance in the tax period up to cessation, consequently either increasing the written-down value carried into the company or affecting the amount of the balancing allowance or charge.

Open market value is used in the case of industrial buildings unless the election to transfer at the tax written-down value is made.

Trading stock (TA 1988, s 100)

27.3   While the legislation requires the transfer of stock to be at market value, the sole trader/partners and the company can normally elect within two years after the transfer date for the greater of the cost or price paid by the company to be used instead if that would give a lower figure. Work in progress prior to incorporation will usually not have included the value of sole proprietor/partner time, although there is no reason why it should not do so, but the unrecovered cost will have to be included in the subsequent year-end valuations of the company.

Unused trading losses (TA 1988, s 386)

27.4   If there are unused trading losses, these cannot be carried forward to a company as such, but they may be relieved against income received by the trader or partners from the company, either in the form of directors' fees or dividends, so long as the business is exchanged for shares and the shares are still retained at the time the loss is set off. Other available loss claims may be made first, e.g. under TA 1988, s 380 against income of the year of loss or the previous year, or terminal loss relief for a loss of the last twelve months against the trading income of the previous three years (see CHAPTER 25), and the relief against income from the company would then be available on the balance of unrelieved losses.

Capital gains tax (TCGA 1992, ss 17, 18, 162, 162A, 286)

27.5   When the transfer takes place, the general rule is that those assets chargeable to capital gains tax which have been transferred are treated as being disposed of to the company at their open market value. Current assets (stock, debtors, etc.) are not chargeable assets. Plant and equipment, even though covered by an election to transfer at the tax written-down value for capital allowances purposes, may be a chargeable asset for capital gains tax and thus treated as transferred at market value. Moveable plant and equipment is chargeable unless valued at £6,000 or less for each item (see CHAPTER 39), but it will not normally be valued at more than cost, so that capital gains tax will not usually apply, leaving the most likely assets on which a liability may arise as freehold or leasehold premises, fixed plant and machinery and goodwill. Although goodwill acquired by a company on or after 1 April 2002 is normally dealt with under the rules for intangible assets rather than the capital gains rules, this does not apply in most cases to acquisitions from a related party, which would include a transfer on incorporation (see 20.21). Such goodwill would accordingly still be a chargeable asset for capital gains in the hands of the company.

An obvious way of avoiding the charge on premises is for the proprietor or partners to retain ownership and to allow the company to use the property either at a rent or free of charge. This also saves the stamp duty land tax that would have been incurred on the transfer (see 27.10). From 1 December 2003 there is no stamp duty charge on any assets transferred to the company except stock and marketable securities, so it is no longer necessary for business debts to be collected by the proprietor/partners in order to save stamp duty.

The only way of not transferring the goodwill is if the sole trader/partners continue to own it whilst licensing the company to carry on the trade, but unless this is commercially practicable, sensible and properly done, the goodwill will automatically follow the trade. The valuation of goodwill depends not only on the size of the profits but also on the extent to which the profits depend on the skills of the proprietor or partners, the nature of the trade and many other factors.

The capital gains effect is considered in Example 1.

Example 1

The net assets of a trader at the time of incorporation of his business in July 2004 were:

	£
Freehold premises at current market value	204,000
Goodwill	120,000
Plant and equipment (cost £320,000)	140,000
Net current assets other than cash	256,000
Cash and bank balances	80,000
	£800,000

The premises had been acquired for £120,000 and the trade newly commenced in 1989. Assume indexation allowance to April 1998 to be £32,000 on the premises.

The potential chargeable gains on incorporation are:

489

		£	
Freehold premises — market value		204,000	
Less: Cost	120,000		
Indexation allowance	32,000	152,000	52,000
Goodwill — market value		120,000	
Less: Cost	Nil		
Indexation allowance	Nil	—	120,000
			£172,000
Chargeable gains after maximum business assets taper relief of 75% for 2 years or more			£43,000

The gain on the premises can be avoided by the trader retaining ownership, but a gain on the goodwill will arise on the transfer of the trade, unless it is possible to retain it while licensing the company to use it and that arrangement is properly made.

There are two main alternatives for reducing or eliminating an immediate capital gains tax charge. One is the rollover relief of TCGA 1992, s 162, which requires *all* the assets (except cash) to be transferred to the company, and defers gains only to the extent that the consideration is received in the form of shares in the company. The second is a combination of retaining some assets in personal ownership and making a claim under the business gifts relief provisions of TCGA 1992, s 165 (outlined at 4.27) to limit the gains on other chargeable assets (notably goodwill) to the amount actually received, the company then being treated as acquiring those assets at market value less the gains not chargeable on the transferor. Under this alternative, any consideration received from the company for the assets that are transferred need not be shares and a credit may be made to a director's loan account or cash taken instead. Another possible alternative if the company is a qualifying unquoted trading company is enterprise investment scheme deferral relief (the rules for which are outlined at 29.3).

Capital gains rollover relief on transfer (TCGA 1992, ss 162, 162A)

27.6   For relief under section 162 to apply in Example 1, all assets other than the £80,000 cash would have to be transferred.

The chargeable gains on the disposal of the business are calculated (taper relief not being taken into account), and they are treated as reducing the tax cost of the shares received in exchange for the business. The lower base cost for the shares will of course increase the potential capital gains tax liability in the future, with taper relief being given at the time of the eventual disposal of the shares and being based only on the period of ownership of the shares (see

4.23). Maximum business assets taper relief of 75% is, however, available after only two complete years, so that after that period the maximum tax on disposal of the shares by a 40% taxpayer is only 10%, with further reliefs possibly being available at that time, for example enterprise investment scheme deferral relief or gifts relief, or total exemption if the shares are still held at death. See Example 2.

Example 2

In consideration of the transfer of the trade in Example 1, the trader receives 700,000 shares of £1 each, fully paid, in the new company, transferring all assets except the cash of £80,000.

The base cost of the shares will be:

700,000 shares (£800,000 assets – £80,000 cash)	720,000
Less gains otherwise arising on premises and goodwill (without taper relief)	172,000
Cost of 700,000 shares for capital gains tax purposes	£548,000

The difference between the £700,000 par value of the shares and the £720,000 assets value in Example 2 represents a share premium. It is almost inevitable that the par value will not correspond with the asset values since those values cannot be precisely determined before the transfer date.

If the transfer is made only partly for shares, and partly for cash or credit to a director's loan account, then only proportionate relief is given. See Example 3.

Example 3

Suppose the consideration of £720,000 in example 2 was satisfied as to £480,000 shares and £240,000 cash. Only two-thirds of the chargeable gains can be deducted from the base cost of the shares.

		Shares	Cash
Consideration		480,000	240,000
Gains	£172,000	114,667	£57,333
Cost of shares for capital gains tax purposes		£365,333	

Unless covered by other reliefs or losses, the £57,333 is reduced by 75% taper relief to £14,333 and is charged to capital gains tax, as reduced by the annual exemption if available.

Obtaining the maximum deferral of gains under section 162 therefore requires the consideration for the shares to be locked in as share capital. If the consideration is provided through leaving money on director's loan account, tax will not be deferred, but the money can later be withdrawn at no personal tax cost.

The section 162 relief is given automatically without the need for a claim, although if the transferor has acquired business assets for use in another trade and wants to claim the business assets rollover relief instead (see 4.26), that rollover relief claim takes priority over section 162. Otherwise section 162 must be applied even if gains would be covered by, say, the annual exemption. To avoid the problem, the appropriate part of the consideration resulting in chargeable gains equal to available exemptions after taking into account any available taper relief could be left on director's loan account, so that a gain would be immediately realised, as shown in Example 3. Using the figures in that example, if £137,300 of the consideration of £720,000 was in cash, the proportionate part of the gain relating to the cash consideration would be £32,800, leaving a chargeable gain after 75% taper relief of £8,200, which is the amount of the annual exemption.

Where assets that are being transferred to the company are depreciating assets against which gains have been held over under the business assets rollover provisions (see 4.26), the disposal to the company *triggers* the deferred gains, but the deferred gains do not actually arise on the transfer, so relief for them is not available under section 162.

See 4.12 for the treatment of disposals that are affected by deferred gains on assets acquired before 31 March 1982.

Where gains have been deferred under s 162, an early disposal of the shares in the company may result in significantly increased gains if the two year period to obtain maximum taper relief has not expired. The taxpayer may *elect* for s 162 relief not to apply, so that gains that would otherwise have been deferred are chargeable in respect of the transfer to the company, as well as any gains on the disposal of the shares. The time limit for the election is two years from 31 January following the tax year of transfer, unless all the shares are disposed of by the end of the tax year following the tax year of transfer, in which case the time limit is one year from 31 January following the tax year of transfer. This enables taxpayers to obtain s 162 relief initially and then make the election later if appropriate (see Example 4).

Example 4

Say the trader in Example 1 had transferred all the assets except cash to the company in July 2004 with full s 162 relief, so that his shares had a base value of £720,000 less gains £172,000 = £548,000 as in Example 2. On 1 May 2005 he accepted an offer of £800,000 to buy the shares.

> Without the election the gain of £252,000 on disposal of the shares would have been fully chargeable, subject to the annual exemption if available, because the shares have not been owned for one complete year, so no taper relief is available. The trader may, however, *elect* for incorporation relief not to apply, the time limit for the election being 31 January 2007. His chargeable gains will then be £43,000 in 2004/05 as in Example 1 plus £80,000 in 2005/06 in respect of the gain on the shares, making £123,000 in total. The gains would be reduced in each case by the annual exemption if available.

Where a business is owned by partners, each partner has a separate right to elect or not in relation to his partnership share.

Gifts of business assets (TCGA 1992, s 165)

27.7   If, in Example 1, the premises were retained in personal ownership, saving capital gains tax and stamp duty land tax, this would leave the gain on the goodwill to be considered. The business gifts relief enables the whole of the gain on goodwill to be deferred providing any consideration received does not exceed the capital gains tax base cost of the goodwill. In Example 1, that cost was nil, so that the full gain on the goodwill could be deferred only if nothing was charged for it. Goodwill will have a capital gains tax cost either if it was purchased or if it had a value at 31 March 1982. As indicated in 27.5, in the hands of the company the goodwill will normally be a chargeable asset for capital gains rather than being within the rules for intangible assets. If, however, the goodwill of the unincorporated business arose after 31 March 2002, either because the business started after that date or the goodwill was purchased after that date from an unrelated third party, it should be possible for the acquiring company to obtain tax relief on its writing off within acceptable accounting principles. This aspect is therefore likely to become more important in the future.

The disadvantage of charging consideration equal to the capital gains tax base cost is that the transferor is only credited in the accounts of the company with that amount (before reckoning any available indexation allowance), not with the market value at the time of transfer, and that lower value (plus any available indexation allowance up to that time or April 1998 if earlier) will be the company's acquisition cost.

The chargeable asset could be transferred at a figure in excess of capital gains tax base cost, but less than market value, any available taper relief and exemptions being set off against the gains arising by reference to the transfer price. This has the advantage of more cash being received on the transfer or a higher credit to the director's account, and in either case a higher base value for the asset in company ownership. The business assets gifts relief eliminates the chargeable gain on the difference between market value and the value used for the transfer.

Deferring gains under the enterprise investment scheme (EIS) (TCGA 1992, s 150C and Sch 5B)

27.8 The disadvantage of the section 162 rollover relief is that all assets must be transferred to the company, whereas it may be preferred to retain premises in personal ownership. The disadvantage of the business gifts relief is the reduced value at which the company is regarded as acquiring the gifted assets. Both disadvantages can possibly be eliminated if the company is a qualifying unquoted trading company for EIS purposes by claiming EIS deferral relief instead (see 29.3), although the rules are extremely complex and it is not certain that the incorporation of the business can be structured in such a way as to enable the relief to be claimed. If the relief is available, you would only need to transfer such assets as you wished, and they would be transferred at full market value. Money need only be locked into share capital to the extent necessary to cover the gains (without any taper relief) arising on the transfer values. If the EIS option is being considered, professional advice is essential.

Value added tax (VATA 1994, s 49; SI 1995/1268, para 5; SI 1995/2518, paras 5, 6)

27.9 On the transfer of a business to a company, VAT will not normally arise on the assets transferred and the company will take over the VAT position of the transferor as regards deductible input tax and liability to account for output tax (see 7.28). This VAT-free treatment does not apply to transfers of land and buildings in respect of which the transferor has opted to charge VAT (see 32.23), or of commercial buildings that are either unfinished or less than three years old, unless the transferee company gives written notification before the transfer that it has opted to charge VAT on future transactions in connection with the land and buildings. In that case any VAT charged by the transferor would be recovered as input VAT by the transferee, leaving Customs in a neutral position, and VAT is not therefore chargeable on the transfer. Otherwise, VAT must be charged. A claim may be made by the trader or partners and the company for the existing VAT registration number to be transferred to the company. It is advisable to contact the appropriate VAT office in good time to obtain the necessary forms and ensure that the various requirements are complied with.

Stamp duty

27.10 From 1 December 2003 stamp duty was abolished except for instruments relating to stocks and shares and marketable securities (and also certain transfers of interests in partnerships, which are not relevant to the incorporation of a business). Stamp duty will not therefore be payable on the transfer agreement unless and to the extent that such assets are included.

From the same date stamp duty on land transactions was replaced by stamp duty land tax (SDLT). The detailed provisions on both stamp duty and stamp duty land tax are in CHAPTER 6.

On the transfer of a business, SDLT will be only be payable if the business premises are transferred. In that event, then since the person transferring the business is connected with the company, SDLT will be charged on the open market value of the premises, regardless of the transfer value (see 6.10). The value on which SDLT is charged includes any VAT on the transaction. Since SDLT is a self-assessed tax, it is up to the taxpayer to calculate the amount of SDLT due. If SDLT was paid on the basis that the transfer of going concern rules applied (see 27.9) and this turned out not to be the case, the additional SDLT would be payable plus interest from the date of the transaction.

Inheritance tax

27.11   There will not usually be any direct inheritance tax implications on the incorporation of a business, but three situations need watching.

The first is the effect on the availability of business property relief where partners form a company. If assets such as premises are owned within the partnership, they form part of the partnership share and 100% business property relief is available. A partner who personally owns assets such as premises used in the business is entitled to business property relief at the rate of 50%. Relief at the 50% rate is available to a shareholder only if he is a controlling shareholder, and no relief is available at all for such assets owned by minority shareholders. Shares of husband and wife are related property and the available rate of relief is determined by their joint holdings. Where the assets are reflected in the value of the shareholdings, business property relief will apply to the value of the shares (see 5.19).

The second situation arises where assets have been transferred using the capital gains provisions for gifts to the company of business assets (TCGA 1992, s 165). Such gifts are not potentially exempt for inheritance tax since they are not to an individual or qualifying trust fund. They may be covered by the 100% business property relief, but if not, the amount of the transfer of value is the amount by which the sole trader's or partner's estate has fallen in value. In measuring that fall in value, the value of the shares acquired in the company (enhanced by the gifted assets) will be taken into account. The result may be that there is no transfer of value. If there is a transfer of value, no tax may be payable, because of annual exemptions and the nil rate threshold. If tax is payable, the tax may be paid by instalments if the company as donee pays the tax.

Thirdly, what was previously a sole trader's or partner's capital/current account which attracted business property relief will, unless converted into appropriate shares or securities, no longer qualify because it will be an ordinary debt due from the company.

See CHAPTER 5 for further information on inheritance tax.

Issuing shares to directors (ITEPA 2003 ss 421B, 421J-421L)

27.12   On the incorporation of the business, the sole trader or partners will usually become directors, and shares in the company will be issued to them (or transferred from the formation agent if the company is bought 'off the shelf'). The issue of such shares is regarded as being by reason of their employment or prospective employment, and details must be reported to the Revenue (usually on form 42) before 7 July following the tax year in which the shares are issued (extended to 7 September 2004 for 2003/04). There are penalties for failing to comply with the reporting requirements. Care should be taken to ensure that shares are issued or transferred at market value, to avoid a potential benefits charge.

National insurance

27.13   If a sole trader or partner becomes a director and/or employee in the company, national insurance contributions on earnings from the company are payable by both the employer and the employee. The burden is significantly higher than the maximum self-employed contributions under Classes 2 and 4. See CHAPTER 18 for further details.

Business rates

27.14   Although the incorporation of a business means a change of occupier for rating purposes, any transitional relief to which the unincorporated business was entitled is available to the company (see 8.12).

Tax points

27.15

● Where you want to claim relief under TCGA 1992, s 162 on the transfer of a business, minimise the amount locked up in share capital by not transferring cash. If the cash is needed to assist the liquidity of the company, it can always be introduced on director's loan account.

- Rollover relief on the replacement of business assets can be claimed on premises owned personally and used in the owner's personal trading company — see 4.26. A personal company is one in which the individual owns at least 5% of the voting rights.

- The payment of rent by the company for property owned personally by the former sole trader or partners does not affect business property relief for inheritance tax (but the size of the shareholding does).

- You cannot get the best of all worlds on incorporation of a business. Maximising the capital gains deferral can only be done at extra cost in terms of stamp duty land tax and with the disadvantage of locking funds into share capital. Retaining premises saves stamp duty land tax, and using gifts relief on those assets that are transferred enables you to fund the company by making loans to it, but your director's account is credited with a lower figure in respect of the gifted assets and that value becomes the company's base value for capital gains. This could also significantly reduce the indexation allowance when the company disposes of the assets.

- When considering how much of the proceeds for the transfer of the business should be locked in as share capital, do not forget that funds may need to be drawn for the payment of taxation relating to the former sole trade or partnership. Unless there are sufficient funds on directors' loan account, it will not be possible to withdraw the required funds from the company without incurring a further tax liability on remuneration or dividends.

- It may be possible to reduce the problems of locking in share capital by using redeemable shares, which can be redeemed gradually as and when the company has funds and possibly using the annual capital gains exemption to avoid a tax charge on the shareholder. There are, however, anti-avoidance provisions, and also a clearance procedure, and professional advice is essential.

- If, when a sole trader or partners transfer a business to a company, shares are issued to other family members, the Revenue may seek to use the settlements provisions of TA 1988, s 660A to tax the income from dividends on the former sole trader/partners rather than the share-holding family members.

- The lack of writing-down allowances in the last tax period before incorporation may cost tax relief at 40% compared with a much lower rate of relief in the first accounting period of the company.

- It is worth considering transferring chargeable assets, such as goodwill, at their full value, with a corresponding credit to your director's account. This will increase the capital gains tax payable at the time (the gains themselves, however, being reduced by taper relief of up to 75%), but will provide a higher facility to draw off the director's loan account at no future personal tax cost.

- But take care not to overstate the value of goodwill. To do so will risk the Revenue seeking to reduce the credit to the director's account, perhaps resulting in its becoming overdrawn, leading to a liability under TA 1988, s 419, or the amount being regarded as a distribution of company profits.

- The private use of motor cars used in a sole trade or partnership will have been dealt with by excluding part of the running costs and capital allowances from the allowable business costs for tax purposes. If the cars are acquired by the company, the private use will be reckoned under the employee benefits rules.

The resulting tax and national insurance costs need to be considered when deciding if the cars should be transferred, or retained in personal ownership, with an appropriate business mileage claim being made.

28
Selling the family company

Background

28.1   There are two ways in which the family company may be sold — selling the shares or selling the assets and either liquidating the company or keeping it and distributing dividends from its subsequent income. The most difficult aspect of the sale negotiations is usually reconciling the interests of the vendors and the purchasers.

The vendors will often prefer to sell the shares rather than the assets to avoid the double capital gains tax charge which will arise on the assets sale and on the distribution to the shareholders if the company is wound up. The purchaser may prefer to buy assets in order to be able to attract tax-efficient investment for their purchase through the enterprise investment scheme (see 29.2 to 29.4), to claim tax allowances on purchases of equipment, plant, qualifying buildings and goodwill, or capital gains rollover relief on the purchase of appropriate assets. Also buying assets is sometimes more straightforward than a share purchase, with consequently lower costs. Stamp duty is charged on share transactions and stamp duty land tax on the acquisition of land and buildings, but the stamp duty land tax rates are much higher. Yet again, the vendors may intend staying in business, so that a sale of assets by a trading company, with the company then acquiring replacement assets, may give an opportunity for capital gains rollover relief. If the vendors plan to invest in another company, then providing that company is a qualifying unquoted trading company for enterprise investment scheme deferral relief (see 29.3), all or any part of the gains on the disposal of the shares in the existing company (and any other gains they may have) may be held over to the extent that shares are subscribed for in the new company. (The relief is not available where the acquisition is of shares already in existence.) The gain is not deducted from the cost of the new shares and the tax payable crystallises when they are disposed of unless further relief is then available.

Not only any known liabilities, but also any latent liabilities and obligations of the company will remain as company liabilities following the sale of the shares, making it most important that extreme care is taken for commercial and taxation purposes (often referred to as due diligence). The purchaser will clearly require indemnities and warranties from the vendors, but the vendors will want to limit these as much as possible, and in any event the purchaser would have the inconvenience of enforcing them or perhaps be unable to do so if the vendor had insufficient funds or was not able to be contacted.

The outcome of the negotiations, including the adjustments each party agrees to in order to resolve points of difference, will depend on the future intentions of the vendor, the relative bargaining strength of each party and how keen vendor and purchaser are to conclude the transaction.

Selling shares or assets

28.2   Part of the sale consideration may relate not to tangible assets but to the growth prospects or the entrepreneurial flair of those involved with the company, and where goodwill is a substantial factor, the valuation placed on it will be an important part of the negotiations, providing flexibility in agreeing a price.

The tax cost of selling the shares can be significantly less than that of selling the assets followed by a liquidation. See Example 1 for a straight comparison of a share sale and an assets sale based on the same values.

Example 1

Trading company was formed in 1987 and 1,000 £1 shares were issued at par. Balance sheet of company immediately prior to intended sale at the end of April 2004 was:

	£		£
Share capital	1,000	Net current assets	50,000
Accumulated profits	99,000	Premises at cost	50,000
	£100,000		£100,000

A sale is now proposed on the basis of the goodwill and premises being worth £350,000.

If the shares are sold:

Assets per balance sheet		100,000
Increase in value of premises and goodwill (350,000 – 50,000)		300,000
Sale proceeds for shares		400,000
Cost	1,000	
Indexation allowance to April 1998, say	600	1,600
		£398,400

Chargeable gain after maximum business assets
taper relief of 75%*   £99,600

Capital gains tax @ 40% (ignoring any set-offs and
exemptions and assuming that the shareholders'
basic rate threshold has been fully utilised)   £39,840

If assets are sold and company is liquidated:

Assets per balance sheet		100,000
Increase in value of premises and goodwill	300,000	
Less provision for corporation tax on sale (£300,000 less, say, £40,000 for indexation to April 2004 on cost of premises)		
Gain £260,000 @ say 30%**	78,000	222,000
Amount distributed to shareholders on liquidation (ignoring liquidation costs)		322,000
Cost of shares	1,000	
Indexation allowance to April 1998, say	600	1,600
		£320,400

Chargeable gain after maximum business assets
taper relief of 75%*   £80,100

Capital gains tax @ 40% (ignoring any set-offs
and exemptions and assuming that the basic
rate threshold has been fully utilised)   £32,040

Amounts received by shareholders:

	Proceeds £	Capital gains tax £	Net £
On sale of shares	400,000	39,840	360,160
On liquidation	322,000	32,040	289,960
Extra cost of liquidation route			£70,200

> *   Assuming that the shares have qualified for the business assets rate of taper relief throughout. See Example 3.
>
> **   The illustrative rate of 30% would probably be somewhere between 19% and 32.75% depending on the profits for the accounting period in which the disposal took place.

Knowing the tax advantage of the share sale to the vendor, coupled with the potential tax liability if the company in its new ownership sells its premises and goodwill, the purchaser may well seek a reduction in price if this route is to be followed. It was for many years common practice to reduce the disadvantage to the vendor of the liquidation route by the company paying a dividend equivalent to the profit less tax on the sale of its assets, and then distributing the remainder of its funds upon liquidation. The shareholder received a tax credit which covered the tax liability for a basic rate taxpayer and left a higher rate taxpayer with a further 22½% to pay on the tax credit inclusive dividend, i.e. a rate of 25% on the cash dividend. Following the reduction of the business assets taper relief period to two years from 6 April 2002, however, the pre-sale dividend does not benefit a higher rate taxpaying shareholder if he is entitled to 75% taper relief, since his effective capital gains tax rate is 25% x 40% = 10%. See Example 2.

A pre-sale dividend out of distributable reserves, with the sale price of the shares themselves being reduced accordingly, is likewise less attractive.

Example 2

		£
Assets on balance sheet per example 1 are £100,000.		
Profit on sale of assets after tax		222,000
Dividend April 2004		(222,000)
Distribution on liquidation		100,000
Indexed cost of shares		1,600
		£98,400
Chargeable gain after 75% taper relief		£24,600
Capital gains tax @ 40%		£9,840
Received by shareholders:		
Dividend	222,000	
Less higher rate tax on (222,000 + tax credit (⅑)		
24,667 =) £246,667 @ (32.5% − 10%)	55,500	166,500
On liquidation	100,000	
Less capital gains tax	9,840	90,160
		£256,660

Comparison of amounts received by shareholders in Example 1 and in this example:

	Share sale	Asset sale/ liquidation	Asset sale/ dividend/ liquidation
	£	£	£
Value of assets	400,000	400,000	400,000
Corporation tax		(78,000)	(78,000)
Shareholders' higher rate tax			(55,500)
Shareholders' capital gains tax	(39,840)	(32,040)	(9,840)
	£360,160	£289,960	£256,660

The availability of 75% taper relief means that the pre-sale dividend route leaves the shareholders with (289,960 − 256,660 =) £33,300 less than they would receive from an asset sale/liquidation (i.e. 15% on £222,000).

Where the company was established before 31 March 1982, the value of its chargeable assets and of the shares at that date may be substituted for cost, and the appropriate amount of indexation allowance also calculated on that value, if it reduces the gains or if an election has been made to use 31 March 1982 value for all assets. Whilst the chargeable gains may be correspondingly less, the principles outlined above still apply.

Other factors

28.3   The disadvantages of selling assets may be mitigated if the company has current (as distinct from brought-forward) trading losses which may be set off against the gains on the assets.

If it is intended that the company shall continue trading in some new venture rather than be wound up, it may be possible to roll over or hold over the gains by the purchase of new assets. Alternatively, if the new trade commences before the old trade ceases, trading losses may arise in that new trade against which the gains may be set under the normal rules for set-off of trading losses.

Goodwill (FA 2002, s 84 and Schs 29, 30)

28.4   Following the Finance Act 2002 provisions relating to goodwill, where goodwill is purchased from an unrelated party, or from a related party that commenced business after 31 March 2002, the purchasing company will be able to claim tax relief over a period on the price paid (see 20.21). The purchase of goodwill is also exempt from stamp duty.

The purchaser in example 1 might therefore be reluctant to buy the shares, but the vendor is seriously disadvantaged if the company has first to sell its assets and then distribute its available cash. This might provide a bargaining opportunity under which the purchaser pays somewhat more for goodwill, the real cost, however, being reduced by the forthcoming tax relief, whilst the vendor accepts that his company must sell assets and pay the appropriate corporation tax, his share proceeds, however, being higher because of the increased amount which the company has received for goodwill.

Capital gains tax taper relief

28.5 As indicated at 28.2, capital gains tax on business assets is now at a maximum effective rate of 10% after only two years of ownership, significantly reducing the tax cost of selling the family company. See, however, 4.19 re the effect on taper relief where shares qualify as business assets only from 6 April 2000.

See also 4.22 for the special rules re the business assets rate of taper relief where assets have been transferred between spouses.

The taper relief rules exclude from the qualifying taper relief period any periods when a close company was not active (see 4.20). A company will usually, however, be active during the time it is being wound up, in that it will be realising its assets.

It follows that the shareholder in example 1 is further disadvantaged if the company first sells its assets and then makes a capital distribution or distributions, since the period between cessation of trading and the distribution will not qualify for the business assets rate of taper relief. See Example 3.

Example 3

Assume that the available funds are distributed to the shareholders in Example 1 on 30 September 2004, the company having ceased to trade upon sale of its assets on 30 April 2004.

		Months
Business asset period (from inception of taper relief on 6.4.98 to 30.4.04)	(a)	73
Non-business asset period (1.5.04 to 30.9.04)	(b)	5
		78

	£
Chargeable gains	320,400

Taper relief at	(a) on 73/78, i.e. on	299,862
	(b) on 5/78, i.e. on	20,538
		320,400

Taper relief is:	(a) 299,862 @ 75%	224,896
	(b) 20,538 @ 25%*	5,134
		230,030

Chargeable gain is	320,400
Less taper relief	230,030
	90,370

rather than as in Example 1	80,100

* Includes pre 6.4.98 'bonus' year

Payments in compensation for loss of office

28.6   Compensation and ex gratia payments are dealt with in detail in CHAPTER 15. There are two aspects, first whether the director/shareholder will be exempt from tax on the first £30,000 of the payment, and second whether the payment will be deductible as an expense against the company profits.

As far as the individual is concerned, in order for the £30,000 exemption to apply, the company must be able to demonstrate that any payments are wholly unassociated with a sale of the individual's shares in the company and moreover do not represent an income dividend. Ex gratia payments may also be challenged as being benefits under an unapproved retirement benefits scheme (see 15.3).

As far as the company is concerned, the company must show that the payments are wholly and exclusively for the purposes of the trade, which is more difficult if the payment is ex gratia rather than compensation for loss of office. Where the company's trade ceases following a sale of the assets, an ex gratia or compensation payment cannot satisfy the 'wholly and exclusively' rule because there is no longer any trade. The part of the company's payment that can be set against the company's trading profits in those circumstances is limited to the amount of statutory redundancy pay to which the director is entitled plus a sum equal to three times that amount, unless the payment is made under a pre-existing contractual or statutory obligation (see 15.8). Where a compensation or ex gratia payment is made prior to a sale of the shares, the company's trade continuing, this restriction will not apply.

Whether there is a sale of the shares or an assets sale followed by a liquidation, the compensation payment will reduce the value of the company's assets, and thus the amount of disposal proceeds on which the shareholder's capital gains tax liability will be calculated.

Payments into a pension scheme

28.7   Prior to selling the shares, the cash resources of the company, and thus, effectively, the eventual sale proceeds, may also be reduced by an appropriate pension scheme contribution, the benefits of which may be taken partly as a tax-free lump sum and partly as a pension. Again, the trading profits prior to the sale are reduced, with a corresponding saving in corporation tax. This is of course only acceptable if the levels of contributions and benefits payable are within the stipulated limits. Company pension schemes are dealt with in CHAPTER 16.

Sale of a trading subsidiary

28.8   Where a single trading company (or member of a trading group) is selling a trading subsidiary (or holding company of a trading group), then so long as the shareholding in the trading subsidiary (or holding company of a trading group) exceeds 10% and has been owned for a continuous period of twelve months within the preceding two years, the shares in the subsidiary (or trading group holding company) can be sold by the parent company to another trading company or group holding company without a charge to corporation tax on the capital gain arising (see 3.25).

Whilst this relieves the selling company of the corporation tax on its gain, it does not remove the issues of lack of tax relief to the purchaser because goodwill has not been purchased, and the effect on the vendor's taper relief of the non-trading period.

Selling on the basis of receiving shares in the purchasing company (TCGA 1992, ss 126–139, 279, 279A–279D and Sch 6, para 2)

28.9   Where, as consideration for the sale of their shares, the vending shareholders receive shares in the company making the acquisition, then each vending shareholder is normally treated as not having made a disposal of the 'old shares', but as having acquired the 'new shares' for the same amount and on the same date as the 'old shares' (known as 'paper for paper' exchanges).

Where the consideration is part shares/part cash, that part received in cash is liable to capital gains tax, whilst the 'new shares' again stand in the shoes of the old. See Example 4.

Example 4

Shares cost £10,000. As a result of an acquisition of the entire share capital by another company, the shareholder receives cash of £40,000 and shares in the acquiring company valued at £60,000. The capital gains position is:

		Cash £	Shares £
Cost of £10,000, divided in proportion to the proceeds		4,000	6,000
Proceeds:			
Cash	40,000	40,000	
New shares	60,000		
Total consideration	100,000		
Chargeable gain (subject to indexation allowance to April 1998, taper relief and available exemptions)		£36,000	
Cost of 'new shares'			£6,000

The shares received in exchange qualify for taper relief from the date of acquisition of the original shares. The deferment of the capital gains charge also applies where the exchange is for loan stock, but in this case the taper relief position depends on whether the loan stock is within the definition of a 'qualifying corporate bond' (see 38.23). If the loan stock is a qualifying corporate bond, taper relief runs to the date of the exchange and the gain at that date is frozen until the bonds are disposed of (the bonds themselves being exempt from capital gains tax). If the loan stock is not a qualifying corporate bond (for example because it is redeemable in a foreign currency), taper relief runs from the date of acquisition of the shares to the date of disposal of the loan stock. Professional advice on this aspect is particularly important.

Where part of the consideration depends upon future performance, say the issue of further shares or securities if a profit target is met, the value of the right to receive further shares or securities (known as an earn-out right) is normally treated as part of the disposal proceeds at the time the original shares are sold. Where the vendor is employed in the business and is to continue in employment in some capacity for a period after the sale, it must be clear that the earn-out right is not linked in any way to the future employment, otherwise the value of shares issued under the earn-out would be charged to tax and national insurance as employment earnings rather than being dealt with under the capital gains rules. Where the capital gains rules apply, the value of the right is treated as a security, so that any capital gains are rolled over until the further shares or securities are sold. The taxpayer may elect for this treatment not to apply, making the value of the earn-out right itself liable to capital gains tax. For rights conferred before 10 April 2003, an election had to be made for the rollover treatment to apply. Finance Act 2003 reversed the elective procedure.

The rollover treatment does not apply if the future consideration is to be cash. In that event, the whole of the value of the right to future consideration is liable to capital gains tax at the time of the sale, with a further liability on the difference between that value and the amount of consideration actually received, or the proceeds of selling the right (such proceeds being a non-business asset and therefore not attracting taper relief unless they arise more than three years after the disposal of the shares). Where cash is to be received, or because of an election the rollover does not apply, then if, after 9 April 2003, the proceeds of deferred unascertainable consideration or of selling the right to receive it are less than the estimated value brought in for the right, and the disposal occurred in a tax year later than that when the original gain arose on the undeferred consideration, the taxpayer may elect for the loss to be carried back to that earlier tax year. The time limit for a carry back claim is the first anniversary of the 31 January following the tax year of the loss, and the year to which the loss is carried back cannot be earlier than 1992/93.

Stamp duty

28.10   Stamp duty is normally payable by the purchaser at ½% on the consideration for a sale of shares. Where there is a sale of assets, then from 1 December 2003 stamp duty land tax (SDLT) is payable on land transactions, the rate of tax being 1%, 3% or 4% depending on the sale proceeds (see 6.11). Stamp duty will not be payable on any assets other than stocks, shares and marketable securities.

The value on which SDLT is payable includes any VAT on the sale. It may not be known when a business is sold whether the VAT 'going concern' treatment will apply (see 28.11). If VAT is excluded from the amount on which SDLT is paid, and the 'going concern' basis proves not to be available, the appropriate amount of additional SDLT would be payable, plus interest from the date of the sale.

Value added tax (VATA 1994, ss 49, 94 and Sch 9 Group 5; SI 1995/1268, para 5; SI 1995/2518)

28.11   Where the family company is sold by means of a share sale, the sale does not attract value added tax because the shares are not sold in the course of business but by an individual as an investment.

Where all or part of the business is sold as a going concern by one taxable person to another, no value added tax is charged by the vendor and the purchaser has no input tax to reclaim on the amount paid (subject to what is said at 27.9 for land and buildings). The going concern treatment only applies, however, where the assets acquired are such that they represent a business which is capable of independent operation.

Where the 'going concern' concept does not apply, value added tax must be charged on all taxable supplies, and any related input tax suffered by the seller is recoverable. Taxable supplies include goodwill, stock, plant and machinery, and motor vehicles (except that cars on which input tax was not recovered when they were acquired will only be chargeable to the extent, if any, that the disposal proceeds exceed original cost). Business premises on which the seller has exercised his option to tax are also included, and the seller can therefore recover any VAT relating to the costs of sale, for example on legal and professional fees. The disposal of book debts, and of business premises over three years old on which the option to tax has not been taken, is an exempt supply and does not attract VAT. For partially exempt businesses there are some complex rules as to how the sale of the business is treated.

It is important to ensure that the purchase agreement provides for the addition of value added tax and that the purchase consideration is allocated over the various assets acquired. If value added tax is not mentioned in the purchase agreement, the price is deemed to be VAT-inclusive.

Tax points

28.12

- When a company ceases to trade, this denotes the end of a chargeable accounting period, and if there are current trading losses these cannot be relieved against chargeable gains arising after the cessation. But gains are deemed to be made on the contract date, not on completion, so if the company enters into the contract for sale of the chargeable assets while it is still trading, the right to set off current trading losses against chargeable gains in that trading period will be preserved.

- Compensation for loss of office and ex gratia payments upon cessation of employment can only be expected to escape Revenue challenge if they are genuine payments for breach of contract or reasonable ex gratia amounts bearing in mind years of service, etc. and even so, ex gratia payments may not qualify for the £30,000 exemption (see 28.6 and CHAPTER 15).

- When selling shares in a family company with significant retained profits, the Revenue may argue that the increased share value as a result of the retained profits represents not a capital gain but sums that should have been paid out as income, and that they are chargeable as such. Although capital gains are charged at income tax rates, taper relief and enterprise investment scheme deferral relief are only available against a capital gain. You should therefore ensure that Revenue clearance is obtained for the proposed sale. On the other hand, income can be sheltered by investment in an enterprise zone building, whereas a chargeable gain cannot.

- When buying the shares in a company, you should look particularly for any potential capital gains liabilities which will be inherited, such as the crystallisation after ten years of gains on depreciating business assets which have been held over because the company acquired new qualifying assets, or, if the company you are purchasing is leaving a group, the crystallisation of gains on assets acquired by it from another group company within the previous six years. Moreover, the accounts value of the company assets may be greater than the tax value because earlier gains have been deducted under the rollover relief provisions from the tax cost of the assets now held or the assets have been revalued for accounts purposes. Thus a chargeable gain may arise on the company even though the item is sold for no more than its value in the accounts. Taxation due diligence is essential.

- If you buy a company with unused trading losses, you will not be able to use them when you restore the company to profitability if the change of ownership takes place within a period of three years during which there is also a major change in the nature or conduct of the business. There is also a restriction on availability of trading losses where the company being acquired has succeeded to the trade of another company without taking over that other company's liabilities (see 26.16).

- Whether shares or assets are purchased, the purchaser will take over the predecessor company's Class 1A national insurance liability for that part of the tax year before the succession. Again, taxation due diligence is essential.

- The purchase consideration may partly depend on the company's future profit performance, sometimes referred to as an 'earn out', and when it is received it may be partly in cash and partly in the form of shares or securities in the purchasing company. The capital gains tax position is complicated and professional advisers have to look very carefully at this aspect, if possible obtaining the views of the Revenue when they apply for clearance on the share sale.

- The carryback to an earlier tax year of a loss arising in relation to deferred unascertainable consideration is not limited to where the original disposal was of shares. It could equally apply to a disposal of goodwill by a sole trader or partners, where further consideration depended upon profit performance, or where the proceeds of land depended on planning consents.

- While the capital gains charge is deferred where, on a disposal of the family company, shares are exchanged for loan stock, the taper relief available when the loan stock is disposed of depends upon the type of loan stock. Professional advice on this aspect is essential.

- A private company may avoid the costs of putting a company into formal liquidation by distributing the assets and then having the company struck off the companies register as a defunct company. Although strictly the distribution of assets in these circumstances is an income distribution on which the shareholders would be liable for income tax, the Revenue will usually agree to treat it as if it were a capital distribution in a formal liquidation (concession C16). It is essential to get the formal approval of the company's tax district, which will require certain undertakings on behalf of the company and by the shareholders. Care is needed where there are non-distributable reserves.

- A possible way of preventing the loss of business assets taper relief when an assets sale followed by winding up is the only way of disposing of the family company is to transfer the shares to an interest in possession trust before the trade ceases, thus crystallising the gain at that time.

- Because there are so many pitfalls and problems when selling or buying a family company, it is essential to get expert professional advice.

29
Encouraging business investment, enterprise and efficiency

Background

29.1   This chapter deals with various schemes that encourage investment in new and expanding companies and other measures to promote business enterprise, efficiency and innovation. CHAPTER 11 at 11.13 deals with the enterprise management incentive share option scheme that is available to small, higher risk companies. See also 3.25 re the exemption for company gains on substantial shareholdings and 20.21 re the new regime for dealing with intellectual property, goodwill and other intangible assets.

Although the aims of the various schemes are reasonable, the provisions are for the most part extremely complex and regarded by some as unnecessarily restrictive. The Government, on the other hand, thinks some of the rules have enabled investors to obtain a guaranteed return, rather than being focused on rewarding risk-taking, and has introduced changes to prevent the schemes being used in this way. This chapter gives only an outline of the provisions, professional advice being essential.

Enterprise investment scheme

Income tax relief (TA 1988, ss 289–312; FA 2004, s 88 and Sch 18)

29.2   Income tax relief at 20% is given where a 'qualifying individual' subscribes for 'eligible shares' in a 'qualifying company' carrying on, or intending to carry on, a 'qualifying business activity'. The subscription must be wholly in cash (other than subscriptions for shares issued to those who are not claiming EIS reliefs) and all the shares must be issued to raise money for a qualifying business activity. At least 80% of the money raised must be used for a qualifying business activity within 12 months after the shares are issued or, if later, within 12 months after the commencement of the trade, with the remainder being required to be used within the following 12 months. The definition of the various terms used is complex, but is broadly as follows.

A 'qualifying individual' is one who is not 'connected' with the company, which mainly excludes someone who is or has been an employee or director, or who controls more than 30% of its capital. (Someone who was not connected with the company before the shares were issued may, however, become a paid director without affecting his entitlement to relief.) Non-residents are eligible, but the reliefs can only be given against UK tax liabilities.

Eligible shares are new ordinary shares that are not redeemable for at least three years (five years for shares issued before 6 April 2000).

A 'qualifying company' carrying on a qualifying business activity is an unquoted trading company (which includes companies on the Alternative Investment Market — AIM) carrying on business wholly or mainly in the UK whose trading activities are not specifically excluded. Companies that do not qualify include those providing finance, legal and accountancy services, leasing (excluding certain ship chartering), property development, farming and market gardening, forestry and timber production, hotels and nursing or residential care homes. A trade of receiving royalties or licence fees is also excluded, except where the income arises from an intangible asset, the greater part of which has been created by the company or a company in the same group. At the time of the issue of the shares there must not be any arrangements for the company to cease to be unquoted, or to become a subsidiary of a company that ceases to be unquoted. The total gross assets of the company (and, where relevant, other companies in the same group) must not exceed £15 million immediately before the issue of the shares, nor £16 million immediately afterwards.

There is a clearance procedure under which the Revenue will give advance *provisional* approval that a company's shares will qualify for relief. The relief is subject to detailed anti-avoidance provisions. Relief is denied where there are arrangements at the time of an individual's investment that protect or guarantee the investment, or set up disposal arrangements for the benefit of the investor.

Claims for relief cannot be made until a certificate has been received from the company, issued on the authority of a Revenue officer, stating that the relevant conditions have been satisfied. Providing the certificates are received in time, claims may be included in tax returns, or amendments to returns. Otherwise claims are made on the form incorporated in the certificate from the company. The overall time limit for claiming the relief is five years from the 31 January following the tax year in which the shares are issued. If any of the requirements for a 'qualifying individual' are breached during a 'relevant period' — broadly three years (five years for shares issued before 6 April 2000) after the issue of the shares, the relief will be withdrawn.

Amount of relief

The maximum amount on which an individual can claim relief in any tax year is £200,000 (£150,000 before 6 April 2004), this limit being available to each of husband and wife. Relief is given in the tax year when the shares are purchased, but one-half of the amount subscribed before 6 October in any tax year can be carried back for relief in the previous tax year, up to a maximum carry-back of £25,000. Although the tax saving from the carry-back claim is calculated by reference to the tax position of the earlier year, it reduces the tax liability of the tax year in which the shares are subscribed for, so that any interest on overpaid tax will run only from 31 January after the end of that tax year — see 9.5. The claim for carry-back must be made at the same time as the claim for relief, and the carry-back cannot increase the relief for a tax year to more than £200,000 (or £150,000 for years before 2004/05). The minimum subscription by an individual to one company is £500 except where the investment is made through an investment fund approved by the Revenue. Income tax relief is given at 20% of the qualifying amount in calculating the individual's income tax liability for the year.

Withdrawal of relief

The shares must be held for a minimum of three years (five years for shares issued before 6 April 2000), otherwise the relief is withdrawn completely if the disposal is not at arm's length and the tax saving is lost on the amount received for an arm's length bargain. Relief is also withdrawn if the individual receives value from the company within one year before or three years after the issue of the shares. 'Value' is exhaustively defined and includes the repayment of loans that had been made to the company before the shares were issued, provision of benefits, and purchase of assets for less than market value. It does not, however, include dividends that do not exceed a normal return on the investment, and receipts of insignificant value are ignored. For shares issued on or after 17 March 2004, the repayment of loans made before the shares were issued does not constitute value received unless the repayment is made in connection with any arrangements for the acquisition of the shares.

An amount received in respect of an option to sell EIS shares will cause the loss of an appropriate amount of relief, but an arrangement to sell them (say to the controlling shareholders) after the qualifying period will not.

Relief is not withdrawn when a shareholder dies.

Where relief is to be withdrawn, the Revenue will issue an assessment outside the self-assessment system. Although tax on such assessments is payable within thirty days after they are issued, interest runs from an earlier date, depending on the event that triggered the withdrawal.

Capital gains reliefs

29.3

Capital gains exemption for EIS shares (TCGA 1992, ss 150A, 150B)

There is no charge to capital gains tax if shares for which EIS income tax relief has been given are disposed of at a profit after the three year retention period (five years for shares issued before 6 April 2000), although deferred gains may become chargeable under the deferral relief provisions outlined below. There is no exemption for disposals within the retention period (and EIS income tax relief will be withdrawn as indicated above). Gains may, however, be deferred if reinvested in new EIS shares or VCT shares (see below). If the disposal results in a loss, relief is available for the loss whether the disposal is within or outside the retention period, but in calculating a loss, the allowable cost is reduced by the EIS income tax relief that has not been withdrawn (see Example 1). A loss can be relieved either against chargeable gains (including deferred gains triggered by the disposal), or against income (under the provisions outlined at 38.21).

Example 1

	£
Cost of shares acquired under EIS	10,000
Income tax relief at 20%	2,000
Net cost of investment	8,000
Disposed of six years later for	6,500
Cost net of EIS relief	8,000
Loss available for relief	£1,500

Where shares have been acquired at different times, disposals are identified with shares acquired earlier rather than later. Where shares were acquired on the same day, disposals are identified first with shares to which neither EIS income tax relief nor capital gains deferral relief (see below) is attributable, then with shares to which deferral relief but not income tax relief is attributable, then with shares to which income tax relief but not deferral relief is attributable, and finally shares to which both reliefs are attributable. The normal capital gains tax identification and pooling rules do not apply.

Capital gains EIS deferral relief (TCGA 1992, ss 150C, 150D and Schs 5B, 5BA; FA 2004, s 93 and Sch 18)

A claim may be made for all or any part of a chargeable gain on the disposal of *any* asset (or a chargeable gain arising under the venture capital trust

515

provisions — see 29.7, or under the now withdrawn reinvestment relief provisions, which enabled gains to be deferred where they were reinvested into shares before 6 April 1998) to be deferred to the extent that it is matched by a subscription for EIS shares within one year before and three years after the disposal. The subscription for the shares must be wholly in cash, the issue must not be part of arrangements to avoid tax, and the shares must be issued to raise money for a qualifying business activity. 80% of the money raised must be used for that purpose within twelve months and the balance within the following twelve months. Gains may be deferred whether or not income tax relief was available on the EIS shares (in particular enabling owner/ directors to obtain deferral relief where they subscribe for shares, with the deferral not being limited to gains of £200,000). The relief is only available if the investor is resident and ordinarily resident in the UK.

Deferral relief is not available where there are guaranteed exit etc. arrangements (the provisions being the same as for the income tax relief — see 29.2).

The deferred gain (as distinct from the gain on the EIS shares, which is dealt with above) becomes chargeable on the disposal of the shares (other than to a spouse), or if the investor becomes non-resident within three years of acquiring the shares (five years for shares acquired before 6 April 2000), or if the shares cease to be eligible shares (as defined at 29.2), or the company ceases to qualify within three years. The deferred gain is not triggered if the investor (or spouse to whom the shares have been transferred) dies. Where the gain is triggered, it may be further deferred by another EIS investment (or investment in a venture capital trust — see 29.7) if the conditions are satisfied.

Except for successive investments in EIS shares as indicated below, taper relief is based on the period of ownership of the asset that gave rise to the deferred gain, so that if the deferral occurred before 6 April 1998 taper relief is not available. Special taper relief rules apply to EIS shares on which either or both of the EIS income tax relief or capital gains deferral relief have been given where the shares were issued after 5 April 1998. Where there are successive investments in such EIS shares (but not where investments are switched between EIS and VCT shares), taper relief is based on the cumulative period of ownership of the EIS shares. This means that the taper relief period in respect of the respective deferred gains arising on the disposal of the first and each successive holding of EIS shares will run from the time that holding was acquired to the time when replacement EIS shares are disposed of without the proceeds being invested in another EIS investment. Any gaps between shares being disposed of and new shares being issued are, however, excluded.

The taper relief in respect of an asset on which a gain was deferred when the *first* EIS holding was acquired is still based on the period of ownership of that asset.

Withdrawal of investment after relevant period

29.4   Potential investors may see a disadvantage in their being locked in as minority shareholders. The company may, however, build up reserves by retaining profits, and use the reserves to purchase its own shares after five years, using the rules described in 29.11. There must not, however, be guaranteed arrangements for this to be done (see 29.2).

Venture capital trusts (TA 1988, ss 332A, 842AA and Schs 15B and 28B; TCGA 1992, ss 151A, 151B and Sch 5C; FA 2002, s 109 and Sch 33; FA 2004, s 94 and Sch 19)

29.5   Those who wish to support new and expanding companies but are unwilling to invest directly in unquoted shares may obtain similar relief to that available under the EIS through venture capital trusts.

VCTs are quoted companies holding at least 70% of their investments in shares or securities they have subscribed for in qualifying unquoted companies trading wholly or mainly in the UK. At least 30% of such holdings must be in ordinary shares, and no single holding may be more than 15% of total investments. Furthermore, loans or securities that are guaranteed are excluded and at least 10% of the total investment in any company must be ordinary, non-preferential shares. 80% of the money invested in a company by the VCT needs to be used for the purposes of the company's trade within twelve months. The remainder must be used within a further twelve months. Companies on the Alternative Investment Market (AIM) count as qualifying unquoted companies providing they are carrying on a qualifying trade. The VCT must not retain more than 15% of its income from shares and securities and must satisfy the gross assets test (see below). VCTs are exempt from tax on their capital gains. There are anti-avoidance provisions to prevent the exemption being exploited by means of intra-group transfers, or by transferring a company's business to a VCT or to a company that later becomes a VCT.

Regulations are to be introduced (having retrospective effect to 27 March 2002) which will enable VCTs to retain their tax approval when they merge and also to treat VCTs as being approved while they are being wound up. This will prevent investors losing their tax reliefs in these circumstances.

The main exclusions from the definition of qualifying trading company are the same as for the EIS (see 29.2). The total gross assets of the company (and, where relevant, other companies in the same group) must not exceed £15 million immediately before the VCT acquired the holding, nor £16 million immediately afterwards.

Individual investors aged 18 or over are entitled to relief from income tax reliefs and two capital gains reliefs as follows.

Income tax reliefs

29.6   When new ordinary shares are *subscribed for*, income tax relief may be claimed on up to £200,000 of the amount subscribed each tax year (£100,000 for shares acquired before 6 April 2004). The rate of relief has been increased from 20% to 40% for shares issued in the tax years 2004/05 and 2005/06. Claims may be made in tax returns.

The relief will be withdrawn to the extent that any of the shares are disposed of (other than to the holder's spouse, or after the holder's death) within three years (five years for shares issued before 6 April 2000). If the disposal is at arm's length and at a loss, relief is withdrawn in the proportion that the consideration received on disposal bears to the amount subscribed. Where shares are acquired from a spouse, the acquiring spouse is treated as if he or she had subscribed for the shares. The relief will also be withdrawn if the VCT loses its qualifying status within the three (or five) year period. Where relief is to be withdrawn, the Revenue will issue an assessment outside the self-assessment system, tax being payable within thirty days after the assessment is issued. Unlike the EIS position (see 29.2), there are no special provisions for interest on overdue tax where VCT relief is withdrawn, and it would appear that interest would run from 31 January following the end of the tax year for which the relief was given.

Dividends from ordinary shares in VCTs are exempt from tax to the extent that not more than £200,000 in total of shares in VCTs are *acquired* each year (£100,000 for shares acquired before 6 April 2004), whether the shares were acquired by subscription or by purchase from another shareholder. Dividend tax credits are, however, not repayable.

The reliefs are not available if avoiding tax is a main purpose of acquiring the shares.

Capital gains position

29.7

Capital gains exemption

Gains arising on the disposal of VCT shares that were acquired by subscription or purchase up to the £200,000 limit (£100,000 limit for shares acquired before 6 April 2004) in any year are exempt from capital gains tax (and any losses are not allowable). There is no minimum period for which the shares must be held. Disposals are matched with acquisitions according to the rules outlined below. Where gains are chargeable, they may be deferred if reinvested in new VCT shares or EIS shares (see 29.3).

Capital gains deferral

A claim may be made for all or any part of gains on the disposal of *any* assets by someone resident or ordinarily resident in the UK to be deferred to the extent that they are reinvested, within one year before or one year after the disposal, in VCT shares on which income tax relief is given and which (where relevant) are still held at the time of the disposal. This deferral relief is not available for gains reinvested in VCT shares where the VCT shares are issued on or after 6 April 2004.

The *deferred* gains (not the gains on the VCT shares themselves) become chargeable if the VCT shares are disposed of (other than to a spouse), or the investor (or spouse who has acquired the shares) becomes non-resident within three years of acquiring the shares (five years for shares issued before 6 April 2000), or the VCT loses its approval, or the income tax relief is otherwise withdrawn. The deferred gain is not triggered by the death of the investor (or spouse to whom the shares have been transferred). Where deferred gains are triggered, they may again be deferred if further reinvested in new EIS shares (see 29.3) if the conditions are satisfied.

Taper relief is not taken into account in arriving at the gain to be deferred, but when the deferred gain is triggered, the taper relief is based on the period of ownership of the asset that gave rise to the deferred gain (see 4.23). If the deferral occurred before 6 April 1998, therefore, no taper relief is available.

Example 2

In May 2003 an investor buys shares in a qualifying venture capital trust from an existing shareholder for £40,000. On 1 August 2003 he subscribes £90,000 for further shares, so that his total investment in the tax year is £130,000.

He will get 20% income tax relief on the £90,000 subscribed for new shares. No relief is available for the purchased shares.

Dividends on the shares bought for £40,000 and on £60,000 of the shares subscribed for will be exempt from tax. Capital gains exemption will apply to the same amount.

Gains of up to £90,000 on *any* assets disposed of between 1 August 2002 and 1 August 2004 may be deferred against the shares subscribed for. If, say, a gain arising in August 2002 was deferred, and it related to a

---

business asset held on 5 April 1998, taper relief of 75% would be available when the gain was triggered.

If the VCT shares had been issued on or after 6 April 2004, deferral relief would not have been available.

Capital gains rules for matching disposals with acquisitions

29.8   Any disposals of shares in a VCT are identified first with shares acquired before the trust became a VCT. To decide whether other disposals relate to shares in excess of the £200,000 (or £100,000) limit in any year, disposals are identified with shares acquired earlier rather than those acquired later. Where shares are acquired on the same day, shares in excess of the £200,000 (or £100,000) limit are treated as disposed of before qualifying shares. Any shares not identified with other shares under these rules qualify for the VCT capital gains exemption on disposal, and they are not subject to the normal capital gains rules for matching disposals with acquisitions.

If a VCT loses its qualifying status, shares eligible for the CGT exemption are treated as disposed of at market value (any gain being covered by the exemption) and immediately reacquired at market value. They are then brought within the normal capital gains rules for matching disposals with acquisitions.

Corporate venturing scheme (FA 2000, s 63 and Sch 15; FA 2004, s 95 and Sch 20)

29.9   A corporate venturing scheme is available to companies in respect of qualifying shares issued on or after 1 April 2000 and before 1 April 2010. The Revenue have produced a booklet IR 2000 giving details of the scheme. It is intended to encourage companies to invest in small higher risk trading companies (defined as for EIS and VCT — see 29.2) and to form wider corporate venturing relationships. 80% of the money invested in the small company needs to be used for the purposes of the company's trade within twelve months. The remainder must be used within a further twelve months. The small company must not be a 51% subsidiary of another company. Financial companies that invest by way of business are not eligible to claim the relief.

Investing companies are entitled to 20% corporation tax relief on cash subscriptions for new ordinary shares of a qualifying unquoted small company providing the investing company has received from the small company a certificate of compliance that the requirements for investment relief are met. Small companies may obtain advance clearance that their shares will qualify.

The relief is given against the corporation tax payable for the accounting period in which the shares are issued. The relief will be withdrawn if the company disposes of the shares within three years, or in certain other circumstances.

When the shares are disposed of, then whether or not the corporation tax relief is withdrawn as a result, tax on any capital gain arising may be deferred to the extent that the gain is reinvested in another corporate venturing scheme holding within one year before or three years after the disposal. If capital losses arise on disposals, then as an alternative to relief against capital gains, relief may be claimed for the amount of the loss (net of the corporation tax relief obtained) against the corporate venturer company's income of the current or previous accounting period.

Relief is not available if the corporate venturer company, alone or with connected persons, controls the small company. Connected persons include the corporate venturer's directors but not its employees. The corporate venturer company's holding must not exceed 30%, and at least 20% of the small company's share capital must be held by individuals. There is no minimum investment requirement.

Relief is not lost if the small company becomes quoted during the three year qualifying period providing there were no prior arrangements to do so.

Community investment tax relief (FA 2002, s 57, Schs 16 and 17)

29.10   Investments made by individuals and companies on or after 17 April 2002 in a community development finance institution (CDFI) qualify for tax relief of 5% per annum of the amount of the investment for a period of five years, so that the total relief is 25%. For an individual, the five-year period commences in the tax year in which the investment is made. For a company the relief applies to the accounting period in which the investment is made and the accounting periods in which the next four anniversaries of the investment date fall. The relief is set against the amount of tax payable. The aim of the relief is to encourage private investment in businesses and social enterprises in disadvantaged communities (referred to as Enterprise Areas) via accredited CDFIs. Investments may be by way of loans or subscription for shares or securities, and CDFIs will supply investors with a tax relief certificate. Claims for relief cannot be made earlier than the end of the tax year or company accounting period in which the investment is made. In the case of loans, the amount of the investment is calculated in each of the five years following the investment date according to the average balance in that year (or, for the third, fourth and fifth years, the average capital balance for the period of six months starting 18 months after the investment date if less).

As with all such schemes, there are detailed conditions that must be complied with, and loss of accreditation by the CDFI in the five years after the investment date will result in investors losing the right to claim further relief. The relief will be restricted, or in some circumstances withdrawn completely, if the investor disposes of all or part of the investment or receives value within the five years after the investment date.

See 6.20 for the exemption from stamp duty land tax for sales and leases of property in Enterprise Areas.

Purchase by company of its own shares (TA 1988, ss 219–229)

29.11   Where an unquoted trading company or the unquoted holding company of a trading group buys back its own shares (or redeems them or makes a payment for them in a reduction of capital) in order to benefit a trade, the transaction is not treated as a distribution, and thus liable to income tax in the hands of the vending shareholder, but as a disposal on which the vending shareholder is liable to capital gains tax. This does not apply if there is an arrangement the main purpose of which is to get undistributed profits into the hands of the shareholders without incurring the tax liabilities on a distribution.

The main requirements are that the shareholder must be UK-resident, he must normally have owned the shares for at least five years, and he must either dispose of his entire holding or the holding must be 'substantially reduced'.

A company may apply to the Revenue for a clearance that the proposed purchase will not be treated as a distribution.

Any legal costs and other expenditure incurred by a company in purchasing its own shares are not allowable against the company's profits.

Where the purchase of its own shares by a company is *not* covered by the above provisions, the purchase is treated as a distribution on which income tax is payable, and the anti-avoidance provisions at 45.7 will apply if the company has purchased its own shares from trustees.

Unless capital gains reliefs were available, it has been common for a purchase of own shares to be deliberately structured so as to breach the capital gains rules, because the effective tax rate on net dividend distributions for higher rate taxpayers is 25% compared with 40% capital gains tax. The introduction of capital gains tax taper relief has changed the position, since the business assets taper relief rate after two years is 75% (giving a tax rate of 10% for a higher rate taxpayer).

Management buyouts

29.12   The provisions enabling a company to purchase its own shares could assist a management buyout team to acquire the company for which they work, in that only shares remaining after those bought in by the company need then be acquired by them.

If only part of a trade is to be acquired, the existing company could transfer the requisite assets into a subsidiary company using the reconstruction provisions of TA 1988, s 343 (see 26.15), the buyout team then buying the shares in the subsidiary.

Alternatively, if the buyout team form an entirely new company and purchase assets from their employing company, capital allowances will be available where appropriate and the new company may be able to raise some of the funds it needs through the enterprise investment scheme, or by attracting investments from venture capital trusts (see 29.5).

Demergers (TA 1988, ss 213–218; TCGA 1992, s 192)

29.13   The aim of the demerger legislation is to remove various tax obstacles to demergers, so that businesses grouped inefficiently under a single company umbrella may be run more dynamically and effectively by being allowed to pursue their separate ways under independent management. The detailed provisions are very complex, the following being an outline.

A company is not treated as having made a distribution for corporation tax purposes (and the members are not treated as having received income) where the company transfers to its members the shares of a 75% subsidiary, or transfers a trade to a new company in exchange for that new company issuing shares to some or all of the transferor company's shareholders.

In order for these provisions to apply, all the companies must be UK-resident trading companies, the transfer must be made to benefit some or all of the trading activities, and the transfer must not be made for tax avoidance reasons.

A qualifying distribution by the holding company of shares in subsidiaries to its members is also not treated as a capital distribution for capital gains tax purposes, and the capital gains charge when a company leaves a group on assets acquired within the previous six years from other group companies (see 45.30) does not apply.

There are detailed anti-avoidance provisions, and there is also provision to apply for Revenue clearance of proposed transactions.

Enterprise zones

29.14   Certain areas in which the Government particularly wants to encourage investment have been designated as enterprise zones. (These are not the same areas as the Enterprise Areas referred to in 29.10.) Those who set up business within an enterprise zone get certain advantages for a limited number of years, such as not paying business rates and entitlement to 100% relief for expenditure on new buildings for use in the trade. The relief for expenditure on buildings is also available to landlords and is dealt with in 22.30 to 22.34. If you are considering buying a new building in an enterprise zone, make appropriate comparisons to ensure that the cost has not been increased unreasonably because of the available tax relief on construction expenditure and the other known advantages of operating from a designated area.

The tax benefit of enterprise zone investment may only be retained by long term investors. If you dispose of your investment in the building either by selling or by granting a lesser interest, such as a long lease, the disposal triggers the withdrawal of the 100% allowance (see 22.30).

Contributions to enterprise agencies, TECs etc. (TA 1988, ss 79, 79A)

29.15   Businesses may claim a deduction from their profits for contributions they make to local enterprise agencies, training and enterprise councils (TECs), Scottish local enterprise companies and business link organisations.

Local enterprise agencies are bodies approved by the Secretary of State that promote local industrial and commercial activity and enterprise, particularly in forming and developing small businesses. TECs are private companies whose directors are mainly local businessmen. They are mainly concerned with Government training programmes. Scottish local enterprise companies are similar to TECs but cover economic development and environmental functions as well as training. Business link organisations are authorised by the Department of Trade and Industry to use the 'Business Links' service mark and provide a single point of access for TECs, local enterprise agencies, chambers of commerce and local authorities.

Revenue expenditure on research and development (TA 1988, ss 82A, 837A; FA 1998, Sch 18 Parts 9A, 9C; FA 2000, s 69 and Sch 20; FA 2002, ss 53, 54 and Schs 12, 13; FA 2004, ss 53, 141; SI 2000/2081)

29.16   Various reliefs are available in respect of revenue expenditure on research and development (R & D), as indicated below. Capital expenditure on research and development qualifies for 100% capital allowances (see 22.37). New DTI guidelines on the meaning of R & D have been introduced. These will apply for accounting periods ending on or after 1 April 2004. The main changes are the inclusion of expenditure on computer software, power, fuel and water.

For accounting periods beginning on or after 1 January 2005, UK companies may prepare their accounts in accordance with either UK generally accepted accounting practice or international accounting standards (see 20.2). From a date to be fixed by statutory instrument, companies that treat R & D for accounts purposes as part of the cost of an intangible asset rather than as revenue expenditure may nonetheless still claim the tax reliefs in this section.

Expenditure by small and medium-sized companies

29.17   Individuals and companies are normally entitled to deduct 100% of their revenue expenditure on research and development in calculating taxable profits (see 20.19). Indeed, small and medium-sized companies as defined can claim R & D tax relief for *150%* of their qualifying revenue expenditure on research and development, providing it amounts to not less than £10,000 (£25,000 for expenditure in accounting periods beginning before 27 September 2003), or pro rata amount for an account of less than 12 months. Expenditure on R & D work subcontracted to them by large companies (see 29.18) is included in deciding whether the £10,000 (or £25,000) threshold has been reached. The R & D relief gives companies liable to small companies' rate a tax saving of 28.5% on the R & D expenditure. Any intellectual property (know-how, patents, trade marks etc.) created as a result of the R & D must be vested in the company (alone or with others).

Companies carrying on R & D before they start to trade may treat the R & D relief as a trading loss. Where a company has an unrelieved trading loss (excluding brought forward or carried back losses), it may surrender the R & D tax relief (or the unrelieved loss if lower) in exchange for a tax credit equal to 16% of the surrendered amount (i.e. 24% of the corresponding R & D expenditure). The credit cannot, however, exceed the company's PAYE and NICs liabilities for payment periods ending in the relevant accounting period. The tax credit will be paid to the company, or used to discharge outstanding corporation tax liabilities.

Small and medium-sized companies are broadly defined as those with fewer than 250 employees, having a turnover of not more than Euro 40 million (about £27 million) and/or assets of not more than Euro 27 million (about £18 million).

Small and medium-sized companies who do subcontract R & D work for large companies may claim relief in respect of their expenditure on such work as indicated in 29.18, in addition to the relief outlined above for other R & D expenditure. There is no provision for companies to be able to claim a tax credit for this relief where they have trading losses.

Expenditure by large companies etc

29.18   Large companies (i.e. those not within the definition of small and medium-sized companies in 29.17) may claim R & D relief of 125% of their qualifying revenue expenditure on research and development, providing it amounts to not less than £10,000 (£25,000 for expenditure in accounting periods beginning before 9 April 2003), or pro rata amount for an account of less than 12 months. Qualifying expenditure includes direct R & D expenditure, expenditure subcontracted by the company to an individual, partnership, university, charity or other qualifying body, and contributions to individuals, partnerships and qualifying bodies for independent R & D which is relevant to the company.

Where a large company subcontracts work to a small or medium-sized company, the small/medium-sized company may claim R & D relief of 125% of the qualifying expenditure, providing the company's total R & D expenditure, including that undertaken independently (see 29.17) is not less than £10,000 (or £25,000 for expenditure in accounting periods beginning before 9 April 2003), reduced pro rata for an account of less than 12 months.

Expenditure on vaccines research

29.19   In addition to the normal 100% deduction for research and development expenditure, or the higher R & D relief available to small/medium-sized and large companies outlined in 29.17 and 29.18, from 22 April 2003 all companies may claim an extra 50% relief for their qualifying expenditure on research and development related to vaccines and medicines for TB and malaria, HIV and AIDS. This is subject to a £10,000 threshold as indicated in 29.17 and 29.18 (£25,000 for expenditure in accounting periods beginning before 27 September 2003). The relief is also available for contributions to charities, universities and scientific research organisations for funding independent research related to a trade carried on by the company. Where the R & D does not come within the provisions of 29.17 and 29.18, the company is still entitled to the extra deduction of 50%.

The same provisions apply as under 29.17 for small/medium-sized companies to treat the relief in respect of pre-trading vaccines research expenditure as a trading loss and for surrendering losses in exchange for a tax credit payment of 16% of the surrendered amount.

Tax points

29.20

- The detailed conditions and anti-avoidance rules in relation to most of the provisions dealt with in this chapter are too extensive to deal with in detail, but should be looked at carefully by interested companies and investors.

- Although qualifying companies or fund managers will issue certificates to individuals investing under the enterprise investment scheme, each individual must make a specific claim for income tax relief to his own tax district within the time limit indicated at 29.2. Capital gains deferral relief for reinvestment in EIS shares must also be claimed within the same time limit.

- When you reinvest gains by subscribing within the appropriate limits for EIS shares, you can effectively get up to 60% tax relief at that time (20% income tax relief on the shares and 40% capital gains relief on the deferred gains for a higher rate taxpayer). Although the capital gains relief is only a deferral, further deferral may be possible when the deferred gains are triggered. The gains may eventually become chargeable if they are triggered before your death.

- Although gains deferred under the EIS provisions may become chargeable as indicated above, gains on the disposal of the shares themselves up to the relevant holding limits are exempt, providing that they were subscribed for and held for the three or five-year period.

- You cannot get EIS income tax relief if you are connected with the company, but the connected persons rules do not apply to the EIS deferral relief enabling you to defer tax on capital gains up to the amount invested.

- Shares in companies on the Alternative Investment Market (AIM) are treated as unquoted, so EIS relief is available providing the company is a qualifying company. The limit on the company's assets of £15 million immediately before the issue of the shares and £16 million immediately afterwards will, however, exclude many AIM companies.

- The Revenue will not usually give a clearance under the demerger provisions where companies in the same ownership are first merged and then demerged so that each company ends up in the ownership of independent people.

30
Your family home

Background

30.1   There are various tax aspects to consider in relation to your family home. Apart from inheritance tax considerations, the most important are the capital gains aspects, but you also need to consider the income tax position when you receive rental income for the property or use it for your employment or business, and the relevant provisions in relation to council tax and business rates.

As far as inheritance tax is concerned, the large increases in property values that have taken place over recent years, coupled with the minimal increases in the inheritance tax nil rate band, have left many people with significant inheritance tax problems in relation to the family home. This aspect is dealt with in 35.6.

Leasehold reform

30.2   As a result of the Commonhold and Leasehold Reform Act 2002, those acquiring property in new developments will be able to buy the freehold of their individual flats and become members of a 'commonhold association' that is responsible for the management and upkeep of the common parts of the property. Commonhold land will be registered with the Land Registry. Leaseholders of existing developments may convert to commonhold if all leaseholders agree.

There are already arrangements to enable leaseholders to acquire the freehold of their flats through a nominee purchaser. The rules relating to such acquisitions have been simplified and leaseholders will be able to acquire the freehold of their units through an RTE (Right to Enfranchisement) company. The rate of stamp duty land tax on the consideration for the acquisition of the freeholds will be arrived at by dividing the total amount payable by the number of flats and the rate on that fractional amount will be applied to the total consideration. Whether or not the leaseholders form an RTE, they may take over the management of the common parts of the development through an RTM (Right to Manage) company.

For those participating in commonhold associations or RTM/RTE companies, various tax points need to be borne in mind, particularly where some tenants buy and some do not. Someone has to be responsible for dealing with the tax on any income, such as interest on the maintenance fund, and there are also capital gains tax considerations. Professional advice is essential.

Capital gains tax private residence relief (TCGA 1992, ss 222–226B; FA 2004, s 112 and Sch 22)

30.3   The basic capital gains treatment on the disposal of your main residence is that any gain is exempt from capital gains tax providing the property has been your only or main residence throughout your period of ownership, or throughout that period except for all or any part of the last thirty-six months. This is subject to various provisions to cover situations such as other periods of absence, owning two or more residences, using part of the property for business or letting and so on, which are dealt with later in the chapter.

Buying and not moving in immediately

30.4   If you do not move into your house immediately, for capital gains purposes the Revenue will, by concession, allow you to treat any non-occupation in the first twelve months as covered by your owner occupier exemption if you do not move in because you are having the property built, or you are altering or redecorating the property, or because you remain in your old home while you are selling it. (See also 30.12 re job-related accommodation).

Empty property may be liable to council tax, but newly built or structurally altered property is not subject to the tax for up to six months after the work is substantially completed, and there is no charge on any unfurnished property for up to six months.

Periods of absence (TCGA 1992, s 223)

30.5   Provided that a house has at some time been your only or main residence, the last three years of ownership are always exempt in calculating capital gains tax, whether you are living there or not. Other periods of absence also qualify for exemption provided that the house was your only or main residence at some time both before and after the period of absence, and that no other residence qualifies for relief during the absence (see 30.10).

These qualifying periods of absence are any or all of the following:

(a)   three years for any reason whatsoever (not necessarily a consecutive period of three years);

(b)   up to four years where the duties of a United Kingdom employment require you to live elsewhere; and

(c)   any period of absence abroad where the duties of employment require you to live abroad.

If these periods are exceeded, only the excess is counted as a period of non-residence. If you have to move to another place of employment, so that it is not possible to have a period of residence immediately after an employment-related absence, that condition is waived.

You can thus have long periods of absence without losing any part of the capital gains tax exemption.

Periods of absence before 31 March 1982 are ignored in calculating the chargeable gain, which depends on the proportion of residence/deemed residence to the total period of ownership after 30 March 1982. The exemption for the last three years of ownership still applies, however, no matter whether the period of residence was before or after 31 March 1982.

If you are going to occupy rented property during your absence, then even if your tenancy has no capital value, the property you are occupying would strictly 'qualify for relief' as a second home (see 30.10). In those circumstances the Revenue will accept a main residence election for your own property, so that the rules for qualifying periods of absence can apply. By Revenue concession D21, where in these circumstances you did not know at the appropriate time that an election was required, the Revenue will accept an out of time election providing you make it promptly as soon as you become aware, the election then taking effect from the time the tenancy was acquired.

If you acquire an interest in a property from your spouse (including an acquisition as legatee when your spouse dies), your period of ownership is treated as starting when your spouse acquired the property, and your tax position would take into account any part of that period when your spouse was not resident in the property.

There are no special council tax provisions about permitted absences, other than the exemptions listed at 8.3 and the discount for a property that is no-one's only or main home.

Dwelling occupied by a dependent relative or under a trust (TCGA 1992, ss 225, 226, 226A, 226B; FA 2004, s 117 and Sch 22)

30.6   If you owned a property on 5 April 1988 that has been continuously occupied rent-free by a dependent relative since that date, the property is exempt from capital gains tax when you dispose of it. Payment of council tax by the relative does not affect the exemption.

The capital gains tax exemption ceases if there is a change of occupant after 5 April 1988 even if the new occupant is also a dependent relative, but the period from 31 March 1982 which did qualify for the exemption reduces the chargeable period when calculating any chargeable gain.

'Dependent relative' is defined as your own or your spouse's widowed mother, or any other relative unable to look after themselves because of old age or infirmity. There is no income restriction.

See 34.6 for a possibly tax-effective way of providing a home for a dependent relative now.

The private residence exemption also applies where trustees dispose of a property occupied by someone entitled to occupy it under the terms of the trust. For disposals on or after 10 December 2003 the trustees are required to make a claim for this relief. Anti-avoidance provisions deny the relief for such disposals where the calculation of the gain would take into account gifts relief (see 4.28) on an earlier disposal, unless the earlier claim is revoked. Where the earlier disposal on which gifts relief was given was before 10 December 2003, the private residence relief is denied only in respect of the period from that date (and the exemption for the last three years of ownership will not include any post-10 December 2003 period). See 33.13 for the use of the trust exemption where couples get divorced.

If your home is let (TCGA 1992, s 223(4); F(No 2)A 1992, s 59 and Sch 10)

Income tax

30.7   A 'rent-a-room' relief is available for owner-occupiers and tenants who let furnished rooms in their only or main residence. The relief is available both where the rent comes under the 'Schedule A business' rules (see 32.3) and where substantial services are also provided, for example guest houses and bed and breakfast businesses, so that the rent is charged as trading income (see CHAPTER 21). (If you let part of your property unfurnished in the same year, however, the relief cannot be claimed.) You must occupy the property as your main home at the same time as the tenant for at least part of the letting period in each tax year or business basis period. No tax is payable if the gross rents for the tax year (or for trades, your accounting year ended in the tax year), before deducting expenses, do not exceed £4,250. If the letting is by a couple, the relief is £2,125 each. The rent taken into account for the relief is the payment for the accommodation plus payments for related goods and services. You can claim for the relief not to apply for a particular year, for example if your expenses exceed your rent and you want to claim relief for a loss. The time limit for the claim is one year from 31 January following the end of the relevant tax year (or longer at the Revenue's discretion). If your rent exceeds £4,250, you can choose to pay tax either on the excess over £4,250 or on the rent less expenses under the normal rules described below. If you want to pay on the excess over £4,250 you must make a claim to do so, and that basis will then apply until you withdraw your claim. The time limit for such a claim is the same as that for electing for the relief not to apply at all.

If the 'rent-a-room' relief does not apply, then unless the letting amounts to a trade (see above), the letting income is chargeable to income tax along with other letting income, if any, after setting off appropriate expenses (see 32.4). It is normally treated as unearned income, but if the letting qualifies as furnished holiday accommodation (see 32.17), the income is treated as trading income.

Capital gains tax

30.8   As far as the capital gains exemption is concerned, the last three years of ownership of your home always count as a period of residence (see 30.5), so if you move out and let the property during that time it will not affect your exemption.

If you continue to live in the property while letting part of it, your capital gains exemption is not affected if the letting takes the form of boarders who effectively live as part of the family. Where, however, the letting extends beyond this, or you let the whole property, other than during the last three years of ownership or during another allowable absence period (see 30.5), the appropriate fraction of the gain on disposal is chargeable but there is an exemption of the smaller of £40,000 and an amount equal to the exempt gain on the owner-occupied part.

Example 1

The gain on the sale of a dwelling in 2004/05 is £80,000. The agreed proportion applicable to the let part is £48,000, the exempt gain being £32,000.

The £48,000 gain on the let part is reduced by the lower of

(a)   £40,000 and

(b)   an amount equal to the exempt gain, i.e. £32,000.

Therefore a further £32,000 is exempt and £16,000 is chargeable (but gain will be reduced by any available taper relief — 25% if the property was acquired before 17 March 1998 — and the £8,200 annual exemption will reduce the gain still further if not already used).

Where a married couple jointly let part of the home, each is entitled to the residential lettings exemption of up to £40,000.

The exemption is not available if the let part of the property is effectively a separate dwelling, such as a self-contained flat with its own access. But where part of the home is let, without substantial structural alterations, it will qualify, even if it has separate facilities.

The Revenue used to take the view that the residential lettings exemption was only available where the letting had some degree of permanence, but they lost a case on the point in the Court of Appeal, where it was decided that the exemption was available to the owners of a small private hotel who occupied the whole of the property during the winter months, with one or two guests, but lived in an annexe during the summer. The exemption can be claimed only if the property qualifies as your capital gains tax exempt residence for at least part of your period of ownership, so it cannot be claimed on a property which, although you live in it sometimes, has never been your only or main residence for capital gains tax purposes. Subject to that, it can be claimed where all of the property has been let for part of your period of ownership, or part of the property has been let for all or part of your period of ownership.

The position of furnished holiday lettings (see 32.17) is not clear. Gains on such property are specifically eligible for rollover relief when the property is sold and replaced, but providing you comply with the rules outlined above, it would seem that if the property is your qualifying main residence the residential lettings exemption could apply instead. To continue to get the other benefits of the furnished holiday lettings provisions, you would have to make sure that you complied with the rules for such lettings (in particular ensuring that neither you nor anyone else normally occupied the accommodation for a continuous period of more than 31 days for at least seven months of the year).

Council tax and business rates

30.9   If the let part of your property is self-contained living accommodation that counts as a separate dwelling, the tenants are liable to pay the council tax. But for any period when it is not anyone's only or main home, for example when it is untenanted, you are liable to pay up to 90% of the council tax (subject to certain exemptions, for example unfurnished property for up to six months — see 8.3). If the let part of your home is not self-contained, you are liable to pay the council tax, but you will usually include an appropriate amount in the rent to cover the proportion applicable to the tenants. If you do not live in the property while it is let, the council tax will be paid by tenants who occupy it as their main home, except for multi-occupied property such as bed-sits, where you will remain liable. If the let part is let as short-term living accommodation, and is therefore no-one's only or main home, you will pay up to 90% of the council tax unless the property is available for short-term letting for 140 days or more in a year (for example self-catering holiday accommodation), in which case you will pay business rates instead. If you offer bed and breakfast facilities in your own home, you are not liable to business rates providing you do not offer accommodation for more than six people, you live in the house at the same time and the house is still mainly used as your home. If part of your home is let for business purposes rather than as living accommodation, business rates are payable on that part.

You may deduct an appropriate part of the council tax, or the business rates, paid on let property from the rent in arriving at your taxable letting income.

More than one home (TCGA 1992, s 222(5)(6))

Capital gains tax

30.10   You may notify the Revenue within two years after acquiring a second home which of the two is to be the exempt home for capital gains tax. The nominated property may be in the UK or abroad. Only a property used as your home qualifies for the exemption, however, and you cannot nominate a property you have never lived in. After nominating the exempt property you may later notify a change of choice from a specified date, which cannot be earlier than two years before the date of the later notification. If you do not make a notification, and a dispute between you and the Revenue is taken to appeal, the main residence will be decided by the Appeal Commissioners as a question of fact. Provided that both houses have been your qualifying main residence for capital gains tax at some time, the last three years of ownership of both will in any event be counted as owner-occupied in calculating the exempt gain. An election is not required where you have a residence that you own and a second residence that you neither own nor lease (e.g. accommodation with relatives, or a hotel room). A property that you occupy as a tenant would, however, need to be taken into account even if your occupation rights have no capital value (see 30.5).

The ability to change your election as to which of two homes is your main residence may be helpful where you have owned two homes for many years, one of which has never been your qualifying main residence, and you sell that property at a gain. See Example 2.

Example 2

A taxpayer has owned and occupied two homes Westcote and Eastcote for many years, and had made an election for Westcote to be his main residence. He sells Eastcote at a substantial gain in December 2004 and on 10 January 2005 notifies the Revenue that Eastcote is to be treated as his main residence from 10 January 2003. On 17 January 2005 he notifies the Revenue that Westcote is to be his main residence from 17 January 2003. The elections enable him to obtain the exemption for the last three years' ownership of Eastcote, at the expense of having one chargeable week in respect of Westcote.

A married couple living together can only have one qualifying residence and where there are two or more residences owned jointly, or each owns one or more residences, the notice as to which is the main residence needs to be given by both. Where both spouses own a residence when they marry, a new two-year period starts for notifying which is the main residence. A new two-year period does not start if on marriage one spouse already owns more than one residence and the other owns no property. If a couple jointly own more than one property before and after marriage, a new two-year period still begins, because the election after marriage must be a joint election.

Council tax

30.11   For council tax, you pay up to 90% of the tax on a property which is no-one's only or main home (see 8.5). The question of which of two or more homes is your only or main home for the council tax is a question of fact, decided in the first place by the local authority, but you may appeal against their decision. In some circumstances, one of the properties might be the main home of one spouse and the other property the main home of the other, in which case the resident partner would be liable to pay the council tax at each property, with a 25% single resident reduction if the property was not also the main residence of anyone else over 18. This could apply, for example, if a wife lived at a house in the country and her husband at a house in town, going to the other house at weekends, etc. But the length of time spent at the property would not necessarily be the deciding factor and all relevant circumstances would be taken into account. If the second home was a holiday property available for short-term letting for 140 days or more in a year, it would be liable to business rates rather than the council tax.

If your second home is a caravan, it will not usually be liable to council tax. The site owner where the caravan is kept will pay business rates, which will be included in his charge to you. Touring caravans kept at your home when you are not touring are not subject to council tax.

Job-related accommodation (TCGA 1992, s 222(8), (8A)–(8D), (9))

30.12 If you live in accommodation related to your employment, for example as a hotel manager or minister of religion, or to your self-employment, for example as the tenant of licensed premises, you may buy a property now that is to be your future home. The property qualifies for capital gains tax exemption, even though you do not live there.

If you let the property, you are entitled to deduct from the letting income interest paid on a loan to buy the property. Relief against the letting income is given at your top tax rate. You may also deduct interest on loans for improvements to the property.

Unless the property is someone's only or main home (for example if you let it long-term), you will pay 50% of the council tax on it (see 8.5).

Moving home (TA 1988, ss 191A, 191B and Sch 11A; TCGA 1992, s 223)

30.13 Owning two houses at the same time is usually covered for capital gains tax purposes by the exemption of the last three years of ownership.

You may need to take out a bridging loan when you move house. Employees earning £8,500 per annum or more and company directors are charged to tax on the benefit of certain low rate or interest-free loans from their employers (see 10.23). This includes bridging loans, but there are specific statutory provisions covering removal and relocation expenses, under which employees are not taxed on qualifying expenses paid by their employers up to a limit of £8,000 (see 10.13). If the £8,000 limit has not been fully used, any balance is available to cover an equivalent amount of the notional interest chargeable to tax on a low rate or interest-free bridging loan from the employer.

See 10.14 for the tax treatment if you sell your home to your employer or to a relocation company.

As far as council tax is concerned, the same points apply as stated at 30.5 for 'Periods of absence'.

Part use for business purposes (TCGA 1992, s 224)

30.14   Interest on that part of any borrowing attributable to the use of part of your home exclusively for business is allowed as a business expense. See 20.3 for other allowable expenses when you work from home.

You will pay business rates on the business part of the property (allowable against your profits for tax). Where part of the property is used for both business and domestic purposes, and the business use does not prevent the continued domestic use, such as a study where you do some work and your children do their homework, business rates are not payable, and you may claim a deduction against your profit for the appropriate proportion of your council tax.

As far as capital gains tax is concerned, the private residence exemption is not available on any part of your property that is used *exclusively* for business purposes. Where a replacement property is acquired that is similarly used partly for business, rollover relief may be available to defer the gain (see 4.26) and see also 30.8 for letting businesses. Any chargeable gain remaining after claiming appropriate reliefs will be reduced by taper relief at the business assets rate. The way in which the taper relief is worked out is, however, anomalous and unfair. See Example 3.

Example 3

Taxpayer sold his private residence in June 2004. He had owned the property for 20 years and had always used 20% of the property exclusively for business purposes. The total gain after indexation allowance was £100,000, so the gain on the business proportion was £20,000.

Even though logically the whole £20,000 should qualify for 75% business assets taper relief, giving a chargeable gain of £5,000, the legislation requires the gain to be split into two gains according to the business/non-business use of the asset over the qualifying period. So 80% of £20,000 = £16,000 is regarded as relating to a non-business asset and 20%, i.e. £4,000, to a business asset. Non-business assets taper relief of 25% (for seven years, including extra year) reduces the gain of £16,000 to £12,000, and business assets taper relief of 75% reduces the gain of £4,000 to £1,000. The overall chargeable gain (subject to any available annual exemption) is therefore £13,000.

Your capital gains exemption is not affected if none of your home is *exclusively* used for business purposes. To avoid the anomaly illustrated in example 3, you should try to ensure that the part of the home used for business is also used as your home. Clearly in some circumstances, such as with a doctor's surgery, this may not be possible.

When an expenses claim against employment income has included part of the home expenses (TCGA 1992, s 158(1)(c); SP 5/86)

30.15   If you use your home in connection with your employment, part of your home expenses, such as rent, insurance, heat and light, may be allowed as an expense against your earnings. If you regularly work at home, reasonable payments by your employer to cover additional household expenses are exempt (see 10.11). The allowance of expenses for income tax does not affect your capital gains exemption unless a substantial part of your home is *exclusively* used for the purposes of your employment. Where there is such exclusive use, a 'just and reasonable' proportion of the gain is chargeable. A claim for rollover relief (see 4.26) is then possible where your employer does not make any payment or give other consideration for his use of the property nor otherwise occupy it under a lease or tenancy, thus making it an investment property. Alternatively, any gain might be wholly or partly covered by your annual capital gains tax exemption. Taper relief would be available at the business assets rate providing your employer carries on a trade (but see 30.14 for the taper relief calculation).

Selling to make a profit, including selling off part of the garden

30.16   The capital gains tax exemption for your main residence does not apply if you acquired the property with the intention of reselling at a profit, and if after acquiring a property you incur expenditure wholly or partly to make a gain on sale, an appropriate part of the gain will not be exempt (TCGA 1992, s 224). The Revenue have stated, however, that expenditure to get planning permission does not affect the exemption.

The capital gains exemption covers grounds not exceeding half a hectare (approximately 1¼ acres), or such larger area as is appropriate to the size and character of the house. If you sell some of the land, perhaps for building plots, the sale is covered by the exemption so long as the land was enjoyed as part of the garden and grounds and is sold before the house and immediately surrounding grounds.

In exceptional circumstances, the Revenue may assert that selling part of the garden, or frequent buying and selling of properties (particularly when accompanied by substantial work on them while owned), amounts to a trade, resulting not only in the loss of the capital gains tax exemption but also in the taxation of the profits as trading income.

Death of home owner

30.17   When the home owner dies, the capital gains and inheritance tax aspects need to be considered. There is no capital gains charge on death, but gains may arise during the period of administration. See 42.5 for the capital gains position of the personal representatives and beneficiaries. The treatment of the home for inheritance tax depends on the terms of the will, as amended by any subsequent variation. For inheritance tax planning in relation to the family home see 35.6.

Tax points

30.18

- Since you cannot claim tax relief for interest on home loans, consider whether you could reduce your home loan and instead borrow for other tax allowable purposes on which relief at your top tax rate is available. For allowable interest, see 2.10. See also 20.10.

- If you acquire a second home, consider carefully which is your main residence for council tax purposes and which you wish to treat as your capital gains tax exempt residence, remembering that the last three years of ownership of a house which at some time has been your main residence for capital gains tax can in any event be counted as years of owner-occupation in the capital gains tax calculation.

- Where you have nominated a property as your exempt residence for capital gains tax, you can notify a change to a different property and backdate the election for two years, and then notify a further change back to the original property if you wish. But if you did not make the election within the permitted two year period from the date of acquiring a second home, you lose the right to make it and the question of your main residence will be decided as a matter of fact.

- If you are living in job-related accommodation, be certain to tell the Revenue about the acquisition of a dwelling for your own occupation, thus avoiding any doubt that you regard it as your main residence for capital gains tax.

- When considering the business proportion of mixed premises for the purpose of claiming relief for expenses, bear in mind the possibility of capital gains tax when the premises are sold.

- To qualify for 'rent a room' relief (see 30.7), you need to live in the property at the same time as the tenant for at least part of the relevant tax year. You can then still claim the relief for that tax year even if you have left the property. But if you do not live in the property at all while it is tenanted, rent a room relief is not available.

- If you take in a lodger under the 'rent a room' provisions, make sure you tell your contents insurer. Even so, you will probably be covered for theft only if it is by breaking and entering. You should also check with your mortgage lender that you are not contravening the terms of your loan.

- The maximum £40,000 capital gains tax exemption where the family home has been let (£40,000 each if jointly let by husband and wife) applies where it is wholly let for residential occupation for part of the period of ownership, or partly let for residential occupation at some time during the period of ownership. Because of the residential requirement, it could not exempt a gain that was chargeable because part of the accommodation was used by the family company for trading purposes.

- Where a house has separate buildings to accommodate staff, they may count for the capital gains exemption if they are 'closely adjacent' to the main property, but not if they are so far away that the house and buildings cannot really be regarded as a single dwelling.

- If you undertake a barn conversion for your own occupation, you can reclaim the VAT on the building materials.

- Each of husband and wife has a separate annual capital gains tax exemption and each can use the 20% savings rate on gains to the extent that income does not exceed the basic rate threshold. Joint ownership of a second home might therefore reduce the capital gains tax on an eventual sale.

- If you are selling off part of your garden, make sure it is sold before the house and immediately adjoining land.

- If your house sale falls through and the prospective buyer forfeits his deposit, this is treated in the same way as an abandoned option (see 4.39), so the person who forfeited the deposit cannot claim relief for a capital loss. You are taxable on the amount received, reduced by the annual exemption if available. Neither private residence relief nor taper relief applies.

- If following your death your home is to be sold by the personal representatives, there may be a significant increase in value before the sale takes place, and personal representatives may not qualify for the private residence exemption. See 42.5 for the circumstances in which the private residence exemption is available and other planning points.

- If you have converted part of your home into a self-contained flat for letting, you will be liable to pay up to 90% of the council tax on it if it is untenanted, except for the first six months if it is unfurnished.

- As a bed and breakfast provider you will not pay business rates providing you do not offer accommodation for more than six people, you still live there as well and the property's main use is still as your home, and because of the 'rent a room' relief there will be no income tax to pay if the gross income does not exceed £4,250 in a tax year.

31
A country life: farms and woodlands

Farming and market gardening profits

31.1   The profits of farmers and market gardeners are calculated in the same way as those of other businesses, but because of the particular characteristics of farming, various special rules apply, some of which are mentioned below.

The Revenue published Business Economic Note 19 on farming stock valuations in 1993, and in their May 1993 Tax Bulletin they gave their view of the treatment to be followed if a change in the basis of valuation was to be made. The valuation of cattle bred on the farm can be included at 60% of market value, and likewise that of home-reared sheep and pigs at 75% of market value, but no reduction is permissible for mature bought-in animals.

There are many different grants and subsidies available to farmers. The general tax treatment is that where the amounts are to meet particular costs, they should be set against those costs (and the costs net of such amounts would then be included, where appropriate, in stock valuations). Where they are to subsidise the sale proceeds of a particular crop they should be recognised as income when the crop is sold. Animal grants and subsidies will normally be taken into account either at the end of the retention period or when they are received. Superlevy payments for exceeding milk quota are an allowable expense, but purchases of extra quota to avoid superlevy are capital expenditure. Amounts received for loss of milk or potato quota are treated as income or capital depending on whether they are compensation for loss of profit or of the quota itself. In the event of receipts for loss of milk and potato quotas being treated as capital, rollover relief (see 4.26) is available. Amounts received by sugar beet growers for the sale of all or part of their contract tonnage entitlement are taken into account in calculating trading profits (see the Revenue's Tax Bulletin of October 2001). See 31.16 for the special rules for companies in relation to agricultural quotas from 1 April 2002. Following the reform of the Common Agricultural Policy, the present system of subsidies is to be replaced from 2005 by a single payment scheme. This payment will initially be based largely on historic receipts from the various schemes, and will be gradually changed to a single flat rate over the period to 2012. The Revenue have stated that the extinguishing of an entitlement to receive agricultural subsidies will be a disposal for capital gains tax purposes, and that the disposal of an entitlement to receive a single farm payment will normally also be a chargeable disposal for capital gains tax.

It is common in farming for members of the family to be employed on the farm. As with all businesses, expenses must be 'wholly and exclusively for the purposes of the trade', and there has been a court decision that a farmer's wages to his young children were pocket money and were therefore neither allowable as an expense in calculating farm trading profits nor to be treated as the children's income to enable their personal allowances to be used. The fact that the children were below legal employment age was taken into account, although it was not conclusive.

It is essential that proper professional advice is sought on the agreement of taxation liabilities.

Farming as a single trade (TA 1988, s 53)

31.2 All farming carried on by one farmer is treated as a single trade, so that several holdings are treated as a single business and a move from one farm to another will not be treated as the cessation of one business and the commencement of another. The single trade treatment applies whether the farmer is a sole trader, a partnership or a company.

Loss relief (TA 1988, ss 380–385, 388, 389, 397)

31.3 The usual reliefs for losses in early and later years and on cessation of trading are available to farming businesses and the usual restriction applies to prevent losses being set against other income if the business is not operated on a commercial basis (see CHAPTER 25). In addition, a loss in the sixth tax year of a consecutive run of farming and market gardening losses (calculated before capital allowances) can only be relieved against later profits of the same trade. The same applies to a loss in a company accounting period following a similar five-year run of losses (before capital allowances). The restriction does not apply if a competent farmer or market gardener could not have expected a profit until after the six-year loss period.

If losses are required to be carried forward, any related capital allowances are similarly treated. Once one year shows a profit, another six-year period then applies to later losses.

Averaging (TA 1988, s 96)

31.4 The results of an individual farmer or market gardener or of a farming or market gardening partnership may be averaged over two tax years if the profit of one year is less than 7/10ths of the profit of the other year, with marginal relief if it is more than 7/10ths but less than ¾.

If profits are averaged, the average figure is then used as the result of the second year and it may again be averaged with the result of the third year and so on. Losses are counted as nil profits in the averaging calculation, with relief for the loss being available separately.

Averaging claims are not made by partnerships. The individual partners may make separate claims on their profit shares if they wish.

The time limit for the claim is one year from 31 January following the end of the second tax year, claims being made in the tax return or an amendment to it. Averaging may not be claimed by farming companies nor in relation to any profits charged to tax under Schedule A (see CHAPTER 32).

An averaging claim cannot be made in the first or last tax year of trading.

Averaging enables farmers to lessen the effect of high tax rates on a successful year when preceded or followed by a bad year. The tax and Class 4 national insurance contributions payable under the various alternatives needs to be calculated, taking into account, if appropriate, the possibility of not claiming plant and machinery capital allowances or claiming a reduced amount (in which case the written-down value carried forward to attract writing-down allowances in later years would be increased).

Under self-assessment, the adjustment to the tax and Class 4 contributions of an earlier year resulting from a farmer's averaging claim is *calculated* by reference to the position of the earlier year, but the adjustment is made in relation to the *later* year. If the adjustment is an increase, it is added to the tax and Class 4 contributions payable for the second year. If it is a decrease, it is treated as a payment on account for the second year. If the adjustment and payments on account for the second year exceed the tax and Class 4 contributions due on the averaged profit for the second year, the excess amount will be repaid (or offset if other tax is due or will become due within 35 days). Interest on overpaid or underpaid tax and Class 4 contributions relating to the adjustment for the earlier year, where relevant, runs from 31 January following the later year (see 9.5).

Averaging does not affect the payments on account for the first of the two years that are averaged, which are still based on the previous year's tax and Class 4 contributions, subject to any claim to reduce them to the amount payable on the unaveraged profits. Payments on account for the second year will initially be based on the unaveraged profits of the first year. Once the liability for the second year can be accurately ascertained, based on the averaged profits, a claim can be made to reduce payments on account if appropriate.

The change to the assessable profit of the second year affects the payments on account for the *next following* year. The increase or decrease in the second year's tax and Class 4 contributions as a result of the averaging adjustment for the first year does not, however, enter into the figure for the second year on which payments on account for the next following year are based. See Example 1.

Example 1

Farmer's profits after capital allowances are as follows:

Year ended 31 December		£
2002	Profit	42,000
2003	Loss	(7,000)
2004	Profit	46,000

The farmer is a single man with no other sources of income. The relevant tax rates and allowances are:

	Basic rate threshold £	Personal allowance £	Income limit for higher rate tax £
2002/03	29,900	4,615	34,515
2003/04	30,500	4,615	35,115
2004/05	31,400	4,745	36,145

Class 4 national insurance contributions are payable on profits between:

		Rate	Chargeable at 7%/8%
2002/03	£4,615 to £30,420	7%	£25,805
2003/04	£4,615 to £30,940	8%	£26,325
2004/05	£4,745 to £31,720	8%	£26,975

In addition, from 2003/04, Class 4 contributions are payable at 1% on profits in excess of the upper limit.

Assessable profits may variously be as follows:

	No averaging £	Averaging 2002/03 and 2003/04 only £	All three years averaged £
2002/03	42,000	21,000	21,000
2003/04	—*	21,000*	33,500*
2004/05	46,000	46,000	33,500

* Loss of £7,000 available for relief

The loss of the year to 31 December 2003 is treated as a loss of 2003/04, for which relief may be claimed under TA 1988, s 380 in 2003/04 or 2002/03. Alternatively it may be carried forward under TA 1988, s 385 and set off in 2004/05. (Losses are dealt with in CHAPTER 25.)

With no averaging, but claiming relief for the loss of £7,000 in 2002/03 to save higher rate tax in that year, higher rate tax would be payable on £485 in 2002/03 and £9,855 in 2004/05, and the personal allowance and starting rate band of 2003/04 would be wasted.

If 2002/03 and 2003/04 are averaged, and the loss is carried forward to 2004/05, reducing the taxable profit of that year to £39,000, the 2003/04 personal allowance would be utilised, and the higher rate tax of 2002/03 would be eliminated, but higher rate tax would still be payable on £2,855 in 2004/05. The 2003/04 averaged figure of £21,000 would be used to calculate the payments on account for 2004/05.

If all three years are averaged, and loss relief is claimed in 2003/04, no higher rate tax would be payable in any year. Following the first claim, the total tax and Class 4 contributions payable in respect of 2003/04 can be ascertained, comprising a reduction in tax payable for 2002/03 and increase for 2003/04. A claim can then be made to reduce the 2003/04 payments on account (which were originally based on the £42,000 profit for 2002/03) to the amount payable on the averaged 2003/04 figure of £21,000 less the reduction for 2002/03. The 2003/04 averaged figure of £21,000 would be used in arriving at payments on account for 2004/05. This would not alter following the second claim, the increase in tax payable for 2003/04 being treated as extra tax due for 2004/05. This extra tax would not, however, be taken into account in calculating payments on account for 2005/06, which would be based on the 2004/05 averaged figure of £33,500.

The third alternative eliminates all higher rate tax and utilises the personal allowance and starting rate band of 2003/04. On the other hand, because of moving profits into 2003/04, it gives a much higher Class 4 national insurance liability, offset by a reduction of £12,500 (£46,000 – £33,500) in the amount charged at the 1% rate in 2004/05. The overall increase in Class 4 national insurance contributions with the third alternative is outweighed by the tax saving. The third alternative reduces the overall liability significantly.

A slightly greater overall saving could be made by setting the loss against the 2004/05 profit instead of 2003/04. This would also result in a £7,000 reduction in the income on which the 2005/06 payments on account were calculated.

Herd basis (TA 1988, s 97 and Sch 5)

31.5   Farm animals and other livestock are normally treated as trading stock. A production herd may, however, effectively be treated as a capital asset if an election is made for the herd basis. The election is irrevocable. In addition to being available to individuals, companies and partnerships the herd basis is available where animals are held on a shared basis, for instance in share farming.

For companies, the time limit for making the election is two years from the end of the first accounting period in which the herd is kept.

The time limit for individuals and partnerships is one year from the 31 January following the tax year in which the accounting period in which the herd is first kept ends (unless it ends in the first tax year of trading, in which case the time limit for individuals but not partnerships is extended by one year). See Example 2.

Example 2

A production herd is acquired in May 2004 by an established business that makes up its accounts to 31 December.

The time limit for the claim is 31 December 2006 for a company and 31 January 2007 for individuals and partners.

The limit would remain the same if the year to 31 December 2004 was the first year of business for a sole trader, because the account ends in the second tax year. If accounts had been made up to 5 April and the year to 5 April 2005 had been the first accounting year of a sole trader, then the relevant account would end in the first tax year, i.e. 2004/05, and the time limit would relate to the following year, i.e. 2005/06, so that it would be 31 January 2008.

A change in the partners in a farming partnership requires a new herd basis election to be made even where the farming business has owned the herd for several years. There are, however, anti-avoidance provisions to prevent the change being used solely or mainly for the purposes of obtaining a benefit resulting from the right to make a herd basis election or flowing from the election. A herd basis election is not affected when a partnership becomes a limited liability partnership.

Under self-assessment, partnerships make a single election for the herd basis, even though partners are assessed separately. The Revenue have stated that they will not require farmers to make a separate written election where it is clear from material submitted that the herd basis has been applied.

A production herd is a group of living animals or other livestock kept for obtaining products such as milk, wool, etc. or their young.

The effect of the election is that the initial purchase of the herd and any subsequent purchases that increase the herd attract no tax relief, but a renewals basis applies where animals are replaced, so that the cost of the replacement is charged as an expense and the sale proceeds are brought in as a trading receipt. Where there is a minor disposal without replacement ('minor' being defined by the Revenue as less than 20% of the herd), profits on the disposal are also brought in as a trading receipt. See the Revenue's Tax Bulletin of April 2003 for their revised view on how the cost of the animals disposed of is arrived at. If the whole or a substantial part of the herd is sold and not replaced, no part of the proceeds is charged as income, because it represents the sale of a capital asset, and capital gains tax does not arise since the animals are wasting assets on which capital allowances are not available and are therefore exempt (see 4.7).

Compensation for compulsory slaughter

31.6   By Revenue concession B11, where compensation is paid for compulsorily slaughtered stock to which the herd basis does not apply, the compensation may be left out of account in the year of receipt and brought in over the next three years in equal instalments.

Farm plant and machinery

31.7   Capital allowances on farm plant and machinery are available in the usual way (see CHAPTER 22). Expenditure should be carefully analysed to make sure that plant and machinery is properly treated as such rather than being treated as part of an agricultural building.

Agricultural buildings allowances (TA 1988, s 379A; CAA 2001, ss 361–393, 570A)

31.8   The owners or tenants of agricultural land may claim agricultural buildings allowances in respect of expenditure incurred by them on the construction of buildings such as farmhouses, farm buildings and cottages, fences and roads, and on the installation of services. In relation to farm-houses, not more than one third of the cost may be included (see 31.14). Any grants received are deducted from the allowable cost. Farm shops count as agricultural buildings, but the allowable expenditure is restricted if the shops also sell bought-in items.

Expenditure is relieved by writing-down allowances at 4% per annum over 25 years. The allowances for sole traders and farming partnerships commence in the accounting period in which the expenditure is incurred. For non-trading agricultural landlords they commence in the tax year in which the expenditure is incurred. For both trading and non-trading companies the allowances commence in the accounting period in which the expenditure is incurred. For companies the allowance is proportionately reduced if the accounting period is less than twelve months. For unincorporated businesses the allowance is proportionately reduced or increased according to the length of the period of account (see 22.3 and 22.4).

Writing-down allowances may be reduced to whatever amount the claimant wishes. The final writing-down allowance at the end of the 25 years is, however, calculated as if all allowances had been taken in full. Claiming a reduced allowance may enable additional allowances to be claimed later where an initial allowance has been taken (see below). Otherwise there would only be a benefit if there was a subsequent balancing adjustment during the writing-down period (allowances then being recalculated on the full amount of the unrelieved expenditure), but such an adjustment is unlikely (see below).

A special 20% initial allowance was available for expenditure under a contract entered into between 1 November 1992 and 31 October 1993, providing the buildings or works were brought into use before 1 January 1995. The taxpayer could claim less than the full initial allowance if he wished. The first writing-down allowance was not given in the same period as the initial allowance unless the buildings or works were brought into use by the end of that period. Unless there is a sale on which a balancing adjustment is made (see below), the 25-year writing-down period will be shortened according to how much of the initial allowance was claimed (subject to any reduction of writing-down allowances claims as indicated above).

A balancing allowance or charge may be made when agricultural buildings or works are disposed of, demolished or cease to exist, but only if an election to that effect is made by the former and new owners, if there is a disposal, or by the owner, if there is no disposal. The purchaser then gets allowances for the remainder of the 25-year period, normally on what he pays or on what the first user paid, whichever is lower. The time limit for making the election for companies is two years after the end of the relevant accounting period, and for individuals one year from the 31 January following the end of the relevant tax year.

The joint election for the balancing adjustment will not usually be made, because it will be to the advantage of one of the parties at the expense of the other.

In the unlikely event that an election is made, anti-avoidance provisions apply where a balancing allowance arises on or after 27 November 2002. Where the sale price has been artificially depressed as a result of a tax avoidance scheme, the seller is not entitled to a balancing allowance, but the buyer's allowances are calculated as if the balancing allowance had been made.

If the election is not made, the seller gets a final writing-down allowance which is proportionate to the length of the part of his basis period up to the date of sale, and the buyer gets the remaining allowances, with his first writing-down allowance depending on the part of his basis period that occurs after the date of sale.

If a farming tenant vacates his holding and does not receive any consideration for his unrelieved agricultural buildings expenditure from the incoming tenant, the landlord is entitled to relief for the balance over the remaining writing-down period.

In the case of a farming trade, the allowances are given in calculating the trading profits and may therefore increase or create a loss, for which the usual loss reliefs are available (see CHAPTERS 25 and 26).

For agricultural landlords, the allowances are treated as expenses of a 'Schedule A business' and the rules of Schedule A determine how losses may be relieved (see 31.11).

Where a building is sold for more than cost, the full cost is taken into account in the capital gains computation, despite any allowances that have been given against income. Where a building is sold for less than cost, there is no allowable loss for capital gains purposes, because the full value is allowed through the capital allowances system.

VAT

31.9   For VAT purposes, most of a farm's outputs are zero-rated, but there may also be standard-rated outputs, such as sales of equipment, shooting rights, holiday accommodation, and exempt outputs such as rents for residential caravan sites, possibly leading to partial exemption restrictions. Some farming subsidies and grants, such as set-aside, are outside the scope of VAT. The usual input tax restrictions for entertaining, private use, etc. apply (see CHAPTER 7). For the treatment of land and buildings and of the farmhouse, see 31.12 and 31.14.

If milk quota is sold separately from land, it is standard-rated. If the sale is linked to a supply of land the VAT liability is the same as the liability for the land.

Flat-rate farmers (VATA 1994, s 54; SI 1992/3221; SI 1995/2518, regs 202–211)

31.10   Farmers may opt to become 'flat-rate farmers' for VAT purposes, regardless of their turnover, providing they satisfy Customs that the total flat-rate compensation they will be entitled to in the year after they join the scheme will not exceed the input tax they could have claimed by £3,000 or more. They do not need to register for VAT and therefore make no VAT returns, but they add a fixed flat-rate compensation percentage of 4% to their sale prices when they sell to VAT registered businesses, which they keep to offset the input tax they have suffered. The registered businesses are able to reclaim on their VAT returns the compensation amount charged to them. Farmers below the registration threshold need not become flat-rate farmers unless they wish to.

Agricultural landlords (TA 1988, ss 53, 379A, 392A; CAA 2001, ss 361–393)

31.11   Income from letting agricultural land is taxed in the same way as for any investment property (see CHAPTER 32).

For individuals, all rental income is charged as the profits of a 'Schedule A business'. If expenses exceed income, the landlord may claim to set the loss off against his total income of the same tax year and/or the following tax year, to the extent that the loss consists of capital allowances (see 31.7 and 31.8) and/or maintenance, repairs, insurance or management expenses (but not loan interest) relating to agricultural land that is managed as one estate. Any part of the loss remaining unrelieved is carried forward to set against later rental income.

Companies are subject to broadly the same 'Schedule A business' rules as individuals. The treatment of losses, however, is not the same. Companies may set Schedule A losses against their total profits of the same accounting period, or alternatively surrender the losses by way of group relief, any unrelieved balance being carried forward to set against the *total* profits of succeeding periods. For further details see CHAPTER 32.

The occupation of land for farming purposes (such as growing crops and raising farm livestock) is treated as a trade. This will apply where an owner receives income from short-term grazing lets, providing the owner's activities in growing the grass, fertilising, etc., and general upkeep and maintenance of the land, can be regarded as farming. In that event, the land will qualify as a business asset on which rollover relief for capital gains tax is available if it is sold and the proceeds reinvested in a qualifying replacement asset within one year before and three years after the sale (see 4.26).

Although gifts relief for capital gains tax normally applies only to business assets or to gifts that are immediately chargeable to inheritance tax (see 4.27 to 4.30), it applies to agricultural property held as an investment providing the conditions for inheritance tax agricultural property relief are satisfied (see 5.19).

Value added tax (VATA 1994, Sch 8 Group 5, Sch 9 Group 1 and Sch 10)

31.12   Grants of long or short leases of agricultural land and buildings, and rents received therefrom, are exempt from VAT, but the landlord has the option to charge VAT. Written notice must be given to Customs within 30 days. VAT is then charged from the day the landlord exercises his option, or any later date he specifies. (If the landlord is not already VAT registered, he will have to become registered to take this option.) If the option is taken, it can be revoked within three months from the time it takes effect, or twenty or more years after it takes effect. Where a landlord has interests in several different estates, an election can be made for specific discrete areas (such as one farm). The landlord may increase existing rents by the VAT charged if the lease allows VAT to be added or is silent as to VAT. If not, the rent has to be treated as VAT-inclusive.

Following the exercise of the option, VAT must be charged not only on rents and lease premiums, but also on any sale proceeds as and when any of the land and buildings are sold (subject to what is said in 32.23). An apportionment will be made in each case, however, to exclude any private dwelling/charitable element. Making the election enables the landlord to recover any VAT he suffers, for example on the acquisition of the property, or on repairs, and the farmer tenants will usually be VAT registered and will therefore be able to recover the VAT charged.

Small agricultural holdings

31.13 The profits of a commercial smallholding are taxed as trading profits, but if losses arise, the Revenue may contend that the trade is not conducted on a commercial basis with a view to profit, so that the losses may only be carried forward against future income from the smallholding and not set against any other income. This is quite separate from their right to disallow farming losses from the sixth year onwards (see 31.3).

The smallholder may seek voluntary VAT registration even though his taxable supplies are less than £58,000 p.a., because he will then be able to reclaim input tax on his expenditure and he will have no liability on his supplies, which are zero-rated. Customs are required to register anyone making taxable supplies who seeks voluntary registration. The smallholder may alternatively join the flat-rate scheme (see 31.10).

The farmhouse (TCGA 1992, ss 222–224; IHTA 1984, s 115(2))

31.14 The restriction for agricultural buildings allowances of the qualifying capital expenditure on a farmhouse to a maximum of one-third recognises that the domestic and business activities overlap. In arriving at the farm profits, an appropriate part of the establishment charges of the farmhouse is allowed, based on the extent to which the farmhouse is used for business.

Customs adopt a similar approach in relation to the recovery of input VAT on farmhouse expenses such as light and heat. They will, however, allow a sole proprietor or partner working full-time to recover 70% of the input VAT on repair and maintenance costs. Where farming is not a full-time business, the allowable percentage will need to be agreed with Customs.

The business expenses deduction will not jeopardise the capital gains tax private residence exemption (see CHAPTER 30) provided that no part of the farmhouse has been used exclusively for business purposes. Where part is so used and a chargeable gain arises, rollover relief may be claimed if the farmhouse is replaced (see 4.26). Where rollover relief does not apply, the chargeable gain will be reduced by taper relief at the business assets rate. The capital gains tax exemption usually extends to grounds up to half a hectare, but for a farmhouse a larger area may be allowed because of the situation and character of the farmhouse and immediately surrounding grounds. The capital gains tax exemptions and reliefs are dealt with in CHAPTER 4.

Agricultural property relief for inheritance tax is available on the farmhouse providing the owner also owns the agricultural land, the farmhouse is 'of a character appropriate to the property', and occupation of the farmhouse is ancillary to that of the agricultural land. These conditions are often considered by the Revenue not to be satisfied. In two recent cases before the Special

Commissioners, one (SpC337) went against the personal representatives and the other (SpC336) was decided in the personal representatives' favour. Where there is part business use of the farmhouse, for example for bed and breakfast, business property relief will apply on the business proportion.

Land let by partners to farming partnership, or by directors to farming company (TCGA 1992, ss 152–158, 164 and Sch 6)

31.15   Where land is owned personally by a partner or director, and let to the farming business, any rent paid is allowed as an expense of the business and treated as unearned income in the partner's or director's hands. If interest is paid on a loan to buy the land, it may be deducted from the rent (or any other rent) so long as the letting is on a commercial basis (see CHAPTER 32 for the detailed treatment of let property). The charging of a commercial rent will not prevent business assets taper relief applying on disposal of the land if the other conditions are met (see 4.17).

Capital gains tax rollover relief may sometimes be claimed if the land is disposed of and the proceeds used to acquire a qualifying asset within one year before and three years after the sale. Charging rent as indicated above does not affect this relief. See 4.26.

Capital gains tax (TCGA 1992, ss 152(4), 155)

31.16   Various capital gains tax aspects are dealt with elsewhere in this chapter. As far as rollover relief for replacement of business assets is concerned, some categories of qualifying asset specifically relate to farming, namely milk quota and ewe and suckler cow premium quotas (see 4.26). For companies, agricultural quotas acquired on or after 1 April 2002 come within the intangible assets provisions and are dealt with in calculating income rather than under the capital gains rules. There are transitional provisions in relation to capital gains rollover relief where quota is disposed of on or after 1 April 2002 but a replacement asset was acquired before that date. See 20.21 for the detailed provisions. The following provisions now apply only for individuals.

Quota is treated as a separate asset from land, and where nothing was paid for the quota there is no allowable cost to set against the gain on disposal. The Revenue regard quotas as being non-depreciating assets for rollover relief. Where quota and land is transferred in a single transaction, values have to be apportioned on a just and reasonable basis. See also 31.1.

Where a tenant receives statutory compensation following a notice to quit, or for improvements at the end of the tenancy, the compensation is not liable to capital gains tax.

Farming companies are not qualifying companies for enterprise investment scheme relief (see CHAPTER 29).

Inheritance tax (IHTA 1984, ss 115–124C)

31.17 When agricultural property is transferred, inheritance tax agricultural property relief is given on the agricultural value, and where the property is also business property, business property relief is given on the non-agricultural value. The detailed rules for each relief are in CHAPTER 5. Farmland dedicated to wildlife habitats under Government Habitat Schemes qualifies as agricultural property.

The rate of relief for some tenanted agricultural property used to be 50%, as against 100% for owner-occupied land, but relief at the 100% rate is now available for all qualifying tenanted property where the letting commenced on or after 1 September 1995, including successions to tenancies following the death of the previous tenant on or after that date (see 5.19). The grant of the tenancy itself is specifically exempt from inheritance tax so long as it is made for full consideration. Although tenanted property normally has to be owned for seven years to qualify for agricultural property relief (see 5.19), the period is only two years where the tenant is a partnership in which the donor is a partner or a company controlled by the donor.

The relief applies to lifetime transfers which are not potentially exempt, or which, having been so, become chargeable because the donor dies within seven years, and to transfers on death. The relief is only available in calculating the tax or additional tax payable as a result of the donor's death within seven years if the donee still owns the property (or qualifying replacement property) when the donor dies, or if earlier, when the donee dies.

Where relief at the time of the transfer is at 100%, there will be neither a chargeable transfer nor a potentially exempt transfer at that time, but the transfer will be counted at death if the donor does not survive the seven-year period. Where relief is at the 50% rate, and two years' annual exemptions are available (see 5.3), a combination of the 50% relief and the annual exemptions totalling £6,000 will exempt £12,000 of the transfer.

The 100% rate of agricultural property relief discourages lifetime gifts, because a lifetime gift will attract capital gains tax (although payment can be deferred by claiming gifts relief), whereas on death there is a capital gains tax-free uplift in asset values. There is, of course, no certainty that the present favourable regime will continue.

Stamp duty

31.18   From 1 December 2003 stamp duty land tax is payable on the sale of farm land and buildings. It is not usually payable on a gift, but if say mortgaged farmland was transferred from a farmer to a family farming partnership, or from one family partnership to another, and the transferee took over liability for the mortgage, the amount of the mortgage would be subject to stamp duty land tax unless it fell within the zero rate band.

Woodlands and short rotation coppice

31.19   The tax treatment of woodlands is dealt with below. Short rotation coppice is treated as farming, rather than under the woodlands provisions (see 31.24).

Income tax

31.20   There is no income tax charge on woodlands, so relief for losses incurred and interest paid in the initial planting period cannot be claimed, but as and when profits arise they are not taxed.

Capital gains tax (TCGA 1992, ss 158, 250)

31.21   There is no charge to capital gains tax on trees that are standing or felled. Proceeds of sale of timber are therefore not charged to tax at all. The land is, however, a chargeable asset for capital gains purposes. It is therefore important on acquisition and disposal to establish the different values applicable to the timber and the land.

For commercially run woodlands, gains on sale of the land may be deferred by rolling them over against the cost of replacement assets where the land sale proceeds are reinvested in qualifying business assets within one year before and three years after the sale (see 4.26). If a gain is made on a disposal by way of gift, it will not qualify for gifts relief (see 4.27) unless the woodlands operation is a trade. The same applies in respect of the business assets rate of taper relief.

Where woodlands are owned by a company, the land is a qualifying asset for rollover relief as far as the company is concerned, but an individual will not get rollover relief when he sells his shares and reinvests the proceeds (unless he qualifies for enterprise investment scheme relief — see 29.3). He will not be entitled to gifts relief in respect of the shares unless the company is a trading company and the other conditions for relief are satisfied (see 4.27 and

4.31). Providing the company is a trading company, the business assets rate of taper relief will normally be available on any chargeable gain (see 4.17).

Value added tax (VATA 1994, Sch 1 para 9)

31.22   A commercially run woodland is within the scope of VAT, the supply or granting of any right to fell and remove standing timber being standard-rated. It is possible to register for VAT before making taxable supplies, the intention to make taxable supplies being sufficient for registration purposes even though they will not be made for some years. Having registered, you can recover input tax on goods and services in connection with the woodlands operation.

Inheritance tax (IHTA 1984, ss 125–130)

31.23   Where an estate on death includes growing timber, an election may be made to leave the timber (but not the land on which it stands) out of account in valuing the estate at death. The election must be made within two years after the date of death and is only available if the deceased either had been beneficially entitled to the land throughout the previous five years or had become entitled to it without consideration (for example by gift or inheritance). (Commercially managed woodlands will usually qualify for 100% business property relief, in which case the election would not be made — see below.)

The election may not be made if the occupation of the woodlands is subsidiary to the occupation of agricultural land, but agricultural property relief would be given if the necessary conditions were fulfilled.

Following the election, when the timber is later disposed of by sale or gift, there will be a charge to inheritance tax on the sale price or, if the disposal is for less than full consideration, the market value, less allowable expenses in both cases. Allowable expenses are the costs of sale and expenses of replanting within three years after disposal, or such longer time as the Revenue allow.

The net disposal proceeds or market value are treated as value transferred at the date of death, forming the top slice of the property passing on death, but using the scale and rates current at the time of disposal to find a notional liability on the estate first excluding and then including the timber proceeds, the tax on the timber proceeds being the difference between the two. The tax is due six months after the end of the month in which the disposal takes place, with interest on overdue tax payable from that date. The person entitled to the sale proceeds is liable for the tax. Where there are no proceeds because the disposal is by way of gift, the donee is liable for the tax, which may be paid by instalments over ten years.

A lifetime gift of woodlands not qualifying for business property relief either attracts inheritance tax or is a potentially exempt transfer (see CHAPTER 5). Where the disposal is one on which tax is payable following its being left out of account on an earlier death, the value transferred by the lifetime transfer is reduced by the tax charge arising out of the previous death.

If the person who inherits woodlands on which an election has been made dies before the timber is disposed of, no inheritance tax charge can arise in respect of the first death. Furthermore, a new election may then be made on the second death.

Where woodlands are managed on a commercial basis, despite there being no income tax charge, they qualify for 100% business property relief so long as they have been owned for two years (see CHAPTER 5). Where tax is payable, it may be paid by instalments in the case of a death transfer where the value has not been left out of account and where, exceptionally, a lifetime transfer is not potentially exempt. If an election is made to leave the timber out of account on a death, business property relief is given on the net sale proceeds when it is disposed of, but only at 50% rather than 100%. This will be relevant where the election has already been made, but clearly no new elections will be made where the 100% business property relief is available.

Short rotation coppice (FA 1995, s 154)

31.24   Short rotation coppice, which is a way of producing a renewable fuel for 'green' biomass-fed power stations from willow or poplar cuttings, is regarded as farming for income tax, corporation tax and capital gains tax, and as agricultural land for inheritance tax.

The Revenue consider that the initial cultivation costs of the short rotation coppice are capital expenditure, the net amount of which (after deducting any Woodland Grants offset against the expenditure) may be used to roll over gains on disposals of other business assets. The expenditure (net of both Woodland Grants and any rolled over gains) will be allowable in calculating gains when the land is disposed of, providing the coppice stools are still on the land at that time.

Subsequent expenditure after the initial cultivation will be revenue expenditure. Set-aside receipts are treated as normal farming income (see 31.1), rather than being regarded as income from the coppice.

Council tax and business rates

31.25   Agricultural land and buildings are exempt from business rates. Any buildings or parts of buildings that are for domestic rather than agricultural use attract up to 90% of the council tax if the building or part is no-one's only or main home. If it is someone's only or main home, the residents are liable to pay the council tax. The valuation takes into account the restricted market for the property because of the agricultural use. In Scotland only, unoccupied, unfurnished property previously used in connection with agricultural land or woodlands, etc. is exempt from council tax.

Where farms diversify into non-agricultural activities, business rates are payable, but for property with rateable values up to £6,000, mandatory rate relief of 50% has been introduced (initially for a five-year period from 2001) providing the property was in agricultural use for at least half of the previous year. Councils have the power to increase the relief to 100%.

In small rural communities, post offices and/or village food shops (other than confectionery shops or catering businesses) with rateable values up to £6,000, sole pubs or petrol stations with rateable values up to £9,000, and farm shops etc. on what was previously agricultural land and buildings are entitled to 50% mandatory business rates relief. Councils have the power to increase the relief to 100%, and may also grant relief to other rural businesses important to the community that have rateable values up to £12,000.

Tax points

31.26

- If you have a smallholding which is likely to show consistent losses, you are unlikely to be able to relieve them against other income, and treating the smallholding as a trade may prejudice your capital gains tax private residence exemption. It may be preferable to make a yearly note in your tax return that the working of the holding is not by way of trade but only for the maintenance of the holding and that no profits arise.

- Where a smallholding or market garden is clearly a trade, make sure if possible that no part of the dwelling house is used exclusively for business, to avoid any possible loss of the private residence capital gains exemption.

- If you are making losses and are in danger of falling foul of the six-year rule, see if you can show a small profit in one year, perhaps by delaying repairs or other expenses. The six-year cycle will then start again.

- When buying a holding with agricultural buildings, remember that what you pay for them does not necessarily entitle you to any capital allowances. You cannot get allowances on any more than that part of the original building expenditure for which relief has not yet been given.

- If you are an individual agricultural landlord and have incurred expenditure on agricultural buildings, you may make a claim to set the available allowances against any income to the extent that your total rental income is insufficient. Relief can be given in the tax year itself or the following year. Company landlords may claim to set rental losses (which will include allowances not covered by rental income) against their total profits, including capital gains, of the same accounting period and then succeeding accounting periods.

- Owning agricultural land personally and renting it to your partnership or company will not stop you getting capital gains tax rollover relief (see 4.26) if the land is sold and replaced. Rollover relief is not available to other agricultural landlords.

- Gifts relief *is* available to agricultural landlords if the conditions are satisfied (see 4.27).

- A farmer's averaging claim affects income for two or more years, but the claim has no effect on the dates on which tax is due for payment (see 31.4). Note that the claim affects the permissible levels of personal pension contributions for the years concerned, although you may presently pay contributions for five years based on the earnings of an earlier nominated 'basis year' (see 17.9).

- If you transfer ownership of your farm to the family, but still live in the farmhouse, the farmhouse will not qualify for inheritance tax agricultural property relief. You need to be a partner, with a share, albeit small, in the farm, to remain entitled to the relief.

- There are a number of specialist organisations ready to advise on an investment in woodlands, not only from the taxation point of view but also on the question of cash grants through the Forestry Commission, and on estate management.

32
Investing in land and buildings

Introduction

32.1 This chapter deals with both commercial and private investment properties in the UK. The detailed treatment of let agricultural buildings is covered in CHAPTER 31. The tax advantages of investing in enterprise zone buildings and the special provisions relating to the grant of a lease on an enterprise zone building are dealt with in CHAPTER 22. The treatment of UK property let by those who live abroad and of property abroad let by UK residents is dealt with in CHAPTER 41. Companies may claim relief equal to 150% of qualifying expenditure on cleaning up contaminated land that has been acquired for the purposes of a trade or Schedule A letting business (see 20.22). For anti-avoidance provisions in respect of rent factoring schemes see 45.23.

Income from land and buildings

32.2 Income from UK land and buildings is usually charged to tax as investment income, except for income from furnished holiday lettings, which is treated as trading income (see 32.17). The distinction between trading income and investment income is important to individuals in relation to relief for contributions to provide themselves with a pension, although both earners and non-earners may get tax relief on personal pension contributions up to £3,600 a year, and in addition a 'basis year' may presently be nominated following which contributions may be paid for five years based on the earnings of that basis year, regardless of the earnings of the year of payment — see 17.9. The distinction is also important for capital gains purposes because an investment property does not qualify for the business assets rates of taper relief (see 4.17), nor for rollover relief (see 4.26) when it is replaced (unless it is compulsorily purchased — see 32.18), and gifts relief (see 4.27) will not usually be available either. As far as inheritance tax is concerned, business property relief is not available where the business consists of making or holding investments, which includes land which is let (see 5.19). The relief has been denied in cases before the Special Commissioners even where the owners played a very active role in the letting, management and maintenance of their properties, and one decision by the Special

Commissioners in favour of the taxpayer in a case concerning a caravan site was overruled in the High Court (but see 32.17 re furnished holiday lettings). Agricultural property relief is available to landlords of let agricultural property (see 31.17).

Income tax on rents is usually paid as part of the half-yearly payments on account on 31 January in the tax year and 31 July following, with a balancing adjustment on the next 31 January. Companies pay corporation tax on all their profits under self-assessment, the due date normally being nine months after the end of the accounting period, except for certain large companies who are required to pay their tax by instalments (see 3.18).

The tax treatment of individuals is dealt with from 32.3 to 32.8 and that of companies at 32.9 and 32.10. The capital allowances provisions for both individuals and companies are dealt with at 32.11 to 32.13. The treatment of furnished holiday lettings, which applies both to individuals and companies, is dealt with at 32.17. The treatment of lease premiums, where the treatment is again broadly the same for individuals and companies, is dealt with at 32.14 to 32.16.

Tax treatment of individuals (TA 1988, ss 15, 21, 21A; CAA 2001, ss 15, 16, 35)

32.3   Special rules apply where you let furnished rooms in your own home, and in some circumstances the letting may amount to a trade. This is dealt with in 30.7 to 30.9. Profits from the provision of accommodation in hotels or guest houses are wholly trading income and are not within Schedule A. With these exceptions, all income from UK property (including the right to use a fixed caravan or permanently moored houseboat) is treated as the profits of a 'Schedule A business', whether there is just one letting or a number of lettings, whether the property is let furnished or unfurnished, and no matter whether repairs are the responsibility of the landlord or the tenant (although income from qualifying furnished holiday lettings is kept separate and the provisions outlined at 32.17 apply).

Calculation of Schedule A profits

32.4   The income charged to tax is that of the tax year from 6 April to 5 April. (Different rules apply to partnerships — see 23.4.) Although the income is investment income, the general accounting rules for working out trading profits apply. Allowable expenses are broadly those that are of a revenue rather than a capital nature and are wholly and exclusively for the purpose of the lettings, so that appropriate adjustments must be made where there is part private use of the let property.

Allowable expenses include business rates or council tax if appropriate (see 32.26), rent payable to a superior landlord, insurance and management expenses, including advertising for tenants, and maintenance, repairs and redecorations (but excluding repairs to newly acquired property that were necessary before the property could be brought into use, which form part of the capital cost of the property). Improvement expenditure on, for example, building extensions or installing central heating or double glazing, is not allowable in calculating income, although it is counted as part of the cost for capital gains purposes. Interest payable, including interest payable to a non-resident lender, is allowed in calculating profits, subject to the 'wholly and exclusively' rule. See 32.18 for the treatment of a payment for dilapidations by an outgoing tenant.

In calculating the taxable rent, adjustments are made for rent and expenses in arrear or in advance. (Where total gross rents do not exceed £15,000 a year, the Revenue will accept computations on the basis of amounts received and paid, with no adjustments for amounts in arrear or in advance, providing the cash basis is used consistently and does not give a materially different result from the statutory method.)

Where capital allowances are available, they are calculated in the same way as for trades and are deducted as an expense (see 32.11).

Where your gross rents are below £15,000 a year, you need only include total figures of rent, expenses and net income on your tax return — see 9.17.

Landlord's Energy Saving Allowance (FA 2004, s 143)

32.5 Landlords who incur capital expenditure between 6 April 2004 and 5 April 2009 inclusive to install loft insulation and/or cavity wall insulation in residential property may claim an income tax deduction for the expenditure of up to £1,500 per property in computing their rental income. For new Schedule A businesses, the deduction is available for expenditure incurred up to six months before the business commenced (but not before 6 April 2004). The deduction is not available where the property is let under the rent-a-room scheme (see 30.7) or as furnished holiday accommodation (see 32.17).

Treatment of losses (TA 1988, s 379A)

32.6 If losses arise, they are normally carried forward to set against later rental income. Relief is, however, available against other income of the same and/or the following tax year in respect of excess capital allowances (see 22.7) and certain agricultural expenses (see 31.11).

Interest paid by those in job-related accommodation or working away from home

32.7   Special rules apply to interest paid by someone who lets their home while they live in job-related accommodation (see 30.12) or while they are working away (see 30.5).

National insurance contributions

32.8   Property letting will rarely be regarded as self-employment for national insurance purposes, although if the extent of the landlord's involvement in managing the lettings and looking after the properties is substantial (which might be particularly relevant for furnished holiday lettings — see 32.17), it is possible that the activities will constitute a business, in which case Class 2 national insurance contributions will be payable (see 24.2). Class 4 contributions are only payable where income is taxed as trading income under Schedule D, Case I. Even though rents are now *treated* as being from a business for Schedule A income tax, this is not the same as saying that a business actually exists, and it does not alter the national insurance position.

Tax treatment of companies (TA 1988, ss 15, 21–21C and 392A)

32.9   All rental income of companies is treated as the profits of a 'Schedule A business' in the same way as for individuals, except as indicated below. See 32.18 for the treatment of a payment for dilapidations by an outgoing tenant Interest paid by a company is dealt with under the 'loan relationships' rules (see 32.10). Capital allowances are deducted as expenses in arriving at the rental profit or loss as for income tax (see 32.11). If a loss arises, then providing the business is carried on on a commercial basis, the loss may be set against the total profits of the same accounting period, or surrendered by way of group relief (see 26.13), any unrelieved balance being carried forward to set against future *total* profits.

Relief for interest

32.10   Interest on company borrowings is dealt with under the 'loan relationships' rules outlined at 3.6. Interest relating to furnished holiday lettings (see 32.17) is deducted from the income from those lettings, since expenses may be deducted as if such lettings were a trade. All other interest relating to let property is taken into account in arriving at the overall non-trading surplus or deficit on loans. If there is a deficit, relief is available as indicated at 26.5.

Capital allowances (CAA 2001, ss 15, 16, 35, 172–204, 219; FA 1997, s 82 and Sch 12)

32.11 The capital allowances available on let agricultural buildings are dealt with in CHAPTER 31, and CHAPTER 22 deals with allowances on industrial buildings, hotels and buildings in enterprise zones.

As far as plant and machinery is concerned, capital allowances are not available on plant and machinery let for use in a dwelling house, except for furnished holiday lettings (see 32.17), and subject to the exception outlined at 22.23. For buildings other than dwellings, allowances are available not only on plant and machinery in the let buildings but also on plant and machinery for the maintenance, repair or management of premises. The allowances are calculated in the same way as for trades — see CHAPTER 22. With regard to expenditure on fixtures, the expenditure may be incurred either by the landlord or by the tenant, or the items may be leased from an equipment lessor. There are special provisions to deal with the various possibilities (see 22.23). See also the provisions at 22.2 relating to finance leases and at 22.21 relating to long-life plant and machinery. Although there is no relief for plant and machinery in dwelling houses as indicated above, relief for wear and tear of furniture etc. may be claimed under Revenue concession B47, either on a renewals basis (so that nothing is allowed when furniture, etc. is first bought, but as and when any item is replaced the full cost of the renewal is allowed), or more usually by way of a wear and tear allowance of 10% of rents. Any additions to rent for council tax, water charges and other sums for services which would normally be borne by a tenant are deducted, if material, before calculating the 10% relief. Where the 10% allowance is claimed, no further deduction is allowed for renewing furniture and furnishings, such as suites, beds, carpets, curtains, linen, crockery or cutlery, nor for items such as cookers, washing machines or dishwashers. But an additional deduction may be claimed for renewing fixtures such as baths, washbasins and toilets. To qualify for the concession, the property must be sufficiently furnished to enable it to be occupied without the tenant necessarily having to buy any furniture of his own.

Capital allowances are deducted as a trading expense and are thus taken into account in arriving at the Schedule A profit or loss. See 22.7 for the relief available to individuals for excess allowances. No separate relief for excess allowances is available to companies (see 32.9).

Conversion of parts of business premises into flats (CAA 2001, ss 393A–393W)

32.12 Capital allowances are available for expenditure by property owners and occupiers on the renovation or conversion of empty or underused space above qualifying shops and other commercial premises to provide residential flats for short-term letting (i.e. on a lease for not more than five years). The allowances are deducted as expenses of a Schedule A letting business. The available allowances are an initial allowance of 100%, which may be claimed wholly or in part, and writing-down allowances of 25% of cost per annum (or lower amount claimed) until the expenditure is fully relieved. A balancing charge or balancing allowance will be made if there is a balancing event (sale, long lease, flat ceasing to be available for letting etc.) within seven years from the time the flat is available for letting. There will be no clawback of allowances if a sale, lease etc. occurs after that time. The allowances are not transferable to a purchaser. Anti-avoidance provisions apply where a balancing event occurs on or after 27 November 2002. Where the proceeds have been artificially depressed as a result of a tax avoidance scheme, no balancing allowance may be claimed.

In order to qualify, the properties must have been built before 1980 and must satisfy detailed conditions, including a requirement that the ground floor must be currently rated for business use, there must be not more than four floors above ground level and they must originally have been constructed mainly for use as dwellings, the renovated or converted part of the building must have been empty or used only for storage for at least a year, the new flats must be self-contained with not more than four rooms (excluding bathroom, kitchen, hallway etc.), and the rental value must be within prescribed limits.

Business premises renovation allowance

32.13 In 2005 the Government intends to introduce a Business Premises Renovation Allowance Scheme, subject to state aid approval from the EU. The scheme will provide 100% capital allowances for the costs of renovating business properties that have remained empty for at least a year in designated disadvantaged areas known as Enterprise Areas.

Where a premium is payable (TA 1988, ss 34, 37, 87; TCGA 1992, Sch 8; FA 1999, s 54 and Sch 6; FA 2003, Sch 17A–18; FA 2004, Sch 39)

32.14 Premiums may be payable by an incoming tenant to an outgoing tenant when a lease is assigned. They may also be paid by a tenant to a landlord when a lease or sublease is granted. A third type of payment is a payment by a landlord to induce a potential tenant to take out a lease — usually called a reverse premium.

A payment to an outgoing from an incoming tenant is dealt with under the capital gains tax rules.

Premium paid to landlord on grant of lease or sublease

32.15   The treatment of premiums paid to landlords on the grant of a lease or sublease depends on the length of the lease. If a lease is granted for more than 50 years, it is treated as a part disposal for capital gains purposes. There are both capital and income aspects if the lease is of 50 years duration or less (known as a short lease), in that the premium is partly treated as income and partly as disposal proceeds for capital gains. The income portion is treated as additional rent and is the amount of the premium less 2% for each complete year of the lease except the first. The amount by which the premium is reduced is treated as the proceeds of a part disposal for capital gains, the cost of the part disposed of being the proportion of the total cost that the capital portion of the premium bears to the full premium plus the value of the freehold reversion. See example 1.

The income portion of a premium on a short lease is wholly charged in the year the lease is granted, although the lease may run for anything up to 50 years.

Since the income part of the premium is treated as additional rent, any expenses of the letting can be relieved against it. The premium might in fact have been charged to recover some extraordinary expenses, perhaps necessitated by a previous defaulting tenant.

Where a premium on a short lease is paid by a business tenant, he may deduct the income portion (i.e. after the 2% deduction) as a business expense, but spread over the term of the lease rather than in a single sum (see Example 1). A similar deduction may be claimed by a tenant who sublets, his deduction depending on the length of the sublease. Any deductions allowed in calculating income are not allowed in calculating the capital gain if the lease is disposed of.

Any expenditure on the acquisition of a lease is treated for capital gains purposes as wasting away during the last 50 years (or shorter period for which the lease was granted) and only the depreciated cost (using a special table in TCGA 1992, Sch 8) may be used. If a lease is held for its full term, no allowable loss may be claimed for the unrelieved expenditure on acquisition, so that any expenditure for which relief has not been given in calculating income will not have been allowed for tax at all.

Example 1

Individual charges a premium of £80,000 on granting a lease for 21 years commencing 20 June 2004. The cost of the freehold was £150,000 in 1990. The value of the freehold reversion after the grant of the lease was £240,000.

The amount included in assessable rent for 2004/05 is:

	£
Premium	80,000
Less Treated as part disposal for capital gains (21 – 1) = 20 years at 2% = 40%	32,000
Amount treated as additional rent	£48,000

The chargeable gain (before indexation allowance and taper relief) is:

Capital proportion of premium	32,000
Less Allowable proportion of cost	

$$150,000 \times \frac{32,000}{80,000 + 240,000}$$

	15,000
	£17,000

If the tenant was a business tenant, he could claim a deduction for £48,000 spread over 21 years, i.e. £2,286 per annum, in addition to the deduction for the rent paid. If he assigned the lease within the 21 years, the allowable cost for capital gains would be arrived at by reducing the premium paid of £80,000 by the total annual deductions allowed as a business expense, and depreciating the reduced amount according to the table in TCGA 1992, Sch 8.

Payments from landlord to tenant — reverse premiums

32.16   Where a landlord pays a sum to induce a potential tenant to take a lease (a reverse premium) then, unless the payment reduces expenditure qualifying for capital allowances, it is treated as income for income tax or corporation tax in the hands of the tenant (either trading income or letting income as the case may be). The charge is spread over the period in which the premium is recognised in the tenant's accounts. The charge does not apply where the premises are to be the tenant's main residence or to sale and leaseback arrangements.

A reverse premium is not chargeable to stamp duty land tax.

Furnished holiday lettings (TA 1988, ss 503, 504; CAA 2001, ss 17, 249; TCGA 1992, s 241)

32.17   As with other furnished lettings, the 'rent-a-room' relief exempting gross rent of up to £4,250 a year is available to individuals who let rooms in their homes (see 30.7) and this may be more beneficial than the furnished holiday lettings treatment described below.

Income from qualifying furnished holiday lettings of UK property is broadly treated as trading income, although it remains chargeable under Schedule A rather than Schedule D, Case I. If interest is paid on a loan to purchase or improve the property, it is allowed as a trading expense (restricted if necessary by any private use proportion). Capital allowances (see CHAPTER 22) on plant and machinery, such as furniture and kitchen equipment, and loss relief (see CHAPTERS 25 and 26) may be claimed, and the income qualifies as relevant earnings for personal pension purposes (although non-earners may get tax relief in any event on personal pension contributions of up to £3,600 a year — see CHAPTER 17). Income tax is payable under the self-assessment provisions (see 2.23). Except for instalment paying companies (see 3.18), corporation tax is payable nine months after the end of the accounting period. Despite the trading treatment, individuals do not have to pay Class 4 national insurance contributions, because Class 4 contributions only apply where profits are charged under Schedule D, Case I or II. Class 2 contributions would, however, usually be payable unless already paid by reference to other self-employment or the landlord's activities in managing the properties were insufficient to be regarded as carrying on a business (see 24.3).

Furnished holiday lettings count as business assets for capital gains tax taper relief (see 4.16 onwards). The property is eligible for capital gains rollover relief either when it is itself replaced, or as a qualifying purchase against which gains on other assets may be set, and for business gifts holdover relief (see 4.26 and 4.27). If the property has been the main residence for capital gains tax, it may also be possible to claim the residential lettings exemption (see 30.8).

To qualify, the accommodation must be let on a commercial basis; it must be available as holiday accommodation for at least 140 days in the tax year, and actually let as such for at least 70 of those days. The 70 days test may be satisfied by averaging periods of occupation of any or all of the holiday accommodation let furnished by the same person. The accommodation must not normally be in the same occupation for a continuous period of more than 31 days during at least seven months of the year, which need not be continuous but includes any months containing any of the 70 let days. Where only part of the let accommodation is holiday accommodation, apportionments are made on a just and reasonable basis. Where there is part private use of the property, the normal rules for restricting allowable expenditure apply. In these circumstances, great care must be taken to ensure that the letting can be shown to be commercial, rather than producing income merely to offset costs.

As far as inheritance tax is concerned, property used for holiday lettings does not qualify for agricultural property relief and it may not qualify for business property relief (see 32.2). Business property relief will, however, probably be available if the lettings are very short-term (say a week or a fortnight) and the owner, personally or through someone acting for him, was substantially involved with the holidaymakers' activities (see the Revenue's Capital Taxes Manual).

The letting of holiday caravans is, depending on the scale, either treated as a trade or as a furnished letting. In the latter case, the income may be treated as trading income from furnished holiday accommodation if the conditions are satisfied. Long-term lets would accordingly not qualify. Caravans occupying holiday sites are treated as plant and machinery qualifying for capital allowances, even if they are on hard standings and not required to be moved.

Income from letting caravan sites is charged as unearned income under Schedule A, unless the activity really amounts to a trade, embracing services, shops, restaurants, etc. in which case the whole income will be treated as earned income from a trade.

Even where caravan sites are accepted as trading businesses, inheritance tax business property relief has usually been denied because the rent from caravan pitches was regarded as being from holding investments. The Court of Appeal has, however, recently held that business property relief was available for a caravan park with a wide range of activities, of which the pitch letting was only one.

For the treatment of furnished property, including holiday property and caravans, in relation to council tax and business rates, see 32.26.

Capital gains on sale of investment properties (TCGA 1992, ss 243–248; Revenue Statement of Practice SP 13/93)

32.18   The usual capital gains tax principles apply (see CHAPTER 4), including the relief dealt with in 30.8 where part of the property is owner-occupied, and that dealt with in 32.17 where the property is let as furnished holiday accommodation. Apart from those instances, there is no rollover relief on disposal and replacement of investment properties except where the disposal is occasioned by compulsory purchase. In this case, there is no tax charge if the proceeds are reinvested in another property, provided that the reinvestment is made within the period beginning one year before and ending three years after the disposal. The replacement property cannot, however, be the investor's capital gains tax exempt dwelling house at any time within six years after its acquisition. As an alternative to rollover relief where part of a holding of land is compulsorily purchased, small proceeds (not defined but taken in practice to mean not exceeding 5% of the value of the holding) may be treated as reducing the capital gains cost of the holding rather than being charged as a part disposal.

Compulsory purchase includes not only purchase by an authority but also purchase of the freehold by a tenant exercising his right to buy.

If a lease is surrendered and replaced by a new lease on similar terms except as to duration and rent payable, the surrender is, by Revenue concession D39, not treated as a disposal for capital gains tax so long as a capital sum is not received by the lessee. When the extended lease is disposed of, it will be treated as acquired when the original lease was acquired. There are anti-avoidance provisions to prevent people escaping tax by abuse of this concession — see 45.12.

Where at the end of a lease a tenant makes a payment to a landlord in respect of dilapidations, a decision needs to be made as to whether the amount received by the landlord is a capital or income receipt. If the landlord sells the property, the receipt will probably be regarded as compensation for a breach of the terms of the lease and will be treated as additional proceeds. If on the other hand the landlord carries out the repairs, or relets at a reduced rental, the amount received will be probably treated as Schedule A income.

See 31.11 for the availability of capital gains gifts relief for agricultural landlords.

The Revenue have two separate schemes relating to valuations for large property portfolios. The first applies to taxpayers who dispose of 30 or more interests in land in one tax year or company accounting period. The Revenue use a sampling process in order to avoid, if possible, the need to agree individual valuations for all the properties disposed of. The second, which was originally introduced for a trial period from 21 March 2000, relates to pre-disposal valuations. The Revenue are continuing with the scheme and have announced some relaxations. Companies or groups with a property portfolio including either 30 or more properties held since 31 March 1982 or properties held since 31 March 1982 with a current aggregate value higher than £20 million (previously £30 million) may ask the Revenue to agree 31 March 1982 values for all relevant property. For notes on these schemes see the Revenue's Tax Bulletin of October 2003.

Property dealing, etc.

32.19 Although the income from letting is assessed under Schedule A, any surplus on disposal of a property may even so be liable to income tax or corporation tax, either specifically under TA 1988, s 776 (see 45.21), or as a trading transaction, instead of as a chargeable gain. Whether or not a trade may be inferred is dealt with in CHAPTER 20, but the letting, whilst not conclusive, will at least indicate an investment motive and be influential in the surplus being treated as a capital gain.

Housing investment trusts (TA 1988, ss 508A, 508B, 842)

32.20 Approved investment trusts (see 38.16) may invest in residential property. The property must be either unlet or let on assured shorthold tenancies when acquired, and must subsequently be let on assured tenancies. The property must be either freehold or long lease property at a low rent, costing not more than £125,000 in Greater London and £85,000 elsewhere. Housing investment trusts pay corporation tax at the small companies rate of 19% on net rental income, and any capital gains on the properties are exempt.

VAT (VATA 1994, Sch 7A, Sch 8 Group 5, Sch 9 Group 1 and Sch 10)

32.21   The VAT position on land and buildings is very complex. Sales of new commercial buildings and commercial buildings that are less than three years old are standard-rated. Sales or leases for more than 21 years of new residential properties (including dwellings created by the conversion of non-residential property) and new buildings occupied by charities for charitable purposes are zero-rated. (Shorter leases are exempt and cannot be subject to the option to charge VAT — see 32.23.) The sale of renovated houses that have been empty for ten years or more is zero rated.

Otherwise, unless the vendor has exercised his option to charge VAT (see 32.23), all sales of buildings that are more than three years old are exempt, and grants of long or short leases (other than those mentioned above) are also exempt, except for holiday accommodation (see 32.24). Rents received are exempt unless the landlord has opted to charge VAT.

Most landlords letting domestic property are exempt from VAT. Any VAT they are charged therefore forms part of their costs, and must be taken into account in fixing their rents. Landlords letting commercial property are in the same position, unless they opt to charge VAT (see 32.23). If the expenditure is revenue expenditure, such as repairs, the unrecovered VAT may be claimed as part of the expense against the rent. If it is capital expenditure, such as on property conversion, reconstruction, extension, improvement, etc., no deduction can be claimed against the rent, but the unrecovered VAT will form part of the cost for capital gains purposes when the property is disposed of.

See 7.8 for the reduced rate of VAT of 5% on the installation of energy saving materials, and on central heating systems etc. if funded by Government grants.

Where there is non-business use of commercial land and buildings, it has previously been possible either to claim input VAT in full when the land and buildings are acquired and adjust for the private use as and when it arises, or to claim only the business element of the input VAT at the outset. From 10 April 2003 full input VAT can no longer be claimed and the input VAT must be apportioned to reflect the private use.

Residential conversions and renovations

32.22 VAT is charged at the reduced rate of 5% on the supply of services and building materials for the conversion of non-residential property into dwellings, conversion of residential property into a different number of dwellings, conversion of residential or non-residential property into a multiple occupancy dwelling (e.g. bed-sit accommodation), conversion of non-residential property or one or more residential properties into a care home, children's home, hospice etc. (where the services are supplied to the person who intends to use the property for that purpose), the conversion of a care home etc. into a multiple occupancy dwelling, and the renovation or alteration of dwellings, multiple occupancy properties and care homes etc. that have been empty for three years or more. Constructing a garage, or turning a building into a garage, as part of a renovation also qualifies for the reduced rate. Where someone buys a house that has been empty for three years or more and lives in it while it is being renovated, the 5% rate will still apply to the building work providing it is completed within one year from the date the property was purchased.

Option to charge VAT

32.23 In all situations where exemption applies (other than leases of residential/charitable property for less than 21 years, pitches for residential caravans and mooring facilities for houseboats), the owner/landlord has an option to charge VAT (but if he is not already VAT registered he has to become registered in order to take this option). Customs must be notified in writing within 30 days. The effect of taking the option is that VAT is then charged on rents and lease premiums and also on any sale proceeds when buildings are sold. Although the sale of tenanted property may represent the disposal of part of a business, the provisions relating to the sale of a going concern (see 7.28) do not apply to land on which the seller has exercised the option to tax unless the buyer notifies Customs before the sale is completed that he, too, has exercised the option. For transfers on or after 18 March 2004 there is also a requirement that the buyer must notify the seller that his option to tax will not be disapplied. In the absence of such an election and notification, the going concern treatment is not available and VAT must be charged on the sale.

Making the election enables the landlord to recover any VAT he suffers, and could be particularly beneficial where he has to incur substantial repair expenditure. But if most of his tenants are partially exempt, part of the VAT will be an extra cost to them, so the overall effect needs to be considered carefully. Following the election, the landlord may add VAT to the rent unless the lease specifically prevents him from doing so. In that event, the rent he receives will have to be treated as VAT inclusive until such time as it may be increased on a rent review.

The option may be exercised separately in relation to each building (but not separate parts of a building) and in relation to discrete areas of agricultural land, such as one farm (see 31.12). Once taken, the option can only be revoked by that owner within three months from the date it has effect and before it has had any tax consequences, or twenty years after it has effect. A new owner may or may not exercise the option as he wishes, but if he does not, he will not be able to recover the VAT charge on his purchase.

Anti-avoidance provisions prevent banks, insurance companies and other exempt bodies from manipulating the option to tax in order to reclaim input tax. Even though the option has been exercised, input tax cannot be claimed on buildings subject to the capital goods scheme (see 7.18) or buildings that will later become subject to the capital goods scheme, if the building is not expected to be occupied mainly for taxable business purposes. Further anti-avoidance provisions have been introduced from 18 March 2004 in relation to the use of the option to tax and the transfer of a going concern. They prevent the use of artificial structures either to increase allowable input tax or to spread the VAT cost of purchase or construction of land and buildings over several years.

Holiday accommodation, etc.

32.24   The provision of short-term holiday accommodation in hotels, boarding houses, caravans, etc. is charged to VAT at the standard rate but reduced charges apply if a tenant stays for more than four weeks. If you sell or lease holiday accommodation, including time share accommodation, that is less than three years old, then both the initial charges and any periodic charges, such as ground rent and service charges, are also standard-rated. If the property is over three years old, the initial charges are exempt from VAT but periodic charges are still standard-rated. The standard rate applies to charges for pitching tents and to seasonal pitch charges for caravans (charges for non-seasonal pitches being exempt). If the pitch charges to the caravan owners include water and sewerage services and the landlord can ascertain how much is provided to the caravans as distinct from the rest of the site (shops, swimming pools, etc.), this can be apportioned between the caravans and shown separately on the bills, and VAT need not then be charged on those services. Similarly, separately metered supplies of gas and electricity are charged at the reduced rate of 5%. VAT is not charged on any part of the pitch charge that represents business rates on the individual caravans (but it is charged on any business rates element that relates to the rest of the site).

The sale of building plots for holiday accommodation is standard-rated.

Stamp duty

32.25   Stamp duty on land and buildings was replaced by stamp duty land tax (SDLT) from 1 December 2003. Under the stamp duty land tax provisions, no tax is payable if residential property is purchased for £60,000 or less, or if non-residential property is purchased for £150,000 or less. If the purchase price exceeds the relevant amount, tax is payable on the whole of the purchase price at 1%, 3% or 4% depending on the consideration. See 6.12 to 6.15 for the SDLT provisions in relation to leases. Any SDLT paid forms part of the cost for capital gains tax purposes on a subsequent disposal.

Where VAT is included in the cost of property, SDLT is charged on the VAT-inclusive amount. See 6.16 for the position relating to the option to charge VAT.

Other aspects of SDLT are dealt with in CHAPTER 6. Exemptions apply to certain transfers of land and buildings involving Registered Social Landlords (see 6.19) and to sales and leases of property in designated 'disadvantaged areas' (see 6.20).

Council tax and business rates

32.26   The detailed council tax and business rates provisions are in CHAPTER 8, which outlines the exemptions and discounts available.

When considering liability to council tax and/or business rates, each self-contained unit is looked at separately. Where there is mixed business and domestic use, business rates are payable as well as the council tax, even if there is no separate business part of the property, unless the business use does not materially detract from the domestic use. Any charges that fall on a landlord are allowable according to the normal expenses rules.

Let property that is domestic property and is not someone's only or main home is liable to a council tax charge of up to 90%, unless any other discount or exemption applies (see CHAPTER 8). Where let property is someone's only or main home, that person is liable to pay the council tax and there are no council tax or rates implications for the landlord, unless the property is multi-occupied property, such as bedsits, with rent paid separately for different parts of the property, in which case the council tax is payable by the landlord.

Non-domestic property, such as commercial property, boarding houses, etc., is liable to business rates. Staff accommodation, however, is domestic property. If the owner lives there as well, he is liable to pay the council tax. If he does not live there, the staff are liable to council tax if it is their only or main home. If the domestic accommodation was no-one's only or main home, the owner would be liable to pay up to 90% of the council tax. In the case of self-catering holiday accommodation, business rates are payable if it is available for short-term letting for 140 days or more in a year. This is independent of the number of days for which the property is actually let. Bed and breakfast accommodation is not subject to business rating providing it is not offered for more than six people, the provider lives there at the same time and the bed and breakfast activity is only a subsidiary use of the home. Where holiday property is not business rated, the council tax charge of up to 90% is payable on any self-contained accommodation that is not someone's only or main home.

If someone lives in a caravan as his or her only or main home, he or she pays the council tax. For other caravans, the site owner pays business rates on the caravans and pitches, passing on the charge to the caravan owner in the site rents. (Note that this part of the site rent is not liable to VAT — see 32.24.)

Time shares

32.27   If you buy a time share, you may be concerned with taxation in respect of income from it, or on a capital gain when you sell it.

The nature of the rights acquired depends on the particular agreement, but most time share agreements do not give you any rights of ownership over the property itself, but merely a right to occupy it at a certain time.

If you let your time share, you will be liable to tax on the income less expenses under Schedule A. Where time share property is abroad, income is from a foreign possession charged under Schedule D, Case V (see 41.6 and 41.10). Many people will not have any time share income, but will sometimes exchange time shares. If this is done on a temporary basis, there are no tax implications, but a long-term arrangement could be treated as a part disposal for capital gains tax.

When you sell a time share, you are liable to capital gains tax on the profit, after taking into account the cost, indexation allowance to April 1998 and any available taper relief in the usual way. If the time share has less than 50 years to run, a depreciated cost must be used (on a straight line basis).

Time share property in the UK is usually subject to business rates. The owner of time share property charges value added tax on the selling price for the time share if it is less than three years old and on any service charges made, including business rates. If the property is over three years old, the sale proceeds for the time share, but not the service charges, are exempt from VAT.

The Revenue apparently regard timeshares as leases for stamp duty land tax, although no tax would be payable unless the £60,000 nil threshold was exceeded.

Tax points

32.28

- If interest paid cannot be relieved against rents, individuals cannot set it against a capital gain on disposal of the property but investment companies can — see 32.9 and 26.5.

- Management expenses are allowed as a lettings expense. This covers a landlord's expenses of travelling to his properties solely for the purposes of property management. The expenses are not allowable if the travelling is for mixed business/private purposes.

- If you hope to benefit from the furnished holiday lettings treatment, make sure you can demonstrate the commercial viability of the lettings and that all the various conditions are satisfied. Taking a very large mortgage such that letting income will not cover costs in the reasonably near future may prevent relief being available for losses.

- The fact that property is being let does not of itself prevent an income tax charge instead of a chargeable gain on a profit on disposal if a trading motive can be proved. There are various possibilities for reducing or deferring tax liabilities, but it is important to establish which tax applies so that the proceeds can be invested in an appropriate purchase (see CHAPTER 29).

- The value added tax provisions relating to property letting, including holiday letting, are extremely complex. Make sure you look carefully at the appropriate Customs booklets relating to your circumstances.

- If you normally let your property for long-term residential use but it is empty for a period of time, you are liable to pay council tax on it, subject to any available discounts and exemptions (see 32.26).

- Bed and breakfast providers can escape business rates if they offer the facility as a subsidiary use of their own homes for not more than six people. Otherwise, business rates are payable.

- If you borrow to buy property for letting abroad, income tax relief is available on the interest.

- An investment in a property in an enterprise zone can be particularly tax-efficient so long as the price is right. See 22.30 and 29.14.

- Under self-assessment, individuals must keep the records relating to their property income for at least 5 years 10 months after the end of the tax year — see 9.6. Penalties of up to £3,000 per tax year apply if they do not. The Revenue have issued a useful booklet SA/BK3 on the record-keeping requirements. The self-assessment provisions for companies similarly require records to be kept for six years, with the same penalty for failing to do so of up to £3,000 per accounting period.

33
Family matters

Introduction

33.1   At present there are many provisions in the UK tax system which apply only to married couples and not to unmarried heterosexual partners or same-sex partners. Under the Civil Partnership Bill currently before Parliament, same-sex couples (but not unmarried heterosexual couples) will be able to have their relationship legally recognised. This will have no immediate tax effect, because any changes will be made in a Finance Bill, but the legislation will affect child and working tax credits (see 2.27).

Married couples

33.2   The incomes of husband and wife are taxed independently. Each is entitled to a personal allowance and before 6 April 2000 a married couple's allowance was also available to all married couples. From 6 April 2000 married couple's allowance is available only where one of the couple was born before 6 April 1935. The detailed provisions are in CHAPTER 34.

A married couple's gains are also taxed independently, each being entitled to the annual exemption, currently £8,200. Losses of one spouse may not be set against gains of the other, but transfers of assets between husband and wife who are living together are not chargeable to capital gains tax, the acquiring spouse taking over the other's acquisition cost. (This has no relevance to assets acquired on a spouse's death, which are treated as acquired at probate value.) Any indexation allowance arising to the date of transfer (or to April 1998 if earlier) increases the original cost for the purpose of calculating the gain on an eventual disposal (subject to rules to ensure that the indexation allowance does not create or increase a loss when the other spouse disposes of the asset — see 4.5). Taper relief (see 4.16 onwards) is given according to the combined period of ownership. Section 4.22 deals with the availability of the business assets rate of taper relief where assets have been transferred between spouses. The capital gains rules enable couples to plan in advance and make appropriate transfers one to the other before negotiating disposals to third parties, so that, for example, one spouse does not have gains in excess of the exempt threshold while the other has unrelieved losses, or so that tax is charged at a lower rate where one spouse's tax rate is higher than the other's. Such transfers must, however, be outright gifts (see 33.4). If capital losses are brought forward from before the introduction of independent taxation on 6 April 1990, each spouse's losses must be separately identified so that they are set only against that person's gains.

Husband and wife are each responsible for completion of tax returns and for payment of the tax.

Despite the fact that married couples are treated independently for tax purposes, their joint income is taken into account for working and child tax credits and the credits are claimed on a single form. (The same will apply to registered same-sex partnerships when the Civil Partnership Bill becomes law.) Tax credits are social security benefits, although they are administered by the Revenue. The detailed tax credits provisions are in 2.27 to 2.34.

For inheritance tax purposes, husband and wife are taxed separately and have separate exemptions and a separate nil rate threshold. Transfers between the two are exempt unless one of them is not domiciled in the United Kingdom, in which case the transfers to the non-domiciled spouse are exempt up to £55,000, and potentially chargeable on the excess over that amount should the donor not survive for seven years. For the meaning of domicile, see 41.4.

Stamp duty/stamp duty land tax is not normally charged on the value of assets transferred between husband and wife, but see 33.5 re mortgaged property.

Using available allowances and lower rates of tax

33.3   Some people on low incomes need to make sure that they make the best use of their allowances and the 10% starting rate band.

You will get a cash flow advantage if you receive income equal to your available personal allowance and starting rate band in full, without tax being deducted by the payer. Investments that always pay interest gross are national savings bank accounts and offshore accounts with banks and building societies. The fact that tax is not deducted does not mean that the income is tax free. The tax payable must be worked out according to your circumstances. If you will not be liable to tax *at all*, you can claim to receive interest from other banks and from building societies without tax being deducted rather than having to reclaim the tax later (see 37.2). The claim to receive it in full cannot be made if you expect some of your income to be liable to tax, even if you will be entitled to reclaim all or most of the tax deducted by the bank or building society.

Transferring property from one spouse to another (TA 1988, ss 282A, 282B, 660A, FA 2004, s 91)

33.4   In order to take best advantage of being taxed separately, it may be sensible for property to be transferred from husband to wife or vice versa. Any such transfers are fully effective for tax purposes providing the transfer is an outright gift of the property with no question of the transferring spouse controlling it or deriving a benefit from it, and providing the gift is not substantially a right to income. The Revenue have recently used the settlements legislation to contend that certain gifts between spouses are caught by this proviso, particularly where shares in family companies are concerned. See 12.9, 18.2 and 23.21 for further comments.

It is not possible to transfer a right to income while retaining a right to the capital (but see 33.5 re jointly owned property). The rules do not prevent the spouse who gave the property getting it back later as a gift, or after the other spouse's death, providing there were no 'strings' on the transfer in the first place. And where property is transferred into the joint names of husband and wife and they own it under the normal 'joint tenants' provisions, the Revenue do not regard this as breaching the 'outright gift' rules, even though the property goes automatically to the survivor when one dies (see 33.5).

Such transfers will be beneficial where a wife or husband would otherwise waste their personal allowance or 10% starting rate band, or where one spouse would be paying higher rate tax while the other did not fully use the basic rate band. You must make sure you have evidence of transfers in the proper legal form.

Stamp duty/stamp duty land tax is not charged on gifts (except possibly in relation to mortgaged property — see 33.5).

Where husband and wife are living together and one spouse acquires the other's interest in the family home in lifetime or on death, the joint period of ownership after 31 March 1982 is taken into account for the purpose of the capital gains private residence exemption (see 30.5).

Jointly owned property

33.5   Husband and wife are normally treated as owning joint property as 'joint tenants', which means that each has equal rights over the property and when one dies, it goes automatically to the other. The joint tenancy can, however, be severed, and replaced by a 'tenancy in common', in which the share of each is separate, and may be unequal, and may be disposed of in lifetime or on death as the spouse wishes. If you do this, make sure you have proper documentary evidence of what you have done. Severing the joint tenancy may be particularly relevant if couples separate. Otherwise one spouse's share of the property would automatically go to the other in the event of their death.

Where property other than shares in a close company (see 3.21) is in joint names, it is treated as being owned equally for income tax purposes unless it is actually owned in some different proportions *and* you make a declaration to that effect. Such a declaration takes effect from the date it is made, providing notice of the declaration is given to the Revenue (on form 17) within 60 days. The form only covers the assets listed on it. Any new assets must be covered by a separate form. The treatment of jointly owned property as being owned in equal shares for income tax purposes unless form 17 was submitted used to apply to *any* jointly owned property, but from 2004/05 onwards it does not apply to dividends on shares in family companies.

The tax treatment of joint ownership may be useful to overcome one practical difficulty of maximising the benefits of being taxed separately — that the richer spouse may be unwilling to make a significant transfer to the other. The reluctant spouse could transfer an asset (other than close company shares) into joint ownership as tenants in common, retaining 95% ownership and giving the spouse a 5% share; if no declaration of the actual shares is notified to the Revenue, the tax law treats the income as being shared equally.

This treatment applies to transfers of any sort of property other than close company shares — land and buildings, non-close company shares, bank accounts, etc. When you open joint bank and building society accounts, you normally declare that they are in your joint beneficial ownership. You can still later change your ownership to tenants in common, but this must be done formally, for example by deed. The Revenue have stated that evidence of such a change in the way bank etc. accounts are owned must be provided with form 17. The bank or building society are still likely to act on the basis of your original declaration, so that they would treat the account as belonging to the survivor when one dies. In that case your personal representatives need to be left clear instructions so that they can deal properly with your estate. Another point that needs to be watched is in relation to mortgaged property. If the spouse to whom the property is transferred takes over responsibility for the mortgage, the mortgage debt is treated as consideration for the transfer and is liable to stamp duty land tax unless covered by the £60,000 limit (see 6.11). This will not apply if the spouse who is transferring the property undertakes to pay the mortgage. (See also 33.13 re separation and divorce.)

Regardless of the way income is treated for income tax purposes, it is the underlying beneficial ownership of assets that determines the capital gains tax treatment. Again, it is essential to have evidence of the proportions in which property is held. See 4.22 for the taper relief rules where assets are transferred between spouses and 38.9 for the treatment of disposals of joint holdings of shares where there are also individual holdings of shares in the same company.

For inheritance tax purposes, there are special 'related property' rules which require transfers of assets owned by husband and wife to be valued as part of their combined value (see 5.16). This applies in particular to unquoted shares and freehold or leasehold property. There are also 'associated operations' rules to link a series of transactions as a single transaction (see 5.18). The combined effect of these two sets of provisions prevents husband and wife obtaining an undue advantage by using the exemption for inter-spouse transfers to route a transfer to their children via the other spouse.

Children

Child tax credit

33.6   Child tax credit is a means tested social security benefit paid to the main carer. Although independent taxation of husband and wife has been in operation for many years, it has no relevance for tax credits, and a joint claim form must be completed. For further details see 2.27 to 2.34 and 33.2.

Children's income (TA 1988, s 660B)

33.7   The income of your children is theirs in their own right, no matter how young they are, and they are entitled to the full personal allowance and lower rate tax bands. For a child under 18 and unmarried, this does not apply to income that comes directly or indirectly from you (including income from ISAs for 16- and 17-year olds — see 36.23), which is still treated as your own income with the following exceptions.

(a)   Each parent can give each child a capital sum (say a bank or building society deposit) from which the child receives no more than £100 gross income per annum. (But if the income exceeded the limit, the whole amount and not just the excess over £100 would be taxed on the parent.)

(b)   The national savings 'children's bonus bonds' for under 16-year olds (see 36.11) can be given in addition.

(c)   A parent may pay premiums (maximum £270 per annum) on a qualifying friendly society policy for a child under 18 (see 40.15).

(d)   A parent may pay personal pension contributions of up to £3,600 a year on behalf of a child under 18, such contributions being paid net of basic

rate tax, which is retained whether or not the child is a taxpayer (see
CHAPTER 17). The pension fund is, of course, not available to the child
until he/she reaches pension age.

(e)   From 6 April 2005, parents may contribute up to £1,200 to a Child Trust
Fund account for their children, in addition to any gifts under (a)
above (see 33.8).

(f)   A parent may establish an 'accumulation and maintenance' settlement
for his children, the income from which is not treated as his in certain
circumstances (see CHAPTER 42).

Gifts within (a) to (e) above are not taken into account as far as inheritance
tax is concerned providing they are regular gifts out of income (see 5.3).

The above rules do not affect gifts to children over 18, but the inheritance tax
provisions need to be borne in mind for children of any age. There would be
no inheritance tax effect if any gifts were covered by the regular gifts, family
maintenance, small gifts or annual inheritance tax exemptions (see 5.3).
Otherwise the gifts would be potentially exempt transfers and would not
attract inheritance tax unless the parent died within seven years.

Many parents help to fund their children through higher education.
Although student loans are available, one quarter of the available loan is
restricted according to the parents' or child's income, so the student's income
from parental gifts might also affect the available loan. Where parents buy
property for a student child, if they retain ownership they will be treated as
any other landlord (see CHAPTER 32). If the property was given to the child,
the inheritance tax effect would need to be considered, but if other students
shared the property the child might be able to claim rent a room relief (see
30.7) and so long as it remained the child's main residence the property
would be exempt from capital gains tax on disposal. See 10.25 and 10.26 re
tax-exempt payments to employees for work-related training. Students in
further education may wish to pay Class 3 voluntary national insurance
contributions to maintain their benefits entitlement — see 13.3.

Child Trust Funds (SI 2004/1450)

33.8   Child Trust Funds (CTFs) will be available from April 2005 for all
children born after 31 August 2002 for whom child benefit is payable and
also for children born on or after that date who are in care. The Government
will provide vouchers of £250 for each child, which may only be invested in
CTF accounts in the beneficial ownership of the child. An additional £250
will be provided for a child who is part of a family with a household income
below the income threshold for child tax credit (presently £13,480). The
contributions will be slightly increased for children born between 1 September
2002 and 5 April 2005 to compensate for the shorter accumulation period

before age 18. The Government intends to make further contributions when children reach age seven (the first payments being made in 2009). Parents will not need to claim the awards, which will be made automatically following the award of child benefit. Where vouchers are not used to open an account within twelve months (or before the child reaches age 18 if sooner), and also for children in care, accounts will be opened by the Revenue.

CTF accounts may only be provided by approved account providers. The permitted investments will be similar to those for individual savings accounts (ISAs), i.e. bank and building society accounts, stocks and shares and life insurance. Provision will be made for accounts to be transferred from one provider to another.

Additional contributions may be made to CTFs by family, friends and others, up to an annual limit of £1,200. The limit of £100 income from funds provided by a parent referred to in 33.7 does not apply to CTF accounts. Income and capital gains from CTF investments will be exempt from tax (and capital losses will not be allowable).

No withdrawals will be normally be permitted until the child is 18, and only the child will be entitled to make such withdrawals. Access to the CTF account will, however, be available for children under 18 who receive disability living allowance because they are terminally ill.

Various penalties may be imposed, including a penalty of up to £300 for fraudulently opening or withdrawing funds from a CTF, and a penalty of up to £3,000 in the case of fraud or negligence by account providers.

Death of the husband

33.9   There are no special tax allowances available to a widow in the year of her husband's death. If the married couple's allowance has remained available because one of the couple was born before 6 April 1935, then in the year of her husband's death, the widow can receive the benefit of any of the allowance which has not been used against the husband's tax bill up to the date of death. This might be particularly relevant where the husband died early in the tax year. The husband's executors must notify the Revenue that the surplus married couple's allowance is being transferred to the widow. The widow's income will include any she is entitled to from the assets in her husband's estate.

See 30.5 for the capital gains position when a widow acquires her late husband's interest in the family home.

A woman who is under state pension age of 60 when widowed, or whose late husband was not entitled to the State retirement pension, will get a tax-free bereavement payment of £2,000 from the Department for Work and Pensions (DWP), providing the late husband satisfied the contribution conditions or his death was caused by his job. Widowed parent's allowance or bereavement allowance may also be available. These benefits are taxable, apart from additions to the widowed parent's allowance for dependent children. See the DWP's leaflet GL 14 for further details. A widow who remarries before age 60 may be worse off in terms of her State retirement pension. A widow used to inherit the whole of her late husband's entitlement under the State Earnings Related Pension Scheme (SERPS). The rules were changed from 6 October 2002. See 13.3 for details.

Death of the wife

33.10   Where the married couple's allowance has remained available because one of the couple was born before 6 April 1935, the husband is entitled to the full allowance for the tax year in which his wife dies. If all or part of the allowance has been claimed by the wife, and her income in the year of her death is insufficient to cover her allowances, any surplus married couple's allowance can be transferred back to the husband, providing the wife's personal representatives notify the Revenue accordingly.

Investment income arising on the wife's assets following death will be assessed through her estate and will form part of the husband's income to the extent that he is the ultimate beneficiary.

See 30.5 for the capital gains position when a widower acquires his late wife's interest in the family home.

The bereavement payment of £2,000 and other bereavement benefits referred to in 33.9 are available to widowers, based on the national insurance position of the wife. State pension age for the husband is 65.

Separation and divorce

33.11   For the treatment of the married couple's allowance for the over 65s in the year of separation or reconciliation see 34.2.

The tax position of divorced couples is broadly the same as that of separated couples. There are some provisions, for example the rules for employee benefits and close company associates, that apply up to divorce (but not thereafter) even though the couple are not living together.

For policies entered into before 14 March 1984, a divorced wife continues to be entitled to life assurance relief on a policy on her husband's life taken out before the divorce. If she wishes to protect herself against the loss of maintenance on her husband's death, this can be done with her husband's co-operation if he takes out a policy on his own life in trust for her, or she herself takes out a policy on his life. There will be no tax relief on the premium.

Where all or part of the rights under life policies were transferred from one spouse to another under a divorce settlement, the Revenue previously took the view that the transfers were for money or moneys worth and thus potentially chargeable under the life policies chargeable event rules dealt with in CHAPTER 40. They have now changed their view and have given detailed comments on the changes in their Tax Bulletin of December 2003, including details of the circumstances in which taxpayers may amend their self-assessments to reflect the new treatment.

Maintenance payments (TA 1988, s 347B)

33.12   Tax relief for maintenance payments is only available where one spouse was born before 6 April 1935. The relief is at a fixed amount (currently £2,210) for all eligible claimants. All maintenance received is free of tax. For further notes see 34.4.

The family home (TCGA 1992, ss 222, 223; FA 1985, s 83; FA 2003, Sch 3; Stamp Duty (Exempt Instruments) Regulations 1987 (SI 1987/516))

33.13   For capital gains tax, when a couple separate, the family home will cease to be the main residence of the spouse who leaves it. His or her share of any calculated gain on a subsequent sale will therefore be chargeable to the extent that it relates to the period of non-residence, subject to any available exemptions or reliefs. The last three years of ownership always count as a period of residence, even if a new qualifying residence has been acquired. If the property is disposed of more than three years after a spouse leaves it, part of the calculated gain will be assessable, but only in the proportion that the excess period over three years bears to the total period of ownership since 31 March 1982. Even then the chargeable gain may be covered by the annual exemption, currently £8,200. There is a Revenue concession D6 covering absences of more than three years following separation or divorce, but only where the property is eventually transferred to the spouse remaining in it as part of the financial settlement, and an election for a new qualifying residence has not been made by the spouse moving out in the meantime.

The private residence exemption can be preserved on divorce if a court order known as a Mesher order is made, under which the sale of the home is postponed, with a spouse and children remaining in occupation until a specified event, such as the children reaching a specified age or ceasing full-time education. This is treated as a trust, and occupation of the property by a trust beneficiary qualifies for the private residence exemption (see 30.6). On the sale of the home by the trustees when the trust ends, the proceeds will not be liable to capital gains tax.

If property is transferred from one spouse to another on break-up of a marriage, neither stamp duty nor stamp duty land tax is payable on property of any description, even if the acquiring spouse takes over a mortgage.

Pension schemes

33.14   See 16.10 for the provisions to enable pension rights to be shared on divorce.

Capital gains tax — chargeable assets other than the family home (TCGA 1992, ss 58, 165)

33.15   The capital gains exemption for assets transferred between husband and wife only applies in a tax year when a married couple are living together at some time during the year. For transfers in later tax years, capital gains tax is chargeable in the normal way, and this must be remembered when considering a matrimonial settlement following separation. If qualifying business assets are transferred from one to the other after separation but before the divorce, gains need not be charged to tax at that time if husband and wife jointly claim the 'business gifts relief' (see 4.27), under which the recipient takes over the other spouse's original cost plus any available indexation allowance for the purpose of calculating the tax payable on an eventual disposal. Taper relief on an eventual disposal is, however, given only according to the period of ownership of the acquiring spouse (see CHAPTER 4). Business gifts relief has not previously been available on assets transferred after divorce since such transfers were regarded as being for consideration and therefore not eligible for gifts relief. Where, however, assets are transferred under a court order (even a 'consent' order ratifying an agreement made by the couple), the Revenue now accept that gifts relief will be available. This applies to claims from 31 July 2002 and earlier claims that were unsettled at that date.

Inheritance tax (IHTA 1984, s 18(1))

33.16   The spouse exemption for inheritance tax is not lost on separation but continues until the time of divorce. Even then there is an exemption for transfers to former spouses for the maintenance of themselves and the children. See CHAPTER 5.

Living together without being married

33.17   Child tax credit is available to an unmarried couple living together as husband and wife in respect of children under 16 according to the same rules as for married couples (see 33.6). As for married couples, a single claim showing the incomes of both must be made for tax credits.

Where the home is in the name of only one of the cohabitees, but they regard it as their joint property and want the survivor to have the property when one of them dies, it is important to ensure that the other cohabitee's rights in relation to the home are safeguarded. This may be done by the property owner making a declaration that the property is held in trust for them both as joint tenants in equal beneficial shares. The lifetime declaration of trust would not be reckoned for inheritance tax to the extent that both parties had contributed, directly or indirectly, to the cost. If a transfer of value remained, it would be potentially exempt and (subject to the transferor not retaining any benefit in respect of the share transferred — see 5.8) would only become chargeable if the property owner died within seven years. The declaration would ensure that once the seven years had elapsed, the property owner's estate for inheritance tax would only include the market value of his half share, which would be discounted because the co-habitee would still occupy the property. If such a declaration was not made, then even if both parties contribute to the cost and upkeep, the Revenue may treat the whole property as part of the owner's estate at death. The exemption from inheritance tax for property passing from one spouse to the other does not apply to cohabitees, so that an unwelcome charge to tax will arise when the inheritance tax threshold is exceeded.

Council tax

33.18   Couples who are living together as husband and wife, whether married or not, are jointly liable for payment of council tax. This only applies for any part of the year when they are living together, and would not apply after separation or divorce. A partner is not liable unless the authority has issued a bill to him or her.

Tax points

33.19

- The Revenue require a married couple to send in a separate form 17 (notification of unequal shares — see 33.5) for any new jointly owned assets. This needs to be borne in mind if you have a joint share portfolio, where there may be frequent changes. See also 38.9 for the special matching rules where there are both joint and separately owned shareholdings.

- If you change your ownership of bank and building society accounts so that you hold them as tenants in common rather than joint tenants, make sure you have proper evidence that you have done so.

- Although the capital gains tax private residence exemption applies only to your qualifying main residence, if you own a second home jointly you will be entitled to two annual exemptions when you sell it (unless used against other gains). See also 30.10 re changing your qualifying main residence.

- In a bona fide husband and wife partnership where both play a significant role in the business, profits can be shared so as to maximise the benefit of being taxed separately.

- If your joint wealth is substantial, you may be able to save inheritance tax by rearranging the ownership of assets between you. See CHAPTER 35 for details.

- If you are cohabiting, remember that social security regulations are different from those relating to tax. They should be researched before making financial arrangements between you, and for children.

34

Especially for the senior citizen

Personal allowances (TA 1988, ss 256, 257, 257A, 257BA, 257BB)

Personal allowance

34.1   Personal allowances based on age are available both to single and married claimants. They are deducted from taxable income and save tax at the payer's highest tax rate. The allowances are, however, reduced if income exceeds a certain limit (£18,900 for 2004/05 — see 34.3). The allowances for 2004/05 are as follows:

Under 65	£4,745
65 to 74	£6,830
75 and over	£6,950

Note that even if a woman gets State pension at 60, she does not get the higher tax allowance until she is 65.

Married couple's allowance

34.2   Married couple's allowance is available only for couples one of whom was born before 6 April 1935. It will also become available to someone born before 6 April 1935 who is single but later marries. The allowance is based on the age of the older spouse. The allowance is given as a reduction of your tax liability and saves you tax at only 10%, the allowances for 2004/05 being as follows:

		Tax saving @ 10%
Elder 67 to 74	£5,725	£572.50
Elder 75 or over	£5,795	£579.50

As with the personal allowance, these amounts are reduced where income exceeds a specified limit (see 34.3).

The available allowance (after taking into account the income limit where appropriate) is reduced in the year of marriage by 1/12th for each complete tax month before the wedding date (see 2.15 for further details). The allowance is given in full in the year of separation or death of either spouse. If a separated couple become reconciled in a later tax year, the full married couple's allowance is available in the year of reconciliation (unless they had divorced). If the reconciliation takes place in the same tax year as the separation, they will usually be taxed as if they had not been separated.

The married couple's allowance is normally given to the husband. A married woman may, however, claim £1,105 of the married couple's allowance for 2004/05 as of right, and the couple may jointly claim for the wife to get £2,210 of the allowance, providing in each case the claim is made *before* the tax year in which it is first to apply (except in the year of marriage when the claim may be made within that year). A claim in respect of 2005/06 must therefore be made by 5 April 2005. Claims must be made on form 18, available from the Revenue. The allowance will then be allocated in the chosen way until the claim is withdrawn, or, where a joint claim has been made for £2,210 to go to the wife, until the husband makes a fresh claim for half of that amount. The withdrawal or the husband's claim must also be made before the beginning of the tax year for which the revised allocation is to take effect.

A wife can use the transferred allowance to reduce any of her tax for the year, even if the tax relates to income arising before marriage or after the date of separation or of her husband's death.

If your tax bill is too low to use the tax reduction available to you, you may notify the Revenue that you want to transfer the surplus allowance to your spouse. The whole of any surplus allowance may be transferred, and not just the part of the allowance that may be claimed by either spouse. There is a box to tick on tax returns if you want to apply for a transfer notice form (form 575). The time limit for making a claim to transfer the surplus is five years from the 31 January following the tax year.

Since the allowance is given as a fixed amount of tax saving, transferring all or half of the specified amount to the wife does not save tax unless the husband has insufficient income to pay tax, or he has dividend income and his tax bill would otherwise be lower than his available dividend tax credits. A transfer to the wife may, however, improve cash flow if, say, the husband would get the reduction in the tax on self-employed profits that he pays half-yearly as part of his provisional and balancing payments under self-assessment whereas the wife is an employee who would reduce her PAYE tax from the beginning of the tax year.

Income limit for age allowances (TA 1988, ss 257, 257A; FA 1990, s 25)

34.3 The benefit of higher personal allowances is withdrawn to the extent that income exceeds a specified limit, £18,900 for 2004/05. Each of a married couple has his or her own limit. The personal allowance is reduced by half the excess of income over that limit until it reaches the normal personal allowance level, currently £4,745.

The married couple's age allowance is similarly subject to the income limit, but the amount available depends on the husband's income only, even if the extra allowance is being given because of his wife's age rather than his. For 2004/05, after the personal allowance has been reduced to £4,745, the married couple's allowance is similarly reduced by half of the excess of his total income over £18,900 which has not already been taken into account to reduce his personal allowance, until it reaches the minimum allowance of £2,210 (which may have been transferred to the wife).

Once income reaches a certain level, therefore, all the benefit of the increased personal allowance, and the excess above £2,210 of the married couple's allowances, is lost.

The reduction of the age allowance by £1 for every £2 of income over £18,900 is sometimes called the age allowance trap, because it has the effect of costing you tax at 1½ times the relevant tax rate on the excess income over £18,900. The tax rate on the excess income depends on the mix of dividends, savings income and non-savings income and may be as high as 33%, i.e. 1½ times 22%, where the extra income is wholly within the basic rate band. This is illustrated in Examples 1 to 3.

							(a) £	(b) £
Example 1								
Single person, aged 68, has income in 2004/05 of:								
Pension							11,900	12,100
Savings income (bank and building society interest)							7,000	7,000
							18,900	19,100
Personal allowance (over 65)								
Unrestricted							(6,830)	
Restricted by ½ of £200								(6,730)
Taxable income							12,070	12,370
Tax thereon:								
Non-savings income	2,020/	2,020	@ 10%	202	202			
	3.050/	3,350	@ 22%	671	737			
Savings income	7,000/	7,000	@ 20%	1,400	1,400			
	12,070/	12,370		£2,273	£2,339			

Additional tax payable on extra £200 income is £66, i.e. 33%, which is 1½ times 22%.

Example 2

Facts as in Example 1 but extra income is savings income.

				(a) £	(b) £
Pension				11,900	11,900
Savings income				7,000	7,200
				18,900	19,100
Personal allowance as before				(6,830)	(6,730)
Taxable income				12,070	12,370
Tax thereon:					
Non-savings income	2,020/	2,020	@ 10%	202	202
	3,050/	3,150	@ 22%	671	693
Savings income	7,000/	7,200	@ 20%	1,400	1,440
	12,070/	12,370		£2,273	£2,335

Additional tax payable on extra £200 income is £62, i.e. 31%. This is because the extra savings income attracts tax at 20%, but the withdrawal of £100 of the age allowance increases the income charged at 22%, representing a rate of 11% on £200, making 31% in total.

If the pension had been only £7,000 and the remaining income was savings income, the position would be:

				(a) £	(b) £
Pension				7,000	7,000
Savings income				11,900	12,100
				18,900	19,100
Personal allowance as before				(6,830)	(6,730)
Taxable income				12,070	12,370
Tax thereon:					
Non-savings income	170/	270	@ 10%	17	27
Savings income:	1,850/	1,750	@ 10%	185	175
	10,050/	10,350	@ 20%	2,010	2,070
	12,070/	12,370		£2,212	£2,272

Additional tax payable on extra £200 income is £60, i.e. 30%, because the extra £200 income has resulted in an extra £300 being taxed at the savings rate of 20%, so that the effective rate is 1½ x 20%.

Example 3

Facts as in the first part of Example 2, but with the savings income including tax-credit inclusive dividends of £2,000 and the extra £200 income being dividends.

				(a) £	(b) £
Pension				11,900	11,900
Savings income:					
Non-dividend income				5,000	5,000
Dividends				2,000	2,200
				18,900	19,100
Personal allowance as before				(6,830)	(6,730)
Taxable income				12,070	12,370
Tax thereon:					
Non-savings income	2,020/	2,020	@ 10%	202	202
	3,050/	3,150	@ 22%	671	693
Savings income other than					
dividends	5,000/	5,000	@ 20%	1,000	1,000
Dividends	2,000/	2,200	@ 10%	200	220
	12,070/	12,370		£2,073	£2,115

The extra tax of £42 represents 21% on the additional dividend income of £200, made up of 10% tax on the dividends plus a further 11% through the withdrawal of £100 age allowance as in the first part of Example 2.

To the extent that income above the age allowance threshold results in a reduction of married couple's allowance, the extra tax on that part of the excess income is only 5%, because the married couple's allowance saves tax at only 10%, so the tax cost of reducing the allowance by half of the excess income is only 5%.

If you are caught in the age allowance trap, you should consider reducing your taxable income by switching to tax-exempt investments such as national savings certificates and Individual Savings Accounts (ISAs). For details, see CHAPTERS 36 and 37.

Where you are entitled to reliefs against your income, such as donations to charity (see 2.9), the payments reduce your income for age allowance purposes. Your income for age allowances should strictly not be reduced by personal pension contributions, since tax relief for such contributions is given in a different way (see 17.15). By Revenue concession A102, however, the gross amount of personal pension contributions is treated as reducing income for the purpose of calculating age allowances.

Separation and divorce (TA 1988, s 347B)

34.4   Where a couple are separated or divorced, and either was born before 6 April 1935, a spouse making maintenance payments to the other spouse by court order, Child Support Agency assessment or written agreement is entitled to reduce his/her tax bill by a maintenance relief of 10% of £2,210 (or 10% of the maintenance paid if less). Relief is not available in respect of maintenance paid to or for children.

The full relief is available in the year of separation, as well as the married couple's allowance. Payments due after your spouse remarries do not qualify for relief. Maintenance relief is available to qualifying nationals of the European Economic Area (EEA — i.e. the European Union plus Iceland, Liechtenstein and Norway) who are resident in the UK and to qualifying UK nationals paying maintenance by order or written agreement of an EEA country. The relief is given by an adjustment to PAYE codings or in the payer's self-assessment.

All maintenance received is free of tax.

Pensions and State benefits

34.5   There are various points you need to know about pensions, both from employers and from the State. An increase in State pension results in a larger deduction of tax under PAYE from an occupational or personal pension. This is because the State pension increase takes up another slice of your tax allowances, reducing the amount available to set against your occupational or personal pension. You are still better off overall. People with small occupational pensions may not get the full benefit of their allowances and starting rate band through their tax deductions and may need to claim a refund (see Example 5 at 2.26).

Where allowances (in particular married couple's allowance) are restricted to 10%, PAYE codes incorporate an Allowance Restriction, which relies on estimates of your income to adjust the PAYE code so as to charge the correct amount of tax. Variations in income will lead to under- or overpayments and you should let your tax office know if your income varies substantially. Some people may be able to avoid overpaying tax by registering to receive bank and building society interest in full, but you are not entitled to register unless you will not be liable to pay tax at all — see 37.2. You can, however, claim a refund of tax deducted from bank and building society interest without waiting until the end of the tax year if the refund is £50 or more.

Some State benefits are taxable and others are not (see Table at 10.3), so you need to take care where you have a choice. See 13.3 for the changes being made to a widow's SERPS entitlement from 6 October 2002, and 33.9 and 33.10 for the bereavement payment of £2,000 and other bereavement benefits available to widows and widowers. For general points on State benefits, see CHAPTER 13.

Providing a home for a dependent relative (IHTA 1984, s 54; TCGA 1992, ss 73, 225)

34.6   A gain on the disposal of a property provided rent-free for a dependent relative, such as a parent over 65, used to be exempt from capital gains tax but this no longer applies unless the relative was in the property on 5 April 1988 and still lives there. It is, however, possible for you to acquire a property, put it into trust and allow an elderly relative to live in it rent-free for life, the property then reverting to you when the relative dies. There would be no income from the property, therefore no income tax to pay, capital gains tax would not be payable when the property reverted to you (but may be payable on a subsequent sale of the property by you — see 42.32), and providing the relative does not outlive you, inheritance tax would not be chargeable on the value of the property in the trust on the death of the relative, since there is an inheritance tax exemption where the property reverts to you in your lifetime. If the property was already owned for a time before it was put in trust and was not exempt as your private residence, there would be a chargeable gain at that time equal to the excess of the value of the property when transferred to the trust over its cost, taking into account indexation allowance to April 1998 and taper relief if appropriate (see CHAPTER 4). Professional advice is essential.

Purchased life annuities

34.7   A purchased life annuity is where you receive an annual sum for your lifetime in exchange for a capital payment. The characteristic of a purchased life annuity is that part of it is regarded as a return of capital and thus escapes tax; the income element is regarded as savings income and tax is deductible at only 20% (see 2.21 and 2.22). The older you are the greater the tax-free capital element of the annuity. You do, of course, sacrifice the capital required to buy the annuity, and this loss of capital must be weighed against the greater income arising. You may think the loss of capital is worthwhile to enable you to improve your standard of living, particularly if you have no dependants or others you want to leave your capital to. Recent annuity rates have, however, been very low and it is essential to get proper professional advice before making this sort of arrangement. See also 36.21 and 40.3.

Payments for long-term care (TA 1988, s 580C; FA 2004, s 147)

34.8   Payments made under an 'immediate needs annuity' (which is a special form of life annuity) to a care provider or local authority are exempt from tax. The exemption applies where the annuity is provided to fund long-term care for someone who is unable to live independently because of physical or mental infirmity. This applies to payments made on or after 1 October 2004, but in practice such payments were not taxed before that date.

Making the most of the dwelling house

34.9   Your home is often your most significant asset, yet it can be your biggest liability in the sense that you have to maintain it, and in most cases it does not produce income.

If you decide to let part of your home, you will not have to pay income tax on the rent unless it exceeds £4,250 a year — see 30.7. The letting will not cause you to lose any of your capital gains tax private residence exemption (see CHAPTER 30) when you sell the property provided that the gain on the let part does not exceed that on the exempt part, subject to a maximum exempt gain on the let part of £40,000. Taking in boarders who live as part of the family does not affect your capital gains tax exemption at all.

There are numerous life assurance/annuity/loan schemes, some of which are outlined below. Proper financial advice is essential and you must also be sure that the scheme gives you security of income and does not put your home at risk.

Sometimes the money to purchase a life annuity (see 34.7) is raised by a loan secured on your home (a home income plan). If the loan was taken out before 9 March 1999 (or a written offer of the loan had been made before that date), interest on the first £30,000 of the loan is still allowed for tax. Relief may be given under the MIRAS scheme despite the general MIRAS relief having been withdrawn. The rate of relief is 23%. You continue to be entitled to relief for the interest payable even if you remortgage, or move to another property or into a nursing home. The interest paid clearly reduces the extra income from the annuity and careful calculations are necessary to see if the result is a meaningful increase in your spending money. Another possibility is an arrangement whereby no interest is paid on the loan during your lifetime and the compensating interest payable to the lender on your death is fixed in advance.

A further possibility is a home reversion scheme, under which you sell all or part of your house to the reversion company for much less than its value (the discount usually being at least 50%) in return for the right to live in it until you die. Some schemes give you a lower initial sum but give you a share in future increases in value of the property. The initial cash sum does not attract capital gains tax but shares of future increases in value may be liable. The investment of the initial capital sum gives you extra spendable income.

Yet another possibility is a shared appreciation mortgage, where you get an interest free mortgage equal to a percentage of the value of the property in return for giving up a substantial part of any increase in value of the property when you either sell it or die. Unlike some earlier home income plans, you are not risking losing your home if property values fall, because if there is no increase only the amount of the mortgage is repaid.

Certain types of equity release scheme will be subject to regulation by the Financial Services Authority from October 2004 and home reversion plans will be brought within the regulations at a later date.

Helping the family

34.10   You may be in a position to give financial help to your family rather than requiring help from them. Income tax and possibly capital gains tax advantages may be obtained by placing funds in a 'bare trust' (other than for your children) — see 42.14. As far as inheritance tax is concerned, the following gifts may be made without inheritance tax consequences:

(a)   habitual gifts out of income that leave you with enough income to maintain your usual standard of living;

(b)   gifts of not more than £250 per donee in each tax year;

(c)   the first £3,000 of total gifts in each tax year, plus any unused part of the £3,000 exemption for the previous tax year. This exemption applies to gifts on an 'earliest first' basis, so if you gave away nothing last year and give £5,000 in May and £5,000 in June, the May gift is exempt and £1,000 of the June gift is exempt.

Even if the gift is not exempt, there is still no immediate inheritance tax to pay since lifetime gifts (other than to discretionary trusts) are only brought into account for inheritance tax if you do not survive the gift by seven years. In the meantime they are called 'potentially exempt transfers' (see 5.7). If you do not survive the seven-year period, there is still no question of inheritance tax being payable if the gift is within the nil rate band for inheritance tax, currently £263,000. This nil band is used against the earliest gifts in the seven years before death. Any gifts over and above the nil band are chargeable, but the tax is reduced on a sliding scale if you have survived the gift by more than three years. All non-exempt gifts within the seven years before death do, however, affect how much of the nil rate band is available to reduce the chargeable estate at death.

Husband and wife are treated separately for inheritance tax, each being entitled to the available exemptions and the nil rate band.

Tax position on death

34.11   When you die, your wealth at death and the chargeable transfers you have made in the previous seven years determine whether any, and if so how much, inheritance tax is payable (see CHAPTER 5). There is no inheritance tax on assets passing to your husband or wife. There is no liability to capital gains tax on any increase in the value of your assets up to the date of your death, and those who acquire the assets are treated as having bought them at their market value at the date of your death. Further details on the position at death are in CHAPTERS 33 and 35.

If capital gains have been made in that part of the tax year before your death, they are chargeable if they exceed the annual exemption, currently £8,200. Any capital losses in the tax year of death may be carried back to set against gains on which tax has been paid in the three previous tax years, latest first, and, in that event, tax will be repayable to the estate. Interest on the repayment runs from the payment date for the tax year of death (see 9.5).

As far as income tax is concerned, the income to the date of death is charged to tax in the usual way, and a full personal allowance is available. In the case of a married couple, the married couple's allowance, where still available, is given in full in the year of the wife's death but not in later years. If all or part of the allowance has been claimed by the wife, and her income in the year of death is insufficient to cover it, the balance may be transferred back to the husband (see 33.10). If the husband dies first, any part of the tax saving on the married couple's allowance that is not used against his tax bill may be transferred to the widow, and she can use it against any of her tax for the year, on income arising both before and after her husband's death (see 33.9).

Council tax

34.12   Your property is exempt from council tax if it is left unoccupied while you are a long-term hospital patient, or are being looked after in a residential care home, or are living elsewhere to receive care (see 8.3). You may qualify for a one-band reduction for council tax if your home has special features because you or another resident is disabled (see 8.6). Other discounts may be available (see 8.5).

People on low incomes are entitled to council tax benefit of up to 100% (see 8.7).

Tax points

34.13

• The present structure of tax rates will be very confusing to many people, particularly pensioners. The 10% tax credit on dividends is not repayable, so if your other income does not cover your allowances the dividend credits are wasted. The 10% starting rate band of £2,020 may be used against both non-savings income and savings income from banks, building societies etc. Those whose income is not fully covered by allowances and deductions cannot, however, register to receive bank etc. interest in full, so they may overpay tax and be required to claim a refund. Many pensioners will not be aware of their entitlement.

• The Revenue are launching a major campaign to get pensioners entitled to refunds to make repayment claims. They are using a new database (Pensioner Tax Back System — PTBS) to identify likely claimants. Their forecast is that 60,000 pensioners will make a claim during 2004/05, with tax refunds amounting to approximately £25 million.

• The marginal tax rate for those over 65 with income over £18,900 can be as high as 33%, so that investments that produce tax-free income or capital gains should be considered in those circumstances.

• In reckoning your income for age allowances, any investment bond withdrawals over the 5% limit have to be taken into account even though there is no tax to pay on that excess at the higher rate (see CHAPTER 40). Conversely, the gross amount of a properly recorded donation to a charity reduces your income when calculating whether age allowances are to be restricted. The same applies to a personal pension contribution (see 34.3).

• There is no point in increasing available income now if this jeopardises your capital and causes worry and uncertainty for the future.

• If you have a pre-9 March 1999 life annuity 'home income plan' and you have to leave your home, you can still get tax relief for loan interest for a limited time providing the property is put up for sale. You will not get the relief if you are not trying to sell it.

• Since lifetime transfers are potentially exempt from inheritance tax and do not have to be reported, it is most important to keep accurate records of gifts out of income and capital so that there can be no doubt about dates and amounts of gifts. Personal representatives are responsible for dealing with the inheritance tax position of lifetime transfers and carefully kept records are essential for the avoidance of doubt.

- If, because of disability, you have to provide, adapt or extend a bathroom, washroom or lavatory in your private residence, the cost is not liable to VAT. There is, however, no income tax relief on the cost or on money borrowed to finance the work.

- If your spouse does not have enough income to cover his/her personal allowance for income tax, you should consider transferring some of your assets to him/her if this is practicable, so that the income from them will then be his/hers and not yours (see 33.4). Interest on national savings bank accounts is paid gross, and the spouse's personal allowance can be used to cover interest from such accounts. Interest on other bank and building society accounts can only be paid gross to those who are able to register because they will not be liable to tax at all (see 37.2). If this does not apply, there will be a cash flow advantage with national savings bank interest, but the rates of interest on offer need to be compared as well. Remember that the personal allowance increases after age 65.

- If it is not appropriate to transfer assets from one spouse to the other, placing them in joint ownership but in unequal shares will still have the effect of the income being split equally even if the ownership share of the one spouse far exceeds that of the other (see 33.5). From 6 April 2004 this will no longer apply to dividends on shares in family companies.

- The income limit for married couple's allowance depends on the husband's income, even if the allowance is given because of the wife's age. It does not matter how high the wife's income is.

- If a husband's income is too low to use the married couple's allowance, the unused amount can be transferred to his wife and the full amount transferred is available to her, no matter how high her income is.

35
Making a will and post-death planning

If you die without making a will

35.1   If you die intestate, that is without making a will, the law divides your estate in a particular way. If you are married, your spouse automatically acquires the matrimonial home, and indeed any other assets (for example bank accounts), if they are owned as joint tenants (see 35.5), and the intestacy rules apply only to the remainder of your estate. If, on the other hand, the house and other assets were owned either by you alone or jointly with your spouse as tenants in common (see 35.5), your share would form part of your estate and would be subject to the intestacy rules. The intestacy rules applicable in England and Wales are set out in the following table. The spouse will not inherit under these rules unless he/she survives the deceased spouse by at least 28 days.

Where there is a surviving spouse Are there any:			Spouse takes:	Remainder
Children and their issue*	Parents	Brothers and sisters and their issue*		
No	No	No	Whole estate	
Yes			Personal chattels + £125,000 + life interest in half of residue	Children (or their issue*) share half residue and take spouse's share on his or her death
No	Yes		Personal chattels + £200,000 + half of residue absolutely	Parents share half of residue absolutely
No	No	Yes	''	Brothers and sisters (or their issue*) share half of residue absolutely

Where there is no surviving spouse

If there are children, or their issue*, they take the whole estate absolutely.

If there are no children or their issue*, the whole estate goes to surviving relatives in the following order of precedence, each category taking the whole estate to the exclusion of any later category:

Parents
Brothers and sisters (or their issue*)
Half brothers and sisters (or their issue*)
Grandparents
Uncles and aunts (or their issue*)
Parents' half brothers and sisters (or their issue*)

If there are none of these relatives, the estate goes to the Crown.

*   'Issue' means children and their children, grandchildren, great grandchildren etc., each such person being entitled to an appropriate proportion of the deceased parent's share.

The share of anyone under 18 is held on trust to age 18.

It is possible for those entitled under an intestacy to vary their entitlement (see 35.10), but the shares of beneficiaries under 18 cannot be reduced without court consent.

General considerations

35.2   In making the best arrangements from a taxation point of view, you should not forget that the prime objective is to ensure that those left behind are properly provided for in a sensible, practical and acceptable way. There are important tax implications, which it can be expensive to ignore, but they should not be allowed to override the main aim.

It should be borne in mind that wills need to be regularly reviewed to ensure that they remain appropriate. In particular, the effect of marriage, separation or divorce needs to be borne in mind. A will is generally revoked by marriage. It is not revoked on divorce, although bequests to the former spouse would no longer apply, nor any appointment of the spouse as executor. Separation has no effect on a will. If the family home is held as joint tenants, the joint tenancy will not be affected by either separation or divorce, so it will usually be appropriate for separating couples to sever the joint tenancy in order to ensure that if one dies before the couple's affairs are settled, the property does not automatically go to the other (see 35.5).

Where the court considers that the terms of a will or the intestacy rules do not make reasonable financial provision for certain people, such as a spouse, former spouse who has not remarried, child, or cohabitee, they may make an appropriate order, for example for the payment of a lump sum or maintenance. Such orders take effect as if they had applied at the date of death and override the provisions of the will or intestacy rules.

Inheritance tax: spouse exemption (IHTA 1984, s 18; TCGA 1992, s 58)

35.3   Gifts between husband and wife are exempt from inheritance tax for both lifetime and death transfers (unless the donee is not domiciled in the UK, in which case gifts are exempt up to a limit of £55,000 — see CHAPTER 5). Transfers between husband and wife in a tax year when they are living together are also exempt from capital gains tax, and there is no stamp duty or stamp duty land tax on gifts.

Since husband and wife are each entitled to the inheritance tax nil rate threshold (currently £263,000) before transfers become chargeable, it is clearly sensible for the joint wealth to be arranged in such a way that each takes advantage of it. The tax advantage may, however, be lost on death if the estate is then left to the surviving spouse. If, say, each had £263,000 wealth and made no transfers in the seven years before death, no tax would arise if each left the wealth to the next generation, because it would be covered by the nil rate threshold. But if the wealth were left to the surviving spouse, that spouse would then have £526,000 (ignoring any capital variation in the meantime) which would attract a tax liability of £105,200 (at current rates) on the second death.

Bypassing your spouse will not be practicable if he/she is left with inadequate assets to maintain his/her standard of living. The surviving spouse can still have the benefit of the joint capital during his/her lifetime whilst preserving the family wealth for the next generation through the use of life insurance to cover the tax liability on the second death. This is dealt with later in the chapter.

Providing the nil rate threshold is used by each spouse, there is no inheritance tax incentive to equalise estates in lifetime, and indeed it may be better on death to leave the excess over the nil rate threshold to the surviving spouse so that tax would be paid later rather than earlier, and the surviving spouse would be able to make further tax-exempt gifts and gifts within the nil rate threshold as it increased year by year. But for income tax, it is tax-efficient for each spouse to have sufficient capital to produce enough income to use the starting and basic rate bands, capital gains also being charged at income tax rates, so the overall position needs to be looked at.

Use of discretionary trusts

35.4 It is possible, in order to use up the nil threshold, to leave £263,000 or other appropriate amount to a trust where the trustees have a discretion as to what they do with the income and capital. You could include your wife/husband as one of the beneficiaries. The supporting capital is thus not transferred to your spouse directly to swell his/her estate for tax purposes on eventual death, but any unexpected need may be made good by the trustees exercising their discretion to pay amounts to him/her.

A discretionary trust is also useful where there is some uncertainty at the time of making the will as to who should benefit. A transfer of the capital to one or more individuals by the trustees within two years after your death (but not within the first three months of that two years) is treated for inheritance tax purposes as having been made by your will, and has the same effect. Capital gains tax may, however, be payable (see 35.10).

Discretionary trusts are dealt with in more detail at 42.18 to 42.25. The use of discretionary trusts in tax planning is a complicated area, and professional advice is essential.

Jointly owned assets

35.5 There are two ways in which assets may be held jointly — as joint tenants or as tenants in common. If you hold an asset with someone else as a joint tenant, it automatically passes to the other joint tenant(s) when you die. With a tenancy in common, each has a separate share which can be disposed of in lifetime or on death as the person wishes. Husband and wife are presumed to own assets as joint tenants, and other people are presumed to own them as tenants in common, but if they want to vary the normal presumption this can be done. It must, however, be done in the proper legal manner appropriate to the asset.

The appropriate share in a jointly held asset still forms part of a person's estate for inheritance tax whether the asset is held on a joint tenancy or as tenants in common, but where assets are held jointly by husband and wife, any assets passing to the spouse are covered in any event by the spouse exemption. Holding as joint tenants has the advantage in the case of a joint bank or building society account that when your spouse dies, all that is needed to enable you to take over sole ownership of the account is production of the death certificate. You do not have to wait for grant of probate or administration. But a joint account has other tax implications, particularly in relation to income tax since the shares of income accruing to each spouse may not give the best income tax position.

The joint ownership principles must be borne in mind when planning the use of the nil rate threshold for inheritance tax, and action taken to vary the normal presumptions where necessary (see 33.5).

The family home

35.6   Although most taxation aspects relating to the family home are dealt with in CHAPTER 30, there are various points which are of particular importance when making a will, albeit the taxation considerations should never be allowed to get in the way of the security and comfort in body and mind of the surviving spouse or other dependants.

Whatever is done will have an impact not only on inheritance tax but also on capital gains tax, income tax and stamp duty land tax, so it is essential that no aspect is considered in isolation. The possibility that the spouse or dependant who would normally occupy the property might need to go into care should not be forgotten, bearing in mind that the house value might have to be realised to pay fees which might otherwise be subsidised by the authorities if the spouse or dependants did not have an entitlement to occupy the house or receive the sale proceeds.

Where the will provides that the home is left to a surviving spouse or dependant outright, or that he/she is entitled to occupy it for his/her life, then on the death of the surviving spouse or dependant, the value of the home at that time will be reckonable for inheritance tax, but no capital gains tax will be payable on the increase in value to that time, with that value becoming the cost for a future disposal.

A problem might, however, arise when the first spouse dies in that while it is clearly sensible for inheritance tax purposes to use the £263,000 threshold by leaving sufficient wealth away from the surviving spouse, with a potential 40% saving on that amount at the second death, there may not be enough wealth to enable that to be done without taking into account the value of the house or of a share in it. Not only might the surviving spouse be unhappy that he/she has to rely for his/her continued occupation on the co-operation of the family who have inherited the house or a share in it, but family members who do not occupy the house might face a capital gains tax charge on any increase in value, whereas that increase would have escaped capital gains tax had the occupant either owned the house outright or been entitled to occupy it under an appropriate trust.

Again, a spouse who inherits the house and is considering giving it away must not fall foul of the clear rule that he/she must not retain a benefit after doing so if the value is not to be reckoned for inheritance tax at his/her death. This could be avoided by the surviving spouse paying a commercial rent to the donee upon which the donee would pay income tax (but perhaps in the process reducing any income surplus of the surviving spouse which would otherwise increase the donor's wealth on eventual death). The gift would drop out of the inheritance tax reckoning after seven years.

If, having given away the property, instead of paying rent the surviving spouse paid a lump sum for the right to occupy the property for life, the value of the spouse's estate for inheritance tax would deplete at once by the purchase price of the lease for life, with the gift of the property dropping out of the reckoning after seven years.

A variation on this theme might be the next generation purchasing the house from the surviving spouse with a commercial loan, the interest being funded by the rent received from the spouse and income tax only being paid on the net surplus. This would provide cash to the former house owner who could either use it to produce income or to make capital gifts, the value of the house in the meantime increasing in the hands of the next generation.

But none of the arrangements in the previous three paragraphs would protect the increasing value of the home from capital gains tax, since the property at the time of death of the surviving spouse would neither be owned by him/her nor occupied under the terms of a trust.

Mention has been made in 35.4 of the use of a discretionary trust to use up the inheritance tax nil threshold, but with the surviving spouse being a beneficiary under the trust. Where the family home is included in the trust, the surviving spouse could be allowed to occupy it. If instead, the spouse is not a beneficiary under the discretionary trust, he/she could purchase it from the trustees, thus having the comfort and security of ownership, with the capital gains tax uplift applying at his/her death. If he/she had insufficient resources for the purchase, the trustees could allow the purchase price to remain on loan from them. This would effectively leave the present value of the house out of the estate of the surviving spouse, but the increase would be within it, albeit attracting capital gains tax private residence relief on that increase.

A number of more sophisticated arrangements might be considered, but with these and indeed the others outlined in this section, a word of caution is necessary in that what might be attractive for one purpose is often not so for another, with savings on the one hand sometimes being eroded by costs on the other, and the Capital Taxes Office also being able to challenge arrangements which might be considered to be artificial.

Professional advice is essential.

Legacies and their effect on the spouse exemption

35.7   Unless a will states otherwise, legacies are payable out of the residue of an estate, after inheritance tax has been paid, reducing the amount available to the person entitled to the balance of the estate — called the residuary legatee. The legacies are not themselves reduced by inheritance tax unless the will specifically says so. It follows that the amount available to a residuary legatee is often less than is apparent at first sight.

If the residuary legatee is the surviving spouse, this has an effect on the tax payable because the exempt part of the estate (which goes to the spouse) is first reduced by the tax. In Example 1, out of a gross estate of £400,000, A's children receive legacies totalling £280,000, leaving an apparent residue of £120,000 for the widow. She does not, however, get £120,000, but only that amount less the tax on the rest of the estate. This is calculated by working out the tax on a figure sufficient to leave the legacies intact, called grossing-up. The tax amounts to £11,333 as shown in the example, leaving the widow with £108,667. If the will had provided that the children should pay the tax on their legacies, the widow would have received £120,000 and the total tax payable by the legatees on £280,000 would have been £6,800 (40% of the £17,000 excess over £263,000). The children could have provided for this liability by insuring their father's life, using the proceeds of the policy to pay the tax on the legacy.

Example 1

A has made no transfers in the seven years before his death in 2004/05. He leaves an estate of £400,000 as follows:

£70,000 to each of his four children = £280,000
Residue to his wife

The inheritance tax position on A's death is as follows:

	Gross £	Tax £	Net £
Net legacies up to the nil threshold	263,000		263,000
Balance grossed up at 100/60	28,333	11,333	17,000
	291,333	11,333	280,000

The estate will accordingly be divided as follows:

Gross estate	400,000
Legacies to children	(280,000)
Inheritance tax payable out of residue	(11,333)
Remainder to widow, covered by spouse exemption	£108,667

Where there are deaths in quick succession (IHTA 1984, s 141)

35.8   Where at the time of someone's death, his estate has been increased by a lifetime or death gift made to him within the previous five years, the tax charge on the second transfer is reduced by quick succession relief. Although the relief is deducted from the tax payable on the second transfer, it is calculated as a percentage of the tax paid on the earlier transfer (see CHAPTER 5).

Quick succession relief is therefore not relevant in the case of assets acquired from a spouse, in lifetime or on death, or where they have been acquired in lifetime but no tax has been paid by reference to that transfer. While not losing sight of the overriding principle of family provision, there are cases where it is clearly not sensible to increase a person's estate by incoming transfers, if they have adequate resources already. Thus it will often be more tax-efficient to leave to grandchildren instead of to children. This gives the added advantage that the income arising is then that of the grandchildren in their own right, on which they will not have to pay tax if it is covered by their available income tax allowances.

Simultaneous deaths and survivorship clauses (IHTA 1984, s 92)

35.9   Where two closely related people die at the same time, or in circumstances in which it is impossible to decide who died first, neither estate has to be increased by any entitlement from the other in calculating the inheritance tax payable. This is not so if it is clear who died first. It is therefore often advisable to include a survivorship clause in a will making a bequest conditional on the beneficiary outliving the deceased by a given period, and this is effective for inheritance tax providing the period does not exceed six months. This is particularly useful to a husband and wife who wish to leave their estates to each other to make sure that there is adequate provision for the survivor's lifetime. If the wills include an appropriate survivorship clause, then if they both die within six months, the estate of the first will not pass to the second, inheritance tax being payable at each death on the value of the separate estates. This will often attract less tax than if no tax was paid on the first death, but tax was calculated on the combined estates for the second, with the second spouse to die having had little or no benefit from the assets in the meantime. The assets in each estate and the extent to which the inheritance tax nil rate band is available need to be taken into account.

A 28-day spouse survivorship period is also prescribed under the intestacy rules (see 35.1).

Variations and disclaimers etc (IHTA 1984, ss 17, 142–144, 218A; TCGA 1992, s 62)

35.10   It is possible for those entitled to a deceased's estate (either under a will, on an intestacy or otherwise) to vary the way in which it is distributed, or to disclaim their entitlement, provided that they do so within two years after the death. The variation or disclaimer then takes effect as if it had applied at the date of death. For variations (but not disclaimers) this applies only if the variation contains a statement by those making it, and by the personal representatives if additional tax is payable, that they intend the variation to have that effect. Where additional tax is payable, then within six months after the date of the variation the personal representatives must notify the amount of additional tax to the Revenue and send a copy of the variation. Court consent is needed for a variation that adversely affects the shares of beneficiaries under 18. If an original beneficiary has died, his personal representatives can act in his place but there may be restrictions on what they are able to vary. Following the variation or disclaimer inheritance tax is charged as if the revised distribution had operated at death.

Such a variation or disclaimer can also be effective for capital gains tax purposes (subject to what is said below about trusts) providing, in the case of a variation, the document specifies that it is to apply for capital gains tax. The ultimate beneficiary then takes the asset at the market value at the date of death, so that any increase in value since death is not charged to capital gains tax until the beneficiary disposes of the asset. The original entitlement under the will, while the estate is in administration, is itself a right (a chose in action), and but for the specific application of the variation to capital gains tax, the variation might itself be regarded as a disposal of that right, causing a liability to capital gains tax. As far as income derived from the assets is concerned, the personal representatives will have paid income tax on it at the appropriate rate (i.e. either the basic rate of 22% on non-savings income, the lower rate of 20% on savings income other than dividends and 10% on dividend income), but the income is regarded as having been received not by the person who actually receives it following the variation but by the original beneficiary, and any tax due in excess of the amount paid on the income up to the date of variation or disclaimer will be calculated by reference to the original beneficiary's tax rates. It may be appropriate for the person actually receiving the income to agree to pay any income tax at excess rates. Where a variation includes the setting up of a trust, those whose entitlement but for the variation goes into the trust are regarded as settlors of the trust fund for income tax and capital gains tax, so that, for example, parents whose share is given up in favour of infant children will still be taxed on the income so long as the children are under 18 and unmarried, and trustees' capital gains may be treated as the original beneficiary's gains if that person is a beneficiary under the trust.

A deed of variation or disclaimer could be used to advantage where, for example, an estate has been left to the surviving spouse without the deceased's nil rate threshold having been used. If the surviving spouse is already adequately provided for, part of the estate could be diverted to, say, the children. It could also be useful where, for example, children have sufficient assets of their own and would prefer legacies to go to their own children, subject to what is said above about trusts.

Where quoted shares fall in value within the twelve months after death and are sold, cancelled, or dealings are suspended within that period, the lower value may be substituted in calculating tax on the death estate (see 5.15). The reference to cancellation is apparently intended mainly to apply to liquidations, but it may be that the liquidation is not completed within the twelve-month period, so that the relief cannot be claimed. One way of avoiding the tax liability on the higher death value of the shares would be to use a deed of variation to re-direct the shares to an exempt beneficiary, such as a spouse, so that there would be no tax payable on that higher value.

Deeds of variation and disclaimer can be used to lessen the overall tax burden on death, but it is necessary for all concerned to consent to the arrangement, and they should usually be regarded as something in reserve rather than a substitute for appropriate planning.

Two other ways of building flexibility into a will are worth consideration. It is possible for someone making a will to leave a 'letter of wishes' asking the personal representatives to give effect to the requests in the letter. This is particularly useful for dealing with chattels and personal effects, and is treated for inheritance tax purposes as if it had been part of the will. The letter of wishes is not, however, binding upon the personal representatives, as distinct from being useful guidance to them. The other useful provision is the ability to create a discretionary trust by will, out of which the trustees can make distributions within two years of the death, which are again treated as having been made by the will, providing they are not made within the first three months after the death. This can, however, have capital gains consequences if the assets have grown in value since the date of death because the trustees would be taxable at 40% on that increase (subject to any available annual exemption) unless business assets gifts relief applied (see 4.27). The gifts relief normally available for transfers out of discretionary trusts does not apply because inheritance tax is not chargeable on the distribution. It is possible for the capital gains charge to be avoided if the trustees appoint assets out of the trust to beneficiaries *before* the personal representatives transfer the assets to them. This is a complex area and professional advice is essential.

Insurance

35.11   Life assurance may often be useful in planning for inheritance tax. It is not always possible to reconcile making adequate provision for the family with reducing the tax liability, and insurance may then be used to cover the anticipated liability.

There is no point in insuring your own life for the benefit of your estate, because the proceeds would then form part of the estate and attract inheritance tax. Furthermore, they would not be available until the grant of probate or administration is obtained. If, however, a policy on your life is arranged by someone with an insurable interest, say your children, or you take out a policy yourself and pay the premiums, with the proceeds in trust for someone else, again say your children, the funds will not be taxable in your estate. If you pay the premiums on a trust policy, each payment is a separate gift, but you will usually be able to show that it is normal expenditure out of income, and thus exempt from inheritance tax, or, if not, covered by the annual exemption of £3,000 for transfers out of capital.

Tax points

35.12

- Since inheritance tax is charged at a single 40% rate on the excess of the estate over the exempt threshold, currently £263,000, no extra inheritance tax savings will be made by transferring assets from one spouse to the other once each has used that nil threshold. It may be better to leave most of the excess over the nil threshold to the surviving spouse, to avoid tax on the first death and give maximum flexibility for the future. The income tax and capital gains tax position needs to be looked at as well.

- Where tax at death cannot be avoided, consider covering the liability through life insurance, the policy being written so that the proceeds belong to those who will have to bear the tax.

- If you leave your entire estate to your spouse, he/she can make lifetime transfers out of your combined wealth to an extent which he/she sees as sensible depending on the family circumstances from time to time. Those transfers may be completely exempt if they are covered by annual or marriage exemptions, or potentially exempt, becoming completely exempt if your spouse survives for seven years after making them (and where they exceed the nil rate threshold any tax arising would be subject to tapering relief on survival for three years). Unless you use appropriate trust provisions, you cannot ensure that your spouse will carry out your wishes, since if your estate is left to him/her unconditionally, it is up to the spouse what he/she does with it.

- Although those entitled to your estate have the right to vary the way it is to be distributed, it is sometimes useful for your will to contain authority for a deed of variation, since this may help the beneficiaries to accept that they would not be acting against your wishes.

- If you are apprehensive about leaving outright bequests to certain people, but still want them to benefit, you could leave an amount in trust for them to receive the income it produces, and in certain circumstances, the capital. There are only minimal, if any, taxation disadvantages and it may give you the comfort of knowing that, for example, an adult child, whilst able to benefit immediately from the income, does not have an outright capital sum until a later stage when he/she is better able to manage it.

- Since all gifts to your spouse are exempt from inheritance tax, it is often more tax effective to leave agricultural and/or business property to someone else, otherwise agricultural and business property relief will be wasted. The tax position should not, however, override family and commercial considerations.

- Where inheritance tax business property and agricultural property reliefs are at the rate of 100%, deferring gifts of such property until your death avoids any charge to capital gains tax and also any problems of the inheritance tax relief being withdrawn at death because the donee has disposed of the property. But today's reliefs may not be available tomorrow, and you may still prefer to make lifetime gifts now, deferring any capital gains tax under the gifts relief provisions (see 4.27).

- Although wealth left to the next generation is liable to inheritance tax on your death, whereas it is not liable if left to your spouse, inheritance tax is avoided on any increase in value between your death and that of your spouse, if the next generation inherits at the death of the first rather than the second parent.

- Changing legislation, as well as family circumstances, make it important to review wills regularly.

- If you hold shares through a nominee holding with a broker, he has the legal right to sell them after your death before probate is granted. The broker may be willing to do this at the executors' request in order to raise sufficient funds for the executors to pay the inheritance tax due without borrowing. See also 42.1 for provisions enabling personal representatives to arrange for banks etc. holding the deceased's funds to pay inheritance tax direct to the Revenue.

- It will make your executors' task far easier if you keep an up-to-date schedule of your investments, mortgages, pensions etc., with your will, showing where all the relevant documents are kept. Any potentially exempt gifts for inheritance tax (see CHAPTER 5) should also be recorded.

- For further post-death planning points see CHAPTER 42, which deals with the administration of a deceased's estate.

36
Tax on your investments

Introduction

36.1 This chapter outlines the tax position on the main forms of investment available to the majority of taxpayers. More detailed information is given in CHAPTER 37 on investing in banks and building societies and in CHAPTER 38 on stocks and shares. The following investments are not dealt with in this chapter but are covered in the chapters indicated:

(a) Industrial buildings (CHAPTER 22).

(b) Unquoted trading companies through the enterprise investment scheme (CHAPTER 29).

(c) Single premium life assurance policies — investment bonds (CHAPTER 40).

(d) Chattels and valuables (CHAPTER 39).

The information given on each type of investment is so that you can see the effect of taxation on the income and capital growth. It is not intended to replace advice on the investments themselves, which you should seek from appropriate sources.

If you make investments through an authorised investment adviser, and you suffer loss as a result of bad advice, poor investment management or the adviser going out of business, you may claim compensation under the Financial Services Compensation Scheme of up to 100% of £30,000 and 90% of the next £20,000, giving an overall maximum compensation figure of £48,000.

Tax on investment income

36.2 For individuals, most investment income is currently charged to tax at 10% if it is dividend income and at 20% otherwise, unless taxable income exceeds the higher rate threshold of £31,400, in which case dividends are taxed at 32½% and other income at 40%. In many cases tax at the 20% rate is deducted at source and dividends carry a 10% tax credit. Higher rate taxpayers then have further tax to pay and non-taxpayers are entitled to a repayment (other than on dividends). See 36.19 for further points on dividends. Tax on interest received gross, and higher rate tax on taxed income, is included in the half-yearly payments on account on 31 January in the tax year and 31 July following for continuing sources (unless covered by the de minimis limits — see 9.7), with any balance being part of the overall balancing payment due on 31 January following the tax year. For employees or pensioners with small amounts of untaxed interest, the tax may be collected by adjusting their PAYE codings.

Where income tax is deducted from a company's income, the company still has to pay corporation tax on the income, but gets a credit against its tax payable for the income tax deducted. Income tax is no longer deducted from many payments made by and to companies (see 3.17). See also 36.16 re interest on government stocks.

Investing in building societies and banks (other than the National Savings Bank)

36.3 Most people who invest in building societies and banks invest in normal interest-bearing accounts. The interest on such accounts is received after deduction of tax at the lower rate of 20%, unless you are able to register to receive interest in full because your total income is expected to be covered by your personal allowances (see 37.2). If after the end of the tax year the tax deducted is more than your liability, you may claim a repayment of tax from the Revenue. You can claim a repayment before the end of the year if it amounts to £50 or more. If you have received interest in full and it is found at the end of the tax year that some tax is due, the tax will have to be paid. There are other types of investment on offer — for example mini and maxi cash Individual Savings Accounts (ISAs) (see 36.22). For details on the tax treatment of bank and building society accounts other than ISAs, see CHAPTER 37.

National Savings Bank accounts

36.4 The National Savings Bank operates both ordinary and investment accounts, although after 31 July 2004 ordinary accounts will become dormant and holders will only be able to access the accounts either to close them or to transfer them to the 'easy access savings accounts' which have replaced them (see below). So long as ordinary accounts remain open, however, the account balances will continue to earn interest. Interest on both types of account is credited annually on 31 December without deduction of income tax (see 36.2 for the way in which tax is collected). The National Savings Bank also operates accounts that are eligible for the cash component of ISAs (see 36.22).

The first £70 of interest on ordinary accounts is and will continue to be exempt from tax (for husband and wife, £70 each). The rate of interest at 1 June 2004 is 0.7% on balances of £500 or more and 0.6% on lower balances.

The investment account pays interest at varying rates depending on the amount invested and gives you a cash flow advantage compared with investing in other banks or building societies if you are not entitled to register to receive your bank and building society interest without having tax deducted. Receiving the National Savings interest in full to start with saves you having to wait for a tax repayment. One month's notice is required for withdrawals.

From 29 January 2004 a new easy access savings account was introduced to replace the ordinary account. It is card based and account holders will receive quarterly statements. Accounts may be opened and operated by telephone, by post, on the internet, or at post office branches and may also be operated via ATM machines. The minimum balance is £100 and the maximum holding £2 million (£4 million for joint accounts). Deposits are subject to a £10 minimum, and up to £300 may be withdrawn daily. Interest rates are variable and paid gross on 31 March annually. Unlike the ordinary account, there is no exempt slice of interest and the full amount earned must be declared on tax returns.

Fixed interest National Savings certificates

36.5   These certificates may be attractive to those paying income tax at the higher rate, since the interest, at rates guaranteed for either two or five years, accumulates over the period of the investment, and when the certificates are cashed the increase in value is totally free from income tax and capital gains tax. They may also be attractive to someone whose income would otherwise exceed the age allowance income limit (see 34.3). The minimum purchase is £100. New issues are made fairly frequently, so you need to check the details of the issue currently on offer. A maximum holding of certificates is prescribed for each issue, that for the 77th five-year and 27th two-year issues being £15,000, but in addition an unlimited amount may be reinvested from matured certificates (including index-linked and yearly plan certificates). The certificates may be wholly or partly repaid before maturity, so that regular withdrawals could be made to provide an effective tax-free income, although at a lower rate of return. The certificates are repaid at their purchase price in the first year (except for reinvested certificates, which carry interest for each complete three months in the first year), but after that, the tax-free yield rises each year, with the increases biased to discourage early repayment. The compound tax-free interest rate for the 77th five-year issue if held for the full period is 3.65% per annum and for the 27th two-year issue 3.5%. On maturity, the certificates may be rolled over for the same term at new rates of interest, or reinvested for a different term or into a different type of certificate, or cashed in. Some of the earlier issues attract only the lower general extension rate on maturity. Holders need to check interest rates to ensure they obtain the best available terms.

National Savings index-linked certificates

36.6   As with the fixed interest certificates, index-linked certificates are subject to a minimum purchase of £100. They provide inflation proofing over a three or five-year period, plus guaranteed extra interest on an increasing scale each year, but biased to discourage early repayment. The original purchase price is index-linked in line with the increase in the retail prices index, and the index-linking and extra interest are earned monthly from the date of purchase (subject to the rules for early encashment). At the end of each year, the index increases and extra interest are capitalised, and the total amount then qualifies for index-linking and extra interest in the following year. The compound extra interest over the full term in addition to the index linking is 1.35% for the 35th five-year issue and 1.25% for the 8th three-year issue.

The certificates may be wholly or partly repaid. If they are cashed within the first year, only the amount invested is repaid (except for reinvested certificates, which earn index-linking and interest for each complete month). If they are cashed after the first year, they qualify for the index increases plus extra interest for each complete month they have been held since the date of purchase. Although the extra interest rates are guaranteed for only three or five years, the certificates may be held for longer, and after the end of the fixed period they attract interest at an indexed extension rate unless they are reinvested or cashed in. The same maturity options apply as stated above for fixed interest certificates. Any increase in the value when the certificates are cashed is free of income tax and capital gains tax.

There is a limit on the maximum holding of certificates in each issue, which has been increased from £10,000 to £15,000 from 29 April 2004, but an unlimited additional amount may be reinvested from matured certificates (including fixed interest and yearly plan certificates).

These certificates are suitable for taxpayers who are prepared to forgo immediate income to protect their capital in real terms, and the extra interest improves the return and is itself fully index-linked once earned. Those who want regular income could make partial withdrawals of their investment, but at a lower rate of return on the certificates cashed.

National Savings capital bonds

36.7   Capital bonds may be purchased by investing £100 upwards, with an upper limit of £1 million. The bonds are for a five-year period at a guaranteed rate of interest, which works out at 5% per annum compound on Series 19 if you hold the bonds for the full five years. The interest is added to the bond each year. They may be cashed in early but there is no interest if they are repaid in the first year, and you earn a lower rate unless you hold the bonds for the full five years.

Although the interest is taxable, it is received in full and tax is accounted for as indicated at 36.2. The disadvantage for taxpayers is that tax is payable every year even though no income is received from the bond until the end of the five-year period, unless it is wholly or partly cashed in, in which case lower interest rates apply.

National Savings income bonds

36.8   National Savings income bonds are intended for those who wish to invest lump sums at a reasonable rate of interest, and to receive a regular income from their capital. At the time of writing, the rate of interest is 3.95% gross on up to £25,000 and 4.2% gross on £25,000 and over. Interest is paid by monthly instalments, either by post or direct to a bank account. Although the interest is taxable, it is received in full and tax is accounted for as indicated at 36.2. The bonds are particularly beneficial for those whose income is not high enough for tax to have to be paid. The minimum holding is £500 and the maximum £1 million, for either an individual or joint holding. Three months' notice is required to obtain repayment. Alternatively the bonds may be cashed without notice subject to the loss of 90 days' interest.

National Savings pensioners' bonds

36.9   National Savings pensioners' guaranteed income bonds are similar to the ordinary income bonds, but ordinary income bonds carry a variable interest rate. Pensioners' bonds enable those over 60 to invest between £500 and £1 million in bonds carrying interest fixed either for five years, two years or one year. The five-year bonds carry interest at 4.9% per annum gross (on the current Series 40 issue) for the first five years. The two-year bonds (Series 31) carry interest for the first two years at 4.7%. The rate of interest on the one-year bonds (Series 25) is 4.55%. The interest is paid monthly direct into a building society or bank account. Repayment may be made without notice at maturity, or after 60 days' notice (no interest being paid during the notice period), or with no notice and 90 days' loss of interest. Although the interest is taxable, it is received in full and tax is accounted for as indicated at 36.2.

National Savings fixed rate savings bonds

36.10   Fixed rate savings bonds offer fixed rates of interest depending on the amount invested, guaranteed for a period ranging from one to five years.

Unlike other National Savings products, tax is deducted from the interest (at the 20% lower rate), the net interest being added to the bond annually. Those liable to higher rate tax will have further tax to pay, and those not liable to pay tax may claim a refund (see 36.2). The minimum holding is £500 and the maximum £1 million, and bonds can be held indefinitely or cashed at full term without penalty. Bonds cashed other than at full term carry a 90-day interest penalty.

Children's bonus bonds

36.11   National Savings children's bonus bonds for children under 16 are in units of £25 and the maximum holding per child is £1,000 in each issue. The current issue 15 carries a guaranteed return over the first five years of 4.7% per annum compound. The bonds may be cashed in before the end of the five years, but no interest is earned if they are cashed in the first year and only 3% per annum is earned on later early repayments. At the end of five years they may be held for a further five years at revised guaranteed rates of interest, except that they mature at the holder's 21st birthday and no further returns are earned after that time.

All returns are exempt from tax, and parents may provide the funds without affecting their own tax liability.

National Savings Treasurer's Account

36.12   The National Savings Treasurer's Account is for non-profit-making organisations such as charities, clubs and societies. Interest is paid gross. The minimum deposit is £10,000 and the maximum £2 million. Funds may be withdrawn on 30 days' notice without penalty, or without notice with the loss of 30 days' interest. The rates of interest at the time of writing range from 3.1% to 3.65% depending on the amount invested.

National Savings Guaranteed Equity Bonds

36.13   National Savings and Investments offer Guaranteed Equity Bonds, which are five-year investments with a guaranteed return linked to the increase in the FTSE 100 index. Eight issues of the bonds have been made at the time of writing, each issue being available only for a limited period or until fully subscribed if earlier. The 8th issue guarantees a return at the end of the five-year term equal to 75% of the growth in the FTSE 100 index, or a minimum return of 15%, whichever is higher. Even if the FTSE 100 falls during the five-year period the amount invested will be repaid in full. At the end of the term, in addition to any return on the bond, investors receive interest for the period from the time of their investment to the issue of the bond. Both the FTSE return and the interest are paid in full, but are liable to tax. Special provisions apply if the investor dies before the bond matures.

Premium savings bonds

36.14   Any person over 16 can buy these bonds and an adult can buy them for a child under 16. The minimum purchase is £100, and the current maximum holding is £30,000. They do not carry interest, but, once a bond has been held for a clear calendar month, it is included in a regular monthly draw for prizes of various amounts. All prizes are free of income tax and capital gains tax and the bond itself can be encashed at face value at any time. This gives you the chance to win a tax-free prize, but at the cost of not receiving any income or protection of the real value of your capital.

Local authority stock, bonds and loans

36.15   Some local authority stocks are listed on the Stock Exchange and interest on the stocks is paid to individuals after deduction of income tax. Local authorities also raise money by unlisted temporary loans, mortgages and non-negotiable bonds. Interest on these items is usually paid to individuals after deduction of 20% income tax, although if your income is not more than your available personal allowance you can register to receive interest gross in the same way as with bank and building society interest (see 37.2). Interest paid by local authorities to companies is paid gross (see 3.17).

Local authority stocks, bonds and loans that are transferable are subject to the accrued income provisions described at 36.18. They are also within the definition of 'qualifying corporate bonds' and are exempt from capital gains tax. See 38.23.

Income, gains and losses relating to a company's holdings of local authority stocks, etc. are taken into account in calculating the company's income, and disposals are not within the capital gains regime (see 3.6 and 38.22).

Government stocks (TA 1988, s 50; TCGA 1992, s 115; F(No 2)A 1997, s 37)

36.16   These represent borrowings by the British government, and they vary considerably in terms of interest. Some are issued on an index-linked basis so that the interest paid while the stock is held and the capital payment when it is redeemed are dependent on increases in the retail prices index. From 6 April 1998 interest is paid gross on *all* government stocks acquired on or after that date, unless application is made for net payment. Payment will also be made gross from that date on taxed stocks acquired earlier, but only if the stockholder makes an application. Otherwise those who acquired taxed stocks before 6 April 1998 will be treated as having applied for net payment. See 36.2 for the way in which tax is accounted for. Special rules apply to companies (see below).

Government stocks are exempt from capital gains tax. Some stocks have a redemption date upon which the par value, or index-linked value as the case may be, is paid to the holder, so if you buy them below par you will have a guaranteed capital gain at a given date. The gain on non-index-linked stock is fixed in money terms whereas on index-linked stock it is fixed in real terms. In the meantime, the value of the stock fluctuates with market conditions, so that there may be opportunities to make tax-free capital gains before the redemption date. If, however, you make losses they are not allowable for set-off against chargeable gains.

Government stocks can be useful as a means of providing for future known commitments, such as school fees, and if you are inclined to overspend, the government stock is not as readily accessible as a building society account.

Looked at on a pure money return basis, however, a purchase for capital growth may sometimes be no better for a higher rate taxpayer than an investment producing a greater income with no growth prospects. It depends upon the rates of interest being paid from time to time, and the price at which government stock can be purchased.

For individuals (but not companies), interest on government stocks is subject to the accrued income scheme (see 36.18).

As far as companies are concerned, capital gains on government stocks are not exempt from corporation tax (with two exceptions — see 38.22) and both the income from the stocks and profits and losses on disposal of them are taken into account in calculating a company's income. In the case of indexed government stocks held other than for trade purposes, the index increase in each year is not taxed as part of the company's profits at that time, and tax is chargeable on disposal only on the increase in capital value excluding the index increase over the period. Other indexed securities are normally treated in the same way as other loan stock.

Companies receive interest on government stocks in full, accounting for the tax along with the tax on their other profits.

Company loan stock

36.17   Company loan stock is normally within the definition of 'qualifying corporate bonds' and exempt from capital gains tax in the same way as government stocks, although for companies holding such stock, their gains and losses are brought into account when calculating the company's income (see 38.22). Most company loan stock is a less attractive investment than government stocks for the individual taxpayer, because it may not be so readily marketable, there is a greater degree of risk, brokers' commission charges are higher and it is not possible for individuals to receive interest without deduction of tax. For individuals, trustees and personal representatives, the 'accrued income' rules for reckoning interest on a day-to-day basis apply (see 36.18). Company loan stocks may be held in an Individual Savings Account (ISA) — see 36.22.

Accrued income scheme (TA 1988, ss 710–722)

36.18   The accrued income scheme applies to interest-bearing marketable securities such as government stocks and to most local authority and company loan stock. It also applies to building society permanent interest bearing shares (see 37.4). It does not apply to ordinary or preference shares in a company, units in unit trusts, bank deposits or securities within the 'discounted securities' provisions at 38.25.

The accrued income scheme does not apply to companies because they are already taxed on interest accrued due under the 'loan relationships' rules (see 3.6). Nor does it apply to an individual if the nominal value of all accrued income scheme securities held does not exceed £5,000 at any time either in the tax year in which the next interest payment on the securities falls due or in the previous tax year. If, for example, you bought or sold securities in February 2004 on which interest is paid in June and December, the two tax years to look at are 2004/05 (in which the June interest date falls) and 2003/04 (the previous year). If the interest had been payable in March and September the two tax years to look at would have been 2003/04 (the interest date year) and 2002/03.

Where the scheme applies, interest received is included in income according to the amount accrued on a day to day basis, so that selling just before an interest date does not enable income tax to be avoided on the interest by effectively receiving it as part of the sales proceeds. If you sell before a security goes 'ex dividend', you are taxed on the accrued interest to the settlement date and the buyer's taxable income is correspondingly reduced. If you sell ex dividend (so that you get the full interest at the payment date), your taxable income is reduced and the buyer's increased by the interest applicable to the period between the settlement date and the interest payment date. The accrued income adjustments are made in the tax year in which the next interest payment date falls, the savings income charged at 20% (or 40% for higher rate taxpayers) being increased or reduced accordingly. See Example 1.

Where a sale is through a bank or stockbroker, the accrued interest is shown on the contract note.

The accrued income scheme applies not only to sales but also to any other transfers, except that it does not apply on death.

Accrued income charges and reliefs must be shown in the investor's tax return (see 9.22). Most securities covered by the accrued income scheme are exempt from capital gains tax (see 38.23).

Example 1

An individual investor who is a higher rate taxpayer sells £10,000 12% stock (on which interest is payable half-yearly on 10 June and 10 December) to a buyer who is a basic rate taxpayer. Stock goes ex dividend on 2 June 2004.

If sold for settlement on 27 May 2004 (i.e. sold cum dividend)

Buyer receives the full 6 months' interest on 10 June 2004, but effectively 'bought' part of this within his purchase price. The interest accrued from 11 December 2003 to 27 May 2004 is:

$$£1,200 \times \frac{169}{366} = £554.10$$

Seller's taxable income is increased (by an accrued income charge) and buyer's taxable income reduced (by accrued income relief) of £554.10.

If sold for settlement on 2 June 2004 (i.e. sold ex dividend)

Seller receives the full 6 months' interest on 10 June 2004, but effectively 'bought' part of this by receiving reduced sale proceeds. The interest from 3 June 2004 to 10 June 2004 when he did not own the stock amounts to:

$$£1,200 \times \frac{8}{366} = £26.23$$

Seller's taxable income is reduced (by accrued income relief) and buyer's taxable income increased (by an accrued income charge) of £26.23.

The accrued income adjustments are made in the tax year in which the next interest payment date falls, 2004/05 in this example, and are recorded in the tax returns for that year. In the first instance (sale for settlement 27 May 2004), the seller will pay tax at 40% on the accrued income charge of £554.10 and the buyer will save tax at 20% on that amount. In the second instance (sale on 2 June 2004), the seller will save tax at 40% on the amount of £26.23, by which his income is reduced and the buyer will pay tax at 20% on that amount.

Ordinary shares in listed companies

36.19   Ordinary shares are 'risk capital' and investors have to be prepared to accept the risk element in return for seeking rising income and capital appreciation. Although listed shares are readily marketable, the price can fluctuate considerably, as recent movements in stock market prices have demonstrated, so they are not recommended if you may need to make an unplanned sale to meet unexpected commitments or if the risk of loss of capital is unacceptable.

Dividends attract a tax credit amounting to 1/9th of the cash amount. This represents a rate of 10% on the tax-credit inclusive dividend. Basic rate taxpayers have no further tax to pay, and higher rate taxpayers are taxed at 32.5%, i.e. an extra 22.5% (which is 25% of the cash dividend). Non-taxpayers cannot claim repayment of the tax credits.

Dividends are included in your income as they arise and are not subject to the 'accrued income' provisions that apply to government, local authority and company loan stocks.

Investment in ordinary shares can be free of income tax and capital gains tax if you invest in an Individual Savings Account (see 36.22). Dividends on shares held in Personal Equity Plans (PEPs) are similarly tax exempt (see 38.29).

The detailed treatment of shares, and further information on company loan stock and government stocks, is in CHAPTER 38.

Unit and investment trusts and venture capital trusts

36.20   The tax treatment of investments in unit and investment trusts is dealt with at 38.15 to 38.18. Venture capital trusts are dealt with at 29.5.

Purchased life annuities

36.21   If you pay a lump sum to a life assurance company to get a fixed annual sum in return, the annual sum is partly regarded as a non-taxable return of capital, thus giving a comparatively high after-tax income, and the after-tax income is even higher for basic rate taxpayers since they only pay tax on the income element of the annuity at 20%. You have, however, spent capital to secure the annual income and thus there is less capital left in your estate when you die.

Purchased life annuities are therefore often acquired in conjunction with life insurance policies, part of the annual income being used to fund the life insurance premium so that at the end of the annuity period the life insurance policy proceeds can replace the purchase price of the annuity. There are numerous variations on this sort of arrangement — see CHAPTER 40.

Individual Savings Accounts (ISAs) (SI 1998/1870)

36.22   Since 6 April 1999 you have been able to invest in tax-free Individual Savings Accounts (ISAs), which have replaced TESSAs and PEPs. There is no requirement to switch existing PEPs into ISAs and their tax advantages continue. TESSAs opened before 6 April 1999 were allowed to run their course and could then be transferred to ISAs (see below), but no further PEP subscriptions may be made. See 37.5 and 38.29 for notes on TESSAs and PEPs respectively.

ISAs are available to individuals aged 18 or over who are resident and ordinarily resident in the UK. Cash ISAs are also available to 16- and 17-year-olds (see 36.23). If you become non-resident, you may retain the tax-exempt benefits of existing ISAs but no further investments may be made. Joint accounts are not permitted. ISAs are guaranteed to run for ten years, although there is no statutory minimum period for which the accounts must be held. There is no lifetime limit on the amount invested. The annual investment may presently be split into three components: a cash component (bank and building society accounts and designated National Savings products), life insurance, and stocks and shares. The maximum annual investment for years up to 2005/06 is £7,000, of which under the present rules not more than £3,000 can be invested in cash and not more than £1,000 in life insurance. The whole amount may be invested in stocks and shares if the saver wishes. The Government plans to make changes to the ISA provisions from April 2005, the main change being to relax the rules for qualifying investments for the stocks and shares element so that various medium-term 'stakeholder' products and all qualifying life insurance products will be embraced within the stocks and shares element. The life insurance element will then no longer be limited to £1,000. There will, however, be a test to limit investments that provide a 'cash-like' return to the ISA cash component. This will apply where the investment is not exposed to a significant risk of loss through fluctuations in capital value.

From 2006/07, the maximum annual investment will be £5,000, with not more than £1,000 in the cash element. There is no statutory minimum subscription, although interest rates on the cash element may vary according to the amount invested.

Although there is no minimum holding period for an ISA, this does not mean that you can make withdrawals and deposits as you wish. If any part of the amount invested in a year is withdrawn, that part of the limit for the year is not available for further investment. If, for example, you deposited the full

£3,000 in a cash ISA in 2004/05, and unexpectedly needed to withdraw £2,000, you could not replace the funds in that tax year, and you can only reinvest in a later year by using the cash limit for that year. If you had only deposited £2,000 in 2004/05 and withdrew it, you would be able to reinvest £1,000 into the account in order to use up the remainder of the £3,000 limit.

Savers have a choice of ISA managers each year, and may make their annual investment through a single manager (a maxi ISA) or may choose separate managers for each of the three components of the account (mini ISAs), and accounts may later be transferred to a different manager. If, however, you take out a mini ISA, say, by investing cash, this prevents you from taking out a maxi ISA in the same year, and furthermore limits the amount that can be subscribed in a mini ISA for the stocks and shares component to £3,000, even if you have not invested the maximum available £3,000 in the cash component and you have not taken out an insurance component. If you take out a maxi ISA, you cannot take out a mini ISA in the same year, although you may have a TESSA only account, as indicated below.

The last TESSAs matured during 2003/04. The capital (but not interest) from maturing TESSAs could be paid into an existing cash ISA or a separate TESSA only ISA within six months of maturity. TESSA capital transferred in this way did not affect the annual ISA limits. If you are not resident and ordinarily resident in the UK you were not eligible to transfer the capital from a maturing TESSA to an ISA.

ISAs are free of income tax and capital gains tax, and where ISA investments are in shares, dividend tax credits were paid into the account for the period to 5 April 2004. Now that the dividend credits have been taken away, the benefits of acquiring shares through ISAs will disappear for many taxpayers, since the capital gains exemption will often not be relevant and in the current climate many shares are showing large capital losses, for which no tax relief is available. The ISA tax exemption ceases on the death of the investor.

The stocks and shares component may broadly be invested at present in shares and securities listed on a recognised stock exchange, gilts, units in qualifying authorised unit trusts, shares in qualifying open-ended investment companies and investment trusts, and cash held temporarily for the purpose of investing in qualifying investments. Interest on such cash is not tax free and the account manager has to account for tax at 20% to the Revenue. There is, however, no effect on the investor, who is neither treated as having received taxable income nor entitled to a tax refund. In the case of rights issues, managers may use cash held within the stocks and shares component to take up the rights, or the investor may make further cash subscriptions up to the annual limit. Alternatively an investor may pay cash to enable the manager to take up the rights outside the account, providing the investments are transferred to the investor to be held outside the account.

Certain funds, known as UCITS (undertakings for collective investments in transferable securities) have not previously been qualifying investments for ISAs. UCITS use derivatives to protect all or part of an investor's capital. Under the changes to be made to the ISA provisions from April 2005, the Government proposes to allow UCITS that guarantee to return at least 95% of the investor's original capital to qualify for cash ISAs, and UCITS guaranteeing a lower return to qualify for stocks and shares ISAs (and also for PEPs, as to which see 38.29).

Shares received from approved profit sharing and savings-related share option schemes and approved share incentive plans (see CHAPTER 11) are also qualifying investments and may be transferred within 90 days into the stocks and shares component of the ISA free of capital gains tax, so long as, together with any other investments, they are within the annual subscription limit of £7,000 for years up to 2005/06 and £5,000 thereafter. There is no facility to transfer shares acquired under a public offer or following demutualisation of a building society or insurer into an ISA.

The shares component of an ISA is kept separate from any other holdings of the investor for the purpose of the capital gains rules for matching disposals with acquisitions. If the investor withdraws his investments, their base cost for capital gains tax is the market value at the date of withdrawal.

If tax relief on an ISA is found to have been wrongly given, the Revenue may make a direct assessment outside the self-assessment system on either the account manager or the investor to recover the relief. In limited circumstances, and with the approval of the Revenue, invalid ISAs may be 'repaired' rather than being closed, although any tax relief up to the date of the repair will still be forfeited.

The Government has introduced CAT marks for ISAs, indicating that the account on offer complies with stipulated conditions as regards Charges, Access and Terms. CAT marks are not a quality standard and do not guarantee that you will get good returns from the investment. The Government's aim with ISAs is to encourage more people to save. It seems inappropriate to insist that the larger part of the permitted investment be in equities, because equities are not normally considered suitable for those who do not have a firm underlying core of low risk investments. Non-taxpayers cannot benefit from a tax-free account, and basic rate taxpayers, having lost the benefits of receiving dividend tax credits, may find any other benefits being eroded by the account charges.

16 and 17-year-olds

36.23   Up to £3,000 a year may be invested in cash ISAs (but not stocks and shares ISAs or life insurance ISAs) by those who are 16 or over at the end of the tax year but under 18. The investment may be made using either a cash mini ISA or the cash component of a maxi ISA. In the tax year in which the investor attains age 18, not more than £3,000 may be invested before the 18th birthday but the normal ISA limits apply thereafter. If parents give their children money to invest in ISAs, then unless the income within the ISA is not more than the £100 limit per parent for income from all capital provided by the parent, it will be treated as the income of the parents until the child reaches age 18 and must be reported on the parents' tax returns (see 33.7).

Tax points

36.24

- If you have spare personal allowances, National Savings Bank accounts still have a cash flow advantage over other bank accounts and building society accounts unless you can register to receive the bank or building society interest in full, without tax being deducted. This needs to be weighed against the interest rates on offer. See CHAPTER 37.

- Index-linked national savings certificates offer inflation proofing plus a minimal amount of guaranteed extra interest, the best return being available if you invest for the full term.

- Although investing for the full term shows the highest returns with National Savings certificates, they can be repaid gradually over the period, giving the opportunity to draw an effective tax-free income.

- Some of the National Savings products are attractive to higher rate taxpayers because of the tax-exempt income. National Savings and Investments (NS&I) frequently changes its products, and you can keep up to date with what is on offer by telephone and on the internet.

- The cash component of ISAs can be invested in accounts at building societies and banks, including the National Savings Bank and super-market banks. Once you have invested in a cash mini ISA, however small the amount, your permitted investment in stocks and shares is restricted to £3,000.

- Make sure that you don't take out a maxi ISA (i.e. an account with one manager covering all three ISA components) and a mini ISA (covering just one of the components) in the same tax year. If you did, you would not only lose the tax exemption but if you had been fraudulent or negligent you would be liable to a penalty.

- There can appear to be a disproportionate extra tax charge on divi-dends or other savings income if an increase in other income takes the total income over the basic rate threshold. For an illustration, see 2.22.

- If you are a small investor, you can benefit from a wide range of investments through a unit or investment trust. The trust is exempt from tax on its gains. You pay tax on income and gains in the normal way, unless the investment is through an ISA or was made before 6 April 1999 into a PEP. See 38.15 to 38.18.

• For those who are liable to tax, capital bonds (see 36.7) have the disadvantage of tax being payable every year even though no income is received until the end of the investment period.

• If you have children under 16, you can invest the maximum £1,000 in *each issue* of children's bonus bonds — see 36.11.

• You are eligible to acquire pensioners' bonds if you are over 60. Although the interest is taxable, you will not pay more than 20% tax unless your taxable income exceeds the basic rate threshold of £31,400 (but see 34.3 if you are over 65 and have income above the age allowance income limit of £18,900).

37
Investing in banks and building societies

Investing in building societies and banks (other than the National Savings Bank) (TA 1988, ss 477A, 480A, 481, 482)

37.1   Investing in building societies and banks is regarded as a low risk investment. If the bank or building society should fail, however, compensation is payable under the Financial Services Compensation Scheme. The maximum compensation is 100% of the first £2,000 and 90% of the next £33,000, giving an overall maximum of £31,700. The compensation scheme does not cover investments in building society permanent interest bearing shares, as to which see 37.4. Nor does it cover investments in offshore banks and building societies in the Channel Islands and Isle of Man, although some UK banks and building societies may offer their own protection for those who save with their offshore subsidiaries.

Building societies and banks, including the National Savings Bank, notify the Revenue how much interest has been paid to customers, no matter how small. This includes interest payable to those who are not ordinarily resident in the UK (see 41.11).

Income tax is not deducted from bank and building society interest paid to companies (see 3.6), Individual Savings Account managers (see 36.22), Personal Equity Plan managers (see 38.29) and charities (see 43.3). Nor is tax deducted from interest on building society permanent interest-bearing shares (PIBS — see 37.4), because they are within the definition of quoted Eurobonds (see 3.17).

Apart from interest on PIBS and tax-exempt accounts such as SAYE accounts (which are only available when linked to an employee share option — see 11.11) and Individual Savings Accounts (see 36.22), interest paid to individuals by building societies and by banks other than the National Savings Bank is paid after deduction of 20% tax, unless either you can register to receive it in full (see 37.2) or the interest is paid in full because it arises under one of the following headings.

(a)   Certificates of deposit (including 'paperless' certificates) and sterling or foreign currency time deposits, providing the loan is not less than £50,000 and is repayable within five years.

(b)   General client deposit accounts with building societies or banks operated by solicitors and estate agents.

(c)   Offshore accounts, i.e. held at overseas branches of UK and foreign banks and building societies.

(d)   Bank and building society accounts held by someone who is not ordinarily resident in the UK and has provided a declaration to that effect stating their principal residential address.

Interest under headings (a) and (b) is taxed in the same way as national savings bank interest (see 37.6). Interest on offshore accounts under heading (c) is taxed as income from a foreign possession — see 41.6. Interest under heading (d) usually escapes UK tax (see 41.20).

Interest counts as income for tax purposes according to the date when it is credited to your account. It is not apportioned over the period when it accrues. Whether tax has been deducted by the payer or not, you may have to pay some more or claim some back, depending on your tax rate. For the way in which this is done, see 36.2.

Bank and building society interest paid to trustees is also net of tax, unless it is excluded under heading (a) or (c) above or it is paid to non-resident trustees of discretionary and accumulation trusts of which the beneficiaries are not ordinarily resident in the UK, providing the trustees have given the bank or building society a declaration to that effect.

Receiving bank and building society interest in full (TMA 1970, s 99A; TA 1988, ss 477A, 480A, 480B)

37.2   Although tax is normally deducted from interest paid by banks and building societies, you can register to receive the interest in full if you expect your total taxable income to be below your available allowances. The relevant forms R85 may be obtained from banks, building societies and local authorities (see 36.15) or from your tax office. A separate form is needed for each account. A parent can register the account of a child under 16 if the child's total income will be less than the personal allowance (£4,745 for 2004/05), providing not more than £100 income arises from all parental gifts (a separate £100 limit applying to income from gifts from each parent).

You must give written notice straight away to banks and building societies who are paying you interest in full if your circumstances change and you are no longer eligible to receive gross interest. You should also let your tax office know about any tax you may have to pay. Where tax has been underpaid, it will be collected either by adjustment to a PAYE coding or through your self-assessment. A penalty of up to £3,000 may be charged if you fraudulently or negligently certify that you are entitled to register to receive interest in full, or if you fail to notify that you are no longer entitled to receive interest in full.

It is not possible to register some accounts and not others. You must expect to have *no tax liability at all* in order to be eligible. If you cannot register, say because your income is just above your available allowances, you are entitled to a refund of any tax overpaid, and a refund can be claimed as soon as at least £50 tax is owing to you. You do not have to wait until the end of the tax year.

You will be entitled to a refund of part of the tax deducted from the interest to the extent that your other income is below the limit for the 10% starting rate (£2,020 for 2004/05), so that some of the interest is taxable only at 10% rather than 20%.

Building societies: conversion to banks, takeovers, mergers (FA 1988, Sch 12; TCGA 1992, ss 214C, 217)

37.3   Building societies are able to convert to companies under the Building Societies Act 1986. If they do, they are subject to normal company and bank legislation. Possible adverse consequences of conversion for building society members are prevented by specific rules which provide that members are not liable to capital gains tax on rights to acquire shares in the company in priority to other subscribers, or at a discount, or on rights to acquire shares free of charge; these provisions apply whether the rights are obtained directly or through trustees. As and when the shares are disposed of, there will be a capital gain equal to the excess of the proceeds over the amount (if any) paid for the shares plus indexation allowance to April 1998 if relevant. If the shares were free, there is no allowable cost and therefore no indexation allowance. Any gains arising may be reduced by taper relief if appropriate from the date the shares were issued or 6 April 1998 if later, the taper period being increased by one year if the shares were held at 17 March 1998. Any remaining amount may be covered by the annual capital gains exemption if not already used.

Similar rules apply when a building society is taken over by a company rather than being converted.

Where a cash payment is received on a conversion or takeover, the payments are not chargeable to income tax. Cash payments to *deposit* account holders are also exempt from capital gains tax (since such an account represents a loan, i.e. a simple debt, gains on which are exempt — see 4.8). Presumably cash payments to borrowers are also exempt, since they do not derive from an asset. Cash payments to share account holders are not exempt, but the holders may add indexation allowance to the amount(s) deposited from the date of the deposit to April 1998, which in many cases will eliminate any chargeable gain. Such gains cannot be reduced by taper relief. The calculation of the indexation allowance could be very complicated where account balances have fluctuated frequently, but in many cases the amounts concerned will be covered by the capital gains annual exemption in any event so that calculations will not be necessary. If taxpayers are unable to make the necessary calculations for their tax returns, the Revenue will if asked use their computer programme to produce the figures. See the Revenue's Tax Bulletin of April 1998 for detailed comments on both free shares and cash bonuses.

As far as building society *mergers* are concerned, the Revenue view is that any payments on the merger (whether paid in cash or credited to an account) are chargeable to income tax. Such payments would be treated in the same way as other income from the building society. Tax would be deducted at 20%, higher rate taxpayers would have to pay a further 20% and non-taxpayers would be able to claim a repayment. Taxpayers need to make appropriate entries on their tax returns.

Building society permanent interest bearing shares (TA 1988, ss 477A, 710; FA 1996, s 81; TCGA 1992, s 117)

37.4   Building societies may issue a special type of share — permanent interest bearing shares (PIBS). These shares are acquired through and listed on the Stock Exchange and are freely transferable, dealing charges being incurred on buying and selling. You are not entitled to compensation if the building society fails, and the PIBS are irredeemable, so what you get back on sale will depend on prevailing interest rates and the soundness of the building society. Interest on PIBS is paid gross. For non-corporate shareholders PIBS are within the definition of qualifying corporate bonds (see 38.23) and are exempt from capital gains tax, so that no allowable losses may be created. They are also within the accrued income scheme (see 36.18), so that adjustments for accrued interest are made when they are transferred.

For companies, the accrued income scheme does not apply. Dividends, interest and capital gains on the PIBS are dealt with under the loan relationships rules (see 3.6).

Where PIBS are issued to existing members in priority to other people the right to buy them does not result in a capital gains tax charge.

Tax Exempt Special Savings Accounts (TESSA) (TA 1988, ss 326A, 326B, 326BB, 326C)

37.5   Before 6 April 1999, anyone over 18 could open a tax exempt special savings account (TESSA) with a bank or building society (or EU authorised institution). No further TESSA investments could be made from that date, but existing TESSAs were allowed to run their course, so that any remaining TESSAs came to an end at latest at the end of 2003/04.

At the end of the five-year period the tax exempt status of the capital element of the TESSA savings (but not the interest) could be retained by transferring that element into an Individual Savings Account (ISA) within six months of the maturity date — see 36.22. The balance of the account, representing accumulated interest, would have to be transferred to other accounts or withdrawn. Any interest credited on the capital between the maturity date and the reinvestment date is not covered by the TESSA exemption and is fully taxable. Such interest is credited net of tax at the 20% savings rate, so additional tax is due only from higher rate taxpayers.

Investing in the National Savings Bank (TA 1988, s 325)

37.6   The main investments offered by the National Savings Bank are outlined in CHAPTER 36. National Savings certificates, children's bonus bonds, premium savings bonds and National Savings ISAs are exempt from tax. Fixed rate savings bonds (see 36.10) are taxable, but unlike other National Savings investments, the interest is paid net of tax and is treated in the same way as interest from other banks and building societies, so that you may have to pay more tax or claim some back, depending on your tax rate.

Interest on other accounts with the National Savings Bank and on capital and income bonds, including pensioners' bonds, although received in full, is chargeable to tax. The first £70 of interest received on *ordinary* accounts is exempt from tax. Husband and wife get an exemption of £70 each. Any unused part of the £70 exemption cannot be transferred to the other spouse, but interest up to £140 is exempt when the account is in joint names. From 31 July 2004 ordinary accounts will become dormant and holders will only be able to access the accounts either to close them or to transfer them to the 'easy access savings accounts' which have replaced them (see 36.4). The accounts will continue to be entitled to the £70 exemption up to that point.

Tax points

37.7

- If you do not register to receive bank and building society interest in full, even though you are entitled to do so, you will still get the overpaid tax back. You can claim before the end of the tax year if you are owed £50 or more. If you do not know your tax office, fill in form R95 in leaflet IR 111 (which is obtainable from any tax office or tax enquiry centre).

- Make sure you do not register to receive bank and building society interest in full unless you expect all your income to be covered by your available allowances. Even if some tax will be repayable, you are not eligible to register unless you will have no tax liability at all.

- Even if most of your bank and building society interest will be covered by your allowances, you cannot register some accounts and not others. It is all or nothing.

- If you have registered to receive bank and building society interest in full there is no difference in tax treatment between investing in the National Savings Bank and investing in other banks and building societies. You need to compare the rates of interest on offer. If you cannot register but have allowances available to set against interest, you will still get a cash flow benefit from a National Savings Bank account, because for other accounts you will usually have to wait for a tax refund.

- When filling in your tax return, don't forget to show any interest you have received on your bank current accounts, as well as interest on your savings accounts.

- If you receive a cash windfall on a building society takeover/ conversion, it is liable to capital gains tax, but tax is not payable if it is covered by your annual exemption (£8,200 for 2004/05). A cash windfall on a building society *merger* is liable to income tax, and will be received net of 20% tax, but you will not have any more tax to pay unless you are a higher rate taxpayer and you may be entitled to a refund if you pay tax at less than 20%.

- If you have a building society ISA, you are a member of the building society and will thus qualify if there is an offer of free shares on the conversion of the building society to a company.

- Although the capital from a maturing TESSA may be invested within six months into an ISA, any interest credited after maturity and before reinvestment is fully taxable and must be declared on your tax return. Higher rate taxpayers will have to pay a further 20% tax in addition to the 20% tax already deducted.

- It is only the general client deposit accounts maintained by solicitors and estate agents on which interest is received without tax being deducted, and not their normal accounts for office monies.

- A joint bank or building society account of husband and wife is normally treated as owned in equal shares, with the survivor automatically entitled to take over the whole account when the other dies, and it is unlikely that banks and building societies would be prepared to vary this treatment. It is, however, possible for the underlying beneficial ownership to be altered by taking specific action to sever the joint tenancy and the account could then be held as tenants in common in whatever proportions you wish, providing the spouse giving up part of his or her share does so as an outright gift. The Revenue will require you to provide evidence of the change to tenancy in common on form 17 (see 33.5). If the account continued to be treated as a common pool from which each could and did draw freely, the Revenue would be unlikely to accept that an outright gift had been made.

- If you do take specific action to hold a bank or building society account as tenants in common, then although the bank may regard the account as going automatically to the survivor when the other died, the survivor would have to account to the personal representatives for the deceased spouse's share.

38
Investing in stocks and shares

Background

38.1   The term 'quoted securities' has in general been replaced in the tax legislation by 'listed securities'. For EU countries (and Iceland, Liechtenstein and Norway) listed securities means securities listed by a competent authority and admitted to trading on a recognised stock exchange. For other countries it means securities admitted to trading by a recognised stock exchange. AIM securities are unlisted.

Many of the provisions in the capital gains legislation deal with stocks and shares acquired many years ago, in respect of which the old terminology may still apply. For simplicity, the terms 'quoted' and 'unquoted' have been retained in this chapter.

When you invest through the Stock Exchange, the principal securities you may acquire are company shares or loan stock, government stocks, local authority loan stock and building society permanent interest bearing shares (see 37.4). You may also invest in unquoted company stocks and shares and unquoted local authority loans. Gains and losses made by a company in relation to loans (both ordinary debts and loan stock) are taken into account in calculating the company's income, and the capital gains provisions generally do not apply (see 38.22).

Unquoted local authority loans are dealt with at 36.15. Unquoted company stocks and shares are dealt with in this chapter. The treatment of foreign stocks and shares is dealt with in CHAPTER 41 at 41.5 (capital gains) and 41.6 (income), 'foreign' meaning that the issuing company is not resident in the UK.

There are various special provisions relating to trading on the Stock Exchange by broker/dealers, including provisions for stock lending and manufactured payments. Where shares are held as trading assets (either by dealers or others such as banks), dividends and other distributions received, and also manufactured payments treated as received, are treated as trading profits (and manufactured payments made are deducted as trading expenses). The chargeable (or allowable) amount excludes tax credits.

Tax treatment of income from stocks and shares

Dividends (TA 1988, ss 1A, 1B, 20, 231; F(No 2)A 1997, s 30; FA 1998, s 76)

38.2   Dividends paid by companies on their shares represent a distribution of profits to the members. The shareholder receives a tax credit of 1/9th of the cash amount of the dividend, representing 10% of the tax credit inclusive amount. Someone whose income does not exceed the basic threshold has no further tax to pay and higher rate taxpayers have to pay a further 22.5% (25% of the cash dividend received). Non-taxpayers cannot, however, claim a refund. Tax credits were previously paid into personal equity plans (PEPs — see 38.29) and Individual Savings Accounts (ISAs — see 36.22), but this does not apply after 5 April 2004. Tax credits were similarly reclaimable by friendly societies on their exempt dividend income up to that date (see 40.15) and tax credits may be available to non-residents under the terms of double tax treaties (see 41.25). See 36.2 for the way tax is collected.

Scrip options (TA 1988, ss 249, 251)

38.3   If you take scrip shares instead of a cash dividend from a UK resident company (a scrip dividend option), the cash dividend forgone is treated as your income, unless it is substantially different from the market value of the shares, 'substantially' being interpreted by the Revenue as 15% or more either way. In that event your deemed income is the market value of the shares on the first day of dealing. You are treated as having a notional tax credit of 1/9th, which is treated in the same way as an actual tax credit. If scrip dividend options are taken up by personal representatives, the gross equivalent is treated as income of the estate. The gross equivalent is treated as income liable to the 40% rate of tax where scrip dividend options are taken up by trustees of discretionary trusts (except trusts in which the settlor retains an interest). The capital gains tax effect is dealt with at 38.14. Where scrip dividends are issued to a company, or to a trust in which the settlor retains an interest, they are not treated as income, and have a capital gains base cost of nil. This also applies to scrip dividends issued to a life interest trust unless the scrip dividend is income of the life beneficiary under trust law. If the trustees take the view that the scrip dividend belongs to the life tenant, the shares are effectively treated as acquired directly by the life tenant outside the trust's holding of shares (except in Scotland, where the rules are different — see Revenue Statement of Practice 4/94), and the life tenant would be treated as having notional income in the same way as if he had acquired the shares directly. Some companies have established dividend reinvestment plans (DRIPs), under which shareholders use their dividends to acquire shares bought on the market by the company on their behalf. There is, however, a cost to the shareholder because part of the dividend is used to cover the cost of brokers' fees and stamp duty.

Interest (TA 1988, ss 1A, 18, 50, 348, 349–349D; F(No 2)A 1997, s 37)

38.4   Interest paid by companies and local authorities on quoted stocks is paid gross. Companies and local authorities may also pay other interest to another company or local authority without deducting tax (see 3.17 for details). Other interest is paid after deduction of lower rate tax. Interest on government stocks is paid gross unless the holder applies to receive it net. Where lower rate tax is deducted, those with income below the basic rate threshold have no further tax to pay, non-taxpayers can recover tax at the 20% rate and higher rate taxpayers have a further 20% to pay. See 36.2 for the way tax is collected and 36.18 for the special accrued income scheme provisions that may apply to individuals in relation to interest-bearing securities. The treatment of interest received by companies is dealt with at 3.6.

There are some special provisions for discounted securities held by personal investors (see 38.25).

Capital gains treatment of stocks and shares

38.5   For capital gains purposes, shares and interest-bearing stocks are treated differently. Furthermore, companies are subject to different rules from other taxpayers in relation to interest-bearing stocks. The rules have been changed so frequently that this area has become one of the most complicated in the tax legislation, and it is not possible for this book to deal with all the complexities.

As far as individuals, personal representatives and trustees are concerned, government stocks, qualifying corporate bonds and local authority stocks are exempt from capital gains tax, so that there are neither chargeable gains nor allowable losses when they are disposed of (subject to some special rules for losses on qualifying corporate bonds — see 38.24). Other interest-bearing stocks are chargeable to capital gains tax and are subject to the same rules for identifying disposals with acquisitions as those relating to shares.

For companies, virtually all gains and losses on the disposal of interest-bearing assets, are taken into account in calculating the company's income. The capital gains treatment of shares is outlined below, and the rules for dealing with disposals of interest-bearing stocks are outlined at 38.23.

Capital gains when shares are disposed of (TCGA 1992, ss 2A, 35, 53–55, 104–110A and Schs A1, 2)

38.6   When shares are disposed of, a capital gains computation is made. The general rules for calculating capital gains and losses outlined in CHAPTER 4 apply. There are, however, special problems associated with shares (scrip and rights issues, takeovers, mergers, etc.), and there are also different rules for shares on hand when capital gains tax started in April 1965, those acquired before April 1982, and those acquired after that time. From 6 April 1998 the position has been further complicated by the freezing of indexation allowance and the introduction of taper relief. Neither of these changes applies to companies, however, so it is now necessary to have two separate sets of rules running side by side. Calculating gains and losses is therefore very difficult for most shareholders and their tax advisers.

Many of the complexities outlined below will not, however, affect individuals with modest holdings. If you do not regularly buy and sell, you may acquire shares in a company by a single purchase and sell them by a single sale, so unless there have been rights issues, takeovers, etc., the calculation merely requires you to add indexation allowance to the cost from the date of acquisition to April 1998, and compare the indexed figure with the sale proceeds. You may then need to consider taper relief (see 4.16 onwards), but if the sale proceeds of all disposals in the tax year are such that any gains arising will be below your annual capital gains exemption, taper relief is not relevant and you may not have to show calculations of gains in your tax return (see 9.20). If, however, the transaction produced a loss, you would have to show calculations in order to claim loss relief.

Example 1

Shareholder acquired 2,000 shares in A plc in June 1990 for £8,000 (including acquisition costs) and sold them in May 2004 for £10,500 (net of selling costs). He had no other capital transactions in 2004/05. Since the 2004/05 annual exemption is £8,200, any gains arising are clearly exempt.

If the proceeds had been £6,500 there would have been an allowable loss of £1,500.

Shares acquired before the commencement of indexation

38.7   If a general rebasing election has been made (see 4.12), all shares of the same class in the same company held on 6 April 1982 (1 April 1982 for companies), including any acquired before 6 April 1965, are treated as acquired at their 31 March 1982 market value and are regarded as a single asset. (No special provision is made for acquisitions by individuals from 1 to 5 April 1982, but logically such acquisitions should be included at cost.) Any such holding is called a '1982 holding' in the legislation, but it is referred to in this chapter as a pre-1982 pool.

If the rebasing election has not been made, then unless some of the shares in the company concerned were acquired before 6 April 1965, the single asset treatment still applies but there are two values for pre-1982 pools, namely cost and 31 March 1982 value. If some of the shares were acquired before 6 April 1965, then they must be kept separate from the pre-1982 pool. This does not apply to *quoted* shares if an election had been made (under provisions introduced in 1968) to treat them as acquired at their market value on 6 April 1965, in which case they are included in the pre-1982 pool at that value. The treatment of unpooled pre-6 April 1965 acquisitions is dealt with at 38.12.

Where the rebasing election is not made, the 31 March 1982 value is still used to calculate the gain or loss unless using the cost would show a lower gain or loss. If one calculation shows a loss and the other a gain, the transaction is treated as giving neither gain nor loss. In both calculations, the indexation allowance is based on the *higher* of the cost and 31 March 1982 value.

Where 31 March 1982 valuations of unquoted holdings are needed by several shareholders, the Revenue Shares Valuation Division will open negotiations with the shareholders or their advisers before being asked by a tax office, providing all shareholders with similar holdings will accept the value agreed. Someone with pre- and post-6 April 1965 unquoted holdings may, by concession, have them valued as a single holding, which may give a higher value per share. This does not affect the rules for matching disposals with acquisitions (see 38.9).

Shares acquired after indexation was introduced

38.8 Rules were introduced from 6 April 1985 (1 April 1985 for companies), to treat each holding of quoted or unquoted shares of the same company and class acquired on or after 6 April 1982 (1 April 1982 for companies) as a single asset. This asset is now called a 'section 104 holding' in the legislation, but it is referred to in this chapter as a post-1982 pool. (Shares acquired by an employee that are subject to disposal restrictions are treated as being of a different class from any other shares held.) Post-1982 pools grow with acquisitions and are depleted by disposals (see identification rules in 38.9 and 38.10). For individuals, personal representatives and trustees, however, no further shares are added to post-1982 pools after 5 April 1998 (except for scrip issues and rights shares — see 38.13) and each acquisition of shares after that date is treated as a separate, free-standing acquisition. Acquisitions continue to increase post-1982 pools for company shareholders.

Identification of disposals for individuals, personal representatives and trustees

38.9   When shares are disposed of, there are rules to relate the disposal to specific shares acquired. For the purpose of these rules, all the shares acquired on the same day are treated as having been acquired by a single transaction. See, however, 11.32 for a special rule where some of the shares are acquired under Revenue approved schemes. The matching rules do not apply to disposals of scrip and rights shares, because scrip and rights shares are treated as acquired when the original shares were acquired, so that the appropriate number of scrip or rights shares is added to pre-6 April 1965 acquisitions, pre-and post-1982 pools and post-5 April 1998 acquisitions (see 38.13). This does not apply to shares acquired under scrip dividend options, which are treated as free-standing issues from 6 April 1998 (see 38.14). Apart from scrip and rights shares, disposals on and after 6 April 1998 (17 March 1998 in relation to heading (b)) are matched with acquisitions in the following order:

(a)   Acquisitions on the same day as the disposal.

(b)   Acquisitions within 30 days after the disposal, earliest first.

(c)   Previous acquisitions after 5 April 1998, latest first.

(d)   The post-1982 pool.

(e)   The pre-1982 pool.

(f)   Pre-6 April 1965 acquisitions that are not included in the pre-1982 pool, latest first.

(g)   Acquisitions more than 30 days after disposal, earliest first.

The introduction of the 30-day rule in (b) prevents 'bed and breakfast' transactions, where shares are sold and bought back on the following day in order either to use the capital gains exemption or to produce losses to reduce chargeable gains. The rules do not prevent a spouse repurchasing the shares on the market, providing the spouse is the beneficial owner of the shares bought. Alternatively, a similar effect could be achieved by acquiring shares in a company in the same business sector. The above matching rules apply not only to shares but also to loan stock that is not exempt from capital gains tax (see 38.22).

Someone who acquires shares from his/her spouse in lifetime is treated as acquiring the shares at the other spouse's cost plus any available indexation allowance, and can count the other's period of ownership for taper relief purposes (see 4.5), but the transferred shares will not qualify for the *business assets* rate of taper relief for the transferor spouse's period of ownership unless the *transferee* spouse satisfied the conditions during that period (see 4.22). The shares are *not* treated as having been acquired when the other spouse acquired them for the purpose of matching the acquiring spouse's disposals with acquisitions, and the normal identification rules above apply (see Example 2). Shares acquired on a spouse's death are treated as acquired at the date of death at probate value.

Example 2

Wife acquired 3,000 shares in ABC plc in June 1987 for £9,000 (the indexed cost to April 1998 being £14,364). Husband acquired 1,000 shares in the company in October 2001 for £18,000. The shares do not qualify for business assets taper relief. Wife gave her husband 1,000 shares in 2003 (the indexed cost being £4,788) and he sold 500 shares in August 2004 for £14,500.

The sale will be matched with 500 of the shares he acquired from his wife, which have an indexed cost of £2,394, giving a gain of £12,106. Taper relief for 7 years (including the extra year for pre-17 March 1998 ownership) is 25%, reducing the gain to £9,080 (which will be further reduced by the annual exemption of £8,200 if available). Had the inter-spouse transfer not been made, the husband would have been treated as disposing of 500 shares that cost £9,000 in October 2001, giving a gain of £5,500 (covered by the annual exemption if not already used but no taper relief being available since the shares had been owned for less than three years).

If husband and wife hold shares in a company both separately and in a joint holding, the Revenue do not consider that the joint holding represents a separate asset for the identification rules. If, therefore, the joint holding is sold but there are later acquisitions by either spouse within the 30-day period (see (b) above), the disposal by each spouse is treated as being a disposal of that spouse's later acquisitions in priority to his or her share of the joint holding.

Identification of disposals for companies

38.10   Disposals are matched with acquisitions in the following order (subject to the same treatment as outlined in 38.9 for scrip and rights shares, except for scrip dividend option shares, which are treated as normal scrip shares (see 38.14)):

(a)   Acquisitions on the same day as the disposal.

(b)   Where the company owns 2% or more of the issued shares of a particular class, acquisitions in the previous month (latest first) then acquisitions in the following month (earliest first).

(c)   Where (b) does not apply, acquisitions within the previous nine days (and no indexation allowance is available on the disposal).

(d)   The post-1982 pool.

(e)   The pre-1982 pool.

(f)   Pre-6 April 1965 acquisitions that are not included in the pre-1982 pool, latest first.

(g)   Acquisitions after disposal (other than those taken into account in (b)), earliest first.

The rules outlined above (except (b) and the scrip dividend option rules) applied to unincorporated shareholders as well as companies before 6 April 1998.

Indexation allowance and taper relief

38.11   For shareholders other than companies, indexation allowance is not given on any acquisitions on or after 6 April 1998 and no further indexation allowance is given on earlier acquisitions. Taper relief is given instead of indexation from that time according to the complete years the shares have been owned from the date they were acquired or from 6 April 1998 if they were held on that day. An extra year is added for shares acquired before 17 March 1998 unless the shares qualify as business assets (see 4.17). Indexation allowance continues to be available for companies, and they are not entitled to taper relief.

For pre-1982 pools of shares held at 6 April 1982 (1 April 1982 for companies), the indexation allowance is calculated by taking the increase in the retail prices index between March 1982 and the month of disposal (or, for unincorporated shareholders, April 1998 if earlier). Where the rebasing election has been made to treat all assets acquired before 31 March 1982 as being acquired at their market value on that date, the indexation allowance is based on that 31 March 1982 value (see Example 8 below). Where the election has not been made, the indexation calculation is based on the higher of the value of the shares at 31 March 1982 and their cost or, for shares held at 6 April 1965, their 6 April 1965 market value when using that value to calculate the gain or loss (see 38.12).

Indexation allowance on post-1982 pools (see 38.8) is worked out from the month in which the expenditure was incurred. The holdings are maintained at both an unindexed value and an indexed value, and the indexed value is uplifted by further indexation every time an event occurs that alters the value of a holding (such as a purchase or a sale). Indexation allowance is not added for events after April 1998 except for corporate shareholders. Unlike other indexation allowance calculations, the indexation adjustment on the post-1982 pool should strictly not be rounded to three decimal places. If the index has fallen since the previous event, no adjustment is made to the indexed value. The post-1982 pool rules were introduced on 6 April 1985 (1 April 1985 for companies) and an opening figure for the indexed value was required at that date, working out indexation allowance on each acquisition from 6 April 1982 (1 April 1982) onwards. (If the calculation was delayed until the time of the first event affecting the value of the holding, it would not significantly affect the figures.)

Where the rebasing election has been made, the pre-1982 pool can be maintained at both unindexed and indexed values in the same way as the post-1982 pool, although this is not provided for in the legislation. This can still be done even if there is no rebasing election, but figures would be required both for indexed cost and indexed 31 March 1982 value, basing indexation allowance in both cases on the higher of those two figures, but not so as to create or increase a loss. (For an illustration, see Example 11 at 38.13.)

Where partly paid shares are acquired, the instalments of the purchase price qualify for any available indexation allowance from the date the shares are issued, unless they are paid more than twelve months later, in which case they qualify from the date they are paid. This does not apply to the privatisation issues, which qualified for indexation from the date of issue even if some instalments were paid more than twelve months later. (Any privatisation issue vouchers that were used to reduce bills were deducted from the allowable cost. Any free shares acquired later are added to the holding and treated as acquired at market value on the first day of dealing in them.)

See Examples 3 to 9 and refer to the general computation rules in CHAPTER 4.

Example 3

An individual investor acquired 5,000 shares in AB plc in May 1987 for £7,500 and a further 2,000 shares in December 1990 for £4,000. The shares do not qualify as business assets. Say he sold all the shares in July 2004 for (a) £18,000 or (b) £13,000 or (c) £10,000. The retail prices index was 101.9 for May 1987, 129.9 for December 1990 and 162.6 for April 1998. The capital gains computation is:

AB plc post-1982 share pool		Number of shares	Unindexed value	Indexed value	Proceeds	Gain (loss)
			£	£	£	£
May 87 Bought		5,000	7,500	7,500		
Dec 90 129.9 − 1 Indexation on £7,500 from May 101.9 87				2,061		
Bought		2,000	4,000	4,000		
		7,000	11,500	13,561		
Apr 98 162.6 − 1 Indexation on £13,561 from Dec 129.9 90				3,414		
		7,000	11,500	16,975		
Sold July 2004: (a)		(7,000)	(11,500)	(16,975)	18,000	1,025
		7,000	11,500	16,975		
(b)		(7,000)	(11,500)	(16,975)	13,000	—
		7,000	11,500	16,975		
(c)		(7,000)	(11,500)	(16,975)	10,000	(1,500)

Note that the gain in (a) is the difference between proceeds and indexed value, i.e. £1,025, the loss in (c) is the difference between proceeds and unindexed value, i.e. £1,500, and if as in (b) the proceeds lie between unindexed and indexed values, the indexation allowance reduces the gain to nil.

Assuming there are no allowable losses, taper relief of 25% = £256 is available on the gain in (a) because the shares have been owned for seven complete years from 6 April 1998 (counting the extra year for non-business assets acquired before 17 March 1998).

Had the investor been a company, there would have been no indexation adjustment at April 1998 and indexation allowance would have been calculated up to July 2004. Taper relief would not have been available.

Example 4

Quoted shares in CD plc are acquired by an individual as follows:

	Number	Cost (£)
1.1.59	2,000	2,000
10.9.64	500	1,000
Between 6.4.65 and 5.4.82 (pre-1982 pool)	5,000	35,000
Post-1982 pool:		
Between 6.4.82 and 5.4.85	4,000	42,000
31.5.85	2,000	24,000
Sales	Number	Consideration (£)
28.11.94	2,000	38,000
16.9.2004	10,000	170,000

The shares do not qualify as business assets. Market value was £3 per share at 6 April 1965 and £8 per share at 31 March 1982. No election had been made to include shares acquired before 6 April 1965 in the pre-1982 pool nor a rebasing election to treat all assets acquired before 31 March 1982 as being acquired at 31 March 1982 value.

The relevant increases in the retail price index are 1.047 between March 1982 and April 1998, .005 between April 1985 and May 1985, .526 between May 1985 and November 1994 and .119 between November 1994 and April 1998.

Sales identified on 'last in, first out' basis (see 38.9).

		Gain
	£	£
Sale of 2,000 on 28.11.94 out of post-1982 pool	38,000	
Indexed cost (see Example 5)	(35,826)	2,174
Chargeable gain on CD plc shares in 1994/95		£2,174
Sale of 10,000 on 16.9.2004:		
Proceeds for sale out of post-1982 pool 4,000/10,000 × 170,000	68,000	
Indexed cost (see Example 5) but cannot create loss	(80,179)	—

	Gain
Sale of 5,000 shares in pre-1982 pool	
Gain (see Example 6)	3,120
Sales of 500 shares acquired 10.9.64 and of 500 shares out of 2,000 acquired 1.1.59, each show gains of £312 (see Example 7)	624
Giving total chargeable gains on CD plc shares in 2004/05 of	£3,744

The same points apply as in Example 3 re taper relief and company investors.

Example 5

CD plc post-1982 pool	Number of shares	Unin-dexed value £	Indexed value £
At 6.4.85 per Example 4 (acquisitions between 6.4.82 and 5.4.85)	4,000	42,000	42,000
If at 6.4.85 the entire holding had been sold, the indexation allowance would have been, say			4,200
Giving indexed value at 6.4.85 of			46,200
May 85 Indexed on £46,200 from Apr 85 (.005)			231
Bought	2,000	24,000	24,000
	6,000	66,000	70,431
Nov 94 Indexed on £70,431 from May 85 (.526)			37,047
			107,478
Cost of shares sold (one-third of holding)	2,000	22,000	35,826
	4,000	44,000	71,652
Sep 2004 Indexed on £71,652 from Nov 94 to Apr 98 (.119)			8,527
			80,179
Cost of shares sold	4,000	44,000	80,179

Example 6

CD plc pre-1982 pool
5,000 shares cost £35,000, value at 31.3.82 £8 each
= £40,000.

	£	£
Sale proceeds 16.9.2004 5,000/10,000 × 170,000	85,000	85,000
Cost	(35,000)	
31.3.82 value		(40,000)
Indexation allowance 1.047 on 31.3.82 value	(41,880)	(41,880)
	8,120 or	3,120
Lower gain		£3,120

Example 7

CD plc

	Number of shares	Cost (£)
Pre-6.4.65 acquisitions per Example 4:		
1.1.59	2,000	2,000
10.9.64	500	1,000

Identified with sales on 'last in, first out' basis.
Sale 16.9.2004 of 500 shares acquired 10.9.64:

	£	£
Using old 6.4.65 rules		
Sale proceeds 500/10,000 × 170,000	8,500	8,500
Cost 10.9.64	(1,000)	
6.4.65 value		(1,500)
Indexation allowance to April 1998 1.047 on 31.3.82 value (500 @ £8 each = £4,000, which is higher than both cost, £1,000 and 6.4.65 value, £1,500)	(4,188)	(4,188)
	3,312 or	2,812
Lower gain is		£2,812

Using 31.3.82 value	
Sale proceeds	8,500
31.3.82 value	(4,000)
Indexation allowance (as above)	(4,188)
Gain	£312
Gain is lower of £2,812 and £312	£312

Sale 16.9.2004 of 500 shares acquired 1.1.59:

Using old 6.4.65 rules	£	£
Sale proceeds 500/10,000 × 170,000	8,500	8,500
Cost 1.1.59 500/2,000 × 2,000	(500)	
6.4.65 value		(1,500)
Indexation allowance to April 1998 1.047 on		
31.3.82 value of £4,000	(4,188)	(4,188)
	£3,812	£2,812
Lower gain is		£2,812
Using 31.3.82 value Gain is as above		£312
Gain is lower of £2,812 and £312		£312

Example 8

Facts as in Example 4, but rebasing election has been made to use 31.3.82 value for all pre-31.3.82 acquisitions.

Treatment of sale of 2,000 shares on 28.11.94 and of 4,000 out of 10,000 shares sold on 16.9.2004 is unchanged, since they comprise the post-1982 pool. The gain in 1994/95 thus remains at £2,174 and there is neither gain nor loss on the disposal of the 4,000 shares in 2004/05.

Since the pre-1982 pool and the shares acquired before 6 April 1965 are all treated as acquired at their 31.3.82 value of £8, the gain or loss on the remaining 6,000 shares sold on 16.9.2004 can be worked out in a single calculation. Since 31.3.82 value was used to work out gains in any case, rebasing would show the same result as follows:

	£	£
Sale proceeds 6,000 shares		
6,000/10,000 × 170,000		102,000
31.3.82 value (£8 each)	48,000	
Indexation allowance to April 1998 1.047	50,256	98,256
Gain in 2004/05 on CD plc shares as in		
Example 4		£3,744

The figures used in the examples are not intended to be indicative of probable values and are used merely to illustrate the rules. In many cases, 31 March 1982 values will be higher than earlier costs and the irrevocable rebasing election will have been or will be made. If the time limit for making the rebasing election has not expired (see 4.12), it needs to be considered in the light of all the chargeable assets held on 31 March 1982 and not just the particular asset sold.

Shares held on 6 April 1965 (TCGA 1992, Sch 2, Parts I and III)

38.12   If the rebasing election has been made to treat all assets acquired before 31 March 1982 as acquired at their market value on that day, gains and losses are computed on that basis for both quoted and unquoted shares (as in Example 8).

Where the rebasing election has not been made, the procedure is as follows.

For unquoted securities, the legislation requires two computations to be made, as follows.

(a)   (i)   Calculate the gain or loss over the whole period of ownership.

(ii)   Adjust for the available indexation allowance based either on cost or 31 March 1982 value, whichever is higher (but not so as to create or increase a loss), then calculate the proportion of the resulting gain or loss that relates to the period after 5 April 1965 (but ignoring any period of ownership before 6 April 1945).

(iii)   As an alternative to the result in (ii), the taxpayer may make an irrevocable election to have the result computed by reference to the value of the asset on 6 April 1965, with indexation allowance based on the higher of 6 April 1965 value and 31 March 1982 value (but the indexation allowance cannot create or increase a loss). If this calculation would give a loss instead of a gain, the transaction is deemed to give neither gain nor loss. The election cannot give a greater loss than the amount by which the cost exceeds the sale proceeds.

(Losses will not usually arise under either calculation because the costs of many years ago are being compared with current sale proceeds.)

(b)   Calculate the gain or loss as if the shares had been bought on 31 March 1982 at their market value on that date. The available indexation allowance is based on the higher of 31 March 1982 value and either cost or 6 April 1965 value according to which was used to give the result in the first computation (but not so as to create or increase a loss).

If both computations show a loss, the lower loss is taken, and if both show a gain, the lower gain is taken. See Example 9. If one computation shows a gain and the other a loss, the result is treated as neither gain nor loss. If, however, the first computation has already resulted in no gain, no loss, that result is taken and the 31 March 1982 value calculation is not made. Where a gain arises it will be obvious in many cases that the lower gain will result from using the 31 March 1982 calculation, without making the alternative calculation. As far as losses are concerned, there can only be an allowable loss if the sale proceeds are below both the cost and the 31 March 1982 value.

For quoted securities, unless a rebasing election has been made, or the shares on hand at 6 April 1965 are included at their value at that date in the pre-1982 pool (see 38.7), two computations are also made. The procedure is similar to that for unquoted securities, except that time apportionment does not apply. In the first computation, the sale proceeds are compared with both the cost and the 6 April 1965 value and the lower gain or lower loss is taken. If one method shows a gain and the other a loss, the computation is treated as giving rise to neither gain nor loss. The available indexation allowance is deducted in each case (based on the higher of the cost/6 April 1965 value and 31 March 1982 value) but not so as to create or increase a loss. The second computation treats the shares as acquired at 31 March 1982 value (but the available indexation allowance is nonetheless based on cost/6 April 1965 value if it exceeds 31 March 1982 value). The lower gain or lower loss produced by the two computations is then taken. If one computation shows a loss and the other a gain, the result is neither gain nor loss. If the first computation has already given a no gain/no loss result, then the second computation is not made. See Example 7 at 38.11. As with unquoted securities, it will often be obvious that the lower gain will result from the 31 March 1982 calculation. Allowable losses will not arise except to the extent that the proceeds are less than the lowest of the cost, 6 April 1965 value and 31 March 1982 value.

The examples show that where a taxpayer has acquired shares at various times before and after 31 March 1982 the rules may require several calculations to be made. If the rebasing election has been made, the position is simpler because for acquisitions before 6 April 1998 (and later acquisitions by companies) there are only two share 'pools' for any class of shares in any company, one covering all acquisitions up to 5 April 1982 (the pre-1982 pool) and the other all later acquisitions (the post-1982 pool). Even so, complications arise through scrip and rights issues, takeovers, etc. The fact that indexation allowance for unincorporated shareholders is frozen at April 1998 will eliminate some of the complexity over time, but in the short term the complexity has increased. The calculations can be simplified by using the Taxation Services of FT Interactive Data to obtain 31.3.82 values and other relevant information.

Example 9

1,500 unquoted shares were acquired by an individual investor on 6 October 1962 for £2 per share. The shares do not qualify as business assets.

Market value considered to be £2.50 per share at 6 April 1965 and £8 per share at 31 March 1982. No rebasing election had been made to treat all assets acquired before 31 March 1982 as being acquired at 31 March 1982 value.

The shares were sold on 6 October 2004 for £15 per share.

Increase in retail prices index from March 1982 to April 1998 is 104.7%.

First computation

Using time apportionment		Using 6 April 1965 market value	
	£		£
Sale 1,500 shares @ £15	22,500	Sale	22,500
Cost 6.10.62 @ £2	(3,000)	6.4.65 MV	
		1,500 @ £2.50	(3,750)
Indexation allowance*	(12,564)		(12,564)
Overall gain	6,936		
Proportion after 6.4.65			

$$\frac{6.4.65 - 6.10.2004}{6.10.62 - 6.10.2004} = \frac{39.5}{42}$$

Gain	6,523		6,186
Lower gain is			£6,186

Second computation

Sale 1,500 shares @ £15		22,500	
31.3.82 value @ £8		(12,000)	
Indexation allowance £12,564 but cannot create loss		(10,500)	
Result is		No gain/no loss	

The overall result is that there is neither chargeable gain nor allowable loss.

*Indexation allowance is 104.7% on March 1982 value of £8 per share.

Scrip and rights issues (TCGA 1992, ss 57, 122, 123, 126–132)

38.13 Scrip and rights shares are treated as acquired at the same time as the shares out of which they arise, although the amount paid for a rights issue (or treated as paid for a scrip dividend — see 38.3) only attracts indexation allowance from the time of payment (or entitlement to the dividend). Taper relief for unincorporated shareholders, on the other hand, is given according to the period of ownership of the original shares. The treatment of scrip dividends is dealt with in 38.14.

If rights are sold nil paid, the proceeds are treated as a part disposal of the holding, unless they are 'small', in which case they are deducted from the cost instead. Proceeds may be treated as 'small' if they are either not more than 5% of the value of the holding or they amount to £3,000 or less (see Example 10). The taxpayer may use the normal part disposal treatment if he wishes, for example if the gain is covered by his taper relief and annual exemption. (The value of the holding is arrived at by taking the ex-rights value of the existing shares plus the proceeds for the rights shares sold. If not all the rights shares were sold, those retained would also be valued at nil-paid price in this calculation.) For post-1982 pool calculations (see 38.11), the indexed pool is increased by the available indexation before making the deduction. For pre-1982 pools and earlier acquisitions (see 38.7), the legislation provides that the available indexation allowance on a later disposal is first calculated on the full cost then reduced by an indexation amount on the rights sale proceeds from the date of receipt (or for unincorporated shareholders, from April 1998 if earlier). This ensures that the correct amount of indexation allowance is given. It is, however, more straightforward to operate pre-1982 pools on an indexed basis (see 38.11), so that the sale of rights nil-paid can be treated in the same way as for post-1982 pools (see Example 11).

Example 10

An individual taxpayer acquired 2,000 shares in EF plc on 23 February 1986 for £2,000. On 10 December 1987 there was a scrip issue of 1 for 2. On 19 October 2004 there was a rights issue of 1 for 6 at £2 per share. The ex-rights value of the shares was £3.00, giving a value of £9,000 for 3,000 shares.

EF plc post-1982 pool
If rights are taken up:

	Shares	Unindexed value £	Indexed value £
23.2.86	2,000	2,000	2,000
10.12.87 Scrip	1,000		
	3,000		
19.10.2004 Rights	500		
Indexed February 1986 to April 1998.683			1,366
Rights cost		1,000	1,000
Pool values carried forward	3,500	3,000	4,366

If rights are sold nil paid for £1 per share = £500, which is 'small' being less than £3,000, even though more than 5% of (£9,000 + £500 =) £475:

	Shares	Unindexed value	Indexed value
		£	£
As above after indexation to April 1998	3,000	2,000	3,366
Rights proceeds		(500)	(500)
Pool values carried forward	3,000	1,500	2,866

Example 11

In addition to the post-1982 pool in Example 10, the taxpayer had acquired 3,000 shares for £1,500 on 11 April 1979. These shares comprise the pre-1982 pool. The 31 March 1982 value of the shares was 75p per share. Rebasing election not made.

EF plc pre-1982 pool

If rights are taken up:

	Shares	Unindexed cost	Indexed cost	Unindexed 31.3.82 value	Indexed 31.3.82 value
		£	£	£	£
At 31.3.82	3,000	1,500	1,500	2,250	2,250
10.12.87 Scrip	1,500				
	4,500				
19.10.2004					
Rights	750				
Indexed March 1982 to April 1998 (104.7% × £2,250)			2,356		2,356
Rights cost		1,500	1,500	1,500	1,500
Pool values cf	5,250	3,000	5,356	3,750	6,106

If rights are sold nil paid
for £1 per share:

	Shares	Unindexed cost £	Indexed cost £	Unindexed 31.3.82 value £	Indexed 31.3.82 value £
At 31.3.82, adjusted for scrip and indexed as above	4,500	1,500	3,856	2,250	4,606
19.10.2004 rights proceeds		(750)	(750)	(750)	(750)
Pool values cf	4,500	750	3,106	1,500	3,856

Although Examples 10 and 11 show small proceeds on a sale of rights being deducted from the value of the holding, if treating them as a part disposal would produce a gain covered by taper relief and the annual exemption, the part disposal treatment would be better. The part of the cost of the holding that is taken into account against the cash proceeds is arrived at in the same way as for cash on a takeover (see 38.26).

Scrip dividend options (TCGA 1992, s 142)

38.14   If individuals, personal representatives or trustees of discretionary trusts take scrip shares instead of a dividend, the capital gains tax cost is the amount treated as their net income (see 38.3), not the grossed up equivalent. Scrip shares issued to such persons used to be regarded as increasing existing holdings in the same way as ordinary scrip issues. Scrip shares issued in lieu of dividends on or after 6 April 1998 are treated as free-standing acquisitions, so that taper relief is based on the date the scrip shares are issued rather than the time the original shares were acquired.

Many enhanced scrip offers have been made where the value of the shares was usually 50% more than the cash dividend alternative, and the offers included an option for the scrip shares to be sold immediately at a set price. Scrip shares sold in this way used to be regarded as purchased for the amount of the shareholder's notional income (see 38.3) and added pro rata to pre- and post-1982 holdings after adjusting for indexation. The shares sold were then treated as sold out of the post-1982 pool in priority to the pre-1982 pool. For shares issued on or after 6 April 1998, the shares sold are directly linked with the shares acquired.

Where scrip shares in lieu of a dividend are issued to a company, they are treated in the same way as ordinary scrip shares, i.e. there is no deemed cost and the shares are treated as acquired when the original shares were acquired.

The same applies if the recipient is a life interest trust unless the trustees treat the shares as income of the life tenant (see 38.3). Where trustees adopt that treatment, the scrip shares do not go into the trust's holding at all, and are regarded as belonging to the life tenant directly, so that the life tenant is treated in the same way as other individuals, even if the shares are held by the trustees (except in Scotland, where the treatment is different).

Unit and investment trusts and open-ended investment companies

Unit trusts and open-ended investment companies (TA 1988, ss 468–469; TCGA 1992, ss 99, 99A, 100; FA 1995, s 152; FA 1996, Sch 10 para 4; FA 2004, s 118)

38.15   Open-ended investment companies (OEICs) are companies in which the shares may be continuously created or redeemed, depending on investor demand. They are treated in essentially the same way as unit trusts, and existing unit trusts may convert into or merge with OEICs if they wish.

Unit trusts enable an investor to obtain a wide spread of investments, within a professionally managed fund. There are various types of funds to suit particular circumstances, for example some aimed at capital growth and some at maximising income. This chapter deals only with authorised unit trusts (i.e. trusts authorised under the Financial Services and Markets Act 2000 or earlier legislation, which places certain restrictions on the investments the trust is able to make).

Authorised unit trusts do not pay tax on UK dividends. They pay corporation tax on their other income at a rate equal to the lower rate of income tax, currently 20%. They are exempt from tax on capital gains. (There are anti-avoidance provisions to prevent the exemption being exploited by transferring a company's business to an authorised unit trust.) Relief for management expenses and interest is given against profits chargeable to corporation tax.

Distributions to unit holders may be dividend distributions or interest distributions. A unit trust can only pay interest distributions where its interest-bearing investments comprise more than 60% of the total market value of the trust fund.

The position of individual investors is broadly similar to what it would have been if they had invested directly. Dividend distributions carry a tax credit of 1/9th of the cash amount, whether they are from equity based funds or from funds that invest wholly or partly in interest-bearing securities. Interest distributions are paid net of 20% tax. (Foreign investors are able to receive interest free of UK tax in some circumstances, or may be able to claim double tax relief. See 41.5 for the inheritance tax treatment of those not domiciled in the UK.) An individual investor's gains are similarly taxed as if the funds had been invested directly, except that gains on sales of gilt units are taxable, whereas gains on gilts themselves are not (see 38.23). 'Equalisation' payments received when you acquire new units are not taxed as income. They reduce the cost of your units for capital gains tax (see 9.22).

Dividend distributions paid to companies from the fund are franked investment income and are not liable to corporation tax, unless part of the fund's income is not dividend income, in which case an equivalent part of the dividend distribution from the fund is treated as interest received net of 20% tax. This amount is stated on tax vouchers. Any such amount is brought into account along with interest distributions as part of the company's income under Schedule D, Case III. The income tax suffered at source is deducted from the tax payable by the company, but if the investor company is claiming an income tax repayment, the repayment cannot exceed the company's proportion of the unit trust's corporation tax liability on the gross income. The trustees are required to state their net liability to corporation tax on the distribution statement sent to the company and this is usually expressed as an amount per unit held so that the company can calculate the maximum income tax available for repayment. Gains and losses on disposals of a company's unit trust investments also form part of the Schedule D, Case III profit or loss (see 3.6).

Investment trusts (*TA 1988, s 842; TCGA 1992, s 100*)

38.16   Investment trusts are actually companies and not trusts, and you buy shares in them in the usual way. Some trusts with a limited life are split level trusts, i.e. they have income shares that receive most of the trust's income and a fixed capital sum on liquidation, and capital shares that receive little or no income but get most of the capital surplus (if any) on a liquidation.

Investment trusts are exempt from tax on their capital gains if they are approved investment trusts (approval has to be given every year by the Revenue) but the gains may only be reinvested and cannot be distributed as dividends. There are anti-avoidance provisions to prevent the exemption being exploited either by transferring a company's business to a company that is, or later becomes, an investment trust, or by transferring assets intra-group to a company that is, or later becomes, an investment trust. Investment trusts are charged to corporation tax in the normal way (except in relation to certain rental income — see 32.20), which puts them at a disadvantage as against unit trusts.

Savings schemes

38.17   Unit trusts, open-ended investment companies and investment trusts operate monthly savings schemes, which give the investor the advantage of 'pound cost averaging', i.e. fluctuations in prices are evened out because overall you get more units/shares when the price is low and fewer when it is high. Such schemes clearly give calculation problems for capital gains tax both in relation to indexation allowance for units/shares acquired before 6 April 1998 and in relation to taper relief from that date.

Individual Savings Accounts (ISAs) and Personal Equity Plans (PEPs)

38.18   Investors can invest up to £7,000 in years up to 2005/06 and £5,000 a year from 2006/07 onwards in unit and investment trusts and open-ended investment companies through the stocks and shares component of ISAs, providing not more than 50% of the fund's investments are redeemable within five years of the date of acquisition.

PEP investments could be made in such funds up to 5 April 1999 but not thereafter, although the funds may remain invested.

For details of ISAs, see 36.22 and for PEPs, see 38.29.

Venture capital trusts

38.19   Individuals may invest in qualifying unquoted trading companies through a venture capital trust (VCT). These trusts are part of the Government incentives to promote investment and enterprise. For the detailed provisions see 29.5 to 29.8.

Shares of negligible value (TCGA 1992, s 24)

38.20   Where shares (or any other assets) have become of negligible value, you may establish an allowable loss by claiming to be treated as if you had actually disposed of them either on the date of the claim or at a stipulated time within the two tax years before the tax year in which the claim is made, providing the shares were of negligible value on the chosen date (see 4.31). Details of quoted shares that are regarded as being of negligible value, and the date from which that applies, are published by the Revenue. In the case of unquoted shares, the fact that the shares are of negligible value has specifically to be agreed with the Revenue. Even though shares are on the Revenue's list, you do not have to make a negligible value claim unless and until you wish to do so. If a claim has not been made before the time when the shares cease to exist, they are treated as disposed of at that time.

Relief against income for losses on shares in qualifying trading companies (TA 1988, ss 574–576)

38.21   Where an individual disposes of shares at a loss, or the shares become valueless, the loss is normally relievable, like any other capital loss, against gains on other assets. Where, however, the shares are in an unquoted UK trading company (and see below re quoted companies), and they were acquired by subscription as distinct from transfer (including shares subscribed for under the enterprise investment scheme — see 29.2), relief may be claimed instead against any other *income* of the tax year of loss or of the previous tax year. Where some shares were acquired other than by subscription, there are rules to identify which shares have been disposed of. The claim to set off such losses takes priority over any claim for relief for trading losses. Claims must be made within one year from 31 January following the tax year of loss (e.g. by 31 January 2007 for a 2004/05 loss).

For shares issued on or after 6 April 1998, relief is available under these provisions only where the trading company would be a qualifying company for the purposes of the enterprise investment scheme provisions (see 29.2), although the relief is not restricted to EIS shares. Relief will remain available for shares in a company that was unquoted at the time they were issued if the company subsequently ceases to be unquoted, providing there were no arrangements at the time of the share issue for this to occur.

There could be a taper relief benefit of such a claim where there are capital gains against which the loss could be set, in that taper relief is set against gains *after* reduction by losses, so setting losses against income instead of gains could increase taper relief on the gains which are taxable.

Capital gains on government, local authority and company loan stocks (TCGA 1992, ss 104–106, 108, 115–117 and Sch 9; FA 1996, s 96; FA 2004, s 52 and Sch 10)

Companies

38.22   A company's gains and losses on disposal of most loan stock are brought into account in calculating the company's income under the 'loan relationships' rules outlined at 3.6. This does not apply to disposals of 3½% Funding Stock 1999/2004 and 5½% Treasury Stock 2008/12, which are outside the 'loan relationships' rules and are exempt under the capital gains rules, so that there can be neither chargeable gains nor allowable losses. Nor do the loan relationships rules apply to disposals of securities linked to a share index and certain convertible securities, so that such disposals are taxable under the capital gains rules. Convertible securities are within the capital gains rules where there is more than a trivial likelihood at the outset that the conversion etc. rights will be exercised, providing they cannot be redeemed for a 'deep' return over the issue price if they are not converted.

For those securities that remain within the capital gains charge, each acquisition is treated as a separate asset. Subject to certain anti-avoidance provisions (including the provision at 38.10 relating to acquisitions within the month before or the month after the disposal), disposals are identified with acquisitions in the previous twelve months on a 'first in, first out' basis, then with any other acquisitions on a 'last in, first out' basis.

As far as loan stock is concerned, the distinction between qualifying and non-qualifying corporate bonds for individuals (see 38.23) does not apply, and the definition of qualifying corporate bond for companies is *any* asset that represents a loan relationship (as to which see 3.6). See 38.26 for the treatment in takeovers where shares are exchanged for corporate bonds or vice versa.

Individuals

38.23   No chargeable gains or allowable losses arise on disposals by individuals of British Government stock and qualifying corporate bonds (with the exception of certain losses as indicated below). Qualifying corporate bonds are quoted or unquoted non-convertible sterling loan stock purchased or issued on commercial terms after 13 March 1984. Building society permanent interest bearing shares (see 37.4) are also within the definition of qualifying corporate bonds for individuals (but not for companies). Profits and losses on certain securities issued at a discount are dealt with under the income tax rather than the capital gains provisions (see 38.25). Index-linked securities that are outside the discounted securities provisions (i.e. those that are linked to the value of a share index) are also outside the definition of qualifying corporate bond and are thus chargeable to capital gains tax.

The capital gains exemption for qualifying corporate bonds cannot be used to avoid income tax by selling just before an interest date, because of the accrued income provisions (see 36.18). There are special provisions for company reorganisations to ensure that the appropriate exemption is given on loan stock converted into shares or vice versa (see 38.26).

Disposals of interest-bearing stocks that are not government stocks or qualifying corporate bonds (i.e. non-sterling loan stock, loan stock that may be converted into shares, loans that are not commercial loans and loan stock acquired before 14 March 1984) are subject to capital gains tax (unless they are discounted securities within the income tax charge). The same matching rules apply as for shares (see 38.9).

Losses on qualifying corporate bonds (TCGA 1992, ss 254, 255)

38.24   Since qualifying corporate bonds are exempt from capital gains tax, no allowable loss can arise under the normal rules. For qualifying corporate bonds issued before 17 March 1998, relief for losses may be claimed according to the rules outlined at 4.32 if the claimant made the loan to a UK resident trader. Someone to whom the bond has been assigned cannot claim the relief. A claim may also be made when the value of such a loan has become negligible (see 4.31). Where unquoted bonds were issued before 14 March 1989 in exchange for other shares or securities, and they do not strictly qualify for this loss relief because the money has not been used in a trade, the relief is given by Revenue concession (D38). The relief for losses outlined above does not apply to individuals for bonds issued on or after 17 March 1998. Nor does it apply to companies, because a company's gains and losses are dealt with under the 'loan relationships' rules (see 3.6).

See 38.26 for the treatment of losses on qualifying corporate bonds acquired on a takeover.

Securities issued at a discount (FA 1996, Sch 13)

38.25   The deep discounted securities provisions outlined below do not apply to companies, because a company's gains and losses are dealt with under the 'loan relationships' rules (see 3.6).

Special rules apply to all securities issued at a discount to private investors. The accrued income scheme (see 36.18) does not apply to securities within these provisions. Securities are discounted securities where their issue price is lower than the redemption price by more than ½% per year between issue and redemption, or, if that period exceeds 30 years, by more than 15%. The provisions do not cover shares, gilt-edged securities (except for gilt strips, for which there are special rules), indexed securities that are linked to the value of a share index, and life assurance policies.

There is no capital gains tax charge on discounted securities, and for securities acquired before 27 March 2003 investors are charged to income tax under Schedule D, Case III (or Case IV for foreign securities) in the tax year of disposal or redemption on the profit made after deducting expenses of acquisition and disposal. If a loss arises on securities acquired before that date, a claim may be made by the first anniversary of 31 January following the relevant tax year to set the loss against the total income of that tax year. Trustees may only set losses against income from discounted securities of the tax year of loss or, if that is insufficient, of a later tax year. Under new anti-avoidance provisions, for discounted securities acquired on or after 27 March 2003, no deduction will be allowed for incidental costs of acquisition, disposal or redemption, and no relief will be available for losses on disposal or redemption of such acquisitions. When someone dies, they are treated as disposing of the securities to the personal representatives at market value at the date of death, income tax being chargeable accordingly. Transfers from personal representatives to legatees are treated as at market value at the date of the transfer, with income tax being charged on the estate on the difference between the value at death and the value at the date of the transfer.

Takeovers, mergers and reconstructions (TCGA 1992, ss 57, 116, 126–131, 135, 136, 138A and Sch 5AA)

38.26   An exchange of new shares for old does not normally involve a chargeable gain, the new shares standing in the shoes of the old both as regards acquisition date and cost. This often happens when one company (whether or not its shares are quoted on the Stock Exchange) acquires another (either quoted or unquoted) by issuing its own shares to the holders of the shares in the company which is being taken over (known as 'paper for paper' exchanges).

Where both cash and new shares are received, a partial disposal arises, in the proportion that the cash itself bears to the cash and market value of the securities acquired in exchange.

When part of a takeover package takes the form of shares or securities to be issued at some future date, the number of such shares or securities depending for example on future profits (known as an earn-out right), the tax treatment has changed for rights conferred on or after 10 April 2003. For the detailed provisions, including the treatment where the future consideration is to be in cash, see 28.9.

Example 12

X owns 10,000 shares in a company, A, which cost him £6,000 in September 1983. The shares do not qualify as business assets.

Company A is taken over by company B on 6 May 2004, indexation allowance from September 1983 to April 1998 being 88.9%.

Scenario (a)

12,000 shares in company B, valued at £15,000, are received in exchange for the 10,000 shares in company A.

No chargeable gain arises on the £9,000 excess value of the company B shares over the cost of the company A shares.

Instead the 12,000 shares in company B are regarded as having the same £6,000 base value as the 10,000 company A shares which they replace.

Scenario (b)

12,000 shares in company B, valued at £11,250, together with £3,750 in cash are received in exchange for the 10,000 shares in company A, the shares in company A having an indexed cost of £11,334. The cash represents ¼ of the total consideration and the shares ¾.

The 12,000 shares in company B have base values as follows:

Unindexed value ¾ × £6,000	£4,500
Indexed value ¾ × £11,334	£8,500

The indexed cost to set off against the £3,750 cash received for the part disposal is ¼ × £11,334 = £2,834 reducing the gain to £916. Assuming there are no allowable losses, this is then further reduced by 25% taper relief to £687, since the shares are non-business assets owned for seven years after 5 April 1998 (including the extra qualifying year for assets owned before 17 March 1998 — see 4.16).

If X had been a company, the treatment would have been the same, except that indexation allowance would have been given up to the month of disposal, i.e. May 2004, and taper relief would not have applied.

As indicated at 38.23, qualifying corporate bonds are not chargeable assets for capital gains tax, and can create neither a chargeable gain nor allowable loss (subject to the special rules at 38.24). Sometimes on a takeover or reorganisation qualifying corporate bonds may be exchanged for shares or vice versa. When qualifying corporate bonds are exchanged for shares, the normal rules outlined above do not apply and the shares are treated as acquired at their market value at the date of the exchange. If shares are exchanged for qualifying corporate bonds, the gain or loss on the shares at the date of the exchange, including any available taper relief, is calculated and 'frozen' until the qualifying corporate bonds are disposed of, when the frozen gain or loss crystallises. No further taper relief applies after the date of the exchange. No gain or loss can be established on the bonds themselves (with the exception stated at 38.24). In some cases, this could mean that a gain is chargeable even if the qualifying corporate bonds have become virtually worthless. One solution is to give them to a charity. The frozen gain on the shares would not then be charged, nor would the charity have any tax liability when it disposed of the bonds. A frozen gain escapes charge if the taxpayer dies. If a frozen gain arises on shares held by personal representatives, however, it is charged when the loan stock is disposed of by the personal representatives, or when disposed of by a legatee following the transfer of the stock to him by the personal representatives.

Where a frozen gain would otherwise become chargeable, it may be deferred if an equivalent investment is made by subscribing for unquoted shares under the enterprise investment scheme provisions (see 29.3). Where shares are exchanged partly for cash and partly for qualifying corporate bonds, deferral relief may be claimed on the gain on the cash element.

If on the takeover an individual exchanges shares for non-qualifying corporate bonds, the bonds stand in the shoes of the shares as regards date and cost of acquisition, with a later disposal of the bond giving a capital gain or loss at that time, taper relief running to the time of disposal.

For company investors, all loan stock is included within the definition of 'qualifying corporate bond' (see 38.22).

Where a company receives shares in exchange for corporate bonds, the gain or loss on the bonds is taken into account in computing the company's income under the 'loan relationships' rules (see 3.6). If a company receives corporate bonds in exchange for shares, the 'frozen gain or loss' treatment outlined above applies, with the frozen gain or loss on the shares being brought in as a *capital* gain or loss when the bonds are disposed of. (Any gain or loss on the disposal of the bonds themselves will be brought into account under the 'loan relationships' rules.)

Disposal by gift (TCGA 1992, ss 67, 165)

38.27 Where shares or securities are disposed of by gift, the proceeds are regarded as being their open market value. If a gain arises, the donor and donee may make a joint election for the donee to adopt the donor's base cost for capital gains tax purposes, as increased by any available indexation allowance, but this right is only available if the gift is made by an individual or trustees and comprises shares or securities in an unquoted trading company, or in a quoted trading company in which the donor owns 5% of the shares, or the gift is immediately chargeable to inheritance tax, or would be if it were not covered by the donor's annual inheritance tax exemption and/or inheritance tax nil rate band (see 4.27 to 4.30). Taper relief on an eventual disposal of the gifted asset is given according to the period of ownership of the donee (see 4.23).

If a loss arises on a gift to or other transaction with a connected person (which broadly means close family of the donor and of his spouse, trustees of family trusts and companies controlled by the donor) the loss is not allowed against gains generally but only against a gain on a subsequent transaction with the same person. This does not apply to gifts between husband/wife, which are treated as made at neither a gain nor a loss (see 4.5).

Stamp duty

38.28 Stamp duty is payable on most transactions in stocks and shares, usually at ½%, but higher rates apply in some circumstances. The provisions are outlined in CHAPTER 6.

Individual Savings Accounts (ISAs) and Personal Equity Plans (PEPs) (TA 1988, s 333; TCGA 1992, s 151; SI 1989/469; SI 1998/1870)

38.29 Individual Savings Accounts (ISAs) have a stocks and shares component enabling tax-free savings to be made on investments of up to £7,000 in tax years up to 2005/06 and £5,000 a year from 2006/07 onwards. If money is invested in the other components, i.e. cash and/or life insurance, the stocks and shares limit is £3,000. From April 2005 the Government plans to make changes to the ISA provisions, including merging the life insurance element with the stocks and shares element. The detailed provisions are at 36.22.

No further investments may be made in Personal Equity Plans (PEPs) after 5 April 1999, but all PEP investments already made at that date may continue to be held tax-free in addition to any ISA investments and investors will still be able to switch fund managers and investments as indicated below. The PEP rules for qualifying investments and administration provisions are the same as those for ISAs.

Any capital gains, dividends and interest on the PEP investments are entirely tax-free, and remain so for as long as the investment is held within the plan. On the other hand, any losses arising on disposals within a plan are not allowable losses. From 6 April 2004 the plan managers can no longer reclaim dividend tax credits from the Revenue. Investments may be switched from one qualifying investment to another or from one plan manager to another without any capital gains tax effect, although there are costs involved, and parts of plans may be transferred between plan managers. See 36.22 for the inclusion of UCITS (undertakings for collective investments in transferable securities) guaranteeing less than 95% capital return to investors in the range of allowable PEP investments.

An investor may withdraw either cash or investments from the plan. If investments are withdrawn, their base cost for capital gains tax purposes is their market value at the date of withdrawal. If an investor dies, the personal representatives are treated as acquiring the plan at its market value at the date of death and the tax exemption ceases to apply.

Plan managers may hold cash on deposit within a plan for a short period before it is invested or reinvested in ordinary shares. Tax is not deducted from any interest received by the plan managers on the cash deposit, and the interest is not subject to tax at all if it is reinvested in shares or unit trusts. Otherwise, it is taxed in full when withdrawn (tax being deducted at the savings rate of 20%) unless it is not more than £180.

Tax points

38.30

- You cannot sell shares and buy them back the next day (bed and breakfast) to use your annual capital gains exemption (currently £8,200), although your spouse could repurchase them on the market (not directly from you). The complicated calculation of potential gains should be borne in mind when working out what can be sold without attracting tax.

- Investment managers frequently prepare capital gains reports for clients at the tax year end. Care needs to be taken with the thirty day rule for matching disposals with acquisitions where disposals take place shortly before the end of the tax year.

- If you are a small investor, unit and investment trusts can be a useful way of getting the benefit of a wide spread of investments, with the added advantage of expert management. Such trusts are exempt from tax on their capital gains. You pay capital gains tax in the usual way when you dispose of your investment in the trust. The investment is particularly tax-efficient when made through an Individual Savings Account (ISA), although in the current climate the tax exemption has often been more than offset by falling investment values.

- Investing regular amounts on a monthly basis into a unit or investment trust evens out the ups and downs of share prices.

- When a PEP or ISA investor dies, his personal representatives should notify the PEP plan or ISA manager promptly, because the tax exemption ceases at the date of the investor's death.

- If you give away shares, they are regarded as disposed of for market value, but tax does not have to be paid at that time if they qualify for gifts relief and a claim is made for the relief to apply. The relief is available on a holding of quoted shares if you control 5% or more of the voting power (see 4.27).

- See 38.26 re avoiding a frozen gain crystallising on qualifying corporate bonds that were acquired on a takeover, etc. by giving them to a charity.

- If your shares have become virtually worthless, you may wish to make a negligible value claim as soon as they have been included on the Revenue's list (see 38.20). But if, say, making the claim immediately would reduce gains and cause annual exemption to be wasted, you should defer it to a later year.

- If there is some control over the time of payment of a dividend, as with a family or other small company, watch that the date of payment does not aggravate an already high taxable income where the income of the major shareholders varies from year to year.

- If you invest in government stocks you will receive the interest in full and pay the income tax later, rather than receiving the interest net as with some other loans. The end result will be the same but your cash flow will be improved.

- If you hold not more than £5,000 nominal value of government stock or other securities to which the accrued income scheme applies, remember that the accrued interest is not charged to income tax (see 36.18). The securities will usually be exempt from capital gains tax (see 38.23). If they are not, the accrued interest is taken into account for capital gains tax in arriving at the cost or proceeds as the case may be.

- If you hold more than £5,000 nominal value of accrued income scheme securities, you will need to consider what adjustment is required when you dispose of any of them. Details must be shown on your tax return. If you deal through a bank or stockbroker, the amount of accrued interest will be shown on your contract note. Accrued income charges or reliefs are taken into account in the tax year in which the next interest payment is made on the stock.

- The rules for splitting shareholdings into post-5 April 1998 acquisitions, post-1982 pools, pre-1982 pools and pre-6 April 1965 acquisitions mean that a disposal of a holding will sometimes be treated as several disposals for capital gains tax purposes. If the disposal qualifies for the business gifts relief, this may give the opportunity of electing for the gifts holdover relief to apply to only some of the disposals, leaving the gain on others to be covered by the annual exemption if not otherwise used.

- Since the rate at which you pay capital gains tax depends on your income, the timing of disposals can be important where your level of income varies.

- Since husband and wife are both entitled to an annual capital gains tax exemption, currently £8,200, it may be appropriate to split share portfolios so that each may take advantage of it. Transfers between husband and wife are not chargeable disposals. If shares are held jointly in unequal proportions, watch the provisions about notifying the Revenue for income tax purposes (see 33.5).

39
Chattels and valuables

What are chattels? (TCGA 1992, ss 21, 263, 269)

39.1   Chattels are tangible movable property, for example coins, furniture, jewellery, works of art, motor vehicles. Although coins come within the definition, sterling currency is specifically exempt from capital gains tax, as is foreign currency for personal use abroad. Furthermore, the special capital gains chattels rules do not apply to currency of any description. Motor cars (other than one-seater cars) are specifically exempt from capital gains tax. One-seater cars and other motor vehicles are exempt as wasting assets unless they have been used in a business (see 39.3).

Income tax

39.2   If you invest in valuable objects, the appreciation in value does not generally attract income tax (nor sometimes capital gains tax), but on the other hand there is no tax relief for expenses of ownership such as insurance or charges for safe custody.

A succession of profitable sales may suggest to the Revenue that chattels and valuables are held for trading purposes rather than investment, particularly where the scale and frequency of the sales, or the way in which they are carried out, or the need for supplementary work between purchase and sale, suggest a trading motive. Indeed, even a single purchase and sale has on occasion been held to be a trading transaction. However, an important indicator of trading is the lack of significant investment value or pride of ownership. Where chattels have those qualities, a trading motive is more readily refuted.

Capital gains tax on sales of chattels (TCGA 1992, ss 44, 45, 262)

39.3   The capital gains tax treatment of a chattel depends on the nature of the chattel, and sometimes on its value.

Motor cars, sterling currency, and foreign currency for own use abroad are completely exempt, as indicated above. If other chattels have a predictable life of 50 years or less (called wasting assets), they are totally exempt from capital gains tax unless they are used in a business and capital allowances have been, or could have been, claimed on them. Plant and machinery is always regarded as having a predictable life of 50 years or less. So privately owned items such as greyhounds and yachts (and even collectors' items if they are 'machinery') are exempt because they are wasting assets. If an asset is exempt, there can be neither a chargeable gain nor an allowable loss. In many cases, therefore, the exemption denies you relief for a loss rather than exempting a gain.

In the case of chattels (other than coins that are currency) that are not wasting assets, and business chattels (whether they are wasting assets or not), any gain is exempt if the chattel is bought and sold for £6,000 or less. If there are joint owners, such as husband and wife, each has a separate £6,000 limit to compare with their share of the sale proceeds. Where the proceeds exceed £6,000, the chargeable gain cannot exceed 5/3rds of the excess proceeds over £6,000. If the chattel is sold at a loss for less than £6,000, it is treated as sold for £6,000 to calculate the allowable loss. This means that there can only be an allowable loss if the chattel cost more than £6,000, and if it is a business chattel there will not be an allowable loss in any event (see below).

See Examples 1 and 2.

Example 1

	£	£
An antique collector's sale proceeds for an antique dresser in June 2004 are		7,200
Cost was	3,550	
Indexation allowance to April 1998, say	1,020	4,570
Chargeable gain		£2,630
But limited to 5/3 × (7,200 − 6,000)		£2,000

Assuming there are no allowable losses, taper relief of 25% = £500 is available, reducing the gain to £1,500, since the dresser is a non-business asset owned for seven years after 5 April 1998 (including the extra year for assets owned before 17 March 1998). The gain would be eliminated completely if the annual exemption of £8,200 had not been used against other gains.

No allowable loss could arise on the dresser, no matter what the sale proceeds, because proceeds of less than £6,000 are treated as £6,000 to calculate a loss.

> **Example 2**
>
> Painting that had cost a collector £11,000 in January 1989 was sold for £8,000 in June 2004. The allowable loss is £3,000. If the painting had been sold for £4,000, it would be treated as sold for £6,000, giving an allowable loss of £5,000 rather than £7,000.

As far as business chattels are concerned, capital allowances are taken into account in computing income liable to income tax or corporation tax. If the chattel is sold for more than cost, the capital allowances will be withdrawn, so that they will not affect the computation of a capital gain. Where a business chattel is sold for less than cost, the capital allowances computation will automatically give relief for the loss on sale in arriving at taxable income, so there will be no allowable loss for capital gains purposes.

Chargeable chattels comprising a set or collection are treated as separate assets unless they are sold to the same or connected persons (as defined in TCGA 1992, s 286 — see 4.27), in which case the sales are added together for the purposes of the £6,000 exemption. Chattels form a set if they are essentially similar and complementary and their value taken together is higher than if they were considered separately. Where the set is sold over a period spanning more than one tax year, the gain is calculated on the total sale proceeds but it is then apportioned between the different tax years according to the respective amounts of sale proceeds in each tax year. Splitting up a set and selling it to different unconnected people would usually not be sensible because it would substantially reduce its value. See 39.5 re chargeable chattels given away by a series of transactions with connected persons.

For Revenue comments on the treatment of wines and spirits see their Tax Bulletin of August 1999. The treatment of shotguns is dealt with in their Tax Bulletin of February 2000.

Coins (TCGA 1992, ss 21, 262, 269)

39.4   Coins may either be currency, i.e. legal tender, or they may be demonetised.

Where a coin is currency, the £6,000 exemption is not available and the coin is chargeable to capital gains tax in the normal way. An example is Kruger-rands, which are legal tender in South Africa. Foreign currency for your own personal use abroad is, however, exempt from capital gains tax under a specific provision. The same applies to sterling currency (which includes post-1836 sovereigns). Demonetised coins (which include pre-1837 sovereigns) are within the definition of a chattel, and if they have a predictable life of more than 50 years, which obviously applies to collectors' items, the exemption for chattels that are wasting assets does not apply, but the £6,000 exemption is available.

Collectors' coins are normally liable to VAT at the standard rate, whether they are legal tender or not, unless they are dealt with under the special scheme for antiques and collectors' pieces or under the global accounting scheme for second-hand goods (see 7.13).

Subject to certain special rules, coins that are 'investment gold' as defined are exempt from VAT and are not eligible to be sold under the second-hand schemes.

Gifts of chattels

39.5   A gift of a chargeable chattel is treated as a disposal at open market value at the date of the gift. In order to arrive at an estimated valuation, some evidence of the transaction in the form of correspondence, etc. is advisable. If the value is below the £6,000 exempt level, no tax charge will arise, but the valuation at the time of the gift counts as the cost of the asset to the donee when calculating the capital gains position on a subsequent disposal by him.

There are provisions similar to the rules for sets of articles in 39.3 where chargeable assets are given away or otherwise disposed of by a series of transactions with connected persons within a period of six years, and they are worth more together than separately. These provisions apply not only to chattels but also to any other assets, particularly unquoted shares and land and buildings. See 4.27 to 4.30 for details.

If the value of the gifted chattel exceeds the £6,000 exempt level and there is a chargeable gain, tax may not even so be payable because the gain, together with other gains, may be covered by taper relief and the annual exemption (currently £8,200). For gifts of business assets, certain other gifts for public benefit, etc. and gifts into and out of discretionary trusts, it is possible for donor and donee to claim gifts relief, so that the donor pays no tax on the gift and the donee acquires it at cost plus indexation allowance to the month of disposal (or April 1998 if earlier) for the purposes of a future sale by him (see 4.27 to 4.30). The donee's taper relief will be based on his period of ownership rather than the donor's.

For inheritance tax purposes, a gift of a chattel may be covered by the annual exemption. If not, it will either be a potentially exempt transfer, or a chargeable transfer if it is to a discretionary trust, but if the donor does not survive the gift by seven years, the value at the time of the gift will be taken into account in calculating the inheritance tax payable at death. The person who received the gift will be primarily responsible for the inheritance tax triggered by the death within seven years, although the Revenue have the right to look to the estate of the donor if necessary. There will not be any potential liability if the gift was within the nil rate band, but, if there is, it may be worth insuring against by a term assurance policy on the life of the donor in favour of the donee.

Tax points

39.6

- The Revenue have the power to require auctioneers to provide details of all chattel sales exceeding £6,000. At present they ask for details only of sales with a value exceeding £20,000.

- Details of chattel acquisitions are frequently required at a later date, perhaps for capital gains tax purposes or to demonstrate that funds for some other investment or business enterprise were available from their sale. Evidence can be provided by purchase invoices that identify the object, and/or by having substantial items included specifically on a household contents insurance policy when they are acquired.

- A profit on the sale of a vintage or classic car is exempt from capital gains tax (unless it is 'unsuitable to be used as a private vehicle') but if you buy and sell with the aim of making a profit rather than holding the car as an investment you are likely to be held to be trading and thus liable to income tax (or corporation tax).

- 'Machinery' is always regarded as a wasting asset and is therefore exempt from capital gains tax unless it is used in a business. A private individual will therefore not pay tax on a gain on a valuable antique machine, such as a clock. The same would apply to a gain by a private individual on a vintage or classic vehicle not covered by the cars exemption.

- Be aware of the trading trap if you regularly buy and sell chattels and valuables.

40
Sensible use of life insurance

Relief for premium payments (TA 1988, s 274)

40.1   Where term assurance is included in a personal pension plan, you get relief at your highest tax rate (see CHAPTER 17). Apart from that, you cannot get tax relief on life insurance premiums unless the policy was taken out before 14 March 1984 and has not subsequently been amended (whether or not by a clause in the policy) to increase the benefits or extend the term. There are, however, still tax advantages for qualifying policies, because of the treatment of the proceeds.

The rate of relief available on a pre-14 March 1984 qualifying policy is 12½% of the premiums paid, subject to maximum allowable premiums of either £1,500 or one-sixth of your total income, whichever is higher. Premiums are paid net of the tax relief.

Qualifying policy (TA 1988, ss 266, 267, 274 and Sch 15)

40.2   The definition of 'qualifying policy' is complex, but broadly the policy must be on your own or your spouse's life, it must secure a capital sum on death, earlier disability or not earlier than ten years after the policy is taken out, the premiums must be reasonably even and paid at yearly or shorter intervals, and there are various requirements as to the amount of the sum insured and sometimes as to the surrender value. Providing these conditions are satisfied, the policy proceeds are tax-free (subject to what is said below as regards early surrender). The offer of a free gift on taking out a policy could breach the 'qualifying policy' rules, but by concession a gift valued at up to £30 will be ignored.

Purchased life annuities (TA 1988, ss 1A, 656–658)

40.3   A qualifying policy is sometimes useful to higher rate taxpayers in conjunction with a purchased life annuity (see 36.21).

Only part of the purchased annuity is liable to income tax, tax being deducted at the savings rate of 20%, with further tax payable or repayable depending on the annuitant's tax position. The remainder of the annuity is regarded as a return of capital.

Instead of making a conventional investment and losing a substantial part of the income in tax, a higher rate taxpayer could purchase a life annuity and use the net income arising to fund a qualifying life policy, the profits on maturity of the policy being tax-free. Whilst the reduction in tax rates has reduced the advantages of this form of investment, it can still be attractive in some circumstances, but specialist advice is essential.

If you are an older taxpayer, a variation is available under which only part of the net annual sum from the annuity is used to pay the premiums on a qualifying policy to replace the initial cost of the annuity, the remainder being retained as spendable income.

Anti-avoidance provisions apply to prevent life insurance companies manipulating the purchased life annuity rules to obtain an excessive deduction against their profits in respect of annuities taken out by financial traders.

Early surrender of qualifying policies (TA 1988, ss 540, 541, 547)

40.4   Where a qualifying policy is varied, surrendered or assigned less than ten years after the policy is taken out (or, for endowment policies, before the expiry of three-quarters of the term if that amounts to less than ten years), any profit arising is charged to tax at the excess of higher rate tax over the 20% lower rate from 6 April 2004 (excess over basic rate before that date) to the extent that the profit falls within the taxpayer's higher rate income tax band (but top-slicing relief is available — see 40.7). See 40.5 under 'Non-qualifying policies' for the way in which the profit is taken into account where there is savings income.

Details of gains must be shown on your tax return, as for non-qualifying policies (see 40.5).

A variation which acknowledges the exclusion of an exceptional risk of critical illness or disability, with a consequent effect upon the future premium or the sum insured, does not cause a policy to lose its qualifying status.

Non-qualifying policies (TA 1988, ss 540–549; FA 2004, s 130)

40.5   If a policy is not a qualifying policy, there is no relief for premium payments, even for policies taken out before 14 March 1984. Whenever the policy was taken out, the proceeds are not wholly tax-free. They are free of capital gains tax so long as they are received by the original policy holder, but such of the capital appreciation that comes within the higher rate tax band when it is added to your income in the tax year of surrender or assignment, is chargeable to income tax at the excess of higher rate tax over the 20% lower rate (excess over basic rate before 6 April 2004) subject to certain special provisions which are outlined below. Although savings income is treated as the top slice of your income for all other purposes (except for calculating tax on payments covered by the 'golden handshake rules' — see 15.6), life policy gains (including any gains chargeable on qualifying policies) are added in last of all in order to calculate any tax liability.

Gains must be shown on your tax return. Your insurance company will normally provide you with the relevant details (see 40.13). If you are calculating your own tax, you should ask the Revenue for their comprehensive tax calculation guide, which deals with the tax on the life insurance gains.

The provisions charging gains on qualifying and non-qualifying policies are not restricted to UK residents. See Revenue concession B53 for the circumstances in which overseas residents will not be charged.

Investment bonds

40.6   A non-qualifying policy usually takes the form of a single premium investment bond. When invested by the life office, the single premium should ideally grow more rapidly than an equivalent amount in the hands of a higher rate taxpayer reinvesting net income from a conventional investment. You are able to make withdrawals of not more than a cumulative 5% per annum of the initial investment in each policy year (ending on the anniversary of the policy) without attracting a tax liability at that time, such withdrawals being treated as partial surrenders which are only taken into account in calculating the final profit on the bond when it is cashed in. The 5% is a cumulative figure and amounts unused in any year swell the tax-free withdrawal available in a later year, which could be useful if you want to save the withdrawal facility for some particularly heavy item of expenditure. If you withdraw more than the permitted 5% figure, you are charged to tax on the excess, but only if, taking into account the excess, and also the top-slicing rules in 40.7, your taxable income exceeds the basic rate limit, so that if the excess occurs in a year when, after adding in the excess, your taxable income does not exceed the basic rate limit, no charge will arise. The same applies to the position when you finally cash in the bond, because if this can be arranged in a year when your income, even with the addition of the appropriate 'slice' of the bond profit, does not attract the higher rate, no tax is normally payable. Thus it may be possible to surrender in a year when your income is low, for example, because of business losses or following retirement. If the bond is cashed in on your death, any mortality element of the profit as distinct from the surplus on the underlying investments is not taxable, and since the income of the year of death will usually not cover a full tax year, even on the taxable portion there may be little tax liability at the higher rate. You can defer any tax liability by extending the period of the policy and thus its maturity. The tax charge could previously also be avoided where a new policy was issued under the terms of an option contained in the maturing policy and the whole of the proceeds under the maturing policy were retained by the insurance company and applied in paying one or more premiums under the new policy. This is not possible from 2003/04 onwards, subject to transitional provisions where the option was exercised before 9 April 2003 or the policy matured before 1 May 2003.

An astute investor will usually want to switch investments from time to time, say from equities to properties, then to gilts and so on. For a small administration charge, a life office will let you switch the investments underlying your bond, and the switch has no adverse tax effect.

To give added flexibility in the timing of bond surrenders, it is possible to take out a number of smaller bonds, so that they need not all be cashed in the same tax year. Not only can the original investment be cashed over a number of years but the amount liable to tax in any year is itself top-sliced in arriving at the tax payable. This type of arrangement may be used as an alternative to a purchased life annuity in order to pay the premiums on a qualifying policy, and also to pay large items of recurrent expenditure such as school fees.

There is no relief if there is a loss when the bond is cashed in, but if any deficiency on the bond in the tax year in which that event occurs exceeds the cumulative 5% tax-free withdrawals from the bond, a higher rate taxpayer may deduct the excess from his income of that tax year in calculating the amount of extra tax payable on income above the basic rate threshold. For policies taken out or varied on or after 3 March 2004, this relief for a deficiency is only available where the earlier taxable withdrawals formed part of the taxable income of the bondholder. This is to counter avoidance schemes where earlier gains were made by a different person.

There is one instance where the cashing-in of a bond, or an earlier chargeable event, may result in a tax charge, even when you are not a higher rate taxpayer. This may occur where you are entitled to a higher personal allowance because you are aged 65 or over, and/or a married couple's allowance because either you or your wife was born before 6 April 1935. Although the bond profit or excess withdrawn is only chargeable to tax if your taxable income exceeds the basic rate limit, taking into account top-slicing relief, the full profit counts as part of your total income for the purposes of age-related allowances. Any loss of age-related allowances thus indirectly results in a tax charge.

Anti-avoidance provisions apply to 'personal portfolio bonds'. These are aimed particularly at offshore bonds, but they also apply to UK bonds. For details see 45.17.

Top-slicing relief for chargeable events (TA 1988, s 550)

40.7   In the tax year when a chargeable event arises on a qualifying or non-qualifying policy (for example when you cash in a bond) top-slicing relief is available to lessen the impact of the charge to income tax at the higher rate. The surplus on the policy is divided by the number of complete policy years (ending on the anniversary of the policy) that the policy has been held, and the amount arrived at is treated as the top slice of your income to ascertain the tax rate, which is then applied to the full profit. The amount chargeable is the excess of higher rate tax over the lower rate of 20% (excess over the basic rate of 22% before 6 April 2004). The longer the policy has been held the smaller the annual equivalent on which the tax charge is based. See Example 1.

Example 1

			£
Taxpayer purchases investment bond in 1997/98 for			10,000
He takes annual withdrawals of £500 for six years			
(covered by 5% rule)		3,000	
He cashes in bond in 2004/05 for		11,800	14,800
Profit liable to tax in 2004/05			£4,800

His taxable income after all allowances and reliefs is £31,000, leaving £400 available within the basic rate limit.

Annual equivalent of bond profit (1/6th × £4,800)		800	
Tax thereon as extra income:	400 @ 20%	80	
	400 @ 40%	160	240
Less lower rate tax on £800 @ 20%			160
Tax at excess rates on £800			£80
Tax charge on full profit of £4,800 is £80 × 6, i.e.			£480

It might be possible to avoid paying higher rate tax on the bond profit by taking steps to reduce taxable income. See Example 2. Note, however, that a gift aid donation to charity does *not* reduce taxable income for top-slicing purposes.

> **Example 2**
>
> Taxpayer in Example 1 makes a personal pension contribution of £312 net, £400 gross, in March 2005, which increases his basic rate threshold to £31,800. The bond profit does not then attract higher rates, saving tax of £480, which is £168 more than the amount of the contribution.

Top-slicing relief is only available when you pay tax at the higher rate. It does not enable you to avoid losing age-related allowances if the taxable profit or excess withdrawal takes your total income above £18,900. You can, however, reduce your income for age allowance purposes by making a personal pension contribution or gift aid donation to charity.

Secondhand life policies

40.8   When a life policy is assigned, the assignee may have an income tax liability as in 40.5 to 40.7 if the policy proceeds exceed the premiums paid. In addition, for assignments on or after 9 April 2003, an assignee who receives a policy as a gift is subject to the capital gains rules if *someone else* has previously purchased the policy. (There is an exception for consideration paid by one spouse to another, or paid in connection with a divorce, or on an intra-group transfer.) The assignee will be deemed under the normal capital gains rules to have acquired the policy at open market value. Furthermore, the loss allowable for capital gains tax cannot be greater than the loss actually incurred by comparing the assignee's proceeds and cost. The assignee might still have an income tax liability on the difference between the amount of the premiums paid by the original policy holder to the insurance company and the assignee's disposal proceeds.

Transferring shares in life policies (TA 1988, ss 540, 546–546D)

40.9   Where a life policy is changed from joint to single names or vice versa, such as in marriage or divorce settlements, the transfers have been treated by the Revenue as part assignments of the policy and thus subject to the 'chargeable events' rules, although no tax was payable where a share in a policy was transferred for no consideration and the rules do not apply to assignments between spouses living together. Following a court ruling, the Revenue have revised their view where rights are transferred under a court order as part of a divorce settlement and no longer consider that the chargeable events rules apply. Affected taxpayers may be able to make claims to reopen their self-assessments. See the Revenue's Tax Bulletin of December 2003 for details.

Trust policies (TA 1988, ss 547, 547A)

40.10   Where someone is entitled as of right to the income from a trust fund (called an interest in possession), the fund itself is regarded as belonging to that person for inheritance tax purposes (see 42.15).

If you take out a policy on your own life in trust for, say, your children, the policy is treated as belonging to them, and, when the proceeds are received by the trustees, there is no inheritance tax charge because the children have held an interest in the trust fund throughout, which now comprises cash instead of a life policy. Nor is there any inheritance tax when the trustees pay the cash to the children, because the trust fund was always regarded as belonging to them. See Example 3.

Example 3

A taxpayer takes out a qualifying policy on his own life assuring £100,000 on his death and pays the first annual premium of £5,000.

The policy is gifted to trustees for the benefit of his son, but he continues to pay the annual premiums of £5,000 out of his income.

The effect is:

The gift of the annual premiums will be covered by the inheritance tax exemption for gifts out of income.

The son will receive the eventual proceeds when the taxpayer dies without any tax charge whatsoever.

This is a useful way of providing for an anticipated inheritance tax liability by putting funds in the hands of those who will inherit the estate.

It is possible for husband and wife to arrange the policy so that the proceeds do not arise until the second death. The surviving spouse can then take the whole of the deceased's estate at the first death without inheritance tax, because of the surviving spouse exemption, and the liability to inheritance tax on the second death will be covered by the policy proceeds in the hands of the policy beneficiaries.

The rules for charging income tax on gains on non-qualifying policies outlined at 40.5 apply to life policies held in trust, but are taxed on the settlor if he is UK resident. If the settlor is either dead or non-resident when the gain is made, but there are UK resident trustees, the gains are taxed on the trustees at 40% (with the trustees receiving a credit for lower rate tax where the policies are UK policies, reducing the trustees' liability to 20%). If the trustees are non-resident, UK beneficiaries are taxed as and when they receive benefits from the trust funds under the anti-avoidance rules re transferring assets abroad (as to which see 45.17).

Specially adapted trust policies

40.11   There are several tailor-made insurance products which seek to mitigate inheritance tax liabilities whilst giving financial comfort in the meantime. These are very specialised areas requiring advice in each case from appropriately qualified advisers, with the insurance companies themselves providing useful explanatory literature. Two examples are as follows.

Gift and loan trust

Under this arrangement you would make a small gift to trustees for the benefit of the family, including your spouse, the amount of which would usually be covered by the £3,000 annual inheritance tax exemption. You would also make a substantial loan to the trustees. The whole amount would be invested by the trustees, with any increase in the value of the investment belonging to them as trustees. The 5% withdrawal facility would be used by the trustees to repay an equivalent amount of your loan. It is possible to vary the amount of the withdrawal.

The arrangement relies on the growth in the investment (in the hands of the trustees and therefore outside your estate for inheritance tax) replacing the loan which is gradually repaid to you and which you use as income.

Whilst the proceeds over and above the amount of any outstanding loan escape inheritance tax, there is a 20% income tax charge on the bond surplus.

Discounted gift trust

The amount invested is divided into two funds within one insurance bond which is held by trustees. The amount provided to each fund depends upon your age and expectation of life.

One fund gives you the right to withdraw each year for 20 years 5% of the amount invested in the bond. This right cannot be varied and ceases on your death.

The second fund is an immediate gift for the benefit of the family, and to which any growth in the bond is to be attributed.

The first fund remains liable to inheritance tax in your estate, but is immediately reduced in value because of the restrictions on it and because it will be exhausted at latest in 20 years. The second is outside your estate and escapes inheritance tax if you survive for seven years.

Endowment mortgages

40.12   Endowment mortgages are a combination of a loan on which you pay interest, plus a life insurance policy which is intended to pay off the loan when it matures, although there have been very many instances recently where the policy proceeds have proved woefully inadequate. No capital repayments are made to the lender, so the interest cost never falls because of capital repaid. The profit element in the policy when it matures is not liable to tax.

Policies taken out before 14 March 1984 still attract 12½% life insurance tax relief on the premiums.

If the mortgage is reduced because capital becomes available, or is repaid early, usually on change of residence, it is worth considering whether the existing insurance policy should be retained, either in order to preserve tax relief on the premiums because it is a pre-14 March 1984 policy or because to cash in the policy would have an adverse effect on its value. If the existing policy were surrendered and a new policy taken out to cover the whole borrowing, no life insurance relief would be available on the premiums.

If the early surrender causes the rules for qualifying policies to be breached, tax may be payable (see 40.4).

Provision of information by insurers (TA 1998, ss 552, 552ZA)

40.13   Where gains on policies are chargeable to tax, insurers are required to inform the policyholder and are also required to inform the Revenue if the chargeable event is the sale of the policy or if the aggregate gains in a tax year exceed half the basic rate limit.

Pension mortgages

40.14   Some lenders will grant mortgages or loans with no capital repayments, but with an undertaking that the borrowing will eventually be repaid out of the capital sum received from a pension plan (see CHAPTERS 16 and 17), the borrowing in the meantime being covered by temporary life insurance.

The lender cannot take a legal charge on the pension contract, but you can give an undertaking to use the lump sum from the plan to discharge the loan.

The effect is that tax relief at your various marginal rates over the period of your pension plan is obtained on the capital repayment since the fund used to make the repayment has been built up from premiums upon which the tax relief has been obtained at the time of payment. Unless these arrangements are part of an overall plan to provide adequately for your retirement, you will, however, have used part of the money that was intended to finance your retirement to pay off your mortgage.

Friendly societies (TA 1988, ss 459–466)

40.15   Whereas the profits of other life insurance companies are taxable, the profits of friendly societies arising from life or endowment business are generally exempt from income tax and corporation tax. The exemption applies where the premiums in respect of the policies issued by the friendly society, generally assuring up to about £2,500 over a ten-year term, do not exceed £270 a year (or £25 a month), or the annuities which they grant do not exceed £156 a year.

Policies taken out by children under 18 qualify for the exemption and payment of the premiums by a parent does not contravene the income tax rules about parental gifts (see 33.7); there is therefore no tax charge on the parent.

The society's tax exemption gives an added advantage to a qualifying policy with a registered friendly society, although the restrictions on premiums and annuities limit the scope accordingly and as with all life assurance products the society's operating charges may significantly reduce the benefit of the tax exemption.

Friendly societies are able to offer the insurance component of Individual Savings Accounts (ISAs — see 40.16).

Although insurance companies cannot generally claim repayment of tax credits on dividends received, friendly societies were able to do so in respect of their tax-exempt business until 5 April 2004.

Individual Savings Accounts (ISAs)

40.16   UK resident individuals are able to invest in Individual Savings Accounts (ISAs) which are exempt from income tax and capital gains tax (see 36.22). Up to £1,000 of the annual subscription limit may presently be invested in life insurance with an insurance company or friendly society.

From April 2005 the Government intends to merge the life element of ISAs with the stocks and shares element, so that the maximum investment will be £7,000 in 2005/06 and £5,000 thereafter, subject to provisions to restrict investments where the investor is not exposed to a significant risk of loss (see 36.22).

Savers must be able to invest on a single premium basis, with no obligation to keep up premium payments, although the single premium may be payable by instalments and insurers may offer policies with recurrent single premiums payable for more than one year.

Demutualisation

40.17   If your insurance company demutualises, and you receive either free shares or cash or a mixture of the two, the tax treatment depends on the circumstances. There will usually be no immediate tax consequences on the issue of free shares, which will have a nil cost, with taper relief applying from the date the shares are acquired. Cash payments are chargeable to capital gains tax and taper relief is not available. Gains may, however, be covered by your annual exemption (currently £8,200) if not otherwise used. See the Revenue's Tax Bulletin of April 1998. The Revenue stated in relation to the Scottish Widows windfall payments that where there were joint holders, then even though such payments were made only to the first-named holder, they could be treated as received equally, with the gain being divided between the joint holders. Presumably the same will apply to any other insurance windfall payments.

Group policies (TA 1988, ss 539, 539A)

40.18   It is sometimes commercially sensible and convenient to insure a group of lives within one policy, e.g. a number of borrowers. From 9 April 2003, gains on such policies which provide only death benefits are generally exempt from a tax charge.

Gains on policies held by charitable and non-charitable trusts

40.19   Before FA 2003, gains on life policies held by charitable trusts could even so be taxed on the donors to the trust, sometimes resulting in a higher rate tax liability which could be recovered by the donor from the trustees. From 9 April 2003 these gains are treated as those of the trustees, liable to tax at the lower rate of 20% from 6 April 2004. Since lower rate tax (or basic rate tax before 6 April 2004) is treated as having already been paid on such gains (except for most non-UK policies), the trustees will not normally have a tax liability.

So far as non-charitable trusts are concerned:

Gains after 8 April 2003 are to be taxed on the trustees if no other person is liable for the tax;

Sums lent to trustees by or at the direction of the insurer are deemed to be part surrenders equal to the amount of the loan.

Compensation scheme

40.20   If an insurance company goes out of business, compensation may be payable under the terms of the Financial Services Compensation Scheme. For long term insurance, such as life insurance, the first £2,000 is fully protected, plus up to 90% of the remaining value of the policy.

Tax points

40.21

- Since there is no tax relief on premiums on life insurance policies taken out after 13 March 1984, those who seek term assurance should consider arranging it under the personal pension provisions (see CHAPTER 17).

- You still get life insurance relief at 12.5% on the premiums on a qualifying policy taken out before 14 March 1984. Whether or not the policy is linked to a mortgage, this should be taken into account in considering early surrender.

- There is little point in taking out a policy on your own life to cover any inheritance tax arising on your death if the policy forms part of your estate. Although it will produce a capital sum, that sum will increase the taxable estate, and moreover will not be available until a grant of probate or administration has been obtained. A policy for the benefit of someone else will escape tax in your estate and the policy monies will be available to that person on production of the death certificate and appropriate claim form.

- A wide range of ways of investing through life insurance and purchased annuities is on offer by the various life offices, and an arrangement can often be tailored to your specific requirements. There are several schemes aimed at mitigating or providing for inheritance tax. Specialist advice on what is available is essential.

- A single premium bond can be a simple and convenient way of investing without the need for any complex records such as those required when you invest on the Stock Exchange.

- Bonds are also a convenient way to get into and out of the property market by choice of appropriate funds, and you can give away one of a series of property fund supported bonds much more easily than giving land itself, with no inheritance tax charge if the gift is covered by exemptions, or if you survive for seven years after making it.

- Many people with endowment mortgages may be considering surrendering their policies because of concerns as to whether sufficient will be realised to pay off the mortgage. The tax consequences need to be taken into account if the surrender is within ten years (or within three-quarters of the term if less). Care also needs to be taken with selling the policy on the open market, because the same tax consequences will occur if the sale is within that period.

- There is no magic way of paying school fees. Sensible use of the types of life insurance contracts mentioned in this chapter will help, but early planning is essential, and contracts should be taken out soon after the child is born.

- There is a limit to the lump sum you can take from a pension fund when you retire. If you undertake to use your lump sum to repay a loan, the lender needs to be satisfied that the level of regular contributions is sufficient to produce a high enough lump sum to discharge or substantially reduce the debt (leaving you to draw the pension itself).

- Friendly society policies for children are a tax-efficient way of using some of your income for your children's benefit, although the relatively high charges may offset the tax advantages. For other tax-efficient parent/child arrangements, see 33.7.

- Your insurance company may rebate commission to you, or net it off against the premium, or invest it on your behalf. The rebated commission does not count as income for tax purposes.

41
The overseas element

Background

41.1   In today's increasingly global business environment, there are many opportunities for wealthy taxpayers, both corporate and individual, to arrange their affairs worldwide so as to take advantage of the most favourable tax treatment, and tax authorities are correspondingly keen to ensure that a taxpayer's liability remains at an appropriate level on profits and gains derived from the country concerned. The treatment of the overseas aspects of the tax affairs of individuals and companies is consequently one of the most complicated and tortuous in the UK system. This chapter can give no more than an overview of the various provisions, and professional advice is essential. The Revenue have recently published a new International Manual giving updated guidance for Revenue staff on international issues.

There are two main aspects to the overseas element: the tax treatment of UK citizens and UK resident companies with income or assets abroad; and the tax treatment of foreign nationals or foreign-resident companies with income or assets in the UK. The overseas element also affects the taxation of trusts. This aspect is dealt with briefly at 41.39 TO 41.42.

In all cases, the tax liability may be affected by double taxation relief, so the relevant double tax agreement needs to be looked at to see if the treatment outlined in this chapter is varied under the provisions of the agreement with the country concerned. Double taxation agreements normally provide for the profits of a trade to be taxed only in the country of residence unless there is a 'permanent establishment' in the other country. In relation to electronic commerce, the Revenue's view is that websites and servers do not of themselves constitute permanent establishments. The UK legislation has previously used the term 'branch or agency' rather than 'permanent establishment'. FA 2003 replaced all such references with 'permanent establishment' and incorporated into UK law various provisions in line with OECD (Organisation for Economic Cooperation and Development) principles. Even so, a branch or agency is the main form of permanent establishment.

An individual's liability to UK tax depends on where he is resident, ordinarily resident and domiciled. For a company, ordinary residence and domicile are not normally significant, and the company's tax liability depends only on its residence. Within the scope of this book it is only possible to give a brief outline of the meaning of residence, ordinary residence and domicile. The Inland Revenue publishes a useful booklet IR 20, 'Residents and Non-residents — Liability to Tax in the United Kingdom', covering the provisions for individuals in more detail.

The Revenue have a special office – the Centre for Non-Residents – to give help to non-residents and their agents on various aspects of UK tax (and national insurance) liabilities.

Where UK tax is payable, the normal provisions for charging interest and penalties and allowing interest on overpaid tax apply.

To counter tax evasion both nationally and internationally, the Revenue have the power to obtain relevant tax information from taxpayers and third parties and for such information to be exchanged with, or obtained for, other EU states and countries with whom the UK has made either a double taxation agreement or a tax information exchange agreement. EU states provide mutual assistance in collecting taxes and one EU state may require another state to take proceedings to recover both direct and indirect taxes owed in the first state. In order to implement an EU Savings Directive, regulations have been introduced to require paying agents to report details of savings income payments made to certain non-residents. See 7.35 for new civil penalties relating to those who import or export goods from or to countries outside the EU. There are numerous anti-avoidance provisions relating to specific over-seas aspects. See CHAPTER 45 for brief details.

Residence and ordinary residence of individuals (TA 1988, ss 207, 334–336; TCGA 1992, s 9)

41.2   Residence is a question of fact and usually requires physical presence in a country. The residence of husband and wife is determined independently. It is possible for an individual to be resident in more than one country for tax purposes. Ordinary residence is broadly equivalent to habitual residence. You are regarded as remaining resident and ordinarily resident in the UK despite a temporary absence abroad unless the absence spans a complete tax year. The Revenue take the view that mobile workers who usually live in the UK but make frequent and regular business trips abroad will continue to be regarded as resident and ordinarily resident unless there are special circumstances (see their Tax Bulletin of April 2001).

Strictly you are either resident or non-resident for the whole of a tax year, but by Revenue concession A11 a tax year may be split for income tax purposes into resident and non-resident periods as indicated below (see 41.12 for concession D2 relating to split year treatment for capital gains).

If you leave the UK to take up full-time employment abroad for a period which will span a complete tax year, you are regarded as not resident and not ordinarily resident from the day after you leave and as a new resident when you return, providing your UK visits do not overstep the limits for visitors (see below).

If you leave the UK for any other purpose you may be provisionally treated as not resident and not ordinarily resident if you can produce evidence of leaving the UK permanently, e.g. selling your house here and buying one abroad, and the provisional ruling will be confirmed when your absence has spanned a complete tax year. If evidence is not available at the start of the absence, you will provisionally be treated as remaining UK resident for a period of up to three years, and if your UK visits have averaged less than 91 days a tax year, you will be treated as not resident and not ordinarily resident from the time of leaving. If you have property in the UK available for your use, you will need to be able to show that retaining the property is consistent with your stated intention of living permanently abroad.

New permanent residents and those who intend to stay for two years or more are regarded as resident from the date of arrival in the UK, although this treatment might be revised if the circumstances changed and the UK stay was in fact short-term. Those whose intended stay was less than three years would not initially be regarded as *ordinarily* resident. Someone who does not know how long he is going to stay will be regarded as ordinarily resident from the beginning of the tax year after that in which the third anniversary of his arrival falls, or earlier if it becomes clear before then that he intends to stay on a long-term basis, or if he remains in the UK and purchases accommodation in the UK or leases it for a period of three years or more.

Those who visit the UK for a temporary purpose are not regarded as UK resident, even if they have accommodation available here. Visitors are, however, regarded as resident in any tax year in which their visits add up to 183 days in total. If UK visits, while not amounting to 183 days a year, average 91 days a year or more for four consecutive tax years (but excluding any days spent in the UK because of exceptional circumstances beyond the individual's control), a visitor is then regarded as becoming both resident and ordinarily resident in the UK. If it was clear at the outset that he was going to make regular, substantial visits, he may be regarded as resident and ordinarily resident from the start.

Residence of companies (FA 1988, s 66 and Sch 7; FA 1994, ss 249, 250)

41.3   Under UK tax law, any company that is incorporated in the UK is treated as being UK resident no matter where it is managed and controlled. Companies incorporated abroad are regarded as UK resident if they are managed and controlled here. If a non-resident company transfers its central management and control to the UK it is treated as resident from the time of the transfer. Where, however, a company is treated as non-resident under the terms of a double tax treaty, this overrides these rules and the company is regarded as not being UK resident.

A company may have more than one country of residence. Anti-avoidance provisions apply to dual resident companies (see 45.13).

Domicile

41.4 Domicile is different from nationality and residence and a person can only have one domicile at any one time. An individual's domicile is usually the country in which he has his permanent home. A domicile of origin is acquired at birth and under UK law this is the father's domicile for legitimate children and the mother's domicile for illegitimate children. A wife's domicile is ascertained independently of her husband's.

The domicile of origin may be abandoned and a domicile of choice acquired. This necessitates positive action, e.g. changing residence, making a will under the laws of the new country, obtaining citizenship of the new country. A high standard of proof is required to establish a change of domicile.

Domicile sometimes has an extended meaning for inheritance tax — see CHAPTER 5. It has no relevance for companies.

Registration to vote in the UK as an overseas elector does not affect domicile for UK tax purposes (FA 1996, s 200).

The Government is reviewing the residence and domicile rules in relation to individuals. The main area of concern is the ability of long-term resident non-domiciled individuals to pay little or no UK tax because on overseas income they are taxed only on amounts remitted to the UK (see 41.6).

Effect of residence, ordinary residence and domicile on UK tax position for individuals

41.5 Income tax is charged broadly on the world income of UK residents, subject to certain deductions for earnings abroad and for individuals who are not ordinarily resident or not domiciled in the UK. Individuals are normally charged on the full amount of foreign income arising abroad, whether it is brought into the UK or not. Someone resident in the UK who is not UK domiciled, or not ordinarily resident in the UK, is, however, charged only as and when income is brought into the UK (referred to as the remittances basis — see 41.6). Where tax is charged on the amount that arises abroad, the income to be brought into account is the sterling equivalent of the overseas amount at the date it arises. An average exchange rate for the year may be used, using rates published by the Revenue. Non-residents are liable to income tax only on income that arises in the UK and even then special rules apply (see later in this chapter, in particular 41.13 and 41.20). Where the UK chargeable income is high enough they pay higher rate tax. Non-residents are not entitled to personal allowances except as indicated at 41.13.

Individuals who are resident *or* ordinarily resident in the UK are liable to capital gains tax — on world gains if domiciled in the UK, and on gains arising in or remitted to the UK if domiciled elsewhere. The gain or loss on the disposal of property abroad is arrived at by comparing the sterling equivalent of the cost at the date of purchase with the sterling equivalent of the proceeds at the date of sale (subject to any available indexation allowance). Foreign stocks and shares are subject to the same provisions as UK stocks and shares (see CHAPTER 38), so that the capital gains tax matching rules for identifying disposals of stocks and shares apply. Non-residents carrying on business in the UK through a UK permanent establishment are charged to tax on gains on assets used in the permanent establishment — see 41.20. Other non-residents who are not ordinarily resident in the UK are not charged to capital gains tax on the disposal of UK assets. See 41.12 for the capital gains position if you leave and then return to the UK.

For the capital gains position on your private residence when you are absent abroad, see 30.5.

If you are emigrating and you sell qualifying business assets (see 4.26) in a tax year when you are UK resident, investing the proceeds in qualifying replacement assets abroad within three years, the gains on the UK assets may be rolled over against the cost of the replacement foreign assets (whether or not you are resident in the UK at the time of acquisition of the replacement assets). If the replacement assets are then sold in a tax year when you are not resident and not ordinarily resident in the UK (and are not carrying on a business in the UK through a permanent establishment), you will escape UK tax on the rolled over gains (unless you return to the UK and become liable under the rules outlined at 41.12). You may have a liability in your new country of residence.

If you become not resident and not ordinarily resident within six years after receiving a gift on which capital gains tax was deferred under the gifts relief provisions, the deferred gain is chargeable to tax (and taper relief is not available — see 4.27). Becoming non-resident within a specified period also triggers gains deferred under the enterprise investment scheme or venture capital trust provisions (the relevant period being three years in each case — see 29.3 (EIS) and 29.7 (VCTs)).

There are provisions to prevent someone who is ordinarily resident in the UK avoiding tax by transferring assets abroad while retaining a right to benefit from them (see 45.17). These provisions cover benefits to both children and grandchildren. They also apply to certain life policies held in trust (see 40.10).

Residence has no bearing on inheritance tax, which applies to your world-wide property if you are domiciled in the UK and to your UK property if you are domiciled elsewhere. Holdings in authorised unit trusts and open-ended investment companies (see 38.15) are, however, not liable to inheritance tax for those not domiciled in the UK.

Where you have property abroad, this may lead to problems on your death, because foreign probate may be required before the assets can be dealt with by your executors. For jointly held assets this will normally occur only on the second death, because the ownership normally passes by survivorship to the other joint owner. The costs involved should be borne in mind when considering investing abroad.

Basis of charge for foreign income of individuals (TMA 1970, s 17; TA 1988, ss 18, 65, 65A, 391; ITEPA 2003, ss 20–41, 573–576)

41.6   Non-residents are not charged to UK tax on foreign income.

For UK residents, foreign income is taxed as part of an individual's total income at the starting, lower, basic and higher rates as the case may be. Certain individuals are taxed only according to the amount they remit to the UK (see below). Foreign savings income is taxed at the same rates as UK savings income, i.e. the 10% rate on dividends and the 20% rate on other savings income, except for higher rate taxpayers. This does not apply where the recipient is charged to tax only on the amounts remitted to the UK, such remittances being taxed at the same rates as non-savings income.

The basis of charge for income from employment is the earnings received in the tax year (or remitted to the UK in the tax year as the case may be). Deductions are available as indicated at 41.7.

Most foreign pensions used to be taxed under the provisions of Schedule D, Case V, but from 6 April 2003 all pensions are dealt with under the provisions of the Income Tax (Earnings and Pensions) Act 2003. For individuals who are resident, ordinarily resident and domiciled in the UK, tax is charged on only 90% of foreign pensions (except where the pension is paid as a result of Nazi persecution, in which case it is not chargeable at all). See below for the position for those who are not resident in the UK, or not ordinarily resident or not domiciled in the UK.

Other income from abroad may be charged under Schedule D, Case IV (covering foreign securities such as foreign government stocks and foreign debentures) or Schedule D, Case V (covering foreign 'possessions', which includes all other non-employment and non-pension income, such as from shares in foreign companies, bank accounts abroad, foreign businesses and foreign property). Income from self-employment abroad is dealt with at 41.9. Property income from abroad is dealt with at 41.10 (but see 32.27 for foreign time shares). Other investment income from abroad is dealt with at 41.11.

Tax under Schedule D, Cases IV and V other than on the profits of a foreign business is charged on the income arising in the current tax year (or remitted to the UK in the tax year as the case may be) in the same way as for Schedule D, Case III (see 37.1). Where a business is carried on wholly abroad, tax under Schedule D, Case V is charged according to the same rules as for Schedule D, Case I, i.e. on the profits of the accounting year ending in the tax year rather than on the profits of the tax year itself.

If you are resident but not ordinarily resident or not domiciled in the UK, you are not charged to tax on income from abroad unless you remit it to the UK. If you do remit it, you are charged on the full amount remitted (with no percentage deduction for foreign pensions) and tax is payable on remittances of foreign savings income at non-savings income rates (see above). There are rules to decide whether you are remitting income or other sums.

Where you are charged on the amount arising abroad, there are special provisions to treat income that is locked into a foreign country as not arising until it can be brought to the UK (but as and when you are able to extract it, it is taxable at that time whether or not you do in fact bring it to the UK).

UK citizens with earnings from employment abroad (ITEPA 2003, ss 378–385)

41.7 If your employment abroad is full time and spans a complete tax year, and all your duties are performed abroad, you are normally treated by concession as non-resident from the date of leaving and as a new resident when you return. Otherwise you will remain UK resident.

Notice that it is not the length of the absence but whether it spans a tax year that is important, so that if you were working away from 1 April 2003 to 30 April 2004, a period of thirteen months spanning a tax year, you would be non-resident for that period, but if you were working away from July 2003 to December 2004, a period of eighteen months that does not span a complete tax year, you would remain resident throughout.

If you are non-resident, you escape UK tax on all earnings abroad. If you are resident, you are liable to tax on your earnings both in the UK and abroad unless you are a seafarer. Seafarers are entitled to a deduction of 100% in respect of earnings abroad during a qualifying period of at least 365 days. A qualifying period is one consisting either wholly of days of absence or of days of absence linked by UK visits that do not exceed 183 consecutive days and also do not in total exceed one-half of the days in the period. A day does not count as a day of absence unless you are absent at the end of it, i.e. midnight.

If a seafarer who satisfies the 365-day qualifying period rules has both overseas earnings and UK earnings, i.e. for work during his UK visits, the 100% deduction applies only to the overseas earnings. The 100% deduction also applies to earnings in a period of paid leave at the end of the employment, but if the paid leave is spent in the UK it cannot be counted as part of the 365-day qualifying period.

The 100% deduction is given where possible through the PAYE system, but where this is not possible the relief due is taken into account in the employee's self-assessment.

Travelling and board and lodging expenses (ITEPA 2003, ss 341, 342, 370, 371, 376)

41.8   For an employee resident and ordinarily resident in the UK, the costs of travelling from and to the UK when taking up and ceasing an employment wholly abroad are allowed as a deduction from earnings, and also the costs of travelling between a UK employment and a foreign employment and between foreign employments. The costs of any number of outward and return journeys whilst serving abroad are also allowed so long as the expense is met by the employer (thus offsetting the tax charge on the employee in respect of the employer's expenditure). If the employer pays or reimburses the employee's board and lodging costs for an employment wholly abroad, the amount paid or reimbursed is also offset by an equivalent expenses allowance, but no deduction is given for board and lodging payments that an employee bears himself.

If an absence lasts for 60 days or more (not necessarily in one tax year) an employee can claim a deduction for the travelling expenses of two outward and two return journeys per person in any tax year for his wife and children (under 18 at the start of the journey) to visit him, but only where the travelling expenses are paid or reimbursed by the employer (so that the deduction offsets the benefits charge on the expenditure) and not where the employee bears them himself.

A round sum expenses allowance cannot be treated as payment or reimbursement of your expenses by your employer, so care must be taken that the expenses are paid in a way that entitles you to an equivalent deduction.

Earned income from self-employment abroad (TA 1988, ss 80, 81, 110A, 112, 391)

41.9   Where a business is carried on wholly abroad, the expenses of travelling to and from it are allowed in computing profits. A deduction is also allowed for board and lodging expenses at any place where the trade is carried on and, where the trader's absence spans 60 days or more, for not more than two visits in any tax year by wife and children (under 18 at the start of the journey). Expenses of travelling between two or more overseas businesses are similarly allowable, provided that either the business at the place of departure or that at the destination is carried on wholly abroad.

If a business is controlled in the UK, the profits are taxed under the rules of Schedule D, Case I or Case II even though some of the profits are earned abroad.

If a sole trader is resident in the UK, it would be highly unlikely for him to be able to show that his business was carried on *wholly* abroad. The main instance would be where he was only technically resident in the UK and normally lived and carried on the business abroad. If, exceptionally, that was the case, the profits would be charged under Schedule D, Case V as income from a foreign possession. If such a business made a loss, similar loss relief claims could be made as for a UK business (see CHAPTER 25) but the loss could be relieved only against the profits from the same or any other foreign business, and against foreign pensions and, if the trader is not domiciled in the UK, any employment earnings from a foreign employer.

As far as partners are concerned, the profit shares of UK resident partners are charged under Schedule D, Case I or Case II, both on UK profits and profits earned abroad, whether or not the partnership is controlled abroad. For a foreign-controlled partnership, this does not apply to a UK resident partner who is not ordinarily resident and/or not domiciled in the UK. Such a partner is charged under Case I or II on the full amount of his share of UK profits, and under Case V on the part of his share of foreign profits that is remitted to the UK. (Non-resident partners are taxed under Case I or II on their shares of UK profits — see 41.16.)

The UK tax on a UK resident partner's share of the profits of a partnership resident abroad cannot be reduced or eliminated by double tax relief, even though the terms of the double tax agreement exempt the profits of the foreign partnership.

In order to charge residents on their worldwide profits and non-residents on their UK profits, when someone who carries on business wholly or partly abroad changes his country of residence, he is treated as ceasing one business and starting another. This does not prevent the carry-forward of any losses before the change if they cannot otherwise be relieved.

Where profits are charged under Case V rather than Cases I or II, Class 4 national insurance contributions are not payable.

Income from overseas property (TA 1988, ss 65A, 379B)

41.10   If you buy investment property abroad, rents are income from a foreign possession and are charged under Schedule D, Case V (see 41.6). Foreign rental income is calculated in a similar way to UK rental income (see CHAPTER 32), but the special rules for furnished holiday lettings (see 32.17) do not apply. Profits and losses for all foreign let properties are aggregated, any overall profit being treated as the profits of an 'overseas property business'. The profit or loss for properties in different countries needs to be calculated separately, however, in order to calculate the amount of double tax relief available (see 41.23). Allowable expenses include interest on borrowings to buy or improve the foreign property. If there is an overall loss, the rules at 32.6 apply, so that the loss is normally carried forward to set against the total foreign letting profits of later years.

If you are a UK resident but are not UK domiciled, or are not ordinarily resident in the UK, you are chargeable on rental income only when it is remitted to the UK (see 41.6).

Other sources of foreign income (TMA 1970, s 17; TA 1988, ss 1A, 1B, 584)

41.11   Other sources of foreign income apart from business profits and rents are taxed under Schedule D, Case IV or V as outlined at 41.6.

Offshore bank and building society accounts have the advantage that tax is not deducted at source from the interest, although for those required to make half-yearly payments on account under self-assessment, those payments are based on the net amount of tax paid directly for the previous tax year, so an amount is included for continuing sources of untaxed interest.

Interest on foreign government stocks, and also some other interest under Schedule D, Case IV and some dividend income under Schedule D, Case V, is received through a UK paying or collecting agent, such as a bank. UK tax is not deducted from such income, so the full amounts received will be charged to UK tax, subject to any claim for double tax relief (see 41.24). Under arrangements with the EU and various other countries, individuals may also receive interest in full from overseas paying agents. Alternatively a special withholding tax may be deducted. The gross amount is chargeable to UK tax, subject to any claim for double tax relief (see 41.24).

Foreign fixed interest stocks are subject to the accrued income scheme (see 36.18), unless you are only liable to tax on income remitted to the UK (see 41.6). The special rules for scrip dividends (see 38.3) do not apply to scrip dividends from non-UK resident companies. There are anti-avoidance provisions to counter the rolling-up of income in an offshore fund with the intention of realising it in a capital form. The provisions are dealt with briefly at 45.16.

Banks, building societies and other paying and collecting agents are required to provide information to the Revenue on interest paid to investors, including investors who are not ordinarily resident in the UK. The Revenue exchange information on savings income on a reciprocal basis with other countries.

Leaving and returning to the UK (TCGA 1992, s 10A)

41.12   If you go to live abroad, you should obtain from and send back to your tax office a form P85 (Residence or employment abroad). You will also need to complete the 'non-residence etc.' pages in your self-assessment return. Similarly, form P86 and the 'non-residence etc.' pages in the return should be completed when you return to the UK.

In the tax year when you leave the UK to take up permanent or long-term residence abroad, you are treated as non-resident from the date of departure and get a full year's personal allowances against your income for the part of the year prior to your departure. See 41.20 for the provisions exempting certain income of non-UK residents from tax.

If you are abroad for a period that includes a complete tax year and then become UK resident again, intervening visits not having exceeded 183 days in any tax year and not having averaged 91 days or more a year, you are treated as resident for income tax from the date of arrival, with a full year's allowances on your income for the remainder of the year (concession A11). See 41.20 re disposing of foreign sources of income before your return.

If you have been away since before 17 March 1998, capital gains in excess of the annual exemption are charged to tax only if they are realised after your return (subject to certain anti-avoidance provisions). Different rules apply if you become 'temporarily' non-resident on or after 17 March 1998. If you have been resident or ordinarily resident in the UK for any part of at least four of the previous seven tax years and become not resident and not ordinarily resident for less than five tax years, you will be liable to tax on gains on the disposal while you are abroad of assets owned before you left the UK. All such gains in the tax year of departure are chargeable in that year. Gains on such assets arising while you are away will be charged in the tax year when you again resume UK residence. Losses are allowed on the same basis as gains are taxed. If you have an interest in a non-resident trust, you will also be taxed when you return on gains during your absence that would have been taxed on you as settlor had you not been non-resident (see 41.41). Gains on assets acquired while you are resident abroad that are realised in the years between the tax year of departure and the tax year of return are exempt (subject to certain anti-avoidance provisions). These rules are subject to the provisions of double tax treaties. Under Revenue concession D2, a split year treatment applies to the tax years of departure and return under which gains in those tax years after your departure and before your return respectively are exempt. This split year treatment is not available to those who become 'temporarily non-resident' on or after 17 March 1998 as indicated above, nor is it available to someone who left the UK before 17 March 1998 but returns on or after 6 April 1998 after an absence of less than five complete tax years.

If you accompany a spouse who goes abroad to work full-time but do not work full-time yourself, your liability for the tax years in which you leave and return is based on the time spent in the UK in each year, in the same way as for your employed spouse, providing your absence spans a complete tax year and subject to the same rules for intervening UK visits (concession A78).

Inheritance tax will continue to be chargeable on both UK and overseas assets so long as you remain or are regarded as UK domiciled (see CHAPTER 5).

As far as VAT is concerned, when returning from a non-EU country, you may bring your personal possessions into the UK free of VAT and Customs duty providing you have been abroad for at least a year, you paid VAT or duty on the items abroad and have owned and used them for at least six months prior to your return. If you are returning from an EU country, you will have paid VAT abroad when you bought your possessions, except for new motor vehicles, boats, aircraft, etc., on which you pay UK VAT when you return.

Non-residents — tax position and personal allowances (TA 1988, s 278; FA 1995, s 128)

41.13 Non-residents cannot claim UK personal allowances unless they are UK, Commonwealth or Republic of Ireland citizens or EEA nationals (which covers European Union countries plus Iceland, Liechtenstein and Norway), or are resident in the Isle of Man or the Channel Islands, or come under certain other categories. Additionally, a claim for allowances may be provided for by the terms of a double tax agreement. Where allowances are available, they are given in full against the UK income, regardless of the level of the overseas income.

Non-residents are exempt from UK tax on UK government stocks (see 41.20) and may be exempt on other sources of income under a double tax agreement. Tax is not usually deducted from bank and building society interest (see 41.20), or from social security benefits (see 41.17), although such income is not actually exempt from tax. The 10% tax credit rate normally applies to dividend income (see 41.20). If the other income is from property, tax may have been deducted at the basic rate (see 41.19). The *maximum* tax payable by a non-resident is the tax, if any, deducted from interest, dividends and social security benefits (dividend credits being treated as tax deducted) plus the tax on any other taxable income, calculated as if personal allowances were not available. If a claim is made for personal allowances, all non-exempt income is taken into account. This may limit or eliminate the benefit of making a claim.

Example 1

In 2004/05 a non-resident British citizen who is a single person has untaxed income from UK banks and building societies amounting to £1,500 and a State pension of £3,500. No UK tax will be payable, since the maximum tax on such income is the tax, if any, deducted from it.

If the non-resident also had rental income of £2,200, from which tax of £484 was deducted, his maximum liability would be tax on that income as if it were his only UK income. £2,020 of the income would be within the starting rate band, so that tax of (2,020 @ (22 − 10)% =) £242 would be repayable. He could not benefit from a claim for personal allowance, because his untaxed income of £5,000 would have to be taken into account in such a claim and that income exceeds the allowance of £4,745.

If in addition to the rental income of £2,200 the only untaxed income had been the pension of £3,500, the position would be:

	£
Total income	5,700
Personal allowance	4,745
	955
Tax at 10%	95
Tax deducted at source	484
Tax repayable	389

Husband and wife

41.14   As stated at 41.2, the residence and ordinary residence status of a husband and wife is determined independently. If a wife remains in the UK while her husband is working abroad for a period which spans a tax year, she will be taxed as a UK resident on her UK and foreign income, and her husband will normally be exempt as a non-resident from UK tax on income arising outside the UK and will be able where appropriate (see 41.13) to claim personal allowances as a non-resident against his UK income.

If a non-resident husband is entitled to personal allowances but his UK income is insufficient to absorb the married couple's allowance (if available – see 2.14), he may transfer the surplus to his wife providing she is entitled to allowances either as a resident or a qualifying non-resident.

Earned income of visitors to the UK and non-residents (TA 1988, s 18; ITEPA 2003, ss 20–41, 373–375)

Income from employment

41.15   The treatment of a visitor's earnings depends on the length of his visit. A visitor to the UK who does not remain long enough to be classed as resident is nonetheless liable to UK tax on UK earnings (although sometimes he may be exempt under the provisions of a double tax treaty — see 41.25). Non-residents cannot normally claim UK personal allowances (except as described at 41.13).

Expenses of travel and of visits by wives and children are allowed if they are paid or reimbursed by the employer (thus offsetting the benefits charge) in the same way as described at 41.7 for a UK resident working abroad. This only applies, however, where the employee was either not resident in the UK in either of the two tax years before the tax year of his arrival in the UK, or was not in the UK at any time during the two years immediately preceding his arrival. Where this condition is satisfied, the expenses are allowed for a period of five years beginning with the date of arrival in the UK to perform the duties of the employment.

If a visitor is classed as resident but not ordinarily resident, he is still liable only on UK earnings unless he has earnings from abroad which he remits to the UK, in which case he is taxed as well on the full amount remitted. It is important for visitors to keep records (for example, separate bank accounts for capital and for different sources of income) to enable them to demonstrate whether or not remittances out of foreign earnings have taken place.

Once a visitor has been in the UK long enough to be classed as ordinarily resident (or where he is ordinarily resident from the outset because of the length of his proposed stay — see 41.2) he is charged to tax in the same way as a UK citizen. Employers may, however, have made special PAYE arrangements for foreign national employees (known as tax equalisation) under which the employers meet all or part of the employees' tax. Details are in Revenue Help Sheet 212.

See the Revenue's Tax Bulletin of December 2000 for comments on benefits and expenses provided to employees sent on secondment by overseas employers for 24 months or less.

Income from a UK business

41.16   Non-residents who carry on business in the UK either on their own or in partnership are charged to tax on the UK business profits in the same way as UK residents, the charge being under Schedule D, Case I for trades and under Schedule D, Case II for professions or vocations. Tax due on the profits is dealt with under the self-assessment rules and is paid by the non-resident or, where the business is carried on through a UK permanent establishment, by the permanent establishment.

State pensions and other taxable social security benefits, occupational and personal pensions

41.17   Non-residents receive state pensions and other relevant social security benefits in full, and tax is not charged on them (but see 41.13 in relation to tax repayment claims). As far as occupational and personal pensions paid to non-residents are concerned, such pensions are chargeable to UK tax unless (as will usually be the case) they are exempt under a double taxation agreement. Tax is deducted from such pensions under PAYE where the payer has been instructed to do so by the tax office. In this event, the code number may take personal allowances into account.

Non-resident entertainers and sportsmen (TA 1988, ss 555–558)

41.18   Basic rate tax may be deducted by the payer from the UK earnings of non-resident entertainers and sportsmen. Royalty payments received from the sale of records are excluded (as they are already exempt under many double taxation agreements).

Tax need not be deducted where the person making the payment does not expect to pay more than a total of £1,000 to the individual in question during that tax year. Where tax is deducted, the Revenue may agree a rate below the basic rate. The tax deducted is set against the final tax liability for the year, or repaid to the extent that it exceeds that liability.

The rules are administered by the Foreign Entertainers Unit of the Revenue.

Rental income of non-resident landlords (TA 1988, s 42A; SI 1995/2902)

41.19   Where UK property is let, the rental income from all let properties is treated as being from a single Schedule A business, as outlined in CHAPTER 32. There are, however, special regulations dealing with the taxation of rental income of non-resident landlords. The reference to a non-resident landlord is not in fact accurate, because the legislation refers to someone whose 'usual place of abode' is outside the UK, the aim being to make it easier to collect tax from someone who is usually abroad. The Revenue's interpretation is to regard an individual as having a usual place of abode outside the UK if he is away for more than six months. Companies will not be so treated if they are UK resident for tax purposes. References to non-residents in the remainder of this section should be read accordingly.

A UK agent handling let property for a non-resident landlord, or the tenant where there is no such agent, must notify the Revenue's Centre for Non-Residents (CNR). The agent or tenant must then deduct basic rate tax from the property income (net of allowable expenses paid by the agent or tenant and net of VAT on the rent where this has been charged), and pay it over to the Revenue within 30 days after the end of each calendar quarter. The agent or tenant must give the non-resident an annual certificate showing the tax deducted by 5 July following the tax year and must also send in a return to the Revenue by the same date. These provisions apply whether the non-resident landlord is an individual, trustees or a company, except that they do not apply to the rental income of a UK permanent establishment of a non-resident company (see 41.29).

Tax does not have to be deducted at source if the agent or tenant receives written notice to that effect from CNR. Tenants paying rent of £100 a week or less do not have to deduct tax unless told to do so by CNR. The non-resident landlord is required to pay any excess of tax due over the tax deducted at source (or claim a refund) under the self-assessment provisions, so that unless the net tax paid directly to the Revenue for the previous tax year was below the de minimis thresholds, payments on account should be made on 31 January in the tax year and 31 July following, with the balance due at the same time as the tax return on 31 January following the end of the tax year (see 9.7).

A landlord may apply to CNR to receive his rental income in full providing his UK tax affairs are up to date, or he has never had any UK tax obligations, or he does not expect to be liable to UK tax. He must undertake to complete tax returns if required and pay any tax due on time. Unless covered by the de minimis thresholds, the non-resident landlord will be required to make payments on account in the same way as landlords who receive taxed rent (see above). CNR have stated that they will not normally issue self-assessment returns to non-resident individual landlords who have no net tax liability, although returns may still be sent occasionally to ensure that the tax position remains the same.

Where non-resident landlords receive rent from, or pay interest to, persons with whom they are associated, they need to consider the implications of the transfer pricing legislation (see 45.18). For the Revenue's comments on the implications for landlords see their Tax Bulletin of April 2000.

Treatment of other income, capital gains and gifts for visitors to the UK and non-residents (TA 1988, s 349E; TCGA 1992, ss 2, 10, 12, 25; FA 1995, s 128)

41.20   Non-residents have no liability to UK tax on foreign income. If they are not ordinarily resident in the UK they are also exempt from tax in respect of UK income from government securities. The interest on government securities is paid gross. Other UK income is not exempt but special provisions apply as indicated below.

Interest on quoted Eurobonds (i.e. interest-bearing stock exchange listed securities issued by a company) is paid gross. UK bank and building society interest is also paid without deduction of tax to those who provide the bank or building society with a declaration stating that they are not ordinarily resident in the UK and giving their principal residential address. As far as UK dividends are concerned, under the terms of most double tax agreements, non-residents are entitled to reclaim the excess of the tax credits over 15% of the tax credit inclusive dividend. Since the tax credit rate on dividends is only 10%, very few non-residents will be entitled to any repayment (see 41.25). Non-residents are not liable to pay tax on investment income other than rents, except to the extent that tax is deducted at source (tax credits on dividends being treated as tax deducted at source). Non-residents therefore escape UK tax altogether on interest received in full as indicated above, and do not have to self-assess, unless they have other taxable income and are claiming a repayment. In calculating how much tax is repayable, however, any UK income that is not exempt from tax may have to be taken into account (see 41.13). Tax is normally deducted at the basic rate of 22% from patent royalties paid to overseas companies and individuals. A paying company may, however, pay royalties gross, or deduct tax at a reduced rate according to the terms of the double tax agreement, if it believes the recipient to be entitled to double tax relief (see 41.25). The company will have to pay the tax shortfall, plus interest and possibly penalties, if its belief turns out to be incorrect.

Those completing tax returns must show any non-exempt income, whether tax is payable or not, otherwise the return will be incomplete. (The UK tax liability of someone who is non-resident for only *part* of a tax year — see 41.2 — is calculated by reference to *all* taxable income of the year and the treatment indicated above does not apply.)

As far as bank accounts are concerned, if you replace your UK bank and building society accounts with foreign accounts, the interest will be free of UK tax while you are non-resident, and will not be taken into account in calculating relief under a non-resident's personal allowances claim. Closing foreign accounts before you return will prevent any of the foreign interest being subject to UK tax. If you have invested in offshore roll-up funds (see 45.16), you escape UK tax if you dispose of the investment before you resume UK residence. See 45.17 for the anti-avoidance provisions in relation to personal portfolio bonds.

If you have an individual savings account (ISA — see 36.22) or personal equity plan (PEP — see 38.29), you do not lose your tax exemption on the investment when you become non-resident but you cannot contribute further or take out a new ISA.

You do not escape liability to capital gains tax unless you are both not resident and not ordinarily resident in the UK. Even then, if you carry on a trade, profession or vocation in the UK through a permanent establishment, you are charged to capital gains tax on the disposal of assets in the UK used for the business or by the permanent establishment. See 41.12 for the capital gains provisions for those who leave and later return to the UK.

If you cease to carry on the UK permanent establishment, you are treated as if you had disposed of all the assets, and charged to capital gains tax accordingly. If, while continuing to carry on the permanent establishment, you remove any of the assets from the UK, you are treated as if you had disposed of those assets.

If you are in the UK long enough to be classed as resident, you are liable to income tax on foreign as well as UK sources of income. If, however, you are non-UK domiciled, or you are not ordinarily resident in the UK, you are only liable on foreign income if you remit it to the UK. You may therefore think it appropriate to invest abroad and leave the income there. An alternative for those of foreign domicile who are resident and ordinarily resident in the UK is an individual savings account (ISA) (see 36.22). (See 41.15 for the position on income from employment.) As a resident, you are also liable to UK capital gains tax, but if you are non-UK domiciled you are only liable to tax on chargeable gains arising in or remitted to the UK.

A gain on the disposal of your only or main residence is, subject to certain conditions, exempt from tax.

The treatment of income and gains may be varied by the provisions of a double tax treaty (see 41.25).

The normal inheritance tax provisions apply to gifts of UK assets (see CHAPTER 5).

Social security and national insurance contributions

41.21   If you leave the UK for permanent or semi-permanent residence abroad, your liability to pay national insurance contributions normally ceases when you leave, unless you work abroad for an employer who has a place of business in the UK, in which case Class 1 contributions continue for the first 52 weeks. Where you are not liable to pay Class 1 contributions, it may be to your advantage to pay Class 3 voluntary contributions. Alternatively if you are employed or self-employed abroad, you may maintain your contributions record for certain benefits by paying the lower Class 2 contributions, providing certain conditions are satisfied. See the Revenue's leaflet NI 38 for details. Following the reduction in the Class 2 contributions rate from April 2000, the Revenue's National Insurance Contributions Office International Services (now part of the Revenue Centre for Non-Residents) gave people the wrong advice about paying Class 2 contributions instead of Class 3 contributions. Anyone affected may claim to have the Class 3 contributions converted to Class 2 contributions and the excess payment will be refunded.

If you are working temporarily abroad, or moving from one foreign location to another, you may be required to continue to pay Class 1 contributions. The position is different if you go to a country with which the UK has a reciprocal social security agreement, when home country liability may sometimes continue for several years. The position is also different if you go to a country in the European Economic Area (EEA, i.e. the European Union plus Iceland, Liechtenstein and Norway), when you are usually liable in the country of employment from the outset, except for a short-term visit of up to 12 months (although this may be extended to a maximum of five years, providing the other country agrees), during which you remain liable in the UK. If you work in more than one EEA country, but continue to be habitually resident in the UK, UK liability can continue. Employers should ensure that where UK liability continues, they account for the appropriate amount of contributions on all relevant pay and benefits.

If you leave the UK and are self-employed abroad, you are not normally *required* to pay Class 2 contributions but you may be *entitled* to pay them in some circumstances to maintain your contribution record. Again, the position is subject to variation if you work in the EEA or in a country with which the UK has a reciprocal social security agreement. A self-employed person who is not resident in the UK in a tax year is not liable to pay Class 4 contributions.

Class 4 contributions apply only to profits charged under Schedule D, Cases I and II, so they would not be payable by UK residents who are charged on foreign profits under Schedule D, Case V (see 41.9).

Child benefit is not normally payable unless both parent and child are UK resident, but it continues during a temporary absence of up to eight weeks, and may be paid for longer in some circumstances. From 7 April 2003, subject to transitional provisions, child benefit claimants and children must be both present and *ordinarily resident* in the UK. Also from that date, an absence must be unlikely, when it starts, to exceed 52 weeks for it to be regarded as temporary.

Visitors to the UK and new permanent residents who are employees are normally not liable to pay Class 1 national insurance contributions for the first twelve months. This does not apply to those coming from an EEA country or a country with which the UK has a reciprocal social security agreement, who will either be liable to UK contributions from the outset or remain liable under their home country's rules. Where an employee is liable, the employer is liable to pay employer's secondary contributions. This applies to all overseas employers, subject to special rules for EEA countries and countries with which the UK has a reciprocal social security agreement.

People coming to the UK who are self-employed are only *required* to pay Class 2 contributions if they are ordinarily resident in the UK, or have been resident in the UK for 26 or more weeks out of the last 52. They are *entitled* to pay Class 2 contributions if they are *present* in the UK for the relevant contribution week. Again, the general rules are varied for EEA countries and countries with which the UK has a reciprocal social security agreement. Class 4 contributions are payable where relevant unless the person is not resident in the UK for the tax year concerned.

The detailed provisions are complex, so whether you are leaving or coming to the UK, it is advisable to contact the local tax and social security offices to establish your own liability to make contributions and your benefits position.

As far as State pension is concerned, if you emigrate, you are normally entitled to a pension based on the contributions you have made, but it is frozen at the rate payable when you leave the UK or when you first become entitled to it if later. This may be varied by the provisions of reciprocal social security agreements. Again, the position needs to be checked with your social security office.

Council tax

41.22   Even though you spend time abroad, you are liable to pay council tax on property you own in the UK if it is still your only or main residence. If it is not your home, but it is the only or main home of someone else, that person is liable (see 8.4). If property owned by a non-resident is not anyone's only or main home, the owner is liable to pay up to 90% of the tax.

Double taxation relief for individuals (TA 1988, ss 788–791, 804, 806; TCGA 1992, s 277)

41.23   Where the same income and gains are liable to tax in more than one country, relief for the double tax is given either under the provisions of a double tax agreement with the country concerned or unilaterally. The relief is calculated separately for each source of income or capital gains.

UK residents with foreign income and gains

41.24   Where there is a double tax agreement, it may provide for certain foreign income and gains to be wholly exempt from UK tax. If not, UK tax is charged, but a claim may be made for a credit to be given against the UK tax for the lower of the overseas tax liability and the UK tax liability.

UK paying and collecting agents do not deduct UK tax from foreign interest and dividends (see 41.11). Taxpayers must therefore pay any amount by which the UK tax exceeds the foreign tax. If the foreign tax exceeds the UK tax, the double tax relief will be restricted to the amount of the UK tax. Where the overseas company pays dividends with tax credits, as in the UK, the tax credits are not eligible for double tax relief unless specifically provided for by the double tax agreement. If the agreement does not so provide, the amount charged to UK tax is the net dividend paid.

As stated in 41.11, UK taxpayers will sometimes receive interest in full from overseas paying agents in the EU and certain other countries. Alternatively, from a date to be fixed (not earlier than 1 January 2005), a special withholding tax may be deducted. In that event double tax relief may be claimed. The withholding tax will not be deducted if the UK taxpayer authorises the foreign paying agent to report information about the payments made or provides him with a certificate from the Revenue.

Where there is no double tax agreement, you may claim unilateral relief against the UK tax of the lower of the UK tax and the overseas tax. If double tax relief is not claimed, the income or gain, net of the overseas tax suffered, is charged to UK tax but this would rarely be advantageous.

Additional tax credit relief is given for overlap profits arising when a business starts and on changes of accounting date, and the additional relief is recovered as and when overlap relief is given.

If the amount of foreign tax payable is later adjusted, the amount of double tax relief claimed is similarly adjusted. If an adjustment to foreign tax results in too much relief having been claimed, the Revenue must be notified within one year after the adjustment.

Non-residents with UK income and gains (TA 1988, ss 232, 233; F(No 2)A 1997, s 30; FA 2004, ss 107–115)

41.25   Income or gains may be exempt from UK tax under a double tax agreement.

As far as earned income is concerned, many treaties provide that someone working in the UK on a short-term basis will be taxed only in their own country. The Revenue broadly operate a '60 day' rule in this connection (see their Tax Bulletin of December 2003 for detailed comments).

Sometimes a double tax agreement may provide for income that is not exempt from UK tax to be charged at a reduced rate, for example, interest may be taxed at only 10%. The tax on dividends is frequently restricted in the agreement to a maximum of 15%, but as the UK tax credit rate on dividends is only 10% repayments will rarely arise.

Non-residents who claim UK personal allowances (see 41.13) are entitled to dividend tax credits in calculating tax payable whether or not they are entitled to them under a double tax agreement. If no claim for personal allowances is made, and there is no entitlement to a credit under a double tax agreement, a non-resident is liable to UK tax on the amount of the dividend plus the credit, but only to the extent of the excess, if any, of higher rate tax over the lower rate.

UK companies with interests abroad (TA 1988, ss 70A, 392B, 403E, 765–767, 788–795A, 797–799, 801, 806–806M; TCGA 1992, s 140; FA 2003, s 148; SI 2001/1163)

41.26   If a UK resident company has interests abroad, the company is liable to corporation tax on income received, before deduction of foreign taxes, the income being included either under Schedule D, Case I (profits of foreign permanent establishment), Case III (foreign loans) or Case V (foreign possessions, which would include foreign let property and foreign subsidiaries), and also on any capital gains on the disposal of foreign assets. A company's income from all property let abroad is treated as the profits of an 'overseas property business' and computed in broadly the same way as for individuals (see 41.10), i.e. under the 'Schedule A business' rules that apply to UK lettings, but with the profit or loss computed separately for properties in different countries in order to calculate the amount of any available double tax relief (see below). The profits are, however, still Schedule D, Case V profits. Interest on any borrowing to acquire foreign property is deducted under the 'loan relationships' rules in the same way as for UK property (see 32.10). Providing the lettings are on a commercial basis, any losses arising may be carried forward to set against later profits from the overseas property business.

If a UK resident company carries on a trade abroad through a permanent establishment, it is usually charged under Schedule D, Case I on all the profits of the permanent establishment, unless exceptionally the trade is carried on wholly abroad, in which case the charge would be under Case V. Where the charge is under Case I, the normal loss reliefs are available, except in relation to group relief. Losses of a foreign permanent establishment are not available for group relief to the extent that the loss could be relieved for foreign tax purposes in the country in which it arose. If a loss arises in a trade charged under Case V it may only be carried forward to set against later profits from that trade. Other loss reliefs are not available. For accounting periods starting on or after 1 January 2003 new rules apply to the calculation of branch profits (see 41.29), which may alter the amount of double taxation relief available. Where business is carried on through a foreign subsidiary, the UK company's liability will arise only on amounts received from the subsidiary by way of interest or dividends, which will be charged under Schedule D, Case III or Case V.

If an overseas permanent establishment is converted into a subsidiary, Treasury consent is required unless the permanent establishment is in a European Economic Area country (defined in 41.21) — but in that event the transaction may need to be reported to the Treasury. Stock has to be valued at open market value on the transfer, and there are balancing adjustments for capital allowances. Capital gains on assets held at the time of transfer may usually be deferred until the parent company disposes of its shares in the subsidiary. Alternative reliefs are available where the subsidiary is resident in another EU country (see 41.35).

Double tax relief is available in respect of the foreign tax suffered on both income and gains. Normally, only direct foreign taxes are taken into account for double tax relief but if a UK company receives dividends from a foreign company in which it owns 10% or more of the voting power, underlying taxes on the profits out of which the dividends are paid are taken into account as well. In this case the amount included in UK profits is the dividend plus both the direct and underlying foreign taxes. Double tax relief is also available both for direct and underlying foreign tax suffered by UK permanent establishments of non-resident companies, other than tax paid in the taxpayer company's home state.

Unrelieved foreign tax on permanent establishment profits and foreign dividends may be carried back to the previous three years or carried forward indefinitely for offset against tax on income from the same source (providing, in the case of underlying tax, that the required 10% interest continues to be held). Unrelieved foreign tax may also be surrendered within a group of companies (including group companies that are dual-resident).

Anti-avoidance provisions prevent companies entering into schemes deliberately to obtain relief for underlying tax, and restrict the ability of companies to use overseas 'mixer' companies to increase the relief available. There are also anti-avoidance provisions to prevent financial traders getting excessive relief for foreign tax paid on overseas interest. See 45.15.

Double tax relief is given either unilaterally or under the provisions of a double tax agreement.

The relief on overseas income cannot exceed the UK corporation tax payable on the overseas income, after all deductions other than advance corporation tax (which may only be set off under the provisions of the shadow ACT system). It is, however, provided that in deciding how much corporation tax is attributable to the overseas income, any available deductions may broadly be set against any source of profits in the most beneficial way (although not so as to turn profits into a loss for which loss relief is claimed). The main point to bear in mind on interest relating to the trade is that it should be set against UK trading profits in priority to foreign trading profits. As far as non-trading interest is concerned, if there is a non-trading deficit for which relief is claimed against total profits (see heading (a) at 26.5), the deficit must be set against the same profits for both loss relief and double tax relief. Any non-trading deficit brought forward (see 26.6) must be regarded for double tax relief as reducing non-trading profits.

Double tax relief in respect of foreign tax paid on chargeable gains is limited to the UK corporation tax payable thereon.

If double tax relief is restricted because it exceeds the UK tax, then, apart from the provisions mentioned above in relation to unrelieved tax on permanent establishment profits and foreign dividends, the unrelieved foreign tax is wasted and cannot be carried forward or back.

If the amount of foreign tax payable is later adjusted, the amount of double tax relief claimed is similarly adjusted. If an adjustment to foreign tax results in too much relief having been claimed, the Revenue must be notified within one year after the adjustment.

Controlled foreign companies and dual resident companies

41.27   The controlled foreign company legislation provides that in certain circumstances tax is charged on a UK company in respect of profits of a foreign company in which the UK company has a stake of 10% or more. They are outlined very briefly at 45.14. There are also anti-avoidance provisions in relation to dual resident companies, which are outlined at 45.13. Companies are required to declare amounts taxable under the controlled foreign companies rules in their tax returns.

European Economic Interest Groupings (TA 1988, s 510A)

41.28   A European Economic Interest Grouping (EEIG) is a form of business entity that may be set up by enterprises of states in the European Economic Area (i.e. the European Union plus Iceland, Liechtenstein and Norway) for activities such as packing, processing, marketing or research.

The EEIG's profits are taxable and losses allowable only in the hands of the members. The EEIG cannot be formed to make profits for itself. Any trade or profession carried on by the members is treated as carried on in partnership, with the normal rules of income tax, corporation tax and capital gains tax applying.

The 'fiscal transparency' of the EEIG does not apply to provisions other than those charging tax on income and gains, so that an EEIG registered in the UK is required to collect and account for tax on interest, etc. and under PAYE.

Non-resident companies with interests in the UK (TA 1988, ss 6, 11, 13, 13AA, 100; TCGA 1992, ss 25, 171)

41.29   If a non-resident company carries on a trade in the UK through a permanent establishment, it is liable to corporation tax on the trading income from the permanent establishment, income from property or rights held by the permanent establishment and capital gains on the disposal of assets situated in the UK used for the trade or by the permanent establishment. Any rental income from such property is calculated under the 'Schedule A business' rules (see 41.19). For accounting periods starting on or after 1 January 2003, a permanent establishment is treated as having the amount of equity and other capital it would need if it were operating as a separate company. This will restrict the amount of interest that may be deducted in calculating taxable profits. The profits of a permanent establishment are charged to corporation tax at the full rate and the small companies' rate and starting rates do not apply. The permanent establishment is responsible for dealing with the UK tax liabilities on the company's profits. The rules relating to non-resident landlords at 41.19 do not apply. The company is liable to income tax on any UK sources of income not connected with the permanent establishment in the same way as companies not operating through a permanent establishment (see below).

If the UK trade ceases, or the assets are removed from the UK, the company is treated as if it had disposed of the assets, and gains are charged to tax accordingly. If, however, the permanent establishment is converted into a UK subsidiary, the assets are transferred from the parent to the subsidiary on a no gain/no loss basis. The subsidiary may also take over stock at cost, and be treated for losses and capital allowances as if there had been no change.

If a non-resident company does not trade in the UK through a permanent establishment, it is not liable to corporation tax but is liable to income tax (at the basic rate) on UK sources of income, e.g. under Schedule A on rental income from UK property. The charging provisions for rental income are the same as those for individuals (see 41.19). A gain on the disposal of such a let property would not be charged to tax. For companies liable to income tax, interest paid is dealt with under the income tax rules rather than the loan relationships rules.

Group relief for losses etc. (TA 1988, ss 402–413; FA 2000, s 98 and Sch 28)

41.30   A UK permanent establishment of an overseas company may claim group relief against its UK profits in respect of losses surrendered by UK resident subsidiary companies of the overseas parent, and may surrender its losses as group relief to such companies, providing the losses relate to UK activities and are not relievable in the overseas country.

Tax payable by a non-resident company within a group that remains unpaid for six months after the due date may be recovered from another company within the same group.

UK subsidiaries of foreign companies (TA 1988, s 231)

41.31   A UK resident subsidiary of a foreign company is liable to corporation tax in the same way as any other resident company. An overseas parent is not normally entitled to a tax credit on dividends, although some double tax treaties provide for a limited credit. See 41.30 re group relief for losses.

Company ceasing to be resident (TA 1988, ss 765–767; TCGA 1992, ss 185, 187)

41.32   A company incorporated in the UK cannot cease to be resident in the UK for tax purposes, no matter where the business is carried on (see 41.3), unless it becomes unincorporated by a private Act of Parliament, or it is treated as non-resident under the provisions of a double tax treaty (see 41.3). If a foreign-registered company that is resident in the UK ceases to be so resident, it is charged to tax as if it had disposed of all its assets at that time, unless they are retained in a UK permanent establishment. The tax charge is postponed if the company is a 75% subsidiary of a UK resident company and the two companies so elect within two years. The parent company is then charged to tax on the net gains on the deemed disposal as and when the subsidiary disposes of the assets, or ceases to be a subsidiary.

Transfer pricing and thin capitalisation (TA 1988, s 770A and Sch 28AA; FA 1999, ss 85–87; FA 2004, ss 30–37 and Sch 5)

41.33   The transfer pricing provisions require non-arm's length transactions between associated persons to be adjusted for tax purposes to the normal arm's length price. Similarly, the thin capitalisation provisions require non-arm's length interest payments between connected companies to be treated as distributions and therefore not deductible in arriving at profits. Neither of these sets of provisions has normally applied where the companies are wholly within the charge to UK tax. Changes have been made in FA 2004 to bring the two sets of provisions together and to introduce exemptions for most small and medium-sized companies, but also to make the provisions applicable between UK companies. They are covered briefly in 45.18.

Computations relating to foreign exchange matters (see 41.38) are in any event made using arm's length principles and are outside the transfer pricing rules. Taxpayers may make 'advance pricing arrangements' with the tax authorities that their transfer pricing arrangements are acceptable to those authorities. Such agreements are mainly made by multinational companies.

European Union

Possible future developments

41.34   The European Commission has brought forward a two-track strategy for company taxation in the EU, comprising various proposals for extending existing EU directives and laying the foundation for a consolidated tax base for companies' EU wide activities. Obviously any such changes would take a considerable time both to devise and implement, and indeed they may never come to fruition.

Provisions relating to companies (TCGA 1992, ss 140A–140D; FA 2004, ss 97–106)

41.35   From 8 October 2004, under the European Company Statute, a new form of company known as a 'European Company' (Societas Europaea or SE) may be formed by businesses operating in more than one member state — see 3.1.

Under an EU Directive, provisions have been introduced from 1 January 2004 to allow companies to pay interest and royalties without deducting tax where the payments are made to an associated company in another EU state. Companies are associated where one directly owns 25% of the capital or voting rights in the other or a third company directly owns 25% of both. For interest, but not for royalties, the paying company must apply for an exemption notice from the Revenue. Certain EU countries will be allowed to continue to apply a withholding tax to such payments for a transitional period.

A claim may be made for the transfer of all or part of a UK trade between companies resident in different EU states, in exchange for shares or securities, to be treated as a no gain/no loss disposal for capital gains purposes provided certain conditions are satisfied. There are similar provisions to prevent a capital gains charge, or allow a tax credit for any tax paid, on the transfer of a non-UK trade between companies resident in different EU states.

Value added tax

41.36   The VAT treatment of transactions between European Union countries is outlined at 7.32, with comments about the internet and e-commerce in 7.33. From 1 May 2004 the ten countries who joined the EU are subject to the EU VAT provisions, so that transactions with those countries will no longer be 'exports and imports' and UK businesses with customers in those countries will need their customers' VAT numbers.

If a trader suffers VAT in another EU state on goods or services bought and used there (say while participating in a trade fair), it cannot be treated as input VAT in the UK, but it may be recoverable from the other EU state. Details are in C & E Notice 723.

Single currency — the euro (FA 1998, s 163; SI 1998/3177)

41.37   Businesses may pay their taxes and national insurance contributions in euros, although liabilities will still be calculated in sterling and under- or overpayments may arise because of exchange rate fluctuations before payments are actually credited by the tax authorities.

There is legislation to prevent unintended tax consequences arising as a result of the adoption of the euro by other EU states.

Foreign exchange (FOREX) transactions (FA 1993, ss 92–94A; FA 1996, ss 100, 101; FA 2004, s 50)

41.38   Both trading and non-trading companies use the currency of their accounts (or branch financial statements) to calculate their taxable profits and determine their exchange gains and losses, so long as the use of that currency follows generally accepted accounting practice. For accounting periods beginning on or after 1 January 2005, generally accepted accounting practice means either UK generally accepted accounting practice (GAAP) or, where appropriate, generally accepted accounting practice in accordance with international accounting standards (IAS). There are provisions to prevent groups of companies gaining a tax advantage through one company using UK GAAP and the other using IAS.

For UK resident companies, the treatment of profits and losses arising from exchange rate fluctuations is broadly as follows. Foreign exchange gains and losses on monetary assets and liabilities (such as cash, bank deposits and debts), and on forward contracts to buy or sell currency, are taxed as income or allowed as deductions as they accrue. Exchange differences on monetary items are taken into account as they accrue. Unrealised gains above certain limits on long-term capital items may be partly deferred. Exchange differences on borrowing that 'matches' a non-monetary asset are deferred until the asset is disposed of, and then dealt with under the capital gains tax rules. See the Revenue's Statement of Practice 2/02 for the detailed provisions.

Gains and losses on certain financial instruments for managing currency risk are also taken into account in calculating income profits and losses.

For accounting periods beginning on or after 1 October 2002 the separate legislation that previously dealt with foreign exchange transactions has been incorporated within other areas. The provisions relating to loan relationships and other monetary debts are contained within the loan relationships rules. Exchange differences on currency contracts are dealt with in the legislation relating to derivative contracts. See 3.6 and 3.7.

As far as VAT is concerned, foreign exchange transactions are exempt supplies, with no right to recover input VAT on supplies within the EU but with a right to recover related input tax on supplies outside the EU. This needs to be taken into account in partial exemption calculations.

Trusts (TCGA 1992, ss 2, 10A, 13(10), 69–73, 80–98, and Sch 5)

41.39   A trust is treated as not resident and not ordinarily resident in the UK if the general administration of the trust is carried on abroad and a majority of the trustees are not resident and not ordinarily resident in the UK.

Non-resident trusts are dealt with by the Revenue's Centre for Non-Residents. Special provisions apply to reduce or eliminate the tax advantages of offshore trusts as indicated below. See 40.10 in relation to the income tax charge on gains on offshore life policies held in trust and 45.28 for brief notes on other anti-avoidance provisions.

Exit charge when trust becomes non-resident

41.40   Where a trust becomes non-resident, all the trust assets (except any that remain within the scope of UK tax, for example assets that continue to be used in a UK trade) are treated as disposed of and reacquired at market value, and gains are charged to capital gains tax. The charge is at the settlor's rate if he has a present or future right to the income or property of the trust (see 42.16). Rollover relief on replacement of business assets (see 4.26) cannot be claimed if the new assets are acquired after the trust becomes non-resident and are outside the UK tax charge. These provisions also apply to dual resident trusts that are exempt from UK tax on gains because of a double tax treaty.

The acquisition cost of a beneficiary's interest in an emigrating trust for capital gains tax is normally uplifted to the market value at the time of the trust's emigration. This uplift is, however, prevented by anti-avoidance provisions where the trust has a stockpile of gains that have not been attributed to beneficiaries.

Charge on settlor

41.41   Where gains are made by a non-resident trust (or a dual resident trust outside the UK capital gains charge), the settlor may be taxed on the gains. This applies where the settlor has an interest in the trust in the tax year in which the gains arise, and in that year he is UK domiciled and is either UK resident at some time during the year or is ordinarily resident.

Before 2003/04, the gains taxable on the settlor were not reduced by taper relief, because the gains were already tapered in calculating the trust gains, nor could the settlor's own losses be set against the trust gains. The settlor's annual exemption was, however, first used against any trust gains charged on him, before applying the rules at 4.24 in relation to losses brought forward, so that his brought forward losses were used to reduce his own untapered gains only to the extent that such gains remained after setting off any balance of the annual exemption not used against the trust gains. Any gains on which the settlor would have been charged to tax by reason of the 'temporary non-residence' rules outlined at 41.12 were left out of account if beneficiaries had already been taxed on the gains under the provisions outlined at 41.42. The settlor had the right to recover any tax charged on him from the trustees.

Revised rules apply for gains taxed on settlors in 2003/04 and later years. With one exception, trust gains will be calculated without being reduced by taper relief. Any personal losses of the settlor that cannot be set against his personal gains will be set against the untapered trust gains, and taper relief will apply to the amount remaining. The rate of taper relief on the trust gains will be the same as that which would have applied to the trustees. This does not apply where gains are taxed on a settlor under the temporary non-residence rules after being reduced by gains already taxed on beneficiaries. The amount on which the settlor is taxable in respect of any such gains will still be the tapered amount, and he will not be able to reduce such gains by his personal losses. Settlors may *elect*, not later than 31 January 2005, for the revised treatment to apply for any or all of the years 2000/01, 2001/02 and 2002/03. If the election would result in an increase in the total tax that the trustees would have to reimburse to the settlor for those years, the trustees would have to join in the election.

A settlor is treated as having an interest in a trust if his wife, children or their spouses have an interest, or an interest is held by a company controlled by him and/or them. These provisions used to apply only to trusts created on or after 19 March 1991 and to trusts existing at that date if funds were subsequently added or the beneficiaries were changed. Subject to certain exclusions, they apply to pre-19 March 1991 trusts from 6 April 1999 and they also apply to trusts set up for grandchildren on or after 17 March 1998.

Charge on beneficiaries

41.42   Where gains are not charged on a settlor as indicated above, UK domiciled beneficiaries are charged to capital gains tax on their share of the gains of a non-resident trust if they receive capital payments from the trust when they are resident or ordinarily resident in the UK. The tax on a capital payment to a beneficiary is increased by a supplementary charge if gains are not distributed to the beneficiaries in the tax year in which they are made or the following year. The charge runs from 1 December in the tax year following that in which the trustees' gains arose to 30 November in the tax year after that in which the gain is distributed to the beneficiary. The charge is at an annual rate of 10% of the tax on the capital payment, with a maximum of six years, giving an overall maximum possible rate of 60% × 40% = 24%, in addition to the capital gains tax of up to 40% already payable. Gains realised by beneficiaries on *disposal* of their interests in a non-resident trust are taxable if the trust is, or has at any time been, an offshore trust.

In arriving at the gains to be attributed to beneficiaries under these provisions, the trustees' gains are reduced by any available taper relief according to the time the assets have been owned by the trustees. The beneficiaries' own losses cannot be set against such gains.

Various schemes have been devised to avoid the tax charge on the beneficiaries and specific anti-avoidance legislation has been introduced to counteract them. See 45.28 for brief details.

Tax points

41.43

- If you are an employee and your work is wholly carried out abroad, try
  to arrange for your employer to meet the cost of overseas board and
  lodging, so that the taxable benefit can then be offset by an expenses
  claim; otherwise, even though you bear the cost yourself, you will get
  no tax relief on it.

- If you let out UK property, you don't have to be *non-resident* to be
  within the rules requiring tax to be deducted from the rents. The rules
  apply if your 'usual place of abode' is abroad — see 41.19.

- If an overseas property is being purchased through a company in order
  to prevent problems with overseas rules on inheritance, care must be
  taken that an unwelcome UK benefits charge does not arise because of
  the occupation of the property by the family. Professional advice is
  essential.

- If you are resident, ordinarily resident and domiciled in the UK, you
  have to pay tax on all your income wherever in the world it arises. You
  don't escape income tax by investing in offshore roll-up funds — see
  45.16.

- Many people invest in offshore bank and building society accounts to
  get the benefit of receiving gross income (although tax is still payable
  unless covered by reliefs and allowances). Much of the cash flow
  benefit is lost for those making half-yearly payments on account under
  self-assessment. There are also problems in the event of death, because
  of the possible need to take out probate of the will abroad. These points
  need to be borne in mind when considering whether the investment is
  worthwhile.

- If you are taxed on the amount of income or gains you remit to the UK,
  keep funds abroad separate where possible, supported by detailed
  records, so that you can demonstrate, where appropriate, that remittances do not represent either chargeable gains or income.

- The Revenue produce useful booklets IR 20 for the liability to tax of
  residents and non-residents, IR 138 for those living or retiring abroad,
  IR 139 for those with income from abroad and IR 140 for non-resident
  landlords, their agents and tenants.

42
Trusts and estates

Background

42.1   A trust, sometimes called a settlement, arises when someone transfers assets to trustees who hold them and the income from them for the benefit of one or more persons.

A trust can be created in lifetime, or on death by a will or under the intestacy rules where a person does not leave a will (sometimes referred to as a statutory trust). See CHAPTER 35 for additional points relating to trusts created by will, in particular the tax points relating to discretionary trusts. CHAPTER 35 also deals generally with planning points relating to a deceased's estate.

The overseas aspect of trusts is dealt with at 41.39 to 41.42. See also 40.10 in relation to the income tax charge on gains on offshore life policies held in trust.

See 45.7 for the special tax provisions where trustees receive a distribution arising out of the purchase by a company of its own shares and 45.28 for other trust anti-avoidance provisions.

New anti-avoidance provisions in relation to gains on the disposal of a private residence occupied under the terms of a trust are dealt with in 30.6. Other new anti-avoidance measures include a charge to income tax on benefits received by those who continue to enjoy a benefit from property they have disposed of, including the disposal of property to a trust. These are dealt with briefly in 45.27.

The Revenue's work on UK resident trusts and the administration of deceased's estates is dealt with by Inland Revenue Trusts (IR Trusts), except for some small estates where no trust is involved, which are dealt with in local tax offices. Non-resident trusts are dealt with by the Revenue's Centre for Non-Residents.

The tax law and practice relating to estates and trusts can be extremely complicated except in the most straightforward of cases, and it is essential to seek appropriate professional advice.

The Government has been having discussions with representative bodies and other interested parties on modernising the income tax and capital gains tax treatment of trusts. Many of the proposed changes are extremely wide-ranging. Draft legislation is to be produced during 2004 and it is intended that the changes will come into effect from 6 April 2005.There will be a basic rate band of £500 for discretionary trusts, the income within the band being taxed at the basic rate, lower rate or dividend tax credit rate depending on the type of income. Special rules will apply to trusts for the vulnerable (such as disabled people and orphaned minor children), which will be backdated to 6 April 2004. Common definitions and tests will be introduced to make it easier for trustees to determine their tax status.

Administration of an estate

42.2   Where a trust is created on death, the personal representatives must first complete the administration of the estate. They need to deal with the deceased's tax position for the year of death (and earlier years if returns have not been submitted) and also their own tax position as personal representatives until the administration of the estate is completed. Under self-assessment, the normal time limit for enquiring into a tax return is twelve months from the due date for the return (see 9.9). To minimise delays in winding up estates and trusts, and distributing estate or trust property, the Revenue will, on request, issue tax returns before the end of the tax year of death, or of winding up an estate or trust, and will give early confirmation if they do not intend to enquire into the return. See 9.49 re limits in relation to Revenue enquiries into the tax position of a deceased taxpayer.

The personal representatives will not usually be able to settle the deceased's tax liabilities until probate is obtained, and the inheritance tax due must be paid before probate is granted. There is a recent agreement between the Revenue and the British Bankers' and Building Societies' Associations that participating institutions will accept instructions from personal representatives to transfer sums standing to the credit of the deceased direct to the Revenue in payment of inheritance tax before the issue of the grant. This will be of considerable practical help where the personal representatives do not have ready access to other funds outside the estate, such as insurance policy proceeds written in trust. The deceased's tax district should be asked to arrange for the Revenue Accounts Office not to issue any further Statements of Account in the meantime, which can often cause needless distress to the family. By Revenue concession A17, interest on tax falling due after death will not start to run until thirty days after the grant of probate.

The administration period during which the personal representatives deal with the collection of assets and payment of liabilities and the distribution of the estate may last some months or even years if the estate is complex.

42.3   Personal representatives deal with the estate of a deceased either under the terms of the will, according to the rules of intestacy where there is no will, or under a deed varying the will or entitlement in the intestacy. (For the way an intestate person's estate is distributed see 35.1.) Income tax is payable on the income of the deceased up to the date of death, with a full year's allowances, any unused married couple's age allowance of the deceased spouse being transferable to the other if the personal representatives notify the Revenue (see 33.9 and 33.10). There is no capital gains tax on the increase in the value of assets held at death. If the deceased had chargeable gains in excess of the annual exemption in the tax year of his death, capital gains tax is payable. If there are capital losses in the year of death, they may be carried back to set against gains of the three previous tax years, latest first (ignoring any gains already covered by the annual exemption), and tax will be repaid accordingly (but interest on the repayment will run from the payment date for the tax year of death — see 9.5).

Inheritance tax is payable if transfers of wealth by the deceased in the seven years before death which were either then chargeable or potentially exempt, together with the amount chargeable at death, exceed the threshold (currently £263,000). See 9.30 for further details, including the provisions under which an inheritance tax account does not have to be submitted for small estates. Assets to which a surviving spouse becomes entitled either absolutely or to enjoy the income are not chargeable to inheritance tax at that time, but will be included in the spouse's estate for inheritance tax upon the spouse's death or earlier lifetime transfer. The value of business and agricultural property can be eliminated from the calculation of inheritance tax in some circumstances. The way in which the tax is calculated is dealt with in CHAPTER 5.

Personal representatives need to be aware that the Revenue have recently taken a harsh stance in relation to provisional figures in inheritance tax accounts. Before including such figures, personal representatives are required to make 'the fullest enquiries that are reasonably practicable in the circumstances' and in a case before the Special Commissioners the Revenue sought (although without success) to exact a penalty despite the fact that accurate figures were submitted long before the inheritance tax was due for payment.

Where property is transferred to those entitled under a will or intestacy, neither stamp duty nor stamp duty land tax is payable. Nor will stamp duty land tax be payable (from 22 July 2004) when personal representatives dispose of a deceased's home to a property trader.

Income during the administration period (TA 1988, ss 364, 695–701)

42.4   Personal representatives are liable to income tax at 10% on dividend income, at the lower rate of 20% on savings income and at the basic rate on other income. Personal representatives are not taxed at the starting rate or the higher rate, nor can they claim personal allowances. Where the personal representatives have borrowed to pay inheritance tax on property, other than freehold land and buildings, preparatory to obtaining a grant of probate, interest payable for up to one year from the date of the loan may be deducted from the estate income of the tax year of payment. If the interest exceeds the estate income of that tax year, it may be carried back against estate income of preceding tax years, and any remaining amount may be carried forward against future estate income.

The income during the administration period will be distributed to the beneficiaries entitled to it either because they are entitled absolutely to the assets or because, while the assets remain in trust, they are entitled to the income (known as a life interest or an interest in possession). Any payments to a beneficiary on account of income during the administration period are net of the 'applicable rate' of tax, i.e. the Schedule F ordinary rate of 10% on dividends, the lower rate of 20%, or the basic rate (currently 22%) according to the income they represent. The gross equivalent is included in taxable income in the tax year when it is received by the beneficiary from the personal representatives. Payments to beneficiaries are treated as being made first out of brought-forward and current income charged at the basic rate, then brought-forward and current savings income charged at the lower rate, then dividends carrying a non-repayable tax credit at the Schedule F ordinary rate of 10%. Dividend income includes normal dividends, scrip dividends, loans written off by close companies and bonus issues of redeemable shares or securities. The total income will first have been apportioned between beneficiaries on a just and reasonable basis. The rate of tax treated as deducted from payments to beneficiaries is not necessarily the same as that borne by the personal representatives, since the relevant rate is the applicable rate in force at the time of the payment to the beneficiaries, rather than the rate in force when the income was received. When the administration period is completed and the final amount of income due to each beneficiary ascertained, the beneficiary is treated as having received the balance due to him in the tax year in which the administration is completed (or, for someone with a life entitlement whose interest ceased earlier, say because of his death, in the tax year when the interest ceased). The amount due is grossed up at the relevant rate in force at the time of payment according to the income it represents. On a written request from the beneficiaries, the personal representatives must supply them with details of payments made and the rate of tax on the payments.

Capital gains during the administration period (*TCGA 1992, ss 3(7), 4, 62, 225A; FA 2004, Sch 22.5*)

42.5   No capital gains tax arises on the transfer to legatees of assets comprising specific legacies, the legatees acquiring them at market value at the date of death. Assets that pass to the personal representatives (out of which they pay debts due and distribute the residue of the estate) are also acquired by them at market value at the date of death. Any gains arising on a disposal by the personal representatives are calculated by reference to their sales proceeds less the value at death, the gain being reduced by any available taper relief, calculated by reference to the date of death, not the date when the asset was acquired by the deceased. The personal representatives are entitled in their own right to the annual exemption, currently £8,200, against any gains on their disposals in the tax year of death and the next two tax years, but not thereafter. Gains in excess of the exempt limit are taxed at 40% (34% for disposals before 6 April 2004). If any losses arise, they may only be set against gains of the personal representatives and cannot be transferred to beneficiaries.

If the private residence is to be sold by the personal representatives, a chargeable gain may arise between death and sale. For disposals on or after 10 December 2003, the private residence exemption is available following a claim by the personal representatives where the property has been used immediately before and after death as the main residence of individuals who are entitled to at least 75% of the net sale proceeds either absolutely or for life. For disposals before 10 December 2003 a similar relief was given by Revenue concession D5. Where the relief does not apply, it may be appropriate for personal representatives to assent to a transfer of the property to beneficiaries, so that the gain may be charged at their personal tax rates rather than the 40% rate (34% for disposals before 6 April 2004) applicable to the personal representatives on gains above the annual exemption.

Personal representatives do not qualify for gifts holdover relief, but trustees do. Where the residue of the estate is left on trust, the personal representatives should ensure that assets on which gifts holdover is available and is appropriate to be claimed have been formally appropriated to the trustees (which will usually but not necessarily be themselves, but then acting in a different capacity) before being gifted.

End of administration period

42.6   The administration period ends either when the whole estate is finally distributed if no trust has been created, or when the residue of the estate after payment of debts and legacies is transferred to a trust fund. There is no chargeable gain on personal representatives when they transfer assets to beneficiaries or trustees, the assets transferred being regarded as acquired by the beneficiaries or trustees at market value at the date of death or the cost to the personal representatives if acquired later.

Tax liability on setting up a trust (IHTA 1984, s 200; TA 1988, ss 660A–660G; TCGA 1992, ss 165, 169B–169G, 260 and Sch 4; FA 2004, s 116 and Sch 21)

Inheritance tax

42.7   A deceased's estate is charged to inheritance tax where appropriate before property is transferred to a trust created by his will.

Lifetime transfers to trusts for the disabled, to accumulation and maintenance trusts for the settlor's children (see 42.26), or to trusts in which someone is entitled to the income (known as an 'interest in possession') are potentially exempt from inheritance tax and will only be reckonable if the settlor dies within seven years. For trusts created in lifetime in which no-one has a *right* to the income (known as 'discretionary trusts') the settlor is liable to inheritance tax on the property transferred to the trust at one-half of the scale rate, except to the extent that the transfer is within the nil rate threshold. The transfer has to be grossed up if the settlor also pays the inheritance tax (see CHAPTER 5). If the settlor dies within the next seven years, tax on the lifetime transfer is recalculated using the full rate and scale applicable at the date of death less a credit up to the amount of any tax already charged in lifetime.

It is possible for the settlor to settle sums on himself/herself and/or his/her spouse (rather than making an outright gift to the spouse with no strings attached, which would not be treated as a settlement). The transfer into the trust does not in these circumstances have to be reckoned for inheritance tax since the settlor or his wife is still enjoying the benefit of the capital. (Any income in the trust is taxed on the settlor, or his wife after his death.)

Capital gains tax

42.8   As indicated in 42.6, no capital gains tax arises when property is transferred to trustees by personal representatives.

When assets are placed into trust in lifetime, they are treated as disposed of at market value for capital gains tax, but gains may sometimes be held over under the gifts holdover relief provisions where the assets are business assets or where the gifted assets have immediately to be reckoned for inheritance tax, which principally applies to gifts to a discretionary trust (see 4.27 to 4.30).

Where gifts holdover relief has been claimed, the effect is to increase the chargeable gain when the donee disposes of the asset. (Taper relief is given according to the *donee's* period of ownership — see 4.23.) Where, however, the holdover occurred between 6 April 1981 and 31 March 1982 (the relief being available on any asset between 6 April 1981 and 13 March 1989), the heldover gain escapes tax because of the uplifting of values for capital gains tax on that day, and the donee's acquisition cost is not reduced. If the holdover occurred after 31 March 1982 and before 6 April 1988, and the relevant asset was acquired before 31 March 1982, the reduction in the donee's acquisition cost is halved when calculating tax on the disposal of the asset.

42.9   The gifts holdover relief used to apply to qualifying assets transferred into a trust in which the settlor retained an interest. For disposals on or after 10 December 2003, gifts relief is not available on disposals to a trust in which either a settlor (who need not be the transferor) has an interest or there are arrangements under which a settlor will acquire an interest. Gifts relief is also denied in respect of a gain on a disposal to a trust on or after 10 December 2003 if the expenditure allowable in calculating the gain is reduced by gifts relief on an earlier disposal (whether before or after 10 December 2003), and immediately after the disposal the transferor has an interest in the trust, or there are arrangements under which he will acquire an interest. Where gifts relief is not available, the transferor will be entitled to taper relief where appropriate and the annual exemption.

Where a disposal is made on or after 10 December 2003 to a trust that is not initially a settlor-interested trust, any gifts relief on the disposal is clawed back if the settlor acquires an interest within six years after the disposal. Taper relief on the clawed-back gain will be given according to the original transferor's period of ownership.

Types of trust

42.10   There are basically four types of trust:

(a)   'bare' trusts, where the trustee is effectively a nominee for the beneficial owner of the trust assets;

(b)   trusts with an interest in possession, i.e. where someone has a right for the time being to receive the income of the trust (whether or not the trustees have the power to appropriate any of the capital to that beneficiary), often called a life tenant (although the interest may in fact end during lifetime, for example when a widow is only entitled to the income until she remarries);

(c)   discretionary trusts, in which no-one has a right to the income and/or the trust assets; and

(d)   accumulation and maintenance trusts, under which income is, broadly, accumulated for minor children until they reach a specified age, with the assets then being distributed amongst the beneficiaries.

Powers over trusts (IHTA 1984, ss 47A, 55A, 272)

42.11   Trusts may include a general power for the settlor to dispose of trust property as he sees fit. Powers over trusts are normally not treated as part of a person's property for inheritance tax purposes. This is subject to anti-avoidance rules where such powers are purchased.

Stamp duty land tax (FA 2003, s 105 and Sch 16)

42.12   For stamp duty land tax purposes, the acts of bare trustees are treated as those of the person who is absolutely entitled as against the trustees. For trustees other than bare trustees, the stamp duty land tax provisions apply to acquisitions of land and buildings by the trustees as if they had acquired the whole interest in the property, including the beneficial interest. If trustees receive consideration for exercising a power of appointment or a discretion in relation to a land transaction, the consideration is treated as chargeable consideration for stamp duty land tax.

Trusts in which the settlor retains an interest (TA 1988, ss 660A–660G; TCGA 1992, ss 76A–79 and Schs 4A–4C; FA 2000, s 44)

42.13   The tax position of the trustees under the various types of trust is outlined below. Under headings (b), (c) and (d) in 42.10, however, the settlor remains liable for income tax on the trust income if he or his spouse retains a present or future right to the income or assets of the trust, or where the settlement transfers income but not capital (see 12.9, 18.2 and 23.21 for detailed comments). 'Spouse' does not include a future, former or separated spouse or the settlor's widow or widower. Further, even though a settlement is of capital in which the settlor does not retain an interest, if income of the settlement is paid to or for the benefit of an unmarried child of the settlor who is under 18, it is treated as the settlor's income, subject to the exceptions at 33.7 (see also 42.14 and 42.27). The settlor is entitled to recover the tax paid by him from the trustees, or from the person who received the income. The income tax liability on the settlor does not apply to the extent that the trustees give the income to charity, or a charity is entitled to the income under the trust.

As far as capital gains tax is concerned, any gains made by the trustees of settlor-interested trusts are taxed as if they were the settlor's personal gains rather than being allowed the trust's exemption and being taxed at the trust's tax rate. The settlor may, however, recover from the trustees any capital gains tax paid by him. For years up to 2002/03, the trustees' gains were calculated in the normal way, taking into account any available indexation allowance and taper relief based on the period of ownership of the trustees, and subject to the special rules at 42.8 for assets acquired before 31 March 1982. The settlor could not reduce any such gains by his own losses. The settlor's annual exemption was, however, first used against any trust gains charged on him, before applying the rules at 4.24 in relation to losses brought forward, so that his brought forward losses reduced his own untapered gains only to the extent that such gains remained after setting off any balance of the annual exemption not used against the trust gains.

Revised rules apply for gains taxed on settlors in 2003/04 and later years. The trust gains charged on the settlor are calculated without being reduced by taper relief. Any personal losses of the settlor remaining after set-off against his personal gains are then set against the trust gains, and taper relief will apply to the amount remaining. The rate of taper relief on the trust gains is the same as that which would have applied to the trustees. Settlors may *elect*, not later than 31 January 2005, for the revised treatment to apply for any or all of the years 2000/01, 2001/02 and 2002/03. If the election would result in an increase in the total tax that the trustees would have to reimburse to the settlor for those years, the trustees would have to join in the election.

Where a beneficiary disposes of an interest in a trust in which the settlor has an interest (or had an interest at any time in the two previous tax years, excluding any pre–6 April 1999 period), there is a deemed disposal and reacquisition by the trustees at market value, and the settlor is charged on the resulting gains. Gifts holdover relief is not available.

Further anti-avoidance provisions apply to counter a tax avoidance device known as the 'flip flop', which had the effect either of reducing the tax rate on gains on disposals from the settlor's rate of 40% to the trustees' then rate of 34% (now 40%) or of eliminating entirely a tax charge on a UK settlor or UK beneficiaries of an offshore trust. These are outlined at 45.28.

Bare trusts (TA 1988, s 660B)

42.14   A bare trust is one in which the beneficiary has an absolute right to the assets and income, but the trustees are the legal owners and hold the property effectively as nominee. The transfer to the bare trust is a potentially exempt transfer for inheritance tax, becoming completely exempt if the donor survives the seven-year period.

A bare trust could simply be a bank or building society account in the settlor's name as trustee for the beneficiary, and in that event the trust income would not be depleted by administration expenses.

The tax position of the trust depends on the beneficiary's circumstances rather than those of the donor or the trustee, so that the trust income is included with that of the beneficiary in calculating how much of the beneficiary's income tax personal allowances and starting rate band are available. Likewise the question of whether any capital gains tax reliefs and exemptions are available on the disposal of chargeable assets depends upon the circumstances of the beneficiary. Under self-assessment, beneficiaries must show their income and gains from a bare trust in their own tax returns and trustees are not required to complete returns. The Revenue have, however, stated that the trustees may, if they wish, send in a self-assessment return of income (but not capital gains). This will not affect the liability of the beneficiaries to send returns of both income and gains. Any tax deducted at source will be refunded if covered by reliefs and allowances.

The income tax treatment described above applies to bare trusts created before 9 March 1999 even if such a trust was made by a parent in favour of a child (and the parent could be the trustee), providing the income is not actually paid to or for the benefit of the child while the child is unmarried and under 18. If it is, the income would then be treated as the parent's under the provisions at 42.13. The child cannot be prevented from having the property put into his own legal ownership at age 18.

For bare trusts created by parents in favour of their children under 18 on or after 9 March 1999, and for income on funds added to existing trusts on or after that date, income is taxed as that of the parent, unless covered by the £100 limit dealt with at 33.7. Bare trusts created by a parent's will are still effective to treat income as that of the beneficiary, and also bare trusts created by other relatives, although it is not possible to make a reciprocal arrangement for someone to create a trust for his relative's children and for the relative to do the same for his children.

Bare trusts created by parents are effective for capital gains purposes, so that it is possible to use such trusts to acquire investments for children that produce capital growth rather than income. Where capital gains are made, a bare trust is entitled to the full annual exemption (currently £8,200) rather than half of that amount as applies to other trusts (or proportionate amount where several trusts are created by the settlor).

Trusts with an interest in possession

Income tax (TA 1988, ss 1A, 689B)

42.15   Where there is an interest in possession, one or more beneficiaries has a right to the trust income.

The trustees are charged to tax on dividend income at the Schedule F ordinary rate of 10%, on savings income at the lower rate of 20% and on other income at the basic rate (currently 22%). Trustees are not liable to higher rate tax. Income is calculated in the same way as for an individual. There are, however, no deductions for personal allowances. There is no relief in calculating the tax payable by the trustees for expenses of managing the trust, which are therefore paid out of the after-tax income. They are treated as paid out of savings income in priority to non-savings income and out of dividend income before other savings income.

The income beneficiaries are personally liable to income tax on that income less the trust expenses, whether they draw the income or leave it in the trust fund (except where the settlor has retained an interest and the tax is payable by him — see 42.13). They are entitled to a credit for the tax paid by the trustees on that part of the trust income that has not been used to pay trust expenses, but in relation to dividends the credit is non-repayable.

Example 1

Trust's income in 2004/05 comprises rents of £3,200 gross, £2,496 net after tax of £704. The trust expenses are £156. The beneficiary will receive (2,496 − 156 =) £2,340, which is equivalent to gross income of £3,000. If he is a basic rate taxpayer he will have no further liability and will retain the £2,340. If he is not liable to tax he will reclaim tax of (3,000 @ 22% =) £660, and if he is a higher rate payer he will have an additional liability of 18% of £3,000, i.e. £540.

If instead the trust's net income comprised rents of £1,248 after tax of £352, and cash dividends of £1,248 with tax credits of £139, the trust expenses would reduce the dividend income to £1,092, with a tax credit of £121. The beneficiary would still receive £2,340, but the gross income would be (1,600 + 1,213 =) £2,813. A basic rate taxpayer would retain the £2,340. A non-taxpaying beneficiary would be able to reclaim only £352. A higher rate payer would have to pay 18% of £1,600 = £288 plus 22½% of £1,213 = £273, giving a total of £561.

The need to pay expenses out of the taxed income of the trust may be minimised if specific income is paid direct to the beneficiary, for example, by a mandate to a building society to pay interest direct, with a consequent saving in administration expenses. This will improve the position of a beneficiary who is entitled to a tax repayment, but for a higher rate taxpayer it will deny relief on the trust expenses at the excess of the higher rate over that paid by the trustees.

Capital gains tax (TCGA 1992, ss 4, 71–74, 79A, 165 and Schs 1, 7)

42.16   If the settlor transfers chargeable assets to the trust, he is liable to capital gains tax, unless the gifts holdover relief is available. The relief is not available if the settlor retains an interest in the trust (see 42.9).

When the trustees dispose of any chargeable assets they are treated as the settlor's gains if he has retained an interest in the trust (see 42.13). Anti-avoidance provisions apply to counter a tax avoidance device known as the 'flip flop', which aimed to reduce or eliminate the tax on disposals from a trust. These are outlined at 45.28.

Where gains are not taxed on the settlor, they are reduced by an annual exemption (£4,100 for 2004/05). The remaining gains are taxed at 40% (34% before 6 April 2004). Where there are a number of trusts created by the same settlor, the annual exemption of £4,100 is divided equally between them, subject to a minimum exemption of £820 for each trust. Trusts for the disabled qualify for the full annual exemption of £8,200, reduced where the same settlor has created several disabled trusts, with a minimum exemption for each disabled trust of £820.

Where losses arise on disposals by the trustees, they cannot be set against any gains made by the trustees on assets that had been transferred to the trust if the transferor or someone connected with him had bought an interest in the trust and had claimed gifts holdover relief on the transferred assets (see 45.28).

When a beneficiary becomes absolutely entitled to trust property following the death of the person entitled to the income, the trustees are regarded as disposing of the property to the beneficiary at its then market value, but no capital gains tax liability arises. Any increase in value up to that time escapes capital gains tax (and any losses are not allowable). A tax-free uplift for capital gains tax also occurs on property that remains in the trust after the death of the person entitled to the income. In both cases, however, where the capital gains tax cost of the property had been reduced by gifts holdover relief (see 4.27 to 4.30), there is a chargeable gain equal to the heldover amount (subject to the special rules at 42.8 where gains relate wholly or partly to a period before 31 March 1982). Any available taper relief is based on the time for which the property has been held by the trustees (see 4.23). If the property is still qualifying business property for gifts holdover relief, a further claim to defer the tax liability may be made by the trustees and beneficiary, so that the gain will be treated as reducing the acquisition cost of the beneficiary. Taper relief will then not apply at the time of the deferral and will depend on the subsequent period of ownership of the beneficiary.

When a life interest terminates other than on death, for example because a widow remarries, but the property remains in trust, there is neither a chargeable gain nor any change in the base value of the property for future capital gains tax disposals by the trustees.

When, however, a beneficiary becomes absolutely entitled to trust property other than on the death of the person entitled to the income, this is regarded as a disposal at market value at that date, and capital gains tax is payable on the increase in value, subject to any available indexation allowance and taper relief, and subject to the special rules at 42.8 for assets acquired before 31 March 1982 on which gifts holdover relief had been claimed. The same provisions for deferring the gain apply as stated above if the property still qualifies for business gifts holdover relief, with the same effect in relation to taper relief. Where the deemed market value disposal to the beneficiary results in an allowable loss that the trustees cannot use against gains arising at the time of the transfer or earlier in the same tax year, the loss is treated as made by the beneficiary who has become absolutely entitled to the asset, but the beneficiary can use the loss only to reduce a gain on the disposal of the asset, or in the case of land, an asset derived from the land, thus restricting his chargeable gain to that which would have arisen had he adopted the base value of the trustees as his own (see 45.28).

If when a life interest ends, the property goes back to the settlor, the trustees are only chargeable to tax to the extent that gains have been held over, and even then, the special rules at 42.7 may apply. The settlor is treated as acquiring the property at its cost plus any available indexation allowance (and as having held it on 31 March 1982 if it was settled before that date, enabling him to use 31 March 1982 value to compute a gain if appropriate). Any indexation allowance incorporated into cost cannot, however, be used to create or increase a loss when the settlor disposes of the property. Taper relief would not be taken into account until the settlor disposed of the property, and would be based on the settlor's period of ownership from the time he reacquired the property.

If a beneficiary under a trust transfers his interest to someone else, this is not normally treated as a chargeable disposal for capital gains tax, whether he is transferring a life interest or a reversionary interest (i.e. the right to the capital of the trust when those with life interests die or give up their interests). There is a chargeable disposal if the beneficiary had bought the interest from someone else, or had acquired it by gift from someone who had bought it.

See 42.13 for the position where a beneficiary sells an interest in a settlement in which the settlor has an interest (or has had an interest at any time in the two previous tax years). See also 41.42 for disposals of an interest in an overseas trust.

Inheritance tax (IHTA 1984, Pt III)

42.17   Someone entitled to the income for the time being from a trust fund is regarded as entitled to the underlying capital, so that he is treated as making a chargeable transfer of the underlying capital on his death. If he ceases to be entitled to the income in lifetime, with the trust assets passing either to another individual for life or absolutely, or to an accumulation and maintenance or disabled trust, the transfer is potentially exempt. It only becomes chargeable if he dies within seven years. Although any tax is calculated by reference to his own chargeable position, it has to be paid by the trustees. The fact that trust funds are treated as belonging to the beneficiary entitled to the income prevents wealth being protected from inheritance tax through the use of an interest in possession trust. It may also result in inheritance tax being paid on the income beneficiary's own estate whereas his estate would have been below the nil band if the trust funds had not been included.

Example 2

A taxpayer died on 30 September 2004, having made no transfers in lifetime other than a potentially exempt transfer of £170,000 after annual exemptions of £6,000 in June 2002. At his death, his own assets less liabilities (called his free estate) were valued at £100,000. He was also entitled to the income from trust funds, the value of which were £50,000 and to which his daughter became absolutely entitled. He was a widower, his estate being left to his son.

The inheritance tax payable on his death is:

		Gross	Tax	
Lifetime transfer*		170,000	—	
Free estate at death	100,000			
Trust funds at death	50,000	150,000	22,800	**
		£320,000	£22,800	

** $(320,000 - 263,000) = £57,000$ @ 40% = £22,800

The tax is payable as follows:

From free estate	$\dfrac{100,000}{150,000}$ × £22,800	15,200
From trust funds	$\dfrac{50,000}{150,000}$ × £22,800	7,600
		£22,800

If the trust fund had not counted as part of the chargeable estate, the inheritance tax on the estate would have been $(270,000 - 263,000) = £7,000$ @ 40%, i.e. £2,800.

> *Although potentially exempt in lifetime, the transfer must be taken into account at death because the taxpayer died within seven years of making it.

Where there are successive inheritance tax charges on the trust property within five years, the tax payable on the later transfer may be reduced by quick succession relief (see CHAPTER 5).

Since the creation of a trust fund in which someone is entitled to the income is potentially exempt from inheritance tax, and only attracts tax if the settlor dies within seven years, such trusts provide the settlor with an efficient means of inheritance tax planning and family provision. By the creation of the trust the settlor has transferred funds without giving the transferee absolute control over them. Any growth in the value of the assets occurs within the trust fund and not in the settlor's personal estate. There is no tax charge if the beneficiary entitled to the income receives a capital sum from the fund, since he is regarded as being entitled to the capital anyway. Tax may be payable if the income beneficiary continues to hold his interest until death, because the funds are treated as part of his estate. Tax is not, however, chargeable if the settled property reverts to the settlor, or if his/her spouse (or widow/widower if the settlor had died less than two years earlier) becomes beneficially entitled to the property and is UK domiciled. If the interest comes to an end in the beneficiary's lifetime, other than by being transferred to a discretionary trust, potential exemption will again be available.

Discretionary trusts

Income tax (TA 1988, ss 686, 686A, 687, 689B, 832)

42.18 Where trustees have discretionary power over the distribution of income and no-one is entitled to it as of right, the trustees are liable to tax at 40% (34% before 6 April 2004) (known as the rate applicable to trusts) on income other than dividend income. Dividend income is charged at the Schedule F trust rate of 32.5% (25% before 6 April 2004), of which 10% is covered by the tax credit, leaving the trustees with an additional 22.5% of the tax credit inclusive dividend income to pay (25% of the cash dividend received). In arriving at the amount chargeable at the 32.5% or 40% rate, trustees are entitled to deduct their expenses. Expenses are set first against dividend income then against other savings income in priority to non-savings income, so that the part of the trust's income used to pay expenses will bear tax either at 10% if it is dividend income, 20% if it is savings income or the basic rate if it is other income. If the trust has any exempt income, either because the trustees are not resident or are treated as being non-resident under a double tax treaty, the allowable expenses are proportionately restricted. The trustees are not chargeable if the income is treated as the settlor's income (see 42.13). In that event the settlor may recover from them (or from beneficiaries who receive the income) the tax he pays.

Any income paid to beneficiaries (other than any that is treated as the settlor's income) is net of 40% tax (34% before 6 April 2004), the beneficiary being entitled to an income tax repayment to the extent that the income is covered by available personal allowances or chargeable at less than 40%.

Even though the trustees pay tax at 32.5% (25% before 6 April 2004) on tax credit inclusive dividend income, the rate of tax regarded as deducted from payments to beneficiaries is still 40% (34% before 6 April 2004), and non-taxpaying beneficiaries will still be able to recover that tax. The trustees cannot, however, count the dividend credit as tax paid by them when calculating how much of the tax deducted from the beneficiaries' income has to be accounted for by them. The result is that unless the trust has a pool of unused tax from earlier years (see 42.30), the maximum gross amount that can be paid out without depleting the trust fund will be the amount of the cash dividend. The position is illustrated in Example 3.

Example 3

The following example ignores the effect of trust expenses.

Dividend of £160 plus tax credit of £18 was received by a discretionary trust in 2004/05 and distributed to the beneficiaries. The tax position is as follows:

	£
Tax on trust income of (160 + (1/9) 18) @ 32.5%	58
Less: Dividend tax credit	18
Tax payable by trustees @ 22.5% of £178 (tax credit inclusive dividend)	40
Leaving net income of (160 − 40) = £120	
Distribution to beneficiaries equal to cash dividend	160
Tax at 40%	64
Net payment to beneficiaries	96
Further tax to be accounted for by trustees (64 − 40)	24

Net payment to beneficiaries of £96 plus further tax payable of £24 = net trust income of £120.

Non-taxpaying beneficiaries could recover the tax of £64, so that their income would be £160.

Capital gains tax (TCGA 1992, ss 165, 260)

42.19   The settlor is chargeable to capital gains tax on any gains on chargeable assets transferred to the trust, but gains may instead be treated as reducing the trustees' acquisition cost under the gifts holdover relief provisions (see 42.8). The holdover relief is not restricted to business and other qualifying assets, the reasoning being that there is an immediate reckoning for inheritance tax (see 42.20). For disposals on or after 10 December 2003, the settlor cannot claim gifts holdover relief if he retains an interest in the trust (see 42.9).

Gains on disposals of chargeable assets by the trustees are calculated in the normal way, with any available indexation allowance and taper relief being taken into account, subject to the special rules at 42.8 for assets acquired before 31 March 1982. If the settlor retains an interest in the trust, gains are taxed on him under the provisions outlined at 42.13. Note the changed position outlined in 42.13 in relation to the treatment of taper relief on a trust's gains from 2003/04 (or possibly earlier if an election is made). Where gains are not taxed on the settlor, they are reduced by the annual exemption of £4,100 for 2004/05 (or proportionate part thereof where there are associated trusts). The rate of tax on any remaining gains is 40% (34% before 6 April 2004), i.e. the same rate as that payable on income. When a beneficiary becomes absolutely entitled to any chargeable assets of the trust, the trustees are treated as disposing of the assets at market value at that date for capital gains tax purposes (subject to the special rules for assets acquired before 31 March 1982), but if a gain arises the trustees and beneficiary may jointly elect for the tax liability to be deferred by treating the gains as reducing the beneficiary's acquisition cost for capital gains tax, unless the distribution from the trust takes place within three months after its creation or within three months after a ten-year anniversary for inheritance tax (see 42.20). If the distribution takes place within such a three-month period, gifts relief will still be available if the assets are qualifying business assets (see 4.28). It may not be possible to defer capital gains tax where a distribution is made out of a discretionary will trust as described in 35.10 (see also 42.28 re accumulation and maintenance trusts).

Inheritance tax (IHTA 1984, Pt III)

42.20   Since no one has a right to the income of a discretionary trust, the underlying capital cannot be reckoned for inheritance tax in the same way as where an individual has an interest in possession (see 42.17). A discretionary trust therefore has its own threshold for inheritance tax, with tax being charged every ten years by reference to the value of the trust funds, and also upon distribution of capital sums to beneficiaries (called an 'exit charge'). The rate of tax is 30% of the 20% scale rate, giving a maximum of 6% on the amount chargeable, and in the case of the exit charge this is discounted pro rata according to how many quarters have elapsed in the ten-year period. The trust may be set up by the will of the deceased or in lifetime.

A useful way of utilising the inheritance tax threshold at death is illustrated at 35.4.

Gifts into a lifetime discretionary trust are not potentially exempt, so that if the nil rate threshold of the settlor is exceeded, inheritance tax is payable at the 20% lifetime rate, increased to the full 40% rate if the settlor dies within seven years.

Business and agricultural property reliefs are available where the trust assets include qualifying property.

42.21   If an exit charge arises within the first ten years, the inheritance tax payable is calculated by reference to the chargeable transfers of the settlor before he settled the funds on the discretionary trust, and the initial value of the trust funds. See Example 4.

Example 4

A settlor, having made a transfer of £55,000 four years earlier that was a chargeable transfer rather than being potentially exempt, settled £300,000 on discretionary trusts on 1 October 1994, personally paying inheritance tax as follows:

Previous chargeable transfer				55,000
1.10.94 transfer to discretionary trust			300,000	
Less: Annual exemption	1994/95	3,000		
	1993/94	3,000	6,000	294,000
				349,000
Settlor's nil rate threshold (1994/95 scale)				150,000
Chargeable transfer				£199,000
Inheritance tax payable by the settlor personally at 20%				£39,800

If the trustees distributed £100,000 to a beneficiary on 10 June 1999, the inheritance tax payable (assuming that the tax was payable out of the £100,000 so that no grossing up (see 5.9) was necessary) would be:

Previous chargeable transfer of settlor	55,000
Initial value of trust fund	300,000
	355,000
Trust's nil rate threshold (1999/2000 scale)	231,000
	£124,000
Inheritance tax at 20% lifetime rate	£24,800

Representing an effective tax rate of $\dfrac{24,800}{300,000} = 8.27\%$

Of which 30% (the rate applicable to discretionary trusts) =	2.48%	
£100,000 @ 2.48%		2,480
Less: $\dfrac{\text{21 quarters remaining in 10-year period}}{\text{40 quarters in 10 -year period}}$		1,302
Inheritance tax payable out of the £100,000 distribution is		£1,178

42.22   The charge at the first ten-year anniversary is found by reference to the settlor's chargeable transfers before he settled the funds, plus the distributions liable to exit charges in the first ten years and the value of the fund at the ten-year anniversary. See Example 5.

Example 5

Say that at 30 September 2004 the value of the trust fund in Example 4 was £500,000. The tax payable by the trustees is calculated as follows:

Previous chargeable transfer of settlor	55,000
Distributions in the first ten years	100,000
Value of fund at 10 year anniversary	500,000
	655,000
Nil threshold at 30.9.2004	263,000
	£392,000
Inheritance tax at 20% lifetime rate	£8,400

Representing an effective tax rate on fund of $\dfrac{78,400}{500,000} = 15.68\%$

Of which 30% (the rate applicable to discretionary trusts) =   4.7 %

Giving tax payable on the £500,000 trust fund of   £23,500

42.23   Following a ten-year charge, exit charges in the next ten years are based on the effective rate at the last ten-year anniversary, that rate, however, being recalculated by reference to the nil rate threshold at the date of the distribution.

Example 6

Say the trustees at Example 5 made a distribution of £100,000 to a beneficiary on 1 April 2006, at which time the nil rate threshold had increased from £263,000 to, say, £270,000.

Rate applicable on
distribution is:

10 year total as in Example 5	655,000
Nil rate threshold	270,000
	£385,000

Inheritance tax at 20% lifetime rate	£79,000

Representing an effective tax rate of $\dfrac{77,000}{500,000} = 15.4\ \%$

Of which 30% (the rate applicable to discretionary trusts) =	4.62%	
£100,000 @ 4.62%		4,620
Less: $\dfrac{34\ \text{quarters remaining in 10 year period}}{40\ \text{quarters in 10 year period}}$		3,927
Inheritance tax payable out of the £100,000 distribution is		£693

42.24   Where the discretionary trust is created at death in order to utilise but not exceed the then threshold, a distribution within the first ten years will not attract any inheritance tax. See Example 7.

Example 7

	£
Initial value of settled fund at death on 31 August 2004	263,000
Trustees' nil rate threshold at time of distribution will not be less than	263,000
Amount on which rate on distribution will calculated	—

So rate on distributions in the first 10 years is 0%

The 10-year charge will apply to the value of the fund at 31 August 2014, and exit charges on distributions in the 10 years after than will be based on the rate at the 10 year anniversary, as reduced by the quarterly discount.

42.25   Another use of a discretionary trust created by a will is to leave the estate on discretionary trusts, with the trustees being aware of (but not bound by) the preferred wishes of the testator as to its distribution. Distributions out of the trust fund within two years after death are regarded as under the will, and not as a distribution from the discretionary trust. The distributions must not be made within the three months after death but must be made before there is an interest in possession in the property.

Accumulation and maintenance trusts

42.26   These are a special sort of discretionary trust giving flexibility to a parent or grandparent in providing funds for the benefit of children.

Income tax (TA 1988, s 660B)

42.27   The rule that a parent remains chargeable to income tax on income from funds settled on his own unmarried children under age 18 does not apply where the capital and income are required to be held on accumulation and maintenance trusts for the benefit of the children, except to the extent that any income is paid to or for the benefit of the child (for example for education or maintenance). Payments of capital to or for the benefit of the child are also treated as income to the extent that the trust fund has any undistributed income. Any such income or capital payments are treated as the parent's income and taxed on him (unless, together with any other income from the parent, they do not exceed £100 in any tax year).

Since the trust is a discretionary trust, the trustees pay tax at 32.5% (25% before 6 April 2004) on tax credit inclusive dividend income and 40% (34% before 6 April 2004) on other income accumulated within the fund. When the accumulated income is transferred when the child reaches the appropriate age, it does so as capital and thus does not attract any further income tax at that time.

Capital gains tax (TCGA 1992, ss 165, 260)

42.28   The capital gains tax position of an accumulation and maintenance trust is the same as that of any other discretionary trust (see 42.19) except as regards the availability of gifts holdover relief. Since the transfer into the trust is potentially exempt from inheritance tax, gifts holdover relief is not available to the transferor unless the gift is of qualifying business assets (see 42.8). There is also a gifts relief problem when assets leave the trust. There is a specific provision enabling gains on non-business assets to be held over and treated as reducing a beneficiary's capital gains tax cost where the assets are transferred out of an accumulation and maintenance trust, but this relief is not available unless the beneficiary becomes entitled to both capital and income of the trust at the same time.

Where, as is often the case, the child becomes entitled to income at 18 and capital at say 25, the relief is only available on qualifying business assets. A possible way of avoiding the problem is for the trust deed to specifically deny the entitlement to income at age 18.

Inheritance tax (IHTA 1984, ss 70, 71)

42.29 Accumulation and maintenance settlements receive favourable treatment for inheritance tax where one or more of the beneficiaries will become entitled to the trust property (or to the income from it) not later than age 25. To qualify for this treatment, the settlement must either terminate as an accumulation and maintenance settlement not more than 25 years after its creation or all the beneficiaries must have a common grandparent. If such beneficiaries do not survive, their children or widows/widowers can stand in their shoes. 'Children' includes step-children, adopted children and illegitimate children.

The advantages of such a settlement are that the transfer into it is a potentially exempt transfer, there is no ten-yearly charge on the trust funds and no exit charges when a distribution is made to a beneficiary or when a beneficiary becomes absolutely entitled to the trust property or to the income from it. The transfer of property from the settlement to the beneficiaries is thus free of tax in these circumstances.

Where the 25-year rule applies, then if the trust does not terminate as an accumulation and maintenance trust before the expiry of the 25-year period, inheritance tax is payable at up to 21% at that time and thereafter the trust is subject to exit charges and ten-yearly charges in the same way as other discretionary trusts (see 42.20).

Example 8

On 1 August 2004 taxpayer transferred £300,000 into an accumulation and maintenance trust for his three children aged 8, 10 and 15, each being entitled to an equal share of the capital upon attaining age 25 but the trustees being able to make advances of capital in the meantime. He had not made any gifts in the previous three years.

The inheritance tax position is:			
Settlor			
1.8.2004	Gift to accumulation and		
	maintenance trust		300,000
	Annual exemption	2004/05	3,000	
		2003/04	3,000	6,000
	Potentially exempt		
	transfer		£294,000
Accumulation and maintenance trust			
Tenth anniversary 1.8.2014		No inheritance tax charge	
Advances of capital to children before		No inheritance tax charge	
they reach age 25			
Distribution of capital entitlement upon			
each child attaining age 25		No inheritance tax charge	

Trusts and estates — self-assessment

42.30   Trustees and personal representatives are subject to the normal self-assessment rules in relation to their tax liabilities (see CHAPTER 9). They are required to make payments on account half-yearly on 31 January and 31 July, based on the previous year's net income tax (unless covered by the de minimis thresholds), and a balancing payment, including any capital gains tax, on the following 31 January (the due date for submission of the tax return).

There is a special tax return (SA900) for trusts and estates. The format of the return broadly follows that for individuals, with supplementary pages for various types of income and gains and a tax calculation working sheet. Only some supplementary pages are sent with returns. Others need to be requested from the Revenue. Trust returns require certain additional information to be provided, such as details of capital added to a settlement, capital payments to minor children of the settlor, discretionary payments to beneficiaries, and changes in personal representatives and trustees.

Discretionary trusts liable at the Schedule F trust rate of 32.5% and/or the 40% rate (see 42.18) have to maintain details of the 'pool' of tax they have paid, which covers an equivalent amount of tax deducted from subsequent payments made to beneficiaries. Details of the tax pool are included in the tax calculation working sheet. Any tax paid directly in respect of the Schedule F rate or the 40% rate enters into the calculation of the half-yearly payments on account for the following year.

Position of infants

42.31   Where income is paid to beneficiaries (and is not treated as a parent's income), it is after deduction of tax at 10% if it relates to dividends,

20% if it relates to other savings income and at the basic rate for other income, except for discretionary trusts where the rate on all income is 40% (34% before 6 April 2004). If the beneficiaries are infants, a repayment of tax is often due because of their personal allowances, although the 10% tax on dividend income is not repayable. The parent or guardian can make the repayment claim, or it may be made by the beneficiary himself in respect of the previous six years on his reaching age 18.

Trust for a dependent relative

42.32   Establishing a trust is a useful way in which the needs of a dependent relative can be provided for by setting aside a capital sum, the income from which is used for that purpose.

The capital sum is put into an interest in possession trust for the lifetime of the dependant, with the capital of the trust reverting to the settlor or his spouse upon the death of the dependant. In the meantime the income is used for the needs of the dependant. Since the settlor has a future interest in the trust, however, the income will be treated as the settlor's and taxed at his or her tax rate.

When a life interest comes to an end, the supporting capital would normally be reckoned for inheritance tax within the tax calculation of the life tenant, but there is an exemption where the capital reverts to the settlor in his/her lifetime or to his/her spouse (see 42.17).

For the purposes of capital gains tax, any gains by the trustees are taxed as if they were those of the settlor (since a future right has been retained) and the assets in the trust are regarded as acquired by the settlor upon the death of the relative at such value as gives neither a profit nor loss for tax purposes to the trustees. The value is not uplifted to market value on the death of the life tenant as it would normally be.

This arrangement can as easily be used to provide a house for the occupation of a dependent relative as to produce spendable income (see 34.6). If the relative remains in occupation of the property until death, then the fact that there is no uplift to market value for capital gains tax when the property reverts to the settlor would mean that the settlor would face a capital gains charge on eventual sale of the property. It may be possible to avoid this charge by creating a successive life interest for the settlor rather than absolute ownership. It is considered that the life interest would satisfy the 'reverter to settlor' requirement for inheritance tax. Whether or not a successive life interest for the settlor is created, if the house was sold during the lifetime of the dependent relative, the private residence capital gains tax exemption would apply to the trustees, producing a tax-free increase in the trust fund, and the funds would then remain in the trust to be used for the dependant's benefit, say for the payment of care home fees.

Stamp duty (FA 2003, Schs 3, 16)

42.33   From 1 December 2003, stamp duty is no longer relevant other than for transactions relating to shares and securities (see 6.1). Under the stamp duty land tax provisions, the trustees are responsible for the tax liability in respect of land transactions (other than for bare trusts), even though they are not the beneficial owners (see 42.12). Stamp duty land tax is not payable where land and buildings are transferred to a beneficiary.

Tax points

42.34

- Personal representatives have to include in their inheritance tax account details of earlier transfers affecting the inheritance tax liability. Providing they have done everything possible to trace potentially exempt transfers made by the deceased in the seven years before his death and disclose them to the Revenue, then once they have received a certificate of discharge and distributed the estate, they will not usually be asked to pay the tax if untraced transfers subsequently come to light.

- Where a person entitled to trust income has unused personal allowances, it is better to arrange for income to be paid direct to him, because the income will not then be depleted by trust expenses, and he will get a higher income tax repayment where tax has been deducted.

- Since inheritance tax is less where the value transferred is lower, it is usually beneficial to transfer assets that are growing in value earlier rather than later, giving the intended beneficiary an interest for the time being in the income through an appropriately drawn trust. A transfer to such a trust is potentially exempt, but even if the donor dies within seven years the benefit of transferring assets when their value was lower is retained. The supporting capital can eventually be transferred free of inheritance tax to the person enjoying the income.

  Assets transferred into or out of the trust may qualify for business gifts holdover relief (see 4.27 to 4.30), but otherwise the capital gains tax effect must be considered. From 1 December 2003 gifts holdover relief is no longer available on gifts to trusts in which the settlor has an interest (see 42.9).

- Where assets are put into a discretionary trust, the trustees may pay the inheritance tax rather than the settlor. If they do, and dependent upon the type of asset, the tax may be payable by instalments (see 5.29). You also avoid having to treat the amount settled as its gross equivalent when calculating the tax.

- If you are entitled to trust income that you do not need and you would like some or all of the underlying capital to go to the person who will eventually be entitled to it, you could disclaim your entitlement to the income on the appropriate amount of capital. Part of the disclaimed amount would be covered by inheritance tax annual exemptions if not otherwise used and the balance would be treated as a potentially exempt transfer, so there would be no immediate tax charge. If the potentially exempt transfer was within your nil rate band, no tax would be payable even if you died within seven years (although in that event the nil rate band available on your death would be correspondingly reduced). If the potentially exempt transfer was above the nil rate band, tax would be payable by the donee if you did not survive the seven-year period, but it would be reduced if you had survived for more than three years (see 5.12).

- For capital gains tax purposes, those entitled to the assets in a deceased's estate acquire them at market value at the date of death. If assets have fallen in value since death, losses made by the personal representatives on disposal cannot be used by the beneficiaries. If, on the other hand, the assets themselves, rather than cash proceeds from their sale, are transferred to beneficiaries, losses on disposal by the beneficiaries will be their own allowable losses for capital gains purposes.

- Where a trust in which a settlor has an interest realises gains that are covered by available losses, there is no charge on the settlor and the trust's available losses will be used only to the extent necessary to leave gains covered by the trust's annual exemption of £4,100. If, however, gains exceed losses, the gains net of the full amount of the available losses will be taxed on the settlor and the trust's annual exemption will be wasted.

- For additional tax points on trusts, see CHAPTER 35.

43

Charities and
charitable trusts

Formation and legal status

43.1   In order to register a charity, it is necessary to satisfy the Charity Commissioners in England and Wales, or the Inland Revenue in Scotland and Northern Ireland, that the purposes or objects of the organisation fall entirely under one or more 'heads of charity'. These are as follows.

The relief of poverty.
The advancement of education.
The advancement of religion.
Other purposes beneficial to the community.

A charity may be a limited company with a separate legal existence independent of its members, or an unincorporated association which has no separate status so that assets must be held on its behalf by trustees.

Although charitable trusts are frequently national organisations, such as the various children's organisations and bodies for medical research and care, there is nothing to prevent individuals creating and registering a charitable trust which remains under their control as trustees, so long as the 'heads of charity' are satisfied.

Tax status

43.2   The tax status of charities is outlined below. Charities are within the self-assessment system, although the Revenue issue returns only to a sample of charities each year. If a charity that does not receive a return has a tax liability, it is under the usual obligation to notify the Revenue.

Income tax and corporation tax (TA 1988, ss 505, 506; FA 2000, s 46)

43.3   Registered charities are exempt from tax on investment income used only for charitable purposes.

Trading profits are exempt where the trading is in the course of actually carrying out the charity's primary purpose. This includes trading that is mainly carried on by the beneficiaries of the charity. Charities are also exempt from tax on other trading income used solely for charitable purposes if it is less than the smaller of £50,000 and 25% of the charity's income, or in any event if it is less than £5,000 (the amounts of £50,000 and £5,000 being reduced pro rata for accounting periods of less than twelve months). This may remove the need in some cases for charities to have a trading subsidiary (as to which see 43.15), although charities must still consider their position under charity law. By concession C4, the profits of fundraising events such as bazaars, jumble sales, etc., by the charities or by voluntary organisations are exempt providing the conditions set out in the concession are satisfied. The concession covers all events covered by the VAT exemption (see 43.5), providing the profits are used for charitable purposes.

If a charity deposits money with a bank or building society, the bank or building society will pay the interest in full without deducting income tax.

See 36.12 for details of National Savings Treasurer' Accounts for non-profit-making bodies.

See 40.19 for the provisions relating to life policies held by charitable trusts.

Charities, along with other non-taxpaying shareholders, are no longer entitled to repayment of the tax credits on dividends. To cushion the impact of the change, charities were able to claim compensation from the Revenue for years up to 2003/04 by way of a payment equal to a percentage of dividends received, the relevant percentages for 2002/03 and 2003/04 being 8% and 4% respectively.

Capital gains tax (TCGA 1992, s 256)

43.4   A charity is not liable to capital gains tax on gains arising on the disposal of assets where the gains are applied for charitable purposes.

Value added tax (VATA 1994, Sch 8 Groups 4, 12 and 15)

43.5   The general tax exemption for charities does not extend to VAT, and the detailed provisions need to be looked at carefully to ensure that the rules are complied with.

Where a charity makes taxable supplies it must register for VAT, subject to the normal rules relating to exempt supplies and taxable turnover (see CHAPTER 7). If a charity has a number of branches which are virtually autonomous, each branch having control over its own financial and other affairs, each branch is regarded as a separate entity for VAT purposes and is required to register only if its taxable supplies exceed the VAT threshold of £58,000 (£56,000 before 1 April 2004).

Income from one-off fundraising events, including admission charges, is normally exempt. Exemption is also available in respect of a series of events, providing not more than 15 events of the same kind are held in any one location in any year. (Small events do not count towards the limit providing aggregate takings for such events do not exceed £1,000 a week.) Where income is exempt, there is a corresponding restriction in the recovery of VAT on purchases and expenses for the event. Except for fund-raising events, admission charges are normally standard-rated. Where a charity supplies goods or services consistently below cost for the relief of distressed persons, for example, meals on wheels, such supplies are not regarded as being made in the course of business and hence are not liable to VAT. Sales of donated goods to the general public at charity shops etc. and donated goods sold only to disabled people or people receiving means tested benefits are zero-rated. Sales of bought-in goods are standard rated.

Membership subscriptions to 'bodies with aims of a political, religious, patriotic, philosophical or philanthropic nature' are exempt from VAT if the conditions are satisfied. Exemption does not apply where free admission is provided in return for the subscription. Where the members receive publications as part of their subscriptions, the relevant part of the subscription is treated as zero-rated, enabling the bodies to recover an appropriate part of their input VAT.

Certain national museums and galleries who offer free admission are able to claim a refund of the VAT they incur in connection with the provision of the free admission.

Certain supplies to charities may be zero-rated in specified circumstances, such as media advertising, building work (see below), motor vehicles, mechanical products and equipment supplied to those who provide care for the handicapped, aids for disabled people, medicinal products, and bathrooms provided for disabled people in day centres and other charity premises.

As far as buildings are concerned, zero-rating does not apply to new buildings bought by charities or to services provided in the construction of buildings for charities, unless the charity uses the building solely for charitable purposes (which means otherwise than in the course of a business), or as a village hall, or to provide social or recreational facilities for a local community. Any other use strictly falls foul of these provisions (for example, allowing someone to rent a room for a children's party), but by concession business use can be ignored where the non-business use of the building covers 90% or more of the time the building is normally available or of the available floor space, or where 90% or more of the people using the building are engaged solely on non-business activities. Even if zero-rating applies, it does not apply to the services of architects and surveyors, which are standard-rated.

As far as repair and maintenance work is concerned, the EU are presently looking at the UK's proposal to apply a reduced rate to repairs to listed places of worship, but it seems unlikely that the proposal will be accepted. In the meantime the UK had introduced a special grant scheme (the Listed Places of Worship Grant Scheme) enabling churches to receive a payment equivalent to a reduction in the VAT rate on repairs from 17.5% to 5%. The Chancellor has now announced that grants will be paid from 1 April 2004 to March 2006 to cover *all* VAT on the repair and maintenance of listed places of worship.

When buildings are rented, landlords have the option to charge VAT on rents except for buildings or parts of buildings used for charitable purposes (but the exception does not cover the charity's offices). The landlord is entitled to add VAT to existing rents unless the agreement specifically prevents him from doing so. In that event, the rent would have to be treated as VAT inclusive until such time as the landlord has a right under the agreement to increase it.

Customs have leaflets (701/1 and 701/6) on the subject of charities, which are available from local VAT offices.

Stamp duty (FA 1982, s 129; FA 2003, s 68 and Sch 8; FA 2004, s 302)

43.6   No stamp duty is payable on documents transferring assets to charities. Exemption also applies to the stamp duty land tax transactions of charities from 1 December 2003, providing the land is to be held for qualifying charitable purposes and is not being acquired for tax avoidance reasons. From 22 July 2004, exemption from stamp duty land tax will also apply to acquisitions by trusts and unit trusts where all the beneficiaries or unit holders are charities. The relief must be claimed in a stamp duty land tax return or amendment to a return, and it will be withdrawn if within three years the purchaser ceases to be a charity or the land is used other than for charitable purposes.

National insurance

43.7   Charities receive no special treatment. Employers' national insurance is dealt with in CHAPTER 13.

Business rates

43.8   There is both mandatory and discretionary relief from business rates on premises occupied by a registered charity and used for charitable purposes. 'Charitable purposes' includes shops used for the sale of goods donated to the charity. The mandatory relief is 80% and discretionary relief can increase this to 100%, so that no rates are payable. Discretionary relief up to 100% may be awarded by local authorities to various non-profit-making organisations such as schools and colleges, societies concerned with literature and the arts, and recreational clubs and societies.

Giving to charity

Gift aid donations by individuals, including covenanted payments (TA 1988, s 660A(9); FA 1990, s 25; FA 1998, s 48; FA 2004, s 83; SI 2000/2074)

43.9   Tax relief at the payer's top tax rate is available for charitable donations under the gift aid scheme. The scheme covers both single donations and a series of donations, including covenanted payments. There is no minimum limit for gift aid payments, although charities may stipulate their own minimum limit for donations to be brought within the scheme. Gift aid relief is available not only to UK residents but also to non-residents who are liable to UK tax. The Revenue remind taxpayers about gift aid when sending them their self-assessment returns, also indicating that a claim may be made in the return for relief to be given in the tax year to which the return relates for gift aid payments made between 6 April following that tax year and the date the return is submitted (see 43.10). Taxpayers expecting a tax repayment for 2003/04 or a later year will be able to indicate on their tax returns that they want a nominated charity to have all or part of the repayment. They will also be able to indicate that gift aid should apply to the donation. The donation will be regarded as made when the charity receives the payment and it is not possible to treat the gift as made in the tax year to which the return relates.

Donations do not qualify for relief if the donor receives a benefit from the gift (such as membership benefits), unless the benefits come within stipulated limits (broadly 2½% of the donation up to a maximum of £250). Benefits consisting of the right of admission to the property of a heritage or wildlife conservation charity (such as the National Trust) are presently ignored. This provision has, however, enabled such charities effectively to turn one-off admission charges into gift aid payments. The Government intends to restrict the application of the concession to rights of admission for not less than a specified period, with no restriction on the number of visits. They propose to make these changes at a later date (not earlier than April 2005) after consultation with affected charities.

To qualify for gift aid relief, donors are required to make a declaration. The declaration may cover any number of donations already made or to be made. The declaration need not be written, and may be made by telephone or over the internet, providing the donor's name and address is obtained. Where a donation is given by oral declaration, however, the charity must send the donor a written record of the oral declaration, which will explain that in order to retain the tax relief the donor must have a tax liability equivalent to the tax deducted from the donation. The charity must include a note that the donor may cancel the declaration within 30 days.

In view of the fact that tax relief on gift aid donations is given at the payer's top rate of tax, a higher rate taxpayer may be persuaded to increase his donation, thus making a larger contribution to the charity. See Example 1.

Example 1

Higher rate taxpayer makes a cash gift to charity of £1,000. The tax position is:

	£	£
Cash gift	1,000	1,000
Basic rate tax treated as deducted (22/78)	282	282
Amount received by charity	1,282	1,282
Tax saved at 40%		513
Net cost to donor		769

If the donor was prepared to contribute £1,000 out of his after-tax income, he could increase the cash gift to £1,300 as follows:

	£	£
Cash gift	1,300	1,300
Basic rate tax treated as deducted (22/78)	367	367
Amount received by charity	1,667	1,667
Tax saved at 40%		667
Net cost to donor		1,000

Thus the charity would receive extra income of (1,667 – 1,282 =) £385 at an extra cost to the donor of £300.

In fact the tax saving to a higher rate taxpayer may be even higher than 40% where the donations are paid out of savings income, the possible saving being 42% on donations paid out of interest and 44.5% on donations paid out of dividends (see Example 3).

Donations are treated as being net of basic rate tax, but in order to retain the tax relief, donors must be liable to pay an equivalent amount of income tax (including tax at rates below the basic rate) and capital gains tax. In order to put this into effect, donations are not deducted from income in calculating the tax position for the year. Instead the basic rate threshold is increased by the gross amount of the donations. (The gross charitable donations are, however, regarded as reducing income for age-related allowances — see 34.3.)

Where the amount of income tax and capital gains tax chargeable after deducting personal allowances does not cover the tax deducted from the donation, the personal allowances are restricted accordingly. If despite the restriction of personal allowances there is still insufficient tax payable, the donor is liable to pay tax equal to the shortfall. (For this purpose the amount of tax taken into account is before deducting the 10% relief on married couple's age allowance and dividend tax credits. Any unused married couple's allowance is available to transfer to the wife.) See Examples 2 to 4. The Revenue have the right to issue an assessment to collect the tax due. They may not do so if the amount involved is small but where a tax repayment is being claimed, the repayment is restricted to cover the amount due because of the charitable payment.

In addition to cash gifts, relief is also available where shares and securities or land and buildings are given to charity (see 43.12). This relief is given by deducting the value of the gifted assets from income, rather than extending the basic rate band.

Example 2

In 2004/05 unmarried taxpayer aged under 65 has income as shown below and makes charitable donations of £780 net, £1,000 gross.

				£
Interest				12,745
Dividends (tax credit inclusive)				2,000
				14,745
Personal allowance				4,745
Taxable income				10,000
Tax thereon:	Interest	2,020	@ 10%	202.00
		5,980	@ 20%	1,196.00
	Dividends	2,000	@ 10%	200.00
		10,000		1,598.00

Since the tax chargeable exceeds the £220 retained out of the donations, the taxpayer is entitled to keep that amount, even though no basic rate tax is chargeable on his income.

Example 3

In 2004/05 unmarried taxpayer aged under 65 has income as shown below and makes charitable donations of £2,340 net, £3,000 gross.

	£
Earnings	28,745
Interest	5,000
Dividends (tax credit inclusive)	7,000
	40,745
Personal allowance	4,745
Taxable income	36,000

Tax thereon:		£		£
	Non-savings income:	2,020	@ 10%	202.00
		21,980	@ 22%	4,836.00
	Interest	5,000	@ 20%	1,000.00
	Dividends (part)	5,400	@ 10%	540.00
		34,400	*	
	Dividends (balance)	1,600	@ 32.5%	520.00
		36,000		7,098.00

* Basic rate band extended by £3,000 because of charitable donation.

The extension of the basic rate band has saved tax of £3,000 @ 22.5% = £675, in addition to the £660 basic rate relief given by deduction, because an extra £3,000 of dividend income is below the basic rate threshold. The net cost of the gift is therefore (3,000 – 660 – 675 =) £1,665. The tax saving amounts to 44.5%, i.e. basic rate tax 22% + Schedule F tax (32.5% – 10% =) 22.5%.

Had the savings income been wholly interest of £12,000, with no dividends, £3,000 of interest income would have moved below the basic rate threshold and the tax saving would have been 42%, i.e. the basic rate of 22% plus the reduction from 40% to 20% in the tax charged on the interest.

Had all the income been earned income, the tax saving would have been 40%, i.e. the basic rate of 22% plus the reduction of 18% in the tax on the earnings (40% – 22%).

Example 4

In 2004/05 married taxpayer aged 72 whose wife is 69 has income as shown below and makes charitable donations of £780 net, £1,000 gross.

			£
Pensions			9,200
Dividends (tax credit inclusive)			500
			9,700
Personal allowance			6,830
Taxable income			2,870

		£		£
Tax thereon: Non-savings income:		2,020	@ 10%	202.00
		350	@ 22%	77.00
Dividends		500	@ 10%	50.00
		2,870		329.00

	£
Less: Married couple's allowance 5,725 @ 10% = 572.50, but restricted to	109.00
Tax chargeable (being equal to tax deducted from covenant)	220.00
Less: Dividend tax credits	50.00
Net tax payable	170.00

Surplus married couple's allowance transferred to wife (572.50 – 109.00 =) £463.50.

Carryback election for gift aid payments (FA 2002, s 98)

43.10   For gift aid donations made on or after 6 April 2003, a taxpayer may claim to be treated as if the donation had been made in the previous tax year. The claim must be made on or before the date the tax return for the previous year is sent in and not later than 31 January in the tax year in which the gift was made. Provision is made in tax returns for the claim to be made (see 9.27 and 43.9). The relief for the carried back amount will reduce the tax payable for the previous year and the normal treatment of backdated claims in 9.5 will not apply.

Gift aid donations by limited companies (including covenanted payments) (TA 1988, ss 338, 339)

43.11   The gift aid provisions enable companies to obtain tax relief when they make payments to charity. As for individuals, payments under the gift aid provisions by companies include covenanted payments. Companies are not required to deduct tax from any of their charitable payments and the full amount of the payment is deducted from the profits of the company in calculating corporation tax payable for the accounting period in which the payment was made. (See 43.15 for the special provisions for payments by a company owned by a charity.)

The same provisions apply as for individuals (see 43.9) where the company receives a benefit from the gift. Additional restrictions apply where the company is a close company to prevent the company receiving a repayment of the gift or either the company or a connected person receiving benefits in excess of stipulated limits.

See 43.12 for the treatment of gifts in kind.

The after-tax cost to the company in the year to 31 March 2005 depends on whether the company is paying tax at 30%, 19%, the marginal small companies' rate of 32.75%, or the marginal starting rate of 23.75%. The cost may indeed be 100% if the company's profits are £10,000 or less, because the starting rate for such profits is 0%, or if the company has no taxable profits, because in that case loss relief cannot be claimed for charitable payments (except within a group of companies by way of group relief).

Gifts in kind, including stocks and shares and land and buildings (TA 1988, ss 83A, 587B, 587C; TCGA 1992, s 257; CAA 2001, s 63, FA 2004)

43.12   If businesses make gifts of their stock or plant and machinery to charities, they do not have to bring amounts into account as trading receipts or disposal proceeds for capital allowances.

Relief is available against income for gifts to charities of shares and securities that are listed or dealt in on a recognised stock exchange (which includes AIM shares), units in unit trusts, shares in open-ended investment companies, interests in offshore funds and gifts of UK land and buildings. The amount of the relief is the net benefit received by the charity (which will normally be the market value of the gifted assets), plus any incidental costs of making the gift. If a gifted building is a business asset on which capital allowances have been claimed, it would be treated as disposed of for market value, which would probably trigger a balancing charge, reducing the value of the tax relief for the gift accordingly. The relief is given to individuals by deducting it in calculating taxable income and to companies by deducting it as a charge on income. If the donor receives a benefit from the gift, the amount deductible from income is reduced accordingly.

Gifts in kind to charities are exempt for capital gains purposes, so neither a chargeable gain nor allowable loss will arise.

Payroll deduction scheme (TA 1988, ss 86A, 202; FA 2000, s 38)

43.13   Employees can authorise participating employers to deduct a stipulated amount from their earnings before tax, for passing on to charities chosen by the employee, through Revenue approved charity agencies with which the employer has made an arrangement. The employee thus receives full tax relief for the contributions made. There is no limit on the amount that may be deducted under the scheme. The charity agencies are required to pass on the donations to the relevant charities within 60 days of receiving them. For the four years from 2000/01 to 2003/04 the agencies added a supplement of 10% to the amounts paid to the charities, recovering the supplement from the Revenue. Voluntary payments to the agency by the employer to cover running costs are allowed in calculating the employer's taxable profits.

Inheritance tax (IHTA 1984, ss 23, 58, 70, 76)

43.14   All gifts to charity are exempt for inheritance tax purposes whether made in lifetime, on death or out of a discretionary trust.

Where the charity is a discretionary trust, inheritance tax is not payable by the trustees unless property leaving the trust is used for a non-charitable purpose.

Companies owned by charities (TA 1988, s 339(7AA)–(7AC))

43.15   Many charities have fund-raising subsidiaries that covenant their entire profits to the charity. As indicated in 43.11, relief is available for gift aid and covenanted payments made during a company's accounting period, but the total profits will not be known until after the end of the period. Special rules apply to charity-owned companies. A claim may be made by such companies for gift aid donations and covenanted payments to be treated as made within an accounting period falling wholly or partly within the nine months before the payment was made.

Employees seconded to charities etc. (TA 1988, s 86)

43.16   The salaries of employees temporarily seconded to charities, local education authorities or other approved educational bodies may be deducted as a business expense even though, because of the secondment, the salaries are not paid wholly and exclusively for the purposes of the trade.

Intermediary charities

43.17   Individuals and companies may want to give regularly to several charities, but may not want to commit themselves to any one of them. As well as making one-off payments under the gift aid provisions (see 43.9 and 43.11), there are two ways of achieving this and still retaining the tax advantages. The simplest way is to make payments to an intermediary organisation such as the Charities Aid Foundation. You can tell the organisation which particular charities you want to benefit. The organisation will, if you wish, make annual payments to your chosen charities by standing order, which may significantly reduce your own administration of your charitable giving. Alternatively, and especially where the size of the donation is more significant, it is possible for individuals or companies to set up their own intermediary charity. A simple charitable trust whose objects include all the four charitable heads (see 43.1) can be set up relatively easily although it is essential to have proper professional advice. Additionally, for small amounts, the payroll deduction scheme may enable the recipient charity to be varied.

Community amateur sports clubs (FA 2002, s 58 and Sch 18; FA 2004, s 56)

43.18   Some sports clubs may be able to satisfy the tests for charitable status. For those who do not, or who do not wish to apply to be charities, they may be able to register with the Revenue as community amateur sports clubs (CASCs), which will entitle them to various tax exemptions and reliefs. Registration is available to non-profit making amateur sports clubs that are open to the whole community and provide facilities for, and promote participation in, one or more eligible sports. CASCs are exempt from corporation tax on all interest and gift aid income, trading income (before expenses) of up to £30,000 (£15,000 before 1 April 2004), property income (before expenses) of up to £20,000 (£10,000 before 1 April 2004) and capital gains on the disposal of assets.

Donations to a CASC qualify for tax relief under the gift aid provisions (see 43.9 and 43.11), and the relief for business gifts of stock or plant and machinery applies (see 43.12). The capital gains exemption for gifts in kind to charities and the inheritance tax exemption for gifts to charities also apply (see 43.12 and 43.14). From 1 April 2004 CASCs are entitled to 80% mandatory relief from business rates.

Abuse of charity tax reliefs (TA 1988, ss 505, 506 and Sch 20)

43.19   A charity's tax relief may be restricted if it uses its funds for non-charitable purposes, or makes payments to overseas bodies without taking reasonable steps to ensure that they are used for charitable purposes, or makes certain loans or investments for tax avoidance rather than for the benefit of the charity. Where a charity receives a grant from another charity, the grant is chargeable to tax unless it is used for charitable purposes.

Tax points

43.20

- If you set up your own charitable trust, the trustees must not profit from their position or allow their duties and responsibilities to conflict with their personal interests. You can, however, appoint a professional trustee, such as a solicitor or accountant, and an appropriate charging clause in the trust deed will enable his fees to be paid.

- Although gift aid donations may be evidenced by a simple declaration (possibly made by telephone or via the internet), you must be a taxpayer to be able to retain tax relief on the donation. If you make an oral donation the charity must send you a written record. They must keep detailed records to enable the Revenue to check that the conditions for relief have been satisfied. Charities receiving regular amounts in cash (notably church collections) must have a system that demonstrates that the donations have been received.

- For the paying company to get relief from corporation tax for an accounting period on a charitable payment, the payment must be made in that accounting period, except for charity-owned companies, who obtain relief for payments made up to nine months after the end of the accounting period.

- 'Charity affinity cards', i.e. credit cards on which some of the money you spend goes to a charity, will not cause the charity to have a tax liability if the money is channelled through a trading subsidiary that donates its income to the charity. For VAT purposes, Customs will usually treat one-fifth of the charity's income as liable to VAT as income from promotional activities and the remaining four-fifths does not attract VAT. Alternatively charities may in some circumstances be able to treat the whole supply as exempt from VAT.

44

Subcontractors in the construction industry

Employed or self-employed?

44.1   Although this chapter deals with the special scheme for contractors and subcontractors in the construction industry, the scheme has no relevance where the worker concerned should in fact be classified as an employee. The IR35 provisions requiring personal service companies to account for tax and national insurance on deemed pay if an employee would have been treated as employed by a client of the company if he had contracted directly with the client (see 19.3) also need to be taken into account. Where the IR 35 rules apply, the tax and national insurance on the deemed payment is due by 19 April following the tax year, whereas subcontractors may also have suffered tax under the construction industry scheme, such tax not being repayable until accounts have been submitted.

The decision as to whether someone is employed or self-employed is often difficult to make (see 19.1), particularly in the construction industry, but the consequences of getting it wrong can be extremely serious. There is a special version of leaflet IR 148 'Are your workers employed or self-employed?' for contractors in the construction industry, which outlines the factors to be taken into account. In the event of reclassification, the worker's self-employed business will cease in the tax year of reclassification. See 10.2 for the treatment of construction industry employees supplied by agencies.

If contractors are found not to be complying with the PAYE regulations for those who should properly be treated as employees, they will have to account to the Revenue for the amount of the agreed underpayment (but not for earlier years unless there is clear evidence of evasion).

The consequences of reclassification are far-reaching and potentially extremely costly for contractors, not only in relation to tax but also in relation to employment law and health and safety law.

44.2   The construction industry scheme has been revised for the third time, the new provisions applying from a date to be fixed, expected to be April 2006 (see 44.11). In the meantime the present provisions continue.

Construction industry scheme (TA 1988, ss 559–567; SI 1993/743)

44.3   The construction industry scheme applies to contractors and sub-contractors — individuals, partners and companies — working in the construction industry.

Meaning of 'contractor'

44.4   'Contractor' has a wider meaning than just a construction company and covers many other businesses involved in construction work, but private householders and non-construction businesses that spend less than £1 million a year on construction work are excluded. Construction work includes installation, repairs, decorating and demolition. Work outside the UK is not included.

Scheme requirements before workers can be paid

44.5   Under the scheme a subcontractor must obtain from the Revenue either a registration card CIS4 or a tax certificate CIS5 or CIS6 in order to be paid by the contractor. The CIS4 cards and CIS6 tax certificates include a photograph of the user. CIS5 certificates are not personalised, but they will only be issued to companies that are plcs or subsidiaries of plcs, or companies or partnerships with a turnover of at least £1 million, or companies or partnerships who submit a satisfactory business case showing that they have a genuine administrative or commercial need for a CIS5 certificate. Even though a subcontractor holds a CIS4 card or tax certificate, contractors must be satisfied that the subcontractor is not to be regarded as an employee (see 44.1).

Tax certificates to enable payments to be made gross

44.6   In order to obtain a tax certificate, subcontractors must comply with detailed conditions, including those stated above for companies and partnerships who want a CIS5 certificate.

They must have complied promptly with their tax obligations for the previous three years, and will not be able simply to get up to date before applying. Even if they meet all other criteria, subcontractors will normally need to have an average turnover (net of materials) in excess of £30,000 per annum over a three year period to be entitled to gross payment. The limit for partnerships and companies is £30,000 multiplied by the number of partners/directors and, for close companies, shareholders, or alternatively £200,000 average annual turnover over a three-year period.

Alternatively businesses may show that their total net turnover over a period of six consecutive tax months in the twelve months before the date of the application is at least £21,000, multiplied by the number of partners or directors (and close company shareholders) where appropriate. This will obviously be the test applied to new businesses, who may apply as soon as their turnover reaches the prescribed level without waiting the full six months. Turnover from all construction activities and not just those within the scheme may be counted for the turnover tests.

Certificates obtained by passing the three-year test are normally valid for three years. Where the six-months test applies the certificate is valid only for one year. The Revenue are taking an increasingly hard attitude to the renewal of CIS6 certificates, and appear to have changed their view as to what constitutes a minor or technical failure. In particular certificates are being denied where PAYE payments have been more than 14 days late, even though no surcharges had been incurred. There is a right of appeal against a Revenue refusal to issue a certificate but the Revenue's view on late payment has been upheld in a recent decision of the Court of Appeal.

The tax certificate enables the subcontractor to be paid gross, providing the contractor satisfies himself that the certificate is valid. Subcontractors with CIS6 certificates should supply the contractor with a CIS24 voucher either for each payment received or on a monthly basis. For companies and partnerships with CIS5 certificates, contractors will record details of payments on a monthly CIS23 voucher. In either case, contractors will send one copy of the vouchers to the Revenue monthly and retain a copy for their records.

Registration cards and deduction of tax

44.7   Most subcontractors will not hold tax certificates. They will be issued with a CIS4 registration card if they complete a form, supply a photograph and attend an interview. They will be paid net of a deduction of 18% on account of tax and national insurance contributions. CIS4 cards may be either permanent or temporary. For temporary cards, contractors must note the expiry date in their records and ensure that payments are not made after that date unless a further valid card or tax certificate is produced. For tax months in which payments are made, contractors will complete three copies of taxed payment vouchers CIS25, one of which is sent to the Revenue, the second being issued to subcontractors within 14 days after the end of the tax month, showing the deductions made, and the third copy being retained.

Contractors' payments and returns etc.

44.8   Deductions under the scheme are normally paid over to the Revenue Accounts Office each month. Payments may instead be made quarterly if contractors expect their average payments of amounts due under the PAYE system and subcontractor deductions to be less than £1,500 a month. Interest is charged on underpayments as for PAYE (see 10.29). Even where payments are made quarterly, vouchers must be submitted monthly.

Contractors must make annual returns of payments made under the scheme. The conditions of the scheme are modified to provide for vouchers and returns to be submitted electronically. Failure to operate the scheme correctly could lead to contractors losing their own certificates, being required to pay the amount that should have been deducted, to the imposition of penalties (including a penalty of up to £3,000 for failing to check the validity of a registration card or tax certificate) and in some circumstances to criminal proceedings.

Subcontractors' accounts and returns – income tax

44.9   The subcontractor's earnings are brought into the self-employed accounts of the subcontractor, and the amount deducted becomes a payment on account of the tax and Class 4 national insurance due. The deduction by the contractor does not absolve the subcontractor from preparing accounts and submitting returns, and if his liability is greater than the amount deducted there is the possibility of interest and penalties if he has not complied with time limits for submission of returns and payment of tax and national insurance. Where tax and Class 4 national insurance has been overpaid, a repayment may be claimed in the subcontractor's tax return. For subcontractors who make up accounts to a date earlier than 5 April, repayment claims may be made before the end of the tax year, but before making a repayment the Revenue will ensure that the subcontractor's tax affairs are up to date and that all tax and Class 4 national insurance due for earlier years has been paid.

Tax position of company subcontractors

44.10   Tax deducted under the subcontractors' scheme from payments to companies is set off against monthly or quarterly amounts due to be paid by the company to the Revenue in respect of PAYE, NICs etc. and, where the subcontractor itself employs further subcontractors, subcontractors' scheme deductions.

New construction industry scheme (FA 2004, ss 57–77 and Schs 11, 12)

44.11   A revised construction industry scheme will come into operation from a date to be fixed by statutory instrument. It is intended that the new scheme will start from April 2006. Although the broad framework will remain the same, some significant changes will be made. The Government's objectives in revising the scheme are to reduce the regulatory burden on construction businesses, to improve compliance with tax obligations and to help construction businesses to get the employment status of their workers right. Much of the detail of the scheme will be in statutory instruments.

A key feature of the revised scheme will be the requirement for an employment status declaration to be made. The intention is to emphasise the seriousness of the contractor's responsibility to ensure whether the worker is a sub-contractor or an employee.

Under the revised scheme, registration cards and tax certificates will no longer be issued. Contractors will instead verify with the Revenue whether the person they are going to pay is registered for gross payment or payment under deduction of tax. The verification may be done by telephone or over the internet. Unlike the present scheme, contractors will be able to pay unregistered sub-contractors, but the deduction rate will be much higher (probably around 30%). There will no longer be any monthly submission of payment vouchers and instead contractors will submit periodic returns.

Tax points

44.12

- Where tax is deducted from the full labour content of a payment to a subcontractor, an overpayment will normally arise because of the expenses of the trade and because individuals will normally have personal allowances and the 10% tax rate band available (although on the other hand, Class 4 national insurance contributions will increase the liability).

- The definition of those covered by the scheme is wide. Fringe trades should check the legislation to see if they are included. If you get it wrong, you may have to pay the tax you should have deducted from the payments to subcontractors plus interest. If the workers should have been treated as employees, the position is even worse (see last tax point below).

- Under the provisions of the present scheme, subcontractors *cannot get paid at all* unless they produce either a registration card or a tax certificate. Furthermore, new businesses will find it very difficult to get a tax certificate, and when they have only a registration card they will be paid net of 18% tax. If the new business's own subcontractors have tax certificates they will have to be paid gross out of net payments received.

- Contractors should be very careful to ensure that the terms under which workers operate bring them within the self-employed category if they are to treat them as subcontractors. If workers are wrongly classified, the contractor could be held liable for the PAYE tax that should have been deducted, plus employers' and employees' national insurance contributions, and possibly penalties as well. Where a sub-contractor company is caught by the IR 35 personal service company rules, it is the subcontractor company rather than the contractor who suffers the burden of employer's PAYE and national insurance.

45

Main anti-avoidance provisions

Background

45.1   In addition to a wide range of specific anti-avoidance measures, the Revenue's powers to counter what they see as unacceptable ways of avoiding tax have been significantly strengthened by various court decisions. Schemes which include steps inserted purely for tax avoidance are almost certain to prove unsuccessful, although bona fide commercial arrangements will usually be effective provided that they do not breach any of the specific provisions.

The legislation relating to tax avoidance, and its interpretation in the courts, is necessarily complex, and what follows is only a brief indication. In addition to these specific provisions, much of the legislation granting reliefs has anti-avoidance measures within it, e.g. demergers, companies purchasing their own shares and the enterprise investment scheme. (These reliefs are dealt with in CHAPTER 29.) Most anti-avoidance legislation enables the Revenue to obtain information from third parties.

As will be seen from the coverage in this chapter, the present anti-avoidance rules are largely piecemeal and targeted at specific areas. The Government has considered introducing a general anti-avoidance provision, but this is not being proceeded with at present. A general provision has, however, been introduced in relation to stamp duty (see 45.29), and the Government is using a different approach in relation to other taxes by requiring 'promoters' to notify avoidance schemes (see 45.2 and 45.3).

A significant part of the present legislation is intended to prevent what is really income being taxed as a capital gain. Despite capital gains now being taxed at income tax rates, the distinction between income and capital remains important (e.g. for capital gains tax, taper relief, exchange of shares when a company is taken over, deferral of capital gains through investment in enterprise investment scheme companies or venture capital trusts etc.). On the other hand, income can be sheltered by, for example, a purchase of property in an enterprise zone, whereas a capital gain cannot, so that in certain circumstances, a capital gain may be less attractive than income, thereby turning some of the anti-avoidance legislation to the advantage of the taxpayer.

As well as measures affecting direct taxes, there are anti-avoidance provisions relating to VAT. Examples include provisions relating to multinational groups of companies, transfers of businesses as going concerns, business splitting, charity reliefs, the option to charge VAT on buildings, the treatment of staff hire, the margin scheme for second-hand goods, cash accounting, the capital goods scheme and exploitation by commercial sports clubs of the exemption for non-profit making organisations. There is also an anti-avoidance provision requiring non-UK businesses that reclaim UK VAT and then dispose of goods in the UK to be registered in the UK regardless of their turnover.

It is important to bear in mind that, despite many statements by the Government and the press that blur the distinction, tax *avoidance* is legal and tax *evasion* is illegal (see 1.5). The Government have to amend the law in order to block effective tax avoidance schemes. They have taken steps in the Finance Act 2004 to enable swifter action to be taken to counter avoidance schemes by requiring promoters and users to disclose them to the Revenue or Customs — see 45.2 and 45.3.

Disclosure of tax avoidance schemes (TMA 1970, s 98C; FA 2004, ss 290–302)

45.2   New rules are to be introduced, broadly from 1 August 2004, requiring 'promoters' who market certain schemes and arrangements to make a virtually immediate disclosure of information about them to the Revenue subject to special provisions allowing a longer period during the transition to new regime. Disclosure will be required where a main benefit of the scheme is obtaining a tax advantage and further conditions (to be stipulated in regulations) are met. The Revenue will register all such schemes and give each a reference number, which promoters must notify to their clients.

A 'promoter' is anyone who provides taxation services in the course of a trade, profession or business if he has responsibility for designing such schemes, or markets or promotes schemes designed by someone else. The provisions do not apply to professional legal advisers in relation to anything covered by legal professional privilege. Taxpayers will have to provide details of schemes themselves where they have purchased the scheme from an offshore promoter who has not made a disclosure or where the scheme has been devised in-house.

Taxpayers using the schemes will usually only be required to include the reference number of the scheme on their tax returns (except where they are required to notify as indicated above).

The taxes covered by the regulations are income tax, corporation tax and capital gains tax. Initially the rules are being used in relation to employment-related schemes and schemes relating to certain financial products. Approved share schemes and enterprise investment schemes are excluded. The financial products to which the rules apply include loans, derivative contracts, and shares other than ordinary shares.

A penalty of up to £5,000 applies for failure to disclose a scheme, or to provide a client with a reference number, plus a further daily penalty of up to £600 for continued failure. A penalty of £100 applies for taxpayers who fail to notify the Revenue of a scheme reference number, rising to £500 and £1,000 for repeated failures.

Disclosure of VAT avoidance schemes (VATA 1994, s 58A and Sch 11A; FA 2004, s 19 and Sch 2)

45.3   A new requirement has been introduced for businesses that use certain VAT avoidance schemes to disclose their use to Customs. There will be a statutory register of VAT avoidance schemes, each of which will have a reference number. Businesses with an annual turnover of £600,000 or more that continue to use such designated schemes must notify Customs. Various provisions associated with avoidance schemes will also be put on a statutory register. Businesses with a turnover of £10 million or more that use arrangements that include such a designated provision and have as a main purpose the obtaining of a tax advantage must also notify Customs. A penalty of up to £5,000 may be imposed for failing to notify use of a designated scheme, and a penalty of up to 15% of the VAT saving for failing to notify use of a scheme that includes a designated provision.

The provisions will come into force in August 2004 in relation to making the necessary regulations and otherwise from a date to be appointed by statutory instrument.

Cancelling tax advantage from transactions in securities (TA 1988, ss 703–709)

45.4   Where in consequence of a transaction in securities a person has obtained a tax advantage, then unless he shows that the transaction was for bona fide commercial reasons or in the course of making or managing investments, and that none of the transactions had as their main object, or one of their main objects, the realising of a tax advantage, that tax advantage may be nullified.

These provisions have been used particularly where elaborate schemes have been devised with the aim of extracting the undistributed profits of companies in a capital form. In view of the far reaching implications there is an appropriate clearance procedure which it is wise to follow wherever shares are being sold in closely controlled companies with significant distributable reserves.

The provisions of sections 703–709 do not apply until the Revenue serve a notice specifying the adjustment to be made, and taxpayers are not required to deal with the liability in their self-assessment returns, nor are the Revenue bound by the self-assessment enquiry time limits. See Revenue Tax Bulletin April 2000.

Avoiding income on securities (TA 1988, ss 730–738 and Sch 23A)

45.5 Someone who habitually times their sales of securities so that income is not received but is reflected in a capital surplus on sale may be treated as having received the income that has accrued on a day-to-day basis, and be charged to tax at the excess of the Schedule F upper rate of 32½% over the Schedule F ordinary rate of 10%. These provisions only apply to equities and preference shares, because interest is in any event treated as accruing on a day-to-day basis where other securities are sold, whether the sales have been habitual or not, under the provisions of the accrued income scheme — see 36.18. There are provisions to ensure that the legislation does not inhibit the properly controlled operation of the financial markets, and dividends on shares held as trading assets by share dealers are not within the anti-avoidance provisions because they are taxed as trading profits. There are provisions to prevent the rules relating to manufactured payments in respect of UK securities (which are largely relevant to companies trading in the financial markets) being used by individuals to generate tax-deductible manufactured payments coupled with non-taxable receipts.

There are also provisions preventing the purchase and sale of securities being used to create tax allowable trading losses or to enable tax-exempt persons to claim repayments.

Securities issued at a discount (FA 1996, Sch 13)

45.6 For private investors, special provisions apply to securities issued at a 'deep' discount. These are outlined at 38.25. The provisions do not apply to companies because separate rules apply to all of a company's 'loan relationships' (see 3.6).

Companies buying their own shares from trustees (TA 1988, s 686A)

45.7   There is a special treatment for shareholders who are trustees if a company makes distributions in the form of payments on the redemption, repayment or repurchase of its own shares, or on the purchase of rights to buy its own shares. The trustees are taxed on the tax-credit inclusive amount of such payments at the Schedule F trust rate of 32.5% (25% before 6 April 2004). This does not apply where trust income is treated as belonging to the settlor, or where the trust is a unit trust, charitable trust, or pension trust.

Change in ownership of a company

Trading losses (TA 1988, 768, 768A, 769)

45.8   Trading losses may not be carried forward where within a period of three years there is both a change in ownership of a company and a major change in the nature or conduct of its trade. The rules also apply where ownership changes after activities have sunk to a low level and before any significant revival. Similar provisions apply to prevent trading losses of an accounting period ending *after* the change of ownership being carried back to an accounting period beginning *before* the change.

There is a Statement of Practice (SP 10/91) giving the Revenue's interpretation of a 'major change in the nature or conduct of a trade'.

Capital loss buying and capital gains buying (TCGA 1992, ss 177A, 177B and Schs 7A, 7AA)

45.9   There are detailed and complex provisions to prevent groups of companies avoiding tax on capital gains by acquiring a company with capital losses and using the intra-group no gain/no loss rules to transfer assets to the purchased company before disposing of them outside the group. The provisions broadly restrict relief for unused losses brought forward at the time the company joins the group, and also for later losses on the disposal of assets owned by the company at that time, to gains on assets owned by the company before it joined the group, or acquired later (other than from a group company) for use in a pre-existing trade.

There are parallel provisions to prevent the reverse procedure, i.e. acquiring a company with realised gains in order to utilise unrealised group losses. Capital gains made by a company before it joins a group may only be reduced by losses made by the company before it joined the group and losses arising later in the same accounting period on assets held by the company when it joined the group.

There are also rules to prevent groups circumventing either the loss buying or gain buying provisions through the use of intermediate groups.

Schemes to avoid corporation tax liabilities (TA 1988, ss 767A, 767AA, 767B, 767C)

45.10   There are provisions to counteract schemes under which a company's trading assets are transferred to another group company prior to the sale of the first company and the new owners strip the company of the remaining cash assets, leaving the company unable to pay its corporation tax. Corporation tax liabilities arising before the sale of a company may in prescribed circumstances be collected from the previous owners. The provisions also apply to corporation tax liabilities arising after the sale if it could reasonably have been inferred at the time of the sale that they were unlikely to be met.

Pre-sale distributions etc. (TA 1988, Sch 18; TCGA 1992, ss 31–33, 170)

45.11   There are provisions to prevent companies reducing or eliminating capital gains by reducing the value of a subsidiary before its sale. Where unrealised gains are distributed by a subsidiary to its parent company as group income prior to the sale of the subsidiary, the parent company is treated as if it had received additional consideration of an equivalent amount. The provisions also cover the transfer of a subsidiary to a non-resident company in the group prior to its onward sale, where the subsidiary leaves the group within six years after being transferred to the non-resident company.

There are also provisions to prevent companies retaining a subsidiary within a group for capital gains purposes by means of issuing special types of shares, while selling commercial control of the company.

Abuse of concessions (TCGA 1992, ss 284A, 284B)

45.12   Where someone defers a gain under the capital gains provisions under a concession first published before 9 March 1999, or a later replacement concession with substantially the same effect, then if the deferred gain becomes chargeable (e.g. on the disposal of the asset) and the person on whom the gain arises seeks to avoid bringing it into charge, he is treated as having made a chargeable gain equal to the deferred gain in the tax year or company accounting period in which the deferred gain should have been brought back into charge. The person on whom the charge arises could be the same taxpayer or another taxpayer to whom the asset had been transferred with the benefit of capital gains deferral.

An example of the sort of abuse these measures counter is where a trader makes a gain on the sale of a business asset and incurs enhancement expenditure on an existing asset rather than buying another asset. Rollover relief to defer the gain (see 4.26) is not strictly available in these circumstances, but concession D22 enables the enhancement expenditure to be treated as the acquisition of a qualifying asset. Since the gain is deferred only by concession, the trader could not previously be compelled to bring it into account on the disposal of the asset on which the enhancement expenditure was incurred.

Dual resident investment companies (TA 1988, s 404; TCGA 1992, ss 171, 175)

45.13   Where an investment company is resident both in the UK and in another country, that company cannot surrender losses, charges, etc. under the group relief provisions (see 3.24). Such companies are also unable to take advantage of the various capital allowances provisions that would normally prevent transfers to them being treated as being at open market value.

For capital gains purposes, assets may not be transferred intra-group on a no loss/no gain basis if the transferee is a dual resident investment company. Nor may business assets rollover relief be claimed within a group in respect of assets acquired by a dual resident investment company.

Controlled foreign companies (TA 1988, ss 747–756 and Schs 24–26; SI 1998/3081)

45.14   A UK resident company is charged to tax in respect of the profits of a foreign company if the foreign company is controlled to a significant extent by companies or individuals resident in the UK, and pays tax in its country of residence at less than 75% of the amount that a UK resident company would pay, where the UK company and associates have at least a 25% stake in the foreign company. Companies paying tax under what are known as 'designer rate' tax regimes are automatically treated as being subject to a lower rate of taxation. The relevant designer rate regimes are specified in regulations and are in the Channel Islands, the Isle of Man and Gibraltar. Subject to what is said below, the controlled foreign companies rules do not apply if the foreign company satisfies one or more of certain tests as to acceptable distribution policy, exempt activities, public quotation or motive, or if its profits for a twelve-month period were less than £50,000. The acceptable level of distributions is 90% of taxable profits net of capital gains and foreign tax. There are provisions to prevent the rules being exploited by artificial schemes. The Revenue have the power to issue regulations designating certain foreign jurisdictions in which all controlled foreign companies will automatically be covered by the rules, regardless of whether one of the exemptions would otherwise apply.

Companies are required to make any necessary adjustments in their self-assessment tax returns. A clearance procedure is available to both trading and non-trading controlled foreign companies, and the Revenue publish comprehensive guidance notes to help companies comply with the rules.

Double taxation relief (TA 1988, ss 799, 801, 801A)

45.15   For UK companies entitled to double tax relief for underlying tax on dividends (see 41.26), the relief available is restricted where the companies have entered into an avoidance scheme aimed at artificially increasing the amount of the underlying tax. Further restrictions prevent the use of foreign 'mixer' companies, i.e. foreign holding companies interposed between a UK parent and overseas subsidiaries, to increase relief for underlying tax. The rate of underlying tax on any dividend passed up to such a foreign holding company will not be regarded as being higher than the UK corporation tax rate of 30%, although there are provisions to give additional relief in prescribed circumstances by allowing dividends to be pooled in a UK company, and also to enable foreign tax to be surrendered within a group of companies.

There are also anti-avoidance provisions to prevent banks and other financial traders getting excessive relief for foreign tax paid on overseas interest that is part of their trading profits.

Offshore funds (TA 1988, ss 756A–756C, 757–764 and Schs 27, 28; FA 1996, Sch 10 paras 4, 7; FA 2004, s 145 and Sch 26)

45.16   Gains on disposals of material interests in offshore funds by persons resident or ordinarily resident in the UK attract an income tax charge under Schedule D, Case VI instead of a capital gains tax charge, unless the offshore fund operates a full distribution policy (broadly 85% of its income). The income tax charge also arises on interests held at the taxpayer's death.

Where an investor switches from one class of investments to another, the switches are treated as disposals, and attract an income tax charge under Schedule D, Case VI or, where the fund operates a full distribution policy, a capital gains tax charge.

The rules for offshore funds have been modified for accounting periods ending after 22 July 2004 to align the calculation of profits against which distributions are measured more closely with profits for corporation tax, unless the offshore fund manager opts to continue with the existing rules. All but one of the investment restrictions applicable to offshore funds have been removed.

Transfer of assets abroad (TA 1988, ss 739–745); personal portfolio bonds (TA 1988, s 553C; SI 1999/1029)

45.17   The purpose of the transfer of assets provisions is to prevent an individual ordinarily resident in the UK avoiding UK tax by transferring income-producing property abroad in circumstances which enable him to benefit from the property either immediately or in the future, such as a transfer to trustees of a foreign settlement made by him, of which he is a beneficiary. The provisions also impose a charge when benefits go not to the transferor but to someone else, such as his children or grandchildren. The provisions apply to life policies held in trust in certain circumstances (see 40.10).

The legislation provides that the individual need not have been ordinarily resident at the time of the transfer, nor is it necessary for the transfer to have been for the purpose of avoiding income tax. This provision was aimed particularly at 'personal portfolio bonds', which are insurance policies where the policyholder or his adviser may select and vary the underlying investments. A broader and more punitive provision now applies to such bonds, bringing them within the 'chargeable events' provisions for life insurance policies. Although particularly aimed at offshore bonds, the revised provisions also catch UK bonds. The effect of the rules is that there will be an annual income tax charge on the bonds for each policy year other than the last year. The annual charge will be equal to 15% of a deemed gain equal to the total of the premiums paid and the total deemed gains from previous years, net of any taxable amounts withdrawn in earlier years. The gains are charged in the same way as other gains on insurance bonds (see 40.6), i.e. on the excess, if any, of higher rate tax over the 20% lower rate (excess over the basic rate before 6 April 2004), but top slicing relief is not available. The total amount of gains taxed under the yearly provisions will be deducted from any gain arising when the policy terminates. If gains arising during the life of a policy are reversed when the policy comes to an end, a compensating deduction will be made from taxable income.

Most bonds taken out before 17 March 1998 are excluded from the provisions, and policyholders who were not UK resident on 17 March 1998 will have at least 12 months after becoming resident to change the terms of the policy so that they are also excluded.

Sales at artificial prices (transfer pricing) and thin capitalisation (TA 1988, ss 770A and Sch 28AA; FA 1999, ss 85–87; FA 2004, ss 30–37 and Sch 5)

45.18   Where any sales take place between persons connected with each other, including partnerships and companies, at a price other than open market value, the sale price of the one and purchase price of the other must be adjusted to the open market value for tax purposes. Similarly, to prevent the excessive use of debt finance between connected companies, the thin capitalisation rules require non-arm's length interest payments between connected companies to be treated as distributions and therefore not deductible in arriving at profits. Both sets of provisions have previously applied only to transactions between UK and overseas companies.

Changes have been made in FA 2004 to bring the thin capitalisation provisions within the transfer pricing provisions from 1 April 2004 and to introduce exemptions for most small and medium-sized companies, but also to make the provisions applicable between UK companies. Any transfer pricing adjustments must be made in self-assessment tax returns. The normal penalties for fraudulent or negligent conduct apply, but the Revenue have announced that there will be a temporary relaxation until 31 March 2006 of penalties for failing to retain evidence to show that a result is an arm's length result.

Transactions between associated dealing and non-dealing companies (TA 1988, s 774)

45.19   This section prevents abuse through transfer of assets by denying relief to one company where no taxable profit arises in the other.

Disguising income from personal activities as capital (TA 1988, s 775)

45.20   This prevents those with high personal earning potential, such as entertainers, avoiding tax by means of contracting their services to a company in which they hold the shares and thereby turning income into capital by later selling the shares at a price reflecting the personal earnings.

Artificial transactions in land (TA 1988, ss 776–778)

45.21   The aim of this provision is 'to prevent the avoidance of income tax by persons connected with land or the development of land'. It enables land transactions to be taxed as trading or other income instead of as a capital gain.

Sale and lease-back of land (TA 1988, ss 779, 780)

45.22   Where land is sold and leased back, the deduction allowed for rent is limited to a commercial rent. A sale at an excessive price (subject to capital gains tax) cannot therefore be compensated by an excessive rent payment allowable in calculating taxable income.

Further, if a short lease (less than 50 years) is sold and leased back for 15 years or less, part of the sale price is treated as income, that part being (16 − n)/15 where n is the term of the new lease.

Rent factoring (TA 1988, ss 43A–43G)

45.23   Rent factoring schemes are in substance equivalent to bank loans but companies sought to treat the amounts received as capital receipts, so that the gains arising could be offset by losses or reliefs. The legislation now provides that lump sums received for giving up the right to future rental income are charged as rent under Schedule A. Exceptions are made so that the provisions do not affect genuine investment in property and capital allowances based finance leasing.

Leases other than land (TA 1988, ss 781–785)

45.24   Capital gains may in certain circumstances be treated as income, and rent payable is limited to a commercial rent.

Leases and capital allowances (TA 1988, s 384; CAA 2001, s 109)

45.25   Losses arising from capital allowances in a leasing trade carried on by individuals may only be set against non-leasing income if the loss arose in a trade to which the individual devotes substantially the whole of his time and which has been carried on for a continuous period of six months.

Where plant and machinery is leased outside the UK, the writing-down allowance is reduced from the normal 25% to 10%. There are also limitations placed on the nature of the lease.

Relief for interest (TA 1988, ss 786, 787)

45.26   There are provisions to block the artificial creation of allowable interest and to prevent tax relief being obtained on interest that would not otherwise qualify for tax relief by means of various devices such as converting the interest into an annuity.

Income tax charge on pre-owned assets (FA 2004, s 84 and Sch 15)

45.27   New provisions will apply from 2005/06 to impose an income tax charge where a taxpayer has the benefit of free or low-cost use of an asset that he has previously owned. The intention of the provisions is to counter schemes which avoid the inheritance tax charge on gifts with reservation, but it is widely considered that the measures are ill-considered and in many instances unfair, particularly as they relate to transactions that may have been undertaken as long ago as 1986.

The provisions will apply to land, chattels and gifts into trusts of intangible assets (which include cash). The charge for land will be based on the rental value and the charge for other assets will be calculated by applying the official rate of interest to the value of the asset, reduced in the case of chattels by any payments made for use of the asset and reduced in the case of intangible assets by any income tax or capital gains tax payable in respect of the assets. There is no charge if the value of the benefit is £5,000 per annum or less.

The provisions do not apply to property:

(a)   that ceased to be owned before 18 March 1986;

(b)   sold for an arm's length price;

(c)   given outright to the former owner's spouse (or former spouse);

(d)   transferred to a trust in which the spouse or former spouse has an interest in possession (providing the interest has not come to an end, other than on the death of the spouse or former spouse);

(e)   that was a cash gift towards the purchase of land or chattels, made at least seven years before the individual occupied the land or had use of the chattels;

(f)   where the transfer is within the inheritance tax annual or small gifts exemptions or the 'gifts for family maintenance' exemption (see 5.3);

(g)   that is still included in the taxpayer's estate for inheritance tax, for example because the property has been transferred to a trust in which the transferor has an interest in possession, or because of the gifts with reservation rules (as to which see 5.8);

(h)   previously owned only by virtue of a will or intestacy which has subsequently been varied by agreement between the beneficiaries.

The provisions do not apply to those who are not resident in the UK, nor to overseas property in relation to someone who is UK resident but domiciled abroad.

Transitional provisions allow taxpayers to elect for the charge on land and chattels not to apply to specified property, but the property will then be treated as remaining in their estate for inheritance tax so long as they continue to enjoy it. The time limit for making the election is 31 January following the tax year for which the income tax charge would first apply.

Avoidance using trusts (TCGA 1992, ss 71, 76B, 79A, 85A and Schs 4B, 4C)

45.28   There are provisions to prevent artificial schemes under which losses generated within trusts are sold to purchasers to reduce their capital gains on other assets. A loss on an asset transferred to a trust beneficiary may be used only against gains on the disposal of the same asset (or in the case of land, an asset derived from the land).

Further anti-avoidance provisions apply to a variation of the above schemes. Losses arising on disposals by trustees cannot be set against any gains made by the trustees on assets that have been transferred to the trust if the transferor or someone connected with him had bought an interest in the trust and had claimed gifts holdover relief on the transferred assets.

It used to be possible to reduce or avoid capital gains tax by using a device known as the 'flip flop'. This applied in two situations. The first was where trustees of a UK or offshore trust in which a UK settlor retained an interest borrowed money on the security of the trust's assets and lent it to a second trust. The settlor then severed his interest in the first trust. The trustees of the first trust then sold the trust assets and repaid the debt, and the settlor received his money from the second trust. For UK trusts the effect of the scheme was that tax on any gains was charged on the trustees at their then tax rate of 34% rather than on the settlor at his rate of 40%. For offshore trusts there was no tax charge at all. The second situation also used an offshore trust in similar circumstances, and enabled UK beneficiaries to receive capital payments from a second trust which had not realised the gains, thus again avoiding tax entirely.

From 21 March 2000, where the trustees of any trust except a UK trust in which the settlor does not have an interest borrow money and advance it to another trust, the trustees are deemed to dispose of the trust assets and reacquire them at market value, thus crystallising the chargeable gains in the first trust. Gifts holdover relief cannot be claimed on the deemed disposal.

Trustees exploited the anti-avoidance provisions introduced in 2000 relating to the attribution of gains to UK beneficiaries by a new variant of the flip flop scheme. Further provisions were introduced from 9 April 2003 to ensure that UK beneficiaries of offshore trusts do not escape capital gains tax on capital payments. Inheritance tax anti-avoidance provisions were introduced from

20 June 2003 to prevent married couples using trusts to get round the rules in 5.8 about retaining benefits from a gift.

Other anti-avoidance provisions relating to trusts are mentioned in CHAPTERS 41 and 42.

Stamp duty (FA 2000, ss 117–122, 128 and Sch 33; FA 2002, ss 111–115 and Schs 34, 35; FA 2003, s 109)

45.29   There are a large number of specific stamp duty and stamp duty reserve tax avoidance provisions, which are mentioned briefly in CHAPTER 6, in particular at 6.7. In addition the Revenue have power to issue regulations to counter stamp duty avoidance devices as they arise, such regulations requiring Parliamentary approval. Similar provisions were introduced from 1 December 2003 in relation to stamp duty land tax. Any such regulations will cease to have effect after a maximum of 18 months unless they have been included in a subsequent Finance Bill.

Other measures

45.30   There are also measures to counter avoidance in the following circumstances.

Companies leaving a group and taking out a chargeable asset acquired intra-group on a no loss/no gain basis within the previous six years (TCGA 1992, ss 178–181).

Group companies seeking to avoid tax by channelling disposals of assets through tax-exempt bodies such as venture capital trusts and friendly societies (TCGA 1992, s 171).

Claiming group relief for losses when arrangements exist where a company may leave the group (TA 1988, s 410).

Transfers of plant and machinery between associated persons in order to obtain capital allowances (CAA 2001, ss 213–233).

Losses arising from depreciatory transactions, e.g. dividend-stripping (TCGA 1992, ss 176, 177).

Loss relief arising from dealings in commodity futures (TA 1988, s 399).

Artificial transactions in futures and options (see CHAPTER 4).

Value passing out of shares, which could have been avoided by a controlling shareholder (TCGA 1992, ss 29–33A).

Individuals realising capital gains abroad through a non-resident close company (TCGA 1992, s 13).

Transferring relief for partnership losses which would otherwise relate to a partner who is a company (TA 1988, s 116).

Annual payments for non-taxable consideration (TA 1988, s 125).

Transfer of chargeable assets on which holdover relief for capital gains tax is obtained into dual resident trusts (TCGA 1992, s 169).

Loans to participators in closely controlled companies (see CHAPTER 12).

Abuse of life assurance reliefs and exemptions, including the use of artificial annuities (see CHAPTER 40).

Non-resident trusts (see CHAPTER 41).

Residence of companies (see CHAPTER 41).

Deemed disposal of assets at time of ceasing to be a UK resident company (see CHAPTER 41).

Deemed disposal of assets when a non-resident carrying on business through a UK permanent establishment removes assets from the UK, or ceases to carry on the permanent establishment (see CHAPTER 41).

Transferring income from parents to minor children (see CHAPTERS 33 and 42).

Subject index

This index lists the main subject matter referred to in the text.

Reference should be made also to the 'Tax points' at the end of a chapter where appropriate.

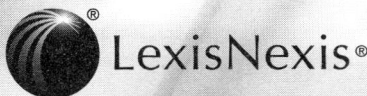